Evagrius of Pontus

Evagrius of Pontus

The Gnostic Trilogy

Translated and annotated by
Robin Darling Young,
Joel Kalvesmaki, Columba Stewart, Charles Stang,
and Luke Dysinger

OXFORD
UNIVERSITY PRESS

Oxford University Press is a department of the University of Oxford. It furthers the University's objective of excellence in research, scholarship, and education by publishing worldwide. Oxford is a registered trade mark of Oxford University Press in the UK and certain other countries.

Published in the United States of America by Oxford University Press
198 Madison Avenue, New York, NY 10016, United States of America.

© Oxford University Press 2024

All rights reserved. No part of this publication may be reproduced, stored in a retrieval system, or transmitted, in any form or by any means, without the prior permission in writing of Oxford University Press, or as expressly permitted by law, by license, or under terms agreed with the appropriate reproduction rights organization. Inquiries concerning reproduction outside the scope of the above should be sent to the Rights Department, Oxford University Press, at the address above.

You must not circulate this work in any other form
and you must impose this same condition on any acquirer.

Library of Congress Cataloging-in-Publication Data
Names: Evagrius, Ponticus, 345?-399, author. | Young, Robin Darling, editor. |
Evagrius, Ponticus, 345?-399. Praktikos English. |
Evagrius, Ponticus, 345?-399. Gnostikos English. |
Evagrius, Ponticus, 345?-399. Kephalaia gnostika English.
Title: Evagrius of Pontus : The Gnostic trilogy / Evagrius of Pontus;
[edited by Robin Darling Young, and 4 others].
Other titles: Gnostic trilogy
Description: New York, NY : Oxford University Press, [2024] |
Includes bibliographical references and index. |
Text in English, Greek, and Syriac.
Identifiers: LCCN 2023033266 (print) | LCCN 2023033267 (ebook) |
ISBN 9780199997671 (HB) | ISBN 9780197744130 (epub)
Subjects: LCSH: Evagrius, Ponticus, 345?-399. |
Theology, Doctrinal–Early works to 1800. |
Gnosticism–Early works to 1800. |
Christian literature, Early.
Classification: LCC BR65.E923 E93 2024 (print) |
LCC BR65.E923 (ebook) |
DDC 299/.932—dc23/eng/20230821
LC record available at https://lccn.loc.gov/2023033266
LC ebook record available at https://lccn.loc.gov/2023033267

DOI: 10.1093/oso/9780199997671.001.0001

Printed by Integrated Books International, United States of America

Contents

The Gnostic Trilogy in Context	1
Abbreviations	22
Praktikos	23
Gnostikos	99
Kephalaia gnostika	146
Bibliography	459
Select Writings of Evagrius	463
Quotations and Direct Allusions	471
Cross References	477
Index	507

The Gnostic Trilogy in Context

This book is the first English translation of the complete *Gnostic Trilogy*, the best-known work of the philosopher, biblical interpreter, and Christian ascetic Evagrius of Pontus (345–399). Although its first part, *The Praktikos*, or *To a Monk*, has appeared six times in recent English translations, the second part, *The Gnostikos*, has never before been published in English translation. Only one of the two extant Syriac versions of the *Kephalaia gnostika* has appeared in English, and its numerous Greek fragments have been untranslated until now.

Because interest in the work of Evagrius has expanded over the past fifty years, his readers need a clear and straightforward translation of this complex and ambiguous trilogy. We have translated all the Greek that survives of the work, as well as the Syriac versions of all three parts, adding explanatory notes.

The trilogy's three parts are noticeably uneven in length, though all consist of an ordered assemblage of kephalaia—short, interconnected, multi-referential, and often deliberately puzzling statements. The *Praktikos* has one hundred *kephalaia*, the *Gnostikos* (alternatively titled *To the One Who Has Become Worthy of Knowledge*) contains fifty; and the *Kephalaia gnostika* (often translated *Gnostic Chapters* or *Gnostic Centuries*) has five hundred forty kephalaia. For reasons discussed below, neither "chapter" nor "sentence" is an adequate or accurate translation for the Greek word *kephalaion* (pl. *kephalaia*).

Evagrius indicates the structure of the trilogy in the preface, a letter to Anatolios[1] that brackets the *Praktikos*: "We have divided concisely matters of the life of practice into a hundred chapters and matters about the life of knowledge into fifty chapters in addition to the six hundred." He presents the trilogy as work of two gradations, treating the *Gnostikos* as a companion to the *Kephalaia gnostika*. The *Praktikos* diagnoses the *pathē*, or disturbances afflicting the soul, and prescribes remedies for *logismoi*—malign thoughts—so that a practitioner may calmly approach with a clear mind the observation of the visible and invisible worlds and the rational beings within those worlds. The *Gnostikos*, the second part of the trilogy, is a collection of fifty

---

[1] An imperial official and associate of Rufinus of Aquileia (344/345–411) and Melania the Elder (ca. 350–410) in Jerusalem.

Evagrius of Pontus. Robin Darling Young, Joel Kalvesmaki, Columba Stewart, Charles Stang, and Luke Dysinger, Oxford University Press. © Oxford University Press 2024. DOI: 10.1093/oso/9780199997671.003.0001

2 EVAGRIUS OF PONTUS

kephalaia for the *gnōstikos*, knower or teacher—the former student now able to instruct others. The third and longest book in the trilogy, the *Kephalaia gnostika*, contains six books of one hundred *kephalaia*; each "century" lacks ten, and the remaining ninety are encoded puzzles for the practiced *gnōstikos*. The ten absent kephalaia in each group may signify the unknowability of God, who is *arrhētos*, not to be spoken (cf. *KG* 1.43), but we should remember as well that the century that constitutes the *Praktikos*, in its first edition, lacked ten kephalaia.[2]

Evagrius meant these *kephalaia* to be a curriculum leading the *gnōstikos* from therapy of the soul to the accurate observation of the created world in its entirety, and then toward the encounter with the divine. Since he thought God was indescribable, Evagrius does not discuss the nature of the Trinity in the *Gnostic Trilogy*. Although he titled each work, and arranged each with great care, Evagrius apparently did not designate a title for the entire trilogy, and in fact the trilogy form seems to have been Evagrius's representation of earlier work (see below). The choice to call it the *Gnostic Trilogy* is ours, because we recognize the author's aim was to prepare the reader's mind for gnōsis. For reasons both internal and external, it is certain that Evagrius meant the work to be a trilogy, signaled by thematic interrelationships, and similar structures.

Overlapping material between the *Gnostic Trilogy* and other works (particularly the *Letter on Faith*, his only securely datable work, written sometime between 381 and 383) confirms that even before his move to Egypt, Evagrius had written the *Kephalaia gnostika*. The *Praktikos* and *Gnostikos* were written later.[3] He does not say when he actually composed any of the works, or how long it took to write them, but he circulated them while he was living in the ascetic settlements at Kellia.

Like other works of Evagrius, the trilogy is meant for ascetics—but not exclusively; *askēsis*, or moral training, had always been part of Christian catechesis. Regardless of their intended audience, the three parts all draw from an older approach to the philosophical life of knowledge and moral practice, rooted in the Platonism of the teachers of Alexandria, beginning with Philo (ca. 20 BCE–ca. 50 CE) and refined in the circles of students taught by the celebrated philosophers Pantaenus and Ammonius Saccas, himself the teacher of both Origen (ca. 184–ca. 253) and Plotinus (ca. 204/5–270), and the generations of students taught by them. In scripture, the books of Wisdom, the epistles of Paul, and the Gospels

---

[2] Claire Guillaumont and Antoine Guillaumont, eds., *Traité pratique, ou, Le moine*, 2 vols., Sources chrétiennes 170–171 (Paris: Éditions du Cerf, 1971), 1:381–84.

[3] Joel Kalvesmaki, "Evagrius the Cappadocian: Redating the *Kephalaia Gnostika*," *Journal of Early Christian Studies* 31, no. 4 (2023): forthcoming.

urge gnōsis or knowledge upon the reader. Dualistic Platonists among early Christians had used the word for their teaching; Clement of Alexandria (ca. 150–ca. 215) was the first to reclaim the term *gnōstikos* for Christian teachers of the non-dualist philosophy that he thought could lead to union with the divine. Although Origen had used the word gnōsis sparingly, Evagrius embraced Clement's approach and revived the word *gnōstikos* as a term for a Christian philosophical teacher.

Following Origen, Evagrius advised the *gnōstikoi* to use *synkatabasis*—the temporary "descent" of a teacher to the intellectual level of a student, hiding more complex truths from the uninstructed. Philosophers had long employed this practice of pedagogical accommodation; now Christian philosophers, raised in the same tradition, employed *synkatabasis* and concealment (often signified by the verb *apokruptō*). In the *Praktikos* prologue, Evagrius tells Anatolios that he has "veiled certain things and obscured others," using the terms *epikrypsantes* and *syskiantes*, "hiding and overshadowing," so that his works could speak to two levels of student at the same time.[4] Christian teachers took as their scriptural model the pedagogy of Jesus and Paul, who could teach moral teachings to the simpler students and hint at complex and hidden truths to the more advanced. The practice of *synkatabasis* and concealment, then, determined both the structure and the content of the trilogy.

In the *Praktikos*, the *kephalaia* are organized in blocks, under subtitles preserved in numerous manuscripts, perhaps expressing Evagrius' original intention. The *kephalaia* of the *Gnostikos* are arranged more subtly, and in the much longer *Kephalaia gnostika* the *kephalaia* are presented in patterns easy to discern but difficult to interpret. Many series of *kephalaia* that belong with each other are staggered, or interwoven, with other series. Their terse style forced students to pay careful attention to every single word. The reader was expected to note relationships, to read the kephalaia slowly and repeatedly, and to draw cross-comparisons, including with other writings.

Education and Exegesis

As a young man, Evagrius had completed the course of *paideia*: a comprehensive education, organized as a consistent system throughout the cities of the late Roman Empire. Often established near municipal or private libraries and financed with public funds through city councils, this system of schools had a public, as well as a personal, purpose—to produce eloquent writers capable

---

[4] Cf. *Letter to Melania* 15.

4 EVAGRIUS OF PONTUS

of using rhetoric in public settings and, at its highest level, philosophers who could communicate with each other, advise leaders of government, and train their successors.[5] Although sometimes women directed such schools,[6] usually women were trained, when they were trained, at home; such was likely to have been the case with Macrina and Gorgonia, and also of Melania the Elder, and of the women who studied with Jerome.[7]

Evagrius' *paideia*, like that of Clement of Alexandria, Origen, Plotinus, and Porphyry, integrated philosophical and mythic or scriptural interpretation into a comprehensive program designed to correct and train a student in moral praxis, to make it possible for that student to avoid and defeat delusions, especially those prompted by demons, and to achieve clear observation of visible and invisible realities. For Christian philosophers of the period, it was expected that angels, the Logos, and the Holy Spirit would assist the thinker in his or her *zētēsis*, or inquiry, leading to the goal of *theōria*. Thus having absorbed the teachings of Christ and other "friends of God" they became capable of pursuing knowledge (*gnōsis*) and *theōria*, after which speech no longer obtained.

Evagrius' scripture was the Greek Bible (for the most part, the Septuagint along with the Greek New Testament); in accord with his training, he used Platonic philosophy as an interpretive tool and second inspired text. Although he wrote four sets of biblical commentaries in the form of scholia, as described below, all Evagrius' works quote and interpret scripture in virtually every line, usually without citation. He often embedded and linked words from different biblical books and wove them together to make new instructions or narratives. Evagrius uses this compositional method in his treatises, scholia, letters, and kephalaia. His biblical exegesis obviously was aimed to attract an audience broader than the monastic foundations with which he is usually connected; in all three sets of scholia, as with the *Kephalaia gnostika*, there is only one mention of a *monachos* or solitary (merely a cross-reference to the *Praktikos*), and descriptions of demonic temptation are vanishingly scarce. Throughout his exegesis, Evagrius concentrated on the moral and the "theoretical" or allegorical interpretations of scripture, showing little interest in the sequence of historical events reported in either testament.

---

[5] See Raffaella Cribiore, *Gymnastics of the Mind: Greek Education in Hellenistic and Roman Egypt* (Princeton, NJ: Princeton University Press, 2001); Lillian I. Larsen and Samuel Rubenson, *Monastic Education in Late Antiquity: The Transformation of Classical Paideia* (Cambridge: Cambridge University Press, 2018).

[6] For instance, the school of Hypatia in Alexandria; see Edward Jay Watts, *Hypatia: The Life and Legend of an Ancient Philosopher*, Women in Antiquity (New York: Oxford University Press, 2017).

[7] See Susanna Elm, *Virgins of God: The Making of Asceticism in Late Antiquity*, Oxford Classical Monographs (Oxford: Clarendon Press, 1996); F. J. LeMoine, "Jerome's Gift to Women Readers," in *Shifting Frontiers in Late Antiquity*, ed. Ralph W. Mathisen and Hagith S. Sivan (Aldershot: Variorum, 1996), 230–41.

THE GNOSTIC TRILOGY IN CONTEXT 5

Following the principle of *synkatabasis* described above, Evagrius expected some readers or hearers to be able to apprehend the text only at a simple level. These were the *haplousteroi* or simpler Christians; in his *paideia*, they correspond to the *praktikoi* among the monks—they are the beginners. The *spoudaioi*, or the zealous, were Christians engaged in serious study and training at the moral and intellectual level. *Gnōstikoi* were those who attained such a level of virtue and intelligence that they could approach or understand the full meaning of scripture and could interpret and reveal that meaning to others—but only to those judged ready to apprehend it. In this approach, he follows not only Origen, but also Philo and Clement before Origen, and Porphyry and Iamblichus after them—and all these writers restricted the deeper meaning of a sacred text to the more advanced reader. Like Origen, Evagrius viewed a triad of scriptural books as an ascending ladder appropriate to levels of understanding along the way to union with the mind of the Logos, and finally of the ineffable Father himself. Origen's extensive homilies and commentaries on Proverbs assisted with the *praktikē*, Ecclesiastes with the *physikē*, and the Song of Songs with the *theologikē*. It is notable, however, that Evagrius did not write scholia on the last of these, but focused on the wisdom literature: Job, Psalms, Proverbs, and Ecclesiastes—the works of David, Solomon, and Job. The last of these had been called a *gnōstikos* by Clement of Alexandria, and Origen devoted a set of homilies to the "righteous man," both precedents that, as well as the contemporary work of Didymus, explain Evagrius' interest.[8]

Unlike Origen, Evagrius seems not to have thought that scripture could contain all three senses in a single passage; rather one passage contained only one sense—ethical, natural, or theological. And whereas Origen wrote about Proverbs, Ecclesiastes, and the Song of Songs through homilies and extensive prose treatises, Evagrius avoided these and wrote tersely, in the genre of scholia. Like Origen, though, Evagrius regarded scripture as unified in vocabulary, in meaning, and in purpose. It has a customary way of expression (*synētheia* or *ethos*), often communicated through symbols (*symbola*) and signs (*gnōrismata*) so that the Logos can, through scripture, express the truth symbolically or figuratively (*tropikōs*). Also like Origen, Evagrius uses this exegetical approach consistently through all his works, often repeating and occasionally altering an interpretive passage from one work to another.

---

[8] For Job as *gnōstikos*, see Clement, *Stromateis* 4.17; as "righteous," Origen, *On Prayer* 29.17; and see Didymus the Blind, *Commentary on Job*.

Writings

Scholars usually divide Evagrius' writings into four types: kephalaia, scholia, treatises, and letters. An exception is his *Antirrhetikos*, or "refutations," an apotropaic collection of scriptural texts to ward off tempting-thoughts, *logismoi*, prompted by demons who constantly attempt to thwart the progress of the solitary.

Apart from fragments of its original Greek, Evagrius' correspondence survives in a Syriac version containing sixty-three letters, and in a shorter Armenian version. Because they lack salutations and valedictions, and because no letters from his correspondents remain in the collection, most addressees can be assigned only hypothetically. Other letters survive as prefatory notes to his other works. Two lengthy letters are well known for their depth and sophistication, and their shared thematic connections to the *Kephalaia gnostika*. One of these, his earliest known work (datable to 382?), *Letter on Faith*, surviving in Greek, presents a defense of faith. The *Letter to Melania*, another theological letter, is likely to have been written after 394.

Although every work of Evagrius contains biblical interpretation, the scholia are direct exegeses of selected verses of four works: Job, Psalms, Proverbs, and Ecclesiastes. These short interpretive passages, surviving in Greek because they were incorporated in later catenae, were meant for readers interested in a philosophical interpretation of the scriptures. Greek literary scholars had long used scholia to discover and state the symbolic meaning of Homeric works and other ancient literature, but Evagrius was one of the first Christian teachers to employ the form, and one of the first to apply it to the scriptures. Thirty-six of the 1,386 scholia on the Psalms, Evagrius' longest extant work by far, are verbatim parallels to the *Kephalaia gnostika*. Five of the 388 scholia on Proverbs do the same. In the use of scholia as exegetical forms, Evagrius may have been inspired by the slightly earlier work of Didymus.[9]

Three of Evagrius' works can be described as prose treatises. Evagrius addressed *Foundations of the Monastic Life* and *To Eulogius* to ascetics in the early stages of their training, and these treatises show thematic overlap with the *Praktikos*. A third prose treatise, *About Thoughts*, which may be part of a trilogy of works including the *Kephalaia on Prayer* and *Skemmata*, has many points of contact with the *Kephalaia gnostika*.

Finally, the majority of Evagrius' works are collections of kephalaia; apart from the trilogy presented here, he employed this form in nine of his works, not all of which, however, bear the title. In this book, we have not translated *kephalaia* as

---

[9] See Richard A. Layton, *Didymus the Blind and His Circle in Late-Antique Alexandria: Virtue and Narrative in Biblical Scholarship* (Urbana: University of Illinois Press, 2004).

"sentences" or "chapters." Evagrius chose his words carefully, and in his thought the Greek term does not mean a numbered and sequential division of a text, in which narrative sections follow each other. Rather, a single kephalaion is a philosophical "summary" (Plato, *Tim.* 26c; *Theaetet.* 3.67; cf. Clement, *Strom.* 7.4.27.6), where an internal logic governs and may refer to entire trains of thought—dialogues, treatises, or biblical books—outside the kephalaion itself but combined and compressed within by way of sophisticated allusion. Evagrius uses these methods of composition throughout his writings.[10]

Evagrius' kephalaia are different from those ascribed to Mani—for example, *The Kephalaia of the Teacher*, where the "kephalaia" reproduce the "question and answer" form of the literary genre of *erotapokrisis*. Mani's followers may have imitated an older Stoic sentence form, but they did not convey Mani's teachings in the aphoristic, summative manner of Evagrius' kephalaia. They, like his scholia, were the first Christian use of the genre to communicate teaching and prompt thinking and observation, and proved an influential model for dozens of later interpreters.

The *Gnostic Trilogy*: Manuscripts, Text, and Ancient Translations

Much of the original Greek text of the *Gnostic Trilogy* perished as a result of the second Origenist controversy in the sixth century, when Evagrius was condemned, along with Origen and Didymus, and many of his works were censored and destroyed. Thus, from the *Gnostic Trilogy*, only the *Praktikos* survived intact in Greek, as being a useful guide to ascetic training and combat with demonic thoughts. As for the *Gnostikos* and *Kephalaia gnostika*, only portions of the Greek remain, and the early Latin translations of all three works have disappeared. Only in Syriac and Armenian can the trilogy be found complete. But even when the works are in the same volume—a rarity—they are never adjacent. Presenting these works as a trilogy is faithful to Evagrius' description of them and recaptures his plan of a complete monastic curriculum.

The Greek fragments of the *Gnostikos* and *Kephalaia gnostika* are of uneven quality. Some reflect the original text exactly, and others only periphrastically. In part, the degree of fidelity relates to the medium of transmission.

---

[10] See the useful remarks in Paul Géhin, "Les collections de *Kephalaia* Monastiques: Naissance et succès d'un genre entre création originale, plagiat et florilège," in *The Minor Genres of Byzantine Theological Literature*, ed. Antonio Rigo, Studies in Byzantine History and Civilization 8 (Turnhout: Brepols, 2013), 1–50; Joel Kalvesmaki, "Evagrius in the Byzantine Genre of Chapters," in *Evagrius and His Legacy*, ed. Joel Kalvesmaki and Robin Darling Young (South Bend: University of Notre Dame Press, 2016), 257–87.

8   EVAGRIUS OF PONTUS

Many of the fragments of the *Kephalaia gnostika* come from Evagrius' other treatises, particularly the scholia on Psalms. This overlap is not unusual for Evagrius, who reused and revised many of his kephalaia for different occasions and genres. Numerous verbatim parallels can be found crossing his letters, scholia, and treatises. Some scholars have argued that the letters were the starting point; others, that the treatises came first.[11] We ourselves regard the scholia, which we believe Evagrius worked on over many years, as representing his initial work and his source of inspiration. Vocabulary specific to the verse being quoted would be substituted for terminology germane to that particular part of the trilogy.[12] Regardless of the sequence of these works, verbatim parallels to the *Gnostic Trilogy* from his other works have significantly different phrasing, reflecting how Evagrius reused his written insights for different audiences. Such fragments cannot always be relied upon to restore the lost Greek.

Other extant Greek fragments are in collections less prone to revision and therefore are more reliable for corroborating the Syriac translations. The most significant collection is the primary anonymous alphabetized collection of Byzantine definitions, published by Furrer-Pilliod in 2000. From Collection A we have nearly half of the Greek fragments for the *Kephalaia gnostika*, and the Greek corresponds strikingly to the translation of S2 (many times against S1). Other fragments survive in anthologies that circulated under Evagrius' name or that of another, less suspect, author. Four manuscripts contain a condensed form of the *Praktikos* (thirty-seven chapters) and *Gnostikos* (nineteen chapters) presented as the work of Nilus of Ancyra. A manuscript now in Moscow (Mosc. 425, sixteenth century) preserves twenty-five chapters from the *Gnostikos* and *Kephalaia gnostika* under the name of Maximus the Confessor.[13] Cod. Ambr. gr. 681 (q 74 sup; tenth century) contains about two dozen kephalaia from throughout the *Kephalaia gnostika*, their original order retained.[14] In other cases, florilegia with excerpts from many authors contain some by Evagrius. Occasionally, however, the Greek exhibits scribal errors. Sometimes entire clauses are missing (e.g., *Gn.* 42), while at other times syntax, word order, or orthography has suffered.[15]

---

[11] Antoine Guillaumont, *Un philosophe au désert: Evagre le Pontique*, Textes et traditions 8 (Paris: Vrin, 2004), 163–70; Evagrius Ponticus, *Scholies aux Psaumes I, Psaumes 1–70*, ed. Marie-Josèphe Rondeau, Paul Géhin, and Matthieu Cassin, Sources chrétiennes 614 (Paris: Les Éditions du Cerf, 2021), 27–31.

[12] For specific examples, see *KG* 1.36, 40; 3.48; 4.46; 5.48-49, 70, 77; 6.46, 49 and corresponding notes.

[13] Irénée Hausherr, "Nouveaux fragments grecs d'Évagre le Pontique," *Orientalia Christiana Periodica* 5 (1939): 229–33; Antoine Guillaumont and Claire Guillaumont, eds., *Le gnostique, ou, A celui qui est devenu digne de la science*, Sources Chrétiennes 356 (Paris: Éditions du Cerf, 1989).

[14] Joseph Muyldermans, *Evagriana: Extrait de la revue Le Muséon*, Vol. 44, *Augmenté de nouveax fragments grecs inédits* (Paris: Paul Geuthner, 1931).

[15] See *KG* 1.69, where most likely ἀρχῶν was changed via dittography into ἐλθὼν, or *KG* 1.14, in which only the first portion was copied.

THE GNOSTIC TRILOGY IN CONTEXT 9

Nearly all such fragments can be checked for accuracy against surviving ancient translations.

Sometimes a fragment survives via quotation. Socrates Scholasticus, Oikoumenios, and Gregory Palamas all quote from *Gnostikos*, and the *KG* appears in the correspondence of Barsanuphios and John (*Letter* 600) as well as in the writings of John of Skythopolis and Dorotheos of Gaza, who cites Evagrius frequently. Two of the fifteen anathemas of the Second Council of Constantinople (553) condemning Origenism appear to quote accurately from the *KG*, perhaps via an intermediary text (see notes at *KG* 2.17, 78; 4.18). Quotations from anti-Evagrian polemic should not be dismissed. Early Christian rhetoric had a long-standing tradition of quoting accurately from one's opponent.

Praktikos

The Greek text of the *Praktikos*, along with its prefatory letter to Anatolios, is well attested in dozens of manuscripts. It is one of the few surviving Greek texts that continued to be attributed to Evagrius. The Guillaumonts, in their masterly critical edition, showed that Evagrius released two editions of the *Praktikos*, the first containing ninety chapters, followed by a second with one hundred.[16] Both editions survive in manuscripts of the tenth to eleventh centuries. Later manuscripts (fourteenth–sixteenth) also present excerpted versions consisting of sixty-three or thirty-seven chapters. Smaller units (e.g., chapters 6–14 on the eight thoughts) or even just individual chapters were often copied in florilegia. Such selection and abbreviation are typical of ascetic literature in general and of the transmission of Evagrius' writings in particular, aided by his choice of the *kephalaion* as his preferred format: a copyist or compiler could easily and selectively extract at will.

The complete form of the *Praktikos* consists of the prefatory letter to Anatolios, a note to copyists urging them to respect the form of the *kephalaia* by presenting them on the page as distinct units, the one hundred chapters, and an epilogue that again addresses Anatolios. The *Praktikos* was translated into Latin, Syriac, Armenian, Arabic, and Georgian.[17] The earliest was the Latin version by Rufinus (Jerome, *Letter* 133.3), but it has not survived. The extant translations into Syriac, Armenian, Arabic, and Georgian have been little studied, and most versions remain unedited. Of these, the Syriac has the greatest number of versions (three)

---

[16] The analysis of the Greek manuscripts was made by Claire Guillaumont in the introductory volume of the critical edition of *Prak.* published in collaboration with her husband, Antoine Guillaumont. Guillaumont and Guillaumont, *Traité pratique*, 1:127–303.

[17] The best overview remains Guillaumont and Guillaumont, 1:318–337, building on the work of Wilhelm Frankenberg, Irénée Hausherr, and Joseph Muyldermans.

10   EVAGRIUS OF PONTUS

and manuscripts.[18] The version most frequently copied was completed sometime before 523, the year of the death of Philoxenus of Mabbug, whose four quotations from the *Gnostic Trilogy* are influenced by or dependent upon it.[19]

Known as S1,[20] this version is attested by eleven manuscripts dating from the sixth to the sixteenth centuries. The earliest is dated 534, and the majority are from before 900, that is, long before the oldest-known Greek manuscripts. The translator joined the *Praktikos* to the *Gnostikos* to make a single work, numbering the chapters 1 through 150. There is neither preface (the letter to Anatolios) nor epilogue, but some of the subheads were retained.

A second Syriac translation from roughly the same period (S2) retains the prefatory letter to Anatolios and the epilogue, lacks the subheads, and presents the *Praktikos* as an independent work (the same translator was most likely responsible for the S2 version of the *Gnostikos*, and thus knew them as distinct works). This version is attested directly in two manuscripts[21] and indirectly in several others that contain only its translation of the letter to Anatolios.[22]

The third version (S3) is only partly preserved in two manuscripts that taken together provide chapters 1 through 43. Both S1 and S2 are direct translations of the original Greek; the translator of S3 seems to have known the two other Syriac versions as well as the Greek.

The Armenian translation, dating from as early as the fifth century for the *Praktikos* and *Gnostikos*, was made directly from the Greek original as was his *On Prayer*, unlike other Evagrian writings translated into Armenian, most of which translated a Syriac translation. The Arabic version, also made directly from the Greek and attested in two manuscripts, could be as old as the eighth century. The Guillaumonts caution that neither dating is certain.

We have translated the Greek text as edited by Claire Guillaumont. Because the complete text securely survives in Greek, we have translated only one Syriac version, the most common, S1, following a manuscript from the British Library,

[18] The number of versions is established by comparison of the extant manuscripts, which reveals substantial differences that go beyond expected variations of orthography or the inevitable scribal errors. We have studied the Syriac versions closely, especially for the *Gnostikos* and *Kephalaia gnostika*, for which we do not have a complete Greek text. Assessing the quality, character, and relationship of these translations, however, is a complex problem, discussed below.

[19] In the *Letter to Patricius* he quotes from *Prak.* 15 and 79, as well as *Gn.* 25 and 36. René Lavenant, *La lettre à Patrikios de Philoxène de Mabboug*, Patrologia Orientalis 30.5 (Paris: Firmin-Didot, 1963), 812, 854–856, 872.

[20] The reader should note that the sigla S1, S2, and S3 are specific to each work. As it happens, all of the S1 versions may well be the work of the same translator, but this is not the case for the versions known as S2 or S3. See the table below for an overview of the Syriac versions of the *Gnostic Trilogy*.

[21] The most ample witness (BL Add. 14616) is missing a few chapters and the endings of some others; the second manuscript (BL Add. 17165) lost the original first eight folios and S2 begins only at ch. 76, the earlier chapters having been supplied at a much later date from a copy of S1. As a result, we have no S2 version of chs. 47 or 62, or of the endings of chs. 5, 14, 15, and 38.

[22] Those manuscripts contain *Prak.* in the S1 version, with the letter to Anatolios presented as a separate work.

THE GNOSTIC TRILOGY IN CONTEXT 11

Add. 14578, which is exceptional because it is completely devoted to the works of Evagrius.[23] The same manuscript contains the prefatory letter to Anatolios, but it is found much later in the manuscript, and, as noted above, it is by the translator of version S2. In our English translation, we have followed the order of the original Greek text, and we ask readers to bear in mind that we translated the letter to Anatolios and the main text of the *Praktikos* from two different Syriac versions.

Gnostikos

There is no longer a complete Greek text of the *Gnostikos*. Its editors recovered about sixty percent of it (thirty-one of fifty kephalaia, some only partially) from manuscripts containing selections from the work.[24] The most extensive fragments come from ascetic florilegia. Some of these contain excerpts from the *Praktikos* and *Gnostikos*, presented as a single work attributed to Nilus. The manuscripts are later than those containing the complete *Praktikos*, dating from the thirteenth through the fifteenth centuries. In one of them (Vienna, Theol. gr. 274, early fourteenth century), an additional kephalaion survives, written in the margin by a slightly later hand, along with its original chapter number (36), a remnant attesting to a complete Greek copy of the *Gnostikos*. Other marginal notes made throughout the manuscript by the same learned person restore to Evagrius the authorship of almost all of his works found therein but ascribed to Nilus.[25]

Additional chapters have been recovered from the works of other authors. The ecclesiastical historian Socrates Scholasticus embeds seven chapters in his *Ecclesiastical History* (written ca. 440), attributing them to Evagrius; the oldest manuscript of this work is from the tenth century. Five other chapters, none of them preserved elsewhere, are presented in a sixteenth-century manuscript along with excerpts from the *Kephalaia gnostika* as a work of Maximus the Confessor. Single chapters are used by Oikoumenios in a commentary on the book of Revelation (there attributed to Evagrius) and by Gregory Palamas in his *Defense of Hesychasts* (attributed to Nilus, and probably gleaned from the excerpted version described above).

The *Gnostikos* was translated into Latin by Gennadius of Marseilles (late fifth century), but this version has been lost. There are three Syriac versions, designated, like those of the *Praktikos*, as S1, S2, and S3. Of these, *Gnostikos* S1 was the work of the same translator as *Praktikos* S1, and they are presented in

---

[23] See Paul Géhin, "En marge de la constitution d'un repertorium Evagrianum Syriacum: Quelques remarques sur l'organisation en corpus des oeuvres d'Évagre," *Parole de l'Orient* 35 (2010): 285–301.

[24] See Guillaumont and Guillaumont, *Le gnostique*, 43–51.

[25] But not the *Chapters on Prayer*.

12   EVAGRIUS OF PONTUS

the manuscripts as a single work with continuous numbering.[26] *Gnostikos* S2 was translated by the same person as *Praktikos* S2 and is found in the same two manuscripts, though not together with the Praktikos. The *Gnostikos* begins with the title "To whomever [or: to the brother who] has become worthy of knowledge," a phrase that resonates with Socrates' description (*Church History* 4.23.36). Each manuscript has lacunae, but fortunately only the last words of a single chapter (21) are missing in both. S3 is a careful revision of S1 on the basis of the Greek, and it survives in a single manuscript, the precious BL Add. 17167, so important for the text of the *Kephalaia gnostika* (see below). The translator's close attention to the original text makes S3 a valuable witness to those portions of the *Gnostikos* that did not survive in Greek. The Armenian version of the *Gnostikos*, like that of the *Praktikos*, was thought by both Irénée Hausherr and Antoine Guillaumont to have been made directly from the Greek in the fifth or early sixth century, and if this is the case, it would also be important for access to the original text and for correcting the Syriac where it seems to have altered the meaning of the Greek.[27] There is no known Arabic translation of the *Gnostikos*.

We have translated the Greek, where it survives, and all three Syriac versions, based on a selection of manuscripts guided by the analysis found in the edition by the Guillaumonts.[28]

Kephalaia gnostika

Only about 25 percent of the *Kephalaia gnostika* survives in Greek, through compilations, quotations, and Evagrius' own reuse of material from his scholia. The fifteen anathemas (see note at 2.78) indicate that in the sixth century a complete version of the *KG* was still available in Greek. Perhaps copies were available even later, as the direct or indirect source of the anonymous Byzantine definitions and the collections of extracts (see above).

The *KG* was translated into Syriac (twice), and on the basis of the Syriac there are Armenian and Arabic versions.[29] The most common Syriac translation,

---

[26] A vestige of the original title remains in a few manuscripts that place *Prak.* 54–100 and *Gn.* under the heading "Book of the *Gnostikos*."

[27] The Armenian version is faithful to the Greek in word order but is not consistent in its handling of technical vocabulary; see Guillaumont and Guillaumont, *Le gnostique*, 71–74.

[28] For S1: BL Add. 14581 (compared with BL Add. 14578, published by Frankenberg); S2: BL Add. 17165 (compared with and supplemented by BL Add. 14616); S3: BL Add. 16167. The transcriptions were made by Columba Stewart and are available at evagriusponticus.net.

[29] Paul Géhin, "La tradition arabe d'Évagre le Pontique," *Collectanea Christiana Orientalia* 3 (2006): 83–104, at 95–96. To the one manuscript mentioned by Géhin, now missing, should be added two more identified by Stephen J. Davis, "Evagrius Ponticus at the Monastery of the Syrians: Newly Documented Evidence for an Arabic Reception History," in *Heirs of the Apostles: The Story of Arabic Christianity*, ed. D. Bertaina et al. (Leiden & Boston: Brill, 2018), 347–392.

THE GNOSTIC TRILOGY IN CONTEXT   13

termed S1, is attested wholly or partially in nine manuscripts,[30] and was the basis for the Armenian translation and for later commentaries on the *Kephalaia gnostika* by both Syriac and Armenian authors.

The second translation, S2, is a revision of S1 on the basis of the Greek, like *Gnostikos* S3, and is contained in the same manuscript. Both versions (*Gnostikos* S3 and *KG* S2) are most likely the work of the same assiduous translator. As with *Gnostikos* S3, most kephalaia have been revised (S2 left intact S1's rendering of about one fourth of the 540 kephalaia). Unlike the *Gnostikos*, in this case the original translation (S1) and its revision (S2) are often dramatically different, with the translator of S2 showing clear intent to reflect the original Greek text, including the restoration of statements that had been softened or simply eliminated by the translator of S1. The single copy of S2 was discovered by Antoine and Claire Guillaumont in a manuscript at the British Museum (now the British Library) and announced in a 1952 article. Antoine Guillaumont's edition of the text followed in 1958, and his crucial study of its significance in 1962.[31] His arguments for the greater fidelity of S2 to Evagrius' original text have gained wide acceptance.[32] The circumstances of the creation of the greatly tamed S1 version remain obscure. It is commonly understood that the translator of S1 aimed to save the Evagrian legacy by eliminating teachings by then judged unacceptable. But there are counter-examples: changes that have no discernible motivation, and retention of speculative theology one might have expected to have been altered (e.g., *KG* 4.51). The expurgated S1 became the dominant version of the *Kephalaia gnostika*, and was the subject of extensive commentaries by Babai the Great (d. 628) and Dionysius Bar Salibi (twelfth century). They and others were aware of S2, but condemned it as a subversive effort to distort Evagrius' teaching.

We have translated the existing Greek fragments as well as both Syriac versions, and have commented selectively on the reliability of individual Greek fragments.

A Profile of the Syriac Translations

As indicated above, the Syriac translations not only are important witnesses to the reception of Evagrius' writings in the East, but in many cases are also the

---

[30] To the eight listed in Guillaumont's edition one can add Diyarbakir, Meryemana Church 205, which contains a fragment from a ?15th-century manuscript containing *KG* 5.39–51 and 76–88. https://w3id.org/vhmml/readingRoom/view/124495.

[31] Antoine Guillaumont, Les *"Képhalaia gnostica" d'Évagre le Pontique et l'histoire de l'origénisme chez les grecs et chez les syriens*, Publications de la Sorbonne série patristica Sorbonensia 5 (Paris: Eds. du Seuil, 1962).

[32] A recent exception is a work by Augustine Casiday, who has argued that S1 is based on a more authentic version of the Greek original, and S2 on a later (sixth-century?) revised Greek text that circulated among Origenist monks. Augustine Casiday, *Reconstructing the Theology of Evagrius Ponticus: Beyond Heresy* (Cambridge: Cambridge University Press, 2013).

14 EVAGRIUS OF PONTUS

only access we have to the lost original Greek text. Because the full Greek texts of the *Praktikos* and much of the *Gnostikos* have survived, they can serve as a benchmark for measuring the Syriac translations against the original text and for comparing them to each other. Such an investigation could be conducted across the entirety of the Evagrian corpus, but we restrict our comments to the *Gnostic Trilogy*.

As we have seen, the *Praktikos* and *Gnostikos* each have three extant Syriac translations, and the *Kephalaia Gnostika* has two. The S1 versions of *Praktikos* and *Gnostikos* each try to render the Greek accurately and intelligibly, though sometimes misunderstanding the often-cryptic original text. Their shared approach to translation, as well as their appearance in the manuscripts as a single work—in every case but one, S1 *Praktikos* is immediately followed by S1 *Gnostikos*—suggests the same translator. That same approach to translation features in the S1 version of the *Kephalaia gnostika*, though here his effort also involved a careful reframing of the content to avoid theologically problematic statements. As a result, the translator of S1 *Kephalaia gnostika* often departed from his Greek source. The many Greek fragments from the *KG* often agree with S2 against S1, or differ from both; 3.62 is the only case we know of a Greek *KG* fragment that agrees with S1 against S2.

The S2 versions of *Praktikos* and *Gnostikos* infrequently appear in the same manuscripts, and even when they do, they are distinct, non-contiguous works. As noted earlier, even S2's translation of the prefatory letter to Anatolios does not appear with the *Praktikos*. Despite the seeming lack of understanding of the shape of the original corpus, the translator of the *Praktikos* and *Gnostikos* S2 versions revised S1 to make the technical vocabulary so typical of Evagrius more accessible to the reader. This is done by using pleonasm or glosses, as in *Gnostikos* 2. The more literal S3 version of chapter 2 reads:

> The practiced one is he who possesses the impassioned part of his soul without passion (*apathes*).

The S2 version avoids both the Platonic notion of divisions of the soul and the Stoic resonances of *apatheia*, a term central to Evagrius' thought, by rendering the chapter in this manner:

> The practiced one is he who has caused the evil passions of his soul to cease, and possesses health of mind by means of steadfast disciplines.

Using "health of mind" to represent *apatheia* is not unlike John Cassian's choice of "purity of heart" (Mt 5.8) for the same purpose. The translator's graceful

THE GNOSTIC TRILOGY IN CONTEXT   15

"steadfast disciplines," characteristic of this version, suggests a pastoral concern to focus on asceticism and not to venture into abstract contemplation.

An example of pleonasm can be found in *Gnostikos* 16, which in the more literal S3 version reads:

> It is necessary that you have material for the interpretation of things that are said, that all these matters suffice for us, even if one of the little things escapes us. For only an angel would not forget one of those things upon the earth.

The translator of S2 has added the italicized phrases:

> We need *testimonies from Scripture and knowledge of the* matters *of the world for the sake* of interpretation of those things that we teach *to a disciple*. And *every vision of created things* will suffice for us. But if a little from the *knowledge of natures* escapes us, *and it is difficult for us to understand, let it not grieve us*, because it belongs to the angels to understand perfectly everything on the earth.

The pleonastic alterations aim at a more general monastic audience by way of *synkatabasis*.

Another set of translations are revisions of the S1 version made for the sake of greater fidelity to the Greek. Confusingly, version numbers differ among the works. The S3 version of the *Praktikos* seems to be a revision of both S1 and S2; the S3 of *Gnostikos* is a revision of S1; the S2 of *Kephalaia gnostika* is a revision of S1. S3 *Gnostikos* and S2 *Kephalaia gnostika* are further comparable in that the sole witnesses come from the same manuscript, and each version tries to respect Evagrius' philosophical vocabulary and speculative thought. S3 *Praktikos*, on the other hand, appears with no other version of the *Gnostic Trilogy*.

In our opinion, the eight versions are the work of at least four but no more than six different translators, as outlined in Table 1. Syriac manuscript witnesses to the *Gnostic Trilogy* are listed in Table 2.

About This Edition

References

Biblical quotations follow the chapter and verse numeration of the Septuagint. A reference in parentheses points to the corresponding chapter or verse number in modern English translations. To reduce clutter, and to aid in reference to the 2021 edition of the scholia on the Psalms, we have avoided double numeration for the Psalms, most of which differ by one chapter (e.g., Ps. 50 LXX = Ps. 51 English).

16   EVAGRIUS OF PONTUS

Table 1 Translators

		Pr	Gn	*KG*
A	Translator of unknown background; tendency toward literal translation technique. This set of translations became the most influential, and so are sometimes called the "common version." May be the same person as translator E.	S1	S1	
B	Translator intent on making the text accessible to a broad audience. The translation tends to be loose, in service to clearer Syriac syntax and semantics, and employs euphemisms or glosses for the sake of comprehension. There is no evidence that he used any other translation.	S2	S2	
C	Translator of unknown background. Seems to have worked from both S1 and S2 as well as the Greek text.	S3		
D	Translator of unknown background. Adjusts the work of translator A. May be the same person as translator F.		S3	
E	Translator of unknown background. Literal translation technique, much like translator A, except for metaphysical or speculative passages that are edited or eliminated. May be the same person as translator A.			S1
F	Translator of unknown background who revised A's translation of the *Kephalaia gnostika*. The style is literal, adhering closely to the Greek, and respecting the philosophical vocabulary and speculative thought of Evagrius. May be the same person as translator D.			S2

References to the *Epistula fidei* follow Bunge's numeration system (1–40), which is better at pinpointing specific passages than is the older system (1–12); references to the *Letters* and the *Letter to Melania* follow Bunge's system as well. For other works of Evagrius, we follow the numeration adopted in the Sources chrétiennes edition, if available.

Annotations

Several principles have guided us as we have commented on the *kephalaia* of the *Gnostic Trilogy*. Our primary goal has been to help readers study the work for themselves and gain their own understanding of it. To that end, we have frequently refrained from interpreting or explaining Evagrius' meaning and have instead emphasized intertextual relationships. In addition to the verbatim quotations from scripture, we provide references to other biblical verses that resonate with Evagrius' vocabulary. When he appears to invoke the philosophical tradition directly, we offer select references to Plato, Aristotle, Porphyry, and

Table 2 Manuscript Witnesses to the Syriac Versions of the *Gnostic Trilogy*

MS	Praktikos			Gnostikos			*KG*	
	S1	S2	S3	S1	S2	S3	S1	S2
BL Add. 12175	96v–98v	101r-*		99r–101r			81r–96r	
BL Add. 14581	12v–23r			23r–27v				
BL Add. 14578	2v–11v	152r–153v*		11v–16v			119r–144r	
Berlin Syr 27	22r–28v	41v–42v*		28v–29v				
BL Add. 14582	125r–141v			141v–146v				
BL Add. 18817	35v–49r			49r–53r				
BL Add. 12167	84v–94v			94v–98v				
BL Add. 14579	20r–27v			27v–31v				
BL Add. 17165	1v–7r	9r–15r**			26r–34v			
Vat. Syr. 126	224r–227v			224r–227v				
London BM Or. 2312	53v–61v	104r-*		61v–65r			173r–182v	
BL Add. 14616		2v–26r**			33r–40r			
BL Add. 14621		127r*						
BL Add. 14541		50*						
London BM Rich 7190		65r*					57v–59v, 69v	
BL Add. 14650			6v–8v					
BL Add. 17166			22r–24v, 25r–27r					

(*continued*)

Table 2 Continued

MS	Praktikos			Gnostikos			*KG*	
	S1	S2	S3	S1	S2	S3	S1	S2
Mingana Syr. 68	1r–11r***			11v–14v				
BL Add. 17167						8v–13r		18r–56r
BL Add. 14615							23r–60r	
Vat. Syr. 178							22v–205r	
Berlin Syr 37							1r–77r	
BL Add. 14635							12	

* = Prefatory letter to Anatolios only

** = Lacks prefatory letter to Anatolios

*** = assumed to be S1; not discussed in SC 170

THE GNOSTIC TRILOGY IN CONTEXT   19

other earlier writers. The same applies to early Christian writers: references to Clement, Origen, Didymus, Gregory of Nazianzus, Gregory of Nyssa, and others are meant to exemplify, not delimit, Evagrius' engagement with his Christian library. Our cross-references are diagnostic examples, to help readers conduct more exhaustive studies on any particular topic.

As for cross-references to Evagrius' own corpus of writings, we have emphasized primarily passages in the *Gnostic Trilogy* itself. For topics and themes that are of a manageable scope, we provide select cross-references to other writings that seem particularly appropriate. Our references are not exhaustive, but should provide a solid starting point for anyone who wishes to conduct more thorough research.

Because we have been working closely with the Greek and Syriac versions, we have registered a number of philological observations, primarily for those readers who are interested in Greek and Syriac terminology. When we comment on the Syriac translations, we have relied upon comparisons with related Greek texts, such as the New Testament (Peshitta), and the Syriac translations of the *Epistula fidei*, *Letters*, and the *Letter to Melania*.

We have avoided references to secondary studies, with some exceptions for complex topics that require discussion beyond the average length of note we have adopted. Attentive readers will notice that many of our notes reproduce references or observations made by previous commentators, particularly the Guillaumonts and Géhin. We have been selective in these choices as well, and focused on those references best suited for brief annotations. Those who wish to do more systematic study of the *Gnostic Trilogy* should consult other translations and editions, as noted in our bibliography.

Reading the *GT* today

For the first time since late antiquity, this book gathers and presents the entire *Gnostic Trilogy* bound together, complete, and in order, as Evagrius intended. Readers can use this translation of the *Gnostic Trilogy* in several different ways: as an entry point into Evagrius' writings and thought; as a collection, in one volume, of a work crucial to understanding the entire Evagrian corpus; and as a case study in Evagrius' complicated legacy, especially in the Syriac tradition. Our translations of the Syriac will help some to think about and reconstruct the lost Greek; it will help others gain some appreciation for how Syriac speakers encountered Evagrius. Some readers may wish to read from beginning to end. Others may wish to read selectively, for example according to topic or scriptural verse. To that end the index and specific notes will be most useful. Whether this book is read sequentially or selectively, it should be read carefully, and repeatedly.

20 EVAGRIUS OF PONTUS

It is not unusual to need several minutes—or even years—before beginning to understand a single kephalaion.

Accordingly, we have tried to provide a usable, reliable translation of the surviving ancient versions for those who are unfamiliar either with the Greek language of the original texts or with the languages into which they were translated in the late ancient world. For readers with a working knowledge of Greek and Syriac, on the other hand, our translation renders Evagrius' thought, and his precise vocabulary, into a consistent English translation that allows consultation of the critical editions (where they exist) or of the various manuscripts. We have tried to place in the hands of scholarly readers a book that enables them to enter the continuing discussion of this puzzling writer. In translating both the Greek and the Syriac, we have attempted to replicate syntax, word order, and ambiguity. The works are full of Greek technical terms—both philosophical and exegetical—that are conveyed in the Syriac in different ways, sometimes in common words, sometimes in transliteration. We have followed this lead, in that we adopt for *praktikos, gnostikos,* and *theologikē* the English terms *practitioner, knower,* and *theological* (and cognates for other forms of those words), but we include the transliteration of the underlying Greek term in parentheses or in our notes. In this way, readers who can access neither the Greek nor the Syriac can apprehend in a clear English style the underlying mechanisms of the text.

Evagrius used four words that we have decided to transliterate because each is capable of differing meanings in different contexts.

Apatheia, technically "the absence of [emotional] disturbance," and a favorite term in Stoic ethical discourse, is better understood in the context of Evagrius' writings as "absence of *pathē,*" or "calm" as a positive state.

Akēdia, sometimes translated "depression," or "dejection," refers instead to lack of effort, or boredom with a task; but may or may not signal a state of mind.

Thēoria was a case in which the translators could not agree on one meaning; some preferred the traditional "contemplation," but others favored "observation." There are good arguments for each, and the reader can decide which meaning better fits the particular context in which the word appears.

Finally, there is *logos,* a word with an ample set of meanings, ranging from word, to speech, to discourse, to reason, or to the inner structures crucial to any being or object in the cosmos—or outside the cosmos, as when logos means Word of God.

In our translations of the Syriac versions, when we encounter a word that certainly or likely corresponds to one of the Greek words above, we may or may not use the transliteration.

* *

The idea for this translation arose at the 2011 meeting of the Syriac Symposium. In ensuing years the translators gathered to work in several locations: the Institute of Christian Oriental Research at the Catholic University of America; the University of Notre Dame; Dumbarton Oaks, where we held a symposium on "The Legacy of Evagrius"; St. Andrew's Abbey in Valyermo, California; the Cenacle in Chicago, Illinois; and at the Institute for Advanced Study in Princeton, New Jersey. We thank those institutions. We have worked both separately and together, in person and later, during the pandemic, through videoconference between the hours of Matins and Lauds—between Gaithersburg and Washington. The Text Alignment Network version of the parallel Greek, Syriac, and English texts and translations—developed by Joel Kalvesmaki—has been essential. The underlying Greek and Syriac texts for every version translated in this book are available at the *Guide to Evagrius Ponticus*, http://evagriusponticus.net, in both HTML and master TAN-TEI XML versions.

We thank Ian Gerdon, then a student at Notre Dame, for his assistance at our meeting on that campus; Carl Vennerstrom and Nathan Tilley for reading drafts of the work and catching errors; Margaret Mullett, former Director of Byzantine Studies at Dumbarton Oaks; Fr. Sidney Griffith, who encouraged the translation project when it began; and our families for their encouragement and forbearance.

Abbreviations

For abbreviations pertaining to the works of Evagrius or books of scripture, see appendixes.

Arm.   Armenian
BL   British Library
BM   British Museum
BnF   Bibliothèque nationale de France
Comm.   Commentary (Commentaries)
CPG   Clavis Patrum Graecorum
CSCO   Corpus Scriptorum Christianorum Orientalium
Frag.   Fragment (Fragments)
Grk.   Greek
Hom.   Homily (Homilies)
LXX   Septuagint
NETS   New English Translation of the Septuagint
Or.   Oration (Orations)
PG   Patrologia Graeca
Sch.   Scholion (Scholia)
Syr.   Syriac

Praktikos

Preface

pr 1

Greek

Dearest Brother Anatolius,

You first wrote to me from the Holy Mountain, requesting that I, living in Scetis, explain to you the symbolic garment of the monks in Egypt, because you believe it neither accidental nor irrelevant that it is so different from the rest of the vestments of human beings. Therefore, I will declare what we have learned about this from the holy fathers.

Syriac

Because you wrote to me earlier from Zion the holy mountain, while I am settled in Sketis, mountain of Egypt, o brother and beloved Anatolius, and [because] you persuaded me to explain to you the interpretation of the habits of the solitaries in Egypt—for you neither see [that habit] as common nor regard it as being some light matter because there are so many more differences between it and the rest of the clothing of human beings—therefore I write and tell you what we have learned from the holy fathers about this habit.

In the Syriac tradition, the prefatory letter does not accompany the dominant version of the *Praktikos*, S1. Our translation of the letter depends upon S2 (whose version of the *Praktikos* is very fragmentary), from Frankenberg's transcription of BL Add. 17142.

HOLY MOUNTAIN: Is 27.13, Jerusalem. SCETIS: near Wadi Natrun, about 40 km south of Nitria and Kellia, by about 50 km; note S2's addition of "mountain." ANATOLIUS: possibly the wealthy imperial notarius/archon mentioned in the Coptic version of *Lausiac History* 2. Grk. *symbolon* is a perceptible object that signifies, or represents higher realities; cf. pr.4, pr.8; 38, 47, 55, subtitle before 63; *Prayer* preface (symbolic number). This is the first attested description of monastic garb; it influenced later versions, e.g., Cassian, *Institutes* 1.1–11.

Evagrius of Pontus. Robin Darling Young, Joel Kalvesmaki, Columba Stewart, Charles Stang, and Luke Dysinger, Oxford University Press. © Oxford University Press 2024. DOI: 10.1093/oso/9780199997671.003.0002

24 · EVAGRIUS OF PONTUS

Compare elsewhere the description of the high-priestly garments: *KG* 4.48, 56, 66, 29, 72, 75; Clement, *Stromateis* 4, drawn from Philo and Aristobulus (Van den Hoek 1988; Philo, *Life of Moses* 2.109–135, *Questions on Exodus* 2.107–124). But Evagrius also alludes to Origen's interpretation, preserved in a fragment of his *Letter* 2 (Eusebius, *Church History* 6.19.14) and in *Contra Celsum* 5.50 on the legendary visit of Alexander to the Temple, where the schema seems to have the power to induce dreams: "They say also that at that time the high priest put on his sacerdotal vestment and that Alexander bowed before him, saying that he had had a vision of a man in this very clothing (schema) who proclaimed to him that he would bring the whole of Asia under his rule." See also Origen, *Hom. on Ex* 9.4.

pr 2

Greek

The cowl is a symbol of the grace of God our Savior; it shelters their ruling faculty and nourishes their infancy in Christ against those who continually attempt to strike and wound it. Those bearing it on their head powerfully chant, "Unless the Lord builds the house and guards the city, the builder and watchman have labored in vain." Such voices produce humility, and uproot pride, the ancient evil that cast down to earth the Daystar, who rose at dawn.

Syriac

The cowl is a symbol of the grace of God our Savior, that which covers their ruling faculty, hovering over and warming their infancy in Christ and warding off those demons who wish always to smite and strike them and to hinder them from the path of life. Those who cover their heads with this cowl earnestly sing and say in their mind these things: "If the Lord does not build the house and if the Lord does not guard the village, whoever builds and tries to guard [it] labors in vain." Chants like these, then, teach them humility and remove from them pride—which is the first evil [and] which cast down to earth the star rising in the morning.

Ps 126.1; Is 14.12

1 Cor 15.10. GRACE OF GOD OUR SAVIOR: Origen, *First Principles* 2; "infancy in Christ": 1 Cor 3.1 and Origen, *Comm. on Mt* 13.6. THOSE WHO SEEK: demons. RULING FACULTY: the *hēgemonikon*; in Stoic thought, the governing part of the intellect and of the cosmos. For the human *hēgemonikon*: Clement, *Strom.* 2.11; Origen, *Contra Celsum* 4.64; it is accessible to demons from which it needs

protection; Clement, *Strom.* 4.6. CHANT: on singing Psalms: Athanasius, *Letter to Marcellinus* 12. Cf. *Prak.* 40, 69; Sch. 3 on Ps 107.5. Psalmody a preparation for prayer: *Prayer* 82–85. DAYSTAR/Lucifer: Is 14.12; Sch. 2 on Ps 109.3 (the birth of Christ and the morning star is impossible for us to work out more deeply). COWL: Grk. *koukoullion*, hood: Latin *cucullus* (Juvenal, *Sat.* 3.170); Athanasius, *Virg.* 11: worn by female ascetics. Garments for athletic contests: If the hood-wearing monks are engaged in a contest, their opponents are "those who attempt to strike." TEACH (Syr): see also pr.5, pr.8, pr.9; *Gn* 26, and *KG* 2.56 (mind teaches the soul; the soul teaches the body); 4.7 (skills). HUMILITY: 33, 57, 58; *KG* 4.73, 79; 5.5. PRIDE: 14.

pr 3

Greek

Bared hands show the absence of hypocrisy within their society. Vainglory is clever at veiling and overshadowing the virtues, always hunting for the glories that come from human beings and chasing faith away. For, "How can you believe," it is said, "when you receive glory from one another, and you do not seek the glory that comes from the one who alone is God?" The good should be chosen for itself, and nothing else. Unless this is conceded, it would seem that anything that moves us to the accomplishment of the good would be far more honorable than the good itself—and nothing could be more absurd than to think and say that something is better than God!

Syriac

The nakedness of their hands is a sign of the candor of their firm disciplines. For they practice them, not as if they would please people, but for their benefits. For proud thinking hides good disciplines, as it always [seeks] empty praise from people. And "when you desire empty praise from people, you do not seek the glory that is from God alone." For it is fitting that the good be desired not for anything else but on account of the good alone. If this were not so, we would practice the good on account of some cause given to us, a [cause that] would be greater than the good. But it is unjust if we either say or think that a matter is greater than God.

Jn 5.44

BARED HANDS: imply the sleeveless tunic called the *kolobion* (Cassian, *Institutes* 1.4). Hands in general symbolize the practice: Sch. 26 on Eccl 4.5; Sch. 203 on Prv 19.24; Sch. 20 on Ps 118.47. A pair of hands could represent the

26 EVAGRIUS OF PONTUS

practice joined with knowledge: Sch. 5 on Ps 143.7. On hand of the Lord: *KG* 2.12. ABSENCE OF HYPOCRISY, Grk. *anupokriton*, also "without dissimulation, unfeigned": cf. Clement *Who Is the Rich Man* 41, *Paidagogos* 2.10, and (in the fourth century) Gregory of Naz., *Or.* 23.13 and Chrysostom, *Hom. on 2 Tm* 6.1. SOCIETY, Grk. *politeia*: Plato, *Republic* 10 (619c); Eph 2.12; Clement, *Protr.* 10; *Strom.* 1.1; Origen, *Contra Celsum* 8, Eusebius, *Church History* pref. 1, and Gregory of Nazianzus, *Letter* 42. As a description of monastic settlements, Athanasius, *Life of Anthony* 14 and Phil 3.20. GLORY: 1 Thes 2.6 forbidding glory to be sought from anyone but God. THE GOOD CHOSEN FOR ITS OWN SAKE: Aristotle, *Nicomachean Ethics* 1.5 and *Rhetoric* 1.7. VAINGLORY: *Prak.* 13. GLORY THAT IS FROM GOD ALONE: Jn 5.44. MOVEMENT: here toward salvation; as primordial cause of fallen natures, see *KG* 1.50–51.

pr 4

Greek

And again, the cloth wound around their shoulders in the form of a cross is a symbol of the faith in Christ that lifts up the meek, always removes hindrances, and permits them unimpeded activity.

Syriac

The cloak, made for them from a thin rope and wrapped around their shoulders like the cross, is a symbol of the faith of Christ, which cloaks the humble and removes obstacles from their practice, like that cord [that] removes what hinders the work of their hands.

CLOTH: *analabos*: "support, contain" as a *symbolon*. Likely refers to Job 17.9, and is an invented term. The Syriac version adds the description of a thin rope (echoed by "cord" later in the sentence), perhaps reflective of conventions in the fifth century. THE MEEK: on meekness/gentleness: 20; *KG* 4.31; *Monks* 12, 34, 53, 85, 99, 111–112, 133; *Thoughts* 27 (with psalms, quell rage); Sch. 1 on Ps 131.1 (gentleness is the undisturbance of the soul that comes at the deprivation of corruptible pleasures).

pr 5

Greek

The belt constricting their loins cuts off every impurity and proclaims: "It is good for a man not to touch a woman."

Syriac

The belt tied around their kidneys and guarding against their impurities keeps from them every defilement and teaches them, saying: "It is good for a man not to touch a woman."

1 Cor 7.1

BELT: Grk. *zonē*, refers to girding for warfare or athletic contest, since *Iliad* 23.685. On the belt/girdle see *KG* 4.79. CONSTRICTING THEIR LOINS/TIED AROUND THEIR KIDNEYS: cf. Moses and Aaron in Ex 12.11. Cf. Philo, *Questions on Exodus* 1.19, girded loins vs. passions; Origen, Hom. on Luke fragment 80. KIDNEYS as *epithumētikon*: Sch. 14 on Ps 72.21; Sch. 1 on Ps 25.2; Basil, *Hom. on Ps* 7.6; Gregory of Nazianzus, *Or.* 40.40; and Gregory of Nyssa, *Life of Moses* 2.108.

pr 6

Greek

They have the sheepskin, for they "always carry around in the body the death of Jesus." They muzzle all the irrational passions of the body, circumcise the wickedness of the soul by their participation in the good, love poverty, and flee greed, the mother of idolatry.

Syriac

They wear sheepskins—those who "always carry in their bodies the death of Jesus" and [always] kill every evil passion of their soul and body, and who love poverty and flee from greed as from the mother of idolatry.

2 Cor 4.10

Athanasius, *Life of Anthony* 91; cf. cloak of Elijah in 3 Kgdms/1 Kgs 19.13, 19; 4 Kgdms/2 Kgs 2.8, 13 and 14; Heb 11.37. SHEEPSKIN as mortification: Origen, *Hom. on Ex* 13.5; Gregory of Nyssa, *Catechetical Oration* 8.4; *Life of Moses* 2.187. DEATH OF JESUS: 2 Cor 4.10; Cf. Basil, *Longer Rules* 22. CIRCUMCISE: cutting: *Thoughts* 7; cf. Jn 15.2. Circumcision: *KG* 4.12. GREED: Col 3.5. The Syriac version lacks a finite verb.

pr 7

Greek

The staff is "a tree of life to all who hold it, trusty for those who lean on it, as on the Lord."

28 EVAGRIUS OF PONTUS

Syriac

The staff they bear in their hands is the cross "of life for all those who hold it, and [for all] those who trust in it," their good things.

Prv 3.18

STAFF: 4 Kgdms/2 Kgs 4.29, where Elijah's staff raises a child from the dead; also a "tree of life," Gn 2.9; Sch. 32 on Prv 3.18 on Wis 1.4; *KG* 5.69; staff as the practice: Sch. 3 on Ps 22.4 and *Eight Thoughts* 8.23–25; staff as correction: Sch. 319 on Prv 26.3; Sch. 364 on Prv 29.18. Elsewhere: Clement, *Strom.* 2.8.39. The Syriac version of Prv 3.18 differs significantly from the LXX; the translator has followed Evagrius for nearly the entire quotation, but concludes with the last word of the Peshitta version.

pr 8

Greek

The vestment, then, is a symbol epitomizing these things. And these are the words the fathers always say to them: "The fear of God, O child, makes faith firm, and self-restraint in turn makes firm [the fear of God]. Patience and hope make self-restraint steadfast: from these two, *apatheia* is born, and love is its offspring. Love is the door to natural knowledge, which is succeeded by theology and the last blessedness."

Syriac

I have made known to you that all these good things they carry in their souls are revealed through the outer habit. It is also fitting for me to tell you the living words that the fathers said to them—those [words] that always teach them and say, "Children, the fear of God secures faith, and the prohibition of foods again [secures] the fear of God. And hope and faith secure restraint from foods. And from them are born health of the soul, whose offspring is love. Love is the door to knowledge about the natures of creatures, after which proceed divine words that concern firm faith, from which we seek victories and last blessings."

EPITOMIZING: epitome as summary of practical philosophy: Epicurus, *Letter* 1. SUCCEEDED BY: succession of virtues: 81, *Monks* 3–5, 7–9; cf. Rom 5.4–5; Gal 5.22–23; Clement, *Strom.* 2.31.1. OFFSPRING: *Prak.* 81; LOVE: *KG* 1.86; chain from SELF-RESTRAINT to LOVE, *KG* 3.35. The phrase HEALTH OF THE SOUL is a common Syriac translation for Grk. *apatheia*. NATURAL KNOWLEDGE: *KG* 1.71, 88. THEOLOGY: 1. LAST BLESSEDNESS: *Letter on Faith* 21.

pr 9

Greek

For now, let these things we have said concerning the priestly vestment and the teaching of the elders suffice. But concerning the life of practice and the life of knowledge, we will now relate not what we have heard or seen, but only what we have learned from them to tell others. We have divided concisely matters of the life of practice into a hundred chapters and matters about the life of knowledge into fifty chapters in addition to the six hundred. We have concealed some things and obscured others, lest we "give holy things to dogs, or cast pearls before swine." But these things will be clear to those who have set forth on their [the same] path.

Syriac

We have said that which was right for us to say concerning their holy habit and concerning the teaching of the blessed elders, and it is something fitting to say. Now I will tell you, my friend, about [their] disciplines, steadfast and shining, those things that they perfect by practice of the commandments and by true knowledge. It was something that we not only have seen or heard, but have brilliantly learned from them. And so we will teach them to others. But we have written and divided one hundred passages that have been spoken about the practice of the commandments, and fifty that are about knowledge. Some of these we have declared openly, and others we have hidden, so as not to "give something holy to dogs and not to cast pearls before swine." These things will be clear to those who intend to proceed valiantly on this very trail of monastic life.

Mt 7.6

PRIESTLY: The term *hieros*, holy or priestly, usually signifies "belonging to a temple/the Temple": cf. Philo, *Special Laws* 3.40 and 1 Cor 9.13a. See Clement, *Protreptikos* 6, for Moses; Origen, *Comm. on Jn* 2.29 of apostles; of the clergy, Athanasius, *Apology* 2 quoting Constantius; of Christians Eusebius, *Church History* 10.1.2. TEACHING OF THE ELDERS: *didascalia ton gerontōn*, "teaching of the ancients": Ac 5.21 *gerousia*; Clement, *Paidagogos* 3.3, God as *aidios gerōn* and *didaskalos*. BUT CONCERNING: The Greek phrasing of the second sentence balances inside a *men . . . de* clause the chapters relevant to the *Praktikos*

30   EVAGRIUS OF PONTUS

and *Gnostikos*. The six hundred (i.e., of the *KG*) are tersely inserted in an unusual phrase, *pros tois hexakosiois*, "in addition to the six hundred" (absent from the Syriac) as if Anatolius already knew about and had a copy of the *KG*, and the two works being sent were to be added to it. The terse prepositional phrase may imply that the *KG* was circulated (and therefore was written) before the *Praktikos* and *Gnostikos*. It may also explain why so many copies of the *Prak.* and *Gn* are treated as parts of a single treatise (see introduction). HUNDRED: *Prayer* pr. and *KG* 4.42. The enumeration of the chapters is similar to that in the preface of *Prayer*, which divides its 153 kephalaia into numbers described as a square, circle, and triangle. CONCEALED: Mt 7.6 and *Gn* 23–27, 36; cf. Origen, *Contra Celsum* 6.26 (hiding the higher teaching on Gehenna). Concealment: cf. Clement, *Strom.* 1.1.1; Origen, *Comm. on SS*, prologue; Gregory of Nyssa, *Catechetical Oration* 32; Chrysostom, *Hom. on Ps* 49.3. PATH/ TRAIL: The Syriac translator calls it monastic, *ihidayutho*.

Title

Greek

The Praktikos

Syriac

Further, the teaching of the same [Evagrius], as it came to him [and] which is unto the brother monks in the desert, one hundred . . . sayings.

At this point, our translation of the Syriac turns from S2 to S1. The Syriac reader would have begun here, not with the prefatory letter to Anatolius, which survives separately. SAYINGS: *memrē*, which implies a discourse.

Copyist's note

Greek

I ask the brothers who encounter this book and wish to transcribe it not to connect kephalaion to kephalaion, nor to place in the same line the end of one kephalaion and the beginning of one to be written, but each to have each kephalaion begin with its own line just as we have marked them via numerals. For in this way the rule of the kephalaion would be preserved and what is said be made safe. We begin the first kephalaion from what is Christianity, which, in our

PRAKTIKOS   31

defining, we have given to be the teaching of Jesus Christ our Savior, consisting of the practical, the natural, and the theological.

Three Greek manuscripts of the *Praktikos* preserve the copyist's note. There is no reason to doubt that it was written by Evagrius himself. The RULE OF THE KEPHALAION, *kephalaiōdēs . . . kanōn*: rules or conventions that governed the relatively new literary genre.

1

Greek

Christianity is the teaching of Christ our Savior, consisting of the practical, the natural, and the theological.

Syriac

Christianity is the teaching of Christ our Savior constituted from works of virtue and from knowledge of natures and from the true faith owed to God.

CHRISTIANITY: the term *Christianismos* is parallel to *Ioudaismos* and *Hellenismos* and signifies an attitude or intellectual commitment instead of a group. After Ignatius and the *Martyrdom of Polycarp*, the term *Christianismos* was used by Clement, *Strom.* 7.1; Origen, *Contra Celsum* 3.12; Eusebius, *Preparation of the Gospel* 1.5.12; Athanasius, *Against the Arians* 1.1; Basil, *Letter* 199; Epiphanius, *Panarion* 69.1; and Chrysostom, *Hom. on Jn* 28.2. On the tripartite division into *praktikē*, *physikē*, and *theologikē*, see *Letter on Faith* 15 (4.24–25), *Monks* 118–120; *KG* 1.10; Sch. 247 on Prv 22.20; and Sch. 2 on Ps 126.1 (not all who undertake *praktikē* graduate to natural observation and theology); cf. Clement and Origen on the *haplousteroi*, or simpler Christians: Clement, *Paidagogos* 1.7, *nēpioi*; Origen, *Contra Celsum* 3.49. The tripartite schema resembles the Stoic division of philosophy into three parts; Seneca, *Letters to Lucilius* 89.9. Cf. Philo, *Life of Moses* 1.76: the patriarchs Abraham, Isaac, and Jacob symbolize the pedagogical triad: teaching, nature, and moral-ascetical practice. Clement describes an ascent from ethics to the contemplation of nature, and then to theologikē, or metaphysics (*Strom.* 1.28.176.1–2). Origen depicted the three biblical wisdom books of Proverbs, Ecclesiastes, and the Song of Songs as exemplars of the three progressive stages of purification, discernment, and love (*Comm. on SS* 3.16) as the ascent from ethics (moral practice) to physics (nature) and finally to epoptics

32 EVAGRIUS OF PONTUS

(contemplation, "looking toward") (*Comm. on SS* 3.1–3). Cf. the triad of repentance in Anthony, *Letter* 1.

2

Greek

The kingdom of heavens is a soul's *apatheia*, together with true knowledge of beings.

Syriac

The kingdom of heaven is the *apatheia* of the soul with true knowledge of those things that are.

This kephalaion forms a pair with the next. In form, they resemble Evagrius' scholia, many of which define a key word or phrase in scripture in other terms. This kephalaion has very close analogues in the following, which also define something as freedom from passion and knowledge of true beings: Sch. 2 on Ps 1.1 (blessedness); Sch. 11 on Ps 36.11 (abundance of peace); Sch. 10 on Ps 38.14 (liberty of God). See also *KG* 5.30 (≈ Sch. 6b on Ps 134.12); Sch. 20 on Ps 9.37 (his kingdom is the observation of all *aeons* that have come into being and will come into being). Cf. the comparable phrase, observation of beings: *KG* 1.73. KINGDOM OF HEAVEN: *KG* 1.44; 2.77 (S1); 4.30, 40; 6.22; *Letter on Faith* 24, 27, 37. Numerous passages in the New Testament use the phrase "kingdom of heaven" (32) and "kingdom of God" (68). The succession of the kingdom of heaven and the kingdom of God may be likened to the attainment of the promised land, then Zion. See *KG* 1.31; 5.30, 36, 68, 71; 6.47, 49. Freedom from passion, Grk. *apatheia*, is a major topic here and elsewhere: pr.8; 33, 53, 56, 58-60, 64, 67, 81, 83, 91; *Gn* 37; *KG* 1.37 (spiritual sense : rational soul :: apatheia : soul), 70, 81; 5.82, 86; *Reflections* 16. For apatheia, see Clement, *Strom.* 6.9 and elsewhere; Aristotle, *Physics* 217, *Metaphysics* 1046.13, Epicurus, *Letter* 1. In Clement's system, *metriopatheia*, regulation of the passions, yields to *apatheia*, the removal of the passions, in the true *gnōstikos*; *Strom.* 7.84.2, 7.13.3. Cf. Porphyry, *Launching Points to the Intelligibles* 7. True gnosis vs. false gnosis: *Monks* 43.

3

Greek

The kingdom of God is knowledge of the Holy Trinity coextensive with the structure of the mind and surpassing its incorruptibility.

Syriac

The kingdom of God is knowledge of the glorious Trinity, considered analogous to the power of the mind, because it is more exalted than its incorruptibility.

> This kephalaion forms a pair with the preceding one. The KINGDOM OF GOD as a state beyond apatheia: *KG* 4.23; 5.30 (≈ Sch. 6b on Ps 134.12); *Virgin* 55. Cf. Mt 6.33; Origen, *Contra Celsum* 3.40.21; Gregory of Nazianzus, *Or.* 40.45 and *Poem* 1.2.34.258. KNOWLEDGE OF THE TRINITY: *KG* 1.52, 70; 2.16; 3.6, 33, 41; 6.29. See also *KG* 1.77 on knowledge of the unity. INCORRUPTIBILITY and KNOWLEDGE OF THE TRINITY: *KG* 3.33; 4.49. COEXTENSIVE WITH THE STRUCTURE, Grk. *symparekteinomenē tē sustasei* (also composition): *KG* 1.54; 4.35, 49; Sch. 123 on Prv 10.30 (an *aiōn* coextensive with the *sustasei* of its life). This technical phrase is first attested in Basil of Caesarea, *Against Eunomius* 5 (PG 29:560): "Time is the interval coextensive with the constitution of the world, in which all movement is measured, whether of stars or animals or of anything moved at all" (χρόνος ἐστὶ τὸ συμπαρεκτεινόμενον τῇ συστάσει τοῦ κόσμου διάστημα, ἐν ᾧ πᾶσα παραμετρεῖται κίνησις, εἴτε ἀστέρων εἴτε ζῴων, εἴτε οὑτινοσοῦν τῶν κινουμένων;). The saying is credited to Evagrius in the Definitions collection: Furrer-Pilliod ed., 210, A.χ.25. INCORRUPTIBILITY: *KG* 3.33.

4

Greek

Whatever someone loves, this he seeks in every way. And what he seeks, this also he struggles to obtain. And while desire initiates all pleasure, sensation begets desire. Thus what has no part in sensation is free from passion.

Syriac

That thing that someone loves, he desires. And what he desires he also works to attain, that through toil it might be his. For every pleasure that exists has its origin in desire, and sensation is a begetter of desire. Anything without sensation is also free from the passions.

> Cf. *Prayer* 42: prayer "with *aisthēsis*" recommended, "with brothers or alone." WHATEVER SOMEONE LOVES: Plato, *Phaedrus* 237d. On senses and sense perception: *KG* 1.34. WHAT HAS NO PART IN SENSATION, Grk. *aisthēseos amoiron*: a technical phrase for insensible objects, perhaps going back to Democritus, frag. 77 (concerning number, *arithmos*). See Themistius, *Paraph. de anima* 5.3:123.9 (plants and stars); Greg. Nyssa, *Hom. on SS* 6:221.3 (characteristic of the dead).

34 EVAGRIUS OF PONTUS

5

Greek

Against the anchorites, the demons wrestle naked, but against those striving for virtue in monasteries or fellowships, they deploy the more careless of the brothers. The second battle is much lighter than the first, since it is impossible to find people on earth more bitter than the demons, or able to undertake all their incessant villainy.

Syriac

The demons wrestle with the solitaries in solitary manner, with no intermediary. But as for those who are in the assembly of the community, perfecting the practice of virtue, the [demons] agitate against the weaker brothers. Of the two, the latter battle is much less intense than the former, because one cannot find upon the earth humans more bitter than demons, or who will fully undertake all their wickedness.

> Conflict with Satan and demons: Mt 4.1–11, temptation of Jesus in the wilderness, and in numerous scenes of exorcisms, e.g., Mt 11.18, 7.22, 9.34, and parallels; demonic power Jn 10.1, Rev 16.14; 1 Cor 10.20ff.; Jas 2.19. They are objects of worship among the nations: Dt 32.17. Final battle with "the devil and Satan," Rev 20.1–10. A DEMON is a rational being, not innately evil (*KG* 4.59), that succumbed to anger and fell from service to God (*KG* 3.34). Demons consist largely of air (*KG* 1.68; 4.37) and interact with the human world (*KG* 3.78) by imitating colors and other bodily attributes (*KG* 5.18). They are cold (*KG* 6.25-26; *Antirr.* 4.22) and have the power of observation (*KG* 6.2), but not of the angelic realm (*KG* 6.69). Some humans can detect them via odor (*KG* 5.78). On the relationship between demons and humans: *KG* 1.22, 57, 68; 2.14; 3.4, 50, 76, 78; 4.13; 5.11; 6.69, as well as various kephalaia throughout *Prak*. Legitimate hatred of demons, *KG* 5.47; *Thoughts* 19; cf. Sch. 50 on Ps 118.113; Sch. 57 on Ps 118.128. Porphyry, *On Abstinence* 2.39: demons convince people that the divine is the source of not only good but confusion and disorder. Battles with demons: 21, 34, 48, 54, 58, 63, 73, 83; *Gn.* 25, 44; *KG* 3.41; cf. *Prak.* 24 & 76; *Antirr.* 4.22. Remijsen 2015. The Syr. for SOLITARY, *ihidi'*, is generally translated elsewhere as "monk." NAKED: alludes to athletes in the gymnasium, and refers to pr.3 (naked hands of the monk). IN SOLITARY MANNER (Syr.): one by one. ANCHORITES . . . IN MONASTERIES

OR FELLOWSHIPS, Grk. *Anachōrētais . . . koinobiois ē synodiais*: the former, "withdrawn from the world," in Origen, *Hom. on Jer* 14.16; later, solitary ascetics: Athanasius, *Life of Anthony* 7; Epiphanius, *Panarion* 64.4 and 70.1; the latter a community of monks, cf. Basil, *Letter* 23 and *Longer Rules* 1.3, 2.1. The distinction between monasteries or fellowships may reflect a distinction between larger and smaller communities. FIND . . . ON EARTH: cf. Lk 18.8. BITTER: *Antirr.* pr.4; *Eulogius* 22. Bitterness and anger: Aristotle, *Eudaemonian Ethics* 2.3 and *Nicomachean Ethics* 4.11.

Subtitle 1

Greek

Concerning the Eight Thoughts

Syriac

Concerning the Eight Thoughts

This is the first of several subtitles marking a block of thematically related kephalaia.

6

Greek

Eight in all are the most generic thoughts; in them every thought is encompassed. The first is that of gluttony, and with it, the thought of sexual lust; the third is the love of money; the fourth, of sadness; the fifth, of anger; the sixth, of *akēdia*; the seventh, of vainglory; the eighth, of pride. It is not up to us whether these thoughts are able to trouble the soul or not trouble it; but whether they linger or do not linger, and whether they move the passions or do not move them, is up to us.

Syriac

There are eight types of evil thoughts, in which every thought of the passions is reckoned. First, gluttony; second, sexual lust; third, love of money; fourth, sadness;

36   EVAGRIUS OF PONTUS

fifth, rage; sixth, listlessness; seventh, vainglory; eighth, pride. All these, whether they trouble the soul or do not trouble [it] is not up to us. Whether they linger or do not linger, or whether they agitate the passions or they do not agitate, is up to us.

EIGHT . . . GENERIC passions: Clement, *Paidagogos* 1.101.1; Philo, *Special Laws* 1.59.

Movement: below, 12, 37, 38, 43, 51, 71, 89. The canonical eight *logismoi* on occasion appear in slightly different forms or order. See Guillaumont 1971, 1:90–93. For ease of reference, the terms for the eight passions are as follows:

Greek	Syriac	English
gastrimargia	*laʿbuthā*	gluttony
porneia	*zāniuthā*	sexual lust
philargyria	*rehmat kespā*	love of money
lypē	*ʿaqthā*	sadness
orgē	*rugzā* or *rigzā*	anger
akēdia	*maʾinuthā*	akēdia
kenodoxia	*šubḥā sriqā*	vainglory
hyperēphania	*rmúthā*	pride

Of these, only sexual lust, sadness, and anger are mentioned explicitly in the *Gnostikos*, and sexual lust, anger, and vainglory in the *KG* (references below). TROUBLE . . . MOVE: Zeno, *On the Passions*, passim. The movement of thoughts: *Letter* 39.3 (Grk. fragment): "the thoughts of sense-perceptible matters lingers in us." The role of the mind in the duration of thoughts, UP TO US: Epictetus, *Manual* 1.2.

7

Greek

The thought of gluttony suggests to the monk a rapid fall from the discipline. It depicts stomach, liver, spleen, acute swelling, chronic sickness, lack of supplies, and scarcity of physicians. It often leads him to recall some brothers who have fallen into these maladies. Sometimes it even prompts those who have suffered them to visit those practicing self-restraint and to drone on about their misfortunes, and how such things resulted from their discipline.

Syriac

The thought of gluttony proposes to the solitary a sudden fall from the discipline, as it frequently pictures before his eyes the sickness of the stomach, and of the liver, and of the spleen, and of acute swelling, and of lengthy illnesses, and of the lack of a doctor and necessities, and of a corpse—and remembering brothers who have fallen into these maladies. But sometimes these very things happen to them. [The thought] makes them go to those ascetics, to tell them their sufferings, as [if] such things happened from the ascetic life.

> GLUTTONY: Ti 1.12; *Gn.* 31; *Antirr.* 1; *Eight Thoughts* 1–3; *Prayer* 134. Clement, *Paidagogos* 2.1. SUGGESTS, Grk. *hypoballei*: an *aisthēsis* "whispers" Epicurus, *Letter* 1.2; cf. below, 9, 22; angelic suggestion 24. ACUTE SWELLING: hydropsia (dropsy) or edema. Palladius, *Lausiac History* 38.13: Evagrius himself suffered stomach ailments.

8

Greek

The demon of sexual lust compels [the monk] to desire a variety of bodies. It violently attacks those practicing self-restraint so that they will give up, as if accomplishing nothing. And defiling the soul, it makes it stoop to these kinds of actions: to make it say and then to hear certain words, as if the deed were actually visible and present.

Syriac

For the thought of fornication compels us to desire various bodies, and it rises more strongly against ascetics so that they are unable to complete anything. They desist from their labors when they have defiled the soul, inclining it to a vile act and forcing it to say and hear words, as if that act were nearby and visible.

> SEXUAL LUST, Grk. *porneia*: Mt 6.18, 1 Cor 6.18, 10.18, 1 Thes 4.3, Rev 19.2; as hostility to God, Rev 19.2. *Gn.* 20; *KG* 1.66, 84; *Antirr.* 2; *Eight Thoughts* 4–6. VARIETY OF BODIES, Grk. *somatōn . . . diaphorōn*: *Antirr.* 2.21; Origen, *On Prayer* 28. STOOP, to bend down, Grk. *katakamptei*: *Eulogius* 19. THESE [unmentionable] ACTIONS; cf. 46.

38   EVAGRIUS OF PONTUS

9

Greek

The love of money suggests a long old age and hands unable to work; imminent famines and the diseases that follow; as well as the bitterness of poverty and the shame of having to receive [life's] necessities from others.

Syriac

Love of money suggests a long old age with the weakness of the hands for work, and hungers that will be, and illnesses, and the bitterness of poverty, and the disgrace of a man's receiving something necessary to him from others.

> LOVE OF MONEY, avarice, Grk. *philargyria*. An avaricious person, Lk 16.14, 2 Tm 3.2; avarice, 1 Tm 6.10; *Antirr.* 3; *Eight Thoughts* 7–8; *Letter* 16.4; 25.4; 39.3; 52.3, 6; Plato, *Republic* 347b. SHAME, Grk. *eponeidiston*: Plato, *Laws* 633e. Reflects Evagrius' audience as one that has previously been wealthy; poverty is bitter, and receiving charity is a disgrace. Cf. *Foundations* 4. *Antirr.* 3.2.

10

Greek

Sadness sometimes occurs because of a deprivation of the desires, and sometimes also accompanies anger. In the case of the deprivation of desires, it occurs in this way: certain thoughts first lead the soul toward memory of home and parents and its previous way of life. And when they see it not resisting, but following, and slipping into pleasures of thought, then they take and plunge it into sadness, for these former things are gone and cannot be regained, because of the present way of life. Then the miserable soul, to the degree that it was dissipated by the first set of thoughts, just so far is it drawn in to be humbled by the second set.

Syriac

Sadness is when there is a deprivation of desires, but sometimes it will accompany rage. Through deprivation of desires the thoughts present to the soul a memory of a house, and family, and way of life. [. . . not] standing against them, but seeing that the [soul] has gone after them and is dissipated in the desires of its understanding, [the thoughts] take [the soul] and baptize it in sadness, since these former things are no more and will not be found, because of the form of

PRAKTIKOS 39

[the monk's] life. And the soul, as if it had been leveled by the pleasure of these previous thoughts, so also by these battles it is humbled and brought low.

SADNESS, sorrow, Grk. *lupē*: 2 Cor 2.1,7; Jn 16.6; *Prak.* 13, 14, 19, 22, 25; *Gn.* 10, 28; *Antirr.* 4; *Eight Thoughts* 11–12; *Eulogius* 7; frustration of desires, *Prak.* 19. MISERABLE SOUL: *KG* 3.79. The translation for Syriac FORM represents Grk. *schēma*. DISSIPATED BY . . . DRAWN IN, Grk. *diechuthē . . . sunestalē*: two contrasting verbs; see Athanasius, *Life of Anthony* 14. OF THOUGHTS, Grk. *kata dianoian*. The *dianoia* was generally regarded as the understanding, a mental faculty higher than the sense perceptions but lower than the mind. See 23, 48.

11

Greek

Rage is the speediest passion. It is said to be a boiling up and movement of the angry part against one who has injured, or is thought to have. It makes the soul savage all day long, but especially during prayers it seizes the mind, reflecting back the face of the person who has caused distress. Sometimes it lingers and is transformed into wrath, causing disturbances at night; weakness and pallor of the body; and attacks from poisonous beasts. These four that follow wrath may be found accompanying many other thoughts.

Syriac

Rage is a sharp passion. For it is called a boiling of anger and a movement against the one who wronged him, or was thought to have wronged him. All day long it hardens his soul and makes it savage, and especially in the moment of prayer it seizes his mind, as one who sets before him the face of him who grieves him. Sometimes it lingers and turns him to wrath and it brings him disturbances in the night, and wastes his body and [gives] him a detestable color, and casts upon him a disease of flowing vomit; but these four things occur after rage. One finds that they follow many thoughts.

RAGE, wrath, Grk. *orgē*: Eph 4.31, Col 3.8, 1 Tm 2.8; divine wrath Ps 93.11 and Heb 3.11, 4.3; Rom 1.18, and judgment Lk 21.23, etc. Anger: *Gn.* 4, 5, 10, 45; *KG* 4.47; 6.63; *Antirr.* 5; *Eight Thoughts* 9–10; *Eulogius* 6, 9, 18; *Thoughts* 19, 42; *Reflections* 23, 24. As movement in the soul and mind, see *Gn.* 5 (easily moved to anger); *Thoughts* 16, 24, 25, 34; cf. *Reflections* 9: "The mind engaged in contemplation is like a dog, for through the movement of the irascible part it chases away all impassioned thoughts." IT IS SAID: Aristotle, *On the Soul* 1.1.403;

40 EVAGRIUS OF PONTUS

Seneca, *On Anger* 2.18; Gregory of Nazianzus, *Poems* 2.25.35–40. Wrath and sadness linked: *Prak.* 22, 23. Sadness comes before wrath (Prv 15.1); *Reflections* 43; wrath as desired antidote for sadness *Antirr.* 5.32. Images forming at the time of prayer, due to anger, 23; *Thoughts* 27; *On Prayer* 45. Cf. *Antirr.* 5.6; *Thoughts* 2. Dreams and fear at night springing from the angering part: *Antirr.* 5.12 and *Eight Thoughts* 10. Sadness is placed after anger: *Antirr.* 5 and 8; *Thoughts* 9–10. Further discussion at 20.

12

Greek

The demon of *akēdia*, also called the "noonday demon," is the most burdensome of all the demons. It attacks the monk at around the fourth hour, and circles his soul until the eighth hour. First, it makes the sun seem to move slowly or even not at all, so that the day seems to be fifty hours long. Next, it makes him keep looking out of the windows and darting out of the cell to peer intently at the sun, [considering] how long it is to the ninth hour, and then to look around in case any of the brothers might be present. Then it suggests hatred for the place, his own life, and manual labor, and makes him think that love has disappeared from among the brothers and that there is no one to comfort him. And if someone has recently grieved the monk over the course of these days, this too the demon adds to increase his hatred. It also leads him into a desire for other places, in which he can easily find what he needs and switch to an easier, more convenient trade. And the demon adds that pleasing the Lord is not a matter of place; after all, it is said that the divine is to be worshipped everywhere. [The demon] joins to these things the memory of his family and his former way of life, and depicts for him a long lifespan, setting before his eyes the difficulties of the discipline. And so it deploys, as they say, every possible mechanism so that the monk abandons his cell and flees the stadium. No other demon succeeds this demon right away: after the contest follow a peaceful state and unspeakable joy.

Syriac

The demon of listlessness, he who also is called "midday," is harsher than all the other demons. It opposes the solitary from the fourth hour and encircles his soul until the eighth hour. And it proposes to him that the sun either has not been moved from its place or resists being moved. And the day seems to him to be fifty hours long. And it makes him look out the window every hour and compels him, that also he will leave his cell and his eyes will search for the sun and he will

PRAKTIKOS 41

consider how many hours away from nine. And that he will look here and there lest someone of the brothers might come. And again it puts hate on him, hate for the place, and for the habitation, and manual labor; that love has ceased among the brothers, there is no consolation. Then if it happens among them in these days that a brother should grieve a solitary, this very demon accomplishes in him an increase of hatred. For it produces in him a desire for other places in which his need is easily filled and he might cultivate a craft easier and more profitable than this. And it shows him that a man does not please God in one place, for indeed God is worshipped in every place. For it proposes these things to him along with the memory of his beloved family members and of his previous ways of life, and it sets before his eyes long life and the labors of the continent life. And it puts in motion every strategem against the solitary, that he will leave his cell, and flee from his contest. But another demon does not follow this one right away; but rest that is full of peace and unutterable joy after this contest, filling his soul.

Ps 90.6; cf. Jn 4.21–24

AKĒDIA, literally, the inclination to cease to work; cf. Sch. 13 on Ps 118.28: " 'My soul has slumbered through *akēdia*: strengthen me in your words': *akēdia* is a long-lasting movement in it of anger and desire: anger at those present and desire for those not present. Drowsiness is the carelessness of the rational soul for the virtues and for the knowledge of God; sleep is the willing separation of the rational soul from true (ontos) life. Wherefore the wise Solomon exhorts neither to give sleep to the eyes, nor to let the eyelids become drowsy (Prv 6.4)." See also Sch. 70 on Prv 6.4. *Akēdia* in scripture: Ps 60.3; 101.1; 118.28; Sir 22.13; 29.5; Is 61.3; Bar 3.1; Dn 7.15. NOONDAY DEMON: below, 36; Ps 90.6 and Sch. 6.2 on Ps 90.6; Sch. 3 on Ps 139.6. Fourth to eighth hour: from 10 a.m. to 2 p.m. Eyes looking toward windows [or doors, in some ms witnesses]: *Eight Thoughts* 6.14. Aversion to the place the monk lives: *Antirr.* 6.26. Prompts accusations among monks: *Antirr.* 6.30. Desire for other places: *Antirr.* 6.33; change of place advisable: *Antirr.* 6.1. Remembrance of kin: *Antirr.* 6.7; over-long life, *Antirr.* 6.25; to flee the cell and leave the [wrestling] match, *Antirr.* 6.52. On memory, see *Prak.* 7, 10, 12, 34, 36, 71, 97; *Gn.* 14; *KG* 4.73; 5.61. Demon following upon the first: Sch. 1 on Ps 139.3. STATE: *katastasis*: 23, 43, 57; *KG* 4.38 (angelic), 46 (human); and in numerous other works, e.g., *Thoughts* 9, 11, 39; *On Prayer* 2, 3, 27, 48, 52, 53. The frequency with which Evagrius uses the term is to be contrasted with the complete absence of the derivative term *apokatastasis*, so prominent in Clement, Origen, Eusebius, Didymus the Blind, and Gregory of Nyssa—a term that led to the condemnation of Origen, Didymus, and Evagrius in the sixth century. On state as Grk. *hexis* see *KG* 6.21. UNSPEAKABLE JOY: 1 Pt 1.8.

42 EVAGRIUS OF PONTUS

13

Greek

The thought of vainglory is most subtle, and it easily stands alongside the virtuous, wishing to publicize their contests and to chase the praise that comes from people. It fabricates shrieking demons and healed women and a crowd of people touching his garments. It predicts he will then gain the priesthood, and makes people appear at his gates seeking to lead him away captive, as if he were unwilling. Then, raising him high with empty hopes, it flies away and abandons him to be tempted either by the demon of pride or by that of sadness, which also brings to him thoughts contrary to his hopes. Sometimes it also hands him over to the demon of sexual lust—this man who, just a moment before, was taken captive to be a holy priest!

Syriac

The thought of vainglory is subtle, and it easily rises against those who are becoming perfect, to bring to the fore their contests to seek out glory from people. As it creates before their eyes: demons wailing among them, a woman whom they heal, a great people squeezing together to approach his garments, and a priesthood predicted for him, setting at his gate many who are seeking him, and as he who as if unpersuaded in a bond it elevates him and thus enchained, he submits himself, against his will. And thus as [the thought] elevates him with an empty hope, departing from his side it abandons him to the demon of pride, who will tempt him further to the demon of sadness, who brings to him thoughts contrary to his first hope. There is another time when it betrays him to the demon of sexual lust—he who a little before was a saint led bound to the priesthood.

cf. 1 Thes 2.6

A revised version of part of this keph. is at *Thoughts* 21. VAINGLORY, Grk. *kenodoxia*: 13, 58; *KG* 5.86; *Antirr.* 7; *Eight Thoughts* 7, 8, 15–16; *Prayer* 73; *Eulogius* 8, 21, 23, 28; *Vices* 7; *Thoughts* 14, 15, 21, 28; *Reflections* 57; *Letter* 8.1; 9; 17.3. To publish your battles: *Antirr.* 7; buying human glory: 1 Thes 2.6; Jn 5; Clement, *Paid.* 2.1; *gnōstikos* is free of it, Clement, *Strom.* 7.13; Origen, *Comm. on Jn* 28.13; Gregory of Naz., *Or.* 2.51; Athanasius, *Life of Anthony* 55; fantasy of healing: *Antirr.* 7.35, 42; fantasy of priesthood: *Antirr.* 7.8, 26. PRIESTHOOD, Grk. *hierosynē*: in the fourth century, *hieros* generally signifies *episkopos* (bishop) as the chief liturgical official. Evagrius speaks of bishops both because of terminology (cf. John Chrysostom, *On the Priesthood*, meaning on the episcopacy) and because of the context: the bishop as an admired *euergetēs* (benefactor, doer of good).

14

Greek

The demon of pride is for the soul an agent of the harshest kind of fall. For it urges it not to profess God as its help, and to reckon itself as responsible for its own upright deeds, and to look down on the brothers as stupid, because not all of them recognize this about it. Anger and sadness dog [the soul], as does the ultimate evil: derangement, madness, and a hallucination of a crowd of demons in the air.

Syriac

The demon of pride is the cause of a harsh fall for a soul, persuading it that the confession of God was not its help, but that the soul itself was the cause for perfection, and that it is made higher than the brothers, as over fools, because all of them are not convinced of this. After this follow anger, sadness, and the final evil: a concealment of the mind, madness, and an assembly of demons seen in the air.

PRIDE, Grk. *hyperēphania*: Mk 7.22 and Prv 3.34; Plato, *Symp.* 219c; Sch. 39 on Prv 3.34 (Christ opposes his humility to pride); Sch. 102 on Prv 8.13; Sch. 23 on Eccl 4.1; *Antirr.* 8; *Eight Thoughts* 17; *Monks* 61–62; *Thoughts* 1, 14, 18, 21, 23; *Reflections* 40, 44, 49, 57; *Exh. Monks* 1.6. DERANGEMENT, Grk. *ekstasis*: defined in *Thirty-Three Chapters* 9: "An ekstasis is the relapse into evil of the rational soul after virtue and the knowledge of God," representing the fall from the human *katastasis* into a lower state resulting from pride, with symptoms of insanity, described in *Thoughts* 21, 23. For the neutral sense, see Gn 2.21, 15.12, Ac 22.17 (Paul) and 10.10 (Peter). Galen, *Protreptikos* 29.462, defined as "a mania of short duration." Plotinus, *Enn.* 6.9.11; Origen, *Contra Celsum* 7.3.39. Cf. Athanasius, *Life of Anthony* 4.34; Palladius, *Lausiac History* 25 and 26. An *ekstasis* is a type of *katastasis*, on which see 12 above.

Subtitle 2

Greek

Against the Eight Thoughts

44 EVAGRIUS OF PONTUS

Syriac

Again, against These Eight Thoughts, by Evagrius.

This section (through 33) discusses remedies for the eight thoughts.

15

Greek

Reading, vigils, and prayer stabilize the wandering mind. Hunger, toil, and withdrawal quench flaming desire. The singing of Psalms, patient endurance, and mercy check seething anger. And these things are done at the proper time and in proper measure. What is done without measure or at the wrong moment does not last long, and what does not last long is more harmful than useful.

Syriac

The mind that wanders is brought together by reading, and by vigil, and by prayer. And again, desire that burns: is withered by hunger, toil, and withdrawal. Singing, longsuffering, and mercy calm the madness of anger. These things will be in proper times and measures, for things done without measure last for a short time. These are harmful, and not beneficial.

> This kephalaion follows the tripartite structure of the soul (see 89). Reading scripture: cf. parallel in *Monks* 1.3; *Eulogius* 19. WANDERING MIND: *KG* 1.85; *Thoughts* 26; and *Letter* 43; on the wandering demon, *Thoughts* 9. TOIL, Grk. *kopos*: numerous uses to describe labor: 1 Thes 1.3; Rev 2.2 and 14.13; 2 Cor 10.15, 11.27, etc. FLAMING DESIRE: 22, 23; *Eulogius* 32; cf. inflamed soul: *Prak.* 39. Psalmody: 71, *Monks* 98; Origen, *Hom. on Josh* 20.1; *Hom. on Nm* 18.3; Basil of Caesarea, *Hom. on Psalms* 1.2. Gregory, *Poem* 2.2.8.273. Psalmody is a means of engaging in the "richly-varied contemplation of nature" (*Prayer* 86; Sch. 8 on Psalm 44.10; Sch. 1 on Psalm 122.1; cf. Eph 3.9–10), to which the soul responds in "hymnody with glorification" (Sch. 4. on Ps 39.4). Proper time, measure: *Letter on Faith* 40. Short-lived practice damaging: Plutarch, *De communibus notitiis adversus Stoicos* 8. Remedies: *Gn.* 47 (ascribed to Serapion); *Virgin* 40-41; *Thoughts* 27; *Prayer* 83. MERCY: *KG* 1.40; divine mercy: *KG* 1.73.

16

Greek

When our soul covets a variety of foods, let it then be reduced to bread and water in order that it might become grateful even for a simple morsel. Surfeit desires various dishes, but hunger considers even a surfeit of bread to be blessedness.

Syriac

But when our soul desires a variety of foods, then it should be restrained by bread and water, so that it will give thanks even for simple bread—for fullness desires various foods, but hunger thinks the surfeit of bread is blessedness.

SOUL COVETS A VARIETY OF FOODS: *Antirrhetikos* 1; *Thoughts* 25. Food giving rise to shameful fantasies: *Monks* 11; *Thoughts* 1, 3, 6, 13, 21 (associated with the *ekstasis* of a bishop); *Maxims 1* 18. SURFEIT, "satiety," Grk. *koros*: 94 (sleep); *Eulogius* 18.26; *Eight Thoughts* 1.17, 33; 2.4, 11–12; *Thoughts* 35, 43.

17

Greek

Lack of water contributes to temperance. Let the three hundred Israelites persuade you; with Gideon they defeated Midian.

Syriac

The lack of water is a great help for chastity. Let Gideon's Israelites persuade you—the three hundred who subdued Midian.

cf. Jgs 7.5–7

Continence arising from restriction of water: Philo, *Special Laws* 310 and Hippocrates, *On Generation* 1. Continence opposed to gluttony: Sch. 1 on Ps 45.2; *Monks* 102; *History of the Monks of Egypt*, Evagrius. PERSUADE YOU: 26; *KG* 1.40 (rich man in Hades persuades me).

46 EVAGRIUS OF PONTUS

18

Greek

Just as it is impossible for life and death to meet at the same time in the same person, so love cannot coexist with wealth in anyone. For love is destructive not only of wealth, but even of our transient life itself.

Syriac

Just as it is impossible for life and death to last in a human being person at the same time, so it is impossible for love and money. For love destroys not only wealth, but also life—this short one.

> Cf. *Thoughts* 18, where death with Christ leads to living near him (Rom 6.8); love leads to knowledge. Cf. *KG* 4.62. Love does not coexist with wealth: Sch. 28 on Eccl 4.8, "God, king of the world created by him, metes out affliction to those who have preferred greed and the emptiness of this life to the knowledge of Christ...." On wealth, cf. 99, ascribed to "one of the elders"; *KG* 1.40. "As it is impossible," Grk. *tōn ouk endechomenōn*, Aristotelian logical vocabulary for possible or impossible premises of an argument (e.g., *Prior Analyt.* 1.3), used again at 44, 58; *Gn.* 33; *Disc.* 19. DESTRUCTIVE, Grk. *anairetikē*, also an Aristotelian term, e.g., *Eudaemonian Ethics* 1229a40: "fear . . . a nature destructive of life."

19

Greek

The one who flees all worldly pleasures is a tower unapproachable by the demon of sadness, for sadness is the privation of pleasure, whether present or anticipated. It is impossible to drive away this enemy when we have a passionate attachment to one of these earthly things, for it lays its trap and produces sadness wherever it sees us especially inclined.

Syriac

The one who flees from the pleasures of the world is a strong tower; the demon of sadness cannot approach it. For sadness is the lack of pleasures, either near or expected. It is impossible to drive away this enemy when we have a passion toward one of these earthly things, for he hides a trap and creates sadness in us when he sees that we are inclined to attachment.

Purgos, TOWER: Lk 13.4, Mt 21.33, 12.1; *KG* 4.53; cf. Gregory of Nyssa, *Hom. on SS* 7. Sadness eliminated by flight from world's pleasures: Cf. 10; *Eight Thoughts* 11, 12. TRAP, Grk. *pagis:* 1 Tm 6.9, "trap of the devil"; 1 Tm 3.9; 2 Tm 2.26. See Sch. 3 on Ps 123.7, distinguishing the effective (*kat' energeian*) trap warned about in the Old Testament against the mental (*kata dianoian*) one in the New.

20

Greek

Rage and hatred increase anger; mercy and gentleness decrease its very existence.

Syriac

Rage and hatred increase anger. Compassion and sweetness diminish it, when it is present.

This kephalaion begins a series through 26 dealing with wrath, *thymos,* which moves human beings toward the state of being a demon, i.e., a rational being in which wrath predominates. RAGE . . . HATRED, Grk. *orgē . . . misos:* the pair is contrasted at 76 to mercy and love. Cf. *Prak.* 15 (pity remedies wrath); *KG* 1.68, 3.34, and 5.11; *Letter* 56, quoting Ps 57.5: "their wrath resembles the serpent." Compare Stoic teaching about controlling anger: Epictetus, *Discourses* 2.18.1. Anger is the dominant characteristic of demons: 73; *KG* 3.34; Sch. 60 on Prv 5.9; Sch. 25 on Ps 17.49; Sch. 9 on Ps 73.19. Anger darkens: 23, 24; it blinds: 62; *Gn.* 5; *KG* 4.47; 5.27; 6.63; *Thoughts* 32; Sch. 4 on Ps 6.8 ("nothing so blinds the mind as the temper disturbed," similar at Sch. 6 on Ps 30.9 and Sch. 7 on Ps 30.10). Wrath's darkening of the intellect and soiling its sacrifice of prayer (Mt 5.24): *Prayer* 21, 27, etc.; *Virgin* 6; *Thoughts* 24. On the disturbed angry part: 21–22 and note at *KG* 5.27. Further references at 11.

21

Greek

"Let not the sun go down on our anger," lest the demons, rising up by night, terrify the soul, and make the mind more cowardly for the battle on the coming day. For terrifying apparitions come about naturally from the disturbance of the angry part, and nothing makes the mind more likely to desert the battle than a disturbed angry part.

48 EVAGRIUS OF PONTUS

Syriac

"Do not let the sun set on your anger," lest the demons come at night and frighten your soul, and terrify your mind, and on the next day forcefully approach to fight it—for fearsome images will come about from the turmoil of anger. For there is nothing that makes our mind to retreat from its rank like anger stirred up.

> Eph 4.26
> Athanasius, *Life of Anthony* 55; Basil, *Letter* 22.3, on the duration of wrath during the night; Gregory of Nazianzus, *Poem* 2.25.348. On anger and dreams cf. Plato, *Republic* 9.572a–b. On the disturbed, blind mind see previous kephalaion.

22

Greek

When the angry part of our soul seizes on some pretext and becomes disturbed, then too, the demons suggest to us that withdrawal (*anachōrēsis*) is good, to prevent us from eliminating the causes of the sadness and freeing ourselves from the disturbance. But when the desiring part is enflamed, then they play on our sociability, calling us grim and uncivilized in order to make us desire and encounter bodies. In either case we should not obey them, but do the opposite.

Syriac

But when from some petty cause the angry part of the soul will be disturbed, then also the demons propose to us that it would be useful to get away from here, lest the cause of our grief be resolved and we free our soul from disturbance. But when the desiring part heats up, then they make us bold, and they call us hard and savage. Then they make us desire bodies, and bodies will find us. To flee these is impossible without doing the opposite.

> This kephalaion, with the next two, contrasts the angry part of the soul with the desiring part. Jn 12.17, "now my soul is troubled." DISTURBED soul: see previous two kephalaia. One of the tricks of the demons: to suggest isolation, *anachōresis*, as a cure for wrath. Cf. *Eulogius* 5; *Thoughts* 22. *Philanthropos*: as the katastasis of God, cf. Clement *Paid.* 1.8, or characteristic of the Logos, *Paidagogos* 1.1, 1.7; of Christ, Origen, *Contra Celsum* 2.38. On the dual use of the angry part of the soul cf. *Eulogius* 11.10: "Prepare yourself to be gentle and also a fighter, the first with respect to one of your own kind and the second with respect to the

enemy; for the usage of irascibility lies in this, namely, in fighting against the serpent with enmity (Gen. 3.15), but with gentleness and mildness exercising a charitable patience with one's brother while doing battle with the thought . . ." Inflamed desire: 15.

23

Greek

Do not give yourself to the thought of anger by fighting in your mind someone who has saddened you; nor to the thought of sexual lust by continually imagining pleasure. For the first darkens the soul, while the other beckons it to inflamed passion. Both befoul your mind, and at the time of prayer, imagining the idols and not offering pure prayer to God, you immediately fall victim to the demon of *akēdia*. This demon readily leaps upon such states and rips the soul apart, like a dog with a fawn.

Syriac

Do not give your soul to the thought of anger and in your understanding fight with him who saddens you, and again not to that thought of sexual lust, so that by a lustful desire you fantasize even more. For the former darkens the soul, and the latter makes you desire the heat of lustful desires; both cloud your mind, and at the time of prayer they will make you fantasize with those images, and you will not offer pure prayer to God. Immediately you will fall into the hands of the demon of listlessness, who strongly attacks the [practicing] ones in this condition and seizes their soul like a dog who seizes a gazelle.

> IN YOUR MIND, Grk. *kata dianoian*; see 10. Darkening of the intelligence: Rom 1.21; and 2 Cor 2.14, "the people of Israel" have "hardened minds"; *Prak.* 20, 24; Sch. 10 on Ps 31.14; intellect soiled by wrath: 10 and 48; caused by the thought of the one who has aggrieved it: 11; on anger in general: 11, 20. Inflamed desire: 15. TIME OF PRAYER: *KG* 5.42. *Akēdia*: 12.

24

Greek

The nature of anger is to fight the demons and to struggle on behalf of any sort of pleasure. For this reason, the angels suggest spiritual pleasure to us, and the blessedness it yields, and they urge us to direct the angry part against the

50 EVAGRIUS OF PONTUS

demons. The latter, however, dragging us back toward worldly desires, violently compel our anger, against its nature, to fight human beings, so that the mind, now darkened and fallen from knowledge, becomes a traitor to the virtues.

Syriac

The nature of anger will fight with the demons and will combat any kind of pleasure. For this reason too, the angels exhort us to spiritual pleasure and blessedness; by this they persuade us to turn our anger against the demons. The latter, though, contrary to the former, turn us toward the desires of this world and [direct] our unnatural anger to make us fight with humans, so that our mind darkens and falls from its knowledge; it will be a traitor to virtue.

Angels, also called holy powers (*KG* 2.30), are rational beings (*KG* 5.7) made of corporeal and incorporeal nature (*KG* 6.17), predominantly mind and fire (*KG* 1.68). They can change the nature of the body for necessary services (*KG* 5.18). They can see both humans and demons, but cannot be seen by them (*KG* 6.69). Ever remembering and watchful (*Gn.* 16; *KG* 4.60), their nourishment is knowledge and the observation of beings (56; *Gn.* 40; *KG* 1.23; 2.74; 3.4; 5.6; 6.2, 17; Sch. 3 on Ps 23.6; Sch. 10 on Ps 77.25). They fall in ranks, which include archangels (*KG* 5.4, 11), cherubim (*KG* 3.54), and seraphim (*KG* 3.48). Christ, before his coming, revealed an angelic body (*KG* 4.41; 6.77). Angels interact with humans (*KG* 3.78), who stand between angels and demons (*KG* 4.13). The hand of God (Sch. 7 on Ps 16.13), they minister by raising and healing other rational beings (*KG* 3.46, 65; 6.24, 35, 86, 88, 90) under their jurisdiction (*KG* 2.30), and they assist in spiritual struggles (24, 76, 80). They are agents of providence and judgment (*KG* 5.4, 7; Sch. 7 on Ps 16.13; Sch. 38 on Eccl 5.7–11), in which judgment, humans may inherit an angelic body (*KG* 2.48; 3.48, 76; 4.74; 5.9, 11; 6.24, 90). Other references: *Gn.* 44; *KG* 4.38; 5.39, 47; *Foundations* 9, *Eulogius* 24, 26, 31; *Eight Thoughts* 4.21, 8.12; *Monks* 23, 125; *Virgin* 54, 55; *Thoughts* 6.19; *Prayer* 30, 74, etc.; *Reflections* 46, 62. Guardian angel: Origen, *First Principles* 2.10.7 on Mt 18.10; *On Prayer* 20.

Worldly desires: Ti 2.12; cf. Origen, *First Principles* 1.7.5 (on Rom 8.20–22); 3.5.4. Aristotle is the source of the distinction between the state "according to nature" (*kata physin*) or "against nature" (*para physin*), employed here to describe the struggle against vice and demonic interference, now in the context of Christ's war against Satan: *Thoughts* 17; *Eulogius* 10: "to combat the serpent with hatred." Cf. *Prak.* 86 on the *thymos*' activity *kata physin*. Demons versus knowledge: *KG* 3.41; wrath as darkening the intellect: see 23.

PRAKTIKOS 51

25

Greek

Pay attention to yourself, lest you provoke to flight one of the brothers you have irritated; for throughout your life you will never escape the demon of sadness, which will always be an obstacle for you at the time of prayer.

Syriac

Give heed to yourself, lest you ever stir up the anger of a brother, and he will have a cause to run away and in the whole of your life you will not be able to escape from the demon of sadness, who becomes a hindrance to you at the time of prayer, in every hour.

PAY ATTENTION TO YOURSELF/watch yourself: Dt 15.9, "Be careful not to harbor this wicked thought" and Lk 17.3. Cf. sermon by Basil of Caesarea, "*Pay Attention to Yourself*," PG 31. Perhaps a reference to Socrates' "Know yourself," itself recalling the saying of the Delphic oracle. See also *Gn.* 24 and 45, and Sch. 19 on Prv 2.3; Sch. 154 on Prv 17.4; Sch. 340 on Prv 27.23–24; cf. *Reflections* 22. PROVOKE, Grk. *parorgisas*, with the root *orgē*, wrath: cause to anger. OBSTACLE . . . AT THE TIME OF PRAYER: 2 Cor 12.7; *Prayer* 13; *Monks* 15.

26

Greek

Gifts quench resentment. And let Jacob persuade you of this, for when Esau was coming against him with four hundred men he beguiled him with gifts. But we, though we are poor, at table should compensate for our lack.

Syriac

Gifts quench resentment—and Jacob will persuade you, he who persuaded Esau with gifts when he came to attack him with four hundred warriors. But because we are poor, we should fulfill simple necessity at the table.

cf. Gn 32.7

Jacob and Esau: Gn 32.7 (32.6) + 14 (13). Gifts as quenching resentment: Prv 21.14; *Virgin* 41 citing Gn 32.4–33.16; *Antirr.* 5.1. Hospitality as reconciliation: *Monks* 15; *Antirr.* 5.28. PERSUADE: 17. COMING AGAINST HIM . . . BEGUILED,

52 EVAGRIUS OF PONTUS

Grk. *Hypelthōn . . .hypantēsin*: Evagrius has changed LXX Gn 32.7 *synantesin* to suggest that Esau and Jacob each were attempting to outmaneuver the other.

27

Greek

When we fall in with the demon of *akēdia*, then with tears we should divide our soul in two, making one part the consoler, and the other the consoled, sowing good hopes in ourselves and repeating the [words] of the holy David: "Why are you saddened, my soul? And why do you trouble me? Hope in God, because I will praise him; the salvation of my face, and my God."

Syriac

When falling into the hands of the demon of listlessness, then we should divide our soul into parts and we should make one part the comforting and the other the comforted. As we sow a good hope, we encourage it with the murmurings of blessed David: "Why are you sorrowing, my soul, and why are you troubling me? Hope in God, because I will thank him even more, the savior of my face and my God."

Ps 41.6

Akēdia is treated from here through 29. Tears as a remedy for *akēdia*: *Virgin* 39; *Monks* 10. Psalms of David vs. *akēdia*: *Antirr.* 6.10 citing Ps 6.7, and *Antirr.* 6.19. Evagrius instructs his reader to "sing by way of enchantment," *katepadō*; cf. Gregory of Naz., *Or.* 9.2; "subdue with a song": Plato, *Gorgias* 483e and *Menas* 80a; Plutarch, *Dion* 14; Libanius, *Or.* 64.91. Orpheus as a type of Christ charming with a song: Clement, *Protreptikos* 1; Eusebius, *Praise of Constantine* 14.5. SALVATION OF MY FACE, so rendered to capture how oddly the phrase, from Ps 41, would have struck the reader, whether Greek or Syriac.

28

Greek

It is imperative not to abandon the cell at the time of temptations, whatever plausible pretext may be fabricated; but sit within it, and persevere, and nobly receive all who advance, particularly the demon of *akēdia*. The heftiest of all, it does its utmost to test the soul. Running away from and avoiding such contests teaches the mind to be unskilled, cowardly, and a fugitive.

PRAKTIKOS 53

Syriac

It is not fitting, at the time of our temptation, to abandon our cell and leave, while we produce fitting excuses. But let us sit within, and think, and receive valiantly all those things that come upon us—especially the demon of listlessness, he who, because he is harder than the others, makes our soul bright. For fleeing from these struggles and leaving makes our mind fearful, and fugitive, and accursed—and troubled, it becomes unstable.

Deserting (*katalimpanein*) the cell (as a battle): 12; *Monks* 55; Origen, *First Principles* 3.1.17. Perseverance (*hypomonē*) as remedy pr.8; *Monks* 27, *Eulogius* 8. Making the mind unskilled: 50. *Akēdia* makes the soul "most tested or experienced": *Monks* 55 and see *Prak.* 98 (*dokimōtatos*, "most experienced in the military company [*parembolē*] of the *gnōstikoi*," of Didymus the Blind). For "tested" Christians: Rom 16.10, 1 Cor 11.19 and Gn 32.2.

29

Greek

Our holy and most practiced teacher said, "The monk must always be prepared to die tomorrow, and yet use his body as if he were going to live with it for many years. For the first, he said, cuts back the thoughts of *akēdia* and renders the monk more zealous, while the second preserves the body and maintains its self-restraint."

Syriac

Our teacher, holy and most practiced, used to say, "Thus also the solitary must be ready as one who would die tomorrow but uses his body as if it would live for many years. For the former cuts thoughts of listlessness from it and makes the solitary zealous, but the latter guards in health his body, and an athlete who is disciplined without guile."

OUR . . . TEACHER: Macarius the Egyptian, quoted again at 93. This direct quotation of Macarius predates the practice of collecting the sayings of notable monks in the *Apophthegmata Patrum* (and see the concluding *rhēseis*, sayings, *Prak.* 91–100, with note at 91). "Most practiced" Macarius the Egyptian: cf. Palladius, *Lausiac History* 18. Remembrance of death as an ethical practice: Macarius the Egyptian, *Letter to His Sons* 17; cf. *Life of Anthony* 19, quoting 1 Cor 15.31. Approaching death: Seneca, *Letters to Lucilius* 12

54 EVAGRIUS OF PONTUS

and 61. Thoughts of *akēdia*: 12; shortness of life: *Antirr.* 6.25 (advises recitation of Ps 102.15; cf. Schol 9 on Ps 102.15). Thoughts that cut (here, *perikoptō*; cf. Plato, *Republic* 519a, etc.): cf. *Thoughts* 7; *Letter* 18. MORE ZEALOUS, *spoudaiōteron*: cf. *Life of Anthony* 19 and Basil, *Longer Rules* 2.6, where *spoudaios* is a term equivalent to an ascetic. Preserve the health of the body: *KG* 4.76; self-control (*enkrateia*), *Prak.* 91.

30

Greek

It is difficult to escape the thought of vainglory, for whatever you do to purge it becomes for you the cause of another instance of vainglory. Not all of our upright thoughts are opposed by the demons; sometimes our besetting vices oppose them!

Syriac

It is difficult for a person to escape from the thoughts of vainglory. For whatever someone does to take care of it becomes another cause for vainglory, for not all the thoughts equally belong to the opposing demons, but yet there they contend. Just as they see us, that we are overcome, so also evils.

Kephalaia 30–32 consider effective remedies for vainglory. Evidence of humility, *Prayer* 7, 8; vices as enemy instead of demons: *Reflections* 46. OUR BESETTING VICES, literally "the vices by which we are made," *pepoiōmetha*, reminiscent of *poiotēs*, quality; Origen, *On Prayer* 24.2, *Comm. on Jn* 6.14 and Evagrius, *Letter on Faith* 9, "the divine is free of *poiotēs*," quality. See *KG* 1.22. The Syriac translator understood UPRIGHT, *orthō*, incorrectly as *orthōs* ("fittingly"), diverting the meaning of the sentence. The perplexing ending to our translation of the Syriac reflects the manuscript's reading.

31

Greek

I have learned that the demon of vainglory is trailed by almost all the demons, and then, when they stumble, it approaches shamelessly and depicts for the monk the greatness of his virtues.

PRAKTIKOS   55

Syriac

I have perceived that the demon of vainglory, when he is chased by all the demons, stops at the fall of the pursuers and shows the solitary greatness of virtue.

I HAVE LEARNED, *egnōn*, literally "I have known": Sch. 2 on Psalms 136.3 "I have learned that demons must speak psalms and spiritual songs." Demon of vainglory chased by other demons: 58. Persistence of vainglory and wrath: *Thoughts* 15; *Antirr.* 7; *Eight Thoughts* 15-16; *Eulogius* 14, 20. Return of demons: *Reflections* 57, *Thoughts* 15; see also *Antirr.* 7.5; *Eight Thoughts* 15–16; *Eulogius* 14, 20, 28.

32

Greek

One who has grasped knowledge and harvested its pleasure will no longer be persuaded by the demon of vainglory offering him all the pleasures of the world—for what could it provide greater than spiritual *theōria*? But to whatever extent we have not tasted knowledge, we should eagerly engage in the practice, showing to God that our goal is doing everything for the sake of his knowledge.

Syriac

He who has approached knowledge and delighted in its fruits will not again be persuaded by the demon of vainglory, who brings him all the pleasures of the world. For what does he promise him that is better than spiritual *theōria*? But until we have tasted knowledge, we should practice deeds with good will and we signal God our intent, that everything we are doing is for his knowledge.

Attaining gnosis and the pleasure harvested by it: cf. 1 Cor 9.11; *Prak.* 24; *KG* 3.64; 4.49; see Origen, *Hom. on Ezek* 44.1; and Clement, *Strom.* 6.9.75.1, "to show our aim [*skopos*] to God . . ."; *skopos*, "for the prize," Phil 3.14; Sch. 9 on Ps 24.17–18. THEŌRIA, observation, commonly called contemplation, comes from *theoreō*, which has a range of meanings including view, consider, and observe. The nominal form, *theōria*, is a beholding, an object of

56 EVAGRIUS OF PONTUS

sight, a spectacle. Of all of these, the one that seems to fit Evagrius' thought here is observation, though other translations may be better in specific contexts. Such observations can be natural (i.e., pertain to natures; see note at *KG* 2.2) or spiritual (see note at *KG* 3.24). Natural observation or contemplation is available even to the impure (*KG* 4.6), but not spiritual. Both kinds involve observation of beings (note at *KG* 1.73), corporeal and incorporeal (*KG* 2.71).

33

Greek

Remember your former life and the ancient transgressions, and how, when you were impassioned, you crossed over to *apatheia* by the mercy of Christ, and also how you left the world that humiliated you so often and in so many ways. Consider this, too: who protects you in the desert, and who drives away the demons gnashing their teeth against you? Such thoughts both instill humility and shut out the demon of pride.

Syriac

Remember your former life, and the origin of errors, and how while you were impassioned, you were brought to *apatheia*; and how by the mercy of Christ again you departed from the world that often humiliated you; and also think of the one who guards you in the desert and drives from you the demons who gnash their teeth against you. These thoughts are establishing humility for you, and they will not admit the demon of pride.

> Cure for wrath by remembering first life and past sins: 10, 12. Christ's mercy: Rom 9.16; *Eight Thoughts* 18. Demonic teeth-gnashing: Job 16.10; Ps 34.16; Ac 7.54; cf. *Life of Anthony* 6, 9, 66. Humility: pr.2.

Subtitle 3

Greek

On Passions

Syriac

On Passions

34

Greek

When we have impassioned memories, we have already welcomed the activities with passion, and in turn, we shall also have impassioned memories of whatever activities we receive with passion. So one who has defeated the demons that effect such things disdains the things they effect: for the immaterial war is harder than the material war.

Syriac

A memory of passions that happen to us: also we received their property we received with passion and we receive all the properties of passion. Because he who has moved them to a victory over the demons treats with contempt what [the demons] accomplish—for a spiritual battle is much harder than a bodily one.

> Kephalaia 34–39 discuss the operation of the passions, understood as disturbances. Impassioned memories—those that entail a disturbance of the soul—are an opening for demons in the war of the *praktikē*. Passionate memories: 67; working of demons: 48; memory: 12.

35

Greek

The passions of the soul have their origins from human beings, but those of the body, from the body. The passions of the body are circumcised by self-restraint; those of the soul by spiritual love.

Syriac

The passions of the soul have been born from the soul, and the passions of the body, from the body. And continence cuts off those that are of the body; spiritual love, those of the soul.

58   EVAGRIUS OF PONTUS

Distinction between passions of the soul and passions of the body: *Eulogius* 23; Aristotle, *Nicomachean Ethics* 10.2 (1173b7–9). Passions of the body arise from its inherent needs; of the soul, from interaction with others. On the body, see pref.6; 8, etc. Love: Eph 5.1–2.

36

Greek

Those [demons] governing the passions of the soul persist until we die; those over the passions of the body retreat sooner. Other demons rise and set like the sun, and they touch only one part of the soul; but the noonday demon usually surrounds the whole soul and suffocates the mind. For this reason, withdrawal (*anachōresis*) is sweet after the emptying of the passions; for then our memories are only simple, and the struggle is preparing the monk no longer for battle, but for the *theōria* of it.

Syriac

Those [demons] fighting with the passions of the soul remain until death, but those of the body leave easily. And these other demons resemble the sun when it rises and sets, and touch only one of the portions of the soul. But that noonday one typically seizes the whole soul, and chokes our mind; and because of this their withdrawal is sweet for us, for after we have been emptied of passions, then we have a simple memory of their battles. And it is not for the purpose of the struggle but to prepare the solitary for *theōria*.

Sin "unto death" 1 Jn 5.17; NOONDAY DEMON (Ps 90.6): 12. Memories: 12; *Gn.* 14. After their conclusion it is possible to contemplate such struggles: 79, 83. The Syriac translator, although following the Greek wording closely, has misrepresented the original, mainly by rendering *proestōtes*, "presiding," as an agonistic word, and by eliding the second understood "passions" from the translation.

37

Greek

Whether it is the thought that moves the passions or the passions that move the thought is a matter that requires reflection. Some have taught the first, others the second.

Syriac

Is it the idea moving the passions, or passions moving the idea? For to many, it is considered to be the thoughts; but among others, the passions exist to be moved by the senses.

> First opinion: Epictetus, *Manual* 5; Marcus Aurelius, *To Himself* 8.47; and Nemesius of Emesa, *On the Nature of Humanity* 16. Second opinion, perhaps Aristotle, *On the Soul* 1.1 (403a16–b3). Cf. similar consideration in Plotinus, *Enneads* 3.6.4.

38

Greek

The passions are naturally moved by means of sensations. When both love and self-restraint are present they will not be moved, but if absent they will be moved. The angry part requires more medicine than the desiring part, and because of this, love is called "great," for it is the bridle of anger. That saint, Moses, in his writings on nature symbolically named it "snake-fighter."

Syriac

But when love and self-control are near, [the passions] are not moved. But when anger increases from desire, there is a need for medicines. And because of this, love is said to be great, for it is a bridle of anger; and because of this, divine people teach us that it will bring rest from anger.

> cf. 1 Cor 13.13; cf. Lv 11.22
>
> LOVE: 1 Cor 13.13. For disturbances (passions) moved by sensations: 4; love and abstinence (*enkrateia*): 35, 49, 74, 78, 84; Sch. 1 on Ps 25.2: all disturbances moved by the "passionate part of the soul." Love heals the angry part of the soul: *Gn.* 47; *KG* 3.35. See Gregory of Nazianzus, *Or.* 6.6 and *Letter* 19; Moses and gentleness: *Letter* 56 citing Nm 12.3; on gentleness, *Letters* 27 and 28. The phraseology implies Moses wrote a treatise titled *Physics*; cf. Sch. 13 on Ps 76.17 and Clement of Alexandria, *Strom.* 1.28.176. On Moses, see *Gn.* 46 and *KG* 4.23. Philo, *Special Laws* 114, *On the Creation of the World* 164, and *Allegories of the Law* 105: continence (not love) is the snake-fighter. For the serpent as anger: *KG* 1.57; 5.44; Sch.

60   EVAGRIUS OF PONTUS

3 on Ps 57.5; Sch. 35 on Ps 17.48. The Syriac version has dropped the quotation from Leviticus, and omitted any reference to Moses (cf. *KG* 2.38 with note).

39

Greek

At the stench prevailing among the demons, the soul is accustomed to be enflamed against thoughts, when it perceives them approaching, affected by the passion of [its] tormentor.

Syriac

From the stench of the demons' temptations, the soul is customarily enflamed against the thoughts. And from their approach toward it, it gets angry as it fights the pain in which it has been immersed.

Demonic stench: *Life of Anthony* 63. Bad odor, *KG* 5.78. On smell: Arist., *On the Soul* 2.9. Some passions stem from sensations (*Prak.* 38); others from demons: *Reflections* 59. Inflamed against the thoughts, 42; *Thoughts* 2; cf. inflamed desire, *Prak.* 15. Perception: *KG* 1.36; 2.83.

Subtitle 4

Greek

Instructions

Syriac

Counsels of admonitions of the same Evagrius

Instructions, *hypothēkai*, can imply precepts of a teacher (Clement, *Paidagogos* 1.1, of Christ; Origen, *Comm. on Jn* 13.49).

PRAKTIKOS 61

40

Greek

It is not possible at every moment to accomplish the ordinary rule, but it is necessary to pay attention to the moment, and to try to accomplish the commandments that are practicable. For the demons themselves are not unaware of such moments. When they are moved against us, they prevent us from accomplishing the possible and compel us to undertake the impossible. They prevent the sick from giving thanks for their sufferings and from being patient with those ministering to them. Instead, they exhort the weak and burdened to practice self-restraint and to stand up to sing psalms.

Syriac

We are not always able to complete services of our custom, but it is necessary to observe the moment, and also . . . that we will be diligent as much as possible, for the demons also know them and move us toward those things that cannot be, and they force us to do those things that are not possible. For they hinder the weak brothers from giving thanks concerning their diseases and from being patient with the ones who serve them, and they convince them in their weakness that they will be humble ones, and that when their body weighs them down, they should stand up and sing [psalms].

Kephalaia 40–53 deal with symptoms of disturbance, and their remedies. On Evagrius' illness and subsequent diet, *Lausiac History* 38.8–9. Cf. *Thoughts* 25, citing "those who have observed certain of the realities present in natural beings," namely Aristotle, *On the Soul* 412b, *On Interpretation* 16, both also cited in Clement, *Strom.* 8.13 on names, thoughts, and objects. The Syriac insertion of BROTHERS renders the text more monastic.

41

Greek

When we are required to spend some time in cities or in villages, and consort with those who live in the world, we should hold all the more zealously to our self-restraint, lest our mind, thickened and deprived of its customary attentiveness by

62   EVAGRIUS OF PONTUS

the present occasion, do something thoughtless and become a runaway, tossed about by the demons.

Syriac

When we are required to go into cities and into villages for a short time, and when we are going around with those who live in the world, then we should especially hold on to much self-control—lest our heart and our mind be darkened, and, separated from the customary care, be compelled to do something that it does not will—and it will become a fugitive, hunted by demons.

Evagrius' letters record instances of monks travelling among settlements, and the perils of those travels: *Letter* 6, 7, 13 (reluctance to leave his hermit's cell), 16 (to Loukios). THOSE WHO LIVE IN THE WORLD, Grk. *kosmikoi*, are opposed to monks, Grk. *monachoi*, at 48; at *Gn.* 36 they are paired with youth. Thickened minds: *KG* 1.11; 2.68; 4.36; 6.2. Cf. also *Monks* 48 on the "thickening" effect of sleep, and *Prayer* 50. CUSTOMARY ATTENTIVENESS: cf. customary canon, previous keph. The RUNAWAY or fugitive mind: 21, 28.

42

Greek

When you are tempted, do not pray before you utter some angry words against the one who afflicts you; for when your soul is affected by the thoughts, your prayer cannot be pure. But if you say something against them with anger, you will confuse and banish the representations that come from the enemies. This is the natural use of anger, even for good representations.

Syriac

When you are tempted, do not at first pray until you first say words of anger against the one afflicting you. For when the soul is oppressed by thoughts, then it happens that your prayer is also not pure. But if you always speak something to them angrily, you will continually destroy all the plottings of your enemies. For this is also the effect of anger in the case of excellent thoughts.

Wrath, *orgē*, as a weapon against demons: *Antirr.* pr.5. Demon as one who afflicts, against whom words [of scripture] are deployed: 72 and cf. generally, *Antirr.* Wrath: cf. *Prak.* 23, soiling the intellect; *Reflections* 8, wrath a power of the soul able to destroy thoughts; REPRESENTATIONS: *noēmata*.

43

Greek

It is necessary to recognize the varieties of the demons and to note their occasions. From the thoughts, and the thoughts from the objects, we shall know which of the demons are rare and heavier; which are common and lighter; and which assail us suddenly and snatch the mind away to blasphemy. It is necessary to know these things, so that when the thoughts begin to put in motion their own particular materials, and before we are driven too far from our own state, we may speak against them and declare which one is present. This way we shall, with God's help, readily make progress, and we shall make them fly away in amazement at us, and in distress.

Syriac

We must know the varieties of demons and note down their moments; and we know these demons from the thoughts, and the thoughts, from the matters; for some, from demons, make war with us infrequently, and are very harsh. But others remain and are less intense, and some of them come upon us immediately, and they seize our mind for blasphemy. We must know these things: that when thoughts are beginning to mobilize their forces, before they drive us far from our tranquility, we will speak against them as we learn which one fights against us. For thus with the grace of our Lord we go forth readily to rule them; then they wonder at us because we inflict pain upon them and make them flee from us.

> On the differences among demons, cf. *Thoughts* 2; to distinguish among them by their behavior: 12, 28, 46 (the demon of blasphemy); on the sources of their matters (*pragmata*): *Reflections* 47; on our own state, *katastasis*, *Thoughts* 11, here meaning peaceable, and cf. *Prak.* 57, *eirenikai katastaseis*. "Declare, predict" *sēmainōmen*: Signify, make a signal: if used in a medical sense, "note down, predict."

44

Greek

When the demons are unsuccessful as they fight against monks, they retreat for a little while and watch to see which of the virtues is being neglected in the meantime. On that basis, they suddenly rush in and tear the wretched soul to pieces.

Syriac

When the weakened demons contend with the solitary, then for a short time they are quiet, observing which of the works of virtue he despises, and then they fall upon him immediately, and ensnare the feeble soul.

> Demons who observe monks neglecting one or another of the virtues, *Prayer* 47. Cf. *Prayer* 134, and *Antirr*. Demons "rend" the soul like a wild animal, cf. *Prak.* 23.

45

Greek

Evil demons seek the help of demons even more evil than themselves. Opposed to one another by their dispositions, they agree only about the destruction of the soul.

Syriac

Harsh demons bring to their aid the ones who are harsher than they. While they are opponents in their intentions, they make alliance with each other, in this alone—that they will destroy the soul.

> Malicious demons (Mt 6.13) can cooperate with even more malicious ones (Lk 11.26), although they are usually not united (*Prak.* 58). Cf. also *KG* 4.59. Dispositions, *diatheseis*, are fleeting manners, opposed to conditions, *hexis* (cf. *Prak.* 70; *Letter on Faith* 3). On this distinction see Aristotle, *Categories* 8b28, *Nicomachean Ethics* 2.4, and *Metaphysics* 4.20.1022b.

46

Greek

Let us not be disturbed by the demon who snatches the mind away to blasphemy against God, and toward those forbidden speculations that I myself have not dared to put down in writing—nor let it break our zeal. The Lord is he "who knows the heart" and he knows that even when we were in the world we were not mad with such madness. The goal of this demon is to stop us from prayer, so that we not stand before the Lord our God, nor dare to lift up our hands toward the one against whom we entertained such thoughts.

PRAKTIKOS 65

Syriac

Let us not be disturbed by the demon who carries us off to blasphemy against God, and to unspeakable hallucinations—these things that not even I have dared to finish with a pen—and let not our good will be cut off. For the Lord is a knower of hearts, and also knew that not even when we were in the world, were we driven mad by this madness. The goal for this demon is this: to hinder us from prayer, so that we will not stand before God and not dare to spread out our hands toward him, as we had intended to do.

cf. Ac 1.24

This is the first of several kephalaia treating *phantasiai*, translated Syr. *šragrāgithā* throughout, and how they are to be avoided. Commonly, *phantasia* described the faculty of the soul we call imagination. Evagrius represents the increase in the fourth century of the alternative meaning, that of vivid depictions, synonymous with *phantasmata*. Although Evagrius has a rich vocabulary for parts of the cognitive faculty (e.g., *nous, dianoia, doxa, aisthēsis: Prak.* 48, 54, 64, 71, 76, 89, 91; *Letter on Faith* 38), *phantasia* is rare (Sch. 1 on Ps 102.1, perhaps derived from another author; see note at *KG* 2.9). Possibly, Evagrius made this distinction following scriptural use of the term *phantazō* or *phantasma* as an external appearance: cf. Mt 14.26, Lk 24.37; cf. Philo, *Allegories of the Law* 1.30. Hallucinations: see note at *KG* 4.60. Fantasies suggested by demons: *Thoughts* 7; *Antirr.* 8.21, 29. Snatching/ dragging: cf. 43 and 51; *Antirr.* 8.41. Blasphemy as folly: 14. Blasphemous thoughts against God and his angels: to deny free will, to think that we sin involuntarily and that the judgment to come is unjust: *Antirr.* 8.16, 47; to deny grace and the help of God: *KG* 4.60. WHO KNOWS THE HEART: God as *kardiognōstēs*: Ac 1.24, 15.8; Rom 8.27 (Jesus); Jer 17.10 (God); Heb 4.12 (logos); cf. *Prak.* 47 and many places in the sch. Pss. On the heart in general, see 47, 50; *Gn.* 39; *KG* 6.52, 84 (angering part : heart :: desiring part : flesh and blood), 87 (joined with the mind). The heart is said to be the site of intelligence (*KG* 6.84). On the relationship between heart and other parts of the human, see note at *KG* 6.87. WHEN WE WERE IN THE WORLD: in the state of a *kosmikos*. The demon who stops the monk from praying: *Antirr.* 8.20, 10, 28. The Syriac translator has taken the *kath' ou* literally, as referring to God, not as a conditional marker.

47

Greek

The symbol of the disturbances in the soul is either some word uttered or a movement of the body, through which the enemies perceive whether we have

66 EVAGRIUS OF PONTUS

their thoughts within us and are in great distress, or have cast them out and are focused on our salvation. For only the God who made us knows the mind, and he does not need symbols to know the things hidden in the heart.

Syriac

There is a sign of the passions that are in the soul—either a word uttered, or movements of the body. For from them the enemies sense the thoughts that are inside them, and with which we think. Or we drive them away from us and remember our life. For only God, who made it, knows the mind, and needs no signs to know the secrets of the heart.

> The opening paraphrases Aristotle, *On Interpretation* 16a3: "Those things uttered then are symbols of the passions in the soul, and those things written [are symbols] of what are uttered." In most modern translations of Aristotle *pathē* and *pathēma* are translated "affections," "emotions," or "experiences," which obscures the connection with the *Praktikos*. By *pathēma* Evagrius intended to refer to the same phenomena Aristotle did, although, in reading scripture (Prv 25.20; Rom 1.26, 7.5, 8.18; 2 Cor 1.5; Col 3.5; Heb 2.9; 1 Pt 1.11) he had a very different view on how they were to be explained, regarded, and treated. SYMBOL, *symbolon*, is a visible manifestation of a state or a truth—in this case the true condition of the soul, discernible by demonic enemies either in an audible word or visible corporeal movement. The demons have limited intelligence, but they can interpret such symbols, as can human beings; God does not need them. Cf. *Letter* 16. Demons notice the signs of our thoughts, *Monks* 59; but God knows the intellect directly Ps 32.15. Cf. *Thoughts* 5, 8, 12, and 37 on demonically induced fantasies and demonic ignorance. Knower of what is in hearts: 46.

48

Greek

The demons wrestle with those who live in the world more by means of objects, but with monks even more through the thoughts, for because of solitude they lack objects. And since it is easier to sin by thinking than by acting, the warfare related to thinking is proportionately harder than that arising from objects. The mind is a thing easily moved, and difficult to stabilize in the face of forbidden imaginings.

Syriac

The demons fight with those who live in the world by means of things; but with solitaries, for the most part, by means of thoughts, because they are deprived

PRAKTIKOS 67

of things, because of solitude. And just as someone sins more easily in understanding than in an action, so the battle of the understanding is created much harder than of things. For our mind is small and easily seizes unlawful illusions.

Kosmikoi, those who live in the world, whom demons fight (or wrestle, *palaiousi*) by means of things or actions (*Prak.* 8, 10, 89): *Prak.* 41; *Monks* 34, 78, 113; *Virgin* 24. Cf. *Thoughts* 2; non-monastics are attacked through things or actions; monks by thoughts (43, memories, 34 and 67, or dream-images, 64). To sin in spirit: *Antirr.*, pr.5. OBJECTS translates *pragmata*, rendered *tešbuthā* by the Syriac translator. See note at *KG* 1.78. EASILY MOVED: Grk. *eukinēton*, Aristotle, *On the Soul* 1.2 (405a10; Democritus: being spherically shaped, mind and fire are most easily moved); *Nicomachean Ethics* 6.7 1141a 18–20 and cf. Plotinus, *Ennead* 2.6.2; 3.6.3. DIFFICULT TO STABILIZE: *Thoughts* 25.

49

Greek

We have not been commanded to work or to keep vigil or to fast at all times, but we have been commanded "to pray ceaselessly." For those things that heal the passionate part of the soul need our body for their work, which because of its customary weakness is inadequate for these labors. But prayer prepares a mind to be strong and pure for the struggle, since it is naturally made to pray and even without this body fights demons more than all the powers of the soul.

Syriac

We have not been commanded to work at all times, and to watch, and to fast. But a law is laid down for us, "to pray continually." Because the former heal the passionate part of the soul and need bodily effort, which is inadequate for the . . . because of the weakness of its nature. But prayer strengthens the mind for combat to oppose the enemy; it naturally prays, even without the body.

1 Thes 5.17

Constant prayer: 1 Thes 5; and compare *Virgin* 5 and *Letter* 19; Origen, *On Prayer* 1. The "passionate part of the soul," that is, angry and desiring; *Prak.* 38, 74, 78, 84; *Gn.* 2; *KG* 3.18; Sch. 127 on Prv 11.17; Sch. 230 on Prv 21.23. Weakness, *Thoughts* 25; intellect fortified with prayer, *Prak.* 65; naturally made by prayer, cf. *Prayer* 83 and Sch. 1 on Ps 137.1, *aperispastos*.

68　EVAGRIUS OF PONTUS

Customary weakness: Sch. 310 on Prv 25.17 (of the mind); *Thoughts* 35 (body). To be strong: Acts 15.29, 23.30. Struggle, *palē*, "wrestling-match": cf. *Prak.* 36; Sch. 2 on Ps 141.5. Departure from the body: *KG* 4.70. To combat demons: 24, 89, using the irascible part of the soul. Powers of the soul: *KG* 2.9.

50

Greek

If one of the monks wishes to learn by experience about the savage demons and to become familiar with their technique, let him observe his thoughts and record their intensifications and diminutions, and their intertwinings, and their timing, and which of the demons do a particular thing, and what kind of demon follows another, and which kind does not accompany which kind; and let him seek from Christ the reasons for these things. They are infuriated against those who undertake the practice with a greater level of knowledge, for they wish "to shoot the upright of heart in the darkness."

Syriac

If anyone from the solitaries might wish to receive a trial of wild demons and to learn the cunning of their craft, let him guard his thoughts as he places in his heart their violence and quiescence and their interconnections and their times; and let it be understood which demons do what, and which demon follows another and which does not, and let him seek from Christ concerning the causes about them. Those who wish to perfect virtue with knowledge are very hard upon the demons, because "they wish to shoot in darkness the upright of heart."

Ps 10.2

Demonic skill (*technē*): *Life of Anthony* 11. Contraction, *metemplokē*, tightly woven. For *emplokē*, cf. Plato, *Politics* 282e ("interweaving") and Plotinus, *Enneads* 4.3.15; diminutions: relax, *aneseis*: 2 Thes 1.7 (as "rest"); Plato, *Laws* 4.724a. Demons contract or relax, and are interconnected (all wrestling words; cf. previous keph.). The reasons for these things: *Eulogius* 24, about moving from practice to gnosis (*ekdēmia/endēmia*). Christ knows the *logoi* of demonic attacks and can inform the practicing monk; yet the demons grow even more angry at those who are at the gnostic level (*gnōstikoteron*) in their *praktikē*. In the shadow: Sch. 3 on Ps 10.2: "darkness" (*skotomēna*) is the ignorance of the soul.

PRAKTIKOS 69

51

Greek

After close *theōria*, you will discover that two of the demons are quickest, almost surpassing the movement of our mind: the demon of sexual lust and the one that seizes and carries us away to blasphemy against God. The second does not last for long, but the first, provided it does not move the thoughts with passion, will not impede us from the knowledge of God.

Syriac

If you observe two swift demons, you can see that in their swiftness they are surpassing the movement of our mind—the demon of sexual lust, and the one who drags us to blasphemy against God. The latter lasts a short time, and the former does not hinder us from the knowledge of God, if it does not move our thoughts in passion.

You will discover, *parateresas*, implying observation: 50 and *Thoughts* 7. Demon of fornication: 90. To blaspheme God: 43, 46; *Antirr.* 8.41. Does not last for long, *oligochronios*: 15.

52

Greek

To separate the body from the soul belongs only to him who united them; but to separate the soul from the body belongs also to the one who aims at virtue. For our fathers call withdrawal (*anachōrēsis*) an attention to death and a flight from the body.

Syriac

The body that will separate from the soul belongs to God the creator. But the soul that will separate from the body, to that one who ardently desires virtue. For our fathers called departure from life a study of death and a flight from the body.

Body without spirit: Eccl 12.7; Jas 2.26. *Syndein* is the yoking or joining of the soul to the body: *KG* 1.58; see also *KG* 1.4, 11, 63. See *KG* 5.56 on Plato, *Phaedrus* 67c, and Plotinus, *Enneads* 3.65. Evagrius continues the reference to Plotinus when he forbids violently separating the body from the soul. Porphyry, *Launching Points to the Intelligibles* 8 and 9. It is forbidden to put an end to one's life *KG* 4.33 (see note), 76, or to destroy the body with *askēsis*, *Prak.* 29. Mt 19.6,

70 EVAGRIUS OF PONTUS

"not separating what God has joined"; Origen, *Comm. on Mt* 14.16, 22. The soul cannot separate from the body of its own accord: *KG* 1.47. Distinguishing suicide from the practice of death, *meletē thanatou*: *Eulogius* 19, "to exercise one's own death"; cf. *Prak.* 29. OUR FATHERS: Clement, *Strom.* 5.11.67; Gregory of Nazianzus, *Letter* 31 and *Or.* 27.7, "to make our life an exercise in death." The prohibition against monastic suicide has dropped out in the Syriac translation.

53

Greek

Those who wickedly nourish the flesh and "make provision for its desires" should blame themselves, not the flesh. For they who are obtaining, by means of that body, the soul's *apatheia* recognize the grace of the creator and to some extent are attending to the *theōria* of beings.

Syriac

Those who wickedly nourish their bodies and "make provision for the desires" of the body—let them blame themselves and not their bodies. For the ones who are drawn to the *apatheia* of the soul while they are in the body recognize the grace of their creator—and they attain to the sight of beings as far as they are able.

Rom 13.14

MAKE PROVISIONS FOR ITS DESIRES: Rom 13.14. Body and soul: 35. GRACE OF THE CREATOR: cf. *KG* 4.60 (the body is a gift of the Creator) and 4.62. The body: *KG* 1.11; cf. *Prak.* 49 and *KG* 4.60. To perceive, *epiballein*: 59 and 86. THEŌRIA OF BEINGS: *KG* 1.73.

Subtitle 5

Greek

Concerning Things That Happen during Sleep

Syriac

The book of the Gnostikos.

The Syriac manuscript prematurely signals the beginning of the *Gnostikos*.

54

Greek

When the demons wage war against the desiring part by means of the imaginings during sleep, they show us—and we avidly pursue—gatherings of acquaintances, symposia with family, troupes of women singing and dancing, and other such things made for pleasure; we are sickened in that part of our soul and the passion is strong. But then again, when they stir up the angering part, they force us to walk along the edges of cliffs and raise up armed men, and poisonous and carnivorous beasts. We are terrified of these roads, and we flee, pursued by the beasts and the men. Therefore we should give forethought to the angry part and, calling upon Christ in vigils, employ the remedies mentioned above.

Syriac

When the demons fight us in the desiring part during the fantasies of sleep, at that time they show, and we pursue, such things as these: meeting loved ones, a gathering of kindred, a row of women and other females that engender desires in the part in which we are sick, and passion overcomes them. And when anger is moved, they disturb and force us to walk in stony paths, and bring armed men, and fanged and venomous beasts. But if we are terrified by the road or by the fear of the beasts and of the men who oppose us, if we run from the pursuit we should take care of ourselves and the angry part of the soul, and in our vigil call out to Christ, and use the first medicines.

> This and the next two kephalaia deal with dreams. Fantasies of dreams: cf. 64, suggested by demons; see *Thoughts* 4. On banquets, cf. *Antirr.* 1.36, 39, 40, 41. Dancing women in domestic banquets: Similar in John Chrysostom, *Hom. on Mt* 48.3; Jerome, *Letter* 22. Cf. *KG* 1.38 on the contrast between states of sleep and wakefulness. Passion as a sickness of the soul, 56; and Hippocrates, *On the Regimen* 4.86–93. Terrors of dreams prompted by demons' agitating the wrathful part of the soul, see 11; *Thoughts* 26 and 27. Precipices and wild animals: *Thoughts* 26. Remedies (*pharmakois*): 15, 20, 38.

55

Greek

When the natural movements of the body are free of images during sleep, they show that to some extent the soul is healthy. But the formation of images is a

72   EVAGRIUS OF PONTUS

symptom of illness. Consider blurry faces to be a symbol of an old passion, but
distinct faces that of a fresh wound.

Syriac

Imageless natural movements, moved in dreams, make known how healthy the
soul is; but visible images are an indication of its sickness. Faces unknown to us are
a sign of an old passion; but those that are known are a sign of a passion present in
the soul.

> Seminal emissions: Lv 15.16–17 and Dt 23.11–12; cf. *Didascalia Apostolorum*
> 26; Caelius Aurelianus, *On Chronic Diseases* 5.7; Origen (?), *Select Passages
> on Psalms* 15.7 (PG 12:1216A); Origen, *Hom. on Ps* 2.15; Dionysius of
> Alexandria, *Canonical Letter* 2; Athanasius, *Letter to Amoun*; Anthony, *Letter*
> 1. Good health of the soul is impassibility, *apatheia*; cf. 56. OLD PASSION . . .
> FRESH WOUND: cf. Plato, *Republic* 9.571e–572b and Basil, *Hom. on Julitta* 4;
> *Shorter Rules* 22.

56

Greek

We shall recognize the proofs of *apatheia* during the day through the thoughts,
but at night through our dreams. And *apatheia* is what we call the soul's health;
but its food is knowledge, which alone is able to unite us with the holy powers,
since union with incorporeal beings derives from a like disposition.

Syriac

In the day, you know the indications of advancement toward the soul's *apatheia*
from your thoughts, but at night, from your dreams. And we call the approach
toward freedom of passion of the soul the health of the soul; its nourishment is
knowledge—that which alone is the path carrying us to the holy powers, since
our participation with the incorporeals will become natural from the parity of
our ways of life.

> PROOFS, *tekmēria*. The sense of the word as rhetorical proof: Aristotle, *Rhetoric*
> 1357b4; as "symptom," i.e., medical proof of disease, Oribasius, *Synopsis*
> a.43; Philodemus, *On the Gods* D 3.8; *On Signs*, frag. 2. Cf. *Life of Anthony*
> 43, *ataraxias tekmērion*. *Apatheia* as the health of the soul: Cicero, *Tusculan*

Disputations 3.7, 23; the terminology underlies, e.g., *KG* 1.41; 2.48; 3.46; 6.64. Gnosis as the nourishment of the soul: *KG* 2.32, 88; 3.4. See Plato, *Theaetetus* 176b. Incorporeals: *KG* 1.70. To UNITE US, *synaptein hēmas*: cf. Sch. 189 on Prv 19.4: the impure (*akathartos*) separated from the angel given at birth; the pure ("rich in knowledge") joined to the angels.

Subtitle 6

Greek

Concerning the State Approaching *Apatheia*

57

Greek

There are two peaceful states of the soul: one arises from natural seeds; the other comes about from the withdrawal of the demons. From the former there follow humility with compunction, tears, limitless longing for God, and immeasurable zeal for the work. From the second come vainglory with pride, which capture the monk after the destruction of the other demons. One who perceives the borders of the first state will even more quickly recognize the raids of the demons.

Syriac

The soul has two peaceful habits. One arises from the constitution's natural movements that are blended; another is from the departure of the demons. Humility follows the first, with compunction and tears, and limitless longing for God, and immeasurable eagerness for labors. But the other, from the withdrawal of demons, is followed by pride and vainglory, which seizes the solitary. He who keeps the first's depth of peace will come to know more keenly the attack of the demons against him.

PEACEFUL STATES OF THE SOUL differ from apatheia: *Eight Thoughts* 2; *Reflections* 3. Virtues are "natural seeds": *KG* 1.39; at the retreat of other demons, the demon of vainglory arrives, accompanied by the demon of wrath (*Prak.* 31, 13) and cf. Clement, *Strom.* 1.1 on Mt 1.9–13, 18–23. Cf. *Prak.* 48 for demonic war; here, retreat (*hypochōresis*) implicitly contrasted with ascetic withdrawal (*anachōresis*).

74 EVAGRIUS OF PONTUS

Military retreat: Xenophon, *Cyropaedeia* 2.4.24; political retreat from democracy to oligarchy, Plato, *Republic* 560a. Zeal, *spoudē*: *KG* 1.79; 3.43. LIMITLESS LONGING FOR GOD, "an infinite desire for the divine": cf. *Prayer* 118. The one who has acquired *apatheia* "recognizes" the tactics of the demons; cf. 50.

58

Greek

The demon of vainglory is opposed to the demon of sexual lust, and it is not possible for them to attack the soul simultaneously, since one promises honors, and the other is an agent of disgrace. Thus, if either one comes and presses upon you, then form in yourself the thoughts of the opposing demon. If you are able, as they say, to "drive out a nail with a nail," "know yourself" to be near to the borders of *apatheia*, because your mind has become strong enough to annihilate, with human thoughts, the thoughts of the demons. To drive away with humility the thought of vainglory, or that of sexual lust with that of temperance, would be proof of the most profound *apatheia*. Try to practice this with all the demons that are opposed to each other, and you will immediately know the passion with which you are most troubled. Even so, ask God with all your might to ward off the enemies with the second method.

Syriac

The demon of the love of vainglory is the opposite of the demon of sexual lust, and these two cannot attack the soul simultaneously, because one promises honor but the other is the cause for shame. Thus when one of these approaches and attacks you, let your mind shape the thoughts of the one who is his opposite, and if you are able, as is said in a parable, to drive out a nail with a nail, know that you are near the border of the freedom from passion, for your mind can annihilate the thoughts of demons with human thoughts. This is a sign of the gateway to *apatheia*: when by humility a man can drive far away from him the love of vainglory, or by purity the thought of sexual lust. Take pains to practice this toward all the demons who are opposed to each other, for you learn through them that you were enticed by a certain passion. But with all your might, supplicate God that by this second method you may conquer your enemies.

Demons opposed to each other: 45; IT IS NOT POSSIBLE, cf. 18. The demon of vainglory and of fornication, cf. *Eulogius* 22. TO DRIVE OUT A NAIL WITH A

PRAKTIKOS 75

NAIL: Aristotle, *Politics* 5.11.3; Cicero, *Tusculan Disputations* 4.75; Palladius, *Lausiac History* 26.4. *Tekmērion* of *apatheia*: cf. 56. BORDERS OF APATHEIA, *horoi*: cf. Sch. 38 on Eccl 5.7–11, quoting Mt 13.38 where the kosmos is a field, *agros*, with frontiers, *horoi*. TRY TO PRACTICE THIS ... AND YOU WILL ... KNOW: a diagnostic technique. ASK GOD: Mt 7.7–8.

59

Greek

The more the soul progresses, the stronger are the antagonists that succeed each other against it; for I am not persuaded that the very same demons remain with it. Those who apply themselves most attentively to their temptations know this best—they who see the *apatheia* they acquired being pried away by successive demons.

Syriac

However much the soul strives for the works of virtue, to that degree strong ones always battle it. For I am not persuaded that those very same demons always persevere against the soul. And especially those who are tested most carefully in their temptation know this, seeing that other demons wish to trouble the calming of passion that is theirs.

The advance of the soul prompts a stronger assault from demons. *Prokoptō*: advance in a military campaign, commonly; Xenophon, *Anabasis* 3.1; Phil 1.25, 1 Tm 4.15; in philosophy Clement, *Prophetic Eclogues* 57; Origen, *Comm. on Jn* 6.49. Cf. *Antirr.* 4.3. See *Prak.* 46 for the temptations particular to a gnostic. The "battering" or "wrestling" demon, cf. *Prak.* pr.2; 55; as a struggle, *palē*: 36 and 49.

60

Greek

Perfect *apatheia* comes about within the soul after the defeat of all the demons that oppose the practice. *Apatheia* is said to be incomplete in proportion to the power of the demon still wrestling against it.

76 EVAGRIUS OF PONTUS

Syriac

The perfection of virtue is possible for the soul when it will conquer all the demons who are working in opposition to all the practitioners of virtue. But perfection alone is incomplete, when it will conquer a single enemy.

> Demons opposing the practice attack the passionate part of the soul. Imperfect passion: cf. *Thoughts* 15, where this state is called "little *apatheia*," distinct from "perfect health." The demon of vainglory attacks the soul in the state of imperfect *apatheia*. On the imperfect soul, see *KG* 3.14. See *KG* 3.10 on the mind being imperfect.

61

Greek

The mind will not make progress, nor embark on the good departure and come to exist in the land of the incorporeals, unless it has set right the things within. For the disturbance in matters of its own household makes it prone to turn back to the things it had left behind.

Syriac

Our mind does not go to its beginning, make the beautiful departures, and come into the region of the incorporeals if it does not correct the passions that are in it. But if it is troubled from within, it turns back to those things from which it had departed at one time.

> EMBARK, *apodēmēsei*. *Apodēmia* is entry into the gnostic life. *Eulogius* 24, "He who has accomplished the *praktikē epidēmia* and the *gnostikē endēmia*." Cf. Philo, *On the Migration of Abraham and On the Virtues* 219. In *Prayer* 46, Evagrius shows how the demons are opposed to the *ekdēmia pros theon*. The LAND OF THE INCORPOREALS is spiritual contemplation/observation. Cf. *KG* 1.85. SET RIGHT THE THINGS WITHIN: see 14. To make a return is to arrive at the "frontiers of *apatheia*"; see 58. Cf. Sch. 377 on Prv 31.21.

62

Greek

The virtues and the vices both produce a blinded mind: the former, so that it does not see the vices; the latter so that it does not see the virtues again.

Syriac

Both virtues and evils blind the mind. The virtues, for not seeing the evils and the evils, for not seeing the virtues.

Cf. *Prayer* 120 (also 28, 42, 43); the mind has "perfect insensibility (*anaisthēsia*)" at the time of prayer. Blinding: note at *Prak.* 20; *KG* 4.47, 57; 5.27. Cf. Origen, *On Prayer* 21.2 on Mt 6.6. Turning spiritual eyes away from the vices: *KG* 1.66.

Subtitle 7

Greek

Concerning the Symbols of *Apatheia*

63

Greek

When the mind begins to make prayers without distraction, then all warfare is joined, night and day, around the angry part of the soul.

Syriac

When our mind begins to offer its prayers without distraction, then by day and by night a battle arises toward the angering part of our soul.

Here through 70 deal with higher levels of freedom from passion. To pray without distraction, cf. *Prayer* 17: "Undistracted prayer is the highest activity of the intellect." The angering part of the soul: *KG* 4.47. Disturbances at night: 11, 54.

64

Greek

The proof of *apatheia* is that the mind has begun to see its own radiance, remaining tranquil in the presence of apparitions during sleep, and regarding objects calmly.

78   EVAGRIUS OF PONTUS

Syriac

A demonstration of the approach of the soul to *apatheia*: when the mind begins to see its radiance; is not moved toward the illusions from dreams; and sees all these matters clearly.

THE PROOF OF *APATHEIA*: *tekmērion* as in 56 and 64. When the mind beholds its own radiance: *Gn.* 45; *Reflections* 2, 23; *Thoughts* 39–40. See also *Thoughts* 24; *Prayer* 67, 70, 72, 97. Light of the nous: *Prayer* 73, 74; *Reflections* 25. Visions of sleep: 54 and *Thoughts* 29. To look at things with calm: *KG* 5.64 and 1 Cor 13.12; 2 Cor 13.8: the mind is like a mirror.

65

Greek

A mind has been made strong when it does not imagine the things of this world at the time of prayer.

Syriac

The mind is strong when it does not stumble over something of this world at the time of prayer.

MIND . . . STRONG: resistant to fantasy; cf. 49 (a restatement of the command to pray without distraction), 63.

66

Greek

A mind that is with God, proficient in the practice, and steered toward knowledge, perceives the irrational part of the soul only a little or even not at all, because knowledge has carried it off to the heights and separated it from sense-objects.

Syriac

The mind that with the grace of God perfects the acts of the virtues and is brought to knowledge, is perceiving little from the irrational part of the soul. For its knowledge seizes it to the height and separates it from all things that are in the world.

Cf. *KG* 2.6 and *Thoughts* 29. Proficient, *katorthōsas*, cf. *Prak.* 14 (upright deeds). "Knowledge snatches [the mind] away . . ." Cf. *KG* 2.6 and 3.56.

67

Greek

A soul possesses *apatheia* not only when it is unmoved before objects, but when it remains undisturbed even before memories of them.

Syriac

The soul is perfect, not because it does not suffer things, but because it is not even disturbed by the memory of them.

Memory: 12. For (UN)DISTURBED, (*a*)*tarachos/ē*, see 61, 21 and 22, and for *ektarassein*, 21, 22, 46, and 54.

68

Greek

The perfect one does not practice self-restraint, and the one who is free from passions does not remain patient, since patience is for the one who suffers, and self-restraint for the one who is troubled.

Syriac

[Not extant in this manuscript.]

Enkrateia and *hypomonē* superior to *apatheia*; see *Thoughts* 25 and esp. Clement of Alexandria on self-controlled persons being "in the habit of apatheia": *Stromateis* 4.22.138, and 2.18.81.1.

69

Greek

It is a great thing to pray without distraction, but greater still to sing psalms without distraction.

80 EVAGRIUS OF PONTUS

Syriac

Great it is for someone to pray without distraction; still greater that he will sing psalms without distraction.

1 Thes 5.16-18. "To pray without distraction" cf. *Prak.* 63. To recite/sing a Psalm without distraction, cf. *Prayer* 85 and Sch. 1 on Psalms 137.1 (undistracted psalmody is psalmody in the presence of angels). The reading of the final part of the Syriac has been supplied by Berlin Syr. 27 and BL Add 12175.

70

Greek

The one who has established the virtues in himself and is fully intermingled with them no longer remembers law, or commandments, or punishment, but says and does whatever the excellent habit suggests.

Syriac

He who establishes the virtues in himself and is entirely mixed with them is not doing good because of laws and the judgment which is to come, but because of the mercy of God.

Virtue as state/habit (*hexis*): see 45. Cf. *KG* 6.21, "Virtue is the excellent habit of the reasonable soul. . . ."; Sch. 184 on Prv 18.16, "The intellect's chair (or seat of the teacher) is the excellent habit upon which he who is difficult to move, is seated." NO LONGER REMEMBERS LAW: cf. 1 Tm 1.9, "The law was not established for the just, but for the ungodly and sinners. . . ."

Subtitle 8

Greek

Practical Concepts

PRAKTIKOS 81

71

Greek

Demonic songs set our desire in motion, and hurl the soul into shameful imaginings. But "psalms and hymns and spiritual songs" beckon the mind to the memory of virtue by cooling our boiling indignation and quenching our desires.

Syriac

Demonic songs stir up our desire with impure fantasies cast into our soul; and "psalms, hymns, and songs of the Spirit" call us to remembrance of virtue and cool the anger that makes us rage and the desires that inflame us.

Eph 5.19

DEMONIC SONGS: cf. Clement, *Protreptikos* 1; Basil, *Hexaemeron* 4.1; Gregory of Nazianzus, *Poem* 2.2.8; cf. *Virgin* 48, "Demoniacal odes and tunes of the flute dissolve the soul and ruin its vigor." DESIRE IN MOTION: cf. 6; *KG* 1.50. PSALMS, HYMNS AND SPIRITUAL SONGS: Eph 5.19; Col 3.16. The intellect remembering virtue, cf. 70. BY COOLING, *katapsychontes*, the same verb used in *KG* 6.25 of demons freezing a knower. BOILING INDIGNATION, cf. 11; Psalmody as a remedy, cf. 15. Illegible words in the Syriac have been supplied by Berlin Syr 27 and BL Add. 12175.

72

Greek

If wrestlers use choke-holds and counter-chokes, then when the demons wrestle with us they choke us and they are counter-choked by us. As it says, "I will choke them, and they will be unable to get up" and "My enemies and those who were choking me, themselves grew weary and fell."

Syriac

If those who enter into a contest torment and are tormented, then the demons fighting against us are like them, both when they torment us and when they are being tormented by us.

Ps 17.39; 26.2

This *kephalaion* is a syllogism, on which see *KG* 1.1. CHOKE, *thlibesthai*, "crushing": 2 Cor 1.6, 4.8, 7.5; 1 Thes 3.4, 2 Thes 1.7 and *Prak.* 42. Fighters: pr.2;

36, 48, 49, 60. Being crushed: Origen, Hom. 8.1 on Ex. Cf. Sch. 21 on Ps 17.38 (the one disallowing passioned thoughts in himself "pursues the enemy"). The Syriac omits the Bible quotations.

73

Greek

Repose is yoked with wisdom, affliction with prudence. It is impossible to possess wisdom without warfare, and it is impossible to win the war without prudence. For it has been entrusted with opposing the anger of the demons, forcing the powers of the soul to work according to nature, and preparing the way for wisdom.

Syriac

Rest belongs to wisdom; toil, to prudence. For nobody possesses wisdom without a battle and no one prevails in battle without knowledge. For this is entrusted to withstand the anger of demons who afflict the power of the soul, which accomplish their own purpose so as to possess the road to wisdom.

Repose, *anapausis*, equivalent to *apatheia*: 56; *KG* 4.44, "the Sabbath is the repose of the rational soul"; Sch. 3 on Ps 114.7 (sick person : health :: soul : repose). Wisdom, *sophia*, is the virtue allowing for the gnostic "contemplation of the logoi of bodies and the bodiless"; cf. *Prak.* 86. On yoking see *KG* 1.4. Wisdom (*Prak.* 89) and prudence correspond to Aristotle, *Nicomachean Ethics* 6.5–7. *Thumos*: cf. *KG* 1.68 and 3.34; *Monks* 68. Syriac AFFLICT THE POWER OF THE SOUL: probably plural, "powers"; *seyame* are not evident in the manuscript, but are presumed to have dropped out.

74

Greek

A monk's temptation is a thought that rises up through the passionate part of the soul and darkens the mind.

Syriac

The temptation of a solitary is a thought that rises upon the passionate part of the soul and darkens his mind.

PRAKTIKOS 83

Chapters 74 and 75 are parallel to *Gn.* 42 ("the temptation of the *gnōstikos*") and 43 ("the sin of the *gnōstikos*"). On temptation, see *Prak.* 28, 42, 59; *KG* 6.53; *Eulogius* 2.2; *Monks* 39, 47, 70; *Prayer* 12, 37, 98; *Reflections* 21. To darken the intellect, see note at 20.

75

Greek

A monk's sin is consenting to the forbidden pleasure of the thought.

Syriac

The sin of a solitary happens when in his thought he fulfills the forbidden desire. The angels rejoice when our evils diminish but the demons, when our virtues diminish.

Consent or agreement: 1 Cor 6.16 (with idol worship); *KG* 6.68; *Eulogius* 11.10, *Reflections* 45. Cf. Plotinus, *Enn.* 1.8.14. In the Syriac this kephalaion includes the first sentence of 76.

76

Greek

Angels rejoice when evil decreases; demons rejoice when virtue decreases—for the former are servants of mercy and love, and the latter are attendants of rage and hatred. The first fill us with spiritual *theōria* as they approach; the second cast the soul into lewd imaginings as they draw near.

Syriac

For the angels are servants of love and mercies, but [the demons] are not attendants to them, but to anger and hatred. And when the angels draw near to us they fill us with spiritual vision. The demons in their approach turn the soul to lewd fantasies.

Angels always rejoice: Sch. 3 on Ps 12.5; Sch. 10 on Ps 37.17. Humans between angels and demons: 24; *KG* 3.46; 6.86, 88 and 90; on the approach of demons or angels, *KG* 1.68, 3.78; shameful imaginations, 71.

84 EVAGRIUS OF PONTUS

77

Greek

The virtues do not stop the assaults of the demons, but they do keep us unharmed.

Syriac

The virtues do not restrain the assaults of the demons from us, but they guard us in holiness.

Acquiring the virtues leads to *apatheia*, but temptations continue; cf. 36, 70; nonetheless the soul can remain innocent and impassible, *KG* 5.31, 82.

78

Greek

Practice is a spiritual method clearing out the passionate part of the soul.

Syriac

The practice of virtue is a spiritual method of purifying the passionate part of the soul.

Cf. Sch. 4 on Ps 2.12, "Education is *metriopatheia*, which happens customarily because of *praktikē*; since the *praktikē* is spiritual education purifying the passionate part of the soul." Cf. *Gn.* 1–2. The passionate part of the soul: wrath and desire; when these two are purified through the practice the intellect ceases to be subject to passions. Cf. also *Prak.* 38, 49.

79

Greek

The energies of the commandments are not sufficient to heal the powers of the soul completely, unless the corresponding *theōriai* follow them in the mind.

Syriac

The actions of the commandments do not suffice to perfectly heal the powers of the soul, unless there will be found in it the true faith that makes right the way of life.

PRAKTIKOS 85

Healing of the soul: cf. 54–56. Requires healing of the powers of the soul (become holy and intelligible powers, cf. *Gn.* 44). Perfect impassibility: only gaining contemplations completes the *praktikē*. Cf. 82 and 83; succession: 12 and 59.

80

Greek

It is impossible to resist all the thoughts suggested to us by angels, but it is possible to deflect all those suggested by demons. The former are followed by a state of peace, the latter by a state of turmoil.

Syriac

It is not possible to resist all the thoughts from angels that come to us. But it is possible to turn away all the thoughts that come from demons. And after these thoughts from the angels, there is a return to peace, but after these thoughts of the demons, a return to trouble.

Angelic thoughts irresistible and lead to contemplation (cf. 24, 76). For parallels see *Prayer* 30, 74–75. Angelic intervention: *Antirr.* 2.14.

81

Greek

Love is a child of *apatheia*; but *apatheia* is a flower of the practice. The keeping of the commandments sustains a practice, and their sentinel is the fear of God, which is begotten by the correct faith. Faith is an innate good that exists naturally even in those who have not yet believed in God.

Syriac

Love is the child of *apatheia*. *Apatheia* is the flower of the practice. The practices are established by guarding the commandments. But the fear of God, which is the child of true faith, guards the commandments. But this faith is a good that is in the soul, that is naturally found also among those who do not yet believe in God.

Cf. *Monks* 3–6 and 67–69; Sch. 11 on Ps 24.20 (hope is the daughter of affliction; affliction, the offspring of endurance; rephrased at Sch. 4 on Ps 129.4–5). Offspring: pr.8; *Gn.* 28; *Thoughts* 10; Sch. 256 on Prv 23.18; Sch. 3 on Ps 91.7 (foolishness > evil > ignorance). Cf. *Eulogius* 23. Observance of the commandments: Gregory of Nazianzus, *Or.* 39.8. Faith as *endiatheton agathon*, an imminent good: see Clement, *Strom.* 7.10.55, using the Stoic distinction between Grk. *endiathetos* (innate) and *prophōrikos* (applied); Athanasius, *Life of Anthony* 77. On faith, see pr.4 (symbolized by cloth), pr.8 (established by fear of God), 84 (begins love); *KG* 3.83 (willed good); 4.48 (turban a symbol); Sch. 6 on Ps 44.6 ("arrows of faith").

82

Greek

Just as the soul, working through the body, perceives the sick members, so also the mind, exercising the activity proper to it, recognizes its own powers, and discovers the commandment that can heal what is hindering it.

Syriac

Just as the soul acts through the body, sensing the members that are ailing, so also our mind is brought to know its powers when exercising its activities. And that which is a hindrance may be for it the commandment that heals it.

EXERCISING THE ACTIVITY: cf. 86; *Prayer* 83. RECOGNIZES, begins to know, *epigignōskein*; 43, 56, and 57, where the purified intellect gains discernment. Commandments as remedies, *therapeutikē entolē*: 79, 54.

83

Greek

The mind waging war against the passions will not observe the reasons associated with the war: it is like someone fighting at night. But when it has obtained *apatheia*, it will easily recognize the stratagems of the enemies.

Syriac

Our mind, when waging a war against passion, does not understand the ways of war but resembles those who battle at night. But if it will gain *apatheia*, it will easily recognize the ways of its enemies.

War at night: cf. Sch. 2 on Ps 95.4, "the shield of Christ is true knowledge." The *logoi*—reasons, designs—for war are unclear to the intellect when it is in the middle of war. Only when it obtains apatheia does it understand. Cf. Sch. 72 on Psalms 118.159, "logoi of practical knowledge." STRATAGEMS: "Wiles (maneuvers, *methodoi*) of the enemies": Eph 6.11.

84

Greek

Love is the frontier of practice, theology is that of knowledge. Faith is the beginning of one; natural *theōria*, of the other. Those among the demons who lay hold of the passionate part of the soul are said to oppose the practice; those that harass the reasoning part are named enemies of all truth and adversaries of *theōria*.

Syriac

The end of deeds is love but that of knowledge, to speak to God. But the beginning of them both is faith and *theōria* of natures. But those who war against the passionate part of the soul are said to be the opponents of deeds, and those who attack with the thoughts are called the enemies of all truth and the opponents of higher *theōria*. There is nothing that purifies bodies and remains with those who have been purified after their purification.

Cf. pr.8; *Monks* 3. Love as daughter of impassibility: 81. Demons presiding (*protostatoi*) over the eight thoughts; *Thoughts* 1. Cf. Job 15.14; Ac 2.5. Reasoning part, *logistikon*: 86, 89. Two kinds of demons: Sch. 2 on Psalms 117.10 (encircling the practiced and the contemplative, against which justice and wisdom are deployed). Cf. 89. In the Syriac this kephalaion concludes with the first sentence of 85.

85

Greek

Nothing that purifies bodies afterward persists in those who have been purified; but the virtues both purify the soul and remain in it after it has been purified.

Syriac

But the virtues purify the soul and after its purification remain beside it.

Cf. 70; the virtues purify the soul and continue to assist it: 77. PURIFY: 30, cf. *Prayer* 38; Porphyry, *Launching Points to the Intelligibles* 18, 19, 32.

88 EVAGRIUS OF PONTUS

86

Greek

The rational soul is active according to nature when its desiring part inclines toward virtue, its angering part fights on its behalf, and its reasoning part concentrates on the *theōria* of beings.

Syriac

The rational soul operates naturally when the desiring part longs for virtue, and the angering part fights for it. Its rational [part] understands through the *theōria* of the things that exist.

According to nature, *kata physin*: 24, 42, 73; *KG* 1.64; Plato, *Republic* 444 c–e; *Life of Anthony* 20. Prudence presides over the soul: 73. Beings (Greek) vs. exist (Syriac): cf. 92.

87

Greek

Anyone advancing in a practice decreases the passions, and anyone advancing in *theōria* decreases ignorance. There will be a complete destruction of the passions, but for ignorance they say that in one respect there is a limit, but in another respect, there is not.

Syriac

Anyone who advances in the deeds of virtue diminishes his passions, but anyone who comes to the beginning of knowledge diminishes ignorance and passions. There will be a time when ignorance will be perfectly destroyed, but as they say, there is an ending to it and there is not.

Advance, *prokoptō*, 43, 59. Decreases, *meioi*, 20, 76. Complete destruction, *phthora*: cf. *Thoughts* 23. Limitlessness of the knowledge of God: *KG* 3.63; 1.71; Sch. 2 on Ps 144.3. Limit: *Prak.* 83. Limitless ignorance means that knowledge is incomplete. They say (cf. *KG* 1.71): possibly refers to *Life of Moses*, whether by Philo or by Gregory of Nyssa, or to the anti-Eunomian polemic by Basil of Caesarea in *Against Eunomius* and Gregory of Nazianzus in *Theological*

PRAKTIKOS   89

Oration 2 (Or. 28); cf. also John Chrysostom, *On the Incomprehensibility of God.* On its complement, the limit (*peras*) of knowledge: Aristotle, *Metaphysics* 1022a10; Clement, *Paidagogos* 1.6.29.3 (*anapausis*). Our reading of the Syriac is corroborated here by BL Add. 12175.

88

Greek

Things that are good or bad according to their use produce both virtues and vices; it is left to prudence to use them for one or the other.

Syriac

Actions are goods or evils according to use, but it belongs to prudence to use one or the other of them as appropriate.

GOOD OR BAD: parts of the soul; cf. 86; *KG* 3.59. *Thumos* and *epithumia* are not bad in themselves; they are neutral (*adiaphora*) as in Epictetus, *Discourses* 2.5. On prudence, see 73.

89

Greek

According to our sage teacher, the rational soul is tripartite. When virtue exists in the rational part it is called prudence, understanding, and wisdom; in the desiring part, temperance, love, and self-restraint; in the angering part, courage and endurance; and in the entire soul, it is justice. Now the work of prudence is to lead the war against the opposing powers, to defend the virtues, to draw up the battle lines against the vices, and to manage what lies between the two according to the occasion. It is the task of intelligence to administer harmoniously all things that help us toward the goal. The task of wisdom is to observe the reasons of corporeal and incorporeal beings. The task of temperance is to observe without passion the objects that set in motion irrational imaginings within us. The task of love is to devote oneself to every image of God as if to the prototype, even when the demons undertake to defile them. The task of self-restraint is to cast off joyfully every pleasure of the palate. To have no fear of enemies and to endure terrors readily is the task of endurance and courage. The task of justice is to achieve a certain concord and harmony among the parts of the soul.

90 EVAGRIUS OF PONTUS

Syriac

There are three parts of the rational soul, as our wise teacher said. And when virtue is in the reasoning part of the soul, it is called prudence and wisdom and knowledge; but when virtue is in the desiring part, love, purity, and patience. But when in the angering part, [virtue] is courage and endurance. Throughout our soul it is justice. And the task of wisdom is to stand against the opposing powers and to fight for the virtues, and also to battle with evils, and to manage the things that are neutral, neither good nor evil, according to the moments/opportunities. [The task] of knowledge is to direct appropriately everything suitable for use. [The task] of wisdom is to know the reasons that are corporeal and incorporeal. The task of purity is that one see without the passions things that move in us foolish fantasies; of love is to receive every image of God as the true prototype even if the demons are able to defile them; of patience is to remove from the soul with joy every desire that exists, and not to fear its enemies, and with good will to endure in the face of evils. It is [the task] of justice that it make the soul equal in all its parts.

This kephalaion is a counterpart to *Gn.* 44, which is placed in a similar location (at the end, just before a series of sayings), provides a similar summary of four virtues, and is explicitly credited to Gregory. The text, as a whole, goes back to a treatise, *On the Virtues and the Vices*, which survives under the name of Aristotle (attested in manuscripts, collected by John Stobaeus [fifth century CE], and abbreviated heavily by pseudo-Andronicus of Rhodes). Although it predates Evagrius, probably by centuries, it is datable only generally to late antiquity. Evagrius knew readers would be aware of the earlier text when he wrote this kephalaion, and presumably he invited close comparison.

The two texts differ considerably. Ps.-Aristotle credits the text to Plato and distributes eight virtues and vices to the soul: one to the rational part, two to the *thumos* and *epithumetikon* respectively, and three to the soul as a whole. *Prak.* 89 credits the text to "our wise teacher" (likely Gregory; see below), drops the eight vices, reverses the angering and desiring parts, and extensively revises and redistributes a list of nine virtues, seen best in this table of comparisons, where unique virtues are set in boldface.

Virtue of . . .	ps.-Aristotle	*Prak.* 89
. . . the logistikon	*phronēsis*	*phronēsis,* **synesis, sophia**
. . . the angering part	*praotēs, andreia*	*andreia,* **hypomonē**
. . . the desiring part	*sophrosynē, enkrateia*	*sophrosynē,* **agapē***, enkrateia*
. . . all	*dikaiosynē,* **eleutheriotēs,** *megalopsychia*	*dikaiosynē*

PRAKTIKOS 91

Three virtues are not retained in *Prak.* 89: see note at pr.4 on *praotēs*, gentleness; on *megalopsychia* see Sch. 5 on Ps 100.5 (puffery or pride is an imitation of largeness of soul). Liberality or generosity, *eleutheriotēs*, is absent in the extant Greek corpus. The four virtues in *Prak.* 89 but not in ps.-Aristotle are central to Evagrius' other writings. One is tempted to ascribe authorship directly to Evagrius, but the terminology is common in other fourth-century Christian authors such as Gregory of Nazianzus. OUR SAGE TEACHER: likely Gregory of Naz., widely praised in other places: *Prak.* ep. (righteous); *Gn.* 44 (just); *Letter on Faith* 3 (mouth of Christ). Wise teacher: *Gn.* 48 (Didymus); *KG* 6.51 (unnamed). The tripartite soul goes back to Plato/Socrates (*Republic* 4 passim: the healthy state mirrors the human soul, and so has three gradated parts).

90

Greek

The sheaves are a fruit of the seeds, and knowledge is a fruit of the virtues. And as tears accompany the seeds, so joy accompanies the sheaves.

Syriac

The fruits of seeds are the sheaves, but of the virtues, are knowledge. And as tears accompany seeds, so also joys the sheaves.

cf. Ps 125.6

SEEDS of virtue: 57; *KG* 1.24, 39–40. TEARS: Sch. 3 on Ps 125.5 (sowing : tears : *praktikē* :: reaping : joy : gnosis). Cf. *Prak.* 32.

Subtitle 9

Greek

Sayings of Holy Monks

SAYINGS: *rhēseis*: Clement, Str 3.6; Basil, *Letter* 236. The term does not mean *apophthegmata*, rarely used by fourth-century Christian authors. These ten sayings, none of which are attested in any extant corpora attributed to the person, were added by Evagrius to the first version of the *Praktikos*. Cf. discussion by Guillaumont, *Traite pratique*, 116–125.

92 EVAGRIUS OF PONTUS

91

Greek

It is necessary both to inquire into the paths of the monks who have preceded us uprightly and to be rightly guided upon them, for there is much to discover that was admirably spoken or done by the monks. For instance, one of them said that a dry and regular diet, yoked with love, guides a monk more quickly into the harbor of *apatheia*. The same man freed one of the brothers troubled by apparitions at night by requiring him, while fasting, to serve the sick. When asked, he said that passions of this kind are extinguished by nothing so well as by mercy.

Syriac

It is also right for us to trace and to emulate the paths of the solitaries, they who traveled before us in the right way. We can find many things that were done and said well by them. Among them is this: one of them said that regularly following a diet of dry food, joined with love, easily leads the solitary into the harbor of *apatheia*. This same one, when he saw a brother troubled at night, freed him from fantasies by ordering him to fast and serve the brothers who were sick. When asked, he said that these passions are extinguished by nothing other than mercy.

To INQUIRE INTO THE PATHS: Jer 6.16; THE MONKS WHO HAVE PRECEDED US: cf. *Letter* 17.1. Dietary regimen: *Prak.* 17, 29. Pity: 15, 20; night visions: 11, 21; *Antirr.* 5.12.

92

Greek

One of the sages of that time came to Anthony the just and said, "How do you persevere, father, deprived of the consolation of books?" He replied, "My book, philosopher, is the nature of beings, and it is there whenever I want to read the words of God."

Syriac

One of the sages approached the righteous Anthony and said to him, "How do you persevere, O my father, when you are deprived of the consolation of books?"

PRAKTIKOS 93

But he answered and said, "My book is, O sage, the nature of things that exist, and it is near to me when I want to read the words of God."

> Cf. *Life of Anthony* 72–80, encounter with philosophers. Although Athanasius asserts Anthony's illiteracy, this chapter has Anthony demur by citing a superior knowledge, the direct "knowledge of created things" and the ability to discern from them the "reasons" of God (*anaginōskein tous logous tou Theou*). BEINGS (Greek) vs. EXIST (Syriac): cf. 86. CONSOLATION, *paramythia*: 2 Thes 2.12; 5.14; Clement, *Paidagogos* 1.10. Cf. *KG* 1.14; 2.1–2; 3.57; *Letter to Melania* 35–50; and Sch. 8 on Ps 138.16, "The contemplation of corporeals and incorporeals is the book of God."

93

Greek

That "vessel of election," the old man Macarius the Egyptian, asked me, "Why, when we resent human beings, do we obliterate the soul's power of memory, but remain unharmed when we resent demons?" I was at a loss for an answer, and asked for the reason. He said, "It is because the first is contrary to the nature of anger, while the second is in accordance with it."

Syriac

The "vessel of election," the old man Macarius the Egyptian, asked me, "Why is it that when we hold a grudge against humans, we destroy the soul's power of memory, but when we stay angry at demons we remain unharmed?" And since I was unable to answer him, I asked him to teach me about this. He said to me, "The former is outside the nature of anger, but the latter, which is against the demons, belongs to its nature."

Ac 9.15

> See 29; *Antirr.* 4.45. Remembrance: the nous. See 23, *KG* 3.90 and 6.13. On remembrance and anger: *KG* 4.73. ACCORDING TO NATURE, *kata physin*: 24, 42, 73; *KG* 1.64. On the battle of the *thumistikon* against demons, *Eulogius* 21.

94 EVAGRIUS OF PONTUS

94

Greek

I went to visit the holy father Macarius in the full heat of midday, and burning with thirst I asked for some water to drink. He said, "Make do with the shade; there are many people traveling by road or sailing at this very moment, and they lack even that." Then, while exercising myself beside him with words about self-restraint, he said, "Courage, child; for twenty whole years I have never taken my fill of bread or water or sleep. I eat my bread by weight, I drink my water by measure, and leaning myself against a wall, I snatch a little sleep."

Syriac

I came in the glare of midday to our holy father Macarius. Since I was burning with great thirst I asked for water to drink. But he said to me, "The shade will be enough for you. For there are many traveling on boats on the sea or donkeys who lack even this." As he was instructing me with words about endurance, he said to me, "Take heart my son, and know that in all these twenty years I have not taken my fill of bread, water, or sleep. For I eat my bread by weight, and I drink my water by measure, and leaning myself against the wall I snatch a little bit of sleep."

THE HOLY FATHER MACARIUS: Macarius the Alexandrian. Cf. *Antirr.* 4.23; 8.26; *Disc.* 183. Macarius's practice of eating a small amount of bread and a little water: cf. *Monks* 102 alluding to Ezek 4.10–11. Cf. *Prak.* 16, 17; *Thoughts* 35, citing "the companions of Daniel, their poor life and the grains" (Dn 1.12, 16). The Syriac inverts the middle of this chapter, so that it is Macarius, not the interlocutor, who is speaking. This may go back to a variation in the Greek, where *moi* replaces *mou*.

95

Greek

One of the monks was informed of the death of his father. He said to the one who announced it, "Cease blaspheming, for my father is immortal."

Syriac

Someone notified one of the solitaries of the death of his father. But [the monk] responded and said, "Be quiet, man, and do not blaspheme, for my own Father is immortal."

PRAKTIKOS 95

MY FATHER: Jn 8.19; IMMORTAL, 1 Tm 1.17, Rev 6.8. Cf. Palladius, *Lausiac History* 38.13: a saying of Evagrius himself. Infrequent visits to family, *Foundations* 5.

96

Greek

One of the brothers inquired of one of the old men if he would permit him to eat with his mothers and sisters when he went to a house. He said, "Do not eat with a woman."

Syriac

One of the brothers asked one of the old men if he would allow him to eat with his mother and sisters in the house. But he said to him, "You are forbidden to eat with a woman."

INQUIRED, *punthanomai*: cf. Jn 4.52, Ac 23.20, 17.19, Lk 15.26, etc. and Plato, *Gorgias* 455c, *Laws* 196c. Eating with women: Clement, *Paidagogos* 2.1.

97

Greek

One of the brothers possessed only a gospel-book, which he sold to feed the hungry, offering a saying worth remembering: "I have sold the very word that says to me, 'Sell your possessions and give to the poor.'"

Syriac

One of the solitaries possessed only a gospel book. He sold it and gave [the proceeds] to the poor, and spoke a word that is worthy of remembrance: "This very word that says to me, 'Sell everything that you have and give to the hungry'— this I am selling, doing what suffices to fulfill the commandment."

Mt 19.21

Cf. Lk 18.22. Gospel as a single book: Gregory of Nyssa, *Against Eunomius* 2; private use as a *pharmakon* (charm or medicine): Chrysostom, *On the Statues* 19.4, *Hom. on 1 Cor* 43.4.

96 EVAGRIUS OF PONTUS

98

Greek

There is an island near Alexandria, in the northern part of the lake called Mareotis, where lives a monk who is one of the most distinguished within the camp of the gnostics. He declared that everything done by the monks is done for one of five reasons: for the sake of God, nature, custom, necessity, or manual work. He also said that although virtue is one by nature, it takes form in the powers of the soul. For sunlight, he said, although without form, is naturally given form by the windows through which it passes.

Syriac

Near Alexandria on the north side of the lake called Maria there was dwelling a certain monk who was the most eminent in the encampments of the gnostics. That one was saying, "All things done by solitaries are done for five reasons: for God, for nature, for habit, for constraint, for manual work." The same one was saying, "Virtue is one in its nature, but takes many forms in the various powers of the soul, just as the light of the sun is without shape, but takes various shapes in the form of the windows through which it passes."

> The island is in Lake Mareotis, cf. Strabo, *Geography* 17, 14. A MONK . . . MOST DISTINGUISHED: possibly Didymus; cf. *Gn.* 48, "a great and gnostic teacher." ENCAMPMENT: Heb 13.11, 12 (fortified camp), 11.34 (battle-line); Philo, *Giants* 54. FIVE REASONS: Aristotle, *Nicomachean Ethics* 3.5. Powers of the souls: *KG* 2.9. Virtue as single quality: Philo, *On Sacrifice* 84; Clement, *Stromateis* 1.20.97.3. Cf. *Praktikos* 89.

99

Greek

Yet another of the monks said, "I strip away pleasures in order to cut away excuses for anger. For I know that anger is always fighting on behalf of pleasures, troubling my mind, and chasing away knowledge." One of the old men said that love does not know how to hoard food or money. And the same monk said, "I do not know that I have ever been fooled by the demons twice about the same thing."

PRAKTIKOS   97

Syriac

Yet another of the solitaries was saying, "I remove desires from my soul so that I may cut out the causes of anger. For I know that it is a fighter on behalf of pleasures and troubles my mind, and chases away my knowledge" [100]. And one of the old men was saying, "Love knows not to keep a store of food or money." This old man was saying, "Indeed, I do not know that the demons have deceived me twice in the same matter."

> Three anonymous sayings. FOOD AND MONEY, *brōmatōn ē chrēmatōn*, a phrase distinctive to Evagrius: *Thoughts* 1, 3, 5; *Disc.* 15, 69, 97, 159. FOOLED BY THE DEMONS: *Prayer* 94. On the *thumetikon*, see 24; *KG* 4.47; 6.63.

100

Greek

To love all the brothers equally is not possible, but it is possible to encounter all of them free of passion, freed from resentment and hate. One must love priests after the Lord, because they purify us through the holy mysteries and pray for us. But our old men must be honored like the angels, for they are the ones who anoint us for contests and heal the bites of the wild beasts.

Syriac

It is not possible to love all the brothers equally, but it is possible to meet all without passion when we are free from hatred and resentment [102]. [We are] to love priests after our Lord, those who by means of the holy mysteries purify us and pray on our behalf [103]. [We are] to revere the old men as angels, for they are those who ready us for the contest and heal us from the bites of wild beasts.

> Love as the goal of *praktikē*: 84; *apatheia* and love, 81. PRIESTS: 13; *Thoughts* 21, 37; HOLY MYSTERIES, *Thoughts* 8. Revealing mysteries: Sch. 210 on Prv 20.9; *Disc.* 148 (of knowledge), 150 (of God). Purification: *KG* 3.9; *Thoughts* 19.24; *Prayer* 40; *Letter* 12. Old men like the angels: *KG* 3.46; 6.35, 90; on angels, *Prak.* 24, 76. 102 . . . 103: the Syriac manuscript numeration is disrupted, and continues without break into the *Gnostikos* with 104.

98 EVAGRIUS OF PONTUS

Epilogue

Greek

I have said enough to you now, my dearest brother Anatolius, about a practice. Such things we have found, by the grace of the Holy Spirit, gleaning the ripening grapes from our harvest. But when the "sun of righteousness" will shine on us at its zenith, and the grape cluster becomes fully ripe, then we shall drink its wine, which "gladdens the human heart," thanks to the prayers and intercessions of the righteous Gregory who planted me, and of the holy fathers who now water me, and by the power of Christ Jesus our Lord, who makes me grow, to whom be glory and power for ever and ever. Amen.

Mal 3.20; Ps 103.15; cf. 1 Cor 3.6–7

This brief conclusion is phrased as the conclusion to the letter to Anatolios. It is absent in the Syriac tradition. Grappling, cf. 4 Mc 2.9. The vine: Is 5.1-6 and *Letters* 2, 46. Sun of justice, Mal 3.20, following Origen, *Hom. on Lv* 13.2, *Comm. on Jn* 32.24 and 103.19–22. The grape: knowledge, *KG* 5.32 and wine "rejoices the heart of the human being" (Ps. 103.15) as joy accompanies knowledge, *Prak.* 90. RIGHTEOUS GREGORY, *Gn.* 44 and see Gregory of Naz., *Letter* 6 citing 1 Cor 3.6. Planting: 1 Cor 3.6, and *Letter* 46, probably to Gregory. Now: establishes Evagrius's *cursus honorum*, from Gregory to the "holy fathers" of Egypt = the monks of Nitria and Kellia.

Gnostikos

We follow the edition by the Guillaumonts (Sources chrétiennes 356) for the Greek text. Because S3 revises S1, and S2 seems to know both S1 and S3, the Syriac translations appear in the order S1, S3, then S2. For ease of reference, the corresponding manuscripts are as follows:

S1: BL Add. 14581
S3 (revising S1): BL Add. 17167
S2: BL Add. 17165 and 14616

1

Greek

Practiced ones apprehend practical *logoi*, but gnostics see [the things of] knowledge.

S1

Practiced ones understand practical *logoi*, but gnostics will see questions of knowledge.

S3

Practiced ones understand practical *logoi*, but gnostics will see parables of knowledge.

S2

[Concerning that which relates to knowledge.] The first practiced ones of the commandments will consider the power of God's commandments; the gnostics [will consider] parables about knowledge.

This kephalaion introduces the next two, structurally comparable to *Prak.* 1–3. On the distinction between *praktikoi* and *gnōstikoi*, see *KG* 5.65; *Reflections*

100   EVAGRIUS OF PONTUS

32–33, 38–39; and *Monks* 121, referring to Prv 22.2. A *praktikos* understands (*noesousi*), but the *gnōstikos* sees (*opsontai*). On the *logoi* or reasons of a *praktikos*, see Sch. 72 on Ps 118.159. The term *gnōstikos* used in positive sense: Clement, *Strom.* 6 and 7 passim from Plato, *Politics* 258e, 261b, ref. to theoretical knowledge itself; Aristotle *Posterior Analyt.* 100a11; in negative sense as one possessing "false knowledge," 1 Tm 6.20; versus dualists, Irenaeus, *Heresies* 1.11.1; Epiphanius, *Panarion* 26, 31, and Chrysostom, *Hom. on 1 Tm* 18.2. PARABLES (S3): can also be translated "riddles." CONCERNING THAT (S2): This title was mistakenly incorporated in the text. FIRST (S2): an artifact of the Greek, meaning kephalaion number 1.

2

Greek

The practiced one possesses merely the impassioned part of the soul free from passion.

S1

The practiced one possesses the impassioned part of his soul without passion.

S3

The practiced one possesses the impassioned part of his soul without passion.

S2

The practiced one has caused the evil passions of his soul to cease, and possesses health of mind by means of steadfast disciplines.

This kephalaion is to be contrasted with the next. The *praktikos* has (merely) gained *apatheia* as a necessary condition for *gnōsis*; cf. *Prak.* 78.

3

Greek

The gnostic, however, offers a *logos* of salt to the impure, and of light to the pure.

S1

The gnostic, however, is in the likeness of salt for the impure, and like light for the pure.

S3

The gnostic however, is in the likeness of salt for the impure, and as light for the pure.

S2

The gnostic is salt for the rotten and light for the pure.

cf. Mt 5.13–14

This kephalaion is to be contrasted with the previous one. SALT: Mt 5.13–14. Contrast between classes of Christians: Clement, *Who Is the Rich Man* 36. According to the Guillaumonts, Evagrius is the first to distinguish in this way between salt and light. On light and the *gnōstikos* see *KG* 1.74, 81; 5.15; Sch. 9 on Ps 89.17 (illumination is knowledge of God); Clement of Alexandria, *Strom.* 7.12.79.5.

4

Greek

The knowledge that happens to us from the outside tries to make proof of materials through the[ir] *logoi*. But the innate [knowledge] that comes from the grace of God presents matters directly to the understanding, [so that as] the mind looks toward them, it receives their *logoi*. Error is opposed to the first; rage, anger, and the things that keep company with them [are opposed] to the second.

S1

Knowledge that comes to us from outside of us shows its material by means of reasons; but that which is within us from the grace of God shows those matters directly to the understanding, and our mind beholds them and brings forth the *logoi* about them. Error is the opposite of the knowledge that is from outside, and rage and anger and the things joined to them are [the opposite] of the second [knowledge].

102 EVAGRIUS OF PONTUS

S3

Knowledge that comes to us from outside shows us its materials by means of reasons, but that which is within us from the grace of God shows the matters nakedly to the understanding, so that when the mind beholds them it is receptive to their *logoi*. Error is opposed to the first; to the second, rage and anger, and those things joined to them.

S2

When we seek the instruction that is outside, we receive it by wise reasons. But true knowledge exists in us from the grace of God that shows the matters to our understanding simply, and our mind will see those matters simply and take pains to arrive at their truth. Error casts out the first knowledge from us, in that we stray from its teaching. Rage and anger and whatever is born from them make the second knowledge vanish from us.

KNOWLEDGE ... FROM THE OUTSIDE, *exōthen* ... *gnōsis*, was commonly used in the fourth century to signify all knowledge not specifically Christian: Sch. 19 on Ps 104.37 (silver and gold symbolize outside knowledge); Sch. 37 on Ps 118.85 (the verse to be applied to teachers of outside knowledge). On that knowledge FROM THE GRACE OF GOD see 45; *KG* 4.90; 6.22; *Prayer* 63; *Letter* 62. MIND WILL SEE THOSE MATTERS SIMPLY AND TAKE PAINS TO ARRIVE AT THEIR TRUTH (S2): BL Add.: "that sees those matters is changed according to their truth."

5

Greek

All the virtues guide the gnostic, but above all freedom from rage. For the one who has touched knowledge but is easily moved to rage is like someone who gouges out his own eyes with an iron awl.

S1

All the virtues lift up the path before the gnostic. But greater than all of them is that of not yielding to [lit., "ascending"] one's anger. For the one who has drawn near to knowledge and is easily moved by anger resembles someone stabbing his eyes with an iron needle.

GNOSTIKOS 103

S3

All the virtues show the path before the gnostic, but greater than all of them is that of not yielding to [lit., "ascending"] one's anger. But the one who has drawn near to knowledge and is easily moved by anger resembles someone sticking an iron needle in his eyes.

S2

The gnostic is guided to knowledge by means of all the established ways of conduct. But greater than all of them is not being easily enraged. For someone who has received knowledge and is quickly stirred to anger resembles a man piercing his eyes with a needle.

Negation of anger (*aorgēsia*) is gentleness (*prautēs*) and freedom from wrath (*ataraxia*) in Sch. 1 on Ps 131.1 and close to love at *Prak.* 38. *Letter* 27: *aorgēsia* the "mother of knowledge." On iron cf. *Monks* 109; Sch. 4 on Ps 106.10. Anger and the knower: 10; *KG* 4.38; 5.27, 6.63; *Prayer* 64; *Eight Thoughts* 9; Sch. 4 on Ps 6.8; Sch. 7 on Ps 30.10. Anger blinds: see *Prak.* 20; anger hinders the teacher: *Masters and Disciples*, esp. 30–35. To KNOWLEDGE / EASILY (S2): absent in BL Add. 14616. STABBING / STICKING / PIERCING: the three Syriac translations use different verbs.

6

Greek

Let the gnostic be careful when accommodating [students], lest accommodation inadvertently become a habit. And let him endeavor to establish all the virtues equally and constantly, so that they are reciprocally working in him too, because it is natural for the mind to be betrayed by what is inferior.

S1

Let the gnostic take care in his accommodation, lest he go astray and become immersed in it himself. Let him strive to perfect all of the virtues equally so that they come one after the other. For it is natural for our mind to be betrayed by what is inferior.

S3

Let the gnostic take care in his accommodation, lest he go astray and become immersed in it himself. Let him strive to perfect all of the virtues equally so that

104 EVAGRIUS OF PONTUS

they accompany one another in him. For it is natural for the mind to be betrayed by what is inferior.

S2

Let the gnostic take care in his simplification, lest he be stolen away by it and it becomes for him like a habit. Let him therefore strive valiantly to complete all victories in harmony, and may they complete one another in him. For the mind grasping an inferior success is being handed over to sin.

> First mention of discretion in teaching; see also 12. From this point forward, many kephalaia are phrased as admonitions. ACCOMMODATION corresponds to *synkatabasis*, a technical term describing the temporary condescension of a teacher to the student, and applied to the incarnation, when God in Christ came down to the human level. Cf. Sch. 241 on Prv 22.11–12: "It must be noted that Christ as king is said by *synkatabasis* to shepherd us …"; Sch. 4 on Ps 22.5; Sch. 118 on Prv 10.3. See Philodemus, *Rhetoric* 2.25. A quality of the gods, Julian, *Or.* 5 171b; Clement of Alexandria, *Strom.* 7.12.80.8 and 7.9.53.3–4, the latter commenting on Paul's circumcision of Timothy as an example (Ac 16.1–5). S2 prefers the less nuanced SIMPLIFICATION. HABIT, *hexis*: *Prak.* 45. IMMERSED, lit. "dipped," in S1 and S3 may reflect underlying Greek manuscripts that had *brexis* (wetting) instead of *hexis* (habit). Practicing all the virtues as a means of improvement (*katorthoun*): *Prak.* 14. Betrayal of the intellect: *Prayer* 1. Cf. *Gn.* 33 on healing oneself by healing others; *KG* 2.81; *Letter* 47.

7

S1

Let the gnostic at all times train himself in almsgiving and be prepared to do good things. But if he is lacking money, let him make use of the instrument of his soul. For everything, even without money, is by nature for almsgiving, which those five virgins were not doing, and so their lamps were extinguished.

S3

Let the gnostic at all times train himself in almsgiving. But if he is lacking money, let him make use of the instruments of his soul, for all of these are by nature for almsgiving. When it was lacking from those five virgins, their lamps were extinguished.

S2

Let the gnostic devote himself unceasingly to alms, and let him prepare himself for generosity toward the poor. And if he has no possessions that he can use to extend his hand and from them give to the poor, let him work with his hands and do good, which is mystically held to be the oil that was lacking to the virgins, and so their lamps were extinguished.

cf. Mt 25.1–13

THE INSTRUMENT OF HIS SOUL: an Aristotelian phrase; see *KG* 1.67; 2.80; 6.72; *Thoughts* 4. BY NATURE FOR ALMSGIVING, rendered in S2 as oil, an explicitation of the biblical allusion. Given the uncertainty of the original Greek (this is the first chapter in *Gnostikos* for which the Greek is lacking) and the similarity of mercy (*eleos*) and oil (*elaion*), each Syriac translator may simply have been following the text at hand. On the mercy and generosity of the *gnōstikos*, see *Prak.* 91, as well as Clement of Alexandria, *Paidagogos* 62.3. Lack of mercy while fasting: *Letter* 27, *Antirr.* 3. Oil (as in S2): mercy (*KG* 4.25) and knowledge (*KG* 4.21 and Sch. 11 on Ps 88.21). Wise and foolish virgins: *Virgin* 43.

8

Greek

It is shameful for a gnostic to be involved in a legal dispute, whether as the one wronged or the one who did wrong. If as the one wronged, [it is shameful] because he did not endure; if as the one who did wrong, [it is shameful] because he did wrong.

S1

It is disgraceful for a gnostic to speak in a dispute, whether as the one wronged or the one doing wrong: if he was wronged, [it is disgraceful] because he did not endure it, and if doing wrong, then [it is disgraceful] because of the wrong itself.

S3

It is disgraceful for a gnostic to speak in a dispute, whether as the one wronged or the one doing wrong: if he was wronged, [it is disgraceful] because he did not endure it, and if doing wrong, then [it is disgraceful] because of the wrong itself.

106 EVAGRIUS OF PONTUS

S2

It is shameful for a gnostic to enter into a dispute because of transitory matters, whether he did wrong or was wronged. If he did wrong, [it is shameful] because he caused hurt; if he was wronged, [it is shameful] because he did not endure it.

> The *gnōstikos* must not go to court (1 Cor 6.1–8): *Letters* 33, 60; *Antirr.* 3.39, where lawsuits are associated with love of money. See also *Thoughts* 32; Basil of Caesarea, *Longer Rules* 9.2 (taking parents to court); Clement of Alexandria, *Strom.* 7.14.84.5.

9

Greek

When knowledge is protected, it teaches the one participating in it how it can be carefully protected and advance even more.

S1

Knowledge that is preserved teaches the one who receives it how it is to be preserved, and how it will advance beyond itself.

S3

Knowledge that is preserved teaches the one possessing it how he will be preserved and advance beyond himself.

S2

Knowledge when it is preserved teaches the one possessing it how it will be preserved and will increase in him.

> *Exh. Monks* 2.25; cf. *Gn.* 33; *Letter* 48; and *KG* 2.81.

10

S1

Let the gnostic understand [that] at the time of interpretation he should be free from anger, hatred, sadness, bodily suffering, and anxiety.

GNOSTIKOS 107

S3

If the gnostic at the time of interpretation is free from anger and hatred and sadness, and from suffering of the body and from anxiety, let him interpret.

S2

If at the time of teaching the gnostic is free from anger and from hatred and from sadness, and from anxiety and from bodily suffering, he will confidently expound and teach.

> Anger impedes knowledge: 4, 5, 31. On the interconnections of anger, hatred, and sadness, see *Prak.* 11, 23. INTERPRETATION, Syr. *poṣāqā*: 13, 16, 20 (S2), 22 (S2), 26, 34, 40 (S2), 42 (S2); *KG* 4.61; 6.ep. The preface to the *Praktikos* in the Syriac: "Concerning the *poṣāqā* of the garments ('eskímē) of the monks in Egypt."

11

S1

It is not fitting to be meeting with many people until we are immersed in goodness, nor to have the habit of being among many people, lest our mind be filled with apparitions.

S3

Before perfect virtue, do not have familiarity or the habit of being with many people, lest our mind be filled with apparitions.

S2

Before perfection let us not allow ourselves to be seen by many people, nor to have the habit of being among many people, lest our mind be filled with their likenesses and lose pure prayer.

> On caution about encounters, see *Letter* 25; *Foundations* 5. On imaginations and fantasies, see *Prak.* 23, 46, 48, 54, etc.; *Virgin* 6; *Prayer* 1. The addition of S2, TO LOSE PURE PRAYER, shows the translator had closely read *Prak.* 23. HABIT, Syr. *'id'*: 19, 26; *Letter to Melania* 32–34.

108 EVAGRIUS OF PONTUS

12

S1

Anything that is useful for the living from the work of virtue (*praktikē*) or from nature (*physikē*) or from knowledge of God (*theologikē*) is fitting to say and do until death. But one must not say or do things from them that are irrelevant because of those who are easily scandalized.

S3

Everything that is from practice (*praktikē*) or from nature (*physikē*) or from words about God (*theologikē*) and is useful for our salvation, these things it is right for us to say and to do until death. But if from irrelevant things, one must not say or do [them] because of those who are easily scandalized.

S2

Whenever a matter that is from the commandments (*praktikē*), or from intellection of nature (*physikē*), or from words about the divine (*theologikē*) is useful to us for our salvation, these things it is fitting to do and to speak, and to stand firm in them until death. But when they are irrelevant things, with neither benefit nor harm in them, it is not fitting to say or do them because of those who are easily scandalized.

For the three stages of *praktikē, physikē, theologikē*, see *Prak.* 1. *Gnostikos* continues the *praktikē*; see *Prak.* 70, which clarifies the ambiguity of 68. IRRELEVANT THINGS, translates Grk. *ta mesa* (the middle things), a Stoic commonplace found also in *Prak.* 89. S2 captures the meaning of the term by adding WITH NEITHER BENEFIT NOR HARM IN THEM.

13

Greek

It is right [for the gnostic] to converse with solitaries and those who live in the world about a right way of life, and even in part to explain teachings about nature and theology, "without which no one will see the Lord".

GNOSTIKOS 109

S1

It is right to speak about works of virtue (*praktikē*) to youths and adolescents, and to explain a little something about the teaching of God and of nature (*theologikē* and *physikē*), for "without these things a person cannot see the Lord."

S3

It is right to speak about works of virtue (*praktikē*) to youths and to those who live in the world, and to explain a little something about the teaching of nature and words about God (*physikē* and *theologikē*), for "without these things it is not possible to see the Lord."

S2

It is right for us that we speak about established disciplines (*praktikē*) to those who live in the world and to those who are newly instructed, and that we explain to them a little something about matters of natures and divine words (*physikē* and *theologikē*), those things "without which we cannot see God."

Heb 12.14

See *Prak.* 41and 48 on those who live in the world (*kosmikoi*), and 74–75 on monks who are not yet *gnōstikoi*. On RIGHT WAY OF LIFE (*politeias orthēs*) as a synonym for the *praktikē*, see Sch. 15 on Ps 76.21. The YOUTHS of S1 and S3 and the NEWLY INSTRUCTED of S2 are to be understood as those in the early stages of monastic life. The ADOLESCENTS of S1 may reflect a confusion of two similar Syriac words, *ʿalaimē* (adolescents) and *ʿalmāyē* (seculars).

14

S1

Give an answer only to the priests—to those diligent in the fear of God—when they ask you about the mysteries that are accomplished by them and purify our inner person, and about the receptacle and crucible that are in us. It is a demonstration of the impassioned and the rational parts of the soul, and their inseparable mingling, and of when one part overcomes another part. And every one of the actions is the accomplishment of one type. Then tell them the mystery of who is the one doing these things, and of who are those with him chasing off those who prevent us from living in purity; and of which among the living beings have memory and which do not.

110   EVAGRIUS OF PONTUS

S3

Give an answer only to the priests when they ask you, and especially to the better among them, about the allegories that are served by them and purify the inner person, and about the vessels for receiving. They are a demonstration of the impassioned and of the reasoning part of the soul, and their inseparable mixture, and the power of each of them, and the completion of the actions of every one of them for one end. And then tell them the mystery of who is the one doing these things, and of those with him who are chasing off those who prevent pure ways of life; and of which among the living beings have memory and which do not.

S2

Give an answer to the priests alone when they ask you, and then not to all of them, but to those chosen from them, about the mystery of their rites, those things that purify the inner person. And then tell them about the powers of the soul that receive this mystery, which are those from the part of knowledge that is naturally in us, and which are from the part of the passions of the soul. And you will show them the inseparable joining of the two parts, and the victory of each, and the completion of the activity worked by them in harmony. Then you will tell them the model of [those] who are the priests who accomplish this mystery, and who are those with them who are fighting off from us the unclean demons, they who stand against purity of conduct.

> Cf. Mal 2.7 for the secrecy of a priest. A rare discussion of the Eucharist, here interpreted mystically. The three Syriac translators differ in their handling of this difficult chapter (not extant in Greek). One of the manuscripts of S2 simply omits it and the following chapter (BL Add. 14616). Hiding: Sch. 39 on Eccl 5.12, citing Prv 2.1; cf. Mt 11.25. On purification, cf. *Prak.* 100, where priests (see note *Prak.* 13: bishops) "purify us through the holy mysteries," presumably (but perhaps not only) the Eucharist. S3 more clearly indicates that VESSELS likely refers to the chalice and paten used in the Eucharist, whereas S1's THE RECEPTACLE AND CRUCIBLE THAT ARE IN US misses the point (as does S2). For other references to the Eucharist, see *KG* 2.44; *Monks* 119–120; *Letter on Faith* 15; Sch. 15 on Ps 67.24. RITES (S2): or "practices," "ministries." RATIONAL PART, presumably *logistikon*: *Prak.* 38, 84, 86, 89; Sch. 1 on Ps 25.2. INSEPARABLE MINGLING is a symbolic interpretation of the mixture of water and wine in the chalice (cf. *KG* 5.32). On the respective powers of the parts of the soul, and their proper activities, see *Prak.* 86; *Monks* 119–120. Those who help the priests are the angels, contrasted with those who prevent us from living in purity, the

demons (made explicit in S2; cf. *Prak.* 78). LIVING BEINGS: animals generally; cf. Aristotle *Metaphysics* A.1 (980a.29) and *KG* 1.53; 4.37. Memory is discussed elsewhere (e.g., *Prak.* 10, 12; *Thoughts* 4), but not regarding non-human animals. S2 omits this phrase. "Living beings" may refer to the figures in Rev 4.6–9, etc., and Ezek 1.10 and Is 6.2, signifying the cherubim. The reference to memory may point to 1 Cor 11.24–25, the words instituting the Eucharist. See Sch. 61 on Prv 5.11; Origen, *Hom. on Nm* 4.3, 4.5–18.

15

Greek

Learn the *logoi* and the laws of times (*kairos*), lives, and pursuits, so that you will readily have beneficial things to say to each person.

S1

Understand the time of words, deeds, and laws, so that you will speak those things that are helpful.

S3

Understand the reasons and the laws of times, customs, and deeds so that you will speak easily to everyone those things that are helpful.

S2

Know the definitions of laws, times, words, customs, and practices, so that you will be able to teach everyone something that will help him.

See *Prak.* 40 and Gregory of Nazianzus, *Or.* 2.18 on the diagnostic skills of a doctor.

16

S1

It is necessary that you have materials for the interpretation of the things that are said, and that all these matters suffice for you, even if one of their parts will escape us. For only an angel would not forget one of the things on earth.

112 EVAGRIUS OF PONTUS

S3

It is necessary that you have materials for the interpretation of the things that are said, and that all these matters suffice for us, even if one of the little things escapes us. For only an angel would not forget one of the matters on the earth.

S2

We need testimonies from the scriptures and knowledge of the matters of the world for the sake of interpretation of those things that we teach to a disciple. And every vision of created things will suffice for us. But if a little from the knowledge of natures should escape us, and is difficult for us to understand, let it not grieve us, because it belongs to the angels to understand perfectly everything on the earth.

> Material for interpretation may point to a Greek original of *hylē* or *hylas*, referring to underlying matter. On what is said (in scripture) see Origen, *First Principles* 3.1.2. VISION (S2): perhaps *theōria*, "observation." The Guillaumonts suggest that the phrase about all matters sufficing is likely a misconstrual of the Greek *chōrein*, inverting subject and object. The meaning should rather be "that you/we take in all things." Cf. Sch. 250–251 on Prv 23.1–3. Knowledge of the angels: 40; *KG* 1.23; *Thoughts* 8.

17

S1

It is necessary to know definitions of matters, and even more of virtues and vices, for these are the sources and beginnings of knowledge and of ignorance, and of the kingdom of heaven and of punishment.

S3

It is necessary also to know the definitions of things, especially of virtues and vices. For these are the source and beginnings of knowledge and of ignorance, and of the kingdom of heaven and of torment.

S2

It is necessary for us then to know the definition of matters, especially of established ways of conduct and evil deeds, because "there is to every matter a time,

GNOSTIKOS 113

and measures, and definitions." For in our time these are for us causes of knowledge and of ignorance, and of the kingdom of heaven and of torment.

Eccl 3.1 (S2); cf. Wis 11.20 (S2)

Definitions: used in teaching, like the *horoi* ascribed to Plato and later Byzantine collections (ed. Furrer-Pilliod); see Diogenes Laertius, *Lives of the Philosophers* 7.7 (Chrysippus). S2 invokes Eccl 3.1 and Wis 11.20 as congruent with this philosophical approach. On source/principle, see Plato, *Phaedrus* 245c. On knowledge and ignorance, cf. Sch. 23 on Ps 88.49; Sch. 4 on Ps 138.11. Kingdom of heaven: *Prak.* 2; *KG* 1.44.

18

S1

We must understand both the allegorical and the simple mysteries, and whether they are about practices of virtue (*praktikē*), or about natures (*physikē*), or about knowledge of God (*theologikē*). And if they are speaking about practices, we must understand whether they are speaking about rage or about those things that arise from it; about desires or about those things that follow them; or about our mind and its movements. But if they are about these things of nature, we must consider whether they are signifying something about the doctrines of nature and about which of them. But if it is said to be a passage about the divine, we must inquire as much as it is in our power whether it is making something known of the Holy Trinity, and that simply, or is making known the name of something else known with. But if it is not either of these, [if] it is a simple *theōria*, or is making known a prophecy.

S3

We must understand figurative [texts] both allegorical and simple, and whether they are about ways of life/conduct (*praktikē*) or natures (*physikē*) or about words about God (*theologikē*). If they are about practice, let us understand if they are speaking about rage or about those things that arise from it; or about desire or those things that accompany it; or about the mind and its movements. And if they are about nature, it is necessary to consider whether they are making known something from the doctrine of nature and which one it is. And if it is an allegory that is a *theōria* of words about God, to inquire as much as it is in our power if it is making something known of the Trinity, and whether simply or contemplated in the unity. But if not one of these, it is a simple intellection, or announcing a prophecy.

114 EVAGRIUS OF PONTUS

S2

It is necessary for us that we know the allegories and the subjects of the scriptures, those that are said with a mystery and those that are known openly and simply: and that we understand when it is [about] the practices of the commandments (*praktikē*) or nature (*physikē*) or words about divinity (*theologikē*). And if it is about our practice, we must see if it is about rage, and relates [what] flows from it; or about desire and what comes after it; or about the understanding and its turnings. But if the subjects are about natures, we must pursue which aspect of created natures they are. And if they are about words of divinity, let us investigate as much as we can whether they are telling us something about the Holy Trinity, and if they are showing it to us openly or hiddenly. And if neither one of those things, perhaps they are making known a simple *theōria* or a prophecy.

> Tripartite soul: cf. 14; *Prak.* 89. Tripartite pedagogical framework: 12; *Prak.* 1. On movements of the *nous*: *Prak.* 48, 51; *KG* 1.50, 51; 6.75. Unity: *KG* 3.1; 4.21. Trinity: *Prak.* 3.

19

S1

It is good to know the habit of divine scripture, and to establish it as we can by means of testimonies.

S3

It is also good to know the habit of divine scripture, and to establish it as much as possible by means of testimonies.

S2

It is also good for us to know the habit of the scriptures, so that we can easily and aptly bring forth the testimonies that are sought.

> On the HABIT OF THE SCRIPTURES, an exegetical term drawn from the Stoics and used widely by Origen (e.g., *Contra Celsum* 6.70) and Evagrius, see Sch. 4 on Ps 15.9 (*ēthos*), Sch. 5 on Ps 64.10; Sch. 12 on Ps 83.12 (*synēthes*), Sch. 5 on 142.8 (*ēthos*); Sch. 7 on Prv 1.9 (*synētheia* of the Spirit [in scripture]). Further on custom: 11.

GNOSTIKOS 115

20

S1

And this too we should know: that not every text of exhortation (*praktikē*) has an intellection of exhortation with it, nor does every one of nature (*physikē*) have an intellection of nature, but the hortatory one [can] make something known about nature, and that of nature about exhortation. And this also applies to divinity. [For example, the texts] that speak about the adultery and fornication of Jerusalem; and about the animals of the dry land and of the seas, and the birds both clean and unclean; and the sun "rising and setting and going off to its place." It seems that the [texts] are saying these things in order to make something else known, for their intellection is about something else. For the one speaking about the fornication of Jerusalem seems to be about exhortation, but is making something known about theology. And the one about the clean and unclean animals seems to be about nature, but is a text of exhortation. The one about the sun *is* about nature. So the first text seems to be an exhortation, but the [other] two about nature.

S3

And this too we should know: that not every text about exhortation is also an intellection about exhortation, nor is [one] about nature an intellection about nature, but the one about exhortation can have [an intellection] about nature, and that about nature [can have an intellection] about exhortation; and so also for divinity. [For example, the texts] that speak about the adultery and fornication of Jerusalem; and about the animals of the sea and the dry land, and of the birds, both clean and unclean; and about the sun "rising and setting and returning to its place." The first makes known about theology, but the second applies to intellections of exhortation, the third relates to intellections of nature. But the first text is about exhortation, the two others about nature.

S2

This too we should understand: that a text that is spoken about practices (*praktikē*) does not always show an interpretation about practices, nor does a passage about exalted natures (*physikē*) also have an intellection about natures in it. But what is said about practices shows about natures, and then what tells about natures makes known about practices and about divinity (*theologikē*). As for what is in the intellection applied to the scriptures, it reads: the adultery and fornication of Jerusalem; the animal that is on dry land and in the waters, and the bird that is clean or unclean;

116   EVAGRIUS OF PONTUS

and then about the sun that "rises and sets and returns to its place." Let us compare and interpret and call to mind: the first is about divinity, and the second imparts practices, and the third [imparts] natures. But the first text [speaks] about practice, and the two others that followed it speak about natures.

cf. Lv 11.2–19; Eccl 1.5; cf. Ezek 16.15–34

Ezek 16.15–34, adultery and fornication of Jerusalem; Lv 11.2–19, animals and birds; Eccl 1.5, sun rising and setting. Tripartite pedagogical theory: 12, 18. "Word of exhortation" (*pethgamā d-martinuthā*) emphasizes the moral dimension of the *praktikē* and may, as the Guillaumonts suggest, translate *rhēton ēthikon*. On intellection (*sūkālā*, likely Greek *theōria*), see *KG* 2.30. Our translation of S2 and S3 preserves their muddled sequence at the end of the chapter; S1 reflects the correct sense of the passage. The Guillaumonts suspected a failure in the Greek manuscripts rather than a misprision by the translators. S1's avoidance of referring to items simply by number is not unique to this passage: see *Gn.* 45 for a similar repetition of content for the sake of clarity. Syr. and Arm. for "word" likely points back to Grk. *rhēton*. Cf., e.g., Sch. 182 on Prv 18.13.

21

Greek

Do not allegorize the words of blameworthy persons, nor investigate anything spiritual in them, unless God acted by virtue of economy, as in the case of Balaam and of Caiaphas, so that the one would predict the birth, and the other, the death of our Savior.

S1

Do not suppose that there are mysteries in the words of disgraceful people and do not seek anything spiritual [in them], unless God is working with forethought as with Balaam and Caiaphas: the former foretold the birth of our Savior, and Caiaphas his death.

S3

Do not suppose that there are mysteries in the words of disgraceful people and do not seek anything spiritual in them unless perhaps God is working with forethought, as with Balaam and Caiaphas: one of them spoke about the birth of our Savior and the other about his death.

S2

Do not receive words spoken by disgraceful people as allegories, nor seek in them anything spiritually, unless God used them to advantage, as through Balaam....

cf. Nm 24.17–19; cf. Jn 11.49–51

On Balaam as a negative exemplar, see 2 Pt 2.15–16; Jude 11; Rev 2.14. Ambivalent figure: Origen, *Hom. on Nm* 13.7 and 15.1. Caiaphas: see Jn 11.49–51 and Origen's comparison of him with Balaam, *Hom. on Nm* 14.3.

22

Greek

The gnostic must not be sullen or aloof; the first [is typical of] one ignorant of the *logoi* of things, and the latter of someone not wanting "all people to be saved and to come to the knowledge of the truth."

S1

It is not fitting for the gnostic to be sad or unfriendly toward those who approach him. The one who is sad is like a man who does not know the reasons of existent things, and he will not be joyful among those who approach him, like a man who does not want "everyone to be saved and to come to true knowledge."

S3

It is not fitting for the gnostic to be sad or unfriendly toward those who approach him. For the one is like a man who does not know the *logoi* of existent things, and the other like the one who does not want "all people to be saved and to come to true knowledge."

S2

It is not fitting for the gnostic to be either [sad] or forbidding to those who want to consult him. For if he is saddened he shows himself to be ignorant of the true *logoi* of the interpretation of the things about which they are consulting him. But if he will not readily receive those who are asking him, then he will be found

118 EVAGRIUS OF PONTUS

to be like a man who does not want "people to be saved and turned toward true knowledge."

1 Tm 2.4

On the approachability of the *gnōstikos*, see Clement of Alexandria, *Strom.* 7.7.45. One of the manuscripts of S1 (BL Add. 12175) omits the phrase about not knowing the *logoi* of existent things. In the Greek transmission of selected chapters, this text is attached to ch. 15 as its conclusion.

23

S1

It is sometimes necessary that we present ourselves as ignorant because those who ask are not worthy to hear. You are correct if you say that you are embodied, and you do not yet have accurate knowledge of matters.

S3

It is sometimes necessary that we say about ourselves that we do not know, because those who ask are not worthy to hear. For you are correct, in that you are yoked to a body and do not yet have true intellection of things.

S2

Sometimes the gnostic must refrain from an answer to questions and say that he is not learned about what was asked, because they are not worthy to hear. And when he does this he is correct and does not deceive, because he is bound to a body and truly is not yet skilled in the answer.

From here through 27: the discretion of the *gnōstikos*, who must take care not to reveal higher mysteries before the hearers are ready, to give way to hubris or vainglory, or to engage in pointless disputes. On feigning ignorance, cf. *Disc.* 87 and 155; on rebuking those who neglect the knowledge they have received, Sch. 269 on Prv 24.11. Discussion of the practice of "economy," i.e., concealing information or even lying for the good of another, using the example of a physician who lies to the patient for the sake of healing, dates at least to Plato, *Republic* 3.389b; see also Philo, *That God Is Unchanging* 60–69; Origen, *Hom. on Jer* 20.3; Clement, *Strom.* 7.9.53.2. Evagrius compares the *gnōstikos* to a physician in *Gn.* 33. Cf. *Disc.* 155.

GNOSTIKOS 119

24

Greek

Pay heed to yourself, lest for the sake of gain, enjoyment, or the delight of passing glory you say something about things that are not to be spoken, and are cast outside of the sacred precincts as if you yourself were selling baby doves in the Temple.

S1

Watch yourself that you never say anything that must not be spoken for the sake of gain, or advantage to yourself, or passing glory, and you be cast out from the divine precincts like the one who was selling baby doves in the temple.

S3

Watch yourself that you never say anything from the hidden things for the sake of gain, or advantage to yourself, or passing glory, and you be cast outside the divine precincts like the one who was selling baby doves in the temple.

S2

Watch yourself that you not say anything for the sake of gain, or worldly benefit, or because of passing glory that must not be revealed, and be driven outside the temple and the holy enclosure.

cf. Mt 21.12–13

On the admonitory opening words, see *Prak.* 25. Evagrius warns against indiscreet sharing of mysteries for personal benefit. ENJOYMENT, *eupathein*, can also have the sense of advantageous treatment, as the Syriac clearly expresses; cf. *Thoughts* 22; Sch. 214 on Prv 20.10 with ref to Mt 7.12 on reciprocity in benefaction. Temptation to seek passing glory: *Eulogius* 24. "Sacred precincts," of the Temple: alludes to 2 Mc 6.4; cf. Sir 50.2; with reference to Jesus' cleansing the Temple of moneychangers and those selling votive doves in Mt 21.12–13 and parallels. THAT ARE NOT TO BE SPOKEN: *aporrētōn*, "must not be spoken," an admonitory cognate to *arrētos*, ineffable, on which see 41.

120 EVAGRIUS OF PONTUS

25

S1

Those who are disputing without knowledge should be brought to the truth not from the end but from the beginning. And to the young ones do not speak any of the things of knowledge, nor allow them to touch books like these. For they cannot withstand the perils accompanying that *theōria*. Because of this, it is not right to speak words of peace to those who are attacked by the passions, but rather how they might take vengeance on their enemies. For "there are not glad tidings on the day of war," as Qoheleth said. Therefore, those who are attacked by the passions and investigate the reasons of corporeals and incorporeals resemble sick people who discourse about health. The tasting of these honeycombs full of the sweetness of knowledge is fitting for us, however, whenever we are not disturbed by the passions of the soul.

S3

Those who are disputing without knowledge should be brought to the truth not from the end but from the beginnings. But to the young ones do not speak anything from the things of knowledge, or allow [them] to touch books like these, for they cannot withstand the perils accompanying that *theōria*. Because of this, it is not right to speak words of peace to those who are attacked by the passions, but rather how they might take vengeance on their enemies. For "there are not glad tidings on the day of war," as Qoheleth said. Those, then, who are attacked by the passions and investigate the reasons of incorporeals and corporeals resemble sick people who discuss health. The tasting of these honeycombs is fitting, however, whenever the soul is sorely disturbed by the passions.

S2

You cannot persuade those who stand in disputation without knowledge of books from the end of the things that they might ask [about], but rather you should bring them to the truth from the beginning. To those who are now beginning in the solitary life/state, do not respond to them using arguments spoken in a mystery and do not allow them to read books whose power they are unable to understand, for they cannot withstand the attacks that arise from the readings of the books. And because of the passions of desires that excite them, you must not respond to them with words of calm and peace, but tell them that they with difficulty will stand in battles and vanquish the enemies that arise from the passions of desires. And those who want to investigate spiritual things or anything that is invisible resemble sick people who liken themselves to the healthy. It is good for someone to taste of the sweetness of this depth when [needed] to strengthen the armor of the soul against the passions of desires that rage in him.

Eccl 8.8

On those who argue or dispute, see the next keph. YOUNG ONES: 36 and the Syriac versions of 13. The books forbidden here are not specified; perhaps books permitted only to the *gnōstikoi*, e.g., the *KG*; cf. Philoxenos of Mabbug, *Letter to Patrikios*. If alluding to *First Principles*, it may explain why this kephalaion disappeared from the Greek tradition; but Evagrius may also mean philosophical treatises. ENEMIES, possibly *antikeimenoi*; cf. *Prak.* 42. REASONS/*logoi*: *Prak.* 56. TASTING OF ... HONEYCOMBS: *KG* 3.64; *Monks* 72 and frequent in scripture (Ps 18.11; 118.103). Cf. Sch. 270 on Prv 24.13 ref. Origen, *First Principles* 4.2.6; cf. Sch. 72 on Prv 6.8.

26

S1

The time of discussion is not [the time] of interpretation. Because of that we must rebuke those who are discussing the word, for this is the custom of heretics and disputers.

S3

The time of discussion and of interpretation is not the same. Because of that we must rebuke those who are discussing out of turn, for this is the custom of heretics and disputers.

S2

The time of explanation is not [the time] of inquiry. And because of that we must rebuke those who are preventing the explanation of these things by posing a question of inquiry to us, for this is the custom of heretics and disputers.

Two levels of teaching: the first, explanation of biblical texts useful for the *praktikē*, the second reserved for advanced students capable of investigation and discussion of open questions and other matters, the *zētēseis* of which Evagrius writes in Sch. 34 on Ps 118.75 (investigate the *logoi* of judgment); Sch. 48 on Ps 118.109 (investigate how the soul of David can be always in the hands of God). Cf. Plato, *Republic* 7.539 on the danger of students prematurely

122 EVAGRIUS OF PONTUS

admitted to dialectic and becoming argumentative. *Dialegomai* as controversial: Mk 9.34. In a bad sense: Clement, *Strom.* 1.28. Argumentation ascribed to Eunomians: Basil, *Against Eunomius*; Gregory of Nyssa, *Against Eunomius*; and especially Gregory of Nazianzus, *Theological Or.* 2 (*Or.* 28). HERETICS AND DISPUTERS: Neo-Arians, or/and Hellenic philosophers belonging to distinct schools and practicing *dialektikē*; cf. Porphyry on Plotinus as a dialectical philosopher, *Enn.* 1.3.3; Julian the Emperor, *Letter to the Athenians* 268–270; and Clement, *Strom.* 1.9. Palladius, *Lausiac History* 38: Evagrius is *dialektikotatos*, "most skilled in dialectic," for which reason he remained in Constantinople with "the blessed [archbishop] Nectarius."

27

Greek

Do not speak about God thoughtlessly, and never define the divine. Definitions, after all, are for things that come into being and are composite.

S1

Never say something thoughtlessly about the divine, and never define it in any way: for definitions pertain to things that exist and are composite.

S3

Do not speak about God without consideration and never define the divine, for definitions pertain to things that are composite and existing.

S2

Do not say anything about the divinity without caution, nor apply measurements and definitions to anything that is infinite, because measurements and definitions pertain to composite and created things.

THOUGHTLESSLY, *aperiskeptōs*: Sch. 35 on Eccl 5.1. Definitions apply only to what is composed (*sunthētos*); cf. Antipatrus, *On Definitions*, preserved in Diogenes Laertius, *Lives of the Philosophers* 7.60; Aristotle, *Metaphysics* Z.12–13; *Nicomachean Ethics* K 8. The Trinity cannot be analyzed because it has neither matter nor shape, nor is it subject to properties that admit opposites: *KG* 1.2–3; 5.62; *Letter on Faith* 9. God is "simple and non-composite," *haplous* and *asynthetos*. The theme is prominent in the

Theological Orations of Gregory of Nazianzus: *Gn.* 41. CONSIDERATION (S3): alt. "demonstration."

28

Greek

... the one who has experienced evil hates evil, for experience is an offspring of abandonment...

S1

Be mindful of the five kinds of comprehension so that you will be able to direct the faint of heart and those brought low by their adversities: for hidden virtue is revealed by comprehension, and what is neglected is restored to its place by punishment. [Comprehension] is the cause of salvation for others, and whenever the virtue of deeds is found with knowledge, it teaches humility to those who possess it. For the one who has experienced it hates evil, but experience is the offspring of comprehension, and comprehension is the offspring of *apatheia*.

S3

Be mindful of the five causes of abandonment so that you will be able to direct the faint of heart whenever they fall in their adversities. For hidden virtue is revealed by abandonment, and if neglected is restored by punishment. Abandonment is the cause of redemption/ransom for others, and when it precedes virtue, it teaches humility to those who possess it. The one who experiences it hates evil, for experience is the offspring of abandonment, but abandonment is the offspring of disobedience.

S2

Be mindful of the causes by which a person comes into temptation. Thus you will be able to support those who fall into distress from temptation or from evil attacks. For the victory hidden in a person is made known by the suffering that afflicts him. If he rejects and overcomes it, that is a victory. He is restored by instruction and grace, and then the temptation becomes the cause of salvation for many. And if what was previously temptation becomes a victory, it teaches humility to the one who experiences it. For one who was tested by it hates evil; but experience of evil begets health of soul (*apatheia*), and the offspring of health of soul is temptation.

124 EVAGRIUS OF PONTUS

The Greek fragment of this chapter reads *enkataleipsis* (abandonment); but the translator of S1 apparently read *enkatalēpsis* (comprehension). S2 takes a theme from Evagrius (see *Prayer* 37) and associates abandonment with temptation. For more discussion, particularly in readings in Maximus and in Palladius, see the Guillaumonts' commentary in their edition of *Gn.*, 135–138. On abandonment revealing hidden virtue, cf. Sch. 20 on Ps 36.25; Sch. on Job 40.8. On restorative punishment, see Sch. 8 on Ps 37.12 (= *Antirr.* 6.17); *Letter* 42; and cf. Rom 5.3–4. On abandonment teaching humility, see Sch. 1 on Ps 89.3; *Eight Thoughts* 18; *Monks* 62; Basil, *Homily* 7.7. On this line of argumentation see Sch. 11 on Ps 24.20; Sch. 12 on Ps 138.22; *Thoughts* 10. For other texts on abandonment, see *Antirr.* 5.8; Sch. 4 on Ps 70.11; Sch. 22 on Ps 88.46; Sch. 9 on Ps 93.18; *Prayer* 37; see also Origen, *First Principles* 3.1.12. The concluding phrase of this kephalaion is difficult, as it is not extant in the Greek, and the three Syriac versions disagree. On offspring, *engonos*, see *Prak.* 81. This is a rare case of inaccuracy in S3, perhaps because of a faulty Greek reading of *apeitheia* (disobedience) for *apatheia*. HATES EVIL: *KG* 3.87.

29

Greek

Let the students always say to you: "Friend, go up higher." For it is shameful that after going up you would be brought down by those who are listening to you.

S1

Let those who are learning from you be always saying to you: "My friend, go up higher," for it would be shameful if you went up higher in your teaching but then were brought down by your hearers.

S3

Let those who are learning from you be always saying to you: "My friend, go up higher," for it would be shameful if you went up higher in your teaching but then were brought down by your hearers.

S2

Let those who are learning from you be always saying to you: "My friend, go up higher," for it would be shameful for you after going up to be brought down by your hearers.

Lk 14.10

Instruction should be paced, lest the gnostic have to backtrack; cf. *Gn.* 6, 23, 25, 26. Necessity of rising higher (*anabasis*): *Prayer* 36.1; Origen, *Hom. on Lk* 1.14.

30

Greek

The avaricious person is not the one who has money, but the one who desires it: for they say that "the treasurer is a rational purse."

S1

The avaricious person is not the one who has money, but the one who desires to possess it. For they call the treasurer a "rational purse."

S3

The avaricious person is not the one who has money, but the one who desires to possess it. For they call the treasurer a "rational purse."

S2

The avaricious person is not someone who has money, but the one who loves it and is devoted to possessing it. For the one who possesses money and manages it in the fear of the Lord is called a "rational purse."

Aristotle, *Eudaemonian Ethics* 3.4.1232a is the source for the definition of *philargyria*. On the monastic treasurer (*oikonomos*) see Palladius, *Lausiac History* 10. See also *Thoughts* 12; *Monks* 74–76. The *oikonomos* is a symbol for the *gnōstikos*; cf. 1 Cor 4.1; *KG* 5.33; Sch. 153 on Prv 17.2; Sch. 4 on Ps 111.4. See also Clement of Alexandria, *Who Is the Rich Man* 3.

31

Greek

Persuade the old men to control anger, and the young men the belly: for demons of the soul battle the former, while for the most part demons of the body, the latter.

126 EVAGRIUS OF PONTUS

S1

Persuade the old men to restrain their rage, and the young men to conquer their bellies, for passions of the soul fight with the old men, and most of the time bodily ones [fight] with the young men.

S3

Persuade the old men to restrain their rage, and the young men to conquer their bellies, for passions of the soul fight with the old men, and most of the time bodily ones [fight] with the young men.

S2

Persuade the old men not to be overcome by rage or the young men by gluttony. For demons of the soul attack the old men, while bodily demons especially fight the young.

Passions of the soul and those of the body: *Prak.* 35, 36, and 38; cf. *Letter* 25. On fighting against demons, see *Prak.* 59. S1 and S3 have "passions" instead of "demons," but these terms (along with *logismos*) are typically synonymous for Evagrius. Paired instruction: *Prak.* 36 and *Letter* 25. Fight demons: *Prak.* 59.

32

Greek

Shut the mouths of those who slander in your hearing, and do not wonder at being defamed by many: for this is a temptation from the demons. The gnostic must be free from hatred and resentment, even if they do not want it.

S1

Muzzle the mouth of those who slander their companions in your hearing, and do not be surprised if many revile you: for this is a trial of the gnostic from the demons, who do not want the perfect man to be free from hatred and resentment.

S3

Muzzle the mouth of those who slander their companions in your hearing, and do not be surprised if you are condemned by many: for this is a trial from

GNOSTIKOS 127

the demons, those who do not want the gnostic to be free from hatred and resentment.

S2

Shut the mouth of those who are slandering one another before you, and do not be surprised when they speak many things against you: for this is a temptation from the demons since they do not want the gnostic to be free from resentment and hatred.

> Cf. *KG* 3.90; *Prayer* 12. The *gnōstikos* should avoid anger: 5, 10, 31. *Antirr.*
> 5: anger caused by slander. Cf. *Letter* 25; Clement, *Strom.* 5.27.10.

33

Greek

Without knowing, the one healing human beings for the Lord's sake heals himself, for though the medicine that the gnostic furnishes heals the neighbor as much as it possibly can, of necessity it heals himself.

S1

The one who heals other people for the sake of God quietly brings healing to himself, for the medicine that the gnostic administers to his neighbor heals as much as it can, but necessarily [heals] himself completely.

S3

The one who heals other people for the sake of God is unaware of healing himself, though the medicine that the gnostic administers to his neighbor heals as it can, but himself necessarily.

S2

The one who by instruction heals people for the sake of the Lord will know [how] to help himself by the medicines that he administers to others. He either benefits them or does not benefit them, but himself he carefully cures.

> Cf. 9 and *Letter* 47. The *gnōstikos* is a physician who heals passions, the illnesses of the soul, to restore *apatheia*, the health of the soul. See also *Masters and Disciples*

128 EVAGRIUS OF PONTUS

78.30–35, *Disc.* 155. The *gnōstikos* imitates Christ, the doctor of souls; see *Thoughts* 3 and 10 and also Clement of Alexandria, *Paidagogos* 1.2 and 6. The final phrase reads "himself even more than the other person" (*mallon ekeinou*) in the Greek manuscripts, but S1 and S3 seem to be translating *anagkaiōs*, "necessarily," which the Guillaumonts adopt as a preferred reading, citing Sch. 194 on Prv 19.11 on the opposition between *anankaiōs* and *endechomenōs* ("as possible").

34

S1

Do not interpret spiritually all words that are used allegorically, but only those relevant to the matter. If you do not do this, you will spend a lot of time discoursing about the ship of Jonah, compelled to consider each and every thing on the ship, but you will not benefit your listeners. Instead, you will receive laughter from them since all those listening will remind you of the pieces of the ship's rig and fittings and with much laughter bring up whatever was forgotten.

S3

Do not interpret spiritually everything that is included in an allegory, but only those that are relevant to the matter. If you do not do this, you will spend a lot of time babbling on about the ship of Jonah. While you seek to explain each and everything on the ship, you will create laughter among your listeners rather than benefit, when all those around you recall the rig and fittings and with laughter bring up whatever was forgotten.

S2

You should not take up everything that is suitable to mystery that is in allegories, but only those things that contribute and are relevant to the matters. If you do not do this, you will spend much time sitting on the ship of Jonah, and you will want to assess everything on the ship. And there will be much laughter and no benefit for the listener, for everyone sitting around you will bring to you all the rig and fittings that you forgot to assess, and with great laughter put it before you as a question.

cf. Jon 1.5

Evagrius followed Origen in seeing a spiritual sense in every biblical text (*Contra Celsum* 4.49, *Hom. on Gn* 10.2, etc.) but also recognized the danger of becoming lost in speculation, especially when teaching. Jerome has the same caution, using another boat as his example (*Comm. on Ezek* 8, 263B). See the allusion to the ship of Jonah in *Thoughts* 3, where the boat's cargo and tackle tossed overboard in the storm represent the passions, but here they signify anything that might make the ship capsize, its "rig and fittings." Clement of Alexandria recognized the same problem with philosophical allegory, *Strom.* 5.9.58.6.

35

S1

Persuade the solitaries who come to you that each speak with you only about the seemliness of fear of God and the practices of virtue, and not about the teaching of the knowledge of God, unless someone is found who is able to speak about the one as much as the other.

S3

Persuade the solitaries who come to you to speak about virtue and not about doctrines, unless someone is found who is able to inquire into a matter like this.

S2

You should be persuading the brothers who come to you that they learn and speak about faith. As for investigation, do not encourage any of them to speak unless you find someone among them able to advance toward that height of instruction.

Cf. 13 and 36 on levels of instruction.

36

Greek

Let the higher discussion about judgment remain hidden from the worldly and from the young, since it easily engenders disdain: for they do not understand the pain of the rational soul condemned to ignorance.

S1

Let the highest reason about judgment be hidden from the worldly and from youths because it easily begets laxity, for they do not understand the suffering of the rational soul that is to receive ignorance as a punishment.

130 EVAGRIUS OF PONTUS

S3

Let the highest *logos* about judgment be hidden from those in the world and youths because it easily begets laxity, for they do not understand that the suffering of the rational soul that has been condemned is to receive ignorance.

S2

Do not reveal to the worldly and to the immature of mind the highest *logos* about judgment, because it easily begets negligence in them, even if they know the sufferings of the rational soul that receives darkness and gloom of the mind as punishment.

WORLDLY, "those who live in the world," Grk. *kosmikoi*: *Prak.* 41. In Evagrius' period, *kosmikos* does not mean "secular"; rather, as in Clement, *aisthētos*, or as in Didymus, "visible," operating as a symbol of the metaphysical. At *Prayer* 44 *monachos* and *kosmikos* are contrasted "at the moment of prayer." Pain of the rational soul condemned to ignorance: cf. *KG* 6.57, as well as 2.79 and 4.53. Only one who has tasted knowledge knows its happiness: *Prak.* 32; *KG* 3.64. Caution in speaking of judgment and punishment: cf. Origen, *Contra Celsum* 6.26. Presumably the lower account of judgment was one that promised a more understandable form of pain (*odynē*); the higher account of judgment is naturally hidden: *KG* 5.23. Literal presentation of the torments of hell: *Foundations* 9.

37

Greek

Saint Paul enslaved his body by bruising [it]: do not neglect the dietary regime in your life, nor insult *apatheia* by humiliating it with a massive body.

S1

If Saint Paul was punishing and subduing his body, do not neglect your ways of conduct in your life lest you disgrace the *apatheia* that you are humiliating with a body that has not been enslaved.

S3

If Saint Paul was punishing and enslaving his body, do not be negligent about food in your life and disgrace *apatheia* and humiliate it with a stout body.

S2

If Saint Paul was constraining himself and subduing his body with holy disciplines, do not neglect punishing your body all your days, and do not disgrace health of soul (*apatheia*) when you humiliate it by means of the weight of the body.

cf. 1 Cor 9.27

Cf. *Exh. Monks* 2.12. On the regimen: *Prak.* 91; cf. *Eight Thoughts* 1; *Thoughts* 16. For humiliating the body, the Greek has *thanatōsas*, mortifying or putting it to death, which the Guillaumonts corrected to *tapeinōsas* in light of the Syriac translations.

38

Greek

Do not concern yourself with food or clothing, but remember Abner [Abeddara, Obed Edom] the Levite, who after receiving the Ark of the Lord became rich after being poor, and esteemed after being dishonorable.

S1

Do not be anxious about your nourishment or garment, but remember Obed Edom the Gittite and Levite, who received the ark of the Lord and was made rich from his poverty and was glorified from his disgrace.

S3

Do not be anxious about your nourishment or clothing, but remember Obed Edom the Levite, he who received the ark of the Lord and became a rich man from a poor man and was glorified from being dishonored.

S2

Do not be anxious about your provisions or clothing, but remember Obed Edom, who when he received the ark of God was poor and blessed the Lord, and from poverty was made rich and from disgrace was glorified.

cf. 2 Kgdms/2 Sam 6.10–11; cf. Mt 6.25 = Lk 12.22

Cf. *Foundations* 3 and 4 on not being troubled about food and clothing, following Mt 6.25; cf. Clement, *Strom.* 7.7.46 on reason as the sustenance of the *gnōstikos*.

132 EVAGRIUS OF PONTUS

Evagrius has confused Abeddara (2 Kgdms/2 Sam 6.10–11), who received the ark, with Abner, a military leader (1 Kgdms/1 Sam 14.50; 2 Kgdms/2 Sam 2–3). The Syriac versions have the Semitic form of the correct name, Obed Edom. Though Evagrius calls him a Levite, this Obed Edom was a Gittite; someone by the same name was listed as a Levite in 1 Paral/1 Chron 15.18 (Josephus made the same mistake, and was perhaps the source of Evagrius' error: *Antiquities of the Jews* 7.4.2). The propitiatory (cover) of the ark symbolizes spiritual knowledge in *KG* 4.63; cf. Origen, *Hom. on Nm* 10.3, with 4.3 and 5.1.

39

S1

The conscience of the gnostic is a harsh accuser and he cannot hide anything from it, because it knows even the hidden things of his heart.

S3

The conscience of the gnostic is a harsh accuser and it is not possible to hide anything from it, because it knows even the hidden things of the heart.

S2

The conscience of the gnostic is a harsh accuser and he cannot hide from it, because it knows even the hidden things of his heart.

The conscience as an accuser (*katēgoros*): Polybius, *History* 18.43.13; Philo, *On the Decalogue* 87 and *That the Worse Attacks the Better* 23; Origen, *First Principles* 2.10.4. No hidden things: Seneca, *On Benefits* 6.42. Conscience (*synesis*): *Eulogius* 7, 10, 14, 32; *Maxims 3* 5. On secrets of the heart see *Prak.* 46, 47 (there known only to God); *KG* 6.52.

40

S1

Understand that you must never assume that there is one cause for all existent things, but rather many: and that they are revealed to someone according to the measure of his disciplines. The holy powers also are given access to many reasons, though not to the primary ones, which are known only to Christ.

S3

Beware not to assume that there is one intellection, but many, for every existent thing: and that it is according to the measure of their intellections that the holy powers approach matters and find true intellections, though not the primary ones and not those that are known only by Christ.

S2

Observe that there is not for each existent thing one aspect or one interpretation in it, but many, and [also for] the measures of the works of creation. But the heavenly powers attain true knowledge, but not that which is primary and elevated, which only the Son knows.

The fifth-century Armenian translation, reflecting the likely Greek word, here gives *ban*, the equivalent of *logos* (cf. Jn 1.1 in the Armenian Bible). The Guillaumonts note the difficulty of interpreting the keph., and the Syriac versions show the translators' struggles with it. Spiritual *theōria* allows one to know the *logoi* of created things (cf. *KG* 5.40). The Word is the principle of all *logoi* (*KG* 4.9) and he alone knows the original or fundamental *logos* of each thing. All other rational creatures (*logikoi*), even angels, know only derivative, partial *logoi*. Cf. 16 on the angels knowing the truth, and *Letter on Faith* 21, on the relative knowledge of the angels, Christ, and the Father. Disciplines (S1): *dúbārē*, "ways of life" or "conduct."

41

Greek

Every proposition has as [its] predicate a kind, a difference, a species, a property, an accident, or the compound of those things: but one cannot accept anything that has been said about the Holy Trinity. Let the indescribable be worshipped in silence.

S1

If every question that exists makes known different classes, or kinds, or differences, or accidents, or what is composed of these, there is not a single one of these in the Holy Trinity. In silence, therefore, let that which cannot be spoken be adored.

134 EVAGRIUS OF PONTUS

S3

A question makes known different classes, or kinds, or differences, or accidents, or what is composed of these, but there are none of these in the Holy Trinity. In silence, therefore, let that which cannot be spoken be adored.

S2

Every single matter has a class, or a *theōria*, or an explanation, or what is natural to it or accidental to it, or it is composed of all these. But the Holy Trinity is above all of these things, and it is not right that we suppose any of these things about it, but rather in silence let us adore what cannot be spoken.

Severus

If every question has attributed to it either a class, or a kind, or a difference, or a property, or an accident, or that which is composed of these, none of these things that were spoken is found in the Holy Trinity. In silence let that which cannot be spoken be adored.

Severus of Antioch, *Letter* 2 to Sergius the Grammarian (CSCO 119, pp. 137.26–138.2)

The first part of this kephalaion adapts the opening lines of Porphyry's *Isagogē*, an influential introduction to Aristotle's *Categories*: Ὄντος ἀναγκαίου, Χρυσαόριε, καὶ εἰς τὴν τῶν παρὰ Ἀριστοτέλει κατηγοριῶν διδασκαλίαν τοῦ γνῶναι τί γένος καὶ τί διαφορὰ τί τε εἶδος καὶ τί ἴδιον καὶ τί συμβεβηκός (Busse ed., 4.1, p. 1 lines 2–4). Cf. Aristotle, *Prior Analyt.* 1.1 (25a1), *Topics* 1.4 (101b17). ACCIDENTS: *KG* 1.20. On the exemption of the Trinity from such analytical categories, see 27 (quoted along with this chapter by the fifth-century church historian Socrates Scholasticus); see *Prak.* 3 on the Trinity in general. CANNOT BE SPOKEN: Gregory of Naz., *Or.* 28.20. See Clement of Alexandria, *Strom.* 5.7.81.5 on distinguishing between the effable and ineffable, *rhēton* and *arrhēton*. Adoration of the inexpressible in silence is part of the Neoplatonic tradition (e.g., Porphyry, *On Abstinence* 2.34.2) and Christian tradition (e.g., Gregory of Nazianzus, *Or.* 29.8; Dionysius, *Divine Names* 1.1–5). Cf. the "Hymn to God," attributed to Gregory of Nazianzus (PG 37.507–508) but now assigned to Proclus: "You who are above everything . . . cannot be spoken (*arrhētos*) by any word." This keph. is noteworthy for being the only Syriac fragment preserved by way of quotation, here in the Syriac translation of the letters of Severus of Antioch, who quotes this passage twice.

42

Greek

A temptation of a gnostic is to have present in the mind a false opinion of the existent <as being non-existent, or the non-existent as being existent, or of the existent> as not being existent in the way it is.

S1

The temptation of the gnostic is a false opinion in the mind [holding] a matter that exists as if it did not, and that which does not exist as if it did, and that which exists not as it exists but as it seems to exist.

S3

The temptation of the gnostic is a false opinion in the mind [holding] those things that exist as if they did not, and those that do not exist as if they did, and those things that exist not in the manner that they are.

S2

The temptation of the gnostic is a false opinion showing his mind an interpretation of some matter that is true and exists as if it did not exist, and some [matter] that does not exist as if it did exist.

This keph. and 43, a pair, correspond to *Prak.* 74 and 75 on the temptation and sin of the monk who is not yet a *gnōstikos*. On the temptation of the latter, see further Sch. 22 on Ps 118.55; Sch. 3 on Ps 139.6; Sch. 1 on Ps 141.4; Sch. 4 on Ps 141.7. PRESENT IN THE MIND: lit., "hanging around." <AS BEING NON-EXISTENT . . . OR OF THE EXISTENT>: editorial supplements based on the Syriac.

43

S1

The sin of the gnostic is false knowledge of matters or of their intellection, either begotten by some passion or because we are not investigating the matters for the sake of good.

136 EVAGRIUS OF PONTUS

S3

The sin of the gnostic is false knowledge pertaining to things or to their *theōria* begotten from various passions or from not investigating the allegory for the sake of good.

S2

The sin of the gnostic is false knowledge about things or about their *theōria* that is begotten from evil passion of the mind or because it is not for the sake of good.

> On false knowledge, cf. *Monks* 126, where it may refer to dualist teachers such as Manichaeans (cf. *KG* 3.47) opposed to true knowledge; cf. *KG* 4.10 (false teaching); Sch. 282B on Prv 30.4; Sch. 84 on Prv 6.30–31. A fallen *gnōstikos* can become a source of heresy: *KG* 5.38. The sin of the *gnōstikos* is thus error engendered by "love of the world" (*KG* 4.25). See also a nearly identical definition in Sch. 5 on Ps 143.7.

44

Greek

We have learned from the just Gregory that there are four virtues proper to *theōria*: prudence and courage, moderation and justice. And he said that the work of prudence is to contemplate the intelligible and holy powers apart from the *logoi*, for he taught that these are revealed by wisdom alone. The work of courage is to persevere with things that are true, and to wage war, but not to get entangled in nonexistents. He replied that the [task] proper to moderation is to receive the seeds from the first farmer and to reject what is sown later. And for justice, to give to each person the reasons he merits, relating some things obscurely, some things with riddles, and making certain things plain for the benefit of the simple.

S1

We learned four virtues of discipline and of glorious *theōria* from the blessed Gregory, which are these: understanding, courage, chastity, and justice. The work of understanding is that a person see the intellectual holy powers [even] when not granted their causes: for the causes are revealed from the wisdom of God delivered to us. The work of courage is persevering toward truth even when they are waging war against us, and that we not be investigating those things that do

GNOSTIKOS 137

not exist. The work of chastity is to receive the seeds that were sown in us by the best cultivator and to reject from ourselves the sowing of weeds. The work of justice is to distribute and to give to every person as he deserves, whether words or things. There is a time for speaking to them obscurely, and to make known its intention by enigmas, and there is a time for speaking its word plainly for the benefit of the simple.

S3

We learned from holy Gregory that four virtues pertain to *theōria*, which are: understanding, courage, chastity, and justice. He said that the work of understanding is to see the intellectual and holy powers apart from their reasons, for these, he said, are revealed by wisdom. [The work] of courage is perseverance in true things even when accompanied by war, and that we not investigate those things that do not exist. The work of chastity is that it receive the seed sown in us by the first cultivator and reject from us the second sowing. The work of justice is to give *logoi* according to the measure of each, showing some of them obscurely, making some of them known by hints, and making some of them plain for the benefit of the simple.

S2

We learned four virtues and their knowledge from blessed Gregory, which are these: wisdom, fortitude, chastity, and justice. And he used to speak in this way: the work of wisdom is that someone know and understand the spiritual battle-lines and elevate his understanding so that he might see the holy powers without the *logoi* that make them known. For these reasons *logoi*, as he used to say, we know only by the true wisdom that is Christ. The work of fortitude is endurance so that a person will persevere in truth, even if there be a struggle for him because of those things [that befall] him in the conflict with the enemy, and that the mind not investigate anything that does not exist. The work of chastity is to receive the good sowing of the first sower and to keep it until the end, and to reject the other sowing that sows weeds. The work of justice is to offer a saying to everyone as he is worthy, and to speak a word to one that obscures, and to another in allegories, and then to others plainly for the sake of the knowledge and benefit of the simple.

cf. Mt 13.25

Counterpart to *Prak.* 89, quoting Gregory of Nazianzus (though without naming him; see note there) and applying the Stoic cardinal virtues to an anthropological structure. Like that chapter from the *Praktikos*, this one

138 EVAGRIUS OF PONTUS

precedes a series of keph. (45–48, all of which survive in Greek) devoted to sayings from those who were Evagrius' teachers or theological sources. It also has a similar function, attaching the virtues to other things (here contemplation). For prudence, the "holy powers" are angels, cf. *Gn.* 16 and 40; their *logoi* cannot be known without divine revelation. For courage and the deception of "things that do not exist," cf. *Gn.* 42. For continence and the theme of sowing, cf. Mt 13.25; Clement of Alexandria, *Strom.* 6.8.67.2; Origen, *Hom. on Jer* 1.14; and Gregory of Nazianzus, *Or.* 21.21. The theme continues through the metaphor of grain at *KG* 1.24; 2.25, 49. For justice and access to instruction and the *logoi* according to one's degree of progress: 12, 13, 23, 25, 35, 36, 40. OBSCURELY: Pauline mysteries, e.g., 1 Cor 4.1; *KG* 4.44. The deliberate obscuring or use of enigmatic instruction recalls Prv 1.6 (LXX), "the sayings of the wise are *ainigmata*," and *Prak.* pr.9. This approach was noted by Plato, *Letter* 11.312, cited by Clement of Alexandria, *Strom.* 5.10.65, within his longer discussion of truth veiled in symbols; cf. the need of the Divine Teacher to elucidate the mysteries of scripture, e.g., *Paidagogos* 2.10.89.1; 3.12.97.2. Evagrius follows Clement, Origen, and others in using the term "simple" (*haplous*, comp. *haplousteroi*) as in Sch. 363 on Prv 29.11, distinguishing what may be said to the simpler from what may be said to the more zealous (*spoudaioi*); cf. *Thoughts* 16.

45

Greek

The pillar of truth, Basil the Cappadocian, said, "Attentive study and exercise strengthen the knowledge that comes from human beings, but righteousness, freedom from anger, and mercy [strengthen the knowledge] that comes from the grace of God. Even the impassioned can receive the first, but only those free from passion are capable of the second—they who also behold the light proper to the mind shining upon them at the time of prayer."

S1

The pillar of truth Basil the Cappadocian used to say: "The knowledge acquired from humans is strengthened by constant meditation and by assiduous study, but the knowledge that is acquired from the grace of God is maintained by justice, not being quick to anger, and mercy. Even those who are under the passions receive the knowledge of which humans are capable, but the recipients of the knowledge of God are those who have risen above the passions, they

GNOSTIKOS 139

who at the time of prayer see the brilliance of the light of their mind shining upon them."

S3

The pillar of truth Basil the Cappadocian said: "The knowledge acquired by us from humans is strengthened by constant meditation and by assiduous study, but that which is acquired from the grace of God, by justice, calm, and mercy." He said that it is possible even for impassioned people to possess the first [kind], but the second is only for those who are without passion, those who at the time of prayer see the brilliance of the light of their mind shining upon them.

S2

The pillar of truth Basil the Cappadocian used to say: "The instruction that we receive from humans is maintained by constant meditation, but the knowledge that is in us from the grace of God [is maintained by] righteousness and quiet as well as mercy. Even those who are in the passions of desires are able to receive the first [kind of] instruction; but the knowledge that is from the first grace, only those who are without passions of desires are able to possess, those who at the time of prayer also see the great light that enlightens their mind."

cf. 1 Tm 3.15

Basil "the Cappadocian," i.e., of Caesarea, who made Evagrius a reader and was a close friend of Gregory of Nazianzus. Basil's father was from Evagrius' home region, Pontus, but his mother was from Cappadocia (Gregory of Nazianzus, *Or.* 43.15). Basil settled there after his studies in Athens and eventually became bishop of Caesarea, its capital. Pillar of truth: see 1 Tm 3.15; Basil himself used the term for bishops (*Letter* 243.4). Although the formula casts Basil as a fighter for orthodoxy, the body of the quotation frames him as a teacher and, later, sponsor of ascetics: "ATTENTIVE STUDY AND EXERCISE": see Basil's sermon *Pay Attention to Yourself*. On righteousness (justice) as the organizing virtue of the soul, see *Prak.* 89 and cf. *Gn.* 44. On mastery of anger, a constant struggle for the *gnōstikos*, see *Gn.* 4 (obstacle to contemplation) and 5 (obstacle to *apatheia*). Mercy (pity) is a remedy for the angering part of the soul (*Prak.* 15). Freedom from passion (*apatheia*) is the health of the soul, and can be marked by the experience of illumination during prayer (e.g., *Prak.* 64, *Reflections* 2, 4; *Virgin* 54; *Prayer* 68, 73, 74, 92, 146; see Stewart 2001, 193–196, for other references). The end of this kephalaion is preserved in Socrates, *Church History* 4.23.

140 EVAGRIUS OF PONTUS

46

Greek

Athanasius, the holy luminary of the Egyptians, said, "Moses was commanded to place the table on the north side. Let the gnostics know who is blowing against them and endure every temptation nobly, and with ready kindness nourish those who approach."

S1

The holy star of Egypt Athanasius used to say: "If Moses was commanded to put the table on the north side, the gnostics should understand who is blowing against them, strongly endure all temptations, and with good will nourish those who come to us."

S3

The holy star of Egypt Athanasius said: "If Moses was commanded to put the table on the north side, the gnostics should understand who is blowing against them, strongly endure all temptations, and with good will nourish those who come to us."

S2

The holy lamp of Egypt the blessed Athanasius used to say: "If Moses was commanded to place the table of the tabernacle to the north, let the interpreters understand who it is that is blowing against them, strongly endure every temptation, and with diligence nourish the strangers who come to them."

cf. Ex 25.23–30; 26.35; 37.10–16

Athanasius as pillar of the church: Gregory of Naz., *Or.* 21. Moses: 37, 41; *Prak.* 38; *KG* 4.23; *Letters* 27, 28, 56 ("gentlest of men"). The table for the showbread was to be placed on the north side of the Temple sanctuary (Ex 26.35). Cf. Origen's commentary on the candelabrum (menorah) placed on the south side facing north in vigilance against the foe coming from that direction (Jl 2.20), which he allegorizes as the devil (*Hom. on Ex* 9.4). Evagrius follows that lead; the one blowing against the *gnōstikoi* is a demon. In Sch. 53 on Prv 4.27, the north wind is said to symbolize evil (quoting Prv 27.16 and following Origen, *First Principles* 2.8.3).

GNOSTIKOS 141

47

Greek

Serapion, the angel of the church of the Thmuites, said, "The mind is perfectly purified when it has drunk spiritual knowledge, but love heals the enflamed portions of the angering part, and self-control stops the flow of evil desire."

S1

The angel of the church of Thmuis, whose name was Serapion, used to say: "The mind that has fully drunk spiritual knowledge is purified, but love heals the fever of the enraged parts, and self-control restrains the flow of evil desires."

S3

The angel of the church of Thmuis, whose name was Serapion, used to say: "The mind that has drunk spiritual knowledge is fully purified, but love heals the fever of the enraged parts, and self-control restrains the flow of evil desires."

S2

The teacher of the church of Thmuis, blessed Serapion, used to say: "The mind that drinks the drink of the spirit is fully purified; but love heals the fever of rage, and fasting cools and extinguishes inflamed desire."

> Serapion (d. ca. 360), a student of Anthony later ordained bishop of Thmuis in the Nile Delta. ANGEL OF THE CHURCH: Rev 2.1, 8, 12; 3.1, 7, 14. As a monk, Serapion had also followed the "angelic life." The chapter follows Evagrius' tripartite anthropology as it outlines therapies for each part. On the drink of spiritual knowledge, cf. *Monks* 119 ("The blood of Christ is the contemplation of beings . . .") and *KG* 5.13; in Sch. 104 on Prv 9.2 and *KG* 5.32, the *kratēr* (cup) is spiritual knowledge and contemplation. On the healing power of love, see *Prak.* 38. This kephalaion and the next may have anti-Manichaean overtones. See note at *KG* 3.55.

48

Greek

Didymus, the great and gnostic teacher, said, "Train yourself always in the reasons about providence and judgment, and try to remember their materials,

142 EVAGRIUS OF PONTUS

for almost everyone stumbles over these things. You will discover the reasons
about judgment in the difference between bodies and worlds, and those about
providence in the ways that lead us up from evil and ignorance to virtue and
knowledge."

S1

"Meditate by yourself on the *logoi* about the providence of God and judgment,"
the great and gnostic teacher Didymus used to say, "and strive to fix them in your
memory, since everyone stumbles over most of them. You will find the reasons
about judgment in the varieties of bodies and worlds. But the providence of God
you will understand from the ways that turn us from evil things to the virtue of
knowledge."

S3

"Ponder at all times in yourself the *logoi* about the providence of God and judgment," the great and gnostic teacher Didymus used to say, "and hold the fullness of them in your memory, since everyone stumbles over most of them. The
intellections of providence and judgment are found in the variety of bodies and
of worlds; those about providence by those dispositions that turn us away from
evil and ignorance toward the virtue of knowledge."

S2

The great gnostic Didymus used to say: "You should be meditating and
investigating within yourself the reasons about providence and judgment, and
recalling testimonies about them in your mind, for everyone is a little wanting
about these two. You are capable of reasons *logoi* about judgment in the distinction of body and of world, but the reasons about providence you see in the understanding when turned away from sin or error toward virtue."

Didymus (known as "the Blind"; d. ca. 398) taught in Alexandria; Evagrius
may have met him there (*History of the Monks of Egypt* 20.15 claims that
Evagrius visited the city often). Palladius notes that Ammonius, whom
Evagrius praised, had read and memorized Didymus' biblical commentaries
(*Lausiac History* 11.4). Evagrius's familiarity with Didymus is corroborated by
verbatim parallels between the scholia of both authors on Prv 1.9; 3.18, 22;
4.21; 5.8, 15, 18; 9.2; 17.6, 9; 19.24; 24.20; 26.15; 30.8; 31.6–7, 22 (for Didymus'
scholia on Prv, see PG 39:1625–1645). In the last of these, Sch. 378 on Prv
31.22, Evagrius credits his scholion to "someone else." TRAIN (*gymnazē*): an

GNOSTIKOS 143

athletic term used here with the sense of study or meditate. *Logoi* of providence and judgment are the object of natural observation (*theōria physikē*); cf. *KG* 1.27; 5.4, 7, 16, 23–24; 6.43, 75. See note at *KG* 6.75 and *Monks* 132 (the *logoi* of providence and judgment difficult to know); Sch. 2 on Prv 1.1; Sch. 8 on Ps 138.16. Cf. Plotinus, *Ennead* 3.3.7, and Origen, *First Principles* 3.5.8; *Contra Celsum* 8.70; Clement, *On Providence* (lost). See honorific titles similar to "great and knowing teacher" applied to unnamed authorities, probably to be identified with Didymus, in *Prak.* 98 and *KG* 6.45. On providence, *KG* 6.57, 59 (twofold: guards and guides). On judgment, see *KG* 1.82; 2.64. On the pairing of vice and ignorance, see *KG* 2.18.

49

S1

The goal of good practice (*praktikē*) is to purify the mind and to make it unreceptive to passions, but the goal of knowledge of nature (*physikē*) is to show the truth hidden in matters. To save the mind from all of these earthly things and to turn it toward the first cause of everything is the gift of the vision of God.

S3

The aim of the practice (*praktikē*) is to purify the mind and to make it unreceptive to passions, but that of nature (*physikē*) is to show the truth hidden in everything that exists. But to withdraw the mind from material things and to turn toward the first cause is the gift of the reasons about God.

S2

The aim of the teaching of the work of the commandments (*praktikē*) is to purify the understanding and to make it a stranger to passions of desires. But the aim of the teaching on intellection of natures (*physikē*) is to show the mind all truth of created things hidden from it. To lead the mind away from all created things, and to turn it toward the first good that is the source and cause of everything, is the great gift of the words that are about divinity.

A reprise of Evagrius' pedagogical sequence (*Gn.* 12; *Prak.* 1), pointing toward the final stage made possible by divine gift instead of the knower's instruction. For God as FIRST CAUSE, see *Letter* 8 and Gregory of Nazianzus, *Or.* 28.13. Transcendent vision: *KG* 3.9 and expanded at *Disc.* 35, 99, 105. On discerning truth inside the essence of matters, see Nicomachus of Gerasa, *Intr. Arithm.*

144 EVAGRIUS OF PONTUS

1.1.2; Iamblichus, *Pyth. Way of Life* 29.159; Clement of Alexandria, *Strom.* 8.22.4; Greg. Nyssa, *On Virginity* 6.2. See also note at *KG* 3.12.

50

Greek

Looking always toward the Archetype, try to engrave the images, without neglecting those things that contribute to gaining the [image] that has fallen.

S1

Endeavor to engrave your image according to the first and primary form, and do not turn away from your abundance when you are engaged with all those who encounter you.

S3

While you are always beholding the primary form, endeavor to engrave the images and do not neglect any of those things that . . . so that you obtain that which fell.

S2

Endeavor to engrave your image according to the first images: and do not neglect anything that can lead you to possess the full benefit. The perfect solitary will be called a city: for perfect is the one who by virtue of Christ was purified in body and soul, and who when he knows himself exalts the will of his creator.

The human being is the image of the divine archetype (Gn 1.26); the teacher is instructed to depict the archetype as in the creation of an image (cf. Plato, *Symposium* 193a) by referring to the model for the knowledge that leads to salvation: cf. Gregory of Nazianzus, *Or.* 28.17; *Letter* 58. The earliest trace of this idea is in Plato, *Timaeus* 29a, where the rational being turns toward the eternal model; cf. Plotinus, *Enneads* 6.4.10. LOOKING . . . TOWARD THE ARCHETYPE: Gregory of Nazianzus, *Or.* 30.11. For image and archetype, see also *Prak.* 89. The knower, then, must remain fixed on the archetype as the model for those being instructed ("drawn") while being attentive to the means needed to restore ("gain") the fallen human image. Comparison to painters (writers) of portraits: cf. Gregory of Nyssa, *De sancto Theodoro* (PG 46:737) on portraits of St. Theodore; and John Chrysostom, *De sancto*

Meletio Antiocheno (PG 50:516) on numerous depictions of the saintly bishop Meletios, his predecessor. On GAINING another: Mt 18.15; 1 Cor 9.19, 22, 1 Pt 3.1. IMAGE: see *KG* 1.43. The fallen-away: Jas 1.11, 1 Pt 1.24; cf. Origen, *First Principles* 2.6.5. Only S3 reads the keph. correctly, placing the benefit with the students rather than the teacher. S2 adds an extra sentence of uncertain origin.

Kephalaia gnostika

Greek

Six Hundred Prognostic Problems

Socrates Scholasticus, *Church History* 4.23

S1

On the Chapters of Knowledge, Said for the Instruction and the Progress of the Monks

A title is lacking in S2, and the different manuscripts of S1 each vary slightly around the common phrase *ríšē dída't'a*, "chapters of knowledge," presumably *kephalaia gnōseōs*, which is more commonly rendered today *kephalaia gnostika*. Evagrius refers to the work only as "the six hundred," *Prak.* pr.9.

KEPHALAIA GNOSTIKA   147

Century One

S2

First Century

S1

[Same as S2]

1.1

Greek

To the first good there is nothing contrary, because it exists according to substance; thus there is nothing contrary to substance.

Milan, Ambr. gr. 681 (Q 74 sup.); tenth century (Muyldermans 1931, p. 56)

S2

To the first good there is no contrary, because it is good in its substance; thus substance has no contrary.

S1

[Same as S2]

cf. Aristotle, *Cat.* 3b24–25

The opening chapter is a syllogism adapted from Aristotle.

KG 1.1 (Muyldermans)	Aristotle, *Categories* 3b24–25 (Minio-Paluello)
Τῷ πρώτῳ ἀγαθῷ οὐδέν ἐστιν ἐναντίον, διότι κατ' οὐσίαν ἐστίν· ἐναντίον δὲ οὐδὲν τῇ οὐσίᾳ.	Ὑπάρχει δὲ ταῖς οὐσίαις καὶ τὸ μηδὲν αὐταῖς ἐναντίον εἶναι. τῇ γὰρ πρώτῃ οὐσίᾳ τί ἂν εἴη ἐναντίον;

Several keph. treat concepts discussed in the *Categories*: e.g., substance, opposition, quality, number; they draw from Aristotle either directly or indirectly, which he assumes his readers know. On the technical term *kat' ousian*, see *Letter*

148 EVAGRIUS OF PONTUS

on Faith 9 (5x), 27, and 30. God as one and good: Dt 6.4, Mk 12.39. On the One, see 1.12; Plotinus, *Enneads* 6.9.6, 5.2.1. In the *Theaetetus*, Plato writes that "there must always be something opposed to the good," namely evil (176a). The opposition of evil to the good, however, is one of *sub*contrareity (*hypenantion*). Evagrius follows Plato here, insisting that the first good, which is good in its essence, has no contrary. Contraries and God: 1.89. On substance, Syr. *'itūtā*, Grk. *ousia*: 1.3, 35; 2.23; 3.72 (S1); 4.59; 5.4 & 7 (angel is a rational substance), 62 (S1); 6.5, 10 (S1), 79 (Syr. *bar 'ītūtā* ≈ Grk. *homoousios*). For other syllogisms: 1.2, 23; 4.9, 59; 5.44; 6.11, 85; *Prak.* 72. The Greek fragments for *KG* 1.1–5 come from the same source (Milan, Ambr. gr. 681 [Q 74 sup.], edited by Muyldermans 1931), and align well with both S1 and S2, except at 1.3, where S1 departs.

1.2

Greek

The contrariety is in the qualities; the qualities are in the created things; therefore the contrariety is in the created things.

Milan, Ambr. gr. 681 (Q 74 sup.); tenth century (Muyldermans 1931, p. 56)

S2

The contrariety is in the qualities; the qualities are in the bodies; the contrariety therefore is in the created things.

S1

[Same as S2]

cf. Aristotle, *Cat.* 10b12–14

Like the previous kephalaion, this syllogism draws from Aristotle's *Categories*:

KG 1.2 (Muyldermans)	Aristotle, *Categories* 10b12–14 (Minio-Paluello)
Ἡ ἐναντιότης ἐν ταῖς ποιότησιν· αἱ δὲ ποιότητες ἐν τοῖς κτίσμασιν· ἡ ἐναντιότης ἄρα ἐν τοῖς κτίσμασιν.	Ὑπάρχει δὲ καὶ ἐναντιότης κατὰ τὸ ποιόν, οἷον δικαιοσύνη ἀδικίᾳ ἐναντίον καὶ λευκότης μελανίᾳ καὶ τἆλλα ὡσαύτως

KEPHALAIA GNOSTIKA   149

Unlike the syllogism in the previous chapter, this one follows the standard order. Opposition occurs at a level lower than the first good, within rational nature or bodies. Opposition is either possible or constitutive (1.4). Material opposition attends to bodies, but existential and epistemic opposition occurs in rational nature, yet not in God (1.89; 5.62). On quality see 1.22.

1.3

Greek

Every rational nature is a knowing substance; but our God is the known itself: indivisibly, on the one hand, he comes to be in those things he has brought into being, like earthly skill; that which is substantial being, on the other hand, differs from this.

Milan, Ambr. gr. 681 (Q 74 sup.); tenth century (Muyldermans 1931, p. 56)

S2

Every rational nature is a knowing substance. And God is knowable. Indivisibly he dwells in those in whom he dwells, like earthly skill. But he surpasses this in that he exists substantially.

S1

Every rational nature is a knowing creature. Thus God alone is knowable, for he is not divided from those in whom he dwells. But how is God known by those in whom he dwells? It is like a skill in those who are skilled. But he is distinguished from this in that he substantially dwells in those in whom he dwells.

On rational nature: 1.89. In each version, including the extant Greek, it is difficult to know whether Evagrius speaks of (a) knowing substances knowing God or (b) God's self-knowledge, as distinguished from how substances know. Cf. Porphyry, *Commentary on Ptolemy's Harmony* 17.13–17: only incorporeal beings are intelligible; or only beings are understood by intellect. THAT WHICH IS SUBSTANTIAL BEING, Grk. *enypostatos einai*: a technical term for the subsistence of each person of the Trinity (see Lampe, s.v. ἐνυπόστατος); Syr. *qnūmāit* is the adverb based on Grk. *hypostasis*, "substance." On skill (*epistēmē*) or art: 1.14, 33 (contrasted with the intellect or knowledge); 4.7 (available to all humans). Unlike 1.1–2, 4–5, in which S1 closely adheres to the extant Greek (as does S2), here S1 alters and expands the text.

150 · EVAGRIUS OF PONTUS

1.4

Greek

Everything that has come into being is either receptive of contraries or is constituted from contraries. But not all things that are receptive of contraries are yoked to those things constituted from contraries.

Milan, Ambr. gr. 681 (Q 74 sup.); tenth century (Muyldermans 1931, pp. 56–57)

S2

Everything that has come into being is either capable of receiving contrariety, or is constituted from contrariety. But not everything that is capable of receiving contrariety is yoked to those things constituted from contrariety.

S1

[Same as S2]

> The first half of this keph. appears in reversed form at *Letter on Faith* 29: Καὶ πάλιν πάντα τὰ κτίσματα ἢ ἐκ τῶν ἐναντίων συνέστηκεν ἢ τῶν ἐναντίων ἐστὶ δεκτικά. On opposition: 1.2. Of the two entities Evagrius contrasts in this chapter, the first is Aristotelian primary substance (*Categories* 4a11–4b17), equated with rational nature (*KG* 1.64; see note at 1.89); the second, Empedoclean elemental mixtures (Empedocles, frag. 33; Aristotle, *On Generation and Corruption* 2.3 [esp. 331a2], *On the World* 396a33), equated with bodies (*KG* 1.68). On the two types of beings see also 1.11. On receptivity (*dektika*) see 1.39, 49, 54, 61, 84; 2.80 (of the Trinity), 85; 3.11 (of corporeal and incorporeal nature), 32 (bodily nature, of wisdom; the image of God, of unity), 53, 69, 74, 76 (of vice and virtue); 6.73. On yoking: *Prak.* 73.

1.5

Greek

The extremes neither produce nor are produced, but the mean both produces and is produced.

Milan, Ambr. gr. 681 (Q 74 sup.); tenth century (Muyldermans 1931, p. 57)

KEPHALAIA GNOSTIKA 151

S2

The extremes neither beget nor are begotten, but the mean both begets and is begotten.

S1

[Same as S2]

Consideration of extremes versus means pervades Greek philosophy in logic, ethics, physics, and other areas; see Arist., *Nicomachean Ethics* 1106b27, 1107a8. In line with that tradition, Evagrius treats virtue as a mean / *mesotēs* between two opposing vices, using Aristotle's example of courage as a mean between rashness and cowardice (Sch. 53 on Prv 4.27; cf. Arist., *Nicomachean Ethics* 2.5–7). But for *akrotēs* as excess see *Eulogius* 31 (PG 79:1137) and *Thoughts* 35 (twice). On mediation: 1.12, 41; producing/begetting: 1.9; 2.81; 3.89.

1.6

S2

In comparison, (i) we are one thing, (ii) and that which is in us is another thing, (iii) and that in which we are is (yet) another thing; but taken together, there is (a) that in which we are, and (b) that in which is that in which we are.

S1

[Same as S2]

This keph. is the first of a set of four (1.6–9, revisited at 1.17), connected by the concept of "being in." See also 1.44. In the act of comparison or reference, the self ("us"), what is in the self, and what the self is in are all separate entities. But when treated together—likely τῶν ἅμα (repeated at 1.7 Greek)—all that remains is what is in the self and the entity the self is in. The metaphysical context is unexplained, but might point to the resurrection, evil thoughts, or the aeons. The rather garbled conclusion of both S1 and S2 may point to dittography in the Greek.

1.7

Greek

When those things are annulled altogether, then number will also be annulled; and when this (number) is annulled, that which (is) in us and that in which we are will be identical.

Milan, Ambr. gr. 681 (Q 74 sup.); tenth century (Muyldermans 1931, p. 57)

S2

When those things that are together are taken away, then number will also be taken away. And when this (number) is taken away, then that which is in us and that in which we are will be one.

S1

When anything from the middle is raised which at the same time has a number, then number is also raised. And when this [number] is raised, that which is in us and that in which we are will be one.

The previous keph. entertained two approaches, one of comparing the self to the things in it and in which it is, the other of treating the three together. This keph. continues the latter scenario (*tōn hama*) and suggests that when it is annulled, so is number, collapsing the distinction altogether between what is in the self and what the self is in. They are one thing, i.e., they are not number. On entities being removed or taken away see 1.8, 15. On this keph.'s relationship to the canons against Origen, see note at 2.17. In antiquity, number, *arithmos*, entailed more than one thing; properly speaking one was not a number (Arist., *Metaphysics* 1088a4–8; further references at Kalvesmaki 2013, 48–49). On the hypothetical elimination of number see *Divisiones Aristoteleae* 64.20; Alexander Aphr., *Comm. Ar. metaph.* 815.36, Anatolius of Laodicea, *Theol. Arithm.* 5.14 (Heiberg). On the topic of number, see 1.8, 15 (symbolism), 29; 2.39–40 (four and five), 47 (Trinity not numbered); 4.19 (of bodily nature); 6.10–13 (Trinity and numbers), ep. (creation and 6). On number as being without substance: 6.13. On number generally, see also *Letter on Faith* 5–7, 25, 32; *Letter to Melania* 22–24. On number being abolished at the appearance of the Monad, Jesus, see *Letter on Faith* 25.

KEPHALAIA GNOSTIKA 153

1.8

S2

When that in which we were going to be was separated, he generated this in which we are; but when that which is in us is mingled, he will take away that which is taken away along with number.

S1

When that in which we were going to be was separated, it begat this in which we are; but when that which is in us is mingled, he will raise from the middle that which separates us by means of number.

> On separation see previous two keph.; 1.16; 2.45; 3.27 (observation separated from the mind, unseparated). One would expect that the mixing of what is inside of us would lead toward number (*arithmos*; see prev. keph.), not away from it (cf. 4.74 and 5.9, which also use "mixes," *ḥlaṭ*, in contexts where intermingling is the basic idea). On engendering, see the next keph. and 1.48–49. On mingling: 4.74.

1.9

S2

When we are in that which is, we see that which is; but when (we are) in that which is not, we beget what is not; but when these things in which we are taken away, that which is not will once again not be.

S1

When we are in that which is, we see its truth as it is; but when we are in that which is not, we beget that which is not. But when this in which we are is raised, then that which is not will once again not be.

> The series culminates in a paradoxical statement that defies simple explanation. It returns to the theme of "in-ness" (1.6). Begetting: 1.5. On seeing, see 1.70; 2.28; 4.68, 90; 5.60–61. Taking away: 1.7. THAT WHICH IS: 2.5.

1.10

S2

Among the demons, some oppose the practice of the commandments; others oppose the meanings of nature; and others oppose the words concerning the deity, because the very knowledge of our redemption is established by these three.

S1

[Same as S2]

Demons: *Prak.* 5. Tripartite division: *Prak.* 1 and *KG* 1.13. Spirits opposed to theology: Sch. 266 on Prv 24.6. Salvation: see 1.25 (demons hinder), 28; 6.88 (angels help). Nature, Syr. *kyānā*, Grk. *physis*, here refers to natures of various kinds, material or immaterial, and it forms, between practice and theology, the second of the three stages of the gnostic (*Prak.* 1; *Gn.* 12–13, 18, 49; *KG* 4.40). Although mentioned in the *Praktikos* (e.g., 24) and the *Gnostikos* (20), nature is a dominant theme in the *KG*, featuring prominently in the concepts of rational natures (on which see 1.89) and corporeal nature (see 3.10). It is also discussed in the abstract: 1.32, 46, 71 (knowledge of natures is knowledge of unity). Nature can be incorporeal or corporeal (1.74–76; 2.60; 3.10–11, 75, 80; 4.11; 5.18, 50; 6.16–17), corresponding to first and second natures (1.77; 2.13, 31; 3.26–27; 5.85); or knowing/rational versus unknowing (1.89; 2.19; 5.76). Nature of names: 2.66; spiritual nature: 5.60, 74; nature of the Trinity: 5.62; knowledge and nature: 5.79.

1.11

S2

All those who now possess spiritual bodies reign over a kingdom of worlds that have come into being; but as for those who are yoked to practicing or oppositional bodies, they will reign over a kingdom of worlds yet to come.

KEPHALAIA GNOSTIKA 155

S1

All those who now possess spiritual bodies reign over worlds that have come into being; but those who are yoked to practicing bodies will reign over worlds that are coming.

BODIES: here and following may correspond to either Syr. *gūšmā* or *pagrā*. For both words, the corresponding Greek, when present, is almost always simply *sōma*, body, without qualification. This pattern holds between the Greek original and the Syriac translations of *Praktikos*, *Gnostikos*, the letters, and the Peshitta New Testament; only the *Letter on Faith* appears to distinguish between the two, using *pagrā* for Grk. *sarx* and *gūšmā* for Grk. *sōma*; the *Letter to Melania* avoids *gūšmā* and repeatedly uses *pagrā*, most likely for Grk. *sōma*. Thus, when one kephalaion uses *pagrā* but another *gūšmā*, the difference does not rest upon a differentiation made by Evagrius, nor would Syriac speakers have recognized such a distinction (*pace* Ramelli 2015, p. lxx and *passim*). See esp. *Prak.* 53, where Grk. *sarx* and *sōma* are both translated Syr. *pagrā*. Concerning bodies or flesh, see 1.25–26, 45–46; 2.5, 56, 66, 82; 3.26, 53 (not evil, not receptive of knowledge); 4.37 (breathing apparatus), 41, 60, 68, 70, 82–83; 6.78, 81. Bodies come to be (1.73–74), and are subject to transfer or abolition (2.25, 62, 73, 77, 79; 3.9, 20, 25, 48, 50, 68; 4.74; 5.18–19; 6.58), both types of events synchronized with judgment (3.66). They are variegated (2.73, 85; 3.36, 37; 6.3) and are apportioned by rank (2.14; 3.20–21, 29, 38, 47; 5.2, 11). They are the *organon* of the soul and have various powers (1.67; 2.80). The body is an object of observation (1.27, 75; 2.71; 4.62; 5.32; 6.49, 72). Special concern is paid to the relative weight or thickness of bodies (1.68; 2.68, 72; 3.68; *Gn.* 37), and the bodies of angels (4.41) and demons (1.22; 5.11, 18, 78; 6.26). At the judgment of Christ, one receives either a spiritual or dark body (3.50; 5.11; 6.57). On oppositional bodies, see 1.4. On spiritual bodies specifically, see 1.90; 3.25, 45, 48 (angelic), 50 (darkened); 4.23, 24; 6.23, 47, 57, 58. On Christ and his body, see 6.14, 18, 39, 79. On the worlds to come, Syr. *'almē d-'atīdīn*, Grk. *aiōn to mellon* (attested at 4.31), see 2.26 (symbols of), 58 (altars given in), 73 (knowledge of); 3.9 (transfers), 51 (transfers); 4.31 (abasement), 34 (escape from), 38 (anger), 39 (rational beings), 49 (transience); 5.3 (visions of); 6.22–24 (knowledge of), 89 (firstborn). Cf. Mt 12.32, Heb 2.5, 6.5 (*to aiōn . . . to mellontōn*) and the Creed of Constantinople, *zoēn tou mellontos aiōnos*. On the number of worlds, see 2.75; on worlds more generally, see 1.70.

156 EVAGRIUS OF PONTUS

1.12

S2

One is he who exists without mediation; and he who by means of intermediaries exists in all things is also one.

S1

[Same as S2]

> Middles contrasted with extremes: 1.5. INTERMEDIARIES, identified with humans: 1.68; 4.13. On the Logos as mediator, see Clement, *Stromateis* 3.1; Origen, *First Principles* 1.2.4. On the concept of one, see 1.1; 3.1; 4.16.

1.13

S2

Among the rational beings, some have spiritual *theōria* and practice; others have practice and *theōria*; and (still) others have hindrance and judgment.

S1

Among the rational, some have spiritual *theōria* and practice; others have practice and *theōria*; and others are bound in hindrance and in judgment.

> Rational nature: 1.89. The keph. refers to three levels of progress in descending order. *Gnōstikoi* engage in spiritual observation and continued *praktikē*; practicing ones primarily in practice, progressing to observation; the third may refer to the struggle against demons. In reverse order it reflects the levels of *paideia* in Origen's *Comm. on SS* prol.3.4: ethics, physics, and epoptics. On similar distinctions see *Gn.* 2–3, 49; *Prak.* 84.

1.14

Greek

You will seek each of the skills only in its proper domain; but you will discover in all these things the knowledge of him who really is.

KEPHALAIA GNOSTIKA 157

Milan, Ambr. gr. 681 (Q 74 sup.); tenth century (Muyldermans 1931, p. 57)

S2

In each one of the skills, you see in it what it is about; but you will find the knowledge of him who is in all these things, if our Lord "made everything with wisdom."

S1

In each one of the skills, you see it and what it is about; but in *theōria* you will find the knowledge of the truth in all these things, because our Lord "created everything with wisdom."

Ps 103.24

On skills (*epistēmē*) see 1.3. The last phrase, from Ps 103, is missing in the extant Greek fragment. Our translation SEEK (Grk. *theōriseis*, lit. "you will observe/contemplate") captures the reference to Mt 7.7–8; the Syriac has "see." On wisdom in the context of Eph 3.10, quoted numerous times, see 2.2. Christ is wisdom: e.g., Sch. 105 on Prv 9.3; Sch. 202 on Prv 19.23; Sch. 11 on Eccl 2.14; Sch. 10 on Ps 76.15; Sch. 3 on Ps 141.6. On wisdom in general, see 2.1 (of God), 46 (God's wisdom contains all), 57 (of the altar), 70 (creates); 3.13 (of the unity), 57–58 (taught), 81 (made everything); 4.1 (grows in rational beings); 5.32 (mixed cup), 51 (two types: essential versus natural); 5.63 (of the creator; in objects), 65 (helped), 77 (and gates of virtue); 6.16 (and wise man), 51 (joined in soul). Cf. Prv 3.19 (Sch. 33 on Prv 3.19–20 compares it to Eph 3.18); 8.22–31.

1.15

Greek

When the four is annulled, the five is also annulled; but when the five is annulled, the four is not also annulled.

Paris gr. 2748; fourteenth century (Muyldermans 1932, p. 93)

S2

When the four will be taken away, the five will also be taken away; but when the five will be taken away; the four will not be taken away with them.

158 EVAGRIUS OF PONTUS

S1

[Same as S2]

This keph. forms a pair with the next. The four is a necessary condition for the five. A medieval interpreter added a comment in the Greek fragment: "For in the enyokement of the soul, when the four elements of the body are annulled, the five senses also are annulled. But when the five senses are annulled in philosophical death, its four elements are not also annulled." Comparison of 4 and 1: see 1.19. On the pairing of 4 and 5 on analogy with Lent and Pentecost, see 2.38–42. For number as it relates to one, see 1.7. On the number 5 and the senses: 2.35; four elements: 1.29; 2.11; annulment: 2.62. Evagrius' reflections on number often reflect Clement's use of Philo's treatises, e.g., *On the Creation of the World*, on the same subject. *Stromateis* 5.34.4: "four" refer to the four pillars of the Temple into which the gnostic enters and leads others; "five" to the five senses that can serve the *gnōstikos'* entry into the Temple. *Stromateis* 1.28.176.1–3: "four" as the divisions of the "Mosaic philosophy"—the source of Plato's philosophy: the historical, the legislative, the liturgical, and the theological, quoted directly in Sch. 15 on Ps 76.21.

1.16

S2

That which has been separated from the five is not separated from the four, but that which has been separated from the four is released also from the five.

S1

[Same as S2]

This keph. forms a pair with the previous one. Separation: 1.8.

KEPHALAIA GNOSTIKA   159

1.17

S2

When that which is in us will be changed, those things in which we are will be changed; and this so much so that eventually he who is will no longer be named in various ways.

S1

When that which is in us abounds in us, that in which we are abounds in us; so the abundance will increase until he who is will no longer be named in various ways.

THAT WHICH IS IN US . . . IN WHICH WE ARE: 1.6–9. Here, the former may be the soul, the latter, perhaps the body or worlds (cf. *Letter to Melania*). On change, Syr. *ḥelpā* or *šaḥlpā*, likely Gk. *metathesis* or *metabasis*, see 1.22; 2.83, 90; 3.7, 25, 48 & 50 (= Sch. 8 on Ps 1.5; *krisis*, the change [*metathesis, metabasis*] to other bodies); 4.54; 5.10, 19; 6.34, 58; Sch. 21 on Eccl 3.19–22; *Thoughts* 24. See also 2.4 on transfer. VARIOUS WAYS, Syr. *pūrsē* (modes), which likely translates Grk. *epinoiai*, a well-established term for scripture phrases designating Christ or God such as "shepherd," "gate," etc. See 1.51; 2.24; 3.29; and especially 6.5, 20, 33; *Letter on Faith* 7–8; Sch. 210 on Prv 20.9a (Christ has the *epinoiai* of both mother and father); Sch. 3 on Ps 105.5; Sch. 9 on 106.20; Sch. 4 on Ps 135.23 ("our God is a burning fire"); Sch. 13 on Ps 138.23; see also Lampe, s.v., ἐπίνοια. Origen, *First Principles* 1.2.1, 4; *Comm. on Jn* 1.9–11, 22–42; *Hom. on Gn* 1.7, 14.1; *Hom. on Ex* 7.8, *Contra Celsum* 2.64ff. and elsewhere. See also 1.51 on names.

1.18

S2

The goal of practice and of suffering is the inheritance of the saints; but the one who is contrary to the first is the cause of the second. And the goal of that one is the inheritance of those who are in opposition.

S1

[Same as S2]

Eph 1.11–18 and Col 1.12. SUFFERING, Syr. *šunāqā*, literally "torment." See 1.44. INHERITANCE: 2.7, 14 (S1), 74–75 (S1), 77 (S1); 3.72; 4.9, 78; 5.36, 68; Sch. 40 on Prv 3.35; Sch. 3 on Ps 82.13; *Monks* 1.

160 EVAGRIUS OF PONTUS

1.19

S2

Knowledge that is in the four is knowledge of the meanings of creatures; but knowledge of the one is knowledge of that one who alone is.

S1

Knowledge that is in the four is knowledge of the intellections of natures of creatures; but knowledge of the one is knowledge of that who alone is.

On the number 4, see 1.15. Number 1: 1.7. MEANINGS, Syr. *sūkālē*, likely Grk. *logoi*: 2.30.

1.20

S2

When only the meanings of all those things that exist by contingency remain in us, then only the one who is known will be known, by the one who alone knows.

S1

When all these words of beings will alone remain in us, then the one who is known will be known, and by one who alone knows; as it is written, "Heaven and earth will pass away, but my words will not pass away."

Mt 24.35 (S1)

BY CONTINGENCY (S2): Syr. *b-gedšā*, ordinarily a common word, here probably corresponds to the Aristotelian *kata symbebēkos* (so translated in Syriac for *Categories* 6c1), "according to accident." See Porphyry *Isagoge* 27.6. On the accidents, see 1.59; *Gn.* 41. Evagrius distinguishes between transitory things and events (*pragmata*) that "pass away" and the observation of both these things and God, who "does not pass away," Mt 24.35 at Sch. 72 on Prv 6.8.

KEPHALAIA GNOSTIKA   161

1.21

S2

Among those good and evil things that are considered unnecessary, some are found inside the soul, and some outside. But as for those things that are said to be evils by nature, it is impossible that they will be outside the soul.

S1

Among those good and evil things that are considered unnecessary, some are found inside the soul, and some outside. But as for those evils that are evil precisely, there is no means for them to be found outside the soul.

> Things UNNECESSARY versus evils by nature: the latter are vices in the soul; the soul has freedom to remove them; therefore vices, like evil, are not necessary; rather, they are a "lack." See Plotinus, *Enneads* 1.8.12–14; Origen, *Contra Celsum* 4.66. Vices in the soul: *Prak.* 47. On "within-ness": *KG* 1.5.

1.22

S2

The bodies of demons have color and form, but they escape our sense perception because their quality is not like the quality of bodies that fall under our sense perception. For when they wish to appear to humans they are changed into the complete likeness of our body while not showing their own bodies to us.

S1

The subtle bodies of demons receive only color and form, but they escape our sense perception because their quality is not like the quality of perceptible bodies. For when they wish to appear to humans they appear in the likeness of perceptible bodies, while not showing their subtle bodies to us.

> Quality (Syr. *mūzāgā*, Grk. *poiotēs*): one of the chief categories, frequently discussed: 1.2, 39; 2.18 (qualities conceal the nature of bodies), 83 (senses are affected by); 4.84 (knowledge is a quality of incorporeals, colors of corporeals); 5.19 (the resurrection brings changes in qualities); 6.3, 45 (the first world came from a principal quality), 72, 78; *Letter on Faith* 9; *Letter to Melania* 27, 29; *Prayer* prologue; *Thoughts* 31; *Letter* 3; *Disc.* 1. This keph. is

162 EVAGRIUS OF PONTUS

paralleled by *KG* 3.23, where the body–quality contrast is applied to worlds. On color and form, see 1.29; 2.18; 3.29; 5.18; on blue specifically see *Thoughts* 39; *Reflections* 2. On form in general, see 3.31; 6.10, 25; *Disc.* 26; and the preface to *Prayer*. On sense perception: 1.33–34. Ancient physics taught that all material bodies are made of one or more of the four elements: earth, water, air, and fire. In this keph. Evagrius extends those physics to the realm of angels and demons, but he argues that a different manner of synthesis or combination exempts them from existing the same way ordinary material objects exist, thereby also affecting how they are perceived. Bodies: 1.11. On the ability to see demons: 6.69.

1.23

S2

The meanings of those things on earth are "the good things of earth." But if the holy angels know these meanings, according to the word of the Tekoite woman, the angels of God eat the good things of the earth. And it is said, "humans eat the bread of angels." Thus it is clear that even some humans know the meanings of that which is on earth.

S1

The intellections of the words for those things on earth are called "the good things of earth." But if the holy angels rightly know these intellections, according to the word of the Tekoite woman, then God's angels eat the good things of earth. As it is written, "Humans eat the bread of angels." But that is to say that some humans also know the words for the intellections of those things on earth.

> Is 1.19; cf. 2 Kgdms/2 Sam 14.20; Ps 77.25

THINGS ON EARTH: *db'ārā*, literally "things in the earth." GOOD THINGS OF THE EARTH: Sch. 1 on Ps 26.2; Sch. 4 on Ps 68.5. The passage is a syllogism employing this definition and two biblical texts: Ps 77.25, "mere men ate the bread of angels;" (cf. Sch. 103 on Prv 9.2) and 2 Kgdms/2 Sam 14.20, where the female slave Tekoah praises David, who possesses "wisdom like an angel of God, knowing all things on earth." (cf. Sch. 7 on Ps 29.8). These texts, and his conclusion that a small number of human beings attain angelic knowledge, recur throughout his biblical scholia: Sch. 7on Ps 4.7; Sch. 4 on Ps 68.5; Sch. 10 on Ps 77.25; Sch. 24 on Ps 88.51; Sch. 8 on Ps 138.16; Sch. 1 on Ps 144.1; and Sch. 38 on Eccl 5.7–11. Cf. also *Gn.* 16, 40. On bread, see 2.44.

1.24

Greek

If the ear of wheat is in the grain *in potentia*, and the end is in the cause *in potentia*, then the grain and things in the grain are not the same, and the ear and the things in the grain are not [the same].

Milan, Ambr. gr. 681 (Q 74 sup.); tenth century (Muyldermans 1931, p. 57)

S2

If it is the case that the ear of wheat exists *in potentia* in the grain, so also the consummation exists *in potentia* in anything capable of receiving it. But if this is so, the grain and that which is in it are not the same thing, nor are the ear and that which is in the grain. But the grain of that which is held by the ear and the ear of this very grain are the same thing. For although the grain becomes the ear, the grain that is in the ear has not yet received its ear. But when it is liberated from ear and from grain, it will have the ear of the first grain.

S1

If it is the case that the ear of wheat is hidden in the grain *in potentia*, so also the consummation is hidden *in potentia* in the things capable of receiving it. But if this is so, the grain and that which is in it are not the same thing, nor are the ear and that which is in the grain. But the grass that encircles the ear and the ear of this very grain are the same thing. For although the grain becomes the ear, the grain that is in the ear has not yet received its ear. But when this grain is liberated from the ear, so it also will receive its head.

cf. Mk 4.28

1 Cor 15, *Letter to Melania*. See Origen, *Contra Celsum* 5.23; *First Principles* 2.10.3. Cf. *KG* 1.5. "In potentia" = *kata dynamin* = *b-ḥaylā*. Elsewhere the Syriac phrase might translate the Aristotelian concept "*in potentia*" (see 1.55) but in others it might refer to actual powers. For other occurrences of this phrase, encompassing both possible translations, see 1.45–47, 55; 2.29, 33, 34 (S1); 4.70 (S1). On seeds of virtue, see 1.39–40. Wheat analogy: 2.25–26; Sch. 5 on Ps 134.7 (citing Mk 4.28–31). See also Origen, *Hom. on Ex* 1.1 (scripture likened to a seed).

1.25

S2

There are those who wish to "sift" us with trials either by interrogating the thinking part of the soul, or by trying to seize the impassioned part of it, or the body or anything around the body.

S1

Those who wish to "sift" us with trials either by interrogating the rational power of the soul, or by trying to seize the passionate part of it, or the body or anything around the body.

cf. Lk 22.31

Letter 51.3 refers to demons seizing a monk by the garment.

1.26

S2

If the human body is part of this world, but "the form of this world is passing away," it is evident that the form of the body will also pass away.

S1

[Same as S2]

1 Cor 7.31

On form (*schēma*), see 1.22. Cf. 2.62, where "the entire nature of the bodies" is removed.

1.27

S2

There are five primary *theōriai*, under which every *theōria* is placed. It is said that the first is the *theōria* of the adored and holy Trinity. The second and third are the *theōriai* of those things without body, and of those things with body. The fourth and fifth are the *theōriai* of judgment and of providence.

KEPHALAIA GNOSTIKA 165

S1

There are five primary *theōriai*, under whose sign all *theōriai* are included. The first, as the fathers say, is the *theōria* of the adored Trinity. The second and third are the *theōriai* of those without body, and of those with body. The fourth and fifth are the *theōriai* of judgment and of the providence of God.

For the second and third types of observation see 4.86. On observation (*theōria*) see *Prak.* 32. For a similar five-fold structure see 1.70; less similar: 6.49. Numbers four and five: 1.15. Trinity: *Prak.* 3; bodies: 1.11; substrates: 4.81, 87 (observation of the Trinity lacks). On bodiless things, see 1.70; 4.81 (*theōria*), 86; 6.59, 73 (mind); *Monks* 110. Providence and judgment are specially paired by Evagrius: *Gn.* 48. This keph. parallels 1.70, but the list of five things differs.

1.28

S2

Among the multitude of ways, there are three ways of salvation. They together succeed in destroying sins. Two of them uniquely succeed in freeing us from the passions. The virtue of the third is that it will be the cause of glory. Glory follows the first (way), psalmody the second, and exaltation the third.

S1

Among the multitude of ways, three are the ways of salvation. They have in common (the capacity) to destroy sins. But singly, two succeed in freeing us from the passions. The singular virtue of the third is that it will be the cause of glory. The glory of psalmody follows the first (way), the praise of psalmody the second, and the glory of praise the third.

On salvation, see 1.10. On glory, cf. Rom 15.17. On one thing following (*lwā'*) another, see 3.33 (knowledge and names) and 6.11 (Trinity and tetrad). The term originally refers to the *levi'im*, the second rank of officiants after the *kohanim* in the Temple in Jerusalem. On glory, see *Prak.* pr.3; on psalmody, *Prak.* 15. The word *exaltation* (*rūmrāmā*) appears only here.

166 EVAGRIUS OF PONTUS

1.29

Greek

As color, form, and number depart together with bodies, so with the four elements matter is destroyed.

Milan, Ambr. gr. 681 (Q 74 sup.); tenth century (Muyldermans 1931, p. 57)

S2

Just as colors and shapes and numbers go away with bodies, so too matter is destroyed with the four elements. For along with the four elements, matter shares this: that it did not exist and that it came into being.

S1

[Same as S2]

This chapter contrasts the pair body + category with the pair elements + matter; see note at 1.5 on this distinction. The four elements (earth, water, air, and fire) have been alluded to already at 1.4, 15, 16, 19, and they appear in his account of angels, humans, and demons (1.68). See also 2.50 (fire and air are associated with knowledge; air and water with ignorance). At *the time of prayer* the monk should not seek form, shape, or color (*Prayer* 114). On coming to be, cf. Gn 1, Jn 1. On matter (Syr *hūlā/hūli'*= Greek *hylē*), see 1.33, 46; 2.20, 61–63; 3.15, 17, 19, 21, 31, 39; 4.81; 5.62; 6.58, 72. In centuries 2 and 3, S1 avoids *hūlā/hūli'*.

1.30

S2

Fire alone is distinct among the four elements, because of what lives in it.

S1

[Same as S2]

On fire, see 1.68 (predominates in angels), 2.29; 2.51, 72 (S1); 3.9 (increased in second world to come), 18, 39 (two types of fire); 6.26 (not in, but a quality of,

KEPHALAIA GNOSTIKA   167

a body). On the special, living quality of fire, see Plotinus *Ennead* 2.1.6–9. On the equivalence of God with fire, see Origen, *First Principles* 2.6.6 and 2.8.3, quoting Heb 12.29/Dt 4.24 ("our God is a consuming fire"); cf. Heb 1.7; Ex 3.2; Rom 12.11; Jer 5.14.

1.31

S2

Just as among people there is Israel, and among lands there is the land of Judah, and among cities there is Jerusalem: so too the intention of the enigmatic meanings is the portion of the Lord.

S1

Just as among peoples, Israel, and among lands, the land of Judah, and among cities, Jerusalem—have been called "the portion of the Lord"—so too among all the words, the sign of the symbols of intellections is the portion of the Lord.

cf. Dt 32.9

Hidden meanings are available to the *gnōstikos*. INTENTION OF THE ENIGMATIC MEANINGS: literally "sign of the enigmas of the meanings," but Syr. *nīšā* (sign) sometimes translates Grk. *skopos*, aim or goal, which makes better sense in this context (as in *Prak.* 46; *Gn.* 49). On Israel, see 1.83; 4.64 (old vs. new Israel); 6.64, 71 (perceptible versus spiritual). On Judah, see 6.49; Jerusalem: 5.6, 21, 82, 88; 6.49; *Letter* 25.5.

1.32

S2

Those who have seen something of what is in the natures have understood only their common appearance. For only the just have received spiritual knowledge of the natures. But the one who disputes this is like the one who says, "I know about Abraham when he traveled on the road with his two wives." What he says is the truth, but he did not see the two covenants. And he did not understand those who are born from each.

168 EVAGRIUS OF PONTUS

S1

Human beings who have seen something from among the natures have beheld only the common *theōria*. For only the just have received spiritual knowledge of the natures. But the one who disputes this is like the one who says, "I was with Abraham when he was with his two wives." He spoke the truth, but he did not see the two covenants. And he did not understand those who are born from them.

cf. Gn 16–17; cf. Gal 4.21–31

On nature, see 1.10, 89. On the two covenants see Sch. 80 on Prv 6.23. On spiritual knowledge, see 1.72; 2.3 (older than natural observation); 3.15 (S1 = immaterial knowledge), 35 (Grk.), 42 (rel. with observation), 56 (wings of the mind); 4.6 (only for pure), 18 (of holy unity), 25 (symbolized), 49 (S1), 63 (mercy seat); 5.34 (intelligible helmet); 6.48 (action of), 51 (S1), 67 (S1), 90; *Gn.* 47; Sch. 1 on Prv 1.1; Sch. 69 on Prv 6.1; Sch. 103 on Prv 9.2; Sch. 153 on Prv 17.2; Sch. 241 on Prv 22.11–12; Sch. 252 on Prv 23.6–8; Sch. 310 on Prv 25.17; Sch. 354 on Prv 28.22; Sch. 15 on Eccl 3.10–13; Sch. 26 on Eccl 4.5; Sch. 41 on Eccl 5.14–15. See also *Thoughts* 25. "All those human beings who have seen (*etheōrēsan*) something of what is in natures also have produced proofs (*apodeixeis*) from the things they have observed. My own proof in most cases is the heart of my reader, especially if it possess understanding and experience in the monadic [not 'monastic'] life." "*Monadikos*" in *Thoughts* signifies "unitary" or "solitary."

1.33

S2

Just as each of the arts needs a sharp sense suited to its own matter, so also the intellect needs a spiritual sense so that it might distinguish spiritual things.

S1

Just as each of the arts needs an acute sense appropriate to it, so also the intellect requires a spiritual sense that it might distinguish spiritual things.

ARTS, likely *epistēmai*: 1.3. This kephalaion, on the spiritual sense, is paired with the next four, extending into sense perception. See 1.37, 2.35 (five spiritual senses, enumerated); as well as *Contra Celsum* 7.34, in which Origen quotes Prv 2.5, "you will find a divine sense."

1.34

S2

Sense perception, naturally by itself, senses sense-perceptible (things). But the mind always rises and waits for whichever spiritual *theōria* will give itself to it as a vision.

S1

[Same as S2]

Whereas the sense perceptions (*aisthēseis*) engage perceptible things directly, the mind requires intermediaries (see 2.35 on vision). Both the mind and sense faculties distinguish perceptible things (2.45), but the mind as sensation and the sense faculties as perceptible objects (5.58). The latter does not distinguish, but the former does (5.59). See also 4.62, 67 (role between mind and objects), 68 (*aisthēseis* : mind :: windows : house of the soul); 5.41 (reproach for failed senses), 57; *Prak.* 4 (begets desire), 38 (move the passions), 66. On other sense perceptions, see 2.35; spiritual observation: 3.33.

1.35

S2

Just as light, while showing us everything, needs no light by which to be seen, so God, showing everything, needs no light by which to be known. For, in his substance, "He is light."

S1

Just as light itself, while showing everything to us, does not need another light by which to be seen, so also God, although he shows everything, does not need another light by which to be known. For, in his essence, "He is light."

1 Jn 1.5

On the question of mediaries in perception, see 1.34. On the knowability of God see 3.80–81; Gregory of Naz. theological orations, esp. *Or.* 31. On knowing and knowability: Aristotle, *Nicomachean Ethics* 1177; Clement of Alexandria, *Stromateis* 5.12 (God unknowable). On light, see 1.59 (and air), 74 (three types), 81 (of mind and life); 2.29 (of the Trinity), 90 (celestial); 3.5 (heavenly powers'

170 EVAGRIUS OF PONTUS

bodies), 44 (sun), 58 (and writing); 4.25 (holy temples); 5.15 (mind, observation of beings), 26 (experience versus discussing), 42 (mind, and daylight); 6.87 (of the head). On God being in essence light cf. Basil of Caesarea, *Letter* 361.

1.36

Greek

Sense perception and the organ of sense perception are not the same, nor is the one who perceives with the senses the same as the object of sense perception. Sense perception is the power by which we have become accustomed to perceive objects of sense. The organ of sense perception is the organ in which this faculty is seated. The one who perceives with the senses is the very living being that has acquired the senses. And the object of sense perception is that which naturally falls under the senses.

Milan, Ambr. gr. 681 (Q 74 sup.); tenth century (Muyldermans 1931, p. 57)

Sense perception is the power by which we apprehend material (things). The organ of sense perception is the organ through which this faculty operates. That which perceives with the senses is that very thing that has acquired the senses. And the object of sense perception is that which falls under the senses.

Paris gr. 2748; fourteenth century (Muyldermans 1932, p. 89)

Sense perception and the organ of sense perception are not the same thing, nor is the one who perceives with the senses the same as the object of sense perception. For the faculty of sense perception is the power by which we have become accustomed to apprehend material (things). The organ of sense perception is the organ in which this faculty is seated. The one who perceives with the senses is the very living being that has acquired the senses. The object of sense perception is that which naturally is subject to the senses. But it is not so with respect to idols, for they are deprived of all these. They have only imitations of the physical organs of sense perception, such as, an eye and an ear and a nose, and the rest.

Rondeau 2021, Sch. 6 on Ps 113.12–15

[44] Sense perception is the power by which we have become accustomed to apprehend material (things). [48] The organ of sense perception is the organ in which this faculty is seated. [49] The one who perceives with the senses is the very living being that has acquired the senses. [50] The object

of sense perception is that which naturally falls under the senses. What falls under the senses are color and form and weight and thickness and firmness and noise and vapors and juices, smoothness and hardness and these sorts of things.

Furrer-Pilliod 2000, p. 74 A.α.44, 48–50

S2

Sense perception is not the same thing as the organ of sense perception, nor is the one who perceives with the senses the same as the object of sense perception. For sense perception is the power by which we apprehend material things. The organ of sense perception is that member in which the faculty of perception resides. The one who perceives with the sense is a living being that possesses the senses (of perception). The object of sense perception is something that falls under the faculty of perception. But it is not so with the mind, for it has been deprived of one of the four.

S1

The faculty of sense is not the same thing as the organ of sense, nor the one who senses the same thing as the object of sense. For the faculty of sense is the power by which we grasp material things. The organ of sense is that member in which the faculty of sense resides. The one who senses is the living vessel who possesses the organs of sense. The object of sense is something that falls under the organs of senses. But it is not so with the mind, for it has been deprived of one of the four.

This keph. is one of the few that provides multiple Greek fragments for the same text. A close comparison shows the proximity of the different types of Greek fragments to a hypotheized *KG* original. The fragment from Sch. 6 on Ps 113.12–15 appears to be nearly identical to S1 and S2, up to the last sentence, where the scholion contrasts sense perception to the insensibility of idols. The scholion's last sentence is appropriate to the Psalm at hand, concerning idolatry; S1/S2's last sentence attends to the preceding keph., *KG* 1.32–35, to consider how all the senses work. Géhin (SC 615, p. 367) regards the scholion to be an application of *KG* 1.36 to the Psalm verse, and therefore "evident proof" that the *KG* antedates the scholia. The mere fact, however, that one version particularly suits the Psalms and the other the *KG* does establishes not a chronology but only a context. The opposite is equally likely, that a meditation catalyzed by his reading of Ps. 113 has been revised to fit the *KG*.

172 EVAGRIUS OF PONTUS

Here the principle of the non sequitur might be used for dating. If one version proceeds logically from its preceding context, but the other version does not follow logically—it seems a non sequitur—then the former (which catalyzes the idea) likely antedates the latter (which offers no such catalyst). In this case the scholion's phrase BUT IT IS NOT SO WITH RESPECT TO IDOLS makes sense, because it is motivated by the paradox of senses in idols discussed in Ps. 113. But S1/S2's BUT IT IS NOT SO WITH THE MIND lacks any context in *KG* 1.32–35 that would motivate such a diversion, aside from hints in *KG* 1.34.

Any chronology must explain the fragment from Furrer-Pilliod's edition, which lacks the initial cautionary sentence, and concludes with another sentence that defines further the provenance of objects of sense, *aisthētōn*. These four sentences, unique among the versions, do not fit easily into the context of the *KG* or the scholia, but they make sense as four independent literary units, written as if designed for a small, independent collection of definitions (cf. his *Thirty-Three Chapters*; *Maxims 1*; *Maxims 2*).

In our opinion, the most plausible explanation for the versions of 1.36 is the following: Evagrius worked on the definitions of "aesthetic" concepts in isolation, writing independent, concentrated definitions. In reading Ps. 113.12–15 he was struck by the paradox, and integrated four of these independent definitions into a single keph., to explain what was lacking in idols. Doing so prompted him to consider other entities that might lack aesthetic components, namely, the mind, hence the version that was incorporated into the *KG*. Evagrius may have been working on parts of the Psalms scholia at the same time he was writing the *KG*, so his notes on scripture became a starting point for the *KG*.

On the contrast of sense and the organ of sense, see Aristotle, *On the Soul* 2.12. The mind, while it has a faculty, a subject, and an object, does not have an organ of sense in which it dwells, comparable to the eye, ear, etc.; cf. 4.62 concerning the mind at the loss of the organ of sense. On the contrast between the senses and the mind, see 2.45 and especially 83, where the manner in which the senses are altered by qualities is compared to mind changing with observations. See also 5.12, 57–59. On objects of sense perception see 1.22.

1.37

S2

The spiritual sense is the *apatheia* of the rational soul, produced by the grace of God.

KEPHALAIA GNOSTIKA 173

S1

[Same as S2]

On the spiritual sense, see 1.33. On freedom from passion see *Prak.* 2. On grace, distinctively emphasized by the translator of S1, see 1.52 (S1), 58 (S1), 79; 2.6, 11 (S1), 24 (S1), 90 (S1); 3.5 (S1), 82, 89 (S1); 4.60, 89; 5.12 (S1), 79 (S1), 81 (S1); 6.17 (S1), 24 (S1), 6.29 (S1), 90 (S1). Elsewhere, see *Prak.* pr.2 (cowl), 53 (of the creator); *Gn.* 4, 45.

1.38

S2

Just as while we are awake, we say various things about sleep, but when we have fallen asleep we learn them by experience, so too all the things that we hear about God while we are outside of him: when we are in him we will receive their demonstration by experience.

S1

Just as while we are awake, we say various things about dreams, but when we have fallen asleep we learn them by experience, so too all the things that we hear about God while we are outside of him: when we are in him we will receive a demonstration by experience.

DEMONSTRATION, Syr. *taḥwītā*, Grk. *apodeixis.* 1 Cor 2.4. Cf. Sch. 3 on Ps 126.2: "Just as sleep withdraws sensation from us, so the observation of God separates us from sensible things." Cf. Origen, *Hom. on SS* 1.10: direct experience of the bridegroom replaces distant knowledge of him through repute, after the soul's long journey toward him. On experience, see *Gn.* 28 and 41 (the Trinity is to be adored in silence). On the contrast between sleep and wakefulness, see Clement, *Protreptikos* 9.8 on Eph 5.14. On sleep in general, see 3.73; 5.13; 6.25; *Prak.* 54–56.

1.39

Greek

We are born having the seeds of virtue, but not of evil. For it is not the case that if we are receptive of something, we also have its power entirely. Since even though

174 EVAGRIUS OF PONTUS

we are capable of not being, we do not have the capability of non-being, since capabilities are qualities, and non-being is not a quality.

Milan, Ambr. gr. 681 (Q 74 sup.); tenth century (Muyldermans 1931, p. 57)

S2

When we came into being in the beginning, the seeds of virtue existed naturally in us, but not (the seeds) of evil. For it is not the case that if we are receptive of something, we also have its power entirely. For although we are able not to be, the power of non-being is not within us. If powers are qualities, whatever does not exist is not a quality.

S1

[Same as S2, with very minor variations]

> This keph. belongs with the next two, treating the relationship between existence and virtue. Two other Greek fragments for this keph (Hausherr 1939, p. 230, Muyldermans 1931: 58), although independent of each other, are nearly identical, hence our single translation; yet another Greek fragment (*Thoughts* 31) begins, "no wicked thought emerges from nature, for we were not wicked from 'the beginning,' since the Lord sowed good seed in his own field," and then runs parallel to 1.39 starting with only the second sentence. This keph. appears nearly verbatim at *Letter* 43.2, without discernible major differences, aside from minor issues of translation technique. See our note in the next kephalaion on the relationship between the letters, the *KG*, and the scholia on Proverbs.
>
> SEEDS OF VIRTUE: used regularly by Philo, Origen, Didymus, John Chrysostom, among others; see the next keph. (= Sch. 62 on Prv 5.14); *Thoughts* 31; *Letter* 59; Sch. 21 on Ps 36.25; Sch. 3 on Ps 125.5; Sch. 3 on Ps 135.6; Sch. 4 on Ps 136.7; Sch. 3 on Ps 147.3. See also *Letter on Faith* 36. On cultivation of seeds, see 1.24; 6.60; *Prak.* 57, 90; *Gn.* 44. IN THE BEGINNING: Gn 1.1, Jn 1.1. Receptivity: 1.4. Non-being: 1.40, 89; *Gn.* 42. QUALITIES: 1.2.

1.40

Greek

There was when evil did not exist and there will be when it will no longer exist. But never once did virtue not exist, and never once will it not exist. The rich man

KEPHALAIA GNOSTIKA   175

who is in Hades on account of evil, and who has mercy on his brothers, convinces me: to have mercy is a virtue.

Milan, Ambr. gr. 681 (Q 74 sup.); tenth century (Muyldermans 1931, pp. 57–58)

There was when evil did not exist and there will be when it will no longer exist. <But never once did virtue not exist, and never once will it not exist.> For the seeds of virtue are indestructible. The rich man who in the Gospels has been condemned to Hades, and who has mercy on his brothers, convinces me: to have mercy is the most beautiful seed of virtue.

Thoughts 31 (Géhin and Guillaumonts 1998, p. 262)

There was when evil did not exist and there will be when it no longer exists. But never once did virtue not exist, and never once will it not exist. For the seeds of virtue are indestructible. That man convinces me—he who was nearly, but not completely (sunk) in every evil, the rich man condemned to Hades on account of his evil and having pity on his brothers—to have mercy is the most beautiful seed of virtue.

Géhin 1987, Sch. 62 on Prv 5.14

S2

Once evil did not exist and once again it will no longer exist. But never did virtue not exist, and it never will not exist. For the seeds of virtue are indestructible. I am also convinced by that rich man who was condemned in Sheol because of his evil, and yet was merciful to his brothers. For to show mercy is the most beautiful seed of virtue.

S1

[Same as S2]

cf. Lk 16.19–20, 31

This keph. has three Greek fragments: *KG* selections (Cod. Ambr. gr. 681 [q 74 sup.]; Muyldermans 1931: 57–58); *Thoughts* 31 (the second sentence, marked above in angle brackets, is missing in all manuscripts; Géhin and Guillaumonts 1998); Sch. 62 on Prv 5.14 (Géhin 1987). There is a nearly verbatim parallel at *Letter* 43.3 (n.b. *KG* 1.39 = *Letter* 43.2), which attests to the phrase IN THE GOSPEL found in *Thoughts*. This passage also appears at *Letter* 59.3, with slight adjustments ("persuade you" instead of "me"; the rich man is tormented, and

176 EVAGRIUS OF PONTUS

the passage is introduced by preliminary thoughts on Lazarus and the rich man, who is tormented by the fire of ignorance).

The Syriac translations of *Letter* 43.3 and 59.3 are nearly identical, and the translation of *Letter* 43.2–3 differs considerably from S1's translation of *KG* 1.39–40 (nearly untouched by S2: at 1.39 S2 added "all" at the end of the second sentence, and made minor adjustments to a handful of words in the third sentence). The comparison calls into question whether the translator of the *KG* S1 should be identified with the translator of the letters (cf. Guillaumonts 1991, p. 162).

This keph. is the only one to appear in a scholion, two letters, a treatise, and the *KG*. Establishing a chronology for the five versions is difficult. In most of these sources, there is no clear motivation for a meditation on the comparative duration of evil and virtue (see 1.36). Prov. 5.14 is about one who falls into woe (*kakō*) and makes no mention of virtue, suggesting that the scholion is not the earliest version. Unlike the scholia on Psalms, which supplies numerous Greek parallels to the *KG*, there are only four such scholia on the Proverbs: here, 3.38; 5.44, 77. No Greek parallels are known from the other scholia, e.g., Ecclesiastes, Job, except for the rather unusual scholion on Acts: 4.46.

THERE WAS WHEN, or "there was a time": 2.84; 6.18. The opening strongly echoes Sch. 30 on Ps 118.70; Origen; frag. on Prv 5. on Sheol, at 1.57. On evil, see 1.41, 51, 59, 79; *Gn.* 17. IMPERISHABLE SEEDS OF VIRTUE: defined in the preceding keph.; points to the possibility of change and healing after death and thus to the possibility of universal restoration of all beings to union with God (commonly called the *apokatastasis*, a term Evagrius is not known to have used; see note at 2.13). See Origen, *Contra Celsum* 4.65. On human mercy, see *Prak.* 15. On the unmerciful wealthy: Sch. 5. on Ps 38.7 ("'... he lays up treasures and does not know for whom he will gather them': this is to be uttered against barren rich people who are greedy and have pity on none of the poor").

1.41

S2

If death follows on life, and sickness follows on health, then it is evident also that evil follows on virtue. For death and sickness of soul are evil. But virtue is also more ancient than the intermediary.

S1

[Same as S2]

See previous keph. on virtue. On mediaries, see 1.5, 12. MORE ANCIENT THAN: on comparative ages of things see 1.50 (knowledge older than first beings), 2.3 (spiritual knowledge older than natural observation), 19 (knowledge of rational beings older than duality; knowing nature older than all natures); 3.45 (no mind older than another; spiritual and *praktikē* bodies).

1.42

Greek

God is said to be there, wherever he acts. And wherever he acts still more, he is more present. And since he acts fully in the heavenly powers, he is fully present there.

Milan, Ambr. gr. 681 (Q 74 sup.); tenth century (Muyldermans 1931, p. 58)

It is said that God is present wherever he acts. And he is present still more wherever he more fully acts. And since he acts fully in the intellectual powers he is fully present in them.

Paris gr. 2748; fourteenth century (Muyldermans 1932, p. 89)

S2

It is said that God is present wherever he acts. And where he acts more, there he is present more. He acts more in rational and holy natures and he is yet more present in heavenly powers.

S1

[Same as S2]

On the heavenly powers, see 2.78, 80; 3.5; 6.76; heavenly powers as angels: 2.30.

1.43

Greek

God is present everywhere and nowhere: everywhere because he inheres all things that have come into being; nowhere because he is other than they.

Milan, Ambr. gr. 681 (Q 74 sup.); tenth century (Muyldermans 1931, p. 58)

178 EVAGRIUS OF PONTUS

S2

God is everywhere and nowhere: he is everywhere insofar as he is in everything that exists by means of his "wisdom full of differences." He is nowhere because he is not one among other beings.

S1

[Same as S2]

Eph 3.10

God as above being: Plato, *Parmenides* 38a; *Symposium* 211a; Clement, *Paidagogos* 1.71.1. The Greek fragment lacks *polypoikilos* (variegated, differentiated), the key phrase that points to Eph 3.10, quoted in S1 and S2's translations. On this verse, which discusses the "heavenly powers," mentioned in the preceding keph., see 2.2. This verse is incorporated also into 2.21; 3.11; 4.7; 5.84, pointing to the varieties of knowledge that can be secured from this world.

1.44

S2

If the kingdom of heaven is known in what is contained and what contains, so the torment will be known by the opposite of those things.

S1

If the kingdom of heaven is known in what precedes all and contains all, likewise the torment also of those who will be judged will be known by that which is the opposite.

On the kingdom of heaven, see *Prak.* 2. On containing and being contained see *KG* 1.6–8 and 1.17. On post-judgment torment, see 1.56–57, 72; 3.18; 5.5 (counterpart to *praktikē*), 9; 6.8; *Gn.* 17, 36 (teaching to be withheld from some); Sch. 268 on Prv 24.9; *Prayer* 144; *Monks* 54; and Origen, *Hom. on Song of Songs* 2.2.21; *First Principles* 2.10.6–7. On torment as purification see 3.18; 5.5. Scriptural background: "aeonic" fire, Mk 9.49, Mt 7.91 and 25.41; torment: Rev 14.11; purifying fire, Rev 3.18, Num 31.23, Is 66.24, 1 Enoch 1.4.

KEPHALAIA GNOSTIKA 179

1.45

S2

There is nothing from among things without body that has power in bodies; for our soul is without a body.

S1

There is nothing from incorporeals that is *in potentia* in bodies; for our mind is incorporeal, when it likens itself to to God.

> On incorporeals, see 1.70. POWER, perhaps Grk. *dynamis*, potentiality; see next keph. and 1.55. Another possible translation: "No body contains in potency (*in potentia*) anything incorporeal." On soul, see *Prak.* 2; on body: *Prak.* 35. On the separability of the soul from the body: *Prak.* 52.

1.46

S2

Everything that is *in potentia* in bodies is also naturally in them in action. They are of the same nature as those things from which they come into being. But the mind is free from both shape and matter.

S1

All that is *in potentia* in bodies, they possess it in action. They are of the same nature as those things from which they have come into being. But the mind is free from imprint and from matter when it observes God.

> This keph., with the next, contrasts potentiality (*dynamei*) with actuality (*energeia*); see 1.55. On cases of potentiality see 1.24. On the contrast between formal and material causes see 3.31; on the contrast between matter and shape see 5.62. On connaturality, see 5.79; 6.14, 79. The term "shape," Syr. *ḥzātā* (literally, "view"), is likely Grk. *eidos*, as at 5.62.

1.47

S2

There is nothing that is *in potentia* in the soul that can leave it in action and subsist on its own. For the soul was made to be in bodies naturally.

S1

There is nothing that is *in potentia* in the soul that also is in action. For by means of freedom it increases, and it is the power of God that perfects it.

This keph. forms a pair with the next. On the inseparability of the soul, see *Prak.* 52. On soul and body see *Prak.* 2 and 35.

1.48

S2

Everything that is joined to bodies also accompanies those from which they are generated, but nothing from these is attached to the soul.

S1

The imprints that are in bodies are the very ones that are in those who generated (the bodies). But the soul, by means of the freedom which is given to it by God, imprints its being as it wills, either to be made like God or to be made like animals.

See previous keph. On engendering, see 1.8–9 and the next keph.

1.49

S2

The unity is not moved in itself, but it is moved by the receptivity of the mind, which through negligence turns its face away from the unity, and because of privation of the unity gives birth to ignorance.

S1

[Same as S2]

Cf. Origen, *First Principles* 2.9.2: "Every intellectual being, neglecting the Good to a greater or lesser extent due to its own movements, was dragged to the opposite of the Good, that is, evil." See also 3.5.8 and 2.9.6, where neglect is the cause of the first movement, leading to *psyxis*, cooling off. See also *Contra Celsum* 6.45. At Sch. 10 on Eccl 2.11, and Sch. 12 on Eccl 2.22, *proairesis* is the choice of the intellect to engage in a movement (*kinēsis*) toward or away from the unity. On the unity (*īḥīdāyūtā*), see 1.65, 71, 77; 2.3, 5, 11; 3.1–3, 11, 13, 32, 61, 72; 4.8, 18, 21, 27, 43, 51, 89; 5.84 (Grk. *monas, -ados*); and especially 3.22 (separation of the mind from its unity), 28 (mind's fall from unity). The Syr. synonym *ḥdāyūtā* appears less frequently, at 2.3; 3.1, 31, 33; 4.21, 57, 89; and 6.4, and may translate *henas, henotēs*, or *henōsis*. At 2.3 and 3.1, *ḥdāyūtā* and *īḥīdāyūtā* are paired, as if translating Gk. *henas* and *monas*, respectively. See Bunge 1989, 2009. IN ITSELF: may also be translated "uniquely"; on the collocation of "unique" and "uniquely," see 2.53. On receptivity, see 1.84; 3.53; 4.35; 6.73; Sch. 127 on Prv 11.17 (mind is receptive of knowledge). On negligence or carelessness, see 3.28; *Thoughts* 34. On ignorance, see 1.59, 69, 71, 76, 80, 84, 89; 2.8, 18, 51, 54–55, 65, 79; 3.9 (bodies of), 49, 53, 63, 68; 4.17, 29, 53; 5.25, 28, 46; 6.19, 24, 35, 57, 59, 64, 90; *Prak.* 87; *Gn.* 17, 36. See also 2.11 on incomprehensibility.

1.50

S2

Everything that has come to be has come to be because of the knowledge of God. But among beings some are first and some are second. But knowledge is older than those beings who are first, and movement is older than those beings who are second.

S1

[Same as S2]

On first and second beings see 1.54; 2.64; 3.61. The distinction is at the root of second natural observation (see 2.2). On second beings specifically, see 1.61–62, 65; 3.8, 61, 68; 5.87. On first and second natures (not to be conflated with first and second beings), see 2.31. For Evagrius, movement is what led to the fall of noetic beings; see 1.51; 3.22 (first movement), 84; 5.23, 24 (paired with providence); 6.19–20, 36, 75, 85; to be contrasted with Origen, *First Principles* 1.6.2; 1.4.1; 1.8, among other places, where negligence is the key factor. The primary movement becomes the archetype for movement within the human mind and soul, on which see *Prak.* 11; Sch. 10 on Eccl 2.11. On the fall, see also *Letter to Melania* 26. On the relationship between movement and knowledge, see 3.22. Time itself is the basis of movement according to a saying of Basil likely familiar to Evagrius; see note at *Prak.* 3.

1.51

S2

Movement is the cause of evil. But the annihilation of evil is virtue. And virtue is the daughter of names and modes. And the cause of these is movement.

S1

Movement is the cause of evil, but the annihilation of evil is virtue. And the names of virtue are in the ways of instructions. And the cause of these is the movement.

On movement, see the previous keph. On virtue and evil see 1.39–40. On modes, see 1.17. On names, see 2.17, 24, 37, 66 (made known by bodies); 3.33, 54; 4.54; 6.20, 27, 33, 54, 67; Sch. 7 on Prv 1.9. See also 1.17 on *epinoia*.

1.52

S2

When the knowledge of those who are first in their origin and of those who are second in their becoming is in the principalities, then only those who are first in their origin will receive the knowledge of the Trinity.

S1

When true knowledge will be in those who are first in their becoming, then they will also, by grace, be equal to the knowledge of the holy Trinity.

On origin (avoided by S1), see 1.54; 4.38. On first and second beings, see 1.50. On the "becoming" or "coming into being" (Syr. *hwāyā*) of things, see 1.54 (S1),

55, 65; 2.19; 4.2–3; 6.18. KNOWLEDGE OF THE TRINITY: *Prak.* 3; knowledge of the unity, see 1.77.

1.53

Greek

Demonic things that struggle against the mind are called "birds," but "beasts" are those that throw into confusion the angering part and "cattle" are the names of those that move the desiring part.

Mosc. 425, sixteenth century (Hausherr 1939, p. 230)

S2

Those demons that fight with the mind are called "birds," but "beasts" are those that disturb the angering part, and "cattle" are those that stir the desiring part.

S1

[Same as S2, with a minor insertion]

Cf. Gn 1.20–27 as well as 2.20; 7.19–20. See Sch. 9 on Ps 73.19, ref. Job 5.23. On the tripartite soul, see *Prak.* 89. THOSE THAT STIR: S1 inserts before this clause "the names of."

1.54

S2

The fullness of those who are first in their origin is without limit, but emptiness is contained within a limit. But the second beings are coextensive with emptiness and they will rest when the fullness leads those receptive to it toward immaterial knowledge.

S1

The fullness of those who are first in their becoming is without limit, but emptiness is contained within a limit. But the second beings are coextensive with emptiness and they will rest as the perfect fullness will escort those receptive to it toward the knowledge of the Unity of the Holy Trinity.

184   EVAGRIUS OF PONTUS

On origin, see 1.52. On the two types of beings, see 1.50. This appears to be the only keph. that deals directly with limit and emptiness. On limit (here Syr. 'ebrā, also *msaykūtā*), see 1.71; 3.37, 63; 4.44; 6.36; *Prak.* 84 and 87. On immaterial knowledge, see 2.63; 3.15, 17.

1.55

S2

Only those who are first in their becoming will be freed from the corruption that is in action. But there is no one from among beings (that will be freed) from that which is *in potentia.*

S1

Those who are first in their becoming will be freed only from the effect of corruption. The liberations of all will be complete when the Lord of all wills.

On corruption, Syr. *ḥbālā*, here likely Grk. *phthora*, see 6.9; *Thoughts* 25. See also 2.17 on destruction (Syr. *ḥbālā*) of worlds. Action (actuality, *energeia*) is frequently contrasted with potentiality (*dynamis*); see 1.24, 46–47; 2.33; and, e.g., Aristotle, *Metaphysics* 6.8 (1049b–1051a).

1.56

S2

Good things are the cause of knowledge and of torment, but evil things, of torment alone.

S1

[Same as S2]

On torment, see 1.44 and the next keph.

1.57

S2

Humans fear Hades, but the demons, the abyss. But there are ones even more evil than these: serpents that cannot be charmed.

S1

Humans fear Hades, but the demons are terrified of the abyss.

SERPENTS THAT CANNOT BE CHARMED: follows the manuscript reading of Sebastian Brock, cited at Ramelli 2015: 58. On Sheol or Hades, the place of the dead, see 1.40; 3.9, 60; 4.80; 6.8. On demons in general, see *Prak.* 5. On the abyss, see Sch. 33 on Prv 3.19–20; *Disc.* 12–13. ONES MORE EVIL THAN THESE: "these" (*hālēn*) is grammatically ambiguous, and may refer to either humans and demons, or to Sheol and the abyss. On serpent-fighting, see *Prak.* 38; on Satan as a serpent, see Gn 3 and *Eulogius* 17. On the association of demons with serpents see *Disc.* 11. On gradations among demons see 4.33 and *Prak.* 45.

1.58

Greek

Mortal is that which has been unharnessed from the body yoked [to it]; but immortal is that which has not been loosed [from it]. For everything bound to bodies is at some time necessarily released.

Milan, Ambr. gr. 681 (Q 74 sup.); tenth century (Muyldermans 1931, p. 58)

S2

One kind of death has birth as its first cause. But another kind comes from the holy ones, against those who persist in unrighteousness. The mother of the third kind is release. But if "mortal" is the one whose nature is to be released from the body that is yoked to him, [then] the one who is "immortal" is that one for whom it is unnatural that this befall him. For everything that is yoked to bodies is also necessarily released from them.

186 EVAGRIUS OF PONTUS

S1

Among deaths, some are caused by the first judgment. But among others the cause is this: liberating grace. The third cause of death is the release that is merciful. The one to whom none of these things happens is immortal.

> Cf. Rev 20.14. On death and immortality see 1.63; 4.65; *Prak.* 6, 18, 36, 52, 95. On the "mother of idolatry" cf. Rev 17.6.

1.59

S2

Just as the light and darkness are accidents of the air, so also virtue and vice, and knowledge and ignorance, are joined to the rational soul.

S1

Just as the light and the darkness are accidents of the air, so also virtue and vice, knowledge and ignorance belong to the rational soul—excellence and knowledge both preexisting in it.

> On accidents see 1.20. On light and darkness see 4.29 (ignorance the shadow of evil); 5.14 and 5.17 (shadows). At 1.74, knowledge is light (cf. 1.81). See also 1.72. On air, one of the four elements (see 1.29), see 1.68 (predominance in demons); 2.51 (chariots of knowledge and ignorance); 3.9 (increase of in second world to come), 37 (earth's shadow); 4.37 (breathing); 6.63 (hallucinations in).

1.60

S2

If today they are receiving the wise steward in their homes, clearly yesterday they sat and changed their bills of account. He is called wise who the more he received, the more he forgave.

KEPHALAIA GNOSTIKA   187

S1

If today they are receiving the wise steward in their homes, clearly yesterday he sat and reckoned their accounts. But he is called wise who gave to his fellow servants from the profits of the holdings.

cf. Lk 16.1–2, 8

Evagrius introduces the parable from Lk 16:1–8 with "if today," drawing from Heb 3.15; Ps 95.8 ("If today you hear his voice, harden not your hearts," where "today" is understood as the day of judgment); Lk 12.42–43, a parable concerning the return of the Son of God to the earth. The next two kephalaia extend the image from the parable, putting knowledge in the role of the wise steward.

1.61

S2

None of the second beings is receptive of knowledge, and none of the first beings was initially in a place.

S1

There is not one of the second beings who is incapable of receiving knowledge, and none of the first beings is contained in a place.

This keph. links with the next and 1.65, with some tension arising from a paradox, which S1 attempted to rectify by negating 1.61. On second beings, see 1.50. This keph. and the next may allude to the teaching, found in the Alexandrian tradition, where minds were created first, and material bodies and their world, later, based on Gen 1.26 and 2.7. This tradition is first attested in Philo, *Allegorical Commentary on Genesis* and *On the Creation of the World*, which interpret the book in light of the *Timaeus*; it continues in Clement of Alexandria (see *Stromateis* 5.9.34) and appears frequently in Origen's interpretation or debate: *Dialogue with Heracleides* 12.4–14; *Comm. on Jn* 20.22; *Contra Celsum* 4.37; *Comm. on Mt* 4.11; *First Principles* 1.2.10 etc. On knowledge and place, see also 2.54; 5.70. On reception and receptivity see 1.4.

1.62

S2

Knowledge is said to be in a place when the one receiving it is composed with something from the second beings that is truly and originally said to be in a place.

S1

Knowledge is said to be in a place when it is occupied with the intellections of creatures, but in no place when it marvels at the Holy Trinity.

See previous keph.

1.63

S2

Whether rational beings always exist or not exist belongs to the will of the creator. But whether they be immortal or mortal is associated with their will, as well as whether they be joined or not joined to this or that.

S1

Whether rational beings should exist or not exist belongs to the will of the creator. But whether they will be mortal or immortal belongs to their will.

On immortality see 1.58. On life, see 2.31 (multiple lives); 5.20. On death as the disentanglement of the body from the soul, see *Prak.* 1.51. On the concept of joining to bodies see 1.58, 67; 3.20, 40, 51; 4.60; 5.11. On the body as integrally involved with the soul, see *Thoughts* 4. On the will, see 4.62; *Prayer* 31–32; Sch. 27 on Eccl 4.6; Sch. 4 on 29.6 (life is born of the will).

1.64

Greek

Life is genuinely the natural activity of beings with souls; death, contrary to nature.

Milan, Ambr. gr. 681 (Q 74 sup.); tenth century (Muyldermans 1931, p. 58)

S2

The true life of rational beings is their natural activity, and their death is their activity against nature. But if the one who naturally pursues true life is made mortal by such a death, which one of the beings is immortal? For every rational nature is receptive to contrariety.

S1

The true life of rational [beings] is their activity in the spirit, and their death is activity outside of nature.

> The distinction between *para physin* and *kata physin* goes back to Plato's *Republic* and Aristotle's *Nicomachean Ethics,* but here advances the treatment of Plotinus, e.g., *Ennead* 5.9.10. Cf. Corrigan 2009: 115–116. See also *KG* 3.75; *Prak.* 86; *Letter to Melania* 3–4, 33 (threefold division: natural, supernatural, unnatural). For the receptivity of contraries, see 1.4. On mortality, see the previous keph. and 1.58. On activity (*energeia*) see also 6.42; *Prayer* 84; *Disc.* 96 and 171. The conjunction of life and actuality/activity may draw from or respond to Aristotelian ideas; see 4.62.

1.65

S2

Various worlds are constituted by the knowledge of those who are second in their being, and inexpressible battles swarm. But none of this happens in the unity; rather, there is inexpressible peace. There are only naked minds always satiated by its insatiability if, according to the word of our savior, "The Father judges no one, but he has given all judgment to Christ."

S1

In the growth of the intellections of creatures there are toils and battles, but in the *theōria* of the Holy Trinity there is peace and inexpressible tranquility.

Jn 5.22 (S2)

> On various worlds, see also 2.65, 74, 85; 4.89; 5.81; 6.33; see also 1.70 on aeons. On creation of new worlds after successive judgments: 2.85. INEXPRESSIBLE BATTLES: Rev 16. See *Prak.* 50, on the demons as conducting battles against the "more knowing" of the practicing ascetics, which requires knowledge of their strategy and tactics, and petition to Christ, seeking to understand "the inner

190   EVAGRIUS OF PONTUS

spiritual principles" of the varieties of demons and battles. Cf. Ps 10.2. On the
naked mind, see 3.6, 13, 15, 17, 19, 21, 70; *Letter to Melania* 26; Sch. 43 on Ps
118.98 (naked of passions). Origen on *koros*: *On Prayer* 29.3, *Contra Celsum*
5.29 and 6.44, and *Philokalia* fr. on Exodus. Jn 5.22 is also quoted at Sch. 275
on Prv 24.22. Insatiability of intellects passing through the heavens (*caelestia*
loca) see Origen, *First Principles* 2.11.7.

1.66

Greek

Before us are said to be the virtues; behind, the vices. Wherefore we are
commanded to "flee fornication," but to "pursue hospitality."

Rondeau 2021, Sch. 6 on Ps 43.11

S2

Virtues are said to be before us, where we possess the faculties of sense, but vices
are behind us, where we do not possess the faculties of sense, for we have been
commanded to "flee fornication" and to "pursue hospitality."

S1

Virtues are said to be in front of us, before the senses that see them, but vices are
said to be behind us because they are accomplished in darkness, for we have been
commanded to "flee fornication" and to "pursue hospitality."

1 Cor 6.18; Rom 12.13
Faculties of sense: 1.34. Fornication: *Prak.* 8. Hospitality: *Prak.* 26.

1.67

S2

Who knows the composition of the world and the activity of its elements? And
who will understand the composition of this instrument of our soul? Or who
will track down how one thing is joined to another, or what is their domain, and

KEPHALAIA GNOSTIKA   191

their participation with one another, so that the practice will be a chariot for the
rational soul eager to attain the knowledge of God?

S1

Who knows the composition of the world and the activity of its elements and the
labor of this instrument? How will it become a chariot by the labor of the commandments and be taken up by an ascension of the spirit to the Holy Trinity?

> On the practice as a means of attaining knowledge, see *Prak.* 66, 68; *Reflections*
> 11 (knowledge depends upon rejection of desires). Porphyry, in *Launching*
> *Points to the Intelligibles* 32, identifies purificatory virtues as the foundation of
> *theōria*. The INSTRUMENT (*organon*) OF THE SOUL is the body (see, e.g., Plutarch,
> *Septem sapientium convivium* 163e2; Eusebius, *Comm. on Ps* PG 23:576.3;
> Nemesius, *On the Nature of Humanity* 5.54). See also 2.48, 80; 3.20; 6.58, 72;
> Plato, *Republic* 527d8 and Aristotle, *On the Soul* 412a, 415b; *Metaphysics* 1035b;
> Clement, *Strom.* 6.18; Origen, *Contra Celsum* 8.30 and *First Principles* 1.8.1;
> body as *organon* for demons: *Clementine Homilies* 9.10. In the final world to
> come, there will be a knowing *organon*: 3.51. On the chariot of the soul see
> Plato, *Phaedrus* 246a–254e. On the constitution or composition of the world,
> see 2.18; 3.36 (Grk. *systēma*); 4.35; 6.59; Sch. 123 on Prv 10.30; Sch. 74 on Ps
> 118.161 (*systēma* of heaven and earth). See also 4.49 (constitution of the mind).

1.68

S2

In the angels there is a predominance of mind and fire; in humans, of desire and
earth; and in demons, of anger and air. Those who are third approach those in the
middle by the nostrils, as they say, but the first approach the second by the mouth.

S1

In the holy angels there is a growth of mind; in humans, a growth of desire,
and in demons, of anger. And the fathers say that the first approach those in
the middle by the mouth, while the last approach those in the middle by the
nostrils.

192   EVAGRIUS OF PONTUS

This keph. names only three of the four elements; cf. 2.51 (fire, air, water). On the four elements more generally see note at 1.29. Fire: 1.30; 2.29; on the fiery nature of angelic bodies, Heb 1.7; Ps 104.4. See 1.33 on the sense perceptions. Tripartite soul: *Prak.* 89. On the related act of yawning, see *Eight Thoughts* 6.15 and *Thoughts* 9.33. On angels, see 2.30; 5.4; *Prak.* 24.

1.69

Greek

The one coming to knowledge has one after him; the one coming to ignorance does not have one after him.

Paris gr. 2748; fourteenth century (Muyldermans 1932, p. 93)

S2

The one who is chief in knowledge has someone after him, but the one who is chief in ignorance has no one.

S1

[Same as S2]

The concord of S1 and S2 strongly suggests an error in the Greek fragment, which appears to have substituted *elthōn* for *archōn*. Our translation ONE AFTER HIM reflects *met' auton*, which appears in the next keph. to refer to priority in knowledge.

1.70

Greek

With God is said to be: first, the one who knows the Holy Trinity; and next after him one who observes the reasons concerning the intelligible [beings]; third, again, is one who also sees incorporeal beings; and then fourth is one who knows the *theōria* of the aeons; while one who has attained *apatheia* of the soul is justly to be accounted fifth.

Rondeau 2021, Sch. 15 on Ps 72.23

KEPHALAIA GNOSTIKA   193

S2

With God the one said to be first is the person who knows the Holy Trinity, and after him is the one who sees the intellections of intelligible things. Then the third is the person who sees the incorporeal beings, and fourth the person who knows the *theōria* of the worlds. And the person who has acquired impassibility of soul will rightly be reckoned the fifth of these.

S1

The perfect image of God is the one who has been made worthy of the knowledge of the Holy Trinity. And after him is the one who has knowledge of the incorporeal beings; then third, the person who has the *theōria* of those who have bodies. Fourth is the one who has the intellection of worlds. And the one who has acquired the health of the soul will rightly be reckoned fifth.

On the Trinity, see 1.88 on knowledge and more generally, *Prak.* 3. On levels of knowledge, frequently put in sets of three, see 1.13, 14, 74; 2.4, 63; 5.52; 6.49; and *Gn.* passim. A similar five-fold structure is at 1.27. On *apatheia* see *Prak.* 3. On intelligible things (*noēta*) see 2.35, 45; 6.55. On the incorporeals, not to be conflated with angels, see 1.45, 85; 2.61, 71, 87; 3.11, 13, 80; 4.11, 62, 81, 84, 86; 5.32, 50, 52, 54, 62, 79; 6.4, 9, 16–17, 20, 49, 59, 73; *Prak.* 56, 61, 80; *Gn.* 25. On comparable treatments of incorporeals see Porphyry, *Isagogē* 19, 10.4–9; 42, 53.6–10 commenting on *Enneads* 2.7.3.7–14 (Remes 2008: 83; Chiaradonna 2007; see *Disc.* 1, 24, 114). Our translation AEONS reflects the Greek (*aiōnōn*), which has both temporal and spatial meanings. The term was significant in Christian discourse from Paul (as noted at Sch. 123 on Prv 10.30) and Philo (*That God Is Unchangeable* 31–33) onward (see Lampe, s.v.). Cf. Origen, fragment 79 on Luke 19.22; as epoch, Origen, Hom 12.10 on Jeremiah. The corresponding Syriac word, *ʿālmā*, cannot always be relied upon for finding an occurrence of *aiōn*: *ʿālmā* in the Syriac translations of the *Praktikos* and *Gnostikos* correspond to *kosmos* (beauty, world) and cognates. On *aiōn* (attested by Greek fragments), most commonly seen in the phrase "world/aeon to come," see 1.73; 3.31, 36 (definition, attested by Greek fragment); 2.14; 4.31, 34, 38; 6.22; Sch. 275 on Prv 24.22; *Eight Thoughts* 7.14. See also 2.14. On the number of worlds, see 2.75; on worlds more generally, see 1.65. On freedom from passion, see *Prak.* 2.

194   EVAGRIUS OF PONTUS

1.71

S2

The end of natural knowledge is the holy unity. But unknowing has no end. As it is said, "His greatness has no limit."

S1

The end of the knowledge of natures is knowledge of the holy unity. But incomprehensibility, as the fathers say, has no end. As it is written, "His understanding has no limit."

Ps 144.3 (S2); Ps 146.5 (S1)

On natural knowledge, see 1.88. On knowledge of the unity, or holy unity, see 2.5 (S1); 3.13, 28, 61, 72; 4.18, 89; 5.81, 84. Our translation "unknowing" for *lā īda'tā* (lit. ignorance) reflects the import of the scriptural quotation. Cf. 4.29, "ignorance is the shadow of evil" is limitless (*apeiron*) (Plotinus, *Enneads* 1.8.9). Incomprehensibility: 2.11. Note that S1 and S2 quote from two different Psalm verses. LXX for 144 (145).3 = "there is no limit (*peras*) of his greatness (*megalosynē*).

1.72

S2

The Lord has mercy on those to whom he gives spiritual knowledge, because it is written: "The just man walks in light but the fool in darkness." But the Lord has pity also on the fool. He does not torment him straightaway, and urges him away from evil toward virtue.

S1

The Lord has mercy on those to whom he gives spiritual knowledge, because it is written: "The just man walks in light, but the fool in darkness." But the Lord has pity also on the fool in that he does not torment him immediately, but establishes for him a pattern so that he repents and lives.

Eccl 2.14

Torment: 1.18, 44. Spiritual knowledge for the just: 1.32.

KEPHALAIA GNOSTIKA 195

1.73

Greek

The life of the human is holy knowledge, but the mercy of the Lord is the *theōria* of things that have come into being. Many of this aeon promise us knowledge, but "the mercy of the Lord is greater than lives."

Rondeau 2021, Sch. 2 on Ps 62.4

S2

The life of the human is holy knowledge, and the abundant mercy of God is *theōria* of beings. For many of the wise of this age promise us knowledge, but "the mercy of the Lord is better than life."

S1

The life of the human is knowledge of the Holy Trinity, and the many mercies of God are *theōria* of beings. For many of the wise of this age promise us knowledge, but "the mercies of the Lord are better than life."

Ps 62.4

The WISE OF THIS AGE are philosophers; for mercy as a form of knowledge, see 72 above. On different types of observation of beings, see 1.27. On divine mercy, see 2.59. On mercy shown by humans as a moral action, see *Prak.* 15. OBSERVATION OF BEINGS (Syr. *teāwriyā d-hwāyē*; Gk. *hē tōn gegonotōn theōria*, confirmed by Greek fragments here and at 4.21, 5.30, and *Letter* 58.4), a technical term for observing things that have come into existence (Gk. *gignomai*), is prevalent throughout Evagrius' writings: 1.74; 2.5, 23; 3.4, 41; 4.21, 42, 70; 5.15, 30, 35, 63 (S1); 6.1, 17, 30; *Prak.* 2 (*ontōn*), 53 (*ontōn*), 86; *Monks* 118; *Thirty-Three Chapters 1, 4, 13*; Sch. 72 on Prv 6.8; Sch. 79 on Prv 6.20–22; Sch. 200 on Prv 19.19; Sch. 378 on Prv 31.22; Sch. 2 on Eccl 1.2; Sch. 19 on Eccl 3.15; *Thoughts* 42; *Disc.* 30; *Letter* 58.2, 4. On observation in general, *Prak.* 32.

196 EVAGRIUS OF PONTUS

1.74

S2

The light of the mind is divided into three: (1) for knowledge of the holy, adored Trinity; (2) for the bodiless nature which was created by it; (3) for *theōria* of beings.

S1

The light of the mind is divided into three: knowledge of the holy and adored Trinity; nature, incorporeal and corporeal; *theōria* of created beings.

> Levels of knowledge and incorporeals: 1.70. Evagrius says that he undertook a journey with Ammonius to consult with John of Lycopolis (or "of the Thebaid") on the question of whether the inner "light of the nous" perceived during observation is a reflection of the divine light, or whether it arises from the inherent luminosity of the nous itself (*Antirr.* 6.16). John (possibly practicing *synkatabasis* and *epikrypsis*!) did not commit himself to a definitive answer. However, in this keph. Evagrius suggests three possible sources of the light: (1) reflection ("knowledge") of or "mixture with" the divine light (cf. 1.35, 2.29; 3.52); (2) the incorporeal nature of the nous (3.44); (3) the act of observing beings (5.15; 1.81). On the light of the mind or nous, see 1.35, 81; 2.29; 3.44, 52; 5.15; *Prak.* 64; *Gn.* 45; Sch. 258 on Prv 23.22; *Prayer* 74–75; *Thoughts* 17, 39, 40 & 42; *Reflections* 2, 4, 23, 25, 27; *Letter* 39.6; *Antirr.* 6.16. Observing incorporeals: Sch. 1 on Ps 83.3.

1.75

S2

If "the crown of justice" is holy knowledge, and the gold that holds the stones also makes known the worlds that have been or will be, then the *theōria* of corporeal and incorporeal nature is the crown that is placed by the "just judge" on the heads of those who fight.

S1

If "the crown of justice" is knowledge of the Holy Trinity, it is evident that at the completion of their race the holy ones will be crowned with it.

2 Tm 4.8

CROWN designates spiritual knowledge: 3.49; Sch. 7 on Prv 1.9; Sch. 44 on Prv 4.9. 2 Tm 4.8: both athletic and priestly crown. Cf. Zec 9.9; 1 Cor 9.24–25; 2 Thes 2.19; 1 Pt 5.4, Rev 2.10. For the paired comparison of corporeal and incorporeal nature, see 2.60; 3.80; 4.11 (vivify rational beings), 86 (observation of, mutually exclusive); 5.50. On gold, see *Eulogius* 29.31; *Vices* 6; *Eight Thoughts* 3.13, 8.20; *Monks* 60; *Virgin* 47; *Thoughts* 4, 8, 17, 19, 24; *Prayer* pr.; *Maxims 1* 6; *Maxims 2* 22; *Maxims 3* 25.

1.76

S2

Ignorance is not opposed to the knowledge hidden in things, but to the knowledge of the intelligibilities of things. For the ignorance that is in bodily nature is not there naturally.

S1

Ignorance is not opposed to the true knowledge hidden in natures but to the knowledge of children. But when children mature, they will prevail over ignorance.

Of knowledge and ignorance, the latter resides in the mind, not the body (*gūšmā*/substance/corporeality). Unknowing: 1.71. Ignorance cannot by nature be in a *gūšmā*; it is a mental quality susceptible to healing: *Prayer* 37: "Pray first to be purified from the passions, second, to be delivered from ignorance and forgetfulness, and third from all temptation and abandonment."

1.77

S2

The sign of the body is the second nature; but the sign of the soul is the first (nature); but the mind is Christ, who is united to knowledge of the unity.

S1

The mind of all the rational beings that are imprinted with the image of their creator is Christ our Savior, and it is he who perfects them in the knowledge of the Holy Trinity.

cf. Phil 2.13 (S1)

198   EVAGRIUS OF PONTUS

First and second natures: 2.31. On the tripartite soul, see *Prak.* 89. Guillaumont (1962, pp. 152–153) cited this keph. as agreeing with those condemned by anathema 6 of the *Anathemas of 553.* On knowledge of the U/unity, see 1.54 (S1); 2.3, 5; 3.72; 4.21, 43; *Prak.* 56.

1.78

Greek

The first renunciation (*apotaxis*) is the willing abandonment of earthly deeds on account of the knowledge of God.

Mosc. 425, sixteenth century (Hausherr 1939, p. 230)

S2

The first renunciation is the abandonment of worldly things that is done willingly for the knowledge of God.

S1

The first renunciation in the world happens in the soul: that with good will one abandons the things of this world for the knowledge of God.

This keph. through 80 (see also 1.85) corresponds to the end of *Thoughts* 26. RENUNCIATION, *apotaxis: Eulogius* 12.10–11; 16.27; *Prayer* 36; *Thoughts* 21, 32; *Vices* 1,4, as well as Eusebius, *Church History* 1.17.5, Epiphanius, *Panarion* 40.1; Basil, *Letter* 207.2. On "freely," *Prayer* 134. THINGS, here Syr. *sū'rānē*, Grk. *pragmata*, means normal everyday business in society, so could also be translated "affairs" or "matters," even "actions," "things," or "objects." The meaning of *pragmata*, which is also translated in the *Prak.* and *KG* as *ṣebwātā* (things or matters), changes with the context. Compare, for example, *Prak.* 48; Sch. 3 on Eccl 1.11 (*pragmata* of the mind). In general, see 2.32–36, 45, 47; 3.82; 4.67, 77, 81; 5.14, 27, 40, 43, 56–58, 62–63, 73, 75–76, 90; 6.22, 52, 54, 63; *Prak.* 8, 64, 67; *Gn.* 4, 23; Sch. 1 on Prv 1.1.

1.79

Greek

The second renunciation is the laying aside of evil, which happens by the grace of God and the zeal of the human.

Mosc. 425, sixteenth century (Hausherr 1939, p. 230)

S2

The second renunciation is the abandonment of evil, which happens by the grace of God and human diligence.

S1

The second renunciation is the removal of evil, which happens by means of human diligence and the grace of God.

See 1.78. This keph. is strikingly close to Sch. 12 on Ps 17.21. Grace: 1.37. Zeal: *Prak.* 57.

1.80

Greek

The third renunciation is the separation from ignorance, which naturally becomes apparent to humans analogous to [their] state.

Mosc. 425, sixteenth century (Hausherr 1939, p. 230)

S2

The third renunciation is the separation from ignorance, which is naturally apparent to humans proportionate to their states.

S1

The third renunciation is the separation from ignorance, which normally appears to humans like apparitions in combat proportionate to their growth.

See 1.78. On states (Gk. *katastasis* = Syr. *taqnūtā*) see 1.86 (Grk. *hexis*); 2.79 (S1); 3.28, 56; 4.22, 56 (ephod); 5.43 (path), 53; 6.21 (= Gk. *hexis*), 77. For more, see 6.21 (Grk. *hexis*); *Prak.* 12 (Grk. *katastasis*). For another translation of *katastasis* see 2.66.

1.81

Greek

The glory and light of the mind, then, is knowledge, but the glory and light of life is *apatheia*.

Mosc. 425, sixteenth century (Hausherr 1939, p. 230)

S2

The glory and the light of the mind is knowledge, but the glory and the light of the soul is *apatheia*.

S1

The glory and the light of the mind is knowledge of the Spirit, but the glory and the light of the soul is its *apatheia*.

On knowledge of God as light see Origen, *First Principles* 4.4.9; on freedom from passion as glory and light, Clement, *Paidagogos* 1.13.102.2. On the light of the nous see 1.74; freedom from passion, *Prak.* 2.

1.82

S2

What perceptible death normally does in us, in the form of "the just judgment of God," happens for the rest of the rational beings at the time that he is ready "to judge the living and the dead" and "reward everyone according to his deeds."

S1

[Same as S2]

2 Thes 1.5; 1 Pt 4.5; Rev 22.12

Perceptibility: 1.36. For the "last judgment" see 2.77; *Foundations* 9; *Eulogius* 7.7, 13.12, 15.16, 19.20, 21.23, 23.24, 27.29; *Monks* 54, 132, 135; *Thoughts* 11.32; *Prayer* 12; Sch. 5 on. Ps 118.7 (examples of logoi of judgment). Divine judgment: Origen, *Contra Celsum* 1.4. Cf. *KG* 6.74. On the judgment before the existence of bodies see 2.64; on the different numbers of judgments, see 2.75; on the pairing of judgment and providence, *Gn.* 48.

KEPHALAIA GNOSTIKA 201

1.83

S2

If the Gihon is the Egyptian river that surrounds the whole land of Kush, from which Israel was commanded by one of the prophets not to drink, we also knew these three other sources and the river from which the four sources were separated.

S1

[Same as S2]

Gn 2.13 and Jer 2.18. The river Gihon was associated with Egypt and Ethiopia/ Kush, and thus was a symbol of sin and vice (Philo, *Allegories of the Law* 1.63, 68; Origen, *Comm. on Jn* 6.47; Didymus, *Comm. on Zec*, 3.158; Athanasius, *Festal Letter* 7.5). But in Origen's *Hom. on Ps* 76.3.2–3, the Gihon is discussed in a positive way; on analogy to the Jordan, it contains a "power." The Jordan and Gihon appear together in Sir 24.26, where the rivers of paradise symbolize the Torah. See Kugel 1998, p. 112 on the connection to the Jordan. Egypt and Ethiopia: 4.64; 5.6, 21, 88; 6.49; Sch. 19 on Ps 67.32. Rivers: *Monks* 64, 128, 129. Four SOURCES: Gn 2.10 (*archas*).

1.84

S2

Knowledge and ignorance are united to the mind, but desire is receptive of continence and lust, and love and hatred normally accompany the angry part. But the first accompanies first things, and second accompanies second things.

S1

The mind of rational beings is receptive of knowledge and ignorance. But desire is receptive of continence and of license, and love and hate follow after anger. That which is first among the first ones is accompanied by that which is first among the second ones. That which is first among second ones [is accompanied by] that which is first among the third ones.

Tripartite soul: *Prak.* 89. The *hēgemonikon* or *nous* is the principal feature of first beings while the *pathētikon* (moved by *epithumia* and *thumos*) is "secondary," material, and intended as a means of spiritual reascent (*Thoughts* 17).

202 EVAGRIUS OF PONTUS

Cf. 1.50 on first and second beings. S1's addition of a third being is perhaps motivated by his interpretation of 2.31.

1.85

Greek

But the mind, when impassioned, circles and becomes hard to hold in when it surveys the material causes of pleasures. Having become free of passion, it ceases from wandering, having encountered the bodiless things that fulfill for it the spiritual desires.

Paris gr. 2748; fourteenth century (Muyldermans 1932, p. 50)

S2

When the mind is impassioned it wanders, and is uncontrolled when it does the material things constitutive of its desires. When it is without passion, it ceases from wandering, and it comes into the company of those who are bodiless, those who fulfill all these spiritual desires.

S1

When the mind is impassioned it wanders, that is to say, it is uncontrolled when it accomplishes different kinds of desires. But it halts from its turbulence and draws back from the error encompassing it when it becomes dispassionate and it is in the company of those who are bodiless, those who fulfill all its spiritual desires.

This passage (like 1.78–80) is replicated in *Thoughts* 26. See, generally, *Prak.* 15, 49; *Thoughts* 17–19. On the incorporeals, see 1.70; *Prak.* 61.

1.86

Greek

Love is the excellent state of the rational soul, according to which it prefers nothing above the knowledge of God.

Furrer-Pilliod 2000, p. 85 A.α.186

S2

Love is the excellent state of the rational soul, in which state the soul cannot love any corruptible thing more than the knowledge of God.

S1

Love is the excellent state of the rational soul, in which state the soul cannot love anything from this world more than the knowledge of God.

> On love, see *Prak.* pr.8; *Prayer* 54. Cf. Origen, *Comm. on Rom* 5.10.195–226: "Love will restrain every creature from a [further] fall, when 'God will be all in all' (1 Cor 15.28)." On states, see 1.80.

1.87

Greek

All things that came into being came into being through the knowledge of God, so that what came to be is known "from greatness and beauty." But everything that came to be because of another is less than that on account of which it came into being. The knowledge of God is more honorable than all.

> Milan, Ambr. gr. 681 (Q 74 sup.); tenth century (Muyldermans 1931, p. 58)

S2

All beings came into existence because of the knowledge of God. But everything that came into existence because of another is less than that on account of which it came into being. For the knowledge of God is greater than all.

S1

Everything that exists came into existence because of the knowledge of God. But everything that came into existence because of another is less than that on account of which it came into being. For the knowledge of God is greater than everything, for everything came into being because of it.

Wis 13.5 (Greek)

> Cf. Origen, *First Principles* 1.8, 2.9. On beauty, see Sch. 15 on Eccl 3.10–13. Wis 13.5 is discussed at *Disc.* 123.

204 EVAGRIUS OF PONTUS

1.88

S2

Natural knowledge is true comprehension of those things that have come into being on account of the knowledge of the Holy Trinity.

S1

Natural knowledge is intellection of the truth of those things that have come into being on account of the knowledge of the Holy Trinity.

> Natural knowledge: 1.71. On knowledge of the Holy Trinity, see 1.70, 1.74, and the next keph.

1.89

S2

All rational nature was created that it might exist and that it might be knowing, and God is essential knowledge. Nonexistence is the opposite of rational nature. Evil and ignorance are opposed to knowledge; but nothing of these things is opposed to God.

S1

All rational nature has been naturally made to teach true knowledge, and God is substantial knowledge. Thus, the reasoning nature that was created has contrariety, that it was not created. The opposite of its freedom, then, are evil and ignorance. But there is not one of these that is opposed to God.

> Rational nature is the knowing substance (1.3) of rational beings (*logikoi*). It should be differentiated from *logikoi* proper, in that the latter are individuals; the former, the substance of those individuals (1.4, 64). Elsewhere (2.18) Evagrius likens rational nature to Aristotelian primary substance by comparing vice/virtue to inherent qualities, to be contrasted with fleshly nature (3.75), while in a world (6.81)—conditions following the judgment (6.57). Its twofold purpose, existence and knowledge, permeate the *KG*. There are a variety of rational natures: demons (3.34), humans (2.88), the sun (3.44), the moon (3.52), the stars (3.62). The archangels and angels may

KEPHALAIA GNOSTIKA   205

also be included (5.4, 7), but the different phrasing there ("rational essence") may suggest a different concept. On the knowledge of rational beings, see 2.17. Cf. *Letter to Melania* 66: "God is essential knowledge, and all rational beings will participate in that knowledge; all knowledge will rise to become the same essential knowledge, in the restoration of the original unity." Cf. Origen on the progress of all minds to God in *First Principles* 2.1, *Hom. on Nm* 11.

On nonexistence, see 1.39. Contraries and God: 1.1. On essential knowledge (likely *ousiōdēs gnōsis*, as attested in the last citations), frequently equated with the Holy Trinity, see 2.11, 47; 3.3, 12, 49; 4.77; 5.55–56 (mixture versus separation of observation and object), 81; 6.10, 14, 16, 28, 34, 73; *Prayer* 69, 74, 132; *Disc.* 2, 19, 24, 30; Sch. 13 on Ps 43.21; Sch. 11 on Ps 88.21; Sch. 3 on Ps 138.7; *Letter* 29.3; 58.4. Cf. Didymus the Blind, *Comm. on Ps 20–21* 52.19. Evil and ignorance are commonly paired, in that order: 5.28; 6.19, 24, 35, 64; Sch. 55 on Prv 5.3–4; Sch. 112 on Prv 9.12; *Disc.* 14, 95, 124. Evil preceded ignorance: Sch. 159 on Prv 17.14.

1.90

S2

If today is that which is called Friday, on which our Savior was crucified, all those who die are the riddle of his tomb, for in them the justice of God has died which will come to life on the third day, and be raised clothed with a spiritual body, if "today and tomorrow he works miracles and on the third day it is completed."

S1

If today is Friday, on which our Savior was crucified, all those who have died in Christ are the riddle of his tomb, for in them the righteousness of God has been entombed; that which was raised on the third day, clothed in a spiritual body. The word of our Savior is true: "Today and tomorrow he accomplishes miracles, and on the third day it is completed."

Lk 13.32

On Friday and numbered days of the week, see 4.26; 5.83 (types of circumcision on Friday, Saturday, Sunday); 6.7. RIDDLE: *pēlētā*, also "image," "proverb." On the sabbatical year, 5.8. Spiritual body (1 Cor 15.44): *Disc.* 27; on clothing with spiritual bodies, see 4.24. On the third day, see also 3.9.

EVAGRIUS OF PONTUS

Epilogue

S2

Completed is the first [century].

S1

Completed is the first century, which is lacking ten chapters.

Century Two

S2

Century Two

S1

[Same as S2]

2.1

S2

The mirror of the goodness of God and of his power and of his wisdom: these initially became something from nothing.

S1

The mirror of the goodness of God, and of his power and his wisdom, is the creation that from nothing became something.

> Cf. 1 Cor 1.24 and Wis 7.25–26. On mirrors, see 4.55; 5.64 (mirror : images :: impassible soul : earthly affairs); *Exh. Monks* 2.5; *Eight Thoughts* 1.17; 8.22; *Vices* 5; *Maxims 2* 7; *Letter on Faith* 22, 37; *Letter* 12 (letters as a mirror). Creation from nothing: 5.50; Origen, *First Principles* 1.2.2; 4.4.6; *Hom. on Gn* 1.1; *Comm. on Jn* 1.17.103.

2.2

S2

In natural *theōria* of second things we see the wisdom of Christ "richly varied," which he uses and with which he creates worlds; but we have been taught concerning his person by the knowledge that concerns rational beings.

208 EVAGRIUS OF PONTUS

S1

In natural *theōria* of second things we see the wisdom of Christ "richly varied," which he uses and with which he creates worlds, but we are taught concerning his person by the knowledge that concerns rational natures.

Eph 3.10

Eph 3.10 ("wisdom full of varieties") is quoted at 1.43; 2.21; 3.11, 81 (S1); 4.7; 5.84. In *Letter to Melania* 65 it is a symbol of God; cf. Sch. 2 on Ps 3.4; Sch. 8 on Ps 44.10 (golden garment). What is normally said to be "second natural contemplation" we have translated "natural observation of second beings" not only because that reflects the Syriac grammatical construction used consistently throughout the *KG* but because the activity can be applied to either first beings or second beings (see 1.50), or to nature itself (see 2.13). On wisdom in general, 1.14. On observation of first, second, and third things, see 2.3, 4, 13, 20, 21; 3.8 (S1 only), 21 (third observation), 26, 61, 67, 84, 86; 4.19, 27 (dove at baptism), 51; cf. Plotinus, *Enneads* 5.3.11; 6.7.15; Porphyry, *On Abstinence* 31. On the distinction between first observation (immaterial) and second (in material) observation, see 3.19. On observation in general, *Prak.* 32. HIS PERSON: *qnomeh*, which may also be translated "his hypostasis," "his figure," "his face," "his essence."

2.3

S2

The first (kind) of knowledge is knowledge of the union and the unity, and spiritual knowledge is older than every natural *theōria*, for this came forth from the creator first; and it arose with the nature that accompanied it.

S1

The first of all knowledges is unitary knowledge of the unity, and spiritual knowledge is older than every natural *theōria*, for this came forth from the creator first; and it arose with the nature that accompanied it.

See previous keph. on observation of second natures. On *monas* and *henas*, likely the pair of Greek words that were contrasted, see 1.49; 3.1; *Letter on Faith* 7. On spiritual knowledge, 1.32; the contrast with natural observation, 4.6.

KEPHALAIA GNOSTIKA 209

2.4

S2

Although the changes are many, we have received the knowledge of only four: of the first and the second and of the last and the one before it. The first is, as they say, the passage from vice to virtue; the second, from *apatheia* to natural *theōria* of second things; the third, from this to knowledge about rational beings; and the fourth is the passage from all these to knowledge of the Holy Trinity.

S1

Although the changes are many, we know a distinction of only four changes. The first is, as the fathers say, the transition from vice to virtue; the second from disobedience to natural *theōria* of second things; the third, the ascent from this to knowledge of rational natures; and the fourth is the transition from all these to (knowledge of) the Holy Trinity.

The underlying Grk. for CHANGE (Syr. root: *šḥlp or ḥlp*, which could also be translated "transfer" or "alteration") may be *metathesis, metabasis, alloiōsis*, or *allagē*. Another reasonable possibility could be *metamorphōsis*, but that noun is not found in Evagrius' extant Greek corpus, and the underlying concept is of transfer, not transformation. When describing a change, Evagrius prefers nouns such as *metathesis* and *metabasis*, which imply moving or migrating from one body to another, and not a body that is itself changed. On such transfers or changes, which figure prominently in Evagrius' system, see 2.59, 69, 73, 77, 79, 83, 87; 3.7, 9, 20, 25, 45, 47, 50–51; 5.10; 6.58. See also 3.48 and 3.50 (see notes there), which has Greek fragments. For the scriptural texts motivating Evagrius' view of transfer, see Mt 17.1–9; 1 Cor 15.51–58; 2 Cor 3.18. This choice of vocabulary parallels that of Didymus the Blind, who did not use *metamorphōsis* and preferred *metathesis, metabasis*, and *allagē*. Cf. the use of *apogenesis* in Gregory of Nyssa, *Catechetical Oration* 39 and Porphyry, *On the Cave of the Nymphs* 31 and 24 (and Plotinus, *Enneads* 3.4.6) for another way of discussing an upward "transfer" of souls.

There is, in fact, a strong case to be made that the term here is Grk. *allagē*. When discussing the inscription to LXX Ps 44—"Regarding Completion. Over those that will be changed (*alloiōthēsomenōn*). Pertaining to the sons of Kore. Regarding understanding." (NETS)—Didymus the Blind discusses extensively (in about two thousand words) the difference between *alloiōsis* and *allagē*. The former, a familiar Aristotelian term (*Physics* 3.1; *On the Soul* 2.5), denotes a change in quality, e.g.,

210 EVAGRIUS OF PONTUS

a newborn becoming a child. The latter is a change that requires destruction or corruption (*phtharton*; see 1 Cor 15.51–53), e.g., clay to a pot, an egg to a bird, or natron and sand to glass. The key biblical example Didymus uses is that of Paul's discussion of the resurrection at 1 Cor 15: "Paul did not say 'we will all be altered (*alloiōthēsometha*)' but 'we will be transformed (*allagēsōmetha*)'" (Gronewald ed. 328.25), and Didymus appeals to the transformation from grain (*kokkos*) to ear (*stachys*) to wheat (*sitos*) as an example of the *allagē* of the "soulish" body to a spiritual one. Although we do not identify a verbatim quotation from Didymus in the *KG*, Evagrius adopts the same metaphors (e.g., *KG* 1.24; 2.25), terminology (here), scriptures (3.25, 33, 37, 40, 47, 54, 71), and approach (e.g., via categories such as quality and events such as destruction) to make what looks to be a very similar argument. Both authors are dealing with Aristotelian concepts still relevant in their own time. But similarity does not entail duplication. For example, Didymus does not relate the *allagai* to the creation of new worlds and bodies.

On other methods of expressing levels of knowledge, see 1.70.

2.5

S2

The body of that which is, is the *theōria* of beings, but the soul of that which is, is knowledge of the unity. And the one who knows the soul, is called the soul of that which is, and those who know the body are named the body of this soul.

S1

The spiritual body of rational natures is this: the *theōria* of all beings. Their true lives are the knowledge of the holy unity.

"That which is" (*haw d-'itawhi*) is a technical term; see 1.9, 12, 17; 2.31. Ex 3.14, "I am who/that I am." On soul observing being, see *Reflections* 24 = *Thoughts* 42. On the anthropological model of body and soul see *Prak.* 89.

2.6

Greek

The soul that has, together with God, accomplished the practice and left behind the body comes into those places of knowledge in which the wing of *apatheia* will bring the soul to rest.

Mosc. 425, sixteenth century (Hausherr 1939, p. 230)

KEPHALAIA GNOSTIKA 211

S2

The practiced soul that by the grace of God has conquered and left the body is in the places of knowledge where the wings of its *apatheia* will lead it.

S1

[Same as S2]

The Greek fragment is attested twice, here from a sixtheenth-century manuscript, and in *Thoughts* 29, which is virtually identical. On ascent to virtue, see 1.32, 72. Regaining the wings of the soul, Plato, *Phaedrus* 246a–254e. Cf. Sch. 2 on Ps 54.7: the "wings of the dove" raise the soul to observation of the ages and rest in knowledge of the Trinity; on wings see 3.56. PLACES OF KNOWLEDGE, see 1.71; 2.54. Release from the body: 1.58; 4.83; *Prak.* 52.

2.7

S2

These are the soul's heirs after death—those helping it toward virtue or vice.

S1

Those inheriting the soul after death are either virtuous or vicious, and they are its encouragers and helpers.

This keph. forms a pair with the next. HEIRS: Heb 1.14, Gal 4.7; Col 2.14; and Sch. 263 on Prv 23.33; Sch. 288 on Prv 30.9; *Monks* 1. On coheirs see 3.72.

2.8

S2

The wealth of the soul is knowledge, and its poverty is ignorance, but if ignorance is the lack of knowledge, wealth is prior to poverty, and the health of the soul to its sickness.

S1

The wealth of the soul is spiritual knowledge, but its poverty is ignorance. But if ignorance is lack of knowledge, it is clear that wealth is prior to poverty, and the health of the soul to its sickness.

212 EVAGRIUS OF PONTUS

Cf. 1 Cor 1.5. On knowledge as wealth of the soul, see Sch. 155 on Prv 17.6a. On literal, economic wealth see *Prak.* 18; the wealth of God, 4.30. HEALTH OF THE SOUL: 1.41; *Prak.* 56. This chapter parallels the end of *Letter* 43.3, and so should be compared to the other kephalaia that make up that letter: 1.39–40, 85.

2.9

S2

Who knows the action of the commandments and who understands the powers of the soul, and how the former heal the second, and [the latter] encourage to *theōria* of beings?

S1

Who knows the operation of the commandments of God, and who understands the powers of the soul, and how the former are healing for the latter, and draw near to true *theōria*?

On the healing efficacy of the commandments see *Prak.* 79, 82. Keeping the commandments: 1.10; *Prak.* 40; *Thoughts* 26, 30. On healing more generally, see 3.35 (knowledge heals the mind), 46; 6.64; *Prak.* 49, 100; *Gn.* 33, 47. On the powers of the soul, see 3.14; 6.51; *Prak.* 49, 73, 79, 98; Sch. 29 on Prv 3.8; Sch. 1 on Ps 102.1: "That which is within the inner human: the *noētikē* power, and the *dianoētikē*, and the *epibleptikē*, and the *hormētikē*, and the *phantastikē*, and the *mnēmoneutikē*." Disc. 93 identifies the soul as having three powers corresponding to the angering part, the desiring part, and the rational part. Other lists would have been better known, such as that of pseudo-Hippocrates, *Letter to Ptolemy* 287.5: "There are five powers of the soul: mind, understanding, opinion, imagination, and sense-perception" (*nous, dianoia, doxa, phantasia kai aisthēsis*). Cf. the fivefold division from Aristotle, *On the Soul* 433b.

2.10

Greek

Pleasurable are things that encounter us through the senses. More pleasurable than all of these by far is *theōria*, but because of our weakness, sensation does not reach knowledge, but itself seems to be more precious than what is not yet present.

Mosc. 425, sixteenth century (Hausherr 1939, p. 230)

KEPHALAIA GNOSTIKA   213

S2

Desirable are those pleasures that come to us by means of the senses. More desirable than those (pleasures) is the *theōria* of them. But because sense perception does not attain to knowledge, due to our weakness, (sense perception) is deemed superior to what has not yet been attained.

S1

Desirable are those pleasures known by the senses, but more desirable than those (pleasures) is the *theōria* of true knowledge; but because sense perception does not attain to knowledge, due to its weakness, (sense perception) is deemed, by virtue of its closeness, superior to what is distant and superior to it.

> On the mind and the pleasure (Syr. *'argīgān*; Grk. *terpna*) of *theōria*, see 4.49; *Thoughts* 26; *Eight Thoughts* 3.8 (PG 40:1153.38–40). For an overview of the senses and matters (*pragmata*) see Sch. 15 on Eccl 3.10–13. On the weakness (*astheneia*) of the mind see Sch. 310 on Prv 25.17.

2.11

S2

Concerning everything constituted of the four elements, whether far or near, it is possible to receive its image. But only our mind is incomprehensible to us, as is God, its creator. Indeed, it is not possible to understand what a nature receptive of the Holy Trinity is nor to understand the unity, that is, essential knowledge.

S1

Concerning everything that is established from the four elements, whether near or far, we are able to receive a *theōria* with the working of the grace of our Lord. But only our mind is incomprehensible, and greater than this [the mind], is God, its creator. For because of this, God is incomprehensible, as is even his dwelling.

> FOUR ELEMENTS: 1.15. On incomprehensibility (not to be conflated with ignorance; see 1.49) see 1.71; 4.2–3. ESSENTIAL KNOWLEDGE: 1.89.

214   EVAGRIUS OF PONTUS

2.12

S2

The Lord's right is also called "hand" but his hand is not also called "right." His hand is receptive of increase or diminution, but this does not happen to the right.

S1

Christ's right is also called "hand" but his hand is not also called "his right," because of the one, its sign is in the gift, and the sign of the other, is in the instruction.

> On the hand of the Lord see Sch. 7 on Ps 16.13 (provident angels); Sch. 1 on Ps 94.4 (providence of God); in contrast, the right hand designates the Son or Christ: Sch. 19 on Ps 17.37; Sch. 5 on Ps 44.5; *Letter on Faith* 11; *Letter to Melania* 7. S1 translates "right" to mean gift (sc. "of the Holy Spirit") and "hand" to mean "instruction," differentiating the pedagogue from those more advanced. On the right hand and the right in general, see 2.89; 4.21 (Monad and Unity, i.e., essential knowledge); Sch. 6 on Ps 47.11 (arm of God); Sch. 11 on Ps 76.16; Sch. 8 on Ps 79.18. In the Bible (e.g., Mk 16.19) the right hand signifies inheritance, favor, possession, power, and goodness; the "sons of the left hand," by contrast, are demons. On hands in the *praktikē*, *Prak.* pr.3.
>
> On receptivity of increase and diminution, see 1.68 and especially 2.85.

. 2.13

S2

The first *theōria* of nature sufficed for the existence of rational nature; [natural *theōria*] of second things also suffices for its return.

S1

The first *theōria* of the spirit suffices for [understanding] the existence of rational natures; the [*theōria*] of second things will be sufficient also to raise them to perfection.

> On the different types of observation, see 2.2. On the return (S2: *pūnāyā*, likely Grk. *epistrophē* [cf. Ac 15.3 Peshitta]), see 3.60; 5.22; 6.19. It is common to ascribe to Evagrius the teaching of the *apokatastasis*, the restoration of all things. The term appears in the New Testament three times (Mt 17.11;

KEPHALAIA GNOSTIKA   215

Ac 3.21; Heb 13.19), and frequently in the writings of Clement, Origen, Eusebius, Didymus the Blind, and Gregory of Nyssa. The term was a focus of the anathemas of 543 (#9) and 553 (#14). There is no evidence, however, that Evagrius used the term: it does not survive in the Greek corpus, and the passages in the *KG* that are suggestive of the concept point to other Greek terms. This is not to say, however, that Evagrius's concept of the *epistrophē* was significantly different.

2.14

S2

Those who are living in equal bodies are not in the same (state of) knowledge, but they are in the same aeon. But those who are in the same knowledge are in equality of body and are in the same aeon.

S1

Those who are equal in perfection of their ways of life are also equal in the retribution of their toils. And those who are equal in their knowledge of the spirit are also equal in the glory of their inheritance.

Aeons: 1.70.

2.15

S2

When the rational nature will receive *theōria* concerning itself, then also all the power of the mind will be strong.

S1

When rational nature receives *theōria* of itself, then also the power of a mind will be fully perfected.

This keph. forms a pair with the next. Our translation WILL RECEIVE (S2) versus RECEIVES (S1): tries to capture the verbal difference between *nqabel* and *qabel*. On healing, see 2.9. POWER OF THE MIND: 5.60, 79.

216 EVAGRIUS OF PONTUS

2.16

S2

Such is the *theōria* of all that is and will be: the nature that will be able to receive it will also receive knowledge of the Trinity.

S1

Such is the knowledge of all that exists: so that participation [in it] brings the soul to knowledge of the Holy Trinity.

> ALL THAT IS: may also be translated "all that was." On observation, see the previous keph. KNOWLEDGE OF THE TRINITY: *Prak.* 3. On the contrast between observation (*theōria*) and knowledge (*gnōsis*), see *Monks* 110 ("Greater is the knowledge of a Triad than knowledge of bodiless things, and [greater is] observation of it than logoi of all the aeons"). On observation in general, see *Prak.* 32.

2.17

S2

Knowledge concerning rational beings is accompanied by the destruction of worlds, the dissolution of bodies, and the annulment of names, while equality of knowledge remains, like the equality of substances.

S1

By an increase of knowledge of the rational beings, worlds are changed and names are annihilated, while the equality of knowledge remains, like the equality of substances.

> On rational beings and natures (here reprising 2.15), see 1.89. On knowledge about them, see 2.2, 4, 19, 80. The three events mentioned point to the *epistrophē*: no more mortal bodies (*pagrē*); *homonoia* of knowledge: all will join the Good. Cf. *Letter to Melania* 23–30 with exegesis of 2 Pt 1.4 (note that the root metaphor is the entry of the High Priest into the Temple). See note to 1.17 on names (*epinoiai*). DESTRUCTION OF WORLDS: 5.89. DISSOLUTION OF BODIES appears in Origen, *First Principles* 2.3.3, *somatōn apothesis* (attested by Justianian's letter to Menas); see also Cyril of Alexandria, *Comm. on Rom*, Pusey ed. 217.26. On the destruction of the world in scripture, to which this kephalaion may allude, see e.g. Jer 51.25; Is 24.1–3; 2 Pt 3.11–12. This keph. is found nearly verbatim in Anathema 14 of the fifteen anti-Origenistic *Anathemas of 553*:

KEPHALAIA GNOSTIKA 217

"If someone says:

that all reasonable beings will be one, when the hypostases as well as the numbers are removed together with the bodies,

and that **the knowledge about the *logikoi* will be followed by the destruction of the worlds, and the removal of bodies and the abolition of names,**

and that there shall be an identity of knowledge, just as of substances,

and that in the mythologized apokatastasis there will be only bare minds, just as also happens in the preexistence ranted about by them,

let him be anathema."

Trans. based on text in Schwartz and Straub 1971, p. 249. It is unclear whether the quotation here is direct or indirect. The first part of Anathema 14 is similar to *KG* 1.7–8. For other verbatim parallels between the anathemas and the *KG*, see 2.78; 4.18.

2.18

S2

Just as qualities that remain in them conceal the nature of bodies, and without interruption pass from one to another, thus also either virtue and knowledge or vice and ignorance conceal the rational nature. It is not right for someone to say that one of these secondary things was made along with the rational beings. Because it [one of these secondary things] will have appeared with the constitution of nature.

S1

Just as qualities or colors that accompany bodies conceal (those very) bodies, so also virtue and knowledge or vice and ignorance conceal rational natures.

Quality: 1.22. Secondary things here refer to vice and ignorance (not second beings, on which see 1.50). Virtue and knowledge are constituents of rational nature; vice and ignorance are secondary. See 1.40–41, *Letter to Melania* 39–40. On the composition of the world, see 1.67. On the pairing of vice and ignorance, see 5.46; *Gn.* 48.

2.19

S2

Knowledge concerning rational beings is older than duality and the knowing nature (is older) than all natures.

218   EVAGRIUS OF PONTUS

S1

Knowledge of the truth is older than all rational natures, because after they have come to be, they grow by means of it, until they arrive at its perfection.

Duality: 6.12. Knowing natures: 5.76. On comparative ages of things, see 1.41.

2.20

S2

Natural *theōria* of second things had been at first immaterial. Later on by means of matter, the creator unveiled it to the nature of rational beings.

S1

The knowledge of the spirit that is before bodies, the creator taught to rational nature after the creation that is in bodies.

On natural observation, see 2.2. On second things, see 1.50. The unveiling may allude to Rom 10.4, Ex 34.33, or Rev 10.2 (Peshitta *glā*). Note the divergence between S1 and S2.

2.21

S2

Everything that has come to be proclaims "the wisdom of God full of varieties." But there is nothing among all of those beings that makes known his nature.

S1

Everything that has come into being is a herald of "the wisdom of God full of varieties." But there is nothing from all that has come into being that will be perceptive of his nature.

Eph 3.10

On "full of variety" (*polypoikilos*) see 2.2.

2.22

S2

Just as the logos has made known the nature of the Father, so also the rational nature has made known that of Christ.

S1

Just as the image of the Father, the word of truth, his Son our Lord Jesus Christ, has caused to appear and shown the rational nature, so also that rational nature has shown his image.

> Jn 1.1–18. See Sch. 4 on Ps 88.2 on how Christ is known. Note here the distinction between Logos, (presumed) Son, and Christ; see 3.1. On the Father, see 1.65; 2.60 (S1), 89; 3.1, 13 (S1); 4.3, 9 (S1), 21, 78, 80 (S1); 6.4, 14, 20, 33, 34, 77, 79. On fatherhood in general, see 6.28–31.

2.23

S2

The image of the essence of God also knows the *theōria* of things that exist. But the one who knows the *theōria* of beings is not entirely the image of God.

S1

The one who is in "the image of the invisible God" is a teacher of knowledge about him, for he is close to every rational nature that is in his image.

> Col 1.15 (S1)
>
> This keph. may be a quotation from Heb 1.3, "and the express image of his person" (*charaktēr tēs hypostaseōs autou*), which in the Peshitta is translated *ṣalmā d-'ītūteh*, the very phrase that begins S2's translation of this kephalaion. Without the original Greek it is impossible to know. Syriac *panṭūs*, "entirely," is a calque on Greek *pantos*. On the image of God, see 3.32; 6.73; *Gn.* 50. The things that exist are things that always are, whereas the observation of beings pertains to things that come into existence. See note at 1.73

2.24

S2

There is one alone who possesses names in common with others.

S1

There is only one who, by his grace, has taken upon himself to gain names borrowed with his titles.

> On names, see 1.51. On S1's insertion "titles," probably alluding to Greek *epinoiai*, see note at 1.17.

2.25

S2

Just as this body is said to be the grain of the ear of wheat that is to come, so also this world that exists will be called the grain of the one after it.

S1

Just as the body of something sown is called the grain of the ear of wheat that is to come, so also this world that exists will be called the grain of that which is to come.

> Cf. 1 Cor 15.36–44. See above, 1.24 on the wheat analogy; on others' sayings that applied it to the body and resurrection, see, e.g., Origen, *Contra Celsum* 5.23; Gregory of Nyssa, *On the Soul and the Resurrection* 46.157. The most striking parallel comes from Didymus the Blind, discussed at 2.4.

2.26

S2

If wheat bears the symbol of virtue, and chaff the symbol of vice, then the world which is to come [bears] the symbol of amber, which will draw to itself the chaff.

S1

If wheat bears the symbol of virtue, and chaff bears the symbol of vice, that world which is to come bears the symbol of a refiner's furnace that separates wheat from chaff.

cf. Mt 3.12

On the wheat analogy, see previous kephalaion. S2's term *sūqinān*, nowhere else attested in Syriac, transliterates *soukinos*, itself a late antique Greek transliteration of Latin *sucinum* (the more common Greek word was *ēlektron*), a resin commonly imported from the Baltic region. The use of amber to attract chaff (*achyron*) is attested in Hippolytus, *Refutation* 5.21; Clement of Alexandria, *Stromateis* 2.6.26; 7.2, among others. Elektron as a symbol of spiritual perfection: Origen *Hom. on Jer* 11.5 (quoting Ezek 1.27).

2.27

S2

The mind, as it gazes upon intelligibles, sometimes receives the sight of them directly but also sometimes becomes a seer of their effects.

S1

The spiritual mind that looks upon intelligibles sometimes receives a sight of them directly but sometimes is an enlightened seer of them.

This keph. forms a pair with the next. On seeing matters or things, see 2.36 and 45 (the nous is an observer, Grk. *theatēs*, one who sees); 3.30 "the observer of the Holy Trinity"; see also 4.7, 4.90; 5.27 (mind as observer cannot "see" the angering part), 84 (observer of unity; observation of Trinity).

2.28

S2

The eye of sensation, when it beholds something visible, does not see it whole. But the intelligible eye either does not see, or when it sees, encompasses all at once from all sides whatever it is seeing.

S1

The perceiving eye, when it beholds something visible, does not see it whole. But the eye of intellection either does not see, or when it sees all at once it encompasses from all sides whatever it sees.

On the seeing of the intellection, see the previous keph. On the noetic eye, see also *Prayer* 27. For another comparison of physical and mental seeing, see 6.63.

2.29

S2

Just as fire possesses its body with power, so also the mind will possess the soul with power when it is mingled entirely with the light of the Holy Trinity.

S1

Just as fire possesses its body with power, so also the mind will possess the soul with power when it is mingled entirely with the light of the Holy Trinity.

On fire, see 1.30, 68; cf. Origen, *First Principles* 2.6.6 comparing the Word in the soul to fire in iron. The power mentioned here is perhaps connected with the next kephalaion (cf. note at 1.24 on the comparable adverbial use of *dynamis*). On the light of the Trinity, see *Thoughts* 42 on SS 4.9. Although the light of the Trinity admits mingling, the Trinity itself does not: 5.55. Cf. *Prak.* 70 on the mixture of the virtues in the soul.

2.30

S2

For all those whose administration they assume, the holy powers also know their intellections, but it is not the case that they have been entirely entrusted with the administration of those whose intellections they know.

S1

Of all those whose direction they assume, the holy powers also know the intellections of their knowledge, but it is not the case that they assume the direction of all those whose intellections they know.

Following Origen, Evagrius understands the holy powers to be angels: 5.18; *Prak.* 56, *Prayer* 81. On holy powers more generally, see *Gn.* 44; *Thirty-Three Chapters* 31, 33; *Thoughts* 4; Sch. 189 on Prv 19.4; Sch. 120 on Prv 10.18 (friends of God and the holy powers); Sch. 184 on Prv 18.16; Sch. 341 on Prv 27.25 (the holy powers encourage repentance and virtue in rational beings); Sch. 2 on Ps 113.4, quoting Mt 6.10 (God is in the holy powers). On the paired contrast between holy and unholy powers, see 5.18. Our phrase "administration" translates Syr. *mdbrnuth'*, likely Grk. *oikonomia* (e.g., Peshitta Eph 1.10; 3.2, 9); both terms had a wide range of meanings, including "guardianship," "divine economy," and "government"; see 3.37, 65; 4.74, 89. On the administration of the angels, see Origen, *First Principles* 1.8.1. The term *sūkālē*, INTELLECTIONS (cf. 1.70, where it translates Greek *logoi*) can also be translated as meanings (see 2.45: *logoi*), observation (4.81: *theōria*), reasons (5.57: *logoi*), or thoughts (4.67 S1). On pedagogy: *Gn.* 20. Three types of intellections: 5.52 (bodies, incorporeals, Trinity). On the *sūkālē/logoi* of material things, see 5.52, 55, 57; 6.22, 23, 72; for an extended discussion of the logos of gold, see *Thoughts* 8.

2.31

S2

Human beings live three lives: the first, the second, and the third. And indeed the first and second life receive the things of the first nature, but the third life receives those that share in the second nature. And the first life, they say, is from that which is, but the second and third are from that which is not.

224 EVAGRIUS OF PONTUS

S1

Human beings live three distinct ways: naturally, above nature, and against nature. Two are according to the will of God, and one is according to the carelessness of their will.

> On first and second nature see 1.77; 3.24, 26; 5.85. On first and second beings (not to be conflated with first and second nature), see 1.50. On multiple lives, see 3.76 (three: plants, animals, angels/demons); 5.5 (two: practice versus torment); *Prak.* pr.9 (two: practice versus knowledge). On life in general, see 1.64.

2.32

Greek

Just as it is not materials but their qualities that nourish bodies, so also it is not actions, but the *theōriai* of them, that makes the soul grow.

> Milan, Ambr. gr. 681 (Q 74 sup.); tenth century (Muyldermans 1931, p. 58)

S2

Just as it is not material things but their power that nourishes bodies, so it is not actions but the *theōria* of them that makes the soul grow.

S1

Just as it is not material things but their power that nourishes bodies, so also it is not things that make the soul grow, but distinctions in the knowledge of things.

> The Greek manuscript preserves a scribal error, *poiotētes* for *dynameis*, attested by both S1 and S2. The latter reading fits the sense better, since it is hard to see how a quality can affect a body in this way (cf. 2.83: qualities alter senses). In addition, the Greek manuscript reading *diastrephousin* ("twist") we have taken as *diatrephousin*, "nourish." On nourishment in general see 2.82. On the soul growing, compare 6.67 (growth of the mind); *Letter to Melania* 51 (nourishment of the soul); Philo, *On Planting* 114; Clement of Alexandria, *Stromateis* 3.4.26 (quoting the traditions of Matthias); 7.6.33. ACTIONS: *pragmata*, on which see 1.78 and the next few keph., where the same word is adjusted in our translation according to context.

KEPHALAIA GNOSTIKA   225

2.33

S2

Of the actions pertaining to material knowledge some of them are first, and some are second. The first are corruptible in power, but the second [are corruptible] in power and in actuality.

S1

The growth of the knowledge of rational beings is in the sight of both corruptible and incorruptible things; its training is in corruptibles; its perfection is in incorruptibles.

On *pragmata*, likely the opening Greek word, see the previous keph. On potency versus actuality see 1.55. On corruptibility, see 1.86; 3.33, 55; 6.58 (S1).

2.34

S2

Just as a magnetic stone by its natural power attracts iron to itself, so also holy knowledge naturally attracts the pure mind to itself.

S1

Just as magnetic stone with the natural power that is hidden in it draws iron to itself, so also holy knowledge the pure mind.

Knowledge like a magnet: Plato, *Ion* 533d–534e; see a comparable analogy at Clement of Alexandria, *Prophetic Eclogues* 27.5. On the pure mind, Syr. *hawnā dakyā* / Grk. *nous katharos*, see 3.28 (S1); 5.17, 52, 84, 90 (Grk.); 6.48, 63; *Prak.* 49; *Letter* 56.2 (mind alone does not see God, but only the pure mind); *Monks* 107; Sch. 31 on Prv 3.18; Sch. 375 on Prv 31.18; Sch. 376 on Prv 31.19; Sch. 378 on Prv 31.22; Sch. 2 on Ps 10.2 (bow); Sch. 3 on Ps 32.2 (psaltērion = Sch. 2 on Ps 91.4); Sch. 19 on Ps 36.23 (way of the Lord); Sch. 4 on Ps 43.6 (horn of the soul = Sch. 5 on Ps 148.14); Sch. 2 on Ps 131.5 (place of the Lord); Sch. 8 on Ps 138.16 (comes to be written through knowledge); Sch. 1 on Ps 144.1; *Thoughts* 41; *Disc.* 31, 115, 124b, 175, 188, 211.

226 EVAGRIUS OF PONTUS

2.35

Greek

The mind also has acquired five divine senses through which it receives its own materials. The act of sight presents simple intelligible things. Hearing admits the words concerning them. The sense of smell enjoys the fragrance that is unmingled with any falsity, and the mouth receives their pleasure. By means of touching is confirmed the accurate demonstration of the things received.

Milan, Ambr. gr. 681 (Q 74 sup.); tenth century (Muyldermans 1931, pp. 58–59)

S2

The mind also possesses five spiritual senses, through which it senses nearby material things. Vision shows it intelligible matters in a simple manner; through hearing it receives *logoi* about them; the sense of smell delights in the fragrance that is a stranger to every deceit; the mouth receives the flavor of these things; by means of touch it is assured when it receives a precise proof of things.

S1

The mind also possesses five spiritual senses, by which it sees and senses the meanings of creatures. And vision shows the beings of things as objects; but in hearing it receives *logoi* about them; through the sense of smell it is sweetened by a holy fragrance that is unmixed with falsehood, while the palate of its mouth is sweetened by them; by means of touch it receives true assurance of exactly what is in them.

On the senses, see 1.33 (spiritual) and 1.34 (physical). On matters, see 2.32. On proof (Greek *apodeixis*) see Sch. 105 on Prv 9.3; Sch. 240 on Prv 22.10; *Thoughts* 25, and our note at 1.32. See also *Thoughts* 33. On delight or enjoyment, see 3.56 (mind, of knowledge); 4.8 (mind, with Christ); 5.43 (of beings); 6.33. On stench, 5.78 (odor of demons' bodies).

2.36

S2

Not all of those who see intelligible matters have also relied upon the true logos concerning them; nor did those entrusted with seeing their logoi also see their matters. But those made worthy of these two discernments, it is they who are called "firstborn of their brothers."

S1

Not all observers of intelligible matters have also relied upon the true reason concerning them; nor did those entrusted with seeing their reasons also see their matters. But those made worthy of these two great discernments are called "firstborn of their brothers."

Rom 8.29

Those WHO SEE INTELLIGIBLE MATTERS: philosophers; cf. *Disc.* 5. TRUE LOGOS: cf. Origen, *Contra Celsum* 1.3 against the *alēthes logos* of Celsus. On intelligible matters (*sū'rānē metyad'ānē*), see previous keph. and 2.52. On the firstborn (Rom 8.29) see also Col 1.15, 18 (*protoktistoi*); Clement of Alexandria, *Excerpts from Theodotus* 10.6–11.2 on the seven first-created angels. Origen also quotes Rom 8.29: the Christian who can both praise the creature and at the same time "see how it shall . . . be [. . .] restored to the glorious liberty of the children of God (Rom 8.19–20); rising "to a blessedness beyond those Paul calls 'gods'" (*Contra Celsum* 8.5).

2.37

S2

There is one among all beings without a name and [from] an unknown place.

S1

There is only one from all beings who has a name, and his place is unknown.

Letter to Melania 26. On names, see 2.17, 66; 3.33; 4.54; 6.20. See also our note on *epinoiai*, divine names, at 1.17. On place, Grk. *topos*, see 2.54; 5.2, 70. Cf. Ps 23.3.

228 EVAGRIUS OF PONTUS

2.38

S2

Whose nature is in the days before the Passion, and whose knowledge is of holy Pentecost?

S1

There is a part of the meaning of the economy in the days before the Passion, and a part signified by Holy Pentecost.

> This and the following four keph. treat the same set of number and festal symbolism, associating the forty days before the Passion (Lent) with the number four and the fifty days between the Passion and Pentecost with the number five. Four and five have already been associated with the elements and the senses; see note at 1.15. On Pentecost, see also 2.42; 4.53–54 (contrasted with Babel); *Monks* 40, 42.

2.39

S2

The five are kin to the fifty, and the former are preparations for the knowledge of the latter.

S1

The number five shares in the mystery of fifty, and the latter are the cause of intellection.

> See 2.38.

2.40

S2

The four are kin to the forty, and the former is the *theōria* of the forty.

S1

The number four shares in the mystery of forty, and in the latter is the *theōria* of the former.

See 2.38.

2.41

S2

There is one who without the four and the five knows the forty and the fifty.

S1

There is one who without the four and the five is able to know the mystery of the forty and the fifty.

See 2.38.

2.42

S2

Who will come to holy Pascha, and who will know holy Pentecost?

S1

[Same as S2]

See 2.38.

2.43

S2

There is one who was left behind in this [place]; and the same one will be found in it.

230 EVAGRIUS OF PONTUS

S1

There is one who was left behind there; and the same one will be found in the same [place].

> LEFT BEHIND, *'eštbeq* may point to Mt 24.2 on the Temple, "There will not be left here one stone upon another." [PLACE]: assumes that the feminine Syriac pronoun reflects an original *tautē*, which would imply locality.

2.44

S2

Not all the holy ones eat the bread, but all drink of the cup.

S1

[Same as S2]

> Cf. Mt 26.39–42, Mk 10.38–39, 14.36; Lk 24.42. HOLY ONES: Ps 87.7, Rom 16.15. On bread, see 1.23; 2.86 (the showbread of Exodus); 4.28, 57; 5.35. On the cup (cf. Ps 116.13 "the cup of salvation"), see 5.32; Sch. 104 on Prv 9.2; *Letter* 29.2. On the eucharistic elements see *Gn.* 14; *Monks* 118–120. On the eucharistic table see 2.60.

2.45

Greek

The organ of sense and the mind divide perceptible things among themselves. The mind alone contains intelligible things, for it itself becomes an observer of things and of reasons.

> Milan, Ambr. gr. 681 (Q 74 sup.); tenth century (Muyldermans 1931, p. 59)

S2

The organs of sense and the mind distinguish perceptible things. But the mind alone has intellection of intelligible things, for it is itself the seer of matters and of intellections.

KEPHALAIA GNOSTIKA 231

S1

The organs of sense and the mind distinguish perceptible things. But the mind alone has intellection of intelligible things, for it is the observer both of their reasons and of the intellections of things.

On the sense-perceptive faculty, see 1.33–34. On the intellect as observer see 2.27, 36. On the things (*pragmata*) the mind observes: 2.32. The Greek *logos* is here translated by S2 as *sūkālē*, hence the difference in our translation. On separation see 1.8.

2.46

S2

The art separately from the artist contains his work; and the wisdom of God contains all. And just as one who through a (single) word separates the art from the artist voids [the artist's] work, so also one who in his thought separates wisdom from God corrupts all.

S1

The artist's art contains his work; and God's wisdom contains all. And just as one who separates the art from the artist breaks his work, so also one who in his thought dares to separate God's wisdom from [God] corrupts all.

ART: *'ūmānūtā*, renders Greek *epistēmē* at 1.3, 14. Here the Greek may be *technē* or *erga*, and point to the work of a craftsman or worker. On the inseparability of the Trinity and wisdom, see Sch. 2 on Ps 144.3. (SINGLE) WORD, *melta'*, equally translatable as "reason," may reflect an anti-Eunomian polemic.

2.47

S2

The Trinity is not placed with the *theōria* of sense-perceptible things and intelligible things, and even less is it numbered among objects. Because the first is a compound and the latter [two] are created things; whereas the Holy Trinity alone is essential knowledge.

232 EVAGRIUS OF PONTUS

S1

The Trinity is not numbered in the *theōria* of sense-perceptible things and intelligible things, because these are corruptible and receptive of alterations. But the Holy Trinity alone is essential knowledge.

> COMPOUND: Syr. *mūzāgā* customarily translates *poiotēs*, "quality" (see 1.22). On the Trinity see *Prak*. 3. On essential knowledge, see 1.89. Cf. *Letter* 29.

2.48

S2

If the mind advances in its particular path, it meets the holy powers; but if [it advances] in that (path) of the instrument of the soul, it falls among demons.

S1

If the mind proceeds along its particular path, it meets the holy powers; but if on the path of the passions of the body, it meets the demons.

> PARTICULAR PATH: alt. "in the path of its essence." On the mind traveling its own path, see Sch. 28 on Prv 3.5; Sch. 59 on Prv 5.8; Sch. 198 on Prv 19.16. The mind traveling a path is attested earlier, e.g., Philo, *On Planting* 97. On the holy powers, see 2.30. On the *organon* of the soul see 1.67.

2.49

S2

The one who first took the ear of the grain is the first of those who have the grain; and the one who took the second ear is the first of those who have the first ear; and the one who took the third ear is the first of those who have the second ear; and so on with all the others, until the one who, being last, does not have the power of the grain [and] will leave the last ear and the first.

S1

The one who is first and received the head/ear of grain became the first of those who receive the grain. And the one who received the second head/ear became the first of those who receive the third. And thus it is in succession until the power of the grain will be removed.

> Cf. Mt 13.31. On the analogy of grain (drawing from 1 Cor 14) see 1.24; 2.25.

2.50

S2

When mothers have ceased to give birth, then also "the guardians of the house will tremble"; then also the two heads will be wreathed with rose and linen.

S1

When midwives have ceased to give birth, then also "the guardians of the house will tremble" and the columns will be weakened and fall down; then the heads of both will also be wreathed with rose and linen.

> Eccl 12.3
>
> MOTHERS, *yalādtā*, may equally be translated "midwives," recalling Ex 1 and the cessation of midwives' services. The two heads refer back to the house, and are likely to be the capitals on columns (which is how S1 renders this through his interpolation). May point to the two pillars built by Hiram of Tyre for the Temple of Solomon (3 Kgdms/1 Kgs 7), named Boaz and Jachin, whose capitals were decorated with lilies (3 Kgdms/1 Kgs 7.8 [7.22]). The Syriac words for rose and linen, *rādā* and *būṣā*, are loanwords from Greek, *rodon/roda* and *byssos*; although each word appears in the New Testament or the Septuagint, they do not appear together.

2.51

S2

The chariot of knowledge is fire and air; but the chariot of ignorance is air and water.

234 EVAGRIUS OF PONTUS

S1

[Same as S2]

CHARIOT: Sch. 12 On Ps 67.18 (= pure souls) and 6 on Ps 17.11, 1 in Ps 79.2 and cf. 4 Kgdms/2 Kgs 2.11. In the late fourth century, merkavah (chariot) mysticism emerges in both the Christian and Jewish traditions (see Elior 1990, pp. 233–249). This keph. names only three of the four elements; cf. 1.68 (fire, earth, air). On fire in particular, see 1.30. On the four elements in general, see 1.29.

2.52

S2

Some demons have called intelligible things "gnostics," but some have taken the knowledge of the intelligible.

S1

Of the demons, some have called intelligibles "gnostics," but some have seized knowledge from the *gnōstikos*.

On demons in general, see *Prak.* 5. On intelligible matters, see 2.36. Porphyry, *On Abstinence* 2.39: demons convince people that the divine is the source of both good and evil.

2.53

S2

There is only one who is worshipped, the one who alone has the only-begotten.

S1

[Same as S2]

Elsewhere in the *KG*, the one worshipped is the Trinity: 1.27, 74; 5.50. Worship directed toward divine powers is not rejected: 4.45, nor is worship of Christ: 5.48. On the collocation of "unique" and "uniquely" (only-begotten) see 1.49.

KEPHALAIA GNOSTIKA 235

2.54

S2

Knowledge does not advance in the regions of ignorance but in the regions of knowledge.

S1

[Same as S2]

On the role of knowledge here, see previous several keph. Knowledge and place: 1.61; 2.6.

2.55

S2

Ignorance—some have attracted it to themselves voluntarily, and others involuntarily. The second are called "captives," and the first are named "captors": "The captors have come, and they have captured them."

S1

Of rational beings, some have drawn ignorance to themselves voluntarily, but others involuntarily. And the second are called captives but the first are named captors, from whom our Savior "has rescued the captives."

Eph 4.8 (S1); Job 1.15 (S2)

S1 Eph 4.8: Christ liberates prisoners during his ascension to heaven. Cf. Col 1.8–15. On captivity and ignorance, see *Disc.* 14; Sch. 7 on Ps 13.7 (rephrased at Sch. 13 on Ps 67.19; Sch. 1 on Ps 125.1). Demons who choose ignorance make their captives ignorant: *Monks* 23–24. The passage from Job does not appear in the extant scholia on Job attributed to Evagrius.

2.56

S2

The mind teaches the soul, and the soul the body; and only the man of God knows the man of knowledge.

236 EVAGRIUS OF PONTUS

S1

The mind teaches the soul, and the soul the body; and only the man of God is able to know the man of knowledge.

cf. Dt 33.1

THE MAN OF GOD: a title used most often of Moses in the OT and applied by extension to other prophets (David, Elijah and Elisha, and Christ): Dt 33.1; Josh 14.6; Ps 90.1; Ezr 3.2; 1 Paral/1 Chron 23.14; 2 Paral/2 Chron 30.16. On teaching in general see *Prak.* pr.2. The man of knowledge may be compared to the prudent person, *phronimos anthrōpos*, frequently mentioned in Proverbs (e.g., Prv 24.5).

2.57

S2

We learned that there are three altars on high, of which the third is simple but the two [others] are composite. The wisdom which is about the second altar makes known the wisdom of the third, and that which concerns the first altar is before that of the second.

S1

We learned that there are three altars in the heights. One of them is single and not composite, but the two others are composite.

THREE ALTARS: in order of proximity to the Holy of Holies: the altar of sin-offering (Lv 16.3), the altar of burnt offering (Lv 1.1–17), the altar of incense (Ex 40.9; Ps 141.2, Rev 5.8, 8.3–4). See the next keph.; 4.88 (regarding circumference); 5.53, 84. This is the first enumerated series to proceed not from simple to complex, but the reverse. On composites, see also 5.18; *Gn.* 27. On the noetic altar, see 4.88; *Prayer* 1: incense prepared for the third altar 147; and esp. Sch. 4 on Ps 25.6: "Our nous is the rational altar of God upon which we burn every irrational thought, that leaps from the master's herd with the fire that our Lord cast upon the earth (Lk 12.49). We say that there is around this altar of sacrifice what one calls 'empsychosis' [animation]. So when the soul looks not toward the things outside but turns itself its center, it 'circles the altar' of God, fashioning no corner receptive of corruption, 'For foolishness waits around the corner,' says the wise Solomon (ref. unknown; cf. Prv 1.21; 7.12; 8.3 LXX). It is possible that he also calls contemplation of corporeals and incorporeals 'altar,' on which the mind is purified, and the person who 'circles' it, that is, knows, 'how to describe all the wonders of God.'" The third uncircumscribed altar is *theologia*. Cf. Origen *Hom. on Nm* 10: the altar "is a symbol of prayer" (3.3). Cf.

KG 4.22 on sacrifices; *Eight Thoughts* 4.19 and 7.16 on vicious thoughts as unacceptable sacrifices.

2.58

S2

To those who now dwell in the breadth, three altars have been given; but to those [who dwell] in the length and in the depth, [the altars] will be given in the world to come.

S1

To those who now dwell in the breadth, three altars have been given; but to those who dwell in the length and in the depth, [the altars] will be given in the world to come.

cf. Eph 3.18–19

Eph 3.18–19 adds "height" (*hypsos*). The triplet "breadth," "depth," and "length" (*platos, mēkos, bathos*) was the standard way to summarize the character of geometrical solids (see, e.g., Apollodorus, frag. 2; Philo, *On the Creation of the World* 102); the theme recurs in Sch. 33 on Prv 3.19–20; Sch. 153 on Prv 17.2 (see note at 2.69).

2.59

S2

"The just judgment" of our Christ is made known by the transfer of bodies, of regions, and of worlds; his patience, [by] those who struggle against virtue; but his mercy especially [by] those for whom he provides even though they are not equal to it.

S1

The witnesses of the patience of Christ our Lord are those who are made in opposition to virtue. The heralds of his great mercies are those for whom he provides while they are unworthy of it.

cf. 2 Thes 1.5 (S2); cf. Jn 7.24 (S2)

Cf. 1.27. On the transfer of mind into bodies, see 2.4. PATIENCE, likely Grk. *makrothumia* (Syr. *nagīrūt rūḥā*). Cf. *Prak.* 15, 40; Sch. 36.3 on Prv 3.24; Sch.

238 EVAGRIUS OF PONTUS

341 on Prv 27.25; Sch. 363 on Prv 29.11; Sch. 23 on Eccl 4.1. On divine mercy see 1.73.

2.60

S2

The table of Christ is God, and the table of the exalted ones is bodily and bodiless nature.

S1

The table of Christ is God the Father, and the table of his brothers in mercy is He, with his Father.

cf. Lk 22.30

Table of Christ: Sch. 189 on Prv 19.4. On the table of hospitality see *Prak.* 26. On the eucharistic bread and wine, and the knowledge of God, see 2.44. On the exalted ones, taken to be angels, see Sch. 38 on Eccl 5.7–11. On the corporeals and incorporeals see the next several kephalaia.

2.61

S2

Whereas we knew the *theōria* of bodiless things in the beginning without matter; we now know (it) as joined to matter; but that which concerns bodies we have never seen without matter.

S1

We see the first spiritual *theōria* in the holy powers, but [we see] the natural *theōria* of second things in humans.

This chapter and the next form a pair, the first concerning the past and the present; the next, the future. On observation (*theōria* in both Greek and Syriac), see *Prak.* 32. On the relationship between observation and matter see 2.20. On matter in general, see 1.29.

KEPHALAIA GNOSTIKA 239

2.62

S2

When the minds receive the *theōria* about (bodies), then the entire nature of bodies also will be taken away; and thus the *theōria* about them will become immaterial.

S1

When the minds of the holy ones receive the *theōria* of themselves then also the thickness of the bodies will be thoroughly removed from their midst, and sight will from that time be spiritual.

> See previous keph. REMOVED, *neštqel*, in other contexts may be rendered "elevated"; the usage here parallels 1.8–9, 15 (with corresponding Greek fragment), regarding the annulment of the elements and senses.

2.63

S2

Among [the kinds of] knowledge, there is one that will never be material, and the other one will never be immaterial; but the one that is material will also be able to become immaterial.

S1

Among [the kinds of] knowledge, some are immaterial, but others are known through materials. But the knowledge of the Holy Trinity is higher than them all.

> See previous two keph. On levels and types of knowledge, see 1.70.

2.64

Greek

Concerning the first things no one discloses; but concerning the second things the one on Horeb has recited fully.

> Barsanouphios and John, *Letter* 600 (Neyt 2001)

240 EVAGRIUS OF PONTUS

S2

Some beings came to be before the judgment and some after the judgment. And regarding the first (beings), no one has related [anything]; but regarding the second (beings), he who was on Horeb did narrate.

S1

The revelation of everything that exists is unwritten and written. The unwritten is that which is revealed to the mind by the spirit, but the written was given by the spirit, on Horeb.

> On this judgment, which has already happened (not to be confused with the judgment after death; see 1.82), see 2.75; 4.4 (knowledge of). Moses was on Horeb (Ex 3.1), the "mountain of God," where he witnessed the burning bush (see *Prayer* 4 and *Thoughts* 17), and he made known the second ones in Genesis 1. On the pairing of judgment and providence, *Gn.* 48; second beings, see 1.50. On the first beings, cf. Is 14.12, Lk 10.18.

2.65

S2

From those who have attained to the perfect fullness of evil it is possible for us to understand the multitude of worlds that have come to be. Indeed it is not possible for us suddenly to be perfected in ignorance, because neither (is it possible for us suddenly to be perfected) in knowledge.

S1

We learn the greatness of the patience of God from those who have reached the perfect completion by their will; we learn the abundant mercy of our Lord from those who with their good will labor to grow in beautiful actions.

> On multiple worlds/aeons, see 1.65; ignorance: 1.49. On the unusual phrase PERFECT FULLNESS OF EVIL cf. Sch. 62 on Prv 5.14. This is possibly a reference to the rich man in Hades (Lk 16.19–31). See 1.39–40 and notes there. ALL AT ONCE, Syr. *men šeli*, usually translates Grk. *exaiphnēs* (see Greek fragment for 6.52), an important word commonly used in Plato, and in Origen and John Chrysostom. See also 2.72; 4.71; 6.52.

KEPHALAIA GNOSTIKA 241

2.66

S2

The coming to be of bodies does not make known the coming to be of the *logikoi*; rather, it introduces the nature of names. The composition of the former shows the differences in rank of the latter.

S1

Through the differences in the increase of bodies, we see a mystery of the difference of the growth of rational beings; and in the designation of the arrangement of the former the difference in rank of the latter.

> On bodies, see 1.11. On the logikoi, see 1.89. On names, see 1.51. Adam giving names, Gn 2.20. On ranks (Syr. *ṭokāsā*, Grk. *taxeis*)—angels, humans, demons ordered according to place—see 2.76; 3.17, 20–21, 28–29, 37 (of stars), 42 (mind raised to first); 4.46; 6.43 (providence : freedom :: judgment : rank of rational beings). Sometimes *ṭokāsā* translates Grk. *katastasis* (e.g., 4.38, 46; 5.11), which reflects the close proximity of rank and state in Evagrius' thought. See, e.g., 2.68. See also 2.78, which uses the related word *tagma*, order.

2.67

S2

Undifferentiated things will become differentiated when they receive the *theōria* of the things that differentiate them.

S1

When human beings are in the *theōria* of those who are undivided, then they will be with them without division.

> UNDIFFERENTIATED could also be translated "not separated" or "not distinct" (Syr. *metparšānā, pāršā*); our version points to 3.36, where the word translates Greek *diaphora*, difference, and anticipates 2.69 (Syr. *pūršānā* = Grk. *diaresis*). In any translation, the paradox remains. See note at 4.50.

242   EVAGRIUS OF PONTUS

2.68

S2

It is said that those who are above possess light bodies, and those below possess heavy [bodies]: and above the former are others who are lighter than they; while below the latter are those heavier than they.

S1

It is said that there are on high those who have light and fiery bodies. But below, they have heavy bodies. And these have dark and impure bodies.

> Angels with fiery bodies: Heb 1.7. Mental thickness: cf. *Prak.* 41; on bodily thickness, cf. *Disc.* 8. On bodies in general, see 1.11. Cf. Origen on angelic and demonic beings: *First Principles* 1.7.1–1.8.4. On the use of vertical position (Grk. *anō* and *katō*) see 2.78; 3.9, 13; 4.17; 5.40; 6.15, 76.

2.69

Greek

The Holy Spirit fully recites neither the first division of the rational beings nor the first being of the bodies.

> Barsanouphios and John, *Letter* 600 (Neyt 2001)

S2

The Holy Spirit has made known to us not the first distinction of the *logikoi* and the coming to be of bodies, but rather it has revealed to us the present distinction among the *logikoi* and the transfer of bodies.

S1

The Holy Spirit by means of Moses did not reveal to us the distinctions of heavenly ones, but has taught us about the distinctions of beings in this world.

> The letter from Barsanouphios preserves in Greek only the first half of the sentence. It aligns well with S2 (against S1). The tantalizing notion of a "first *ousia* of the bodies" is unclear. See 1.1 (and note there) on the First Good that exists

KEPHALAIA GNOSTIKA 243

according to *ousia*. The insertion of Moses in S1 is to be contrasted with the S1 translation of *Prak.* 38, where the mention of Moses is dropped. DISTINCTION, Syr. *pūršānhūn*, corresponds to Greek *diairesis*, which can mean distinction, division, distribution, separation. Cf. Sch. 153 on Prv 17.2, where the breadth, length, depth, and height of Eph 3.18 (cf. *KG* 2.58) indicates the *diaresis* of rational nature. The theme of distinction recurs at 2.73–74. This begins a cluster of staggered kephalaia regarding the transfer of bodies, on which see 2.4. A comparable cluster appears starting at 3.45.

2.70

S2

If God "has made everything by wisdom," there is nothing created by him that does not bear—each one of them—the sign of the luminaries.

S1

If God has "created everything that he created through wisdom," nothing created by him does not each bear the sign of the luminaries.

Ps 103.24

S1 follows the Peshitta reading of Ps 103.24, but S2 adopts Evagrius' rendering of the LXX. On the luminaries, see 2.90 (two); 3.52 ("Sun of Justice" Mal 3.20); 5.3 (of the Trinity); Gn 1.14; Ps 19.1; Cf. Sch. 33 on Prv 3.19–20. See Origen, *Comm. on Gn* 20.

2.71

S2

The *theōria* of the bodiless things remains in the undescended; but it is evident that as for [the *theōria*] concerning bodies, a part is descended and a part is undescended.

S1

The *theōria* of the incorporeals neither lifts itself nor lowers itself. But the *theōria* of bodies both lifts and lowers itself.

244   EVAGRIUS OF PONTUS

Cf. *Thoughts* 3. THEŌRIA OF: alt. "*theōria* among." (UN)DESCENDED, translates Syr. *(lā) mettaḥtyānūtā*, meaning dejection or abasement, appearing only here in the *Gnostic Trilogy*. Perhaps the underlying Greek word is *sunkatabasis*, on which see note at *Gn.* 6. On similar concepts of descent and falling, see 3.11 (S1), 14, 28; 4.36, 38, 80 (to Sheol); 5.6; 6.56. Cf. Eph 4.9.

2.72

S2

If the knowledge of those who were not suddenly emptied is primary, then it is clear that light bodies are prior to heavy ones.

S1

If the knowledge of spiritual beings is before and principal in relation to the knowledge of bodily beings, it is also evident that the bodies of the former are lighter and more luminous than those of the latter.

SUDDENLY, Syr. *men šeli*, likely Grk. *exaiphnēs*; see 2.65. The emptying here points to an emptying of knowledge. The relative weight of bodies features else-where in the *KG* (see 1.68; 2.68, and further references at the note to 1.11).

2.73

S2

Just as the one who by his *logos* has revealed to us the matters of the world to come, so he has not told us about the coming to be of bodies and the bodiless. In the way that he has made known the coming to be of this world, he has not taught the passing of bodies and the bodiless, but he has told of their distinction and their transfer.

S1

Just as he who by his word has revealed to us the matters of the world to come, he has not told us about bodies and the bodiless, just as when he made known to us on Mount Sinai the coming to be of this world, he did not reveal to us the beauty of the world to come.

On the act of revelation, see 2.69. THE ONE WHO: could be Moses (cf. S1's trans-lation), because it points to what is and is not in scripture. On distinctions, see

2.69; transfers, 2.4. What corresponds to the passing of bodies and the bodiless, in contrast to their distinction and transfer, is unclear. This phrase could be equally translated as the limit or goal of bodies and the bodiless.

2.74

S2

Who has known the first distinction and who has seen the coming to be of bodies, or these different worlds from which some of the holy powers have been nourished and have ruled over a blessed kingdom?

S1

Who is the one who has understood the first distinction, and who is it who has known the first movement and how rational beings, by means of their own labor, are returning to their inheritance?

> On distinctions, see previous keph. and 2.69. Posed as a question—is the answer Moses? Cf. Origen, *First Principles* pref.7–8; 2.1–3. For other kephalaia similarly framed as questions, see 1.67; 2.9, 38, 42; 4.89; 6.36, 76; cf. also 3.70. For biblical parallels, see Rom 11.34, 1 Cor 2.16. On worlds, see the next keph.; Sch. 38 on Eccl 5.7–11, where the holy powers by delegation exercise the judgment given to Christ (on which see the next keph.). Nourishment: 2.82.

2.75

S2

As much as the judge has judged those to be judged, so also has he made worlds; and he who knows the number of judgments knows also the number of worlds.

S1

The transgression of the commandment by rational beings has forced God to be a judge for them, and those who are perfectly obeying the laws of love return to the inheritance of adoption.

> The different judgments (cf. 1 Cor 15.28) include that which occurred before second beings came into existence (2.64) and that which will occur after death (the last judgment; see 2.77 and our note at 1.82). The judgments specified at 1.84 and 6.75 may or may not correspond to these two. See, e.g., *Thoughts* 7;

246 EVAGRIUS OF PONTUS

Sch. 370 on Prv 29.26 (judgment of Christ). Pairing of judgment and providence: *Gn.* 48. On the variety of worlds, whose number is never clearly specified (cf. 3.9: three?), see 1.11, 65, 70, 75; 2.2, 17, 65, 85; 3.9, 23, 78; 4.43, 58, 89; 5.7, 10, 21, 81; 6.3, 33–34, 45, 47, 67. World to come: 1.11; on worlds more generally, 1.70. On the correspondence between judgment and world-creation, see Sch. 275 on Prv 24.22 and 370 on Prv 29.26. The form and content of this kephalaion (the more . . . the more . . .) parallels 6.67.

2.76

S2

Just as various ranks distinguish the rational beings from each other, so too do the places which are fitting for the bodies that are joined to them.

S1

Just as the differences in state distinguish rational beings from each other, so also the differences in their ways of life distinguish their bodies from each other.

Rank: 2.66; variety of bodies: 1.11.

2.77

S2

The last judgment does not make manifest the transfer of bodies; rather it makes known their annulment.

S1

The last judgment of the just judge does not accomplish a change of the body, but it takes away their thickness as it adds to them the power so that they will craft an inheritance, either of judgment, or of the kingdom of heaven.

cf. 2 Tm 4.8 (S1)

LAST JUDGMENT: see 2.75 and our note at 1.82. Transfer of bodies: 2.4; on bodies in general, 1.11. ANNULMENT, Syr. *'ṭāyā*, is the same verb at 2.17, concerning the removal of names. If the word means wiping out or destruction, it could refer to Ps 9.6 and 4 Kgdms/2 Kgs 21.13. Note that S1 has incorporated 2 Tm 4.8, avoiding the abolition of bodies after the final judgment; it is one of S1's longest expansions.

2.78 ·

Greek

Each rank of the heavenly powers has been formed either entirely from those below, or entirely from those above, or from both those above and those below.

John of Scythopolis, Sch. on the *Eccl. Hierarchy* 6 (PG 4:173)

S2

Each of the ranks of the heavenly powers has been established either entirely from those above, or entirely from those below, or from those above and those below.

S1

Each of the bands of the heavenly powers is established either entirely from those above, or entirely from those below, and thus it is established either from those above, or from those below.

ORDERS/RANK, Syr. *tegmē* and Grk. *tagmata*. On the comparable term rank (*taxis*), see 2.66. On high: see 2.68. Heavenly powers: 2.42–43. The Greek fragment, like the one at 5.11, derives from a scholion by John of Scythopolis (early sixth century) on Dionysius the Areopagite, *Ecclesiastical Hierarchy* 6—a scholion until recently thought to be by Maximus Confessor; Rorem and Lamoreaux 1998, p. 93. In these quotations (just after two quotations from Origen's *First Principles*), John refers to the two kephalaia by number: 2.78 and 5.11 (but he writes ιθ', 19, instead of ια', 11, perhaps a scribal error). Both keph. are also corroborated verbatim by Anathema 5 against Origen (of 553), which quotes them in reverse order:
> "If someone says:
> From the angelic state and the archangelic state the psychic state comes to be; from the psychic, the demonic and human; but from the human, angels again and demons come into being.
> or
> Each order of the heavenly powers has been constituted either entirely from those below, and that each order of the heavenly powers is com- posed entirely from those above, or from those below or from both those above and those below,
> let him be anathema" (trans. after Schwartz and Straub 1971, 4.1:248).

Minor differences in phrasing show that John and the writers of the anathemas relied independently upon complete or partial copies of the *KG* in Greek. For other verbatim parallels with the anathemas, see 2.17; 4.18.

248 EVAGRIUS OF PONTUS

2.79

S2

The one who advances toward knowledge draws near to the excellent transfer of bodies; but the one who [moves toward] ignorance advances toward the evil transfer.

S1

The one who advances on the road of knowledge advances in restoration from day to day. But the one who advances on the road of ignorance indeed moves away from the state in which he stands.

On transfer, see 2.4; STATE: 1.80.

2.80

S2

The *theōria* of this instrument of the soul is varied; but [the *theōria*] of the instruments of celestial [beings] are more varied; and *theōria* about rational beings is even more [varied], because the former are the dwellings of the gnostics while the latter are receptacles of the Holy Trinity.

S1

Distinct is the *theōria* of the instrument of the soul; but the *theōria* of spiritual instruments is especially distinct; but the *theōria* of the spiritual ones is more so than these, because it is receptive of the knowledge of the Holy Trinity.

On the *organon* of the soul see 1.67. Celestial bodies/beings: Sch. 3 on Ps 135.6; Sch. 113 on Prv 9.13, cf. 1 Cor 15.40–49 commenting on Gn 5.3; see note at 1.89 on rational beings. On stars, see 3.37; sun, 3.44; moon, 3.52. On receptivity see 1.4. This variegation should be compared with variety in bodies; see note at 1.11.

2.81

S2

Knowledge has borne knowledge, but always bears the gnostic.

S1

Knowledge gives birth to knowledge, and continually gives birth to gnostics for knowing.

On begetting, see 1.5.

2.82

S2

It is not the bodies of spiritual powers, but only [those] of souls that are naturally suited to be nourished by the world related to them.

S1

As is the difference of rational beings, so also the difference of their nourishment in their worlds.

On nourishment, see 2.74 (holy powers in other worlds), 86, 88; 3.4 (angels, humans, demons), 7 (regarding changes); 4.25 (by oil); *Prak.* 56 (knowledge is food of the soul). For virtues as food: *Letter to Melania* 52. On food more generally, see *Prak.* 16. On various worlds, see 2.65. RELATED TO, Syr. *aḥin*, is used at 2.39–40 of the relationship of four to forty and five to fifty.

2.83

Greek

Just as the senses are altered in grasping different qualities, thus also the mind is altered always fixing its attention on various *theōriai*.

Mosc. 425, sixteenth century (Hausherr 1939, p. 230)

250 EVAGRIUS OF PONTUS

S2

Just as the senses are changed by the intellections of various qualities, so also the mind is changed as it regards various *theōriai* at every moment.

S1

Just as in the organs of the senses, the sense is changed by differences of qualities and of colors, so also the mind is changed as it regards different *theōriai*.

> ALTERED: Gk. *alloiountai*; see 2.4. On the comparison between sense and mind, see 1.34. On qualities, see 1.22. Contrast the mind's gazing here (Grk. *enatenizein*, Syr. *ḥār*) with *Prak.* 12; Sch. 310 on Prv 25.17. The nous is stamped or imprinted by diverse observations and temptations (*Thoughts* 2). Only elevated, uniform observations do not imprint or change the nous: Sch. 1 on Ps 140.2; *Reflections* 6. VARIOUS *THEŌRIAI*: lit., differences of observations.

2.84

S2

Once the Lord was a judge of the living only, but never once will he be judge of the dead only, and once again he will be judge of the living only.

S1

There was when our Lord was judge of the living only; but never once will he be judge of the dead only, and again there will be when he will be judge of the living only.

> Judge of the living and the dead: 2 Tm 4.1, 1 Pt 4.5. For a similar starting formula, THERE WAS WHEN, see 1.40; 6.18. Judge: Sch. 8 on Ps 138.16 (on the "book of God": God "as demiurge" is known as "judge through the variety of bodies of rational [beings] and through the multiform worlds and ages they contain."). Christ as judge: 1.65, 1.75, 82; 2.59, 75, 77, 84; 3.2, 40, 66; cf. Sch. 3 on Ps 49.4. On judgment, see 2.75.

KEPHALAIA GNOSTIKA 251

2.85

S2

If the living are receptacles of increase and decrease, then they are the opposite of the dead, for it is clear that they are receiving these things; and if this is so, there will be various bodies, and worlds suitable for them will be created.

S1

If the living are receptacles of virtue and vice, then it is clear that they are the opposite of those who are dead, those who in time fell by their own will, from Life.

> The themes of living and dead here bring with it that of the judgment, discussed in the previous keph. On the creation of new aeons (worlds) after successive judgments: Sch. 275 on Prv 24.22; Sch. 9 on Ps 1.5. Cf. Sch. 1 on Ps 16.2; Sch. 3 on Ps 49.4; Sch. 3 and 4 on Ps 49.6; 8 on Ps 93.15. *KG* 3.48; 3.50, 51. On receptivity of increase and decrease, cf. 2.12 (hand vs. right hand). On various bodies, see 1.11. On various worlds, see 1.65, 70.

2.86

S2

For those who are outside, their bread is not showbread and their drink is full of flies. But for those who are inside, their bread is showbread, and their drink is unspoiled.

S1

For those whose way of life is outside: their bread is not showbread and their drink is full of flies. But for those whose way of life is inside, their bread is showbread and their drink is inviolable.

> cf. Ex 25.30; cf. Heb 9.2
>
> The showbread refers to the bread in the temple, at Ex 25.30; Heb 9.2. On flies, perhaps *kunomuiai*, see the plague at Ex 8.20–32. See Sch. 18 on Ps 77.45 and with notes, Sch. 16 on Ps 104.31: "the Hebrews call various hybrid beasts dogfly." The word "flies" seems also to refer to Beelzebul in Mt 10.25, 12.24; Mk 3.20–30, as reflecting Ex 8.20–32 and 2 Paral/2 Chron 1.2–3, 16 LXX: "Baal the fly god." THOSE . . . OUTSIDE . . . THOSE . . . INSIDE: Mk 4.11–12, "To you has been given the

252 EVAGRIUS OF PONTUS

secret/mystery of the kingdom of God, but for those outside, everything comes in parables, that they may indeed look, but not perceive and may indeed listen, but not understand ... " The Greek words *exōthen* and *endōthen* may also signify here "foreigners" and "citizens," in this case with respect to the kingdom of God. The former are Egyptians; the latter, the Israelites. See *Thoughts* 5 (*exōthen sophōn* are "pagan sages") and *Gn.* 4. On Egypt and Egyptians as a symbol of evil, see note at 1.83. The combination of the bread and drink juxtaposes the Exodus imagery with the eucharist, on which see references at 2.44. Testament of Solomon 6.2: Beelzebul introduces himself as the prince of demons, associated with the star Hesperos/Aphrodite. The Hebrew alternation of the name Baʾalzebul, "Lord of Heaven," worshipped by the Philistines, may be the origin of this doublet.

2.87

S2

The movement of bodies is in time, but the transfer of the bodiless is timeless.

S1

The movement of bodies is temporal, but the alteration of the bodiless is atemporal.

On time, see 6.9 (time reckoned with becoming and corruption); *Disc.* 25; *Letter on Faith* 21, 24–25; Sch. 2 on Ps 89.4: "Time (*chronos*) is observed concerning neither knowledge nor what is knowable. For season (*kairos*), days, and time are of bodily nature." Transfer: 2.4.

2.88

S2

The *theōria* of this sense-perceptible world is not given as food only to humans, but also to other rational natures.

S1

The *theōria* of this visible world is given as food not only to humans, but also to other rational beings.

On nourishment and food, see 2.74 and 2.82. Cf. Heb 5.12–14. On rational natures, see 1.89.

2.89

S2

He who alone "is seated at the right hand" of the Father alone possesses knowledge of the right hand.

S1

He who alone "is seated at the right hand" of the Father alone possesses knowledge of the right hand.

cf. Mk 16.19

Right hand: 2.12.

2.90

S2

Those who have seen the light of the two luminaries will see the first and blessed light, that which we will see in Christ when by means of a virtuous change we will rise before him.

S1

Those who have seen the light of the two luminaries of the spirit, are those who will be made worthy to see that first light of the blessed ones which we will see by the grace of our Lord Jesus Christ, when we will be made worthy of the renewal of our bodies.

Cf. Gn 1.15–16; Phil 2.15, and possibly Mt 17.2, referring to Moses and Elijah (cf. *KG* 4.23, 41) at the transfiguration. On the two luminaries, see 2.70. In our phrase rise before the "before" (Syr. *qdām*) could be temporal or spatial, the latter most likely, as pointing to 2 Cor 5.10, appearing before the judgment seat of Christ.

Epilogue

S2

It is finished, the second.

S1

The end of the second century, that lacks ten chapters.

KEPHALAIA GNOSTIKA   255

Century Three

S2

Century Three

S1

[Same as S2]

3.1

S2

The Father alone knows Christ, and the Son alone (knows) the Father; the (Son) as the only-begotten in the unity, but the (Father) as the union and the unity.

S1

Only the Father knows Christ, and Son himself alone knows the Father; the (Son) as the only united one in unity, but the (Father) as the union of unity.

cf. Mt 11.27

The first three keph. of century 3 discuss Christ, often distinguished by Evagrius from the Son, a characteristic captured by S1's translation. The difficulty of determining what Christ knows is treated extensively in the middle section of the *Letter on Faith*, regarding times and seasons. ONLY-BEGOTTEN, Syr. *īḥīdāyā*, cf. 2.53; can also be translated "unique," "united one," "solitary," or "monk" (5.86); see also 4.16. The other two terms signifying unity, *īḥīdāyūtā* and *ḥdāyūtā*, normally correspond to Gk. *henas* or *monas*, interchangeably. See note at 1.49.

Following Origen, Evagrius understands and discusses *christos* in five ways—(1) as the Christ, Jesus Christ, the one and only unfallen nous who enters the world for the purpose of restoration, with his primary purpose of being a pedagogue to rational beings of all levels; (2) as a teacher seen in the example of Moses, leading souls from Egypt to the land of promise; (3) as a fallen rational being who through baptism becomes one of the "anointed" (cf. *KG* 4.18, 21); (4) as a *praktikos* being anointed for battle (*Prak.* 100 and *KG* 6.90); or (5) as a *gnōstikos* likened to Moses and anointing the simple with the "skill [*technē*] of the thoughts." Cf. *Eulogius* 24 on the

256 EVAGRIUS OF PONTUS

baptismal faith/spiritual seal ("The one experienced in the emigration [*ekdēmia*] of the practical life and the immigration [*endēmia*] of the gnostic life [cf. 2 Cor 5.8–9] must beware and not boast about the gnostic life to show his own glory . . .").

At Sch. 1 on Eccl 1.1 the distinction between Christ and a christ is made central: the Ecclesiast can be either Christ (the incarnate Son of God) who engenders knowledge or the one who is the *gnōstikos* (acting as a christ): "The Ecclesiast is Christ the generator of this [true] knowledge, or the ecclesiast is the [christ] who purifies souls through ethical observations and leads them to natural observation." See also *Prayer* 122: "Blessed is the monk who considers all human beings as 'god' after 'God.'" Cf. *KG* 5.81. For Christ (the anointed one, i.e., king) who trains his followers to be christs, see especially Origen, *Hom. on Ps* 80: "Our teacher, Christ Jesus, is a god and if it is sufficient for the disciple that he become like the teacher, the ideal of the disciple is to become a christ from Christ and a god from a god, and he learns from the light of the cosmos. For everything that the Savior is, he calls his disciples to be." See also Origen, *Contra Celsum* 3.28. At times Evagrius will specify which "christ" he means; see 4.21, Greek fragment. Cf. further notes at 3.3; 6.14.

Christ or christ features in the *KG* in numerous ways. In addition to the next two keph., see 1.65 (judgment), 77 (knowledge and unity); 2.2 (wisdom, creation), 22, 60 (table); 3.11 (wisdom), 26 (knowledge, creation), 57 (wisdom), 72 (inheritance, unity); 4.2–3 (knowledge in), 4 and 8–9 (heirs of), 18 (knowledge, unity, logos), 21 (logos, right hand, anointing), 29 (oil of), 41 (body), 43 (unity, appearance to Jacob), 57 (miracles), 58, 78 (inheritance), 80 (descent to Sheol), 89 (unity), 90 (knowledge); 5.1 (Adam), 6 (belief in), 48 (flesh and Logos), 69 (tree); 6.3 (Adam), 6 (sword), 7 (circumcision, resurrection), 14 (rel. to Trinity, Logos), 15 (feet), 16 (knowledge), 18 (body), 20, 33 (knowledge, worlds), 38, 39 (body), 40 (crucifixion), 42 (death), 46 (commandments), 56 (ascension, return), 57, 66 (teaching), 74 (return), 77, 79 (body). Some of the preceding passages, because of the ambiguity of Syr. *mšīḥā*, could refer either to Christ himself or to ones who become a christ (see above): 3.2; 4.18; 6.14. Some of the preceding topics pertain to *epinoiai*, on which see note at 1.17. Evagrius discusses Christ extensively in *Letter on Faith*; *Letter to Melania*; and the scholia (esp. Psalms). It should not be assumed that when Evagrius uses "Christ" he also means "Word" or "Son." See 2.22; 4.9, 21; 6.14.

KEPHALAIA GNOSTIKA   257

3.2

S2

Christ is the only one in whom there is the unity and [who] has received the judgment of the rational beings.

S1

Christ is the one in whom there is complete unity and [who] has received the affliction of rational nature.

Rational beings: 1.89. Unity of Christ: see previous keph.

3.3

S2

Unity is that which now is known by Christ alone, he whose knowledge is essential.

S1

[Same as S2]

Essential knowledge: 1.89. On unity see 3.1 and 1.49. Without a definite article, this keph. could mean "from Christ" or "from a christ," possibly reflecting Gal 3.27 ("have put on Christ"). For this ambiguity, and the notion of becoming christs, see 3.1; *Thoughts* 38; and compare Origen, *Hom. on Ps* 81.1, "the purpose of the student is to become a christ from Christ and a god from God"; Clement, *Paidagogos* 26, and *Stromateis* 7: "And just as Ischomachus will make those who attend to his instructions husbandmen, and Lampis sea-captains, and Charidemus commanders, and Simon horsemen, and Perdix hucksters, and Crobylus cooks, and Archelaus dancers, and Homer poets, and Pyrrho wranglers, and Demosthenes orators, and Chrysippus logicians, and Aristotle men of science, and Plato philosophers, so he who obeys the Lord and follows the prophecy given through Him, is fully perfected after the likeness of his Teacher, and thus becomes a god while still moving about in the flesh."

258 EVAGRIUS OF PONTUS

3.4

S2

It is indeed characteristic of angels always to be nourished by the *theōria* of beings; humans not always; and demons neither at the right time nor the wrong time.

S1

It is indeed characteristic of angels continually to be nourished by the *theōria* of beings; humans sometimes; and demons never.

> Angels: 2.30; 5.4; and *Prak.* 24. On nourishment, see 2.74, 82. See also Sch. 22 on Prv 2.12.

3.5

S2

The minds of the heavenly powers are pure and full of knowledge, and their bodies are lights that shine upon those who come near to them.

S1

The minds of the heavenly powers are pure, as they are full of true knowledge, and their bodies are a light that shine upon those who by grace receive revelations.

> This keph. may identify the angels with stars, on which see 3.37. Holy powers as angels: 2.30.

3.6

S2

The naked mind is that which, by means of the *theōria* about itself, is united to knowledge of the Trinity.

KEPHALAIA GNOSTIKA   259

S1

The naked mind is that which is perfected by the vision of itself and is deemed worthy to participate in the *theōria* of the Holy Trinity.

> Naked *nous*, see 1.65; *epektasis*: 1.65. Cf. Sch. 41 on Eccl. 5.14–15 and Sch. on Job 1.21. On knowledge of the Trinity, see *Prak.* 3.

3.7

S2

Every one of the changes is established to nourish the rational beings. Those which are nourished come to an excellent change; but those that are not nourished [come] to an evil change.

S1

It has been entrusted to the offering to be nourishing for rational beings, and those who are nourished draw near to virtue, but those who that are not nourished return to inadequate changes.

> Changes, see 1.17; nourishment: 2.82.

3.8

S2

The mind that possesses the last robe is that which alone knows the *theōria* of all the second beings.

S1

The mind that possesses the last garment is that which has the natural *theōria* of second things.

> On garments (possibly Gk. *endymata*), see *Thoughts* 6 and 22 and *Gn.* 38 commenting on Mt 6.25/Lk 12.22. Ordinary garments are contrasted with Abner the Levite's poverty before receiving the ark of the covenant. On temple garments, see 4.72. See also the preface to the *Prak.* on the garments of the

260   EVAGRIUS OF PONTUS

monk. Cf. Porphyry, *On Abstinence* 2.46 and 1.31, on the removal of the "last garment" (flesh) in order to enter the Father's temple.

3.9

S2

In the world to come the bodies of ignorance will be surpassed, and in the one after it, the change will receive an increase of fire and air; and then those that are below will be exhorted to knowledge, if "the houses of the wicked receive purification" and "today and tomorrow" Christ "performs miracles and on the third day is finished."

S1

In the world to come, the ignorance of rational beings will come to an end and knowledge of distinctions will increase in them, those (distinctions) from which joy and sadness flow: joy for the zealous and sadness for the feeble.

Prv 14.9 (S2); Lk 13.32 (S2)

This keph. points to the final judgment, on which see 3.40; on judgment in general, see 2.75. On Prv 14.9 (S2 only), Sch. 136 on Prv 14.9 refers to Mt 5.8 (the two good servants) and associates purification with seeing God and the state of final blessedness, on which see *KG* 3.83. The source of the interpretation is Origen, *First Principles* 2.11.2–3: the two good servants represent the just who become angels in the world to come. Cf. *KG* 6.24, Sch. 10 on Ps 48.15. See also *Letters* 23, 36, 37, on being made "heads of five or ten cities" in the world to come. WORLD TO COME: 1.11. IGNORANCE: 1.49; transfer: 2.4. On the four elements, see 1.29; fire specifically, 1.30; air, 1.59. The realm of those below appears to be Hades, on which see 1.57. On purification, see *Prak.* 100. Third day: 1.90.

3.10

S2

The mind that is imperfect is that which still needs the *theōria* known by bodily nature.

KEPHALAIA GNOSTIKA 261

S1

The uncompleted mind is the one that still needs to advance in the intellection of created natures and in the first *theōria*: things it can gain with this lyre.

> This keph. is associated with the next two, and mirrors 3.14–16. See *Prak.* 60 on the soul being incomplete. STILL NEEDS: not that the imperfect mind does not see well, but that it continues to rely upon physical sight, and improve its interpretation of what is seen (as S1's expanded translation suggests). See note at *Gn.* 49. THEŌRIA is here likened to the types of food discussed at Heb 5.13–14 for the immature and perfect, on which see Sch. 103 on Prv 9.2; Sch. 107 on Prv 9.5; Sch. 153 on Prv 17.2; and 210 on Prv 20.9a. See also *KG* 1.23 and Sch. 10 on Ps 77.25, where the verb "eat" "signifies" to "know." On bodily nature, see next keph., as well as 3.32, 53, 57, 74, 80 (contrasted with incorporeal nature); 4.11, 19 (Gk. *sōmatikē physei*), 58 (creation of); 6.50, 82, 85 (shared with animals). On nature in general, 1.10; rational nature, 1.89; the perfect mind: 3.12.

3.11

S2

Bodily nature has received the "wisdom full of distinctions" of Christ; but of him it is not receptive. But bodiless nature both displays the wisdom of the unity and is receptive to the unity.

S1

The body of Christ has received the "wisdom full of distinctions," that one by which he brought down to us the knowledge of the Holy Trinity.

Eph 3.10

> On bodily nature, see previous keph. WISDOM FULL OF DISTINCTIONS: 1.43. Incorporeals: 1.70. Receptivity: 1.4.

3.12

Greek

A perfect mind is that which is capable of easily receiving the essential knowledge.

> Furrer-Pilliod 2000, p. 156 A.v.39

S2

The perfect mind is that which is readily able to receive essential knowledge.

S1

[Same as S2]

PERFECT MIND: cf. Sch. 8 on Eccl 2.10, and Sch. 199 on Prv 19.17: we receive
knowledge in proportion to apatheia but humans cannot gain the entirety of
knowledge; cf. *Gn.* 23 and Sch. on Prv 17.2, where logoi escape human knowledge. Cf. also Sch. 103 on Prv 9.2; only a few humans are able to attain to knowledge surpassing the human, and are assimilated to the knowledge of angels.
Humans are those "bound to blood and flesh"; see Sch. 287b on Prv 30.9. See
also note at *Gn.* 49. On the imperfect mind, see 3.10.

3.13

S2

We have known the wisdom of the unity, united to the nature that is below it; but
the unity cannot be seen when connected to any of the beings; and because of
this the bodiless mind sees the Holy Trinity in those things which are not bodies.

S1

We have known the wisdom of the holy unity in the descent to rational nature, and
by it we have received hidden revelations of the Father and perfect laws of the Spirit.

THE UNITY: 1.49. The wisdom of the Unity is here to be contrasted with variegated wisdom at 3.11. Perhaps the ability of the mind to see the Trinity refers to
its nakedness, discussed in upcoming keph. (15, 17, 19, 21); see 1.65. Vision of
the Trinity: 3.15.

3.14

Greek

A deficient soul is one whose impassioned power has inclined toward vain things.

Furrer-Pilliod 2000, p. 214 A.ψ.18

KEPHALAIA GNOSTIKA 263

S2

The deficient soul is that whose passible power descends to nothingness.

S1

[Same as S2]

> This keph. forms a trio with the next two keph., echoing 3.10–12. The deficient soul is the imperfect soul (cf. 3.16), on which see *Prak*. 60. Emptiness: Sch. 2 on Eccl 1.2. On the powers of the soul, see 2.9. The passible power, Gk. *pathētikē dynamis*, refers to that part of the soul that is acted upon. See, e.g., Alexander, *Comm. Ar. metaph.* 142.20; Plotinus, *Ennead* 4.3.22–23; Porphyry, *On Abstinence* 26. The descent to vanities or emptiness is suggestive of themes in Psalms and Ecclesiastes.

3.15

S2

If the perfection of the mind is knowledge that is immaterial, as they say, but knowledge of the immaterial is the Trinity alone, it is clear that in perfection nothing material remains; and if that is so, the mind from now on naked will be an observer of the Trinity.

S1

If the perfection of the mind is knowledge of the spirit, as the fathers say, its crown is the knowledge of the Holy Trinity. It is evident that one who is deprived of these is distant from perfection.

> On being a beholder of the Trinity: 3.13, 30; 5.84. On seeing, 1 Cor 13.12. On the naked mind, see upcoming keph. (17, 19, 21) and 1.65. As THEY SAY: source unknown. Immaterial knowledge: 1.54. Immaterial *nous* at prayer: *Prayer* 119.

3.16

Greek

A perfect soul is one whose impassioned power acts according to nature.

> Furrer-Pilliod 2000, p. 214 A.ψ.19

264 EVAGRIUS OF PONTUS

S2

The perfect soul is that whose passible power operates naturally.

S1

[Same as S2]

On the passible power, and the imperfect soul, see 3.14. ACCORDING TO NA-
TURE, *kata physin:* 1.64.

3.17

S2

Those who are in immaterial *theōria* are also in the same rank, but those who are
in the same rank are not also now in immaterial *theōria*. It is at least possible that
they will be in the *theōria* concerning intelligibles, which also requires a naked
mind, if it had previously seen [that *theōria*] nakedly.

S1

Those who are in the first *theōria* are also established in the primary state. And
they who are in the second *theōria* are established in the natural state. But those
who are established in the conduct of virtue are in the state of purity and are
called third in rank.

See 3.15, on immaterial knowledge. "Observation," THEŌRIA, here is parallel
with "knowledge," reflecting the pair "to see" and "to know" in 1 Cor 13.12. On
immaterial observation, not specifically mentioned elsewhere in the *KG*, see
Letter on Faith 23 (raised from material knowledge to immaterial observation);
cf. Greg. Nyss., *Hom. on SS* 6; *On Virginity* 5.1. Immaterial observation is the
first of two types of observation discussed at 3.19. Naked mind: 1.65. Rank (Syr.
ṭaksā): 2.66. STATE (S1): 1.80.

3.18

S2

Torment is the fiery suffering that purifies the passible part of the soul.

S1

Torment is the grief by means of fire that purifies with judgment the suffering of the soul.

Cf. 2 Pt 2.4; *Foundations* 9 on the practice of bringing to mind judgment; citing Is 66.24 and Mk 9.4. Fiery suffering as purifying: Zec 13.9; 1 Pt 1.7. On the impassioned part of the soul, see *Prak.* 49. On torment as purification, see Origen, *Comm. on Rom* 8.11.100–111 and 2.6.35–59; *Hom. on Jer* 13.14; and cf. Sch. 355 on Prv 28.28. On torment in general, see 1.44.

3.19

S2

The first and second *theōriai* have something in common: seeing nakedly. But individually one is immaterial, while the other is material.

S1

Just as the first *theōria* requires a naked mind, so also second *theōria* requires its nakedness, though it differs from the first in its sign.

On the different types of observation, and objects of those observations, see 2.2. These two types of observation are not to be conflated with the objects of observation, also termed first, second, and third things (see 3.21). On bare observation, cf. *Letter on Faith* 23.

3.20

S2

The change of *organa* is the passage from bodies to bodies, according to the degree of the ranks of those who are joined to them.

S1

The transfer of practicing bodies is the renewal from the bodily to the spiritual according to the degree of their state.

266 EVAGRIUS OF PONTUS

On the *organon*, see 1.67. On transfer, see 2.4. On rank (Gk. *taxis*), see 2.66. This keph. is grammatically parallel to 3.48, 50, for which we have Greek fragments. STATE (S1): 1.80.

3.21

S2

It is common to both the *theōria* of second things and the third thing that they are material. But only the former has the naked mind and is in the same rank, while the other is with the body and in various ranks.

S1

The *theōria* of second things and of the third thing have in common the knowledge of the intellections of created things, but that which precedes the other has the naked mind.

On first and second natural observation, see 2.2–3; 3.19. NAKED MIND: 1.65. On the second and third "transfers": 2.4; on rank, see 2.66.

3.22

S2

The first movement of the rational beings is the separation of the mind from the unity that is in it.

S1

The first movement of the rational nature is the separation of its mind from the singular knowledge in it.

Primary movement of the *nous*: 1.50; movement in the soul: *Prak.* 11. On unity, see 1.49.

3.23

S2

It is common to all the worlds that they are constituted of the four elements; but individually for each one of them there is a variation of the mixture.

KEPHALAIA GNOSTIKA 267

S1

The rational beings that are under heaven have in common their four elements, but singly a distinction of the mixtures.

> On worlds, see 1.65; the four elements, 1.29. VARIATION can also be translated "change" or "transfer," on which see 2.4. The mixture refers to the ratio of the four elements in a body, but the underlying term, Syr. *mūzāgā*, is customarily used of qualities, on which see 1.22.

3.24

S2

The knowledge of the first nature is the spiritual *theōria* which the creator used and with which he made minds alone receptive of his nature.

S1

The knowledge that is about the first nature of rational beings is a *theōria* of the spirit to which they are promoted after the perfection of their ways of life.

> This keph. is to be contrasted with 3.26. SPIRITUAL *THEŌRIA* (Syr. *teʾawrīyā*, Grk. *theōria*), a species of observation (see *Prak.* 32), is the knowledge of beings on the part of the Son as Demiurge, whether first beings (at this keph.) or second (3.26). This knowledge is now available to us through angelic assistance (1.34; *Prak.* 76); see also 5.16, 40, 74; 6.2, 65; *Prak.* 32; Sch. 282a on Prv 30.4; Sch. 375–376 on Prv 31.18–19; Sch. 15 on Eccl 3.10–13; Sch. 40 on Eccl 5.13; *Thoughts* 40 (used to put aside bare thoughts); Sch. 6 on Ps 4.7 (face of the Lord); Sch. 5 on Ps 142.8 (symbolized by the mercy of God); Sch. 6 on Ps 142.12 (primary way to expel our enemies). On observation in general, *Prak.* 32. On receptivity, see 1.4. S1's insertion OF RATIONAL BEINGS is an astute gloss: see 1.10.

3.25

S2

The spiritual body and its opposite will not be from our limbs or our parts, but from the body. For the change is not a change from limbs to limbs, but from an excellent or evil quality to an excellent or evil change.

268 EVAGRIUS OF PONTUS

S1

The body of the spirit worn by the intermediate rational ones on the last day is nothing other than this body that they strip off. But this very one "that is sown in corruption" is clothed with incorruption when it is corrected and blessed.

1 Cor 15.42 (S1)

On the body, see 1.11. On transfer, see 2.4. "Limb," Syr. *hadāmā*, is likely Grk. *meros* (see *Prak.* 82). This keph. begins a staggered cluster that quotes from or develops terminology drawn from 1 Cor 15 (3.33, 37, 40, 47, 48, 50, 54, 71).

3.26

S2

Knowledge about the second nature is spiritual *theōria*, which Christ used and from which he created the nature of bodies and worlds.

S1

Knowledge about the second nature is spiritual *theōria*, which Christ used and created worlds.

This keph. is to be contrasted with 3.24. On the first and second natures, see 2.31.

3.27

S2

The first *theōria* of nature is capable of being separated from the mind and not being separated. That which is taught is separable, but that which is seen in the mind that knows it is shown to be inseparable.

S1

The first *theōria* of nature is the sign of the movement of the mind, and its immovability.

IT: ambiguous in the Syriac, refering either to the observation or to the mind. Cf. *Prayer* 56–57 on observations that separate the mind from God, as above,

KEPHALAIA GNOSTIKA 269

KG 3.19, for the "imprinting" effect of diverse observations and temptations. Perhaps Syr. *teʾāwrīyā* here corresponds to Grk. *theōrēma* (the result of an observation).

3.28

S2

The soul is the mind that through its carelessness fell from the unity; and from its carelessness has descended to the rank of practice.

S1

The sinful soul is the pure mind that, through its negligence, fell from *theōria* of the holy unity; and it is necessary that by means of much work it will gain the perfect image of the Holy Trinity, that from which it fell.

On the fall of the mind to become a soul, see *Letter to Melania* 26 and cf. *Letter on Faith* 23. On the fall from unity, cf. 3.34; 4.10; 5.56; *Letter on Faith* 31; *Disc.* 35; Sch. 8 on Ps 36.9 (to be exterminated is nothing other than to fall from God; cf. Origen, *Comm. on Ps.* 118.95); Sch. 11 on Ps 49.22 (stolen soul is "completely fallen" from God); Sch. 3 on Ps 67.5 (the settings and the rational natures falling from the sun of righteousness, and see Origen on Judas' eclipse and fall, *On Prayer* 433); Sch. 5 on Ps 16.11 (likening falling to being encircled); Sch. 46 on Eccl 6.1–6; Sch. 60 on Ecc 7.11–12; Sch. 8 on Prv 1.13; Sch. 26 on Prv 2.21; Sch. 183 on Prv 18.14 (demons); Sch. 310 on Prv 25.17. In this context, the term "fall," Syr. *npal* normally corresponds to Grk. *piptō* compounds (*ekpiptō* [*Gn.* 50; *Letter on Faith* 13, 31], *peripiptō* [*Prak.* 23, 27]). Cf. Plotinus, *Enneads* 4.7.14, where the soul is analogous to the mind in this keph. Cf. Porphyry, *Launching Points to the Intelligibles*; Origen, *Comm. on Jn* 2.13.93. Cf. Philo, *On the Creation of the World* 69–70, 134–135. On rank, see 2.66. "Carelessness," Syr. *lā zhīrūtā*, suggests a lack of caution; cf. *Gn.* 27 (Syr. *lā zhīrūtā*, Grk. *aperiskeptos*).

3.29

S2

The sign of the human rank is the human body, but the sign of each rank is greatness and shapes, and colors, and qualities, and natural powers, and weakness,

270 EVAGRIUS OF PONTUS

and time, and place, and parents, and increases, and modes, and life, and death, and those things that are connected to these things.

S1

The mark of the human state is the human body, but the sign of the state of each human is greatness and shape, and color, and natural powers, and weakness, and time, and place, and parents, and increases, and modes, and skills, and life, and death, and whatever there is to know from those things that proceed after these things.

> RANK: 2.66. Most of the thirteen items in the list fall naturally into pairs, likely the following Greek terms: *megethos, schēma* (or *eidos*), *chrōma, poiotēs, dynameis phusikai, astheneia, chronos, topos, goneis* (see below), *auxēsis, poroi, zōē, thanatos*. Some of these relate to Aristotelian categories (see 1.1–2) and others to biblical descriptors (e.g., Rom 8.38: neither death nor life shall separate us). The item "parents" seems out of place compared to the others. Perhaps an original Grk. *genoi* (types) became *goneis* (parents). On modes, see 1.17. CONNECTED TO THOSE THINGS: cf. the conclusion of *Gn.* 4, Grk. *ta toutois parakolouthounta* (Syr. *naqīpān*).

3.30

Greek

A mind is the one who sees the Holy Trinity.

> Furrer-Pilliod 2000, p. 156 A.v.40

S2

The mind is the observer of the Holy Trinity.

S1

The spiritual mind is the observer of the Holy Trinity.

> On the beholder, see 2.27 and Jn 1.14, 1.32; 1 Jn 4.14. The mind is inexpressible, as is the divine; cf. *Gn.* 41; *Thoughts* 33. Cf. Porphyry, *On Abstinence* 2.34.2 and Gregory of Nazianzus, *Or.* 28.20; cf. also the later *Hymn to God* attributed both to Gregory and to Proclus. Cf. Sicherl 1988.

KEPHALAIA GNOSTIKA 271

3.31

S2

It is possible to speak of the unity of the mind; but of its nature one cannot speak, for there is no knowledge of the quality of a thing composed of neither form nor matter.

S1

It is possible to say what is the movement of the mind; but its nature is inexpressible, because it was not constituted from the four elements.

> On unity, in contrast to separability, see 3.27. On qualities, as well as form, see 1.22; on matter, 1.29.

3.32

S2

The image of God is not that which is receptive of his wisdom, for thus also bodily nature would be the image of God; but rather, that which is receptive of the unity is the image of God.

S1

The image of God is not that in which the sign of his wisdom can be represented, which would be possible even in things constituted of the four elements. But this is the image of God, which can receive the knowledge of the Holy Trinity.

> This keph. forms a pair with 6.73. On image see *Gn.* 50 and notes; on wisdom, 1 Cor 1.24: Christ is the "power and wisdom of God." Wisdom: 1.43. Image of God: 2.23. Receptivity: 1.4.

3.33

S2

The name "immortality" makes known the natural union of the mind; but the fact that it exists forever [makes known] its "incorruptibility." Knowledge of

272 EVAGRIUS OF PONTUS

the Trinity follows the first name, and the first *theōria* of nature [follows] the second.

S1

The sign of the living mind is called "immortality." But the sign of its perseverance is that which remains forever. Knowledge of the Holy Trinity accompanies the first sign; and first natural *theōria* the second sign.

cf. 1 Cor 15.53–54

Cf. *Prak.* 3 on knowledge of the Trinity and incorruptibility. IMMORTALITY: 1.58. Names: 1.51.

3.34

Greek

A demon is a rational nature fallen out of the practice by anger's dominance.

Furrer-Pilliod 2000, p. 106 A.δ.102

S2

A demon is a rational nature that because of an excess of anger fell from the practice of God.

S1

[Same as S2]

Anger: *Prak.* 20. Falling: 3.28. PRACTICE/SERVICE, Syr. *pūlḥānā*, points to Grk. *ergasia*, *diakonia*, *latreia*, and other terms for work, but also *praktikē*, which is rendered occasionally as *pūlḥānā* (e.g., *Gn.* 12 [S3], 20 [S2]). The Greek fragment has *thumou* for anger but lacks *theou* or *theiou*. The similarity of the words might have influenced the Syriac to include OF GOD. Alternatively, the Greek version that survives may have lost OF GOD through a scribal error.

3.35

Greek

Spiritual knowledge purifies the mind; love heals anger; and abstinence checks flowing desire.

Paris gr. 2748; fourteenth century (Muyldermans 1932, p. 85)

S2

Knowledge heals the mind; love [heals] the angry part; and continence [heals] the desiring part. The cause of the first is the second, and [the cause] of the second is the third.

S1

[Same as S2]

For similar remedies for the three parts of the soul see *Prak.* 15, 38, 89; *Gn.* 47. On how continence leads to love, see *Prak.* pr.8.

3.36

Greek

An aeon is a natural system, encompassing rational differences of variegated bodies for the sake of the knowledge of God: "They will rejoice forever," [scripture] says, "because an eternal habitation is for themselves."

Rondeau 2021, Sch. 11 on Ps 5.12

S2

A world is a natural constitution that comprises various bodies and differences (among) rational beings for the knowledge of God.

S1

A world is a constitution of natures that has been established from differing bodies and contains different rational beings for growth in the knowledge of God.

274 EVAGRIUS OF PONTUS

Ps 5.12 (Greek)

SYSTEM (Grk. *systēma*) or CONSTITUTION (Syr. *qyāmā*): 1.67. On ages or worlds created to suit the different ranks of logikoi see 1.11; 3.38. Aeons: 1.70. Bodies: 1.11.

3.37

S2

"The stars are greater than one another in glory," and not in bodies, for their greatness, their shapes, their distance from each other, and their courses are varied. The fact that some of them are within the shadow of the earth, and others are outside of it, and some of them are in the separating boundary, makes known their ranks and the economy with which they have been entrusted by God.

S1

"The stars are distinguished from each other in glory," but not also by bodies, because they are equal.

1 Cor 15.41

The quotation from 1 Cor differs between S1 and S2, the latter following the Peshitta and the former the Greek. S2's ECONOMY most likely reflects an original *oikonomia*. On ranks, see 2.66. The shadow of the earth cannot refer to the earth's literal shadow, which is cast only on the moon; it likely refers to the horizon and what is visible and invisible (but not to an observer in the southern hemisphere). Like Origen (*First Principles* 1.7), Evagrius believed the stars to be luminous angelic beings or celestial *noes* (6.88). For variations in the luminosity of stars see 4.31; for their role in enlightening the ignorant, 3.62, 84; for their role in chastising the negligent, 4.29 and 6.88. See also Sch. 113 on Prv 9.13 (*logoi*); Sch. 3 on Ps 135.6 (beings illuminating those in darkness). On the idea that souls become stars, here referenced by Paul, 1 Cor 15.35–49; for precedent in the OT, Dn 12.2–3; and Cicero, *Dream of Scipio* 3. Cf. also Philo, *Allegories of the Law* 1.31 and *Dreams* 1.33.

3.38

Greek

Judgment is the coming to be of a world that distributes bodies in proportion to each of the rational beings.

KEPHALAIA GNOSTIKA   275

Géhin 1987, Sch. 275 on Prv 24.22

S2

The judgment of God is the coming to be of a world, in which he gives a body in proportion to each one of the rational beings.

S1

The judgment of God is the just distinction that he places in the bodies of the rational beings as a reward, or as a judgment. And in each one of them, according to the practice of their works, namely, either glory or torment.

> Regarding the assignment of bodies at judgment, see 1.11; 3.20, 40, 47, 48, 50; 5.11; 6.57. See further references at 1.11 on bodies in general and 2.75 on judgment in general. Sch. 88 on Prv 7.4; Sch. 153 on Prv 17.2 all refer to the role of *krisis* in assigning minds to positions with respect to knowledge.

3.39

S2

One part of fire burns, and another part does not burn. The part that burns is that which burns perceptible matter. But that which does not burn is that which brings to an end the trouble of the troubled ones. The first one does not burn all of the perceptible material, but the second burns all of the material of trouble.

S1

[Same as S2]

> Cf. 1 Cor 3.12–15. TROUBLE, Syr. *šgīšūtā*, which appears at *Prak.* 80 (state of turmoil), has a range of meanings that could include "vexing," "disturbance," or "unstability" (cf. Jas 1.8 Peshitta), and may point to an original Grk. *tarachē*; cf. *Prak.* 11, 61; Sch. 36 on Prv 3.24–25; Sch. 377 on Prv 31.21. The last phrase of this keph. indicates the burning of evil thoughts. On fire, see 1.30.

276 EVAGRIUS OF PONTUS

3.40

S2

The final trumpet is the commandment of the judge who has bound rational beings in good or evil bodies, after which there will be no evil bodies.

S1

The final trumpet is the commandment of the just judge, he who clothes the rational beings in their bodies according to the state of their ways of life.

cf. 1 Cor 15.52; cf. 2 Tm 4.8 (S1)

FINAL TRUMPET: cf. 1 Thes 4.16. On judgment and fire, see previous keph. and 3.9. On bodies and judgment, see 3.38. On the relation between the last and first trumpet, see 3.66 with note. The reference to the trumpet would have conveyed to readers a wide range of associations: Rev 4.1; 8.6–13; 9.1; 10.7; 11.15; Mt 6.2 (trumpets in synagogues). On the trumpet in the Temple: Nm 10.8; 2 Paral/2 Chron 13.12, 14.

3.41

S2

Concerning the *theōria* of beings, and concerning knowledge of the Trinity, we and the demons are aroused in a great battle against each other. The latter wish to hinder us from knowing, while we strive to learn.

S1

Concerning the *theōria* of beings and concerning the knowledge of the Holy Trinity: we and the demons are roused to this entire battle between us. The latter wish to hinder us from knowing, while we strive to learn.

On observation of beings, see 1.73. On battles, see 1.65 (teeming before the Unity); 6.27 (nations); 6.88 (angels against Sisera); *Prak.* 24. On battles with the demons see *Prak.* 5. GREAT BATTLE: Rev 12.7–12. Angels, led by Michael, and demons battle: Dn 10.13, 21; Jude 9; cf. Origen: *Exhortation to Martyrdom* and *On Prayer* for identification of trained and illuminated minds with angels.

KEPHALAIA GNOSTIKA   277

3.42

S2

Theōria is the spiritual knowledge of those things which were and will be, which lifts the mind to its first rank.

S1

Theōria is spiritual knowledge of everything that was and will be, that which enlarges the mind and brings it to the completion of its image, as it was created.

> Things that are and are to come: Rev 1.19; Dn 2.28; Is 48.6. In this context of the *KG*, reference is also made to the judgments and world-creation past and future, on which see 1.65; 2.64. On rank, see 2.66. For a comparable raising up, see 3.46. On ascent/rising/raising, see 4.24, 80, 85; 5.63, 65; 6.56, 76.

3.43

S2

Those who now are zealous to draw close to knowledge possess the water and the perfumed oil in common, but humans possess the oil especially and abundantly.

S1

Those who strive to be perfected in knowledge of the truth possess the water and the perfumed oil in common, but humans possess the oil uniquely.

> Jn 2.17, zeal for your House has consumed me; Ps 68.10 (69.9); and Mt 26.7, Jesus anointed as king and priest: perfumed oil in the Temple, Ex 30.26; and for kings 1 Kgdms/1 Sam 10.1, 16.13; 4 Kgdms/2 Kgs 9.6. On zeal, here analogous to Grk. *spoudē* in *KG* 1.79, see *Prak.* 57. The perfumed oil, Syr. *mešḥā mbasmā*, corresponds to Grk. *myron* (myrrh; see Mt 26.7 Peshitta); see 3.85 (perfumed); Sch. 2 on Ps 132.2 (emptied-out oil = your name); Sch. 4 on Ps 132.2 (heavenly myron is knowledge of God). On oil, Syr. *mešḥā*, possible here simply Grk. *elaion*, see 3.85 (aroma of sacrifice); 4.29 (of Christ); *Gn.* 7 (virgins and lamps); *Letter* 25.4; 28.1; 51.2; 56.8; 57.4; Sch. 11 on Ps 88.21 (holy oil is knowledge of God or essential knowledge [for the latter, see Sch. 13 on Ps 43.21]); Sch. 3 on Ps 140.5 (oil of sinners for glory coming from human beings). See also 4.18 on anointing.

278   EVAGRIUS OF PONTUS

3.44

Greek

An intelligible sun is a rational nature carrying around in itself the first and blessed light.

> Furrer-Pilliod 2000, p. 124 A.η.13

S2

The intelligible sun is the rational nature, that which contains in itself the first and blessed light.

S1

The intelligible sun is the rational nature, which advances to bear the first light of glory.

> This keph. forms a group with 3.52 and 3.62. It is also the first of thirty-one keph. that follow a distinctive formula: "The intelligible X is . . .": 3.44, 52, 62; 4.12, 18, 28, 36, 48, 52, 56, 66, 69, 72, 75; 5.13, 16, 28, 31, 34, 37, 40, 43, 68, 71, 74, 77, 80, 82, 84; 6.38, 53. Keph. expressed in a similar formula, but without "intelligible": 4.40, 79; 5.10; 6.21, 66. On other celestial rational natures, see 1.89. Keph. of the form "The intelligible X is . . ." are peculiar to the *KG* and the scholia and do not feature in Evagrius' other treatises, or indeed in other Greek writings. In addition to fragments that already appear in the *KG*, see Sch. 3 on Ps 27.5; Sch. 1 on Ps 74.4; Sch. 67 on Ps 118.147; Sch. 3 on Ps 148.4; Sch. 3 on Ps 149.8; Sch. 93, 290 on Prv; Sch. 8 on Eccl 2.10. Several additional such scholia, possibly by Evagrius but otherwise unattested, appear in the anonymous Byzantine collection of definitions: α 35, 36, 115; κ 30; τ 35; ω 15 (Furrer-Pilliod ed.). CARRYING AROUND: also "making known." For the sun, see also 3.52; 5.14; 6.63. On the "sun of justice," see 4.29; *Prak.* ep.; Sch. 49 on Prv 4.18; Sch. 122 on Prv 10.27; Sch. 224 on Prv 21.19; Sch. 374 on Prv 31.15; Sch. 3 on Ps 148.4. Cf. Sch. 1 on Ps 112.3 (risings and settings); Sch. 1 on Ps 18.2; Sch. 12 on Ps 54.24; Sch. 1 on Ps 114.2.

3.45

S2

Just as one cannot say that there is a mind that is older than [another] mind, so also it is not the case that spiritual bodies [are older] than practicing bodies if one change was the cause of both instruments.

S1

Just as one cannot say that there is a mind that is older than a mind, so also there are not spiritual bodies that are older than fleshly bodies.

> This keph. begins a staggered series, through 3.51, concerning transfers of practicing bodies; a comparable cluster begins at 2.69. On the comparative age of rational beings, see 1.41. On the *organon* of the soul, 1.67. On *praktikē* versus spiritual bodies see 1.11.

3.46

S2

The judgment of angels is knowledge concerning the maladies of the soul, [a knowledge] that raises up to health those who have been wounded.

S1

The work of angels is the care for sick souls, which will bring them to the fullness of health.

> Although angels attend judgment (see Revelation, passim), they do not exercise it, and are subject to judgment. Cf. 1 Cor 6.3 (do you not know that we shall judge angels?) and Sch. 370 on Prv 29.26: "In the correction we heal the angels." The insertion of this keph. within a cluster devoted to the transfer is suggestive of how Evagrius understood 1 Cor 6.3. On angels in general, see *Prak.* 24.

3.47

S2

There is one change "in the blink of an eye," which affects every person by degree as a result of judgment and establishes the body of everyone according to the degree of their rank. But the one who says that there is a change in parts besides this common one is someone who does not know the *logoi* of judgment.

S1

Single is the renewal "in the blink of an eye" happening to all rational bodies, which is at the command of the just judge, that will distribute to each one in recompense for his labor. But if someone dares to say that there is another renewal

280 EVAGRIUS OF PONTUS

besides this one common to all, that is a sign of ignorance, of someone who does not perceive the cause of the just judgment of God.

1 Cor 15.52; cf. 2 Tm 4.8 (S1); 2 Thes 1.5 (S1)
The criticism here is likely directed against the Manichaeans, who taught gradual, particulate transfer of this body into the divine. This keph. is the first of a series that presents, explicitly or implicitly, teaching that counters Manichaeism, coincident with treatment of 1 Cor 15 (see 3.25). See notes in following keph. Judgment: 1.82. LOGOI translates Syr. *sūkālē*, on which see 2.30.

3.48

Greek

The judgment of the just is the transition from the practicing body to an angelic one.

Rondeau 2021, Sch. 10 on Ps 1.5

S2

The change of the just is the passage from practicing and seeing bodies to seeing or better-seeing bodies.

S1

The spiritual renewal of the just is the ascent from virtue to virtue, and from knowledge to greater knowledge.

Greek fragments for this keph. and 3.50 come from the same scholion on Psalms (Sch. 8 on Ps 1.5). As with comparable fragments from the scholia, Evagrius has here dropped the vocabulary that corresponds distinctively to the verse annotated by the scholion (here *krisis*), and replaced it with a term better suited to the immediate context in the *KG*. We have suggested at 2.4 (see note there) that this is likely *allagē*, here translated Syr. *ḥūlāpā* (S2) and *šūḥlāpā* (S1). Grk. *metabasis* and *metathesis* have each been translated Syr. *šūnāyā* (similar in meaning to *ḥūlāpā* / *šūḥlāpā*). Thus, scholion 8 has here been adjusted to comment on the terminology of 1 Cor 15 (vv. 51–52: "we shall all be changed [*allagēsometha*]"), the scriptural passage that dominates the middle part of century three. See further remarks at 2.4 on parallels with Didymus the Blind. On *metathesis*, see Sch. 249 on Prv 22.28; *Eulogius*

10.17. The substitution of "angelic bodies" for "seeing bodies" is logical, in that angels always see (mentioned numerous times in the Scholia on Psalms, e.g., Sch. 6 on Ps 4.7). The angels that see "more greatly" are seraphim (Is 6.2; Rev 4.8). A short treatise *On the Seraphim* ascribed to Evagrius, but considered among his *dubia*, exists in Syriac and Armenian and has been included as Armenian *Letter* 25 (for an English translation now see Young and Karapetyan 2022). On angels in general, see *Prak.* 24. On practicing bodies, see 1.11 and 3.45.

3.49

S2

The mind is not crowned with the crown of essential knowledge unless it has cast from itself ignorance of the two contests.

S1

The mind is not crowned with the crown of essential knowledge if it does not expel from itself ignorance of the two contests.

Crowns: Cf. 1.75. ESSENTIAL KNOWLEDGE: 1.89, 3.12.

3.50

Greek

The change of the wicked is the transposition from a practicing body to darkened and gloomy bodies.

Rondeau 2021, Sch. 10 on Ps 1.5

S2

The change of sinners is the passage from practicing or demonic bodies to those that are even heavier and darker.

S1

The transfer of sinners is the passage from sins to more (serious) sins and from ignorance to ignorance darker than it.

282 EVAGRIUS OF PONTUS

See note at 3.48. On bodies in general, see *KG* 1.11. On corpulent demonic bodies, fattened by the fumes from the burning meat of sacrificial animals, see Clement, *Protreptikos* 3, and Origen, *Contra Celsum* 8.32–34. Cf. Porphyry, *On Abstinence* and Mani on the (differing) result of eating vegetables instead of meat. Augustine, *Customs of the Manichaeans* 61.

3.51

S2

Of all the changes that happen before the world to come, some are yoked to excellent bodies and some to evil bodies. But those (changes) that will happen after (the world) to come will yoke all to knowing instruments.

S1

In the entire nature of rational beings, knowledge will spread on the day of renewal. But for some of them this will be for happiness, but for others, for punishment.

Transfer: 2.4. *Organon:* 1.67. Yoking: *Prak.* 73.

3.52

Greek

An intelligible moon is a rational nature illuminated by "the sun of justice."

Furrer-Pilliod 2000, p. 189 A.σ.95

S2

The intelligible moon is the rational nature that is illuminated by "the sun of righteousness."

S1

[Same as S2]

Mal 3.20

On rational nature, see 1.89; on celestial bodies, see 2.80; stars, 3.37; sun, 3.44. Cf. Origen, *Hom. on Gn* 1.5: Christ is the light within us that illuminates us like the moon. Cf. Mani, *Kephalaia of the Teacher* 65 "on the sun" for Mani's teaching on the role of sun and moon in effecting an upward transfer of the light. The term BY THE SUN is Grk. *pros tou heliou*, an unusual construction.

3.53

S2

Anyone who was receptive of the knowledge of God but honors ignorance more than this knowledge, this one is said to be evil. But there is no bodily nature receptive of knowledge, nor are any of the bodies said to be evil.

S1

Everyone who by his creation was made receptive to the knowledge of God but honors ignorance more than this knowledge—this one is justly termed evil. But there is no bodily nature receptive to that knowledge and thus they are not speaking justly who say that the body is evil.

Cf. *Letter* 30.3. God has never created anything evil: 3.59 (also parallel to *Letter* 30). The admonition not to call the body evil is anti-Manichaean (see previous keph.). For a parallel among non-Christian Platonists, Porphyry, *Life of Plotinus* 1. On receptivity, see 1.4.

3.54

S2

In the "blink of an eye," cherubs have been named cherubs; Gabriel, Gabriel, and humans, humans.

284 EVAGRIUS OF PONTUS

S1

By the word of the Lord from the beginning, beings were established embodied and bodiless, and there is none among them who, being in the intelligence of the creator, is older than any other.

1 Cor 15.52 (S2)

Cf. 3.47. On names, see 1.51.

3.55

S2

In the beginning the mind had the incorruptible God as a teacher of the *logoi* of the immaterial, but now it has received corruptible sense perception as the teacher of material *logoi*.

S1

In the beginning, the rational mind had as a teacher the revelation of the Spirit. But it turned and became the student of the senses. Then, by its completion in Christ, it again became equal to the first teacher.

On the good and bad teacher, Sch. 128 on Prv 11.21. Raising the topic of teacher continues the theme in this section of polemic against Mani, who wrote a treatise called *Kephalaia of the Teacher*. Cf. *Gn.* 48 on the "great and gnostic teacher Didymos." The previously mentioned teacher in *Gn.* 47, Serapion "the angel of the church of Thmuis," authored a treatise *Against the Manichaeans*. On "the angel of the church of . . ." cf. Rev 2.17ff. On sense perception, see 1.33.

3.56

S2

Spiritual knowledge is the "wings" of the mind; the gnostic is the mind of the wings. And if this is so, then things bear the sign of "trees": (they are) those things upon which the mind perches, enjoying their leaves and delighting in their fruits, while at every moment striving toward the "tree of life."

KEPHALAIA GNOSTIKA 285

S1

Spiritual knowledge is the "wings" of the mind. The gnostic is the mind of the wings. But if this is so, all the things of this world are assigned to be a symbol of "trees," for upon them the mind perches, enjoying their leaves and delighting in their fruits until it will be made worthy to reach the "tree of life."

Gn 2.9

Sch. 2 on Ps 54.7: Wings are observation of bodies and incorporeals, through which the *nous* is elevated to rest in knowledge of the Holy Trinity. Cf. 2.6; *Thoughts* 29; *Reflections* 5. Cf. Plato on desire that arouses the wings of the *nous*, *Phaedrus* 246a–254e. On trees, see 4.1 (God planting); 5.67, 69. Christ is the Tree of Life: *Maxims 3* 17 on Prv 3.18; Sch. 32 on Prv 3.18, the tree of life is the wisdom of God, and cf. Philo, *Allegories of the Law* 1.17.56ff.; Sch. 132 on Prv 11.30: Adam has rejected the "seeds of justice from which the tree of life grow"; cf. *Prak.* pr.7, monastic staff is the tree of life. On the tree of life and the fruit of justice: Sch. 325 on Prv 26.15; Sch. 8 on Ps 117.27; Sch. 5 on Ps 1.3; cf. Sch. 32 on Prv 3.18; Sch. 132 on Prv 11.30. On the tree of life, Mani, *Kephalaia of the Teacher* 10.10–15. On planting, see 4.1.

3.57

S2

Just as those who transmit letters to children inscribe them on tablets, so also Christ when he teaches his wisdom to the rational beings inscribes [them] on the nature of the body.

S1

Just as those who transmit the letters to small children inscribe them on the lines of tablets, so also Christ when he teaches his wisdom to the rational beings inscribes his letters on the nature of the body.

A possible reference, as part of Evagrius' rebuttal of Manichaean teaching, to the account of Mani's birth and illumination: *On the Origin of His Body*. On letters, see 6.37 (cranes make letters). On engraving ("writing" or "painting") the soul, cf. Plotinus, *Enn.* 6.4.10, summarized in *Gn.* 50, both referring to Plato, *Tim.* 29a.

3.58

S2

The one ready to see written things needs light: so also the one who is ready to teach the wisdom of beings needs spiritual love.

S1

The one prepared to receive letters needs the light to see them, and the one who is prepared to teach the wisdom that is in things that exist needs spiritual love in which he will see the light of knowledge.

> On writing and books, cf. previous keph., and 4.1; see also the saying of Antony the Great: "My book...is the nature of beings..." (*Prak.* 92); Sch. 8 on Ps 138.16 (book of God is the observation of corporeal and incorporeal beings). On spiritual love, see *Prak.* 35; *Prayer* 37. The wisdom of beings is wisdom about things that exist (cf. S1). On light, see 1.35. Cf. Origen, *Comm. on Jn* 1.11.68; *Comm. on Gn* 23. For the principle that knowledge requires love, Plato, *Republic, Timaeus,* and *Symposium.*

3.59

Greek

If every evil naturally comes to be from the rational part, the desiring part, or the angering part, and it is possible to use these powers well or wickedly, the evils befall us clearly in contrary use of these parts. If this is so, nothing of the things that have come into being from God is wicked.

> Mosc. 425, sixteenth century (Hausherr 1939, p. 230)

S2

If all evil is born from the reasoning [part] and from the angering [part] and from the desiring [part], and it is possible that we use these same powers for good or for evil, then it is evident that it is in the unnatural use of these parts that evils befall us. If this is so, this also is so: there is nothing that was created by God that is evil.

S1

If all evil is born from the three parts of the soul, i.e., from its reasoning, its desire, and its anger, and if it is possible to use these things for good or for evil, it is clear that evil is born from their improper use. But if this is so, it is the case that also there is nothing that has been created from God that is evil.

> This keph. continues the polemic against the Manichaeans, who taught the independent existence of evil; Augustine, *Customs of the Manichaeans* 1. It appears, along with 3.53, in *Letter* 30.2–3. On the inherently useful and didactic nature of created powers and things, see 3.53, 75; *Prak.* 88; Sch. 1 on Ps 15.2. Cf. 4.59; 5.47: demons are not in their essence evil. On the soul acting according to nature: *Prak.* 73, 86, 93; *Thoughts* 19; *Reflections* 15; Sch. 15 on Eccl 3.10–13; against nature: *Prak.* 24, 88, 93; Sch. 4 on Ps 3.7; Sch. 5 on Ps 20.12, "we decline when we are moved against nature."

3.60

S2

The sign of the East is the symbol of the saints; the sign of the West is (the symbol of) the souls that are in Sheol. But the Holy Trinity is the end of the return course of all.

S1

The symbol of the dawning of day is the symbol of the saints; [the symbol] of the setting is the souls that are in Sheol. The Holy Trinity is the end of the race of all.

> cf. 2 Tm 4.7
>
> Ps 113.3. On the symbolism of east and west, see Sch. 3 on Ps 67.5; Sch. 21 on Ps 67.34; Sch. 1 on Ps 106.3; Sch. 1 on Ps 112.3; Sch. 282 on Prv 30.4; Sch. 284 on Prv 30.4. Souls in Sheol: 1.40. On the completion of the "race" 1.75 (S1); 5.3 (S1); 2 Tm 4.7. Completion: see 2.13 on *apokatastasis* and cf. *Letter to Melania* 26.

3.61

S2

The virtues show the mind the natural *theōria* of second things, and this (natural *theōria*) shows (the mind) the first thing, and the first thing then (shows) the holy unity.

S1

Virtue shows the mind the natural *theōria* of second things, and this establishes it in its first state. And this first state then brings it to knowledge of the holy unity.

On first and second things, see 1.50; natural observation, 2.2; holy unity, 1.71; state (S1), 1.80.

3.62

Greek

Intelligible stars are rational natures entrusted with illuminating those who are in ignorance.

Furrer-Pilliod 2000, p. 85 A.α.187

S2

The intelligible stars are the rational natures that are entrusted with illuminating those who are in darkness.

S1

The intelligible stars are the rational natures that are entrusted with enlightening those who are in ignorance.

On stars, see 3.37; rational natures, 1.89; light, 1.35. The Greek (IGNORANCE) agrees with S1 against S2 (DARKNESS), the only known exception to the general rule that S2 is closer to the Greek than S1 is.

3.63

S2

For the one whose knowledge is limited, his ignorance is also limited, and for the one of whom ignorance is not limited, neither is his knowledge limited.

S1

The one whose knowledge is limited—it is evident that his ignorance also is limited, and for the one whose ignorance is without a limit, it is evident that his knowledge also is without a limit.

> Cf. 1.65, 1.71; Sch. 2 on Ps 144.3. On limit (Syr. ʿebrā [S1], msayaktā [S2]), see 1.54.

3.64

S2

If, then, among things that one tastes there is nothing sweeter than honey or the honeycomb, and it is said that greater than these is the knowledge of God, then it is evident that there is nothing among all the things on earth that gives such pleasure as the knowledge of God.

S1

If, among things that can be tasted, there is nothing sweeter than honey or the honeycomb, and greater than these is the sweetness of the knowledge of God, then it is evident that nothing of all things on earth gives such pleasure to the soul as the knowledge of God.

> cf. Ps 18.11; 118.103
> Sch. 270 on Prv 24.13 (honey for the simple, honeycomb for the "holy prophets and apostles"); cf. Sch. 15 on Eccl 13.10–13; Origen, *First Principles* 4.2.6. On the knowledge and observation of God as "honey": Sch. 72 on Prv 6.8; *Gn.* 25; cf. Sch. 45 on Ps 118.103; *Letter on Faith* 39.

3.65

S2

Angels, they who instructed human beings from the earth, will establish these (humans) as heirs of their administration in the world to come.

290 EVAGRIUS OF PONTUS

S1

All those who in this world have been made students of the holy angels will in the world to come be partakers of their glory, according to the measure of their advancement.

> On the just who in the age to come will "rule over five and ten cities": Sch. 134 on Prv 13.22; Sch. 10 on Ps 48.15; *Letters* 23, 36, and 37. On administration (Syr. *mdabrānūtā*: Grk. *oikonomia*), see 2.30. On angels, see *Prak.* 24; Clement, *Strom.* 7.1, 2; Origen, *Comm. on Jn* 1.165 etc.

3.66

S2

Just as the first trumpet made known the coming-to-be of bodies, so also the last trumpet makes known the destruction of bodies.

S1

Just as the first commandment was the creation of all bodies, so the last trumpet is the renewal of all bodies.

> On the trumpet, see 3.40. Here, the first and last trumpets suggest the juxtaposition of Ex 9.23–25 and Rev 8.6–13: the first trumpet of the angels of judgment and the seventh plague upon the Egyptians. The setting is the heavenly Temple; see 4.25. On bodies, see 1.11.

3.67

S2

Every natural *theōria* of second things bears the sign of milk, but of the first thing, (the sign) of honey. And that is "the land that flows with milk and honey."

S1

Every natural *theōria* of second things bears the sign of milk, but the first, of honey. But the two are "the land running with milk and honey."

Ex 33.3

KEPHALAIA GNOSTIKA 291

Clement, *Paidagogos* 1.103. On second things, see 1.50; natural observation, 2.2; honey, 3.64.

3.68

S2

Just as God's first "rest" makes known the decrease of evil and the disappearance of thick bodies, so also the second ("rest") makes known the destruction of bodies, secondary beings, and the decrease of ignorance.

S1

Just as the first admonition of God separates wickedness from rational nature, so "God's just judgment" will be the destroyer of the entirety of all evil.

cf. Gn 2.2 (S2); 2 Thes 1.5 (S1)
Cf. 3.40, 3.66; first rest: the seventh day of creation, Gn 2.2; second rest: Heb 3.11; cf. Ps 95.11 "they will never enter my rest." On rest, compare the use of psalmody to bring the temper to rest: *Prak.* 15; *Thoughts* 27, 29; *gnōsis* = rest: Sch. 7 on Ps 94.11. The keph. refers here to the disappearance of fat bodies, demons grown corpulent from the smoke of sacrifices; see further references on thickened/heavy bodies at 1.11.

3.69

S2

It is impossible that something else be established by the *theōria* by which the mind was established unless this also is receptive of the Trinity.

S1

Of everything that is, the mind alone is receptive of the knowledge of the Holy Trinity.

Established, Syr. *'etqayam*, points to a Grk. *-istēmi* verb or compound, with a variety of senses. Here, the meaning points not to an observation leading to the creation of a mind, but to the mind's reception of an observation leading to its administration. Cf. 3.65, and the way of angels, who teach humans, and establish them in a new role in a world to come.

292   EVAGRIUS OF PONTUS

3.70

S2

It belongs to the naked mind to say what is its nature, and to this question now there is no response, but at the end there will not even be the question.

S1

[Same as S2]

> Cf. *Letter to Melania* 26 (the naked mind alone can say what its nature is). This keph. alludes to the question-and-answer genre, Grk. *erōtapokriseis*. On the use of questions in keph., see 2.74.

3.71

S2

Just as the human being received the insufflation and "became a living soul," so also the mind, when it receives the holy Trinity, will become a living mind.

S1

[Same as S2]

> Gn 2.7; 1 Cor 15.45
>
> A possible contemporary analogy is *Apostolic Tradition* 21 on baptismal insufflation (Grk. *emphysēma*); Cyril of Jerusalem, *Catech.* 17.12.

3.72

S2

The inheritance of Christ is the knowledge of the unity, and if all become coheirs of Christ, all of them will know the holy unity. It is not possible for them to become coheirs unless they have first become his heirs.

S1

The inheritance of Christ is the unity of the holy essence, and all who become heirs with him will become partakers with him in this holy knowledge, but it is not possible for them to become coheirs with him unless they have become his heirs.

cf. Rom 8.17

An extension of the previous keph.'s commentary on baptism. To be baptized is to become an heir; to become a coheir is to attain the knowledge of Christ; 4.8. On heirs, see 2.7. On the comparison of heir and coheir, see *Monks* 1. On inheritance and being inherited, see 1.18; 4.4, 8–9, 77. Cf. Sch. 288 on Prv 30.9; Sch. 40 on Prv 3.35; 263 on Prv 23.33. Note the contrast with the Holy Trinity in the previous keph. On becoming a christ: 3.3.

3.73

S2

If "the day of the Lord comes like a thief in the night," then no one among all those who are in the house knows at what hour or what day he will rob those who are sleeping.

S1

If "the day of the Lord comes like a thief," it is evident that no one from all that are in the house will be able to know the hour or the day in which he will steal those who are sleeping.

1 Thes 5.2

The quotation of 1 Thes 5.2 is connected with the parable of the wise and foolish virgins. On knowledge of the day and hour, see *Letter on Faith* 19, 21 (Christ does not know that of judgment). On houses, see 2.50 (guardians of); 4.25 (of demons), 68 (body); 6.8 (Hades). Sleepers: Eph 5.14 and Clement, *Protreptikos* 8.84; Origen, *First Principles* 1.6.2 etc.

3.74

S2

Everything from bodily nature and is called holy: this "is sanctified by the word of God." Everything from rational beings (and) is named holy: this is sanctified by the knowledge of God. But there are at least some from the second that are sanctified by the word of God, like children, who are receptive to knowledge.

294 EVAGRIUS OF PONTUS

S1

Everything that is from corporeal nature and called holy is "sanctified by the word of the Lord," but the rational beings are sanctified by the knowledge of God. But there are also some among the rational beings that are sanctified by the word of God. But these are like youths, who also are receptive to knowledge.

> 1 Tm 4.5
> On the goodness of bodily nature, see 3.53. On children, see 3.57 (taught letters); 4.13 (humans versus demons/angels), 15 (world full of). Cf. Sch. 16 on Prv 1.32 quoting Mt 28.20. Cf. *KG* 4.13 and 15.

3.75

S2

What is impure is so either from unnatural use, or from evil. And everything that is lacking use (and) considered to be polluted is from fleshly nature. But that which is polluted by evil they say is from rational nature.

S1

Whatever is impure is so either because it is outside of use or because of evil. And those things which are outside of use are operated by means of the flesh. But those things that are defiled because of evil are operated by the rational nature, as also the fathers say.

> Mt 15.11–20: evil actions arise from evil cogitations: *dialogismoi*. EVIL = *kakia*, Ac 8.22, "turn your mind from evil." Reference is to the body and mind = Temple, 1 Cor 6.19. On acting according to and against nature (Grk. *kata* and *para physin*), see 1.64; *Prak.* 86. See 3.59 on pollution (or sin) arising from different parts of the soul. On the impure and defilement, 3.78; 4.6, 62, 83, 90; 5.9, 19 (S1); 6.53; *Prak.* pr.5; 8, 89; *Gn.* 20.

3.76

Greek

Formed in the womb, we live the life of plants; when born, the life of the living; and having been perfected, that of the angels. The cause of the first life is the ensouled essence, of the second the sense perceptions, but the third, our being receptive of virtue and vice.

Milan, Ambr. gr. 681 (Q 74 sup.); tenth century (Muyldermans 1931, p. 59)

S2

When we are formed in the belly, we live the life of plants; when we are born, the life of animals; but when we have become adults, we live the life of angels or the life of demons. The cause of the first life is ensouled nature; of the second, sense perception; and of the third that we will be receptive to virtue or to vice.

S1

When we are shut up in the womb, we live the life of plants; when we have been born, we live the life of animals; but when we have become adults, we live the life of angels or the life of demons, either because of virtue or because of neglect.

In Aristotelian theory, the soul went through stages of human embryological development: the vegetative or nutritive soul ("like a plant"); the soul capable of sensation, held in common with animals; and finally the rational soul (Aristotle, *On the Generation of Animals* 2.3 [736b]; Galen, *On the Formation of the Fetus* 6.31 [104.19–22]). This embryonic hierarchy of developing souls parallels the successive judgments that put into effect the changing hierarchy of demons, humans, and angels: cf. 4.13, 15; Sch. 16 on Prv 1.32. On receptivity, see 1.4.

3.77

S2

For those whose life and death the Holy Spirit has recounted to us, [the Spirit] has announced to us in advance also the resurrection to come.

S1

For those about whose life and death the Holy Spirit has told us, [the Spirit] has announced to us in advance also the resurrection to come.

296 EVAGRIUS OF PONTUS

On the resurrection, see 5.19 (of body, qualitative change), 22 (of soul, passivity), 25 (of mind, knowledge); 6.7 (eighth day and Christ). See also keph. interpreting 1 Cor 15, listed at note at 3.25. On act of announcing, cf. 6.77 (the annunciation).

3.78

Greek

How do angels and demons approach our world, and how do we not approach their worlds? For we are unable to more greatly join angels to God, nor can we choose to make demons more unclean.

Thoughts 19 (Géhin 1998, p. 220)

S2

Angels and demons approach our world, but we do not approach their worlds; for we cannot draw angels nearer to God, and we cannot imagine making the demons more impure.

S1

Angels and demons approach our world, but we do not approach their worlds; for we cannot draw angels nearer to God, and we cannot imagine making the demons more impure than they are.

Sch. 33 on Prv 3.19–20 "worlds (*kosmoi*) and bodies." This keph. appears also in *Thoughts* 19 and *Letter* 57.2; see 1.38, 40 on the relationship between the *KG*, *Thoughts*, and the letters. On demons, see *Prak.* 5; angels, *Prak.* 24.

3.79

S2

Those who now are under the earth will entice toward immeasurable evil those who now do earthly things—the wretches!

KEPHALAIA GNOSTIKA 297

S1

While all of the demons are evil in their will, evil differs among them. For it is the case that among them are those in whom evil is harder than among their companions.

cf. Phil 2.10; cf. 2 Cor 11.14

UNDER THE EARTH, perhaps Grk. *katachthonia*; if so, it is a quotation from Phil 2.10. The subterranean realm should not be taken as strictly spatial in light of the previous keph. Cf. Origen, *First Principles* 1.2.10; 1.6.2. Cf. *KG* 1.22; 5.18, 78; 6.25.

3.80

S2

Bodily and bodiless nature are knowable, but only bodiless nature is knowing. For God is both knowing and knowable, but he does not know like a bodiless nature, nor indeed is he known like bodily and bodiless nature.

S1

Beneath knowledge are both corporeal and incorporeal nature, but incorporeal nature alone is knowing. God is also knowing and knowable except he is not like incorporeal nature, nor is he like corporeal nature.

On corporeal versus incorporeal nature, see note at 1.10; on knowing and knowability: 1.35 and the next keph.

3.81

S2

The one who knows God has knowledge either of his nature or of his wisdom, that which he used to make everything.

S1

The one who knows God has either knowledge of his nature or knowledge of the "wisdom full of varieties," that which he used also in creating worlds.

Eph 3.10 (S1)

On wisdom see 1.14; on the frequent use of Eph 3.10, see 2.2.

298 EVAGRIUS OF PONTUS

3.82

S2

Blessed is the one who by means of things receives a demonstration of the grace of God, and blessed also is the one who by knowledge is able to scrutinize them.

S1

[Same as S2]

THINGS: on affairs, Syr. *sū'rānē*, see 1.78. On grace, 1.37. For Grk. *zētēsis*, scrutiny or inquiry, cf. Origen *First Principles* 3.1, *Hom. on the Witch of Endor*, and *zētēteon*, "it must be investigated," in the Psalms homilies and *On Prayer* passim. The same term features in *Thoughts* 19, 20, 41; Sch. 5 on Ps 118.7.

3.83

Greek

Faith is a willed good that guides us toward the blessedness that is to come.

Furrer-Pilliod 2000, p. 175 A.π.111

S2

Faith is a willed good that guides us toward the blessedness that is to come.

S1

Faith is a good that from the beginning was established in us by God, that which guides us toward the good that is to come.

On faith, see *Prak.* 81, which parallels the opening of this keph. On blessedness (Syr. *ṭūbtānūtā*, Grk. *makariotēs*), see *Prak.* 16 (blessedness here); *Letter on Faith* 21–23 (final), 37. See also 3.85–87. The Greek fragment is paralleled by another definition perhaps by Diodore of Tarsus. See Furrer-Pilliod, A.π.41, p. 169.

KEPHALAIA GNOSTIKA 299

3.84

S2

All natural *theōria* of second things bears the sign of the stars. For the stars are the ones who have been entrusted with illuminating those who are in the night.

S1

All natural *theōria* of second things is a symbol of the stars, the ones who have been entrusted with illuminating those who are in darkness.

On stars see 3.37; natural observation, 2.2–3.

3.85

S2

All those who are baptized in water receive the perfumed fragrance, but the one who baptizes is the one who has the perfumed oil.

S1

All those who are baptized in water have a share in the fragrance of the Holy Spirit, but the one who baptizes is the one who has the perfumed oil.

Cf. 3.43 on oil and perfumed oil. Fragrance: Syr. *rīḥā*, Grk. *osmē*, the pleasing aroma of sacrifice (Gn 8.21, Ezek 20.28); oil/myron as knowledge: 3.43, Sch. 4 on Ps 132.2, "heavenly perfume." Cf. *Virg.* 17, 55 on Mt 25.2–13; Sch. 7 on Ps 44.8, "anointed with the knowledge of the Monad." The one who baptizes (*mʿamad*) is Christ tarrying with his disciples, Jn 3.23.

3.86

S2

Blessed is the one who has not loved anything from natural *theōria* of second things except *theōria*.

300 EVAGRIUS OF PONTUS

S1

Blessed is the one who has not loved anything from all that bears the sign of natural *theōria* of second things except the *theōria* of them.

> This keph. forms a group with the next two, describing an ascending order of blessedness (Mt 5.3–11; Grk. *makarios*): 3.83; cf. *Thoughts* 11.34; 20.11; 29.7–8 and *Prayer* 117–123, qualities of a *gnōstikos*. On loving nothing in the world: *Eight Thoughts* 16. On love that possesses nothing but God: *Eulogius* 21; *Vices* 3. Natural observation and second things: 2.2–3; 3.19.

3.87

S2

Blessed is the one who has not hated anything from the first *theōria* of natures except their evil.

S1

Blessed is the one who has not hated anything that is from the first *theōria* of natures, except their negligence.

> See previous keph. On the pairing of love and hatred, 1.84. On hatred of evil, *Gn.* 28; in general, *Prak.* 20, 76, 100. Another rebuttal of Manichaean teaching that evil is a substance: cf. *Acts of Archelaus* 14. On natures, see *KG* 1.10.

3.88

S2

Blessed is he who has arrived at infinite knowledge.

S1

Blessed is he who has arrived at infinite ignorance.

> See 3.86. This keph. is quoted by Isaac of Nineveh (Bedjan ed. 175.10–11). See the Xanthopoloi quotation, PG 147:772, relying upon the Greek translation of Isaac. S1's apparent contradiction, IGNORANCE, is the dominant reading, but one manuscript reads KNOWLEDGE, which is reflected in the Armenian

KEPHALAIA GNOSTIKA 301

translation (dependent upon S1), and the original of S1 may have been KNOWL-
EDGE. See Guillamont 1958, p. 134n1 for further discussion. On infinite knowledge, cf. infinite longing: *Prak.* 57.

3.89

S2

Just as our body when it is born from our parents cannot turn around and give
birth to them, so also the soul which is given birth by God cannot repay him
knowledge. "For what will I repay the Lord from all his gifts to me?"

S1

Just as our body when it is born from our parents cannot turn around and
give birth to them, so also the mind born from God by grace cannot give him
knowledge in return. As it is written, "For what will I repay the Lord from all
his gifts to me?"

Ps 115.3

Begetting: 1.5. Cf. *Gospel of Philip* 33; *Thunder—Perfect Intellect* fol. 13 (Nag
Hammadi VI). On the reverse: repaying (*antapodidous*) evil with evil, Sch. 158
on Prv 17.13; *Thoughts* 23.26 (Ps 102.2–4).

3.90

Greek

The demons do not stop slandering the gnostic even when he does not err, in
order to snatch the mind for themselves. For a certain cloud stands around
the mind and leads the mind away from *theōria*, according to the time when it
reproves the demons as slandering.

Milan, Ambr. gr. 681 (Q 74 sup.); tenth century (Muyldermans 1931, p. 59)

S2

Demons do not cease from slandering the *gnōstikos*, even when he does not err,
in order to attract his mind to them. For a kind of cloud settles upon the understanding and chases the mind from *theōria*, just when it is rebuking the demons
as slanderers.

302 EVAGRIUS OF PONTUS

S1

Demons do not cease from slandering the gnostic, even when he does not err, in order to attract the mind to them by means of anger. Like a kind of dark fog it settles in front of the understanding and drives away *theōria* from the mind just when it is rebuking the demons as slanderers.

> On slander, see *Gn.* 32; Sch. 8 on Ps 26.12 (verse to be uttered against calumny, oppression, and extortion; see Sch. 245 on Prv 22.16); *Prayer* 139 (demonic); slander that darkens the nous: *Thoughts* 37; *Eulogius* 16; and Mt 6.19. The demons seek to arouse anger in the contemplative and thus cloud or darken the nous: *Prak.* 23, 24, 80, 90, 93; *Prayer* 128; Sch. 4 on Ps 4.5 citing Clement, *Strom.* 5.28.2; and see *Thoughts* 16; Sch. 4 on Ps 138.11; *Eight Thoughts* 4.6; *Monks* 13. On demonic slander: Mt 8.31. Previous treatment of slander in a monastic setting, Basil, *Letter* 22.3.8; *Longer Rules* 25.

Epilogue

S2

The third century is finished.

S1

The third century, lacking ten chapters, is finished.

Century Four

S2

Century Four

S1

[Same as S2]

4.1

S2

God has planted for himself rational beings; his wisdom has grown further in them as she reads to them books of all kinds.

S1

God has planted for himself rational beings; his wisdom causes them to grow as she reads to them books of all kinds.

> On tree imagery, see 3.56. On planting, *Gn.* 44; cf. Jer 17.8 ("planted beside the waters"); Sch. 132 on Prv 11.30 (Grk. *phyetai*). Christ is Wisdom (refs. at 1.14), and here Wisdom "reads aloud" (Syr. *qr'*) books, evoking Lk 4.17–21, the reading of the messianic prediction of Is 61.1–2, announcing release and restoration of sight. Cf. also Mt 11.19, Lk 7.35, wisdom justified by her children; Sch. 210 on Prv 20.9a: Christ is "mother" of those needing milk and "father" in revealing (*apokalyptōn*) mysteries. On revealing, see 4.5 below. On writing and books, see 3.58; cf. Clement, *Protreptikos* 12 and *Strom.* 1.1.1ff.

4.2

S2

"What is known of God" is in those who are first in their coming-to-be; that which is unknowable of God is in his Christ.

304 EVAGRIUS OF PONTUS

S1

"What is knowable of God" is in those who are first in their coming-to-be; but his incomprehensibility is in his Christ.

Rom 1.19

This keph. begins a series, to 4.9, treating knowledge and inheritance. It also forms a close pair with 4.3, engaging with the fourth-century discussions of the Trinity that also encompass the teaching, shared with Origen, that all minds were fixed steadily upon God before their fall; the one unfallen mind becomes the human nature of Christ who retains that knowledge. Christ's divine nature is the *ousia* of the Son; thus he is both knowable as a created rational being and unknowable as a divine being. Evagrius reads Rom 1.19–20 as establishing that rational beings can know God's eternal power and divine nature through creation; then "what is knowable of God" is to be contrasted to idolatrous substitutes, as in 1QpHab 3–7 and throughout Rev. On knowability of God, see 1.35. On coming into being, 1.52 and next keph. On first and second beings, next keph. and 1.50.

4.3

S2

What is known of Christ is in those who are second in their coming-to-be. But that which is unknowable of him is in his father.

S1

What is knowable of Christ is in those who are second in their coming to be. But the incomprehensibility of Christ is in his father.

See previous keph. KNOWABLE: "faith is knowable," Clement, *Strom.* 2.4 and Aristotle, *Metaphysics* 1016b20.

4.4

S2

The heir of Christ is the one who knows the principles (*logoi*) of all things that have come to be after the first judgment.

S1

The heir of Christ is the one who has been made worthy to become a seer of things that have come to be.

On inheritance, see 1.18; 3.72 and Rom 8.17, amplified by knowledge of "intellections" of beings created after the first judgment (2.64), thus an exegesis of Gn 1. See also 4.8. Judgment in general: 1.82.

4.5

S2

Knowledge has been revealed to the gnostic, partly in the gnostic and partly in the one who does not know.

S1

For gnostics, knowledge is partly in the things that can be known and partly in things that cannot be known.

This keph. should be read closely with the others in this series (4.2–9), esp. the next keph. Cf. also 1.61. The Syr. verb *gly* represents Grk. *apokalyptō* or *epiphaneō*, "reveal": 4.40, 61 (S1); 6.27 (S1), 34 (S1), 64, 77 (S1); *Prak.* pr.8–9 (S2); *Gn.* 40, 44. Cf. *Thoughts* 28, angelic dreams "reveal the wisdom of the Lord." Sch. 2 on Prv 1.1, "The kingdom of Israel is spiritual knowledge containing the logoi concerning God, incorporeals and bodies, the judgment and the providence, or which reveals observation concerning the ethical, natural, and theological." See also Sch. 134 on Prv 13.22 quoting Rom 2.5, "revelation of the just judgment (*dikaiokrisias*) of God."

4.6

S2

Part of what is knowable comes to be in the pure, and part in the impure. That which comes to be in the first is called spiritual knowledge; and that which occurs in the second is named natural *theōria*.

306 EVAGRIUS OF PONTUS

S1

Of knowledge, a part is known to the pure, and a part to those who are impure. That which is known to the pure is called spiritual knowledge, and that which occurs in the second is called simple knowledge of nature.

See previous keph. On the contrast between spiritual knowledge and natural observation, see 2.3 and cf. 3.42, which identifies spiritual knowledge as a species of contemplation in general. At 4.30 the first term becomes "spiritual observation" (cf. S1: spiritual knowledge) = *Prak.* 32; *Gnos.* 47; Sch. 282a on Prv 30.4. On spiritual knowledge generally, 1.32; observation, *Prak.* 32. Cf. Origen, *pneumatikos*, cf. *Comm. on Jn* 13.15.91–97.

4.7

S2

He who placed "wisdom full of variety" in those who came to be also teaches those willing the skill, namely, how someone can easily become an observer.

S1

He who placed "wisdom full of variety" in beings—he was able to teach the diligent the skill, namely, how a person can easily become an observer.

Eph 3.10

On wisdom and Eph 3.10, see 2.2; SKILL, 1.3. *Logos* as *didaskalos*: see *Prak.* pr.2; the observer: 2.27; 3.15. EASILY, Syr. *dlílāith* (also = "quickly"), Grk. *radiōs*: 5.78; 6.76; *Thoughts* 16 and 27: the soul moved "easily" to the passions; 36 easier to purify an impure soul than to restore a purified one that has fallen. *Gn.* 5, 15 (the teacher should speak "easily" to pupils of the things known, e.g., *logoi*, laws, ways of life and occupations); 36 (*kosmikoi* and young men easily discouraged).

4.8

S2

"The co-heir of Christ" is the one who comes to be in the Unity and delights in *theōria* along with Christ.

S1

"The heir with Christ" is the one who comes to be in the Unity, as he delights with him in his *theōria*.

Rom 8.17

On heirship and coheirship, see 3.72; 4.4. On unity, 1.49; delight, 2.35.

4.9

S2

If the heir is one thing and the inheritance is another, the Logos is not the one who inherits; rather Christ [inherits] the Logos, which is the inheritance. Because anyone who thus inherits is united with the inheritance, but the God-Logos is free from the union.

S1

If the heir is one thing and the inheritance another, it is evident that the rational beings created in the image of the Son are themselves his heirs in relation to the Father.

Logos . . . Christ . . . Logos: could also be rendered as lowercase. This keph. refers to the training of "christs," not simply to Jesus Christ (*pace* Ramelli); see 3.1 and note. The God-Logos was not free from the union with Jesus Christ, but it is free of union with christs who become coheirs with Christ, who are united in a way Christ was not. Two scripture verses lie behind the argument: Phil 2.6–11 and Rom 8.13. On heirship and coheirship, see previous keph. and 3.72. On resemblance to the divine after being taught by the *gnōstikos*: *Gn.* 50 image/archetype and Plotinus, *Enneads* 6.4.10; 1.6.9. Cf. Origen, *Comm. on Jn* 6 etc.; Eusebius, *Demonstration of the Gospel* 4.16. Union: ḥwid', nowhere else used in the *KG*.

4.10

S2

Of the writers about true teachings, some have fallen from the first *theōria* of nature, others have fallen from the second [*theōria*], and still others have stumbled from the Holy Trinity.

S1

Of the writers about erroneous teachings ... [rest the same as S2]

The sequence of the three kinds of WRITERS ABOUT TRUE TEACHINGS seems out of order: one would expect Trinity, first, then second. The solution may lie in the Syriac verb choices. The first two are HAVE FALLEN, Syr. *npl*, possibly from Grk. *-piptō*, whereas the third, HAVE STUMBLED, Syr. *šrʿ*, possibly Grk. *ptaiō* (Jas 2.9; 3.2; 2 Pt 1.10 Peshitta; *Prak.* 33 Syr. *šrʿtʾ* = Grk. *paraptōmatōn*). The original Greek cannot be recovered, but a distinction appears to underlie the two classes of writers. The first, treating first and second natural observations, would correspond to writers about first principles (e.g., Anaximander, Parmenides) and writers about the material world (e.g., Thales, Aristotle; some authors employ both first and second observation). The other class is qualitatively different, pertaining to stumbling in Trinitarian doctrine. One might consider Arius and his successors as the primary examples of those who do not understand the Trinity, but dualists are those who have fallen from the *theōria* of nature. True teaching: 4.28, 75; 6.1; cf. Clement of Alexandria, *Strom.* 6.15.124.3; 6.16.147.2; 7.2.11.3; 7.15.89.1. Cf. false teaching: *KG* 4.25, 53; 5.38.

4.11

S2

If God is known by means of bodily and bodiless nature—for both *theōriai* vivify rational beings—then well has it been said that God "is known in the midst of the two living beings."

S1

If God is known between spiritual nature and corporeal nature—for the *theōria* of both ranks vivifies rational beings—then well has it been said to the prophet that God is "known in the midst of the two living beings."

Hb 3.2

Hb 3.2 LXX, "I have understood the report of you and was amazed; in the middle of two living beings you will be known." This text was understood by third-century Christian interpreters as a Trinitarian reference, where the Son and Holy Spirit are lesser beings than God. The "living beings" are angels in the earlier Greek exegetical tradition, cf. Clement, *Paidagogos* 1.7 and especially Origen *First Principles* 1.3.4, where the "living beings" of the text are angels/the Son and Holy Spirit. In the latter, Origen states that his interpretation comes from "my [anonymous] Jewish teacher." Cf. Jerome, *Letter* 61.2 on this, Origen's "heretical" teaching. And cf. Origen *On Prayer* 14.4. Modifying the earlier Alexandrian interpretive tradition through Gregory of Nazianzus, *Paschal Oration* (*Or.* 45.1), Evagrius here corrects the third-century interpretation of the Habakkuk text to make it fit fourth-century teaching, such that "you" is now Christ, alluding to "Christ the true God," who is both the incorporeal "throne of God" and whose "throne is the incorporeal nature" (Sch. 2 on Ps 9.5, where Christ is formed/formless).

4.12

Greek

An intelligible circumcision is a voluntary casting off of passions for the knowledge of God.

Furrer-Pilliod 2000, p. 179 A.π.172

St. Paul called the intellectual cutting-away of the impassioned thoughts "the. circumcision of the hidden Jew."

Thoughts 35 (Géhin 1998, p. 276)

S2

The intelligible circumcision is a voluntary separation from the passions; it is for the knowledge of God.

S1

Spiritual circumcision is a separation from the passions which occurs by means of good will for the knowledge of God.

cf. Rom 2.29

This mental circumcision is a counterpart to the bodily kind: *Prak.* 35; it is discussed further at 4.14. On circumcision, see 5.83 (seven); 6.6, 7 (eighth day), 66; *Prak.* pr.6; 29; *Vices* 2 (chastity a circumcision of thoughts); *Letter* 4.5 (labor circumcises passions). Origen, *Hom. on Josh* 26.2 discusses the stone knife/ sword that is the word of God by which Jesus effects a second circumcision that

310 EVAGRIUS OF PONTUS

circumcises from every uncleanness, cuts back impurities, separates vices from those who hear, and removes each thing by which the strength of the mind (*vis mentis*) and its natural efficiency are covered over. VOLUNTARY SEPARATION: *KG* 3.83 ("voluntary good"). The circumcision/renewal of the seventh day pertains to the (sabbath-) rest of the soul within nature (4.44); the circumcision on the eighth day, the eschaton, is circumcision/renewal in Christ (6.7). Circumcision seems to be understood here as an unveiling instead of a *pars pro toto* sacrifice; it is the beginning of the revelation of God; cf. Gn 38 on Judah and Tamar, and Paul's understanding in 2 Cor 1.22, and 5.5, and Eph 1.14.

4.13

S2

Those who "have shared flesh and blood are children," but everyone who is a child is neither good nor bad. But rightly do they say that human beings are intermediaries between angels and demons.

S1

Those who "have shared in flesh and blood are children." But every child who is young is neither perfectly good nor bad. Well do they say that human beings are intermediates between angels and demons.

Heb 2.14

This keph. forms a pair with 4.15, and has a strong parallel in Sch. 16 on Prv 1.32 ("Just as infants are placed between the just and the unjust, so are all men placed between angels and demons, without either being demons or bearing the title of angels, until the consummation of the age."). On development of the human, eventually to the life of angels or demons, see 3.76. For human beings as "those who share in flesh and blood" cf. Sch. 287b on Prv 30.9; Sch. 8 on Eccl 2.10; *Letter on Faith* 15, 24.

4.14

S2

Just as the pledge of bodies is a small part of the body, so also the pledge that is in [types of] knowledge is a certain part of the knowledge of beings.

S1

Just as the pledge that is in bodies is a small part of the body, so also the pledge that is in [types of] knowledge is a small part of the knowledge of beings.

This keph. applies the theme of pledge (Syr. *rhbon*; Grk. *arrabōn*) to circumcision, at 4.12, and stands in contrast to 1 Cor 1.22, 5.5, which discusses "the pledge of the spirit." Cf. John Chrysostom, *Hom. on 2 Cor* PG 61:418 (Jews have circumcision; Christians have the pledge of the Spirit). On the pledge of the Holy Spirit: Cyril of Jerusalem, *Catechesis* 1.2, Gregory of Nazianzus, *Or.* 14.14; Origen, *Comm. on Eph* 1.14; Didymus, *Trinity* 2.1 "the *arrabōn* of eternal (*aidios*) goods"; on the pledge of a "prize": Origen, *Sel. on Job* 40.7; Gregory of Naz., *Or.* 34.4; cf. Clement, *Paidagogos* 1.6.

4.15

S2

If the whole world of human beings is a world of children, there will be a time when they will come to a full stature appropriate to the righteous or the unrighteous.

S1

If the whole world of human beings is a world of children, there will be a time when they will come to full stature, that which runs before the righteous or that runs before the unrighteous.

See 4.13. On world, see 1.70.

4.16

Greek

An only-begotten is he before whom another has not been born, and after whom another has not come into being.

Doctrina patrum de incarnatione verbi 33 (Diekamp 1907, p. 263)

312   EVAGRIUS OF PONTUS

S2

The only-begotten is he before whom no other has been born, and after whom no one.

S1

The only-begotten is he before whom no other has been born, and after him also no other.

> This keph. forms a pair with 4.20; for unique see also 1.12; 4.1. For a similar division, see next keph.

4.17

S2

It is said that "on high" is where knowledge brings those who possess it; but "below" where ignorance [brings] those who possess it.

S1

The ascent of knowledge is called "on high," but the descent of ignorance, "below."

cf. Jn 8.23

> 1 Cor 15.34. On vertical position, see 2.68. Cf. Sch. 10 on Ps 17.17–18, "Here we learn that before the visit of our savior the demons were stronger, but now we are superiors, whom Christ gave 'to trample down snakes and scorpions and over every power of the enemy'" (Lk 10.19 and Ps 90.13).

4.18

S2

The intelligible anointing is the spiritual knowledge of the Holy Unity. And a christ is he who is united to this knowledge. And if this is so, a christ is not the word at first, just as he who is anointed is not god at first, but rather the former (christ) is anointed because of the latter (word), and the latter (word), because of the former (christ), is God.

KEPHALAIA GNOSTIKA   313

S1

The intelligible anointing is the knowledge of the holy unity, and Christ the Lord is the teacher of this to the rational beings.

This keph. forms a pair with 4.21. On "christ" used of those who become christs, and the distinction between Christ and Word, see 3.1. Cf. 4.21. On anointing, see 4.21 (= Sch. 7 on Ps 44.8); *Prak.* 100; *Eulogius* 23 (*gnōstikos* anoints students). Evagrius also evokes the scriptural theme of anointment for battle against the enemies of God; cf. 4 Kingdoms/2 Kings 9.1–10, the anointment of Jehu against Ahab and Jezebel. See also 3.43 on oil. BUT RATHER . . . IS GOD: quoted in Anathema 8 of 553 against Origen, but grammatical referents to "former" and "latter" in the anathema do not correspond to their meaning in the keph. Likely, the anathema is quoting here another source that has itself quoted or used *KG* 4.18. See 2.17, 78 on other parallels with the anathemas. Cf. Gregory of Nazienzus, *Or.* 10.35; 30.21; Origen, *First Principles* 2.6, where Christ and "the others" (that is, the baptized and chrismated Christian faithful) are "anointed." On the holy oil as "essential knowledge" of God cf. Sch. 11 on Ps 88.21.

4.19

Greek

For number is of quantity, but quantity is connected to bodily nature. Therefore number is of bodily nature.

Letter on Faith 7 (Gribomont 1983, p. 88)

S2

One is a number of quantity, but quantity is [linked] with bodily nature. Number, therefore, is of natural *theōria* of second things.

S1

One by number is said to concern quantity, and to be bestowed upon bodily nature. Thus number pertains to natural *theōria* of second things.

The Grk. conclusion, BODILY NATURE, becomes here NATURAL THEŌRIA OF SECOND THINGS, the latter being the term preferred in the *KG* for bodily nature;

see 2.2. Each version fits its context, so one cannot determine on the basis of this keph. whether the *Letter on Faith* precedes the *KG* or vice versa. On number, see 1.7. Unlike most ancient texts discussing numbers and number symbolism, where one is not treated as a number, this keph. considers one *qua* number, better expressed in S1's translation than S2's.

4.20

Greek

A firstborn is one before whom another has not been born, and with whom others have not come into being.

Furrer-Pilliod 2000, p. 174 A.π.92

S2

The firstborn is he before whom another was not born, but after whom others have.

S1

[Same as S2]

See 4.16. The second half of the Greek version conflicts with both S1 and S2. The phrase *meth' hou ou gegonasin* was likely misread by a scribe as *meth' hon gegonasin*.

4.21

Greek

The entire power of the heavens is anointed with the *theōria* of things that have come into being. But Christ has been anointed beyond all, even his participants, therefore he has been anointed with the knowledge of the monad. Wherefore Christ alone is said to be seated at the right hand of the Father. I mean Christ, the Word with God, the Lord who appears.

Rondeau 2021, Sch. 7 on Ps 44.8

KEPHALAIA GNOSTIKA 315

S2

The anointing makes known either knowledge of the unity or it points out the *theōria* of beings. But if Christ is anointed more than his companions, it is clear that he is anointed with knowledge of the unity. Because of this, he alone is said to be "seated at the right" of his Father; the right that here makes known, according to the law of *gnōstikoi*, the union and the unity.

S1

The anointing is either a mark of knowledge of the unity or a sign of the *theōria* of beings.

cf. Mk 16.19 (S2/Greek); Eph 1.20, Col 3.1, Heb 10.12; Ps 44.8
This keph. forms a pair with 4.18; the latter treats rational beings who become christ, whereas this one treats Christ himself. On the right (hand), see 2.12. I MEAN CHRIST: the somewhat labored phrase shows the importance Evagrius placed on distinguishing between the Christ the incarnate Logos, and those who become christ. See 3.1; 4.18.

4.22

S2

Just as those who offer symbolic sacrifices to God burn up the beast-like movements of the soul by means of the virtues, so also those who sacrifice to demons destroy the natural activities of the soul by means of the vices.

S1

[Same as S2]

Here begins a series of keph. that interpret priestly symbols: sacrifice (4.22); the temple oil-lamp (4.25); the unleavened bread (4.28); the lobe of the liver (4.32); the sacrificial fat (4.36); the turban (4.48); the petalon (4.52); the ephod (4.56); the propitiatory (4.63); the pectoral (4.66); the coat (4.69); the priestly trousers (4.72); the ephod (4.75); and the belt (4.79). Evagrius draws from Clement of Alexandria, *Stromateis* 5; Origen, e.g., *Hom. on Lv, Contra Celsum* 7–8; Philo, *Life of Moses* 2.135, *Special Laws* 1.85–95, etc. On sacrifice, see 4.45; 5.53; Sch. 5 on Ps 4.6 ("A sacrifice of justice is *apatheia* of the rational soul offered to God"). He frequently associates sacrifice with a broken spirit (following David, Ps 50.19): Sch.

316   EVAGRIUS OF PONTUS

222 on Prv 21.3; Sch. 5 on Ps 26.6; Sch. 11 on Ps 33.19; Sch. 6 on Ps 49.14; Sch. 4 on Ps 95.8. See also 2.57 on altars. Cf. sacrifice to demons, e.g., Porphyry, *Letter to Anebo*; *On Abstinence* 2; Iamblichus, *Pythagorean Way of Life* 58. In favor of sacrifice to demons: Evagrius' contemporary Julian the emperor and contemporary practice in Alexandria at the Serapeum; cf. Rufinus, *Church History* 2.19.

4.23

S2

Moses and Elijah are not the Kingdom of God. If the one (Moses) is *theōria*, but the other (Elijah) is the saints, then how, when our Savior promised to the disciples that he would show them the kingdom of God, did he show them himself with a spiritual body, with Moses and Elijah, on the mountain?

S1

Moses and Elijah are not the kingdom of God because the one is a sign of the *theōria* of natural beings but the other, of holy men.

cf. Mt 17.1–8

On the spiritual body see 1.11, 90; 3.25; 4.24; 6.23, 47, 57–58. On bodies in general, see 1.11. On the Kingdom of God: *Prak.* 2–3 and notes ad loc. On the Transfiguration, see 4.41; cf. 2.90 (two luminaries); cf. Origen, *Comm. on Mt* 12.42. On Moses, see *Gn.* 46. This association of Moses with natural (physical) observation is echoed by *Prak.* 38, which refers to *The Physics* by Moses. On mountains, see 5.6 (Zion), 21 (Zion), 40 (intelligible), 88 (Zion). The identification of the mountain of the Transfiguration with Tabor is attested by commentaries on Ps 88.13 by Eusebius (*Comm. on Ps* PG 23:1092) and Evagrius, Sch. 8 on Ps 88.13 (earlier scholarship attributes this text to Origen). On Tabor cf. Origen, *Comm. on Jn* 2.12.87, which quotes the Gospel to the Hebrews. On the mountain as knowledge of God or Christ, 5.40.

4.24

Greek

A "firstborn from the dead" is he who rose from the dead, and was the first to have had a spiritual body.

Furrer-Pilliod 2000, p. 178 A.π.153

KEPHALAIA GNOSTIKA 317

S2

The "firstborn from among the dead" is he who arose from the dead, and was the first to clothe [himself with] a spiritual body.

S1

[Same start as S2] ... from the dead, as he is clothed in a spiritual body.

Col 1.18; Rev 1.5

Cf. 1 Cor 15.4, 23, 44, 53–54. On the verb "clothe" cf. 1 Cor 15.49. On being clothed with a spiritual body, see 1.90; S1 tends to insert "clothe" in his translation: 3.25, 40; 4.67; 6.34.

4.25

S2

Just as the light that shines in holy temples is a symbol of spiritual knowledge, so also that (light) in the house of idols is the sign of false teachings and reasons (*logoi*). And the first is nourished by the oil of holy love, but the second by means of the worldly love that loves the world and the things that are in it.

S1

Just as the light that shines in holy temples is a sign of spiritual knowledge, so also the lights that shine in shrines of idols are a sign of false knowledge. And the light from the first is nourished by means of the oil of love, but the second from the love of the vanity of this world.

Two construals of temple (Grk. *naos/hierōn*), Clement, *Strom.* 7.5: "a temple is large, as a church, but small, as a human being." LIGHT: cf. Gregory of Nazianzus, *Or.* 45.2, baptizands carrying torches signifying divine light. Temple of idols (*eidōleion*): 1 Cor 8.10; and Cyril of Jerusalem, *Catechesis* 19.8. To this point, numerous cases of temple imagery have been introduced, but only now has the temple itself been discussed. See 5.84; 6.49; *Gn.* 24; Sch. 375 on Prv 31.18: "The Lamp is the pure nous, filled with spiritual observations."; Origen, *Hom. on Lv* 13.2, 4–5, on the oil and lamp of love in the temple of the soul. OIL: 3.43. WORLDLY LOVE: 1 Jn 2.15.

318 EVAGRIUS OF PONTUS

4.26

S2

If on the third day Christ "is finished," and on the day before he who was gathering the fragments of wood in the desert was burned, then it is clear that today is [the day] called Friday, on which, "at the eleventh hour," the nations have been called by our Savior to eternal life.

S1

[Same as S2 with very minor differences]

Mt 20.6; Lk 13.32; cf. Nm 15.32–36
Nm 15.32–36 tells of a man who gathered wood on the Sabbath, but says that for his sin he was stoned, not burned. On days and years as eschatological allegory, see 1.90. The wood that is burned symbolizes the coming "fiery" purification of reasoning natures (Sch. 18 on Ps 36.20; cf. Sch. 4 on Ps 91.8; Sch. 2 on Ps 96.3; Sch. 63 on Ps 118.140; Sch. 6 on Ps 139.11). Regarding the nations, see 6.3, 27, 71.

4.27

S2

The symbol that was seen by the baptizer of the baptized—is it in the first *theōria*, or in the second, or in the third? And again, if the Unity can be stamped by an image like this, there is yet a danger about this [symbol], if it is made known openly. But you will examine this symbol among the *gnōstikoi*.

S1

The image of the dove that was visible over the Jordan to the baptizer is a witness to the baptized, that he is the son of the Most High.

cf. Jn 1.32–34
On natural observation, see 2.2. The first observation is spiritual; the second and third, material (3.21). The question here is: under which type of observation was the dove seen by John at the baptism of Christ? (Mt 3.16; Mk 1.10; Lk 3.22; Jn 1.32). DOVE: cf. *Thoughts* 29 and *Reflections* 1.5, where Christ possesses divinity signified by the dove. For related examination of symbols among the

KEPHALAIA GNOSTIKA 319

gnōstikoi, cf. *Gn.* 34–36 and 42–43. Cf. Ramelli 2015, p. 211, citing Sebastian Brock's suggested emendation from *ttrṣ* to *ttbḥn.*

4.28

Greek

Intelligible unleavened bread is a best state of the rational soul, established from pure virtues and true teachings.

Furrer-Pilliod 2000, p. 85 A.α.185

S2

The intelligible unleavened bread is the state of the rational soul that is established from pure virtues and true teachings.

S1

The unleavened bread of the spirit is the state of the rational soul which is established from pure virtues and from true knowledge.

cf. Ex 29.2

Also cf. Gn 18.6. On true teachings, see 4.10. S1 has BREAD in the singular; S2, following the Grk., in the plural. Intelligible azymes: Origen, *Comm. on Jn*, 13.33; *Comm. on Mt* 12.5; *Hom. on Jer* 12.13.

4.29

S2

Just as, if the earth were destroyed, the night would not exist on the face of the firmament, so also when evil is removed, there will no longer be ignorance among rational beings. For ignorance is the shadow of evil in which those who, as if walking around in the night, are illumined by the oil of Christ and see the stars, according to the knowledge that they have been made worthy to receive from him. And even "the stars will fall" for them too if they do not quickly turn back again toward "the sun of righteousness."

320 EVAGRIUS OF PONTUS

S1

Just as if the earth should be taken away from before the sun, the night would not fall on the face of the firmament; so also when the laxity of the rational beings is completely removed, then ignorance will no longer exist.

> Mt 24.29 (S2); Mal 3.20 (S2)
>
> This keph. treats the eschaton, the destruction of the world, and the creation of the world to come. The hypothetical scenario envisions what would happen if the earth were removed, i.e., the sun would illuminate everything, since there is no earth, necessary for any night. See below, 4.31, on eclipses; stars: 3.37. The loss of earth, and reign of the "sun of justice" over the stars, might be likened to the waters being swept into the great ocean, discussed in the *Letter to Melania* 28–30. Removal of ignorance: 3.68 above. Our STARS WILL FALL FOR THEM could be translated "upon," "against," or "on account of" them—those who do not progress from their observation of the "stars" by turning to the sun itself. *Monks* 124 and Sch. 249 on Prv 22.28, vs. denial that the Holy Spirit is divine. On oil, see 3.43; *Virgin* 55, "oil in her vessels."

4.30

S2

If the "wealth of God" which is to come is the spiritual *theōria* of the worlds that will be, those who limit the kingdom of heaven to the palate and the stomach will be ashamed.

S1

If the "wealth of God," that which is to come, is the spiritual knowledge that is in it, those who limit the kingdom of heaven to the palate and to the stomach will be ashamed.

> cf. Rom 11.33
>
> WEALTH: 4.38; Sch. 42 on Eccl 5.17–19; and on mistaken exegesis of kingdom as a material banquet: Origen, *First Principles* 2.11.2–3; *Comm. on Mt* 17.35. Wealth is a symbol of spiritual knowledge: Sch. 2 on Ps 110.3; Sch. 4 on Ps 64.10, and 1 Cor 1.5: "In all things you are made wealthy [. . .] in all knowledge." Cf. Clement, *Who Is the Rich Man* 19. On economic wealth, see *Prak.* 18; wealth of the soul, 2.8. On the kingdom of heaven, see *Prak.* 2.

4.31

Greek

Just as the hidden star is shown to be higher than the star that hides it, so also in the coming aeon the more gentle will be discovered to be more exalted than the less gentle.

Mosc. 425, sixteenth century (Hausherr 1939, p. 230)

S2

Just as a star that is eclipsed in the overshadowing of another is higher than it, so also the one who is much humbler than another will be found more exalted than he in the world to come.

S1

Just as a star that is hidden by the occultation of another is higher than it, so also the one who is much humbler than another will be found higher than he in the world to come.

On eclipses, see also 4.29 (the shadow of the earth); cf. 3.37. Righteous as stars: Dn 12.3; Humility and exaltation: Lk 1.52.

4.32

Greek

A lobe of a liver is the first thought, established from the desiring part of the soul.

Furrer-Pilliod 2000, p. 145 A.λ.43

S2

The lobe of the liver is the first tempting thought, established from the desiring part of the soul.

S1

[Same as S2]

322 EVAGRIUS OF PONTUS

cf. Ex 29.13

Lobe of the liver treated also at 4.36; see also Galen, *Anatomical Procedures* 6.8. Origen on the levitical lobe of the liver: concupiscence (epithumia); anger (*thumos*) *Hom. on Lv* 3.5 and 5.12.4. Thought, Grk. *noēma* (not *logismos*).

4.33

Greek

Merciless demons receive the merciless after death, but the more inhuman of the [demons] receive the more merciless. But if this is so, then it has escaped their attention what kinds of demons encounter those who cause themselves to depart, for there is a saying, "None of those departing due to the will of God will be handed over to such demons."

Mosc. 425, sixteenth century (Hausherr 1939, pp. 230–231)

S2

Merciless demons receive those who are merciless after their death. But [demons] even more evil than they receive those who are more merciless. And if this is so, it has escaped the attention of those who cause their soul to leave the body, how these demons receive them after their death. There is even a saying, "None of those who leave the body by the will of God will be handed to demons such as these."

S1

Merciless demons receive those who are merciless. Demons more evil than they receive those who are even less merciful. And if this so, it escapes the attention of those who kill themselves that the most demonic demons of all receive them.

On mercy, see 1.40. The saying is not attested elsewhere. Merciless "subterranean demons," who are frightening even to other demons whom they torture: Sch. 1 on Ps 55.3; Sch. 5 on Ps 62.11; Sch. 9 on Ps 68.15; Sch. 8 on Ps 70.20; Sch. 8 on Ps 103.9; Sch. 5 on Ps 118.7; Sch. 2 on Ps 134.6; cf. *Prayer* 104. On suicide, see 4.70, 76, 85 (S1); *Prak.* 52.

KEPHALAIA GNOSTIKA 323

4.34

Greek

It is not possible, in the [world] to come, for someone to flee his own prison; for "he will not escape from there," it says, "without paying off the suffering of the last penny."

Vat. gr. 2028, tenth/eleventh century (Géhin 1996, p. 64)

S2

In the world to come no one will be able to escape the prison into which he has fallen; for it is said, "You will not depart from there until you pay the last penny," which is a small suffering.

S1

In the world to come no one is able to escape the prison into which he has fallen, for it is written, "You shall not depart from there until you pay the last penny," for it is the recompense for a small failing.

Mt 5.26; Lk 12.59

On "prison-house," Grk. *phylakē*, see Sch. 351 on Prv 28.17; Sch. 33 on Eccl 4 "the prison-house (*oikos desmiōn*) is the sensible world (*kosmos*) to which each is attached by the chains of his own sins"; on chains (*schoinia tōn daimōnōn*), cf. Sch. 25 on Ps 118.61. For the interpretation of Mt 5.26 and "eternal" punishment, drawn upon by Evagrius, see Origen, *Comm. on Rom* 5.2.170–176; 10.43.76–78.

4.35

S2

If a gift of languages is a gift of the Spirit, and the demons are deprived of this gift, then they do not speak in languages. But they say that they are taught the languages of humans from training. And it is no wonder if they have this by receptivity, inasmuch as the constitution of the world is coextensive with their constitution. Someone said that their languages are also different for the same reason that humans' [languages are different]. Some say that also there are among them languages of the ancient ones, so that those who contest against the Hebrews

324 EVAGRIUS OF PONTUS

use the Hebrew languages, those who are among Greeks speak in the Greek language, and likewise for the rest.

S1

If the gift of languages is the gift of the Holy Spirit, it is evident that demons lack this, for they do not speak in languages; and also no demon knows all languages. But they train themselves in various languages, because they are ancient beings in the world.

> Cf. 1 Cor 13.1; and Pentecost, Ac 2.4–13. On languages, see 4.54; 6.3. For demons' persuasive power in speaking with humans: Porphyry, *On Abstinence* 2.39; demonic speech in Egypt: Athanasius, *Festal Letter* 42; *Life of Anthony* 23.5. See also Sch. 3 on Ps 54.10 (confusion of languages at Babel slowed evildoing). COEXTENSIVE WITH THEIR CONSTITUTION: 4.49; *Prak.* 3.

4.36

Greek

Intelligible fat is the thickness that accumulates in the ruling part because of evil.

> Furrer-Pilliod 2000, p. 189 A.σ.96

S2

Intelligible fat is the dullness that descends upon the ruling faculty because of wickedness.

S1

[Same as S2]

Ex 29.13

> Ex 29.13 is treated also at 4.32. Origen, *Hom. on Lv* 5.4: an inner quality of corruption to be offered on the fire of an altar. On "seep" (Grk. *episumbainō*, also translatable as "insinuate") see *Prak.* 10; *Gn.* 45. The term DULLNESS is the same for THICKNESS; see references relevant to bodies at 1.11.

4.37

S2

They say that among the animals, some draw breath from outside and [others] of them from the inside, and others of them from round about the surrounding area, and others of them from all sides. And they say that those [who breathe] from the outside are human beings and all those who have lungs, but from within, fish and all whose throat is straight. Those who draw breath from round about with the flat of their wings are bees; and from all sides, demons and all those rational ones who possess bodies of air.

S1

Among the animals, some draw breath from outside, and for others their breath is moved from within; those who breathe from the outside live in the air, but those who breathe from the inside live in the water.

THEY SAY: prior philosophical tradition; cf. *Prak.* 89. Theories on breathing go back to Aristotle, who wrote a treatise *On Breathing* (the second part of *On Youth and Old Age, on Life and Death, on Breathing*), and dealt with the topic in other contexts: *On the Soul* 3 (421a); *Sense and the Sensible* 5; *History of Animals* 4 (534b); *Parts of Animals* 2 (659b), frequently preserving earlier theories. Aristotle divides classes of animals into those with lungs (e.g., *On Breathing* 7), those with gills (fish, e.g., *On Breathing* 9), and those with neither (e.g., bees and insects, *On Breathing* 15). Without the Greek, it is difficult to tell what is intended by the distinction made here at 4.37 between the third and fourth classes, but the association of the final group with demons seems uniquely Christian. The concept of breathing is revisited at 4.67. On the predominance of air and anger in demons see 1.68. Origen, *Contra Celsum* 7.6: demons enjoy odors and sacrifices via the air. Porphyry answered Origen regarding demonic respiration of sacrifices: *On Abstinence* 2.36–43; cf. *Letter to Anebo* 5.4.

4.38

Greek

In the coming aeon, the angry human being will not be numbered among the angels, nor will he be entrusted with any rule. Neither, due to passion, will he

326 EVAGRIUS OF PONTUS

behold; and he will easily bridle at the rulers; and he will fall away from the angelic state, and he will lead them into dangers.

Vat. gr. 2028, tenth/eleventh century (Géhin 1996, pp. 64–65)

S2

In the world to come, the angry man will neither be numbered with the angels nor entrusted with rulership. For because of passion he does not see and he is easily irritated by those whom he leads, and he falls from vision and he leads them into danger. But these two [things] are alien to the angelic order.

S1

In the world to come, the angry person is not numbered with the angels, nor is he granted authority, because anger is foreign to angelic conduct.

On the world to come, see 1.11. Limited number of intelligible beings of the first creation: Origen, *First Principles* 1.5–6. On bridling see *Masters and Disciples* 32 (a doctor should heal, not bridle, those unwillingly sick). Rulership: 2.74; 4.51, 65 (life and death rule); 6.24 (rulership over five or ten cities); Heb 2.5: angelic rule in the coming age; Origen, *First Principles* 3.3. On the classical model of rulership (and Evagrius' counterposition), see 4.51. On what happens to the angry, see *Letter* 56.4 (become demonic). The angelic state (Grk. *katastasis*) is one of many; see *Prak.* 12.

4.39

S2

If in the worlds to come God shows his wealth to rational beings, it is evident that he will do this in those who follow the one who is coming, because before this, rational beings are unable to receive holy wealth.

S1

If in the world to come God shows his wealth to rational beings, it is evident that in this world they grasp a part of it.

ONE WHO IS COMING: Mt 3.11; Rev 1.8. On the wealth of God, see 4.30. The act of being able to receive the wealth of God requires humans to become coheirs with Christ and receive an inheritance: Rom 8.17; 1 Cor 6.9; Eph 2.7. HOLY WEALTH as treasure in heaven, Mt 6.20; also "Holy Spirit and fire," Ac 2.2–4.

4.40

Greek

A "key of the kingdom of the heavens" is the spiritual gift partially revealing the reasons concerning the practical, the natural, and the theological.

Furrer-Pilliod 2000, p. 140 A.к.60

S2

The "key of the kingdom of heaven" is the gift of the Spirit that little by little reveals the reasons (*logoi*) of practice and of nature, and of the words about God.

S1

The "key of the kingdom of heaven" is a gift of the Spirit that reveals to the mind the *theōria* of spiritual practice and the variety that is in natures, and the words concerning the Godhead.

Mt 16.19

Key: Mt 16.19; gift of the Spirit: Ac 2.2–4 and 1 Cor 12; Rom 4.1; LITTLE BY LITTLE: Josh 13.6; Ex 23.30; 33.2; Dt 11.23. Kingdom of heaven: *Prak.* 2, "apatheia of the soul together with true knowledge of beings." See also *Gn.* 12–15. Origen on kingdom of heaven: *Comm. on Mt* 13.31. The trio practice, nature, and *theologikē* recurs in the GT; see *Prak.* 1.

4.41

S2

Before his coming, Christ showed an angelic body to human beings, and he has not shown to the last [human beings] the body that he now has. But he has revealed to them that which they will have.

328 EVAGRIUS OF PONTUS

S1

Christ before his coming appeared to human beings with various images. But in his coming he was made visible to them in the truth of their bodies.

Before his birth, Christ appears to Moses, Gn 17.1, 18.1; as an angel to Jacob, Gn 32.22–31; his present body is unknown to "the last," i.e., humans; but humans saw his body on Mt. Tabor (cf. 4.23) and after the resurrection. Origen, *Comm. on Mt* 12.42.

4.42

S2

The promise of the hundredfold is the *theōria* of beings, but eternal life is the knowledge of the Holy Trinity: "This is indeed eternal life, that they will know you, the only true God."

S1

The payment of the hundredfold which our Lord in his gospel promised is the *theōria* of beings, but eternal life is the *theōria* of the Holy Trinity, as it is written, "This is eternal life, that they should know even you the only true God and the one whom you sent, Jesus Christ."

cf. Mt 19.29; Jn 17.3

HUNDREDFOLD points directly to the grain that fell on good soil, and secondarily to the number of keph. in a century; cf. *On Prayer* (pref.). Aeonic life as knowledge, cf. Origen, *Comm. on Rom* 5.10.

4.43

S2

Christ appeared upon the ladder to Jacob. If he is the one who symbolizes natural *theōria*, the image of the ladder makes known the path of practice; but if he makes known the knowledge of the Unity, the ladder is a symbol of all the worlds.

KEPHALAIA GNOSTIKA 329

S1

The ladder that appeared to Jacob, and whose top extended to the heavens, and upon which the Lord was placed, has in it a sign of the two *theōriai*: the ascent of purity, and the virtue of knowledge.

cf. Gn 28.12–13

Levels of knowledge and angelic ranks: Clement, *Excerpts from Theodotus* 10–11 (frags. 5–6). On the ladder, cf. *Disc.* 192: "Ladder of heaven is the revelation of the mysteries of God, advancing through which the mind is raised rung by rung to God." PATH OF PRACTICE: cf. *Prak.* 91, "paths of the monks." On KNOWLEDGE OF THE UNITY, see 1.77; *Prak.* 56, cf. Plato, *Theaetetus* 176b. On WORLDS, see 1.11.

4.44

Greek

A sabbath is the rest of the rational soul, according to which it naturally does not overstep the boundaries of nature.

Furrer-Pilliod 2000, p. 189 A.σ.97

S2

The sabbath is the stillness of the rational soul, in which it is natural that it not transgress the limits of nature.

S1

The sabbath is the stillness of the rational soul, in which it is natural that it not transgress the limits of nature.

Gn 2.3; Ex 20.8–11; Mt 12.12; Heb 4.9–10. Sch. 3 on Ps 114.7, "those turning back to the first place." *KG* 1.90, days and years; 5.8 and 6.66 for significance of the sixth, seventh, and eighth day/year. For the seventh and eighth, cf. *Reflections* 6; Sch. 76 on Ps 118.164.

330   EVAGRIUS OF PONTUS

4.45

S2

It is not those who worship them but those who sacrifice to them whom the divine powers cast away; and we are plainly taught this in Judges, by means of Manoah.

S1

The holy powers reject those who sacrifice to them; they teach that every sacrifice should be offered to the Lord, as it was said to Gideon and Manoah.

cf. Jgs 6.19–24 (S1); cf. Jgs 13.15–21

Evagrius seems to understand the unnamed angel in Judges 13 as another example of the Son's pre-incarnation appearance as an angel; cf. 4.41, 4.43. Note S1's broader application of this principle to Gideon. On WORSHIP (*sged* = bow down, make *proskynesis*), see 2.53; SACRIFICE, 4.22. Jacob foresees Samson: Origen, *Comm. on Jn* 1.23.

4.46

Greek

Four corners disclose the four elements, and the visible vessel signals the thicker cosmos, and the different animals are the symbols of the states of human beings.

Wolf 1722, 3:167–168

S2

The four corners make known the four elements, and the vessel that was seen makes known the thick world, and the various animals are symbols of the ranks of human beings—and this is what was seen upon the roof by Peter.

S1

The four corners make known a sign of the four elements, and the vessel that was seen is a sign of the thickness of this world, and the animals of every kind are a sign of the ranks of human beings.

KEPHALAIA GNOSTIKA 331

cf. Ac 10.11–16

CORNERS: the Grk. *archai* of Ac 10.11. The Greek fragment is a scholion on Acts, the only one known to be attributed to Evagrius from that New Testament book. Cf. Sch. 379 on Prv 31.24: "The sheet that appeared to Peter on the roof is a symbol of the sensible world, and the four animals that it contains reveal the diverse customs of human beings, purified by the cross of Christ." Origen: animals represent human beings; *Hom. on Lv* 7.4. On THE FOUR ELEMENTS, see 1.29. On state see 6.21 (Grk. *hexis*); *Prak.* 12 (Grk. *katastasis*).

4.47

S2

Against those who are approaching obscure matters and wish to write about them there fights a demon of anger, night and day—who is accustomed to blind thought and to deprive it of spiritual *theōria*.

S1

With those who are writing about subtle spiritual symbols, a demon of anger fights, night and day—who is accustomed to blind the thought and to deprive it of spiritual *theōria*.

Demon of anger, 1.68, 3.34, 5.11; *Prak.* 20–26; *Gn.* 5. Anger blinds: 5.27. Obscure matters: Nm 12; 1 Cor 13.12; Clement, *Strom.* 7.12; Origen, *Contra Celsum* 6.22.

4.48

S2

The intelligible turban is unbending faith, which is not receptive to fear.

S1

The crown of the priesthood is unbending faith, which is always unreceptive of the terror of fear.

cf. Lv 8.9; cf. Ex 28.4

332 EVAGRIUS OF PONTUS

The long series of "intelligible X" keph., which started with 3.44, here turns to priestly clothing and equipment: 4.48 (turban, this keph.), 52 (leaf), 56 (ephod), 66 (pectoral), 69 (cloak), 72 (tunic), 75 (ephod), belt (79), drawn from a cluster of verses, Ex 28.4; 36.34–38 (39.27–31); Lv 8.7–9. For background, see Philo, *Life of Moses* 2.71–135, Clement, *Strom.* 5.38–40; Origen, *Hom. on Ex* 6, 9; and *Hom. on Lv* 6. Cf. Gregory of Nyssa, *Life of Moses* 2.190–201. Compare also the preface to the *Praktikos*, which discusses seriatim the garments of the monk.

Determining the original Greek is difficult, because in four of the eight keph. S1 and S2 diverge in their terminology, and several of the Syriac terms are unclear or obscure. In the rest of the "intelligible X" series, S2 does not alter S1's terminology (the one exception is 6.38; see note *ad loc.*). Their divergence in this section is likely because the Greek terminology was itself obscure, and based on passages where the Greek Septuagint and Syriac Peshitta are difficult or impossible to correlate precisely. Here, at 4.48, the original is possibly Grk. *mitra*, based on Peshitta and LXX Lv 8.9. Here faith wards off fear; at *Prak.* pr.8 the fear of God establishes faith.

4.49

S2

One among all the pleasures is coextensive with the constitution of the mind, namely that (pleasure) which follows knowledge, because everything passes away with the world to come.

S1

While all pleasure from the practice of good deeds precedes the world to come, the pleasure of spiritual knowledge persists with the mind in this world, and in the world to come.

PLEASURE, Syr. *argīgan*, see 2.10 (Grk. *terpna*). COEXTENSIVE, Syr. *mtmtḥ'*, cf. 1.54 (second beings coextensive with emptiness); 4.35; *Prak.* 3. The ESCORT here is Syr. *lwi'*, i.e., Levite, reminiscent in the context of a series of keph. on temple garments of the priestly class, on which see *Gn.* 38. On CONSTITUTION (usually Grk. *systēma*) see 1.67; WORLD TO COME: 1.11.

4.50

Greek

One longing is good and eternal, that which desires true knowledge.

KEPHALAIA GNOSTIKA 333

Leontius of Byzantium, *Against Nestorius and Eutychius* PG86A:1285

S2

There is one good longing, which is eternal: that which true knowledge chooses, and they say it is inseparable from the mind.

S1

One good love remains eternally one, that which is the love of true knowledge.

LONGING: Grk. *pothos*. ETERNAL: lit. "for the age," or *aionic*. The fragment derives from a quotation from Leontius of Byzantium, whose introductory formula ("And well has it been said by one of our predecessors, a divinely wise man") implies exact wording. The term LONGING, Grk. *pothos*, does not appear in the New Testament, but appears multiple times in Evagrius' corpus, including *Prak*. 57; *Letter on Faith* 2 (longing to be with Gregory of Nazianzus), 21 (to know the end); *Virgin* 26; *Foundations* 8 (PG 40:1260.14, 28–34); *Eight Thoughts* 5; *Prayer* 62, 118; *Eulogius* 30.14. Clement, *Stromateis* 7.7, 8.1: leading by *pothos* to the discovery of the Good. The mind, smitten by observation of the heavens, gains a love and yearning for knowledge about them: Philo, *On the Creation of the World* 77. On the phrase GOOD LONGING (Grk. *agathos pothos*) see Gregory of Nyssa, *On the Dead* 9.61.22; *Hom. on SS* 15 (6:366.11). Compare Macarius, *Sermon* 15.2 (= 9.52 collectio H): "May the mind not be separated from the yearning for our Lord." THEY SAY: may point to the tradition previously cited, or earlier, e.g., Plato: Diotima in *Symposium* 204–210. Plotinus on Plato, *Ennead* 3.5.50: eros seeks the good; cf. 1.6.4.16; 4.3.1.12, 21.21; 5.3.10.48; 5.5.4.7, 12.6; 6.7.34.1. On INSEPARABLE, Syr. *lā mēthparnishīthā*, also translatable as "undifferentiated" see 2.67; 5.29; 6.14; *Gn.* 14 (impassioned and rational parts of the soul); *Letter to Melania* 66 (rivers and the sea).

4.51

S2

In natural *theōria* of second things, they say that some are rulers and others are subjects, as if predetermined. But in the unity there are neither rulers nor subjects, but all will be gods.

334 EVAGRIUS OF PONTUS

S1

In natural *theōria* of second things, some are masters and some are subordinates. But in the unity there are no masters and subordinates, but all will be gods.

> On rulership, see 4.38. The division between rulers and the ruled is a foundation of early Greek political philosophy, for example in a passage Evagrius seems here to paraphrase (THEY SAY): "To rule and to be ruled is not only of necessity (*anagkaion*) but of benefit, and straight away from birth, some are established to be ruled, others to rule" (Aristotle, *Politics* 5 [1254a21–24]). In the ensuing discussion (*Politics* 5–6) Aristotle argues that being ruled, and by implication being a slave, is rooted in one's particular nature (although not all slaves are necessarily natural). After noting the commonly accepted division between rulers and ruled in this world, Evagrius looks beyond this world and responds in the mode of Paul (Gal 3.28: there is neither Jew nor Greek, slave nor free, male nor female) and then Christ (Jn 10.34–35, quoting Ps 81.6: I said, "You are gods"). Cf. *Thirty-Three Chapters* 19.3 on Prv 30.24–28: "The locusts have no king" (not discussed in Sch. on Prv)—rational souls that are not ruled by death and are nourished by the seeds of God, and 23.8, "The 'king' is the person deemed worthy of the kingdom of heaven and trained to teach others." PREDETERMINED, Syr. 'nnq', Grk. *anagkē*, also translatable as "necessity," points to material determinism; see Aristotle, *Metaphysics* 1026b28; *Physics* 2.9 (200a–b). "Among [the philosopher's] audience were magnates and kings," Porphyry, *Life of Pythagoras* 19; cf. Eusebius *Preparation of the Gospel* 6 passim on Porphyry and necessity. S1 SUBORDINATES reflects Peshitta Mt 8.9, Lk 7.8, "a man under authority." Here, S1 does not avoid issues of unity and deification. On the unity, see 1.49.

4.52

Greek

An intelligible leaf is true knowledge of the Holy Trinity.

Furrer-Pilliod 2000, p. 179 A.π.173

S2

The intelligible leaf is the knowledge of the Holy Trinity.

KEPHALAIA GNOSTIKA 335

S1

The spiritual leaf is the true knowledge of the Holy Trinity.

cf. Ex 28.36

On the leaf/plate, Grk. *petalon*, see Clement, *Strom.* 5.6; *Excerpts from Theodotus* 27; Origen, *Hom. on Ex* 9; Epiphanius of Salamis, *On Gems* 12; John Chrysostom, *On the Priesthood* 3.4. The leaf was a golden plate that sat on the turban, on which see 4.48. On KNOWLEDGE OF THE HOLY TRINITY, see *Prak.* 3.

4.53

S2

Knowledge failed and declined among those who built a tower with wickedness and with false teachings. But they experience ignorance and a Babel of intellections, as did those who were building the tower.

S1

Knowledge failed and declined among those who from evil and opinion were building a tower. But they experience ignorance and a Babel, as did those who were building the tower.

cf. Gn 11.4–9

On true versus false teaching, see 4.10. Sch. 3 on Ps 54.10 also treats Babel and is almost a verbatim parallel to this keph.: "Those who build a city from wickedness and false teaching also cause the confusion of tongues that hinders their evil deeds, just as those in Chalanē likewise erected the tower." On Babel, see Philo, *On the Confusion of Tongues*; Origen, *Contra Celsum* 4.21. On towers in general, see *Prak.* 19; *Letter* 25 (*gnōstikos* is Jerusalem); *Eulogius* 11.10; 14.15 (double wall against evil, fortified with towers); *Vices* 1 (tower of ascetic labors and wall for ways); *Eight Thoughts* 4.2 (soul as a tower fortified against anger); *Exh. Monks* 2.6 laborers building a tower are like warfare gaining the wisdom of God; cf. Rev 21.12, 14, 17. On the confusion of tongues, cf. next keph.

336 EVAGRIUS OF PONTUS

4.54

S2

In all languages words make known names, and then things are known. Thus the words of the apostles that were spoken in the Hebrew language were changed to the names and the words of (other) languages, and because of this all tribes knew what had been revealed.

S1

In all languages names and words are known, and they make things known. Thus the language of the Spirit makes known the differences of the intellections.

> cf. Ac 2.5–13 (S2)
>
> On tongues/languages, see 4.35; Pentecost: 2.38. On the contrast of Pentecost with Babel, see Origen, *Hom. on Gn* 1, *Contra Celsum* 5.30; Gregory Nazianzen, *Or.* 41.16. Problems in translating from Hebrew: Origen, *Comm. on Mt* 15.14; cf. Eusebius, *Church History* 5.8.1–12, quoting Irenaeus on translating from Hebrew.

4.55

S2

The words of virtues are the mirror of the virtues. Thus the one who "hears words and does not do them" sees only as in a shadow of virtue, which is the face of the soul.

S1

The words of the virtues are a mirror of the virtues, but he who "hears the words and does not do them" sees only in a shadow virtue, as in a mirror. But true virtue is the precise "face of the soul."

> Jas 1.22–24
>
> Cf. 1 Cor 13.12, mirror. For the contrast between "word of teaching" and "word of practice" see Sch. 57 on Eccl 7.8; Sch. 27 on Prv 3.1; and Sch. 246 on Prv 22.17. Cf. Sch. 13 on Ps 102.18; Sch. 26 on Ps 118.61. Virtues are the "face of the just": Sch. 353 on Prv 28.21 (cf. Sch. 94 on Prv 7.15, "face of the soul"). On mirrors, see 2.1.

KEPHALAIA GNOSTIKA 337

4.56

S2

The intelligible ephod is the state of the rational soul in which a human being habitually performs his virtues.

S1

The ephod of the spirit is the virtuous state of the rational soul in which a human being has the habit of practicing his virtues.

cf. Ex 28.4

EPHOD: *pedita'* (S2) versus *'epoda'* (S1); see 4.75. On the ephod, Grk. *epōmis* (generically, any garment fastened at the shoulder), see 4.75; Philo, *On Monarchy* 2.5; *Strom.* 5.38.2; Origen, *Hom. on Ex* 13.7 (our rational understanding); *Hom. on Lv* 6.4 (virtue of wisdom and reason); Gregory of Nyssa, *Life of Moses* 2.190, 196 (virtues). The high priest's ephod or logion is the ability "to respond to everyone asking for a reason concerning faith and truth": Origen, *Hom. on Lv* 6.4.3. Another symbol of a state: 5.43 (path). On states, see 1.80.

4.57

S2

Christ has appeared as creator in the bread of quantity, in the wine of union, then in the blind man's natural eyes.

S1

Christ, in the virtues he cultivated, and in signs and in wonders and in the healings he did, has been proclaimed as creator.

Cf. Mt 14.15–21 (S2); cf. Mt 15.32–38 (S2); cf. Jn 2.1–10 (S2); cf. Jn 9.1–7 (S2) Key concepts from each of three miracles are tethered to other topics. On QUANTITY, Syr. *kamyut'ā*, Grk. *posos*, see 4.19; unity, 3.1; nature, 1.10. Origen: the Logos can heal all fallen intellects, *First Principles* 3.6.5; church as a room of healing, *Hom. on Lv* 8.11.10.

338   EVAGRIUS OF PONTUS

4.58

S2

God, when he created the rational beings, was not in anything; but when he created bodily nature and the worlds out of it, he was in his Christ.

S1

God, before creating rational nature, was dwelling in his essence, but after he created, he made his creation his dwelling.

> On rational nature, see 1.89; BODILY NATURE: 3.10; WORLDS: 1.65; CHRIST: 3.1. God creating rational beings: Col 1.15–17; Origen, *First Principles* 2.8; Clement, *Paidagogos* 3.1. Cf. 2 Cor 5.4–21, God "in Christ reconciling the world (cosmos) to himself."

4.59

S2

If a being is not said to be greater or lesser than [another] being, but a demon has been called by our Savior more evil than [another] demon, it is evident that demons are not evil in their being.

S1

If a created being is not said to be greater or lesser than another being, and our Lord in his Gospel made it known that one demon is worse than another, it is clear that demons are evil not by their creation but by their will.

cf. Lk 11.26

> On ESSENCE, Syr. ʿitūthā, likely Grk. *ousia*, see 1.1. Cf. *Prak.* 2: kingdom of heaven is true knowledge of beings (Grk. *ontōn*). Cf. the lack of innate evil in material, see 3.59. For other syllogisms, see 1.1.

KEPHALAIA GNOSTIKA 339

4.60

S2

For those who blaspheme the creator, and speak evil of this body of our soul—who will show them this grace they have received by being subject to the passions, since they are joined to an instrument such as this? But they bear witness to my words—those who are terrified by demons in hallucinations of dreams, and awake to watchfulness like that of the angels, when the body awakens quickly.

S1

Those who blaspheme the creator and speak evil of this body of the soul—who will make known to them the grace of our Lord, which is accomplished in them and which protects them from the demons at every moment? They witness to me about this—those who are terrified by demons in their dreams, and flee to the angels, and thus come to watchfulness, as ones who are aware.

Acts of Archelaus 25.3, alleging Manichaean hatred for the body. Cf. Augustine, On Heresies 46.1–8. Body as an instrument (organon) for the soul: 1.67. The body was not meant to be a pretext for blaspheming the demiurge (creator): 4.62; Sch. 215 on Prv 20.12; cf. Sch. 52 on Eccl 6.10–12; Prak. 53 (the body is a means for gaining apatheia). During the day the body is an instrument for resisting temptation. This contrasts with the terrifying incorporeal struggle with demons in nocturnal visions and dreams. Cf. Praktikos (refs. below); Thoughts 4; Eulogius 28; Monks 52 on the different effects of angelic and demonic dreams. "Hallucinations," Syr. dbšragrāgāthā, translates several possible Greek phrases: 6.63 (Grk.: poikilois chrōmasi . . . horōsin); Prak. 46 (Grk. phantasias), 48 (phantasias), 54 (phantasias), 64 (Grk. phasmata), 71 (Grk. phantasias), 76 (phantasias), 89 (phantasias), 91 (phasmata); Letter on Faith 38 (phantasias). On phantasia, see Prak. 46.

4.61

S2

A sign is the explanation of the commandments for the consolation of the simple.

340 EVAGRIUS OF PONTUS

S1

The revelation of a sign is the explanation of the commandments of God, that which is revealed for the consolation of the simple ones.

> SIGN: Syr. *šudāʿā*: mark, notice appearance (*semasia*), acquaintance, familiarity, predicate. EXPLANATION: Syr. *pūšāqā*, can mean interpretation or translation. On interpretation, see *Gn.* 10. Cf. Sch. 364 on Prv 29.18, keeping the law requires an "exegete"; cf. Justin, *Dial.* 34.1; Eusebius, *Church History* 4.23 *exēgēseis* are explications of commandments. On consolation, cf. *Prak.* 92. On teaching for the simple, Syr. *pšiṭe*, see *Gn.* 44.

4.62

S2

It is necessary for the mind to become wise concerning incorporeals or corporeals, or simply to see objects, for these are its life. But it will not see incorporeals when its will is defiled, or corporeals or bodily things when it is deprived of the instrument that demonstrates sense perceptible things to it. Then what *theōria* will they give to the dead soul—those who both reject the creator and slander this our body?

S1

It is right for the mind to attend either to the *theōria* of the incorporeal, or to the *theōria* of corporeals, or to the *theōria* of objects, for its life is in these things. But when it is defiled in its will, it cannot see incorporeals; nor, when it is deprived of the lyre (i.e., the instrument), corporeals, which it observes by means of the senses. And if these things are so, what moreover will those who deny the creator and also slander this body of ours give to their vision of the soul that is dead?

> Cf. Mt 10.18 "fear the one who can kill body and soul in hell." On "blaspheme the creator": 4.60. This keph. is written against Manichaeans; see 4.59 above. On the will, see 4.62. This keph., coupled with 1.64 (the true life of rational beings is their natural activity [*energeia*]), points to a dictum by Aristotle: "The actuality (*energeia*) of the mind is life, and [god] is that actuality": *Metaphysics* 1072b27; cf. *On the Soul* 3.10. Cf. Eccl 7.25. The instrument that demonstrates

perceptible things to the mind are the sense perceptions, *aisthēseis*, on which see 1.34 and 4.67 below. On slander: 3.90; *Gn.* 32.

4.63

S2

The mercy seat is spiritual knowledge, which directs the souls of those who practice.

S1

The spiritual ephod is spiritual knowledge, which consoles those who practice.

cf. Ex 25.17

THOSE WHO PRACTICE, *praktikoi.* On spiritual knowledge, see 1.32. On the mercy seat, see Origen, *Hom. on Nm* 10.3.4: "The propitiatory is knowledge of the Trinity." Paul, in Rom 3.25 interprets the mercy seat as Christ, a theme followed by many later Christian writers.

4.64

S2

If many who were not from Israel followed ancient Israel, is it not the case with the new Israel that many from the Egyptians will go out?

S1

If many who were not from Israel followed the first Israel, is it not also the case with the new Israel that many from the Egyptians will go out?

cf. Ex 12.38

Ex 12.38, a "mixed crowd." Exodus of the soul: 6.64; Sch. 12 on Prv 1.20; Sch. 99 on Prv 8.3. On Egypt, normally a symbol of evil, see 5.6, 21, 88; 6.49; Sch. 19 on Ps 67.32; Sch. 3 on Ps 135.6. "Egyptians" as body: *Eight Thoughts* 1.32; *Monks* 129/Dt 11.10–11: "More trustworthy the water of heaven than the water of the Egyptian sages (*sophōn*) who drew it from the earth" by irrigation. "Egyptian sages" may refer to followers of Hermes Trismegistos, following Herodotus, *Histories* 2.35–36, connecting Hermes and Thoth. On Israel, see 1.31. Normally Israel of the Old Testament is contrasted with the true Israel, e.g., Origen, *Contra Celsum* 2.5; cf.

342 EVAGRIUS OF PONTUS

Letter to Diognetus 9.1, Christians are a "new *genos.*" The phrase "new Israel" is uncommon; see pseudo-Epiphanius, *Hom. on Resurrection of Christ* PG 43:468.

4.65

S2

All rational nature is divided into three parts: life rules over the first; death and life over the second; and death alone over the third.

S1

Rational nature is divided into three parts: over the first rules life; and over the next, life and death; but over the third, death.

This keph. is in form and content paired with 5.20. On rational nature, see 1.89. The threefold division should be compared to the tripartition of the soul (e.g., *Prak.* 89), of the demonic realm (1.10), and of Christian teaching (*Prak.* 1). On rulership, 4.38, 51. Ruler over life: Clement, *Strom.* 7.16; Origen, *Comm. on Jn* 19.6. Ruler of this world, Mt 9.34; Jn 12.31; Rom 5.14, 17 "death ruled from Adam to Moses"; 21 "grace rules to life eternal"; 8.2 "law of sin and death"; Rev 13.1–10. On death and immortality, see 1.58; life, 1.64. Epiphanius, *Panarion* 66.76 on rule by evil angels.

4.66

Greek

An intelligible tunic is unspeakable knowledge of the mysteries of God.

Furrer-Pilliod 2000, p. 200 A.υ.58

S2

The intelligible pectoral is the hidden knowledge of the mysteries of God.

S1

The pectoral of the spirit is the hidden knowledge of the commandments of God.

cf. Ex 28.31, 33–34; 36.29

Both S1 and S2 have *prāzomā*, a Greek loanword (*perizōma*) that generally means a girdle or apron, but the Grk. fragment attests *hypodytēs*, an undergarment.

KEPHALAIA GNOSTIKA 343

4.67

S2

Things that are subject to the soul by means of the senses move (the soul) to receive their images in itself, because this is the work of the mind—to know, just like animals who breathe from outside. And [the mind] falls into danger unless it works, if, according the saying of the wise Solomon, "The light of the Lord is the breath of human beings."

S1

Perceptible things move the soul to clothe itself in their images; so also intelligible thoughts move the mind to clothe itself with their *theōria*.

Prv 20.27 (S2)

Cf. 4.37. This keph. treats the old problem of how passive material things can exercise an influence on the soul, which should be the higher, and therefore active, agent. See, e.g., Plotinus, *Enneads* 4.2–3. The same verse is treated at Sch. 221 on Prv 20.27: "If the light of the Lord is the knowledge of the Lord, and if the light of the Lord is 'the breath of human beings,' the knowledge of the Lord is thus 'the breath of human beings.' The lamp is the devil who thinks he is brilliant; he empties the mind of good things and changes his appearance into 'an angel of light' (2 Cor 11.14)." See further, *Prayer* 95; *Antirr.* 8.17, 25, 26; *Letter* 2; *Monks* 52. Falling into danger by not working: On laziness, see *Prak.* on *akēdia*, 12 et al.; *Eight Thoughts* 6; *Eulogius* 5.5; *Vices* 8.9. "Thoughts" (S1): Syr. *sukāle*, which we translate elsewhere as intellections. See 2.30. Note the analogy here, air : breath : lungs :: sense perception : ideas : mind. On lungs/breathing, see 4.37; sense perceptions: 1.34; dangers: *Prayer* 139. On Solomon: 6.87.

4.68

Greek

The body of the soul preserves the image of a house, but the senses contain the reason of windows, through which the mind, bending down, sees perceptible things.

Mosc. 425, sixteenth century (Hausherr 1939, p. 231)

344 EVAGRIUS OF PONTUS

S2

This body of the soul is the image of a house, and the senses bear the sign of windows through which the mind is instructed and sees sense-perceptible things.

S1

This body is the sign of a house, and the senses are the sign of windows through which the mind inspects and sees perceptible things.

> Cf. Wis 1.4. HOUSE: Syr. *baita'*, also "temple." On the soul as house, see Sch. 32 on Prv 3.18; Sch. 17 on Ps 88.32; Sch. 69 on Ps 118.155; *Letter* 29; cf. Sch. 292 on Prv 24.27: Because "a house is built with wisdom"; "wisdom does not enter into a soul committing evil." Syr. *kao'e* are holes/windows/apertures or cupboards; Grk. *thyrides*: *Prak.* 12, 98; *Eight Thoughts* 6.14; Sch. 90 on Prv 7.6 (human flesh). On the senses, previous keph. and 1.34.

4.69

S2

The intelligible cloak is the spiritual teaching that gathers those who wander.

S1

The cloak of the spirit is the spiritual teaching that gathers those who stray.

> cf. Ex 28.4
> CLOAK, Syr. *marṭuṭā*, normally Grk. *himation*. This keph. may point not to a priestly garment but to temple furnishings. See Nm 4.6–14, concerning the mantles (LXX *himatia*) for the tabernacle altar. The "wanderers" that must be gathered are temptations to mental wandering and distraction from spiritual tasks: *Thoughts* 8.

4.70

Greek

Not for all is it fitting to say, "Escape from prison, my soul," unless they are able, because of purity of soul, and apart from this body, to undertake the *theōria* of beings.

KEPHALAIA GNOSTIKA   345

Mosc. 425, sixteenth century (Hausherr 1939, p. 231)

S2

It is not for everyone to say, "Depart from prison, my soul," but for those who because of purity of soul are able also to draw near without this body to the *theōria*
of beings.

S1

It is not for everyone to say forcefully: "Take leave, my soul, from prison, that
I may confess your name," but of those who because of purity of soul are also able,
without this body, to gaze upon the *theōria* of beings.

> Ps 141.8
> The Greek of this keph. is also attested at Sch. 5 on Ps 141.8 (variants at PG 12:1668
> and 39:1604, with slight differences: "purity" vs. "purity of heart"). On the prison,
> see 4.34; suicide, 4.33; observation of beings: 1.73; escape from the body: 4.83.

4.71

S2

If one of the senses should fail, it greatly distresses those deprived of it. Who can
endure the deprivation of them all—which happens suddenly, and deprives him
of marveling over bodies?

S1

If one of the senses of the body fails, it grievously distresses the one deprived of
it. Who is able to endure the lack of all of them, which happens instantly and
deprives him of marveling over bodies?

> SUDDENLY, Syr. *men šeli*, likely Grk. *exaiphnēs*; see 2.65. WONDER, *Letter on
> Faith* 1; Sch. 2 on Eccl 1.2, "those who have entered into the intelligible church/
> assembly and wonder at the observation of beings..." Cf. Socrates in *Theaetetus*
> 115d; Aristotle, *Metaphysics* 982b. Senses: 1.34; death: 1.58. Cf. Origen, *Comm.
> on Rom* Scherer 1957, pp. 208–210 ("Since the dead one, deprived of the senses,
> is dead, and has none of the five, why would you not say that a soul that is dead
> is deprived of the aforementioned divine senses?"). Cf. Didymus, *Comm. on
> Eccl* (Kramer 1970, 152.7).

346 EVAGRIUS OF PONTUS

4.72

Greek

An intelligible loincloth is the mortifying of the desiring part for the knowledge of God.

Furrer-Pilliod 2000, p. 179 A.π.174

S2

The intelligible tunic is the death of the desiring part, which came into being for the knowledge of God.

S1

The loincloth of the priesthood is the mortification of evil desire, which came into being for the knowledge of God.

cf. Ex 28.42

Syriac: *tarbānqā*, from Iranian *tanbānak*, close-fitting trousers, corresponds to *periskelē* at Ex 28.42 and 39.28 in the Syro-Hexapla. In those verses the Peshitta uses *pārzoma*, but the LXX and Peshitta do not align well in these parts of Exodus. A rare word, *tarbanqa* can be interpreted as an upper- or lower-body garment; the Greek term preserved in the fragment, *periskelion*, implies a covering of the loins and upper legs. Evagrius, like Origen, associated the priestly garment covering the loins and legs with the virtue of chastity. "This [garment] signifies that first of all the whole man be clothed with chastity . . . that he may be holy in body and spirit and pure in thoughts and deeds" (Origen, *Hom. on Ex* 9.4). Cf. *periskelē*, "leg-bands," in Gregory of Nyssa, *On the Lord's Prayer* 3. This clothing item restrains desire; see 4.79 for the one that restrains anger.

4.73

S2

The one whose mind is near the Lord at every moment, and whose angering part is filled with humility from the remembrance of God, and whose desire is bent toward the Lord—he does not fear those enemies of ours, who circle around outside our bodies.

KEPHALAIA GNOSTIKA 347

S1

Everyone whose mind is always with the Lord, whose zeal is full of his memory, and whose entire desire is stretched toward him—this one is nearly unafraid of those who circle around outside our bodies and are rebellious enemies.

> The demon of *akēdia*, that called the "noonday" (Ps 90.6), "circles the soul at the fourth hour" *Prak.* 12; cf. *Prak.* 36; Sch. 4 on Ps 90.6, "He says the noonday demon is that of akēdia" and Sch 2 on Ps 90.5: "With a shield his truth will encircle you . . ." to which the scholion is "the shield of Christ is true knowledge, and the one encircling it will not terrify [it]."

4.74

S2

Those among the saints who have now been freed of bodies and have been mixed with the choir of angels—it is evident that they have also come to our world for the purpose of the divine economy.

S1

All those who have been perfected by the completion of the commandments of God and have left this world—it is clear that they are not separated from fellowship with the holy angels.

> Rev 5.11, 13. Humans become angels: Cf. *Gn.* 47, "Serapion the angel of the church of Thmuis," to whom a similar teaching in 73 above is credited; Sch. 163 on Prv 17.17 (angels and holy humans are brothers). *Monks* 39, "imitate the way of the angels," and *Reflections* 30 on intercession. Cf. Clement, Jesus as "hidden angel," *Paidagogos* 1.7.59. On Syr. *ḥlḥṭ*, mingling, see 1.8; 4.89 (S1); 5.9 (with herd of demons); 6.63 (Grk. *kekramenōn*); *Letter to Melania* 27–28, 63; *Letter on Faith* 23 (Grk. *sumphuretai*). Cf. a similar type of oversight, that of archangels over angelic worlds, at 5.4, and angels over human, 5.7. On becoming angels: Origen, *Contra Celsum* 7.32; 7.44.

348 EVAGRIUS OF PONTUS

4.75

Greek

An intelligible robe is righteousness of a soul according to which a blameless person is accustomed to offer a response in action and teachings.

Furrer-Pilliod 2000, p. 179 A.π.175

S2

The intelligible ephod is the soul's justice, with which a human being is accustomed to become glorified in blameless deeds and teachings.

S1

The spiritual linen is the justice of the soul, in which it is accustomed to be glorified in the actions of beautiful actions, and in the knowledge of faith.

cf. Ex 28.4

The original Greek, *podērēs*, meaning a robe, was translated by S1 as *buṣa* (linen), which S2 then corrected to *'apodā*, a decision that is difficult to explain, not just because of the Greek fragment, but because this Syriac term had already been explained by S1 at 4.56. See Sch. 299 on Prv 25.2 on the glory of God and the glory of the king. OFFER A RESPONSE: Grk. *chrēmatizein*, which suggests either a teaching setting or a commercial transaction.

4.76

Greek

And Evagrius said, "Anyone who is impassioned and prays that the departure come to him quickly is like a human being summoning a builder to quickly break up the bed of a sick person." For by means of that body the soul is plucked from its passions and encouraged.

Dorotheus, *Didaskaliai* 12 (Regnault and de Préville 1963, p. 126)

KEPHALAIA GNOSTIKA 349

S2

One who is impassioned and prays that his departure from this world will happen quickly, is like a sick man who persuades a carpenter to break up his bed quickly, before he recovers.

S1

One who is full of passions, and prays that his exit from this world will happen quickly, resembles a sick man who persuades a carpenter to break up his bed quickly, before he recovers.

Meditation on death: see *Prak.* 52; man lowered on bed for healing: Lk 5.17–39; Jesus as carpenter, Mk 6.3. On death, see 1.58; suicide, 4.33.

4.77

S2

Objects are outside the mind, but the *theōria* concerning them is established inside it. But it is not so concerning the Holy Trinity, for it alone is essential knowledge.

S1

Perceptible things are outside the mind, but their sight is inside it. But it is not the same way with the Holy Trinity, for it is essential knowledge.

Cf. 2.47. ESSENTIAL KNOWLEDGE: 1.89. On the concept of "being in," 1.6.

4.78

S2

Christ is inherited and inherits, but the Father alone is inherited.

S1

[Same as S2]

350 EVAGRIUS OF PONTUS

On heirship, see 3.72. Note the conjunction is between Father and Christ, not Father and Son. See 3.1.

4.79

Greek

A high-priestly cincture is gentleness of ruling part binding the angering part.

Furrer-Pilliod 2000, p. 123 A.ζ.18

S2

The "belt" of the high priest is the humility of anger, which establishes the mind.

S1

The "girdle" of the priest is his humility of its anger, which strengthens the rule of the mind.

cf. Ex 28.4

Cf. Ps 109.19. The "girdle," Syr. *'esār ḥaṣe* commonly corresponds to Grk. *perizōma*, apron (Prv 31.24) or *zōnē*, belt (Mt 3.4; Ezek 9.2–3), confirmed by the Greek fragment, but the Syr. word is not used in the relevant passages from Exodus and Leviticus Peshitta (Ex 28.4; Lv 8.7: LXX *zōnē*). Cf. 4.72, restraining *epithumia*; here the cincture with humility restrains wrath. *Prak.* pr.5 citing 1 Cor 7.1. ESTABLISHES: *mḥiṣa'*, cognate with *mehitzah*, the partition between men and women in a synagogue, strengthening the (male) worshippers. On humility: *Prak.* pr.2.

4.80

S2

It is not God the Logos who at first descended to Sheol and ascended to heaven, but Christ, he who has in himself the Logos. For weak flesh is not receptive of knowledge, but God is known.

KEPHALAIA GNOSTIKA 351

S1

The descent of our Lord to Sheol and his ascent to the Father is not because of him, but because of us. For his nature did not require this, but his love alone required it of him.

> Cf. Eph 4.9. "Common flesh," Syr. *pagrā šḥimā*, can also be rendered "profane flesh." See 1.11. God IS KNOWN, Syr. *yidi'ā*, can also be translated "recognized." On Sheol, see 1.57; rising from the dead: 4.24; 6.61; Christ: 3.1; receptivity: 1.4.

4.81

Greek

Every *theōria* is immaterial and incorporeal according to its own reason. But they say, again, that the *theōria* that has and does not have underlying actions is material and immaterial.

> Milan, Ambr. gr. 681 (Q 74 sup.); tenth century (Muyldermans 1931, p. 59)

S2

Every *theōria*, by the sign of its intellection, is immaterial and incorporeal. But they say that that (*theōria*) which has, or does not have, things that fall under it, is material and immaterial.

S1

Every *theōria* is immaterial and incorporeal by the sign of its intellection. But that *theōria* that possesses and does not possess the distinction of material things in which it is known is called material and immaterial.

> On the paired contrast between material and immaterial, see *Prak.* 34 and esp. *Letter on Faith* 22–23: "For they say the kingdom of Christ is all material knowledge, but that of God and Father is immaterial and,

352 EVAGRIUS OF PONTUS

as one might say, the contemplation of the divinity itself . . . 'And I will raise him on the last day,' (Jn 6.40) calling the resurrection the transposition to immaterial contemplation, and saying that the last day is that knowledge after which there is no other." The technical term UNDER-LYING ACTIONS, Grk. *hypokeimena pragmata*, begins with Aristotle, e.g., *Metaphysics* 992b1, and continues through the philosophical tradition; it refers to underlying entities, "substrates." There is no known parallel in extant earlier Greek literature for the possibility that an observation may both have and not have a substrate. On substrates, see 4.87. On the phrase "sign of its intellection," Syr. *niša d-sukālāh*, Grk. *logo . . . asōmatos*, see 5.32.

4.82

Greek

A "place of refuge" is a practiced body delivering an impassioned soul from the demons encircling it.

Furrer-Pilliod 2000, p. 208 A.φ.87

S2

The "place of refuge" is the practicing body of the impassioned soul, that which delivers it from the demons that encircle it.

S1

The "place of refuge" is the ensouled body of the impassioned soul, that which protects it and delivers it from the demons that encircle it.

Josh 20.2–3; Nm 35.11

The PLACE OF REFUGE appears in several places: Nm 35.11; Dt 19.1–13; Josh 20.2–3. The last reference seems most relevant because of the next keph. The knowledge of God is a house of refuge": Sch. 2 on Ps 30.3.

4.83

S2

Let the one who escapes from the body when he is impure consider whether the kinsman of the one who was killed is not standing at the door and accusing him.

KEPHALAIA GNOSTIKA 353

S1

Let everyone who is impure and escapes from the body reckon in his mind if the kinsman of that one who was killed is not standing at the door and accusing him.

cf. Josh 20.4–6

At Josh 20.4–6 the fugitive is given refuge and the accuser is the "avenger of blood." This particular set of verses is sequestered in the Septuagint edition by Rahlfs as being unique to codex Alexandrinus. On escaping from the body: 4.70. "Stand at the door," Rev 3.20; "accuser" Rev 12.10.

4.84

S2

Knowledge is not a quality of bodies, nor are colors qualities of incorporeals. But knowledge is [a quality] of incorporeals, though color [is a quality] of bodies accidentally.

S1

The movements of incorporeals are in knowledge. But the movements of corporeals are in colors and in qualities.

Color is an accidental (transient) quality of bodies: Aristotle, *On the Soul* 2.5. On qualities as well as color, see 1.22. On accident, Syr. *gedšānā'ith*, Grk. *sumbebēkos*, see *Gn.* 41.

4.85

S2

Demons overpower the soul when the passions multiply, and they make a person insensible when they quench the powers of his senses, lest when he finds a nearby object, he will make the mind rise as from a deep pit.

S1

The demons overpower the soul when the passions multiply, and they make a person insensible when they quench the powers of his senses, so that he will not at all perceive one of the beautiful causes that exist for his life and that, if he perceives it, will raise him as if from a deep pit.

354   EVAGRIUS OF PONTUS

DEEP PIT, Prv 22.14; cf. Sch. 243 on Prv 22.14 LXX "The mouth of a lawless one is a deep pit, and the one hated by God has fallen into it": "Job has fallen into it not because he was hated by the Lord, but for testing." At Job 40–41, the pit is Leviathan. S1 has inserted a clause tying the chapter to suicide, on which see 4.33.

4.86

S2

The mind that has a body does not see incorporeals and when it will be incorporeal, it will not see corporeals.

S1

When the mind has a body, it is not possible for it to see incorporeal things. And when it will be incorporeal, it will not see corporeals.

> See 1.27: these are the second and third of the five observations. On incorporeals and corporeals, 1.70, 75. *Prayer* 152: attention to the corporeal and the "delights of the outer tent" makes seeing the incorporeal impossible.

4.87

S2

Every *theōria* appears with an underlying object, except for the Holy Trinity.

S1

Every *theōria* is known in its substrates, but not so the Holy Trinity.

> On substrate and contemplation, see 1.27; 4.81.

4.88

S2

Of the three altars of knowledge, two belong to a circle, but the third is seen without a circle.

KEPHALAIA GNOSTIKA 355

S1

Of the three altars of knowledge, two have circumference, but one is without limit.

On the three altars see 2.57; essential knowledge, 4.77, 87.

4.89

S2

Who will tell of the grace of God, and who will investigate the reasons (*logoi*) of providence, and how Christ guides rational nature, by means of varied worlds, toward union with the holy unity?

S1

Who will tell of the grace of God, and who will trace the reasons of the divine economy, and how Christ through the practice of his holy commandments guides rational nature toward mingling with the Holy Trinity?

Cf. Ps 72.15, "Who will tell of your goodness?" On keph. framed as questions, 2.74; HOLY UNITY, 1.49, 71; GRACE, 1.37; providence with judgment, *Gn.* 48; VARIED WORLDS, 1.65. On providence specifically, 6.43, 75–76.

4.90

Greek

The knowledge of Christ does not need a dialectical soul, but a watchful one, because to engage in dialectic pertains to impure souls, but to watch to the pure ones alone.

Milan, Ambr. gr. 681 (Q 74 sup.); tenth century (Muyldermans 1931, p. 59)

S2

The knowledge of God does not require a dialectical soul, but one who sees. For dialectic is customarily found with souls that are impure, but sight only among pure ones.

356 EVAGRIUS OF PONTUS

S1

The knowledge of Christ does not require a dialectical soul, but a watchful one. The impure can have dialectic, but *theōria* exists only among the pure.

Although we have translated both S1 and S2 DIALECTICAL, the latter uses *mlilūthā*, a calque on Grk. *dialektikos*, and the former, *rušt'*, argue. On dialectic, see Sch. 2 on Ps 115.2 (def. dialectical term *aporos*); *Letter* 61; Plato, *Phaedo, Cratylus* 390c, *Republic* 534b3; Aristotle, *Metaphysics* 995b23; Clement, *Stromateis* 1.28 (investigative use of dialectic); 1.20 (quarrelsome). Cf. Origen, *Contra Celsum* 2.20.

Epilogue

S2

Finished is the fourth.

S1

Finished is the fourth, which lacks ten chapters.

Century Five

S2

Century Five

S1

[Same as S2]

5.1

S2

Adam is "a type" of Christ, but Eve of the rational nature, for because of her Christ departed from his paradise.

S1

[Same as S2]

Rom 5.14

Eve: 2 Cor 11.3, "as the serpent deceived Eve by its cunning, your thoughts (*noēmata*) will be led astray from the simplicity and purity which is in Christ." Paul, in Eph 5.22–32, implicitly relies upon the analogy Adam : Eve :: Christ : Church, which Evagrius alters to Adam : Eve :: Christ : rational nature (see next keph. on the relationship between rational nature and the church). Cf. 1 Tm 2.13–14: "Adam was the protoplast, then Eve, and Adam was not deceived, but the woman was deceived and became a transgressor." Cf. Clement, *Protreptikos* 98; *Strom.* 3.74.3; 80.2; 94.1 and *Excerpts from Theodotus* 1.2, reflecting his reading of Philo and, possibly, referring to the Valentinian interpretation of Eve as a "female instructor of life" and a "spiritually endowed woman" in, respectively, *On the Creation of the World* and *Hypotyposis of the Archons*. On Adam, see 6.3. On paradise, 5.72; 6.8 (habitation of the righteous, opp. Hades).

358 EVAGRIUS OF PONTUS

5.2

S2

The hearers of the perceptible church are separated from each other by places alone, but those [hearers] of the intelligible, which is before that, by places and by bodies.

S1

The hearers of the visible church are separated from each other by places, but the hearers of the church that is in heaven are separated by places and by bodies.

> The hearers were those in church who were being catechized, but had not yet been baptized; see Lampe, s.v. ἀκροάομαι (Jas 1.22–25). As "pupil," Origen, *Hom Jeremiah* 14.3. On church, see Sch. on Eccl 1.1, where "Christ is the Ecclesiast," and Sch. 2 on Eccl 1.2, "the church of the mind . . . the observation of created things." *Virgin* 33 and 54: Remain silent with downcast eyes "in the church of the Lord"; "listen, my child to the doctrines of the church of the Lord, and allow no stranger to win you over"; Sch. 8 on Ps 44.10 (church has a golden mantle, knowing in part, prophesying in part); Sch. 3 on Ps 45.5 (the city of God is the Church, the rational soul itself); Sch. 7 on Ps 150.4 (the *organon [instrument]* is the Church of God, composed of practiced and observant souls). On place, see 1.61; 2.37; BODIES, 1.11.

5.3

S2

Just as those who dwell in this world receive a very small vision about the world to come, so those who are in the last world see some bright splendors of the Holy Trinity.

S1

Those who are in this world and yearn for the world to come, see "some measure" of its *theōria*, but when they have finished its beautiful race and arrived, they see it clearly.

1 Cor 13.9, 12 (S1); cf. 2 Tm 4.7 (S1)

KEPHALAIA GNOSTIKA 359

Partial vision: 1 Cor 13.9, 12; "present age," *Prayer* prologue; "little vision of the world to come," "world to come," Mt 12.32; Heb 2.5 and 6.5; and Ps 111.1. "Shining rays of the Holy Trinity," Gregory Nazianzen, *Theological Oration* 5 on the Holy Spirit (*Or.* 31). On THE LAST WORLD: 5.89.

5.4

S2

An archangel is a rational essence entrusted with the reasons concerning providence and judgment, and those of the worlds of angels.

S1

An archangel is a bodiless rational nature, to whom has been entrusted a higher service in the order of angels.

This keph. forms a pair with 5.7. On PROVIDENCE AND JUDGMENT, see *Gn.* 48; rational beings, 1.89. Angels: *Prak.* 24. On archangels overseeing angelic worlds, ·cf. the saintly/angelic overseeing ours, 4.74. ARCHANGEL: Jude 9 (Michael); 1 Thes 4.16 (Christ); *Foundations* 9; *Eight Thoughts* 8.11 (Lucifer).

5.5

S2

Of the worlds, two purify the impassioned part of the soul—one of them by the practice, and the other by severe torment.

S1

Two great ways of life purify the impassioned part of the soul: the practice of the commandments and the humility and affliction of the mind.

On torment, see 1.44. Cf. Sch. 268 on Prv 24.9–10: "Uncleanness is destroyed either by practice (*praktikē*) or by severe torment (*drimeias kolaseōs*)."

360 EVAGRIUS OF PONTUS

5.6

S2

The *theōria* of angels is named heavenly Jerusalem and Mt. Zion. If those who believe in Christ "have approached Mt. Zion and the city of the living God," it is therefore within the *theōria* of angels that those who believe in Christ have been and will be—that (*theōria*) from which their fathers have left and gone down to Egypt, have been and will be.

S1

If the *theōria* of the angels is called heavenly Jerusalem and Zion, it is clear that those who believe in Christ and "approach his holy mountain and the city of the living God" approach the *theōria* of the holy angels.

Heb 12.22

See also Rev 21.10 "Jerusalem coming down out of heaven"; Gn 46, descent of Israel to Egypt. On mountains, 4.23; Jerusalem: 1.31. On Mount Zion, which symbolizes the Father (Sch. 6 on Ps 13.7), see 5.21, 88. This kephalaion may be motivated by Origen's comment that "Sion" means "watchtower" (*skopeutērion*): *Comm. on Jn* 13.13.81; frag. Jer. 13; frag. Lam. 19; noted by Evagrius at Sch. 1 on Ps 86.2 and expanded at Sch. 8 on Ps 101.14 ("Now he says that Sion is the rational nature born to oversee the heavenly things"). See also Sch. 1 on Ps 147.1–2 (the bars of Jerusalem are the *praktikai* virtues; those of Sion the heavenly teachings and the right faith of the Trinity, since Jerusalem signifies the soul and Sion the mind, for "Jerusalem" is translated "sight of peace" and "Sion" "watchtower").

5.7

S2

An angel is a rational essence to whom have been entrusted the reasons concerning providence, judgment, and the worlds of human beings.

S1

An angel is a rational, bodiless nature to whom God has entrusted the service to the saints—those who are about to inherit life.

KEPHALAIA GNOSTIKA   361

This keph. forms a pair with 5.4. Angels administer divine providence to human beings: Sch. 164 on Prv 17.17; Sch. 189 on Prv 19.4; Sch. 7 on Ps 16.13 (angels are the assisting or benevolent [*euergetikē*] hand of God); Sch. 38 on Eccl 5.7–11.

5.8

S2

Those who have worked their land for six years of the practice will support widows and orphans not in the eighth but in the seventh year; for in the eighth year there are no widows and orphans.

S1

[Same as S2]

cf. Ex 23.10–11

Ex 23.10–11 mentions a sixth and seventh year, but not an eighth (reflected in Sch. 208 on Prv 20.4 and *Letter* 41.4). Eight is a symbol of completion and the realm of the fixed stars; Plato, *Republic* 10 (614–621), the Myth of Er. Cf. *Prak.* 12, eighth hour. The exegetical extension of six and seven into eight follows the model of Clement of Alexandria, *Stromateis* 6.138.5, 140.3. See also *KG* 5.83 (circumcision); 6.7 (eight = resurrection, circumcision). "Orphan" has different meanings: Sch. 17 on Ps 9.35 (one who rejects the wicked father); Sch. 4 on Ps 67.6 (one deprived by evil of the heavenly father); Sch. 4 on Ps 93.6 (the mind bereft of the heavenly father); Sch. 7 on Ps 108.9 (wicked thoughts nurturing Satan as father). Likewise, for widow: Sch. 3 on Ps 93.6 (the soul and proselyte mind killed by the one who evilly interprets the divine writings); Sch. 7 on Ps 108.9 (soul not taking seeds from the devil).

5.9

S2

Among human beings, some will make a festival with angels, but some will be mingled with a herd of demons, and some will be tormented with defiled humans.

362 EVAGRIUS OF PONTUS

S1

[Same as S2]

"Bread of angels" Ps 79.24–25; HERD OF DEMONS, Mt 8.28–34; defilement (Mt 15.11 "what comes out of the mouth defiles"), cf. 4.36, wickedness and intelligible fat. Cf. mingling with angels, 4.74. On festival, Syr. *a'dā*, likely Grk. *heortē* or a cognate, see *Monks* 39, 41, 43, 44; *Virgin* 14, 55 (festival with angels); *Eight Thoughts* 2.7; *Thoughts* 23. Torment: 1.44.

5.10

S2

The firstborn are rational natures who in every one of the worlds approach a higher change.

S1

The firstborn are rational natures, those who by their virtue precede their brothers.

cf. Ex 22.29

Cf. 2.36, 4.24; FIRSTBORN: 2.36; 4.20; or *protoktistoi* ("first-created") Clement, *Prophetic Eclogues* 56.7; *Strom.* 5.12.81. On humans between angels and demons, next keph. and 3.48, 50, 76; 4.13. On change, poss. Grk. *allagē*, see 2.4; worlds: 1.70; 2.75.

5.11

Greek

Out of the angelic state and the archangelic state the psychic state comes to be; from the psychic, the demonic, and human; but out of the human, angels again and demons come into being.

John of Scythopolis, Sch. on the *Eccl. Hierarchy* 6 (PG 4:173)

KEPHALAIA GNOSTIKA   363

S2

From the rank of angels is the rank of archangels and [the rank] of the psychic; but from the psychic, that of angels and humans; but from that of the human, again, angels and demons will come to be—if a demon is that one who, because of an abundance of anger, has fallen from the practice and been bound to a darkened and dense body.

S1

Humans have slid down from the state of angels to human conduct and from it, further, they have been brought down to the degradation of demons. But when they rise back up, they pass by degrees the rank from which they fell.

This keph. survives in Greek via two lines of transmission: in the canons against Origen, and in a quotation from John of Scythopolis (whose wording indicates he was working directly with a copy of the *KG*); see 2.78. Cf. Jas 3.15 (this wisdom comes not from above but is earthly, soulish [*psychikē*], demonic [*daimoniōdes*]). On (evil) bodies: 3.1. Evagrius reprises and expands Origen, *First Principles* (2.6.5, the mind of Christ; it remains attached to God as a *nous* through free choice, 2.9.2–8; the fall of all other minds, 2.8.3). Angry humans become demons, *Letter* 56.4. On dense bodies, 1.11; states: *Prak.* 12.

5.12

S2

The mind that has been stripped of the passions, and sees the intellections of beings, does not henceforward receive sights by means of the senses. But it is like another world created by its knowledge, to which it directs its thought, and casts out from it the perceptible world.

S1

When the mind is stripped of passions and, by the grace of our Lord, it becomes one who sees beings, then it also becomes scornful of all perceptible things, because its spiritual existence is built up, and it becomes more immense in itself— more than the entire world—and directs its thought there, far away from the consideration of appearances.

364   EVAGRIUS OF PONTUS

Sᴵɢʜᴛs reflects S2 Syr. *patkrā*, commonly Grk. *eidōlon*, which in the New Testament and early Christian literature means idols (see 4.25), but here it has the older technical sense of a mental image. The nous, no longer subject to passion, creates a different world removed from *aiesthēseis*; see 5.41. Previously, sense perceptions form *eidōla* in the mind; now knowledge creates another aeon with thought appropriate to that aeon. Cf. 5.81, which presents the corresponding opposite of the creation of *eidōla*; and the more expansive treatment in Sch. 15 on Eccl 3.10–13 "He has placed the aion within his heart"; as a teaching of Jesus, Lk 17.21. On *eidōla* as distracting images: *Thoughts* 4.16; 16.28; 25.55; 36.17; *Antirr.* 4.55. Plotinus, *Against the Gnostics*, on *eidōla*, *Enn.* 2.9.10. On intellections of beings, see 5.14, 17, 29, 39. On worlds, see 1.70.

5.13

Greek

An intelligible cloud is a rational nature entrusted by God to water those who are lower.

Furrer-Pilliod 2000, p. 156 A.v.48

S2

The intelligible cloud is the rational nature that has been entrusted by God to water those who are lower than it.

S1

The cloud of the spirit is the bodiless rational nature entrusted by God to give to the innocent to drink.

cf. Ex 19.9

For the cloud, Grk. *nephelē* (cf. 3.90 Grk., *nephos*), Syr. *'nānā*, see Ex 19.9 (God speaks to Moses); 13.21–22 (pillar of cloud); 40.38 (tent of meeting); 3 Kgdms/1 Kgs 18.44 (portent to Elijah); 1 Cor 10.1–4 "baptized into Moses in the cloud and in the sea"; cf. Rev 10.1; 14.14 "cloud like a son of man." Cloud as reasoning nature (cf. Sch. 3 on Ps 4.3; Sch. 3 on Ps 107.5) in Sch. 6 on Ps 56.11, clouds associated with angels; or the holy powers (Sch. 22 on Ps 67.35; Sch. 7 on Ps 96.4; Sch. 4 on Ps 98.7) that are entrusted with the care of various matters or other logikoi (Sch. 3 on Ps 134.7 and Sch. 7 on Ps 16.13 [sensible cosmos]). With opposite meaning: a "clouded" perception or observation 3.90; *Vices* 4; *Eight Thoughts* 4.6; 6.3; *Thoughts* 42;

KEPHALAIA GNOSTIKA 365

Prayer 128. On watering, cf. Jer 17.7–8; Ps 1.3 (cited at *KG* 5.67), 1 Cor 3.6–8 (planting and watering), and see *Prak.* ep. (fathers watered Evagrius); Sch. 15 on Eccl 3.10–13; Sch. 11 on Ps 103.13 (pure natures water those loftier in heart). "Those who are inferior" corresponds to Grk. *hypodeesterous*. S2 rendered this as *ldmkin*, which has often been interpreted to mean "to sleep," but the Greek fragment confirms our translation. On those inferior, see note at *Gn.* 6.

5.14

S2

Just as when the sun rises, those things placed a little higher than the ground cast a shadow, so also to the mind that begins to approach the intellections of beings, those things appear obscurely.

S1

Just as when the sun rises, even small pebbles on the ground cast a shadow, so also things of this world at first appear as a shadow to the mind that begins to shine with knowledge.

On shadows, see 1.59 (light : darkness : air :: virtue : vice : soul) with references; 3.37. Shadow of the things to come: Col 2.17; Heb 10.1, 9.5; sitting in shadow: Lk 1.79, Mt 4.16, and Ps 108.10, shadow of death; shadows in a cave: Plato, *Republic* 514a–20a; *Phaedo* 107a–115a and Porphyry, *On the Cave of the Nymphs* 3. Cf. Basil, *Hexaemeron* 2.5. On INTELLECTIONS OF BEINGS, see 5.12; THE SUN, 3.44.

5.15

Greek

The mind stripped of passions becomes entirely luminous, shining with the *theōria* of beings.

Vat. gr. 2028, tenth/eleventh century (Géhin 1996, p. 65)

366 EVAGRIUS OF PONTUS

S2

The mind stripped of passions becomes entirely like light, because it is illuminated by the *theōria* of beings.

S1

The mind, when it is stripped of passions, shines entirely, like light, and becomes an enlightened eyewitness of all the works of God.

> On observation of beings, see 1.73. LIGHT: 1.35, 59, 74, 81; 2.29; 3.44, 52; 5.15; *Prak.* 64; *Gn.* 45; *Disc.* 78; *Virgin* 54; Sch. 258 on Prv 23.22; *Prayer* 75; *Thoughts* 17, 39, 40, 42; *Reflections* 2, 4, 23, 25, 27; *Letter* 39.5; *Antirr.* 6.16.

5.16

Greek

An intelligible dark cloud is spiritual *theōria* containing the reasons of judgment and providence of those on earth.

> Furrer-Pilliod 2000, p. 96 A.γ.43

S2

The intelligible dark cloud is spiritual *theōria* which contains in itself the reasons of the providence and judgment of those who are on the earth.

S1

The spiritual dark cloud is spiritual *theōria* entrusted with the reasons of the economy and of the judgment of God.

cf. Ex 20.21

> For the dark cloud, Grk. *gnophos*, Syr. *'arpelā*, see Ex 20.21; Heb 12.18 and cf. *KG* 5.4, 7, 13, 23. Providence and judgment (reversed here in the Greek fragment): *Gn.* 48.

KEPHALAIA GNOSTIKA 367

5.17

S2

Just as waves, when they rise up make a shadow, and once again appear without a shadow, so also when the intellections of beings flee from the pure mind, they will be known again immediately.

S1

Just as waves, when they rise and make a shadow and then quickly become still and their shadow disappears, so also before the spiritual mind there will be little hindrances that easily disappear.

> See 5.14. On WAVES, see *Thoughts* 4; Sch. 3 on Ps 64.8 (wind : wave :: demon : soul); cf. James 1.6–7 (waves blown and tossed). The metaphor in this keph. might be unexpected, since waves were normally associated with temptations or passions: *Eight Thoughts* 2.13–14; *Letter* 52.2–3; *Thoughts* 26; Sch. 3 on Ps 65.6; Sch. 3 on Ps 92.4; Sch. 1 on Ps 96.1; Sch. 13 on Ps 106.28–29; Sch. 15 on Ps 106.29; Plato, *Laws* 740e; Aeschylus, *Eumenides* 8.32; Gregory of Nyssa, *Life of Moses* 2.8. On INTELLECTIONS OF BEINGS, see 5.12; PURE MIND: 2.34.

5.18

S2

Demons imitate only colors and forms and size, but the holy powers also know how to change the nature of the body when they arrange it for necessary services. This happens to composites, but of the bodiless nature there are no intellections such as these, so they say.

S1

Demons imitate only colors and forms of the body, but the holy powers, at the command of God, also change themselves in bodily constitution.

> Syr. *dmā*, imitate, of demons, may be translating Grk. *hypokrinomenoi*, Lk 20.20 "dissemblers." On HOLY POWERS, see 2.30; color, 1.22. Inferior and superior (unholy and holy) powers: Clement, *Excerpts from Theodotus* 69 (frag. 11); "holy powers": Clement, *Strom.* 1.17; 5.6; *Excerpts from Theodotus* 72 (frag. 11); Origen, *Comm. on Jn* 10.23, vs. dualist Heracleon; cf. Epiphanius, *Panarion*

368 EVAGRIUS OF PONTUS

66.24. The verb ARRANGE, S2 Syr. *mṭaksin*, is a loanword from Grk. *taxis*, on which see 2.66. SERVICES, Syr. *tešmēštatha'*, is likely Grk. *diakoniai*, also translatable as ministries. Angelic bodies in service: Heb 1.7, 14. On nature, 1.10; composites, 2.57. for angelic assistance: Sch. 7 on Ps 16.13; Sch. 38 on Eccl 5.7–11; for assistance provided by every rank of reasoning being in "varied worlds" to those below them: *KG* 6.76. SO THEY SAY: source not known.

5.19

S2

The resurrection of the body is the change from the evil mixture to the better mixture.

S1

The small resurrection of the body is the change that happens to it from the fall of impurity to the resurrection of holiness.

> This keph. forms a trio with 5.22 (soul) and 25 (mind). On resurrection, see 3.77; quality: 1.22.

5.20

S2

Life at first gives life to the living, but afterward to those who are living and those who are dying; but it also gives, in the end, life to the dead.

S1

True life guards the living, but it also gives life to the dead.

> This keph. is in form and content paired with 4.65. On life and resurrection, see previous keph.; Gn 1.26; Jn 1.3. Christ is Life: Jn 5.24; 11.25; 1 Jn 5.20. Life to the living ones: Gn 2.7; life to the dead: Jn 5.21. Rev 1.8; 22.13–21 "I am the alpha and omega, the beginning and the end." On death, 1.58.

KEPHALAIA GNOSTIKA 369

5.21

S2

Not in all worlds will you find Egypt, but in the last you will see Jerusalem and the mountain of Zion.

S1

In the Jerusalem in heaven, and on Mt. Zion you will discover incorporeal *theōria*.

On Jerusalem: 1.31; Mount Sion: 5.6; Egypt: 4.64; Egypt, Jerusalem, and Sion: 6.49; worlds: 1.70.

5.22

S2

The resurrection of the soul is the return from the order of passibility to the impassible state.

S1

The small resurrection of the soul is the change that is from passibility to the state of impassibility.

This keph. forms a trio with 5.19 (body), and 25 (mind). RETURN, Syr. *punāyā*, is likely Grk. *epistrophē*: 2.13; cf. Plotinus, *Enn.* 5.5.1; 5.3.6; Porphyry, *Launching Points to the Intelligibles* 13; Ac 15.16; 2 Pt 2.21. On order (*taxis*), see 2.66; state: *Prak.* 12.

5.23

S2

Their multiform movement, and the varied passions of rational beings, have compelled the intellections about providence to appear obscurely, but their various orders have made hidden the intellections about judgment.

370 EVAGRIUS OF PONTUS

S1

The abundance of words and of passions obscures and darkens the sign of the *theōria* of the judgment of God and of his economy.

> MULTIFORM, Syr. *sagi'utha d-mut'*, means literally "many of form," probably reflecting a Grk. compound with *poly-*, e.g., *polyeidos* or *polymorphos*; cf. the regular invocation of the "manifold wisdom of God," Eph 3.10 (see 2.2). The movement has produced evident but obscure displays of providence, whereas the passions coincident with that movement have obscured evidence of the judgment. The two pairs are intended to assist in interpreting 5.27, below. On the movement: 1.50–51; providence, 4.89; judgment 3.47, 48; providence and judgment paired: *Gn.* 48. For the logos of judgment cf. note at 3.47.

5.24

S2

The reasons concerning judgment are second, so they say, to the reasons concerning movement and providence.

S1

The fathers say that the reasons of the judgment are second to the reasons of the movement.

> On the pairing of providence and judgment, see *Gn.* 48; on the movement, see previous keph. and 1.50.

5.25

S2

The resurrection of the mind is the transfer from ignorance to true knowledge.

S1

The small resurrection of the mind is the change from ignorance to knowledge.

> This keph. forms a trio with 5.19 (body), and 22 (soul). On ignorance, cf. 4.29; *Letter to Melania* 26.

KEPHALAIA GNOSTIKA 371

5.26

S2

Just as it is not the same to see the light and to speak about the light, so it is not the equivalent to see God and to understand something about God.

S1

The one who has not seen God is not able to speak about him.

> *Letter* 56.2, pure mind sees God. Although a comparison of pairs, the sequence may be A : B :: b : a in light of *Gn.* 1 (seeing greater than apprehension). See also *Reflections* 20; Gregory Nazianzen, *Or.* 29 (Third Theological Oration).

5.27

Greek

The agitated temper blinds the observer, but desire unreasonably set in motion hides visible things.

> Mosc. 425, sixteenth century (Hausherr 1939, p. 231)

S2

Anger when it is aroused blinds the observer, but when desire is stirred up ferociously, it hides visible things.

S1

Disturbing anger blinds the one who sees, and an evil desire hides visible things.

> See 5.23, establishing movement : thumos :: passion : epithumia. Anger blinds the observer (Syr. *hazāyā*): 4.47; *Prak.* 20. The disturbed temper: 6.63; *Prak.* 21;

372 EVAGRIUS OF PONTUS

Sch. 4 on Ps 6.8 ("nothing so blinds the mind as the temper disturbed," similar at Sch. 7 on Ps 30.10). On anger, *Prak.* 20.

5.28

Greek

An intelligible sword is a spiritual logos separating body from soul, or evil and ignorance.

Furrer-Pilliod 2000, p. 181 A.ρ.3

A sword is the rational mind cutting away the soul from evil and ignorance.

Rondeau 2021, Sch. 6 on Ps 7.13

S2

The intelligible sword is the spiritual logos which separates the body from the soul, or evil, or ignorance.

S1

The sword of the spirit is a spiritual word that divides the soul from the body and severs evil and ignorance from it.

cf. Eph 6.17

This is the first of a subsection of the "intelligible X" series (which started at 3.44) treating martial imagery, both armaments and the taking of the land from the Philistines. The Grk. fragment preserves *romphaia* for sword. Because "shield" and "helmet" are the next images, Eph 6.17 is the primary scripture here quoted (cf. *Thoughts* 34). Because the series has so far drawn from Old Testament imagery, this keph. also has overtones of the sword that guards Eden, Gn 3.24, echoed at Rev 1.16; 2.12, 16; 6.8; 19.15, 21. Sch. 6 on Ps 7.13; Sch. 7 on Ps 17.13; Sch. 3 on Ps 45.5; Sch. 2 on Ps 149.6; cf. Sch. 276 on Prv 24.22c; cf. Origen Hom 7 on Num 12.1; Hom 20 on Num 25.1; Hom 6.2 and Hom 9.2 on Judges. The armory of Eph 6 appears in Sch. 9 on Prv 1.13; *Thoughts* 34; *Antirr.* Pr.4.

5.29

S2

Just as those who enter cities to see their beautiful objects pause in admiration of every one of those works, so also the mind, when it approaches the intellections of beings, is filled with spiritual desire, and will not separate itself from wonder.

S1

Just as those who become observers of the beauties of cities linger in wonder over them, so also the mind, when it becomes an observer of the works of God, lingers in wonder so that no one can drag it away.

> On cities, 1.31; 5.74; 6.24; *Gn.* 50 addendum (S2; solitary a city). *Eulogius* 30, "metropolis of the virtues." Frequently they are to be avoided: *Prak.* 41; *Thoughts* 20, 21 (imagining becoming archbishop of Constantinople). Wonder, *semeion* at the mother: Rev 12.1 and wonder, *thauma* at the evil city, Rev 17.6. WONDER: 4.71.

5.30

Greek

If the kingdom of the heavens is the *theōria* of beings, and this according to our Lord "is inside us," but that which is inside is held by demons, the Philistines are well said to possess the Land of Promise.

> Rondeau 2021, Sch. 6b on Ps 134.12

S2

If the kingdom of heaven is the *theōria* of beings, and this according to the word of our Lord "is within" us, but our inner part is held by demons, he has said well, therefore, that the Philistines have taken possession of the land of promise.

S1

If the kingdom of heaven is the *theōria* of beings, and according to the word of our Lord, it "is inside us," and if our interior is held by demons, it is rightly said that the Philistines have taken possession of the land of promise.

374 EVAGRIUS OF PONTUS

Lk 17.21; cf. Mt 12.43–45; cf. Lk 11.24–26

THE LAND OF PROMISE: 5.36; Gn 50.24; Heb 11.9. On KINGDOM OF HEAVEN, see *Prak.* 2; observation of beings: 1.73; INSIDE: 1.6. The specific saying is unknown, but is reminiscent of 1 Kgdms/1 Sam 23.27 (Philistines have attacked the land), and more broadly of the control held by the Philistines during the time of Samson. On the Philistines, see 5.36, 45, 68 (Grk. *allophylos*); *Letter on Faith* 3; Sch. 2 on Ps 26.3 (let the practiced one fight the Philistines through the virtues); *Thoughts* 19–20; *Antirr.* pr.3; *Disc.* 52, 107; *Letter* 58.2. An anonymous definition that quite possibly comes from Evagrius states, "An *allophylos* and *allogenēs* is one who in thought works in faith and action against the truth" (*Definitions*, Furrer-Pilliod ed. A α 197, p. 86). The Philistines represent "vices and sins" in Origen, *Hom. on Jgs* 4.1.

5.31

S2

The intelligible shield is practicing knowledge that guards uninjured the impassioned part of the soul.

S1

The shield of the spirit is practiced knowledge, which protects unharmed the passionless part of the soul.

cf. Eph 6.16

On the martial symbolism see 5.28; although reminiscent of Eph 6.16, it may point as well to the shield of David, 2 Kgdms/2 Sam 22.36; Ps 3.3; 34.2. Cf. 5.34 (guarding the perceptible part of the soul); *Praktikos* pr.2 (guarding the *hēgemonikon*).

5.32

S2

That which is in the first cup resembles wine, which is the knowledge of incorporeals, and that which is in the second bears the sign of water, but I say the *theōria* of corporeals, and this is the cup mixed for us by Wisdom from these two.

KEPHALAIA GNOSTIKA 375

S1

When the exalted wisdom of God has grown in us, its cup is in us in wine and in water. Investigate the *theōria* of these things with diligence.

cf. Prv 9.2

On the cup in general see 2.44. This keph. discusses a total of three cups or vessels, Syr. *kāsā*, likely Grk. *potērion* or *kratēr*. The third, from Prv 9.2, mentions only one cup, into which are poured the contents of the first two. The complex image points perhaps to other passages, e.g., the two cups mentioned in Luke's account of the Last Supper (Lk 22.17, 20); Melchizedek in Gn 14.18 and Heb 7.15; Ex 24.6; Mt 10.42 (cup of cold water); Jn 19.32–34 (blood and water from the side of Christ). See Sch. 104 on Prv 9.2: the "bowl" of mixed wine is knowledge of incorporeals and of providence and judgment. Cf. also *Gn.* 14, and *Letter* 27, on Melchizedek as Christ and Evagrius as Abraham. The phrase "sign of water" follows a stock phrase Syr. *nišā d-* . . . , seen also at, e.g., 4.81; 5.45, whose corresponding Greek fragments point to Grk. *logos*. Hence this second cup bears a *logos* or account of water.

5.33

S2

The unjust steward cannot work the earth, for he has stripped off the virtues of his soul, and further, the wretched one is "ashamed to beg," he who is the teacher of others. And those who are below him still he teaches angrily, he who now has withdrawn to dwell among the disputatious.

S1

The wise steward is the one who justly has managed the distribution of the gift entrusted from God, that is, as is appropriate for the moment.

cf. Lk 16.3 (S2); cf. Lk 16.5–8 (S1)

Although both S1 and S2 use the same term to point to the steward featured in Luke 16.1–13, S1 commends him by pointing to the second half of the account and S2 condemns him through the first half. The STEWARD, Syr. *rabaithā* = contraction of *rab baithā*, master of the house, is Grk. *oikonomos*. Cf. 1 Cor 4.1 "stewards of the mysteries of God" (cf. Sch. 153 on Prv 17.2). WORK THE EARTH, 5.35; Sch.

376 EVAGRIUS OF PONTUS

352 on Prv 28.19 (the one working the earth cleans himself and will be filled with knowledge); cf. Gn 2.5. On anger and the teacher, see *Gn.* 5.

5.34

Greek

An intelligible helmet is spiritual knowledge guarding unassailable the rational part of the soul.

Furrer-Pilliod 2000, p. 179 A.π.176

S2

The intelligible helmet is spiritual knowledge, that which guards uninjured the intelligent part of the soul.

S1

The spiritual helmet is spiritual knowledge that guards uninjured the rational part of the soul.

cf. Eph 6.17

Helmet (Grk. *perikephalaion*): Is 59.17; Eph 6.17; 1 Thes 5.8. See 5.28, 31; Sch. 9 on Prv 1.13; cf. *Prak.* pr.2. On spiritual knowledge, 4.18 (anointing).

5.35

S2

If the bread of the rational nature is *theōria* of beings, and this we are commanded to eat "in the sweat of our faces," it is clear that we eat it by means of the practice.

S1

If the bread of the rational nature is the *theōria* of beings, and we have been commanded to eat it "in the sweat of our faces," it is clear that we eat it in the practice of the commandments of God.

Gn 3.19

On bread: 1.23; 2.44; Gn 3.19. Cf. Sch. 3c on Ps 126.2, "bread of pain." For working of the earth, see 5.33.

5.36

S2

Those who have inherited the land of promise will slaughter with their whole armed force the Philistines in it, lest when Joshua will become old among them he will stop going out with their armed force, and again they will be slaves to the Philistines.

S1

Those who inherited the land of promise slaughter the Philistines with all their might, lest when Joshua will become old among them he will cease to go out with their army and they will again become slaves of the Philistines.

cf. Josh 13.1

Cf. 5.30, 38; *Antirr.* pr.3. LAND OF PROMISE, 5.30; SLAVES OF THE PHILISTINES, Jgs 13.1–5 (on Manoah, his wife, and the angel: 4.45). On the Philistines, see 5.30. The reference to aged Joshua points not only to Josh 13.1 but also 23.1 and the ensuing speech. Origen, Hom. 4 on Genesis 13.4, where Philistines are Marcionites.

5.37

S2

The intelligible fishhook is the spiritual teaching that pulls the rational soul from the depths of evil toward virtue.

S1

The spiritual fishhook is the spiritual teaching that pulls the soul from the depth of evil.

cf. Job 40.25

Job 40.25; 41.1–2; 4 Kgdms/2 Kgs 19.28; Is 37.29 and 27.1, slaughter of Leviathan the "fleeing dragon"; cf. *Letter* 6.3. DEPTHS OF EVIL: Sch. 5 on Ps 140.9. On spiritual teaching, see 4.69 (mantle).

378 EVAGRIUS OF PONTUS

5.38

S2

The one who fights for impassibility will arm himself with the commandments, but he who fights for the sake of truth with knowledge will kill his enemies. The defeat of the first [is] when he does the thing which is forbidden by the law, and of the second, when he will be leader of false teachings and intellections.

S1

The one who fights for the sake of impassibility will arm himself with the commandments of God, but the one who fights for the sake of truth will arm himself with knowledge, and will go out against his enemies. There is a defeat for the first when he will not do something that he is commanded to do, and for the second when he will fall from the truth in his doctrine and will become the head of erroneous doctrines.

> See 5.36 on killing enemies. COMMANDMENTS: *Prak.* 70, 79, 81, 82; *apatheia*, *Prak.* 83; fight for truth, *Prak.* 84; *Monks* 111; Sch. 1 on Ps 143.1 (practiced one battles for knowledge). Law, *Prak.* 49; "according to the law" *Prayer* 1; "teacher" as monastic authority; cf. *Eulogius* 31.33; teaching, *Gn.* 10. False teaching: 4.10.

5.39

S2

In pure thought are imprinted a heaven luminous to behold and a spacious region in which it appears, as intellections of beings and holy angels draw near to those who are worthy. But this sight which is imprinted is seen obscurely, and anger, when it is inflamed, fully destroys it.

S1

"The place of God" is called peace, but peace is the impassible state of rational nature. Thus the one who wishes that his God will live in him will purify his soul carefully from all passions.

> cf. Ex 24.11 (S1)
>
> See 5.41, 42; 6.33 on imprinting, Syr. *ṭbʿa*, Grk. *tupoō*, impress, stamp, mold. The contrast of heaven and region, Syr. *šmayā* and *ʾathrā*, Grk. *ouranos* and (likely) *topos* or *chōra*, points to heaven-earth pairs, e.g., Rev 21.1–4, "new heaven and

new earth" and 15 (angelic informant). See *Thoughts* 39 = *Letter* 39.5, where Syr. *'athrā* corresponds to Grk. *topos*, "place." Cf. Sch. 291 on Prv 24.27 (field). PURE THOUGHT: Plotinus, *Enn.* 6.7.40, cf. *Reflections* 2–4. Thoughts deriving from angels: *Reflections* 52. INTELLECTIONS OF BEINGS: 5.12; obscurity: 5.14, 23. In S2 the word we have translated in 5.39 is *'athrā* —meaning land or earth vs sky; presumably reflecting Mt 24.35, *šmayā w 'athrā*, Grk. *ouranos kai gē*, "heaven and earth will pass away, but my words (*meli*) will not pass away."

5.40

Greek

An intelligible mountain is spiritual *theōria*, placed on high, difficult to approach, arriving at which the mind looks steadily at the reasons of lower things.

Furrer-Pilliod 2000, p. 165 A.o.91

S2

The intelligible mountain is spiritual *theōria*, is placed at a great height, hard to approach; when the mind will arrive near it, it becomes an observer of all the intellections of things beneath.

S1

The spiritual mountain is spiritual *theōria* placed on the height. When the mind arrives there, it becomes an observer of all the reasons about natures.

cf. Ex 19.3

Ex 19.3ff.; Is 40.9; Mi 4.2. Other symbols of spiritual observation: 5.16 (dark cloud), 74 (city). Presence of God analogous to mountain: *Eight Thoughts* 8.4; ascent of the mountain: *Thoughts* 17; Sch. 341 on Prv 27.25; cf. Sch. 23 on Ps 77.54 (holy mountain is knowledge of God). Cf. Gregory of Nazianzus, *Or.* 28.2. Mountain as knowledge of God (Sch. 23 on Ps 77.54) or Christ: Sch. 1 on Ps 14.1; Sch. 3 on Ps 3.5; Sch. 2 on Ps 42.3. Cf. *KG* 2.90; 4.23, 41. Cf. Origen, *Hom. on Ex* 8.1

380 EVAGRIUS OF PONTUS

5.41

Greek

The one bearing the intelligible cosmos imprinted in himself ceases from all corruptible desire; and he is ashamed at those things he first he enjoyed; his thought frequently reproaches him for his earlier insensibility.

Mosc. 425, sixteenth century (Hausherr 1939, p. 231)

S2

The one in whose soul the intelligible world is fully imprinted keeps himself from all corruptible desire, and from now on is ashamed of the things he was enjoying, as his thinking reproaches him for his earlier insensibility.

S1

The one who carries the world of the spirit in the *theōria* of his soul, and thenceforward removes itself from every corrupt desire, and is greatly ashamed by the things he once did and enjoyed—then his thought rebukes him for all his earlier lack of understanding/discernment.

> On imprinting, see 5.39. Note that S2 implies the mind observing the imprinted soul, whereas S1 makes the soul the agent of observation. The intellect that is intelligible and composed of the *logoi* of this world, into which "pure hearts" enter: Sch. 291 on Prv 24.27, ref. Mt 13.36–44 (parable of the weeds of the field). Cf. Sch. 15 on Eccl 3.10–13 (has placed the world/age within his heart; the verse is cited at *Thoughts* 17); Sch. 38 on Eccl 5.7–11; *Reflections* 14, 38, 39. On the creation of a world fashioned by and attended to by the nous, see the next keph. and 5.12, 81; *Reflections* 14, 38, 39. The charge of "insensibility," Syr. *la margašnuthā*, Grk. *anaisthēsia*, is that one of the sense faculties does not work properly (on which see 1.34).

5.42

Greek

The world created in the mind seems to be difficult to know for us in broad daylight, since the senses distract the mind, and because of the perceptible light shining around; but at night it is possible to see it, imprinted luminously at the time of prayer.

Mosc. 425, sixteenth century (Hausherr 1939, p. 232)

S2

The world—that one fashioned in thought—seems difficult to see in the day, since the mind is enticed by the senses and by the perceptible light that shines; but by night it is visible, imprinted luminously at the time of prayer.

S1

The world of the *theōria* of the spirit that is established in the mind and is encompassed by the mind becomes visible, shining in the virtues; it is continuously darkened by a contrary inclination.

On creation of a world in the mind, see previous keph. Of the three sources of the "luminosity of the nous" described in 1.74, the last is here emphasized: luminosity arising from the observation of beings. On the light of the mind, 1.74. On imprinting, see 5.39.

5.43

Greek

An intelligible path is the best state of the rational soul, making its way along which the mind encounters things and understands their reasons.

Furrer-Pilliod 2000, p. 165 A.o.92

S2

The intelligible "way" is the state of the rational soul, on which the mind, when it travels, encounters objects and understands their reasons.

S1

The road of the spirit is the virtuous state of the rational soul, in which the mind progresses and encounters beings, and delights in the sight of them.

cf. Jn 14.6

382 EVAGRIUS OF PONTUS

There is no specific scriptural reference, appealing as it does to Gn 18.19; Is 40.3; Mt 11.10; Jn 14.6 (cited numerous times in Sch. on Psalms). PATH, Syr. *'urḥa*, Grk. *hodos*, is commented on numerous times in the scholia, e.g., Sch. 45 on Prv 4.10; Sch. 59 on Prv 5.8; Sch. 72 or Prv 6.8 (path of practice; path of observation); Sch. 9 on Ps 76.14 (in every holy thing); Sch. 17 on Ps 118.37. Origen, *Comm. on Jn* 6.3. Another symbol of a state: 4.56 (ephod). On states, see 1.80.

5.44

Greek

If anger is the wine of dragons, and their wine is undisciplined, then anger is undisciplined, making humans undisciplined, and anger is insolent. But if this drunkenness comes into being naturally from the boiling of anger, the Nazirite abstain from wine, according to the law, then it is legislated for the Nazarites to be beyond anger.

Version by Procopius: If anger is the wine of dragons, and their wine is undisciplined, then anger is undisciplined, making humans undisciplined, and anger is arrogant. It comes from the boiling of anger. But it is appointed for the Nazirites, abstaining from wine, to be without anger.

Géhin 1987, Sch. 206 on Prv 20.1

S2

If "the anger of dragons is wine," and if the Nazirites stay away from wine, then the Nazirites are commanded to be without anger.

S1

If "the anger of the dragon is" evil "wine," and Nazirites were commanded to abstain from wine; then it is just that the spiritual Nazirites always abstain from anger.

Dt 32.33; cf. Nm 6.3

For this keph., Evagrius took Sch. 206 on Prv 20.1 and compressed it into a syllogism (see 1.1). To the Deuteronomy and Numbers citations should be compared Paul's Nazirite vow at Acts 18.18. On anger, *Prak.* 11. The phrase "wine of dragons" is peculiar to the Septuagint version of Dt 32.33a, which reads "[T]heir wine is the wrath of dragons" (NETS trans.), where the Hebrew has "Their wine is the poison of dragons," and the Peshitta, "The anger of the dragon is their anger." S1's version has translated in light of the Peshitta (singular dragon instead of plural), interpreting it in light of the last half of Dt 32.33, "and the head of the asp is evil." On wine of dragons, see Sch. 8 on Ps 68.13; *Thoughts* 5 (also applied to Nazirites); Sch. 25 on Ps 17.49 (citing Ps 57.5, comparing anger to a serpent); *Letter* 56.4 (citing Ps 57.5). Cf. *Thoughts* 21 (pride and dragons). On Nazirites, see preceding references and the next keph.

5.45

Greek

The mind is called the head of the soul, but the virtues have the term of hair; when stripped of it, the Nazirite will be deprived of knowledge and will be led out in chains by the enemies.

Mosc. 425, sixteenth century (Hausherr 1939, p. 231)

S2

The mind is named the head of the soul, but the virtues are the symbol of hair; when the Nazirite is deprived of them, he is separated from knowledge, and then he will be taken and bound by his accusers.

S1

The mind is called the head of the soul, but the virtues, the hair of his Nazirite condition; when he is deprived of it, he will be surrendered into the hands of his enemies.

cf. Jgs 16.19–21

Jgs 16, Delilah cuts Samson's hair (antitype to Paul, above). On the unusual phrase OFFER THE WORD OF, Grk. *epechousi logon*, cf. Gn. 3; on word or sign of hair, Syr. *nišā d-saʿrā*, Grk. *trichōn . . . logon*, see 5.32. On the Philistines, 5.30.

5.46

S2

The high priest is he who supplicates God on behalf of all rational nature, and separates some of them from evil and others of them from ignorance.

384 EVAGRIUS OF PONTUS

S1

A high priest is the one who supplicates God on behalf of all rational natures, as by his intercession he separates some from evil, and others from ignorance.

> Christ as High Priest (Heb 4.14) offering supplications (Heb 5.7). As prototype of the *gnōstikos*: *Gn.* 48, enabling others to "return from vice and ignorance to virtue and knowledge"; cf. *Gn.* 14. On the pairing of vice and ignorance, see 2.18.

5.47

S2

We honor the angels, not on account of their nature, but on account of their virtue; and we curse the demons on account of the evil that is with them.

S1

We honor the angels not for their nature, but for their virtue, and we curse the demons, for the enormity of their evil.

> On different responses to angels and demons, see *Prak.* 24; demons not evil in nature: 3.59.

5.48

Greek

The footstool for the feet, some have said, is the flesh of Christ, which because of Christ is worshipped; but Christ is worshipped because of the *logos* of God in him.

Rondeau 2021, Sch. 2 on Ps 98.5

We venerate the flesh of the Savior, not because of the nature but because Christ is in it. And his flesh is worshipped, because of God the *Logos* who is in it.

Rondeau 2021, Sch. 5 on Ps 131.7

S2

Alone of all bodies, Christ is worshipped by us, because he alone has in him God the *Logos*.

S1

There is one body more worshipped than all—the body of Christ, because in him alone in a bodily way is God the *Logos*.

This keph. combines and compresses two different scholia on the Psalms. The one from Ps 98 has a parallel in Didymus, Fragm. Pss. 98.5 (Mühlenberg ed. 956), likely going back to an original from Origen. See Origen, *First Principles* 2.6.5 on the singularity of Christ, the unfallen nous; cf. *Contra Celsum* 2.42, *Comm. on Jn* 20.162; on the unity of Christ and God, *Contra Celsum* 6.47. On worship: 2.53.

5.49

Greek

The "recent God" is the one who is unable to cause anything to exist or the one who has been made by evil.

Furrer-Pilliod 2000, p. 179 A.π.177

[Same as above.]

Rondeau 2021, Sch. 4 on Ps 80.10

The "recent God" is the one who is unable to cause anything to exist. Or: the one who has been made by evil and is regarded by the nations.

Pitra 1876, 3:138, Sch. 4 on Ps 80.10

S2

"The new God" is he who is unable to cause something to exist, or he who is united to evil.

386 EVAGRIUS OF PONTUS

S1

"The new God" is the one unable to create something, but is full of hidden evil.

Ps 80.10

In the longer version preserved by Pitra—Πρόσφατός εστι θεὸς, ὁ μηδὲν οὐσιῶσαι δυνάμενος, ἢ (A) ὁ τῇ κακίᾳ πεποιημένος, καὶ (B) παρὰ τοῖς ἔθνεσι νενομισμένος—the second half, marked by "or," is typical of Evagrius adding to one scholion another interpretation. Phrases marked A and B appear to be quotations. Phrase A appears in catenae on Proverbs, situated near Prv 27.22, Hippolytus frag. 29, argued by Richard 1965, p. 287 to be attributable to Didymus. Phrase B is used by Eusebius in his commentary on Ps 80.10 explaining Symmachus' translation (*Comm. on Ps* PG 23:980.19). See also Schol 13 on Ps 43.21. In writing *KG* 5.49, Evagrius apparently took the scholion, dropped the phrase from Eusebius, and adapted the comment from Hippolytus/Didymus, which would not have been applicable in the context of the *KG*, to Grk. *henomenos*, thus bringing the scholion into conversation with other parts of the *KG* dealing with uniting: 1.77; 3.6, 13; 4.18; 6.29–30, 55. Cf. *Letter on Faith* 25, where Grk. *henoi* is translated Syr. *mḥid*, the same word S2 uses here at 5.49.

5.50

S2

Only the Holy Trinity is worshipped on account of itself, for from it, at the end, corporeal and incorporeal nature at the beginning came into being from nothing to something.

S1

Only the Holy Trinity before the ages is adored, from whom, afterward, all beings corporeal and incorporeal have been established from nothing.

AT THE END: Dn 12.13; Rev 2.26; AT THE BEGINNING: Mt 19.4; 1 Jn 2.13, 14; Is 40.21; 41.26. On worship: 2.53; corporeal versus incorporeal nature, 1.10, 75; creation from nothing: 2.1.

5.51

S2

The one who sees the creator according to the equality of beings does not know his (God's) nature as it is, but he knows his wisdom, she by whom he made everything. Yet I say not essential wisdom, but she who is seen in beings, whom they habitually call natural *theōria*—they who are skilled in these matters. And if this is so, what is the foolishness of those who say they know the nature of God!

S1

He who looks at God from the sight of beings does not see his nature, but the *oikonomia* of his wisdom. And if this is so, what is the foolishness of those who dare to say that they know the nature of God.

> Cf. Rom 1.10; "everything made through wisdom," Prov 3.19; 8.22.31. This keph. reinforces a theme that runs through Gregory of Nazianzus' *Theological Orations* (*Or.* 27–31), directed against Eunomians. Cf. Origen, *First Principles* 2.6.1, *Comm. on Jn* 19.6.37–38, *Contra Celsum* 6.65. On wisdom, as well as skill in it, 1.14.

5.52

S2

For a pure mind are required the intellections of bodies; for a purer one, the intellections of incorporeals; and for one purer than all these, the Holy Trinity.

S1

When we seek to see bodies, we require a pure mind. But when for incorporeals, a greater purity; but even greater, when we will draw near to see the Holy Trinity.

> This keph. forms a pair with 5.57. On PURE MIND, 2.34; INTELLECTIONS: 2.30. These three intellections correspond in reverse order to parts of 1.27, 70.

5.53

Greek

A spiritual sacrifice is a pure conscience, placed upon the state of the mind as upon the altar of sacrifice.

388 EVAGRIUS OF PONTUS

Furrer-Pilliod 2000, p. 138 A.θ.76

S2

A spiritual sacrifice is a pure conscience, which is placed upon the state of the mind as upon an altar.

S1

[Same as S2]

cf. 1 Pt 2 5

On GOOD CONSCIENCE, Grk. *syneidēsis*, see Ac 23.1; 24.16; 1 Tm 3.9; 2 Tm 1.3; UPON AN ALTAR, *Prayer* 3, 21, 147. On STATE see 6.21 (Grk. *hexis*); *Prak.* 12 (Grk. *katastasis*); on THE ALTAR, see 2.57.

5.54

S2

Just as it is harder to see intellections of incorporeals than to approach things by means of the senses, so it is more difficult to know the intellections of corporeals than to see corporeals themselves.

S1

Just as it is more difficult to know the intellections of natures than to see their manifestation, so it is more difficult to know the reasons about bodies than to see the bodies themselves.

On INTELLECTIONS: 2.30; corporeals versus incorporeals: 1.10, 75; senses: 1.34.

5.55

S2

The Holy Trinity is not a thing that is mixed with *theōria*, for this happens to creatures alone. Then reverently a human being will call this essential knowledge.

S1

The Holy Trinity is not a thing of qualities; for this belongs to creatures.

KEPHALAIA GNOSTIKA 389

This keph., dealing with the mixing of observation and the object, should be read closely with the next, about their separation. WILL CALL THIS: points to observation unmixed. On ESSENTIAL KNOWLEDGE: 1.89.

5.56

S2

Someone who has been separated from objects has not entirely fallen from the *theōria* that is about them, nor has he lost the *theōria* that is on the outside of objects. But it has not been so concerning the Holy Trinity. For we believe that it alone is essential knowledge.

S1

He who has been separated from things is deprived of *theōria* about them as well, and he who has been removed from *theōria* will also find himself outside the *theōria* of these things. But it is not this way with the Holy Trinity, for we believe that it is essential knowledge.

See previous keph. The last sentence, WE BELIEVE, poss. Grk. *pisteuomen*, points to the beginning of credal formulas such as that of Nicea-Constantinople. On separation, cf. note at *Prak.* 52.

5.57

Greek

Just as now, we approach perceptible things through the senses, but later, purified, we know their reasons, so also first we shall see things themselves, and then, more greatly purified, we shall also enter *theōria* about them, after which it is possible to know finally the holy Trinity itself.

Mosc. 425, sixteenth century (Hausherr 1939, p. 231)

S2

Just as now by means of perceptions we are brought to approach perceptible objects, but at the end, when we have been made pure and we will know their

390 EVAGRIUS OF PONTUS

reasons, thus at first we see objects themselves, and when we are more greatly purified, we also know the *theōria* about them, for then after that it is possible, therefore, also to know the Holy Trinity.

S1

Just as now by means of the senses we see natures, also, when purified, we see their *theōria*. Likewise, when we have been more greatly purified, we gaze upon the *theōria* of incorporeals, and when thrice purified, we are worthy of the sight of the Holy Trinity.

This keph. forms a pair with 5.52. On observation of perceptibles and intelligibles, see Sch. 15 on Eccl 3.10–13; Sch. 5 on Prv 1.7. Here in the Greek fragment, and in the scholia, Evagrius uses the term *epiballein* (translated as Syr. *methqarbinan*) for the first step, and *epopteuein* for the second step (but here, 5.57, *epigignōskein*). The two acts here result in seeing (Grk. *opsometha*) and entering (*eisometha*). On *epigignōskein*, cf. Plotinus, *Ennead* 1.6.

5.58

S2

The mind distinguishes sensation not as an object of sensation, but as sensation, but the sensation discerns what are capable of being perceived by the senses, not as objects [in and of themselves], but as sensible objects.

S1

The faculty of sense distinguishes objects of sense, but the mind their *theōria*.

See next keph. Cf. Porphyry, *Launching Points to the Intelligibles* 16, 22. Sense perception: 1.34. See also 4.77 (objects outside mind, but observation inside); 5.12 (mind's abandonment of senses).

5.59

S2

Sensation does not distinguish sensation, but distinguishes only organs of sense, not as organs of sense but as what are capable of being perceived by the senses. But the mind distinguishes sensation as sensation, and the senses as the senses.

S1

Sense does not distinguish sense, and sensing faculties do not distinguish other sensing faculties, but perceptible things. But the mind distinguishes the sense-faculties from the senses.

> On SENSATION: previous keph. and 1.34. This keph. provides an example of seeing something as itself, on which see *Gn.* 4.

5.60

S2

One thing is the power of the mind that sees spiritual natures, and another thing is that which knows the *theōria* that is about them. But one is the power that sees and knows the Holy Trinity.

S1

One thing is the strength of the mind when it is observing natures, and another is its power when it observes the *theōria* of them. But single is its power when it is worthy to look at the Holy Trinity.

> The unusual phrasing ONE THING . . . ANOTHER prob. reflects an original Grk. *allē . . . allē.* Their separation is to be contrasted with the single unity of the last power. Cf. Sch. 15 on Eccl 3.10–13. On POWER OF THE MIND: 2.15; SPIRITUAL NATURES: 5.74.

5.61

S2

However many times we observe material things, we arrive at the memory of their *theōria.* And when we receive *theōria*, we are further distanced from material things. But this does not happen to us in the case of the Holy Trinity, for it alone is essential *theōria.*

392 EVAGRIUS OF PONTUS

S1

When we observe material objects, we remember the *theōria* of them, and when we receive the *theōria*, then we come to the memory of material things. But it does not happen to us with the *theōria* of the Holy Trinity.

> This keph. assumes a basic understanding of a classical model of cognition, where the perceptions of the *aisthēseis* were deposited in the memory, Grk. *mnēmē*, perhaps via an intermediary such as *dianoia*, understanding, available for retrieval from a higher faculty. "Essential knowledge" is a recurring phrase in the *KG* (see 1.89), but this appears to be the sole instance of ESSENTIAL THEŌRIA.

5.62

S2

The nature of the Trinity is not known by means of ascents and descents. For there are no underlying objects there, and its nature does not admit analysis because that which analyzes the nature of bodies establishes it entirely with matter and with form. If someone will analyze incorporeal nature he will return to natural *theōria* and to substance receptive of opposition. But it is not possible to know in this way the nature of the holy Trinity.

S1

The Holy Trinity is not a thing of composites or of qualities or of lack or of greatness; for it is a singular essence that is entirely equal, perpetually, to itself.

> ASCENTS AND DESCENTS, 4.17 (S1); 5.63 (S1); Plotinus, *Ennead* 1.1, 2, etc. On ascents: 1.67 (S1); 4.43 (S1), 80 (S1); 6.19 (the return); on analysis, the next keph. On substance receptive of opposites, see 1.1–2; Aristotle, *Cat.* 4a–b. On defining the Trinity, *Gn.* 27; 41; *Letter on Faith* 7. The term FORM, Syr. *ḥzatha'* (literally, "view"), is likely Grk. *eidos*, as at 1.46. ESTABLISHES, Syr. *mqim*, likely from a Grk. compound with -*istēmi*, could imply an intellectual or material act; see next note on "analysis."

5.63

S2

Analysis indeed causes us to ascend to the "in the beginning" of objects, and knowledge according to proportion, makes visible the wisdom of the creator, but it is not in these signs that we see the Holy Trinity. For it does not have a beginning, and we do not at all say that the wisdom in these objects is God, if in the *theōria* of nature these beginnings are in accord with the things of which they are the beginnings. For wisdom that is like this is the knowledge that is without substance which appears in objects alone.

S1

In the *theōria* of beings, there are ascents and descents, according to diligence and negligence. But it is not so in the *theōria* of the Holy Trinity. For it is a sight equal in itself, lacking ascent or descent.

> Cf. Gn 1.1; Wis 11.20
> Cf. Wis: 1.14; Col 2.3, "treasures of wisdom and knowledge hidden in Christ."
> IN THE BEGINNING, Gn 1.1; ACCORDING TO PROPORTION, Wis 11.20. ANALYSIS, both here and in the previous keph., is Syr. *šaria'*, perhaps translating a Grk. compound with *-lysis*, which can also mean dissolution, as in 2.17. If so, then the Greek would have been intentionally ambiguous, inviting the reader to think of objects being mentally analyzed and materially dissolved. S1's unique invocation of ascents and descents draws from the previous keph. WITHOUT SUBSTANCE, Syr. *lā qnomā*, likely Grk. *anupostatos* (cf. 1.3): 6.10, 13; *Disc.* 30 (observation of beings is without substance).

5.64

S2

Just as a mirror that remains unpolluted by images seen in it, so the impassible soul from things that are on earth.

S1

[Same as S2, with a minor insertion]

394 EVAGRIUS OF PONTUS

MIRROR: 1 Cor 13.12; 2 Cor 13.8; Jas 1.23. Cf. *Prak.* 64, mind sees objects with serenity. Mirrors: 2.1. FROM THINGS: S1 inserts "all."

5.65

Greek

A practicing one is a recruit of prudence; a gnostic is shield-bearer of wisdom.

Furrer-Pilliod 2000, p. 179 A.π.178

S2

The one who practices is the soldier of discernment, but the gnostic is a shield-bearer of wisdom.

S1

[Same as S2]

Ps 58.12; 4 Mc 3.12; cf. *Gn.* 1. Syr. *puršā* means separation, distinguishing, and departure, but here discernment. The Syriac employs wordplay: *palāḥā* refers to the practiced one, but *pālḥā* is a soldier. Likewise, *ma'drānā* generally means "helper," but in martial contexts, is a shieldbearer, as in Ps 58.12, corroborated by the Greek fragment.

5.66

S2

The mind is not united to knowledge before it has united the impassioned part of its soul to the virtues of its person.

S1

The mind is unable to share in the knowledge of the Spirit before the passionate part of the soul will arrive at health.

On being united, see 5.49. The passionate part of the soul refers to both the angering and desiring parts, so "personal virtues" refer to those befitting either one; see *Prak.* 89.

5.67

S2

If rational natures bear the sign of trees, but these "grow beside the water," it is said correctly that knowledge is called spiritual water that flows from "the spring of life."

S1

If rational natures bear the sign of trees "growing tall beside the waters," it is evident that knowledge is living waters that flow from "the source of life."

Ps 1.3; 35.10

This keph. forms a pair with 5.69. SIGN OF TREES: Gn 2.3, Rev 22.2; SPRING OF LIFE: Jn 4.14; Rev 21.6. Trees: 3.56. SPIRITUAL WATER: cf. 1 Cor 10.4 (*poma*) on Ex 17; Nm 20.2–13. Reasoning natures: 1.89. On water: Sch. 4 on Ps 148.4 (the waters of Genesis, which praise the Lord, signify the holy rational orders distributed in different worlds).

5.68

Greek

An intelligible Philistine is he who stands against those who travel into the land of the promise.

Furrer-Pilliod 2000, p. 85 A.α.188

S2

The intelligible Philistine is he who stands against those who enter to inherit the land of promise.

396 EVAGRIUS OF PONTUS

S1

[Same as S2]

Cf. 5.30, 36. On Philistines (here Grk. *allophylos*), see note at 5.30. The Philistine par excellence is Goliath: 1 Kgdms/1 Sam 17.8, 10, 32–33, 45; 2 Kgdms/2 Sam 21.15–22. Cf. Rev 12.7f. Goliath represented the attempt to drive out the Israelites (see 5.71), not to prevent them from entering, so the reference here may be to the Philistines as a whole, who opposed Joshua. See 5.71.

5.69

S2

The Holy Trinity is the sign of holy water, and the tree of life is the christ who drinks from it.

S1

The Holy Trinity is the holy "waters", beside which is planted the tree of life.

cf. Gn 2.9

This keph. forms a pair with 5.67. On trees: 3.56.

5.70

Greek

A place of knowledge of God. And a mind is a place of knowledge of God.

Rondeau 2021, Sch. 2 on Ps 78.7

S2

Just as our body is said to be in a place, so also the mind is in some kind of knowledge. Because of this, knowledge rightly is called its place.

S1

Just as our body is said to be in this place or that, likewise our mind is in differing kinds of knowledge.

The scholion and S2 are inversions, and the Greek might be better considered a parallel than a fragment. The Greek parallel lacks a finite verb. On being in a place, Grk. *topos*: 1.61–62. On PLACE OF KNOWLEDGE: cf. Sch 332 on Prv 27.8. On knowledge and place: 1.71; 2.6; place in general: 2.37.

5.71

Greek

A noetic Raphaite is the one striving to drive out again those entering into the land of the promise.

Furrer-Pilliod 2000, p. 181 A.ρ.6

S2

The intelligible warrior is the one who strives to drive out from it those who have entered the land of promise.

S1

The rebellious warrior is the one who strives to drive out from it those who have entered the land of promise.

The Greek fragment reads *raphaitēs*, a person from the tribe of Raphaim; cf. Gn 15.20; Dt 2.11, 20; 3.11, 13; Josh 15.8; 2 Kgdms/2 Sam 23.13. The word is nowhere else in Greek literature (a *hapax legomenon*), including the LXX. The Raphaim were reported to be "a nation, great and numerous and rather powerful, just as the Enakim, and the Lord destroyed them from before them, and they took possession and were settled in place of them" (Dt 2.21, NETS). Cf. Origen, *Hom. on Josh* 22.4, who is commanded to "purge the Raphaein from among you" (Josh 17.15, Hexapla), a name Origen takes to signify "languid mothers" (*resolutae matres*) who bear weak and useless thoughts.

5.72

S2

If the four rulers are divided from a single "river", let someone say, "the world in which there was one river," so that a body will understand also the Paradise from which he drinks.

398 EVAGRIUS OF PONTUS

S1

If the four sources are divided from one source, we will understand by means of differentiation their exits and their regions/courses and their countries.

cf. Gn 2.10

Four rivers: Gn 2.10–14; river of life: Rev 22.1–7. Cf. Sch. 9 on Ps 17.16 (founts are the virtues whence knowledge comes). See 5.67, 69 on trees and water. On paradise, 5.1.

5.73

S2

The mind is amazed when it sees objects and is untroubled in the *theōria* of them, but it runs as if toward household members and friends.

S1

The mind is amazed when it sees natures, and is untroubled; it encounters a related *theōria* and is beloved to it.

Those of a household [of God], *oikeioi*, 1 Tm 5.8; Eph 2.19; Gal 6.10; and *philoi*, "friends," Jn 11.11 (Lazarus). Cf. 5.73; Sch. 2 On Eccl 1.2; schol. 5 on Ps 39.4; 79 on Ps 118, 171; 6 on Ps 148.14. Plato, *Phaedrus* 250a6; Plotinus, *Enneads* 6.7.31.7. On observation of objects, 5.56–61, 75–76.

5.74

Greek

An intelligible city containing the intelligible natures.

Furrer-Pilliod 2000, p. 176 A.π.122

S2

The intelligible city is the spiritual *theōria* that encloses spiritual natures.

S1

The city is the *theōria* of the spirit that contains in itself rational natures.

cf. Mt 5.14

The Greek fragment seems to have lost a noun to go with CONTAINING, likely *theōria* as in S1 and S2 (cf. the parallel grammatical construction at 5.16). Although the citation is attributed by Guillaumont to Mt 5.14, it is also, given other keph. of this kind, an Old Testament reference to Jerusalem or to wisdom as a city, as in Sch. 229 on Prv 21.22: Wisdom is a strong city in which the wise dwell, "having destroyed thoughts, and every proud obstacle (*hypsòma*) raised up against the knowledge of God (2 Cor 10.5)." Cf. *Eulogius* 10; *Eight Thoughts* 1.24; 7.13–15; 8.15; *Prak.* pr.2; *Letters* 4 and 15; Sch. 14 on Ps 30.22; Sch. 3 on Ps 45.5; Sch. 2 on Ps 106.4. Origen, *Hom. on Josh* 18.3. For city as a negative symbol: *Thoughts* 9, 14, 15, 20, 21; *Letter on Faith* 3. City as the mirror of the soul: Plato, *Republic* 2.368c–369a. Other symbols of spiritual observation: 5.16 (dark cloud), 40 (mountain). Spiritual natures: 5.60.

5.75

S2

To the degree that the mind is stripped of passions, thus even more is it brought near to objects, and according to the degree of its order it also receives knowledge. Every rank in which it will stand knows *theōria* as its own.

S1

The more the mind is stripped of passions, so much more does it see intellections and the more its zeal presses, so much more is its knowledge enriched.

Rank, *taxis*: Origen, *Comm. on Jn* 2.17. Angelic ranks, cf. 2.66. On observation of objects, 5.56–61, 73, 76.

5.76

S2

Knowing natures examine objects and the knowledge of objects purifies the gnostics.

400 EVAGRIUS OF PONTUS

S1

A gnostic nature examines the knowledge of natures, and the same knowledge purifies the gnostics.

Cf. *Gn.* 9. Examine: 6.58, 73. Purify: *Thoughts* 19, 24; *Prayer* 39.

5.77

Greek

Intelligible gates are virtues of a rational soul prepared by practice and by God's power.

Furrer-Pilliod 2000, p. 179 A.π.180

He says that the gates are the virtues.

Géhin 1987, Sch. 12 on Prv 1.20–21

He says that the gates of the powerful are the virtues of the wise.
Prokopios version: The gates of the wise are the practical virtues through which the wisdom of God enters.

Géhin 1987, Sch. 267 on Prv 24.7

The gates of the wise are the practical virtues through which the wisdom of God enters.

Rondeau 2021, Sch. 4 on Ps 23.7

S2

The intelligible gates are the virtues of the rational and practicing soul, constituted from the power of God.

S1

The intelligible gates are the virtues of the rational soul that have been constituted by the zeal of the mind and by the power of God.

cf. Ps 23.7

Ps 74.7–10; 117.19–20; Jn 10.7–9; Rev 21–22. Five Greek fragments survive. The best is from the collection of definitions, and matches S2 almost exactly, although the latter seems to have had a text where BY (*dia*) and AND (*kai*) were transposed. Other extant Greek fragments come from two different scholia collections and exemplify how Evagrius adapted the same material to different contexts. He depicts the gates here as a pair of sets of virtues, which draws from Sch. 4–5 on Ps 117.19–20, which treats two sets: the gates of righteousness and the (one) gate of knowledge. See also Sch. 1 on Ps 99.4 (gates of wisdom are virtues). POWER OF GOD: *Prayer* 94.

5.78

S2

The bodies of demons do not grow bigger or become smaller, and a sharp smell accompanies them, by which they also stir up the passions. But they are easily known by those who have received from the Lord the power to sense that smell.

S1

The subtle bodies of the demons neither grow bigger nor smaller, and a harsh smell accompanies them, whose odor is perceptible by those who have received from the Lord the power to sense it.

BODIES OF DEMONS: 1.11. SHARP SMELL or stench, Syr. *sriuta'*, likely Grk. *dysōdia*: *Prak.* 39; Job 6.7; Tb 6.17. On good smell: 2.35; cf. 4.37 on breathing. Bad smell of demons: Athanasius, *Life of Anthony* 63.

5.79

S2

Everything that falls under the power of the mind, which sees the incorporeals, is also entirely of its nature. But something that is seen by the other (power), this is unable to be connatural if the same power will know about intellections of incorporeals and about the holy Trinity.

402 EVAGRIUS OF PONTUS

S1

To sense the *theōria* of natures, then, belongs to the power of the mind, but to see the Holy Trinity is not of power alone, but is a better gift of grace.

> On the power of the mind: 2.15; intellections: 2.30; connatural/same nature: 1.46; 6.14, 79.

5.80

Greek

An intelligible deadbolt is a free will unbending because of the good itself.

> Furrer-Pilliod 2000, p. 151 A.μ.78

S2

The intelligible deadbolt is the ruling freedom that does not bend because of the good.

S1

The deadbolt of the spirit is the freedom of a rational nature, which in its zeal does not bend in the face of evil, because of its love of the good.

> The term "deadbolt," Syr. *muklā*, is a loanword from Grk. *mochloi*, which in most contexts denotes a deadbolt, which resonates with the gates in 5.77. But it also fits similar keph. on the tabernacle furnishings: in Ex 28.28 the beams or bars for the tabernacle are *mochloi*. Origen, *Hom. on Ex* 9.3 writes of the tabernacle *made firm by bars*: "One can also defend himself with *bars* when he has bound himself with the unanimity of love." See also Jgs 16.3, Samson. Sch. 1 on Ps 147.1–2: the bars of the gates of Jerusalem are the practicing virtues hindering the enemies from slipping in. It is treated as a symbol of evil at Sch. 7 on Ps 106.16, where the Lord's breaking of the bars symbolizes the unbending character of the *hēgemonikon* as resistance to virtue. FREE WILL/RULING FREEDOM, Grk. *autexousiōtēs*, Syr. *ḥiruthā mšālṭuthā*, points to the *hēgemonikon*, on which see *Prak.* pr.2.

5.81

S2

When the mind will receive essential knowledge, then it will be called "god," because it will also be able to fashion various worlds.

S1

When the mind will be made worthy to be in the *theōria* of the holy unity, then by grace also it will be called "god," because it will be perfected in the image of its creator.

Cf. Ps 81.6. ESSENTIAL KNOWLEDGE: 1.89. On the nous fashioning worlds, see 5.41; use of Ps 81.6: 4.51. Becoming god: 3.1.

5.82

Greek

An intelligible wall is the rational soul's *apatheia*, unapproachable by demons.

Furrer-Pilliod 2000, p. 194 A.т.47

The walls of Jerusalem signify the soul's *apatheia*. After the demons destroy them, the passions of adultery enter in.

Rondeau 2021, Sch. 6 on Ps 50.20

S2

The intelligible wall is the soul's *apatheia*, that to which the demons do not draw near.

S1

The wall of the spirit is the rational soul's freedom, that which protects it from demons.

Ps 50.20. Wall as apatheia: Sch. 293 on Prv 24.31 (here Grk. *phragmos*, fence); Sch. 343 on Prv 28.4; cf. Sch. 14 on Ps 30.22 (a walled city is a soul free of passion). See also 5.77 and 80 on city and deadbolt.

404 EVAGRIUS OF PONTUS

5.83

S2

All circumcisions are seven, we have found: four of them of the sixth day, one of them of the seventh, and the remainder of the eighth day.

S1

According to the word of the fathers, we have found that all circumcisions are seven: four of them are of the sixth day, and one of the seventh, and the remainder, of the eighth day.

> For circumcision, see 4.12. See 1.90 on Friday; days and years as eschatological allegory. On the six and seven years: cf. Sch. 208 on Prv 20.4. See 5.8; 6.66 on the sixth, seventh, and eighth day/year; cf. *Reflections* 6; Sch. 76 on Ps 118.164 (8 = world to come; 7 = this *kosmos*). WE HAVE FOUND: points to personal observation; cf. *Thoughts* 8, 34.

5.84

Greek

An intelligible temple is a pure mind having "the wisdom of God full of varieties" consecrated in itself . . . A temple of God is one who is an observer of the holy unity.

> Furrer-Pilliod 2000, p. 155 A.v.46–47

S2

The intelligible temple is the pure mind that now has in it "the wisdom of God full of distinctions." The temple of God is that one who is an observer of the holy unity, and the altar of God is the *theōria* of the Holy Trinity.

S1

The spiritual temple is the one who is able to become a dwelling for "the wisdom of God full of distinctions," and he will be perfected in becoming a temple for God when he will be worthy of the *theōria* of the Holy Trinity.

Eph 3.10; cf. 1 Cor 3.16–17; 6.19–20

Greek fragments survive for all but the last sentence of this keph. The temple here refers to any number of Old Testament references to the temple(s), and subsequent New Testament references, e.g., 1 Cor 3.16–17; 6.19–20; Rev 21–22. INTELLIGIBLE TEMPLE as Christ: Sch. 4–5 on Ps 5.8; Sch. 8 on Ps 34.11; Sch. 2 on Ps 27.2; Sch. 2 on Ps 126.1; Sch. 4 on Ps 17.7; Sch. 1 on Ps 83.3; and cf. *Maxims 2* 9. PURE MIND: 2.34; OBSERVER: 2.27; WISDOM: 1.14; the frequent use of Eph 3.10: 2.2; HOLY UNITY (Grk. *monados*): 1.49; 3.61; HOLY TRINITY: 1.74.

5.85

S2

The first nature is because of the one; the second is toward the one; and the same is in the one.

S1

[Same as S2]

This keph. forms a pair with 5.87. Origen, *First Principles* 2.1–3. First and second nature: 2.31.

5.86

Greek

A vainglorious one is the one wishing before [attaining] *apatheia* to be glorified by human beings in things that naturally come from *apatheia* and knowledge of God.

Furrer-Pilliod 2000, p. 138 A.κ.37

S2

The single one who loves vainglory is the one who before *apatheia* seeks to be glorified by human beings in the things that do not exist for *apatheia* and the knowledge of God.

406 EVAGRIUS OF PONTUS

S1

The single one who loves vainglory is the one who before *apatheia* tries to be glorified by human beings, but the humble of spirit is the one who, even after the healing of the soul, does not desire the glory that comes from humans.

> Single one: *īḥīdāyā*, elsewhere "only-begotten," here translated as referring to a monk; see 3.1. Sole reference in *KG* to a solitary, i.e., monk, but only in the Syriac versions, not the Greek. THINGS THAT DO NOT EXIST suggests that S2 had a defective version of this text. The three Greek manuscripts exhibit a variety of readings (Furrer-Pilliod, p. 138 no. 38). On vainglory, *Prak.* 13.

5.87

S2

The knowledge of the second [beings] is in the first, and that of the first is in it; but the second is not knowing.

S1

The second knowledge is in the first *theōria*, and this itself in the same.

> This keph. forms a pair with 5.85. THE FIRST: Rev 22.13 and Is 44.6, i.e., Christ (God). On first and second beings, 1.50. Syr. *idu''*, can mean "intimate/acquaintance" or, as in Lv 19.31, wizard, "instructed/skillful."

5.88

S2

Zion is in the first knowledge, but Egypt is the mark of all evil; but the symbol of natural *theōria* is Jerusalem, in which is the mountain of Zion, the acropolis.

S1

Zion is in the first *theōria*, and all evil is signified by Egypt, but the sign of natural *theōria* is Jerusalem, for in it is the mountain of Zion.

On Zion: 5.6; mountains: 4.23; Egypt: 4.64; Jerusalem: 1.31.

5.89

S2

Just as the destruction of the last world will not be accompanied by a creation, so the creation of the first world is not preceded by a destruction.

S1

Just as after the end of the world no generation of human beings will follow, so also no destruction has preceded the genesis of the first nature.

> Origen on aeon: *First Principles* 3.6.3. On destruction of worlds, *KG* 2.17; the last world: 5.3.

5.90

Greek

Things as they are by nature—either the pure mind sees or the spiritual reason clearly furnishes. But the one stripped of both will go forth to the slander of the scribe.

> Mosc. 425, sixteenth century (Hausherr 1939, p. 231)

S2

Things as they are naturally—either the pure mind sees or the logos of the wise men makes known. But the one who is deprived of them both comes to the blame of the writer.

S1

Either the pure mind sees the sight of beings as it truly is, or the word of the sages has made it known. But the one who is deprived of them both comes to the blame of the writer.

> Objects seen by the pure mind: according to the logos of the sages: Plotinus, *Enneads* 1.3.4.1; Plato, *Phaedrus* 248. On spiritual *logos*, see 5.28 (rational sword). The manuscript that attests to the Grk. fragment may reflect a scribal error at *logos pneumatikos*, which may have been *logos tōn philosophōn*, as in

408   EVAGRIUS OF PONTUS

S1 and S2. The Syriac can be read both as "he who" and "that which." SLANDER OF THE SCRIBE/BLAME OF THE WRITER: no known parallel.

Epilogue

S2

The fifth century is finished.

S1

The fifth century is finished, which lacks ten chapters.

Century Six

S2

Century Six

S1

[Same as S2]

6.1

S2

What is *theōria* of beings, the divine book does not make known; but it has taught openly how someone draws near to it by the practice of the commandments and by the true teachings.

S1

What is the *theōria* of beings, the holy book has not made known; but it has taught clearly how we might come to it by the practice of the commandments and by the truth of knowledge. "For who will go up to the mountain of the Lord?," and the rest.

> Ps 23.3 (S1)
> This keph. forms a pair with the next. DIVINE BOOK: see next keph. Bible as teacher "in the Stoa," Origen, *Comm. on Jn* 6.3. S1 has added to his translation a quotation from Ps 23.3, and instructed the reader (AND THE REST) to apply the entire Psalm to the keph.; TRUE TEACHINGS: 4.10; observation of beings: 1.73.

6.2

S2

The *theōria* of this world is double: the first visible and dense; the second intelligible and spiritual. To the first *theōria* are drawn unworthy men and demons. But to the second, righteous men and the angels of God. And to the extent that angels know spiritual *theōria* more than do righteous people, so also the demons know dense *theōria* more than do unworthy people. Some of this the demons provide

410 EVAGRIUS OF PONTUS

to those who belong to them. But we have learned from the divine book that the holy angels also practice this.

S1

The *theōria* of this world is double: the first literally, the second in spirit. Even unjust people approach the first, but only holy people draw near the second.

> This keph. forms a pair with the previous one. VISIBLE, Syr. *galithā*, entails cognition of the senses, contrasted with INTELLIGIBLE, of the mind. Thickness: 3.68; 4.36, 46. Thick teaching and thick knowledge: *Letter on Faith* 22–24. Angelic, human, and demonic observation: *Thoughts* 8; angelic knowledge: Lk 2.8–20.

6.3

S2

The perceptible peoples are distinguished from each other by places, by laws, and by languages and by clothes, and sometimes also by qualities. But intelligible and holy [nations are distinguished] by worlds, and by bodies, by [types of] knowledge, and, they say, also by languages. The father of the first is Adam, of the second, Christ, of whom Adam is a type.

S1

The nations we can perceive are distinguished from each other by regions, and by languages, by clothes, and sometimes also by qualities, but holy nations, by conducts, by [types of] knowledge, and by the gifts of the Spirit.

> cf. Rom 5.14 (S2)
> Perceptible and intelligible nations: 6.71. On Adam as father of peoples: 1 Paral/ 1 Chron 1–25. Languages: 4.35; 1 Cor 13.1; angelic languages, previously in *Testament of Job* 48.3; 49.2; 50.1–2; *1 Enoch* 71.11. CLOTHES, Syr. *'askimē*, loan word from Grk. *schēmata*, may also be rendered "forms" or "shapes." THEY SAY: source unknown. Cf. 5.1, Adam as a type of Christ.

KEPHALAIA GNOSTIKA 411

6.4

S2

The Father is reckoned before the Son as father, but before the Holy Spirit as principle, but before incorporeals and corporeals as creator.

S1

The true father is called the father of Christ and the principle of the Holy Spirit, but he is the creator of beings.

> On the Father: 2.22. The trinitarian relationships are repeated at 6.20. The Father is most frequently described as the source (Grk. *archē*) not of the Spirit but of the Son; Lampe, s.v. ἀρχή D2b. A very similar version of this keph. appears at *Disc.* 29: "The Father is at once father and principle, and father of the Son but principle of the Holy Spirit, not in time but in essence." Cf. John of Damascus, *Dialogues against Manichaeans* 4. Cf. Origen, *First Principles* 1.3.4 and *Hom. on Nm* 11.8; in the background is Gregory of Nazianzus, *Or.* 31.

6.5

Greek

Uncreated is that before whose essential existence nothing of beings has been previously thought.

> Furrer-Pilliod 2000, p. 72 A.α.12

S2

"Uncreated" is that to which nothing is prior, in that it exists in its essence.

S1

[Same as S2]

412   EVAGRIUS OF PONTUS

The Greek is compressed, and difficult: ἀγένητόν ἐστιν οὗ κατ᾽ οὐσίαν ὑπάρχοντος οὐδὲν προεπινενόηται τῶν ὄντων. HAS BEEN PREVIOUSLY THOUGHT, Grk. *proepinenoētai*, cognate with *epinoia*; see note at 1.17.

6.6

S2

Just as the blade circumcised the perceptible Jew, so the practice [circumcised] the intelligible [Jew], that [practice] which Christ symbolically named the sword that he "cast upon the world."

S1

Just as the blade circumcised the perceptible Jew, so also the practice of the commandments of God [circumcised] the spiritual Jew, according to the teaching of our Lord, who said, "A sword I have come to cast upon the world."

Mt 10.34

Syr. *saifā* and *ḥarbā*: in Mt 10.34 it is Grk. *machaira* (Pesh. *ḥarbā*); Heb 4.12 *machaira distomos*; LXX Gn 27.3 *saifā* = Grk. *skeuos*. On circumcision, 4.12 and 6.66 (blade of Christ in the second circumcision). On the contrast between perceptible and intelligible nations: 6.3.

6.7

S2

If the eighth day is a symbol of resurrection, and resurrection is Christ, then those who are circumcised on the eighth day are circumcised in Christ.

S1

If the eighth day is the day of the resurrection, and our resurrection is our Lord Jesus, it is clear that those who are circumcised on the eighth day are circumcised in him.

cf. Gn 17.12; cf. Jn 11.25; cf. Col 2.11

Circumcision on the eighth day: Gn 17.25 and *KG* 5.83. On days and years: 1.90; circumcision: 4.12; resurrection: 3.77.

KEPHALAIA GNOSTIKA 413

6.8

Greek

Just as Paradise is the habitation of the just, Hades is the place of punishment of sinners.

Rondeau 2021, Sch. 7 on Ps 9.18

S2

Just as Paradise is the instruction of the righteous, so also Sheol is the torment of the impious.

S1

Just as Paradise is the delight of the righteous, so Sheol is the torment of the impious.

The Greek fragment has been adjusted, from specific institutions to the abstract activities. INSTRUCTION, Syr. *mardutha*, sometimes translates Grk. *nouthēsia* (admonition; see Pesh. 1 Cor 10.11) but more frequently *paideia* (instruction; see Pesh. Prv 5.23, Eph 6.4); "torment," Syr. *mšanqanitha*, possibly Grk. *basanismos* (torture; Pesh. Mt 8.29) or *kolasis* (chastisement, correction; Pesh. Mt 25.46), but the latter is more common in Evagrius' other works (see below). For instruction and torture, see Sir 4.16. Chastisement (*kolasis*) was, for Evagrius' predecessors, also a form of instruction (*paideia*); see, e.g., Clement, *Strom.* 7.16.102; Origen, *Comm. on Jn* 28.19.165. On torment, see 1.44; 5.5. For *kolasis*, see Sch. 11.1 on Prv 1.17 where Evagrius inverts the "flight of the soul"; Sch. 145 on Prv 16.14; Sch. 268 on Prv 24.9–10; Sch. 319 on Prv 26.3 (the rod, *rhabdos*, is *kolasis*) and 364 on Prv 29.18. Origen, *First Principles* 2.11.6–7, paradise a school; *Comm. on Jn* 1.263 on Is 11.1: "One should know that [Christ] does not make a staff (*rabdos*) and flower (*anthos*) for the same human beings, but a staff for some needing punishment (*kolasis*) and a flower for the saved." On the imagery of the latter, 5.69; *Prak.* pr.7: at the beginning of monastic discipline, the staff is a "tree of life." Cf. Sch. 32 on Prv 3.18; *Thoughts* 8.23–25. Cf. also on the tree of life: Philo, *On the Migration of Abraham and On the Virtues* 8.36–42 and the anonymous *Life of Adam and Eve* 5.

414 EVAGRIUS OF PONTUS

6.9

S2

If time is reckoned with becoming and corruption, then the becoming of the incorporeals is timeless, because corruption is not prior to this becoming.

S1

If corruption is subjected to time, the first becoming is prior to corruption.

On TIME, see 2.87; CORRUPTION: 1.55.

6.10

S2

The Holy Trinity is not like a tetrad, and a pentad, and a hexad. These are numerical, forms without substance, but the Holy Trinity is essential knowledge.

S1

The Holy Trinity is not like a tetrad, and a pentad, and the rest; for they are numbers, but the Holy Trinity is a single essence.

This keph. forms a set with the next three. See Sch. 15 on Ps 76.21, the philosophy of Moses as a tetrachtys (divided fourfold), on Clement, *Strom.* 1.28 commenting on Aristotle, *Metaphysics* 1.28.176. Plotinus, *Enneads* 6.6; Origen, God as triad, *First Principles* 1.4.3. On number, 1.7; ESSENTIAL KNOWLEDGE, 1.89. On the Trinity not going beyond three, see Gregory Nazianzen, *Or.* 23.8; cf. 29.2. Evagrius' assertion that numerical forms lack substance has no known precedent. This peculiar definition of number is used at 6.13. On WITHOUT SUBSTANCE, associated with observation of beings, see 5.63; 6.13; form: 1.22.

6.11

S2

A tetrad follows a numerical trinity, but a tetrad does not follow the Holy Trinity. Therefore it is not a numerical triad.

KEPHALAIA GNOSTIKA 415

S1

A tetrad follows a numerical trinity, but a tetrad does not follow the Holy Trinity. Therefore the Holy Trinity is not a numerical trinity.

> See previous keph.; Iamblichus, *Chaldean Theology* 28 as reported by Damascius, *On Principles* 43 (1:86.6 Ruelle ed.). On other syllogisms, see 1.1.

6.12

S2

A dyad precedes a numerical trinity, but a dyad does not precede the Holy Trinity, for it is not a numerical triad.

S1

[Same as S2]

> See previous keph. and 6.11. This keph. assumes the conclusion of the previous syllogism and introduces a corollary.

6.13

S2

A numerical triad is constituted by the addition of ones without substance. But the Blessed Trinity is not constituted by the addition of single ones such as these, because it is not a triad in numbers.

S1

A numerical trinity is completed by the addition of ones, but the Holy Trinity does not exist by the addition of numbers, also because it is not a trinity of numbers.

> In antiquity, two competing definitions of number existed, one based on the notion of number as a collection of units, and another based upon emanation from a single monad (Moderatus 1.8; Nicomachus, *Intr. Arith.* 1.7.1). This keph. applies the first of these definitions to numerical monads, dyads, triads, etc. For the second definition, applied to the Trinity, see Gregory Nazianzen, *Or.* 23.8;

416   EVAGRIUS OF PONTUS

29.2; but Evagrius does not explicitly follow suit. Rather, he exempts the Trinity from number on the basis of being without substance (presumably *anupostatos*), with the underlying assumption that all agree that the Trinity has *hypostaseis*. On "without substance," associated with observation of beings, see 5.63; 6.10.

6.14

S2

A christ is not homoousios with the Trinity, because he is also not essential knowledge. But he alone always has in him essential knowledge inseparably. But I say that the Christ is the one who came with God the Logos and in the Spirit he is lord, [he] is not separable from his body, and by union he is homoousios with his father, because also [the Father] is essential knowledge.

S1

The body of Christ is from the nature of human beings, he "in whom all the fullness of God willed to dwell bodily"; but Christ is "God who is over all," according to the word of the Apostle.

Col 1.19 (S1); Rom 9.5 (S1)

Ramelli (2015, p. 323) punctuates the first sentence as the words of an unnamed opponent, which Evagrius refutes in the second half of the keph. But such a literary device is not used by Evagrius, and is out of character for the *KG*, which features syllogisms and arguments, but not refutations, and certainly no text that Evagrius disowns. The BUT I SAY construction, marked by Syriac *'amr 'na'*, occurs at 5.32 and 5.51, to separate and distinguish two halves of each keph., but in each case, the two halves are not in contradiction, but rather in contrast. We think the intended contrast here is, following Origen, between the christ of the first sentence and the Christ of the second. Syr. *mšiḥ'* can correspond to either Grk. *ho christos* (Christ) or simply *christos* (a christ). See discussion on Christ versus christ at 3.1. Therefore this keph. begins with the rational being who has become a christ, then contrasts that person with (Jesus) Christ, homoousios to the Father, as the *archēgos tēs sotērias*, "leading many sons to glory," Heb 2.10. HOMOOUSIOS: cf. 6.79; *Reflections* 18. ESSENTIAL KNOWLEDGE: 1.89 and 6.16.

KEPHALAIA GNOSTIKA 417

6.15

S2

The feet of Christ are practice and *theōria*, but if "he will put all his enemies beneath his feet," then all will know practice and *theōria*.

S1

The feet of Christ are practice and *theōria*, and if "he places all his enemies beneath his feet," it is clear that all who obey him are receptive to practice and knowledge.

1 Cor 15.25

S1 has avoided any notion that the enemies of Christ, i.e., the devil and the demons, will be saved; he has also inserted the Aristotelian notion of receptivity, on which see 1.4. Anointing the feet of Christ to prepare him for crucifixion and burial (and resurrection): Mt 26.6–13; Mk 14.3–9; Lk 7.36–50; Jn 12.1–8, and cf. Sch. 11 on Ps 88.21: "The holy oil signifies the knowledge of God; but even more it makes clear the essential knowledge." Sch. 20 on Ps 9.16, Christ makes his enemies friends; cf. Sch. 14 on Ps 21.29 and in the background Plato, *Phaedrus* 246c and Clement, *Stromateis* 7.40.1 (all the unjust will become just); Sch. 1 on Ps 92.1; Sch. 118 on Prv 10.3; and Sch. 3 on Eccl 1.11. In the background of all these is 1 Cor 15.28. Cf. Origen, *Comm. on Jn* 6.295–296.

6.16

Greek

Christ is he who has appeared to us from essential knowledge and from bodiless and bodily nature; but the one saying "two Christs" or "two Sons" is like the one saying "wisdom and the wise one are two wise ones and two wisdoms."

Furrer-Pilliod 2000, p. 211 A.χ.30

S2

Christ is he who from essential knowledge, and from incorporeal and corporeal nature, has shone forth upon us, and he who says "two Christs" or "two sons"

418 EVAGRIUS OF PONTUS

is like the one who calls the wise man and his wisdom two wise men or two wisdoms.

S1

Christ is he who, from essential knowledge and from incorporeal and corporeal nature, has shone forth upon the family of human beings, and the one who says "two Christs" and "two sons" is like the one who calls the wise man and his wisdom either two wise men or two wisdoms.

> On Christ, see 3.1 and above, 6.14. ESSENTIAL KNOWLEDGE: 1.89; SHONE FORTH: Lk 1.78–79; 2 Cor 4.6; Is 60.1. On wisdom: 1.14.

6.17

S2

A holy power is one who has been established from the *theōria* of beings and from incorporeal nature and corporeal nature.

S1

A holy power is a helper who has come into being from the *theōria* of beings, of beings and from the help of the grace of God.

> On holy powers, see 2.30. Angel: Origen, *First Principles* 2.10.7 following Mt 18.10, an angel given to each of the faithful; and *Prayer* 27.

6.18

S2

There was [a time] when Christ did not have a body, yet there was not [a time] when God the logos was not in him. For with his coming to be, also God the logos dwelled in him.

S1

There was a time when there was not a natural body of Christ, but there was not a time when God the Word was not in him. But as soon as he came to be, secretly it dwelt in him, but was revealed at the end of days.

The initial formula THERE WAS A TIME: 1.40; 2.84. On the becoming of an entity: 1.52, 54 (S1), 55, 65; 2.74 (the world); 4.2, 3. CHRIST: may be better translated lowercase "christ," because 4.2–3 imply that the Christ did not have a coming-to-be. On Christ versus christ see 3.1; 6.14. The possibility that Christ's soul preexisted his body or vice versa was condemned by anathemas 2–3 of 543 (Justinian's letter to Menas).

6.19

Greek

If those in the heavens rejoice over one who has had a change of mind, how much more over those countless numbers who will travel from evil toward virtue, and from ignorance to the knowledge of God.

> Rondeau 2021, Sch. 2 on Ps 113.4

S2

The return is the ascent that is from the movement and from evil and ignorance toward knowledge of the Holy Trinity.

S1

The return is the ascent of the rational nature toward the state from which it fell.

> On the return (likely *epistrophē*; see Peshitta Ac 5.13) see 2.13 and the next keph. The Greek fragment corresponds only to the second half of this keph., and loosely at that. On the movement: 1.50–51; pairing of evil and ignorance: 1.89.

6.20

S2

Before the movement, God was good, and powerful, and wise, creator of incorporeals and father of rational beings and pantokrator; after the movement he became creator of bodies, and judge, and governor, and doctor, shepherd, and teacher, and merciful and longsuffering, and moreover, gate, and road, and lamb, and high priest, with the rest of the names that are said in modes. Also he is father

420 EVAGRIUS OF PONTUS

and principle even before the coming to be of the incorporeals; he is father of Christ and principle of the Holy Spirit.

S1

Before the movement God was good, powerful, sage, creator, father, and pantokrator; but after the movement he is judge and doctor and benefactor.

> On modes, Syr. *pursē*, likely Grk. *epinoiai*, see 1.17. These modes are normally associated with God the Son, but this keph. does not make that explicit, and its conclusion seems to be with God the Father (see 6.4). Titles: cf. Origen, *Comm. on Jn* 1.21–23, titles of Christ, here applied to God. On father/principle of Christ/Spirit see 6.4.

6.21

Greek

Virtue is the best habit of the rational soul, according to which it becomes hard to move toward evil.

> Mosc. 425, sixteenth century (Hausherr 1939, p. 231)
> Furrer-Pilliod 2000, p. 211 A.α.111

S2

Virtue is that state of the rational soul in which it is difficult to be moved toward evil.

S1

Virtue is a state of the rational soul in which, when it remains, it stays without movement.

cf. Aristotle, Cat. 8b27–30

> This keph. is attested independently by two Greek fragments, identical everywhere except word order. The first half appears in an anonymous commentary on Aristotle, *Nicomachean Ethics* 1130a5, CAG 20, ed. G. Heylbut, 211 line 21. STATE reflects Grk. *hexis*, the Aristotelian term for a deep-seated condition that is hard to change (e.g., a person habitually irascible), as opposed to *diathesis*, an easily changed condition (e.g., a habitually good-natured person who momentarily becomes angry); Aristotle, *Cat.*

8c27–28. DIFFICULT TO BE MOVED (S2), Syr. 'asqāith mēttazi'na', probably corresponds to a form of Grk. *duskinētos*; see Aristotle, *Cat.* 8c30. Compare to state as *katastasis*, *Prak.* 12. The keph. corresponds as well to Sch. 184 on Prv 18.16: "The seat of the mind is the best state preserving the seated as hard or impossible to move"; and Sch. 1 on Ps 138.2: " 'Seat' is the best state of the reasoning soul, through which one becomes hard to move toward vice." Cf. *Thoughts* 15; Sch. 99 on Prv 8.3.

6.22

Greek

If perceptible words will present things in the aeon to come, plainly the wise of this aeon will receive the kingdom of the heavens. But if the purity of the intelligence sees and the corresponding word signifies [the kingdom], then the wise will be far from the knowledge of God.

Mosc. 425, sixteenth century (Hausherr 1939, p. 231)

S2

If perceptible words make known things in the world to come, it is clear that the sages of this world too will receive the kingdom of heaven. But if purity of the mind sees, and the logos suitable to it makes known, then the sages of this world will be far from the knowledge of God.

S1

If perceptible words are useful also in the world to come, the sages of this world too will inherit the kingdom of heaven. But if the purity of the mind is equal to the sight of the world to come, it is clear that the wise men of this world will be far from the knowledge of God.

Syr. 'almā translates Grk. *aiōn*. Cf. "wise in this world" (*aiōn*) and "wisdom of this world" (*kosmos*) at 1 Cor 3.18–23. See also 2 Cor 6.1. The "perceptible words" are logoi corresponding to sense-perceptible objects, contrasted in the second half with the logos of the intelligence or understanding (Grk. *dianoia*). KINGDOM OF HEAVEN: *Prak.* 2. On the contrast between these two types of knowledge, see *Gn.* 4. On WISE OF THIS AEON, see Origen, *Comm. on 1 Cor* 27.23; *Hom. on Ps* 36.3.6.

6.23

S2

Just as this *logos* makes known concerning things in this world, so also the *logos* of the spiritual body makes known things in the world to come.

S1

Just as this plain word makes matters of this world known, so also the spiritual word makes known about the truth of the world to come.

THIS LOGOS: presumably the logos of the understanding from the preceding keph. SPIRITUAL BODY: 1 Cor 15.44. On the spiritual body and the world to come, 1.11.

6.24

S2

If those who in the world to come are going to be angels, and have authority "over five" or "over ten cities," it is also clear that they receive knowledge that is able to stir up rational souls from evil to virtue, and from ignorance toward the knowledge of God.

S1

Those who in the world to come become as holy angels, and are established "over five" or "ten cities"—it is clear that they receive great power from the grace of God, as if for divine economy.

Lk 20.36 (S1); Lk 19.17–19

AUTHORITY OVER FIVE . . . TEN CITIES: Sch. 134 on Prv 13.22; Sch. 10 on Ps 48.15; *Letters* 23, 36, and 37. On ascent mediated by: (1) angels see Sch. 7 on Ps 16.13; Sch. 38 on Eccl 5.7–11; and (2) every rank of reasoning being in "varied worlds" to those below them, 6.76.

KEPHALAIA GNOSTIKA 423

6.25

Greek

When the demons are unable to move the thoughts in a gnostikos, then they grasp his eyes, and completely freezing them, pull them down toward sleep. For all the bodies of the demons are cold and they are somewhat like ice.

Mosc. 425, sixteenth century (Hausherr 1939, p. 233)

S2

When the demons are not able to move evil thoughts in the gnostikos, then they seize his eyes in a great cold, and they pull them toward a deep sleep, for the bodies of demons are very cold, in the image of ice.

S1

When the demons are unable to move evil thoughts in the gnostikos, then they draw near his eyes and with a great cold they make him sleep, and thus they make him cease from beautiful *theōria*.

Demons manipulating eyelids and causing sleep: *Thoughts* 33. On bodies, 1.11. On clear ice, see Sch. 5 on Ps 147.5: "Snow and clear ice and fog and frost occur through the deprivation of the sun of righteousness."

6.26

S2

Just as fire is not in our bodies, but its quality has been placed in them, so also in the bodies of demons it is not earth itself or water itself but their quality that the creator has sown in them.

S1

In the bodies of human beings, there are not four elements, but their power.

On QUALITY, see 1.22. Although the human body does not have the element of fire in it, it has its primary quality, heat; so too demonic bodies, which are

424 EVAGRIUS OF PONTUS

principally air (1.68), do not have the elements earth or water, but have their qualities (thickness, heaviness, wetness), i.e., this keph. explains the principle underlying the preceding one.

6.27

S2

If "all the nations will come and bow down before the Lord," it is also clear that the "nations who want war" will come, and if this is so, it is evident that the entire nature of rational [beings] will then bow to the name of the Lord, who makes known the father who is in him, for this is "the name that is greater than all names."

S1

The [verse] "all the nations will come and bow to you, Lord," with the revealed [meaning], has also this [meaning] of mystery, that every knowledge will bow down and will submit to the holy knowledge of God.

Ps 85.9; 67.31 (S2); Phil 2.9 (S2)

Cf. Rev 15.4. The notion of the father in Christ, as a kind of mode (see 1.17), sets the context for the ensuing three keph., which treat Christ as father; see Sch. 78 on Prv 6.19. Cf. as a precedent, Melito of Sardis, *On the Pasch* 6; Christ is "father" and "mother" in Sch. 210 on Prv 20.9a, where Christ is father to those possessing the spirit of adoption and mother to those needing milk; Christ is "speaking in Paul," who became father to the Ephesians and mother to the Corinthians.

6.28

S2

The father is the begetter of essential knowledge.

S1

The father is the parent of essential knowledge.

This keph. forms a group with the next two. They are not about God the Father, but primarily about Christ (see previous keph.) and those who become christ. Cf. Gal 3.27 (as many of you who have been baptized into Christ have put on

KEPHALAIA GNOSTIKA   425

Christ); this verse underlies Evagrius' descriptions of the monastic schema and the robe of the High Priest; those who put on these garments "put on Christ" in two phases. On ESSENTIAL KNOWLEDGE, 1.89.

6.29

S2

The father is he who has a rational nature that is united to the knowledge of the Trinity.

S1

The father by grace is he who, by his mercy, has generated rational nature, receptive of his image.

> On uniting/being united see 5.49. The notion of receptivity (see 1.4) has been inserted by S1. KNOWLEDGE OF THE TRINITY: *Prak.* 3.

6.30

S2

The father is he who has a rational nature united to the *theōria* of beings.

S1

The father who "makes grow" is he who makes youths grow, that they become worthy of the knowledge of the Holy Trinity.

cf. 1 Cor 3.7 (S1)

> See previous keph. On observation of beings, see 1.73.

6.31

Greek

Begotten is the one who is begotten from somebody, as if from a father.

> *Doctrina patrum de incarnatione verbi* 33 (Diekamp 1907, p. 254)

426 EVAGRIUS OF PONTUS

S2

The begotten is the one who has been begotten by something as by a father.

S1

Begotten is something begotten by something, as a son by a father.

This keph. forms a pair with the next, and the whole Greek fragment reads: Γεννητόν ἐστι τὸ ἔκ τινος ὡς ἐκ πατρὸς γεννηθέν, γενητὸν δέ ἐστι τὸ ἔκ τινος γεγονός, explaining the distinction between *gennetos* (begotten) and *genetos* (become). Guillaumont suggests (1958, p. 231) that the translator for S2, or the scribe of the manuscript used by S2, incorrectly read *genneton* at 6.32. Although attractive, this hypothesis cannot explain how S2 would also have also mistakenly read *gennethen* (begotten) for *gegonos* (become), nor can it explain the difference in the final words in the two keph., Syr. *ethyalad* versus *yalidā*. Further, the Greek appears to be missing a phrase at 6.32, e.g., *hōs ek demiourgou* ("as from a creator") to balance *hōs ek ktistēs* ("as from a builder"). The florilegium may preserve the *KG* imperfectly, or it may derive from another work altogether, and the differences reflect two different intents, one to differentiate begottenness from becoming and the other, begottenness from a Father from that of a Creator. That is, the original Greek of 6.32 could have been Γεννητόν ἐστι τὸ ἔκ τινος ὡς ἐκ κτίστου γεγεννημένον. Under this scenario, 6.31 considers being begotten as a single act in the past, and 6.32 as a continuous one. The preceding three keph., we have suggested, are primarily about Christ and those who become christ. The present two keph. then would be about Christ as only-begotten from the Father, and (later) christs as begotten from the creator.

6.32

Greek

That which has become is that which has become from something.

Doctrina patrum de incarnatione verbi 33 (Diekamp 1907, p. 254)

S2

Begotten is he who is begotten from someone as engendered from a creator.

S1

Made is something made by something, as a creature by the creator.

> See previous keph. CREATOR: corresponds to Syr. *bruia'*, which commonly translates Grk. *ktistēs* (2 Mc 1.24; 4 Mc 11.5).

6.33

S2

When Christ is no longer imprinted in various worlds and in differing names, then "he also will be subjected" to God, the father, and he will enjoy the knowledge of him alone, that which is not divided in worlds and in the increases of rational beings.

S1

When Christ will no longer appear to rational nature in many ways, then "everything also will be subjected through him" to the true father.

> 1 Cor 15.28
> On the final subjection of all things to God, Sch. 118 on Prv 10.3; Sch. 1 on Ps 92.1; *Letter to Melania* 22–24. On imprinting: 5.39; different names: 1.17. IN INCREASES, Syr. *w-b-tarbita'* (perhaps Grk. *prokopē*), can also translated "in education," "in advancements," or "in growths," i.e., nurturing rational beings.

6.34

S2

By means of worlds, God will "change the body of our humiliation to the likeness of the body of the glory" of the Lord. And after all worlds he will also make us "in the likeness of the image of his son," if the image of the son is the essential knowledge of God the Father.

S1

By means of the practice of his commandments God clothes us with the seal of his purity, and by the revelation of his Holy Spirit he perfects in us his true image.

> Phil 3.21 (S2); Rom 8.29 (S2)

428 EVAGRIUS OF PONTUS

Origen, *Comm. on Rom* 4.5.161–165; *First Principles* 3.6.1.

6.35

S2

By the intellections of instruction, holy angels purify us from evil and free us from passion, and by [intellections] of nature and divine words they free us from ignorance and make us wise, and gnostics.

S1

By the *theōria* of the practice of God's commandments, the holy powers purify us from evil and make us free from passion; in the *theōria* of natures and words about Godhead, they free us from ignorance and make us wise, and gnostics.

On angels, see *Prak.* 24; essential knowledge, and the pairing of evil and ignorance: 1.89.

6.36

S2

"He who was created to be scorned by the angels" of God—was it not he who began the movement? and in the beginning transgressed the limits of evil, and because of this was called "the beginning of the creatures of the Lord"?

S1

"He who was made to be mocked by the angels" of God—is it he who began the movement and in the beginning transgressed the limits of evil, and because of this was called "the beginning of the creation of the Lord"?

Job 40.19; 41.25

Sch. 25 on Eccl 4.4; *Letter* 27. On THE MOVEMENT, 1.50–51. Cf. also *Thoughts* 34 on "movement of the passions," prompted by demons.

KEPHALAIA GNOSTIKA 429

6.37

S2

Just as cranes fly in the image of letters although they do not know letters, so also the demons repeat proverbs about the fear of God, when they do not know God.

S1

Just as cranes fly in the image of letters although they do not know writing, so also the demons recite proverbs about the fear of God, though they do not know the fear of God.

> FEAR OF GOD: Prv 9.10. Demons quoting scripture: *Antirr.* 2.50; 8.1. The chief letter in question is the lambda, Λ. On cranes: Aristotle, *History of Animals* 9.10.

6.38

S2

The intelligible cross is the willing death of the body that perfects the modesty of a christ.

S1

The bed of sleepers is the mortification of the flesh, which with a good will perfects in a human being the continence that is in Christ.

> Guillaumont suggests (1958, p. 232) that the translator of S1 read the uncial *nomen sacrum* for *stauros* as *soros* ("bier": cf. Lk 7.14). But this would not account for the phrase OF SLEEPERS or the missing "intelligible." Further, the uncial of *stauros*, ΣΣ or ΣΤΣ, would likely not be mistaken for anything like *soros*. More likely, S1 opted to ignore the Greek opening and replace it with text of his own, a sometimes seemingly arbitrary occurrence (e.g., just above at 6.35). Cf. Sch. 1 on Ps 109.2. "The day of power is the day of the cross."

6.39

Greek

A birth of a christ is a rebirth of our inner human being, which Christ, like a good housebuilder, laying the foundation upon his cornerstone, has built upon the house of his body.

Furrer-Pilliod 2000, p. 96 A.γ.42

S2

The generation of a christ is the generation of our original inner humanity, which Christ like a good builder has founded and built upon the cornerstone of his body.

S1

The generation of Christ is the right of the firstborn of the new world.

Eph 2.19–22. Cf. 6.18 and the distinction between Christ and "a christ," discussed at 3.1. CORNERSTONE: Eph 2.20 (the Temple); BODY: Col 1.18, 24; Jn 22.19. "His body, the church." On the begetting: Sch. 2 on Ps 109.3: the birth of Christ and the morning star (cf. *Prak.* pr.2) is impossible for us to work out more deeply. Builder/architect: 6.82.

6.40

Greek

A crucifixion of a christ is the mortification of our old human being, or also a nullification of the written judgment against us, and an abandonment bringing back to life.

Furrer-Pilliod 2000, p. 189 A.σ.98

S2

The crucifixion of a christ is the death of the old human being, the release of the written judgment against us, and the dereliction that returns us to life.

S1

The crucifixion of Christ is the death of the old human being, the release of the written judgment that is against us, and the remission that returns us to life.

DEATH OF THE OLD HUMAN BEING: Rom 6.6; 2 Cor 5.17; Eph 4.22–24; Col 2.11–13; amortization: Col 2.14–15; birthright: 1 Cor 3.18–23; written judgment against us: Col 2.14; abandonment (Grk. *enkataleipsis*): Ps 15.10; 36.28; 93.14; remission (Syriac): Col 2.14 (*aphēsis*). The death and decay of the old human being: Sch. 13 on Ps 72.20 and cf. Sch. 7 on Ps 144.20; Sch. 14 on Ps 77.34; Sch. 6 on Ps 102.5; Sch. 1 on Ps 149.1; *Thoughts* 39. On abandonment: Sch. 20 on Ps 36.25; Sch. 4 on Ps 70.11.

6.41

S2

The perfect removal softens the impassioned part of the soul, but hardens the angry part.

S1

The perfect departure from the world quiets the passionate part of the soul and makes its anger all the hotter.

Monks 8; *Thoughts* 23. Separation: 4.12.

6.42

Greek

A death of a christ is the mysterious activity bringing back up to the aeonic life those who have hoped in this life.

Furrer-Pilliod 2000, p. 131 A.θ.75

S2

The death of a christ is the accomplishment of the mysterious activity that leads back to eternal life those who have hoped in him in this life.

432   EVAGRIUS OF PONTUS

S1

The killing of Christ is the accomplishment of the mysterious operation that leads back to eternal life those who have hoped in him in this life.

> Jn 3.16; *Thoughts* 38. On activity (Grk. *energeia*) see 1.64. Accomplishment of the mystery of God: Rev 10.7. The term "action," Syr. *ma'bdānutha'*, implies the potential/actual distinction, e.g., 1.46–47.

6.43

S2

The providence of God accompanies the freedom of the will, but his judgment gives heed to the order of rational beings.

S1

The providence of God follows the freedom of the will, and his "just judgment" follows the conduct of the soul.

> 2 Thes 1.5 (S1)
> Translator S1 has anchored Evagrius' terminology to scripture, but S2 alludes instead to the *logoi* of providence and judgment; cf. Origen, *Philokalia* 21 on providence and free will. On the *logos* of providence see 4.89 and 6.76; the pairing of providence and judgment: *Gn.* 48. ORDER, Syr. *ṭaksa'*: 2.66. GIVES HEED TO, Syr. *ḥā'ar*, suggests anticipation. Hence judgment responds to preceding acts of free will; providence, to coming new ranks of rational beings.

6.44

S2

A spiritual demonstration is the completion of those things that were predicted in a divine way by the Holy Spirit.

S1

The demonstration of the spirit is those things that in the Holy Spirit have also existed previously in prophecy, and have been perfected in the new gospel in their time.

> DEMONSTRATION, Syr. *taḥwithā*, Grk. *apodeixis*: cf. 1.38, 2.35; 1 Cor 2.4.

KEPHALAIA GNOSTIKA   433

6.45

S2

Of the worlds, not one is better than the first world, for it came about from the first mixture, as they say; and an athlete and a *gnostikos* has transmitted to us that in it, all the worlds will be perfected.

S1

This "humanity was in the image of God," is affirmed without restriction, and the diligent will attain it, according to the word of the fathers.

Gn 1.27 (S1)
Syr. *gāzriā* is translated by Guillaumont as "athlete," from the Persian word *gz'r*, yielding the meaning "one who is circumcised" or "Nazirite" or "diviner"; alternatively, *gāzriā* may be translated from the Syr. root *gzar* as "give a decree, determine, proclaim (a fast)." It may reflect Grk. *rhabdouchos*, later meaning "staff-holder," possibly a bishop or abbot, or even an angel. See *Gn.* 48, on the possibility this may refer to Didymus. In *Gn.* 47, "the angel of the church of Thmuis" is bishop Serapion, who is said to have communicated a teaching about "spiritual gnosis." As THEY SAY: perhaps Straton of Lampsacus; see fragments 42–43.

6.46

Greek

A harp is the practicing soul moved by the commandments of God.

Furrer-Pilliod 2000, p. 140 A.к.62

S2

The harp is the practicing soul, that which is moved by the commandments of Christ.

S1

[Same as S2]

This keph. forms a pair with 6.48, each one attested once in the collection of definitions and twice in the Psalms scholia (6.46 = Sch. 2 on Ps 91.4 [*kithara*];

434   EVAGRIUS OF PONTUS

Sch. 3 on Ps 150.2 [*psaltērion*]; 6.48 = Sch. 3 on Ps 32.2; Sch. 2 on Ps 91.4). The definitions version here has manuscript variants between "Christ" and "Lord." On the *kithara*, see Clement, *Protreptikos* 1.5, which likens the harp to the human organ and Gregory of Nyssa, *Inscriptions on the Psalms* 169.26 (and cf. below, *KG* 6.72). On the harp (Grk. *kithara*) and psaltery as symbols for, respectively, the soul and mind, see Sch. 5 on Ps 56.9; Sch. 2 on Ps 91.4 (both); Sch. 2 on Ps 107.3.

6.47

S2

The judgment of God will lead to the land of promise everyone who will have followed Joshua (Jesus), giving him a spiritual body and a world suitable to him. But those who have not been able to attain [the land of promise] because of the abundance of their possessions the [judgment of God] will settle on the banks of the Jordan, according to their rank.

S1

The "just judgment of God" leads to the land of promise everyone who traveled with Joshua (Jesus), with whom he is given an incorruptible inheritance.

> 2 Thes 1.5 (S1); cf. Nm 32.1–5 (S2); cf. Josh 1.14–15 (S2)
> Cf. 5.36; possessions: 1.78; *Prayer* 17; Sch. 161 on Prv 17.16. S1 avoids the concept of a second, lower world for the less worthy. On the variety of worlds, 2.75.

6.48

Greek

A psaltery is a pure mind moved by spiritual knowledge.

> Furrer-Pilliod 2000, p. 214 A.ψ.17

S2

The psaltery is the pure mind moved by spiritual knowledge.

KEPHALAIA GNOSTIKA 435

S1

[Same as S2]

cf. Ps 32.2; 91.4; 107.3

See 6.46.

6.49

Greek

There is hinted, through the Egyptians, the disposition to evil.

Rondeau 2021, Sch. 19 on Ps 67.32

And again, Egypt, being a symbol of evil, is abandoned as the firstborn perish in their understanding.... And Israel hungering, thirsting, and being tested travels through the desert, which is a symbol of the practice.

Rondeau 2021, Sch. 3 on Ps 135.6

The gates of Jerusalem are the practical virtues hindering the enemies from entering; heavenly doctrines of Zion are also the right faith of the worshipped and Holy Trinity.

Rondeau 2021, Sch. 1 on Ps 147.1–2

S2

Egypt signifies evil; the desert, the practice; the land of Judah, the *theōria* of bodies; Jerusalem, that of the incorporeals; but Zion is a symbol of the Trinity.

S1

Egypt is the sign of evil, and the desert is the sign of the practice. And the land of Judah is that of the *theōria* of bodies; and Jerusalem, that of the incorporeals; and Zion that of the Holy Trinity.

In this keph. Evagrius has synthesized and reworked several scholia from the Psalms. Other relevant scholia: the cities of Judah the reasoning souls (Sch. 23 on Ps 68.36); what [are] *Jerusalem above* and the *Zion* from which the Christ is

436 EVAGRIUS OF PONTUS

said to come (Sch. 5 on Ps 118.7); and Zion, God the Father (Sch. 6 on Ps 13.7). This fivefold sequence of advancement differs from those at 1.27 and 1.70.

6.50

S2

Everything that is a part of this world is of a bodily nature, and everything that is from bodily nature is a part of this world.

S1

Everything that is a part of this world is a part of corporeality, and everything that is a part of corporeality is a part of this world.

Corporeal nature: 3.10; Cf 1.73.

6.51

Greek

If the reasoning part is the most honorable of all the powers of the soul, because it alone is made with wisdom, wisdom would be the first of all the virtues. This also our wise teacher has called "spiritual adoption."

Mosc. 425, sixteenth century (Hausherr 1939, p. 232)

S2

If the intelligent part of the soul is more honorable than all the powers of the soul, because only it is joined to wisdom, then the first of all the virtues is knowledge. For also our wise teacher has called this the "spirit of adoptive sonship."

S1

If the rational part of the soul is more precious than all the powers of the soul, because it is that which participates in the wisdom of God, then the gift of the knowledge of the spirit is greater than all gifts—for it is this that the fathers also called "the spirit of adoptive sonship."

Rom 8.15

Cf. Eph 5.1; Sch. 78 on Prv 6.19; Sch. 101 on Prv 8.10–11; Sch. 163 on Prv 17.17; Sch. 169 on Prv 17.25; Sch. 210 on Prv 20.9; Sch. 28 on Eccl 4.8. In *Gn.* 48, the "wise teacher" is Didymus. Powers of the soul: 2.9.

6.52

Greek

Many passions are hidden in our souls; the sharpest of temptations reveal those that elude us. It is necessary "to preserve our heart with every guard," lest that matter is revealed and we are suddenly snatched away by demons toward whatever passion we have acquired, and we do something that is something of those things rejected by God.

Mosc. 425, sixteenth century (Hausherr 1939, p. 231)

S2

Many passions are hidden in our souls, and when they escape our notice, sharp temptations show them to us. And it is "right to guard our hearts with all vigilance," lest when an object toward which we possess a passion appears, we are suddenly led off by the demons and do one of those things rejected by God.

S1

Many passions are hidden in the soul. When they escape our notice then the temptations that arrive show them to us. And it is right "to guard the heart with all vigilance," so that, when the hidden passion suddenly falls upon us, it will not disturb us to move toward an action that God has commanded us not to do.

Prv 4.23

On the heart, see *Prak.* 46.

438 EVAGRIUS OF PONTUS

6.53

Greek

An intelligible arrow is the first thought established from the impassioned part of the soul.

Furrer-Pilliod 2000, p. 92 A.β.33

The arrow is the impassioned thought, the quiver is the worst habit, filled with unclean thoughts.

Rondeau 2021, Sch. 2 on Ps 10.2

A fiery arrow is the impassioned thought.

Rondeau 2021, Sch. 3 on Ps 75.4

S2

The intelligible arrow is the evil thought that is produced by the impassioned part of the soul.

S1

The evil arrow is the evil thought, which first arose from the desiring part of the soul.

This is the final keph. of the "intelligible X" series (see 3.44) and only the third to describe a symbol of vice (see 5.68, 71). On arrows: *Antirr.* pr.2; *Letter* 27.4; *Letter on Faith* 14; *Monks* 70; *Eight Thoughts* 2.5–7; 5.12–13; Sch. 78 on Prv 6.19; 195 on Prv 19.12.

6.54

S2

If the mind distinguishes words, and if names and words make objects known, then the mind distinguishes objects.

S1

If the mind distinguishes words and names, and words and names make things known, then the mind distinguishes things.

Word, *logos*, as a faculty of judging: Sch. 4 on Prv 1.3; Sch. 24 on Ps 36.27; cf. Clement of Alexandria, *Strom.* 2.7.2. See Sch. 4 on Prv 1.3.

6.55

Greek

The mind approaches the intelligible realities whenever it does not at all construct thoughts from the passionate part of the soul.

Mosc. 425, sixteenth century (Hausherr 1939, p. 232)

S2

The mind approaches intelligible things whenever it is no longer united to the thought that comes from the impassioned part of the soul.

S1

The mind then looks at intelligibles when it is freed from the motions of the passions of the soul.

The *poiōtai* in the Grk. fragment may be a later alteration from an original *henōtai*. On uniting, see 5.49. On the mind approaching sense perceptibles, Sch. 5 on Prv 1.7; *Thoughts* 15.

6.56

S2

If vision is called "in perception" and "in thought," and Christ will come in the same way as the disciples saw him ascend to heaven, let someone say how they saw him. Nevertheless, let him know that Christ certainly always ascends in the holy ones, even though he seems to descend to others.

440 EVAGRIUS OF PONTUS

S1

If vision is called "in perception" and "in thought," and Christ will come in the same way that the disciples saw him ascend to heaven, let someone say how they saw him. Nevertheless, for the holy ones, in spiritual souls Christ surely always ascends, even though he descends to others to make them ascend.

cf. Ac 1.11

Cf. Origen, *Hom. on Ezek* 1.7. Descent as *synkatabasis*, *Gn*. 6.1, 2. VISION, Syr. *ḥzāthā*, may be Grk. *blemma* (alluding to the first half of Ac 1.11); see *Eulogius* 27 (inner versus outer *omma / blemma*). On ascent: 3.42; descent: 2.71.

6.57

S2

The reward given to the rational nature before the judgment seat of Christ: bodies, spiritual or dark, and the *theōria* or ignorance appropriate to them. This is why they say that Christ, whom we await, comes to some in one way and to others in another way.

S1

Something that is repaid to the rational nature before the judgment seat of Christ—either incorruptibility or corruption, or knowledge or ignorance.

JUDGMENT SEAT OF CHRIST: 2 Cor 5.10; *Letter* 37.2. Christ as judge has appeared to the fallen *noes*, the *logikoi*. On other titles of Christ see 1.17; 6.20 (judge among others).

6.58

S2

Among the bodies—those that have been attached after the change—they say that they will come forth as spiritual bodies. But if this will happen from matter or from instruments that will come about, you too should truly examine.

KEPHALAIA GNOSTIKA 441

S1

The change of the bodies of the holy ones on the day of resurrection is in the image of the glorious body of our Lord, and corruptibility will not appear in them, because it is swallowed up by incorruptibility.

THE CHANGE (Syr. *ḥulpā*), see 1.17. SPIRITUAL BODIES: 4.23; INSTRUMENTS (*organa*): 1.67. S1 has taken the lead of SPIRITUAL BODIES referring to 1 Cor 15 (see *KG* 3.25), and replaced the second half of the keph. with a meditation on 1 Cor 15.42.

6.59

S2

The providence of God is double. They say that part of it guards the constitution of bodies and the bodiless, and part of it pushes the rational beings from vice and ignorance toward virtue and knowledge.

S1

The providence of God is double, for one part of it guards the state of incorporeal beings, and the other makes the infancy of corporeal beings grow.

1 Tm 2.4. On providence, see 4.89.

6.60

Greek

A sterile mind is deprived of spiritual teaching, or a mind lacking spiritual seeds sown for the Holy Spirit.

Furrer-Pilliod 2000, p. 85 A.α.189

S2

Sterile is the mind deprived of spiritual teaching, or lacking the seeds sown by the Holy Spirit.

442 EVAGRIUS OF PONTUS

S1

[Same as S2]

This keph. forms a pair with 6.62. SEEDS ... THE HOLY SPIRIT, Clement, *Excerpts from Theodotus* 1.1. On STERILE, Syr. ʿaqrā, Grk. *steira*, see Sch. 4 on Ps 112.9 (sterile is the soul when God has departed). Good seed: 1.40; cf. Sch. 3 on Ps 147.3. This is one of the few keph. where Evagrius joins two possible interpretations with "or," a technique he uses frequently in his scholia.

6.61

Greek

If God is "not the God of the dead but of the living" but according to Moses the holy one, the sorcerers question the dead, then the sorcerer of Saul did not raise up Samuel from the dead, since Samuel was not dead but living.

Sch. on 1 Kgdms/1 Sam 28.11–12 (Devreesse 1959, p. 173)

S2

If God is "the God of the living and not of the dead," and according to the word of the holy Moses, necromancers "interrogate the dead," it was not Samuel that the necromancer brought up from the house of the dead, if Samuel was not dead but living.

S1

If God is "the God of the living and not of the dead," but according to the word of the holy Moses, necromancers "interrogate the dead," it was not the soul of holy Samuel that the necromancer brought up, for he was not dead but living, like Abraham, Isaac, and Jacob.

Mt 22.32; Dt 18.11; cf. 1 Kgdms/1 Sam 28.7–20
This keph. is reminiscent of Origen's homily on 1 Kgdms/1 Sam 28, but he does not cite or apply Mt 22.32/Mk 12.27. The Greek fragment appears in only a single manuscript (Paris. BnF Coisl. 8, fol. 31r 31–33; tenth century).

KEPHALAIA GNOSTIKA   443

6.62

Greek

Sterile is the rational soul that always learns, and "does not yet wish to arrive at the knowledge of the truth."

Mosc. 425, sixteenth century (Hausherr 1939, p. 232)

S2

Sterile is the rational soul that is always learning and "is unable to arrive at the knowledge of the truth."

S1

[Same as S2]

2 Tm 3.7

This keph. forms a pair with 6.60, treating the soul instead of the mind, connecting it with 2 Tm 3.7.

6.63

Greek

Just as those who are cleansed in the eyes and, reaching out to the sun, shed tears and see the air mingled with various colors, so also the pure mind, troubled by anger, is incapable of grasping *theōria* and sees certain clouds hovering over things.

Mosc. 425, sixteenth century (Hausherr 1939, p. 232)

S2

Just as those whose sight is diseased, and look at the sun, are hindered by their tears and see hallucinations in the air, so too when the pure mind is disturbed by anger, it cannot receive spiritual *theōria*, but sees as a dark cloud resting on objects.

S1

Just as those whose sight is diseased, and look at the sun, are hindered by their tears and see hallucinations in the air, so also when the pure mind when disturbed

444 EVAGRIUS OF PONTUS

by anger, cannot look at spiritual *theōria*, but sees, as it were, a dark cloud resting over the things it tries to see.

> On the mental eye and seeing, see 2.28. Both S1 and S2 have taken Grk. *kekatharmenoi* as a sign of ailment; the Grk. fragment, from a manuscript collection, describes the eye as in good health. On the mind and anger, see 5.27; *Prak.* 20–23.

6.64

S2

Just as by the perceptible healing of the paralytic our Savior clarified for us the intelligible healing, and by the visible verified the hidden, so by the perceptible exodus of the children of Israel he has shown us the exodus from evil and ignorance.

S1

Just as regarding that paralytic our Lord made known to us the hidden healing by a visible healing, so by means of the visible exodus of the children of Israel from Egypt he made known to us our hidden exodus from evil and ignorance.

> cf. Mt 9.2–7
>
> Concealing: Sch.10 on Ps 39.13, "The remembrance of ancient faults naturally conceals our thought *(dianoia)*"; concealing: Sch. 153 on Prv 17.2 and *Gn.* 36; exodus of children of Israel signifies exodus of the soul: Sch. 99 on Prv 8.3; cf. *KG* 4.64.

6.65

Greek

A mystery is a spiritual *theōria* eluding the grasp of the many.

> Furrer-Pilliod 2000, p. 150 A.μ.68

S2

A mystery is a spiritual *theōria* not perceived by everyone.

S1

[Same as S2]

Mystērion: Sch. 210 on Prv 20.9a.

6.66

Greek

A stony blade is a teaching of our savior Christ by teachings circumcising the mind veiled by the passions.

Furrer-Pilliod 2000, p. 151 A.μ.89

S2

The blade of stone is the teaching of Christ our Savior, [a teaching] which by knowledge circumcises the mind hidden by passions.

S1

The blade of stone is the teaching of our Lord Jesus Christ, [a teaching] which by knowledge of the truth circumcises the mind hidden by passions.

cf. Josh 5.2–3

On circumcision, see 4.12, 5.83, 6.6–7; blade/sword: 5.28; 6.6.

6.67

S2

The more the worlds are increased, the more, too, the names and the intellections appropriate to them make the Holy Trinity known to us.

S1

The more the mind grows in knowledge of the spirit, the more it comes closer to the *theōria* of the Holy Trinity.

446 EVAGRIUS OF PONTUS

Syr. *methrabin* can refer to expansion in size or in number. The form and content of this keph. (THE MORE . . . THE MORE . . .) parallels 2.75. On names: 1.51. Cf. Sch. 275 on Prv 24.22.

6.68

Greek

Submission itself is the voluntary agreement of the rational nature toward the knowledge of God.

Furrer-Pilliod 2000, p. 200 A.υ.59
Rondeau 2021, Sch. 4 on Ps 36.7

S2

Submission is the assent of the will of the rational nature to the knowledge of God.

S1

The enslavement of the rational nature to the knowledge of God is the consent of a good will.

This keph. forms a pair with 6.70. The two Greek variants agree except in minor details. On submission: *Eulogius* 27. AGREEMENT, Grk. *synkatathesis*: *Prak.* 75.

6.69

S2

Angels see humans and demons; humans are deprived of the sight of angels and demons; demons see humans only.

S1

[Same as S2]

On inability to perceive demons: 1.22.

6.70

Greek

Submission is the powerlessness of the rational nature not crossing the boundaries of its own state. For in this way "he has subjected everything under his feet," according to Paul.

Furrer-Pilliod 2000, p. 200 A.υ.60

S2

Subjection is the weakness of the rational nature, which is unable to cross the boundaries of its measure. Indeed, in this way "he has subjected everything under his feet" according to the word of Paul.

S1

Servitude is the weakness of the rational nature, which is unable to cross its boundaries. Indeed, in this way "he has subjected everything under his feet," according to the word of Paul.

cf. 1 Cor 15.27

This keph. forms a pair with 6.68. On the verse quoted, 1 Cor 15.27, see Sch. 118 on Prv 10.3; Sch. 14–15 on Ps 29 and 30; Sch. 1 on Ps 92.1.

6.71

S2

Just as the perceptible peoples are opposed to perceptible Israel, so the intelligible peoples are opposed to intelligible Israel.

S1

Just as perceptible Israel had as opponents the perceptible nations, so for spiritual Israel there are intelligible nations as opponents.

On Israel: 1.31; sensible and intelligible "nations": 6.3.

6.72

S2

One thing is the intellection of matter, and another thing is the quality that indicates it, and another is that of their inwardness proximate to the elements, and another is that of the perceptible elements, and another is the *theōria* of the body, and another is the human instrument.

S1

One thing is the *logos* of matter, and another thing is the *logos* of its power, and another is that of its elements, another is the quality that is inward, and another is that of bodies, and another is that of the "harp" (instrument) of a person.

The six items listed here are three sets of contrasting pairs: matter versus quality; primary substance versus secondary (perceptible) substance; the human qua body and the human qua *organon*, contrasts that assume some familiarity with Aristotle's *Categories*. On the last pair, see 6.46. The concept of the human *organon* was adopted by earlier Christian writers specifically to denote the Incarnation. See Hippolytus, *Determination of the Date of Easter*, frag. 2. On the *organa* in general, 1.67.

6.73

S2

It is not because the mind is without body that it is the image of God, but it is because it has been made receptive of him. And if because it is incorporeal it is the image of God, then it would be essential knowledge, and from its receptivity it would not be the image of God. But examine if this is the same statement, that it is incorporeal and that it is receptive to knowledge, or, alternatively, like [the notion] about a statue and about its bronze [material].

S1

It is not because the mind is bodiless that it is the image of God, but because it is receptive of the knowledge of the Holy Trinity.

This keph., which forms a pair with 3.32, juxtaposes Gn 1.26 with Aristotle, *Physics* 2.3 and *Metaphysics* 5.2, which uses the analogy of a bronze statue to disambiguate four different causes: material, efficient, formal, and final. The relationship of a statue to its bronze (material cause) explains the nature of the mind. The material cause of the mind is its incorporeal essence: the formal cause, its receptivity. The mind being in the likeness of God is due not to its material cause but to its formal one; if the former were the case, the mind would have the same material cause as God—essential knowledge.

6.74

S2

Christ indeed will come before the judgment to judge the living and the dead. But he will be known after the judgment, if "The Lord is known by the judgment he makes."

S1

The Lord is known to the wise before his judgment. And after his judgment he becomes known to the wise and to the unwise, as it is written, "The Lord becomes known by the judgment that he makes."

Ps 9.17

Whereas S2 uses the two moments, before and after the judgment, to emphasize that Christ is known in the second phase (without suggesting anything about the first), S1 takes an Evagrian turn, and fills in the analogy, specifying that the two periods also coincide with two different groups of knowers. On Christ as judge, see 2.84.

6.75

S2

The first knowledge in rational beings is that of the Holy Trinity. After that there came about the movement of freedom, providence that assists and does not abandon, and after that, judgment. And again there will be the movement of freedom, providence, and judgment, and up to the Holy Trinity in such a way that judgment mediates between the movement of freedom and the providence of God.

450 EVAGRIUS OF PONTUS

S1

The first knowledge that was in rational nature is the *theōria* of the Holy Trinity, after which was the movement of freedom and after that the help of the providence of God, by the punishment that returns to life, or by means of the teaching that makes the first *theōria* appear.

S2 lacks a finite verb for our translation THERE WILL BE. We supply the future because the statement envisions a culminating restoration to the Holy Trinity, which has not yet occurred. Thus, this chapter describes both the fall of the rational beings and their restoration, along a series of three steps, arranged chiastically:

The fall from primary knowledge	The return to primary knowledge
Holy Trinity	
↓ movement of freedom ↓ providence ↓ judgment ↓	↑ judgment ↑ providence ↑ movement of freedom ↑
This world	

The last sentence of this keph. is puzzling, because it should be providence, not judgment, that is called the intervening force.

6.76

S2

If "he who has risen above the entire heaven" has "perfected all," it is clear that each of the ranks of the heavenly powers has truly learned the intellections that are about providence, by which they push swiftly those who are beneath them toward virtue and knowledge of God.

S1

If "he who has risen above the entire heaven" has "perfected all," it is clear that he has renewed the ranks of the rational beings, apart from the troop of rebels.

KEPHALAIA GNOSTIKA   451

Eph 4.10

Cf. 6.86. PROVIDENCE: 4.89; HEAVENLY POWERS: 1.42.

6.77

S2

Did Gabriel announce to Mary the coming forth of Christ from the Father, or his coming from the world of angels to the world of humans? Inquire again also, concerning the disciples who went about with him in his corporeal state, whether they came with him from the world seen by us, or from another one, or from others; or some of them, or all of them. And inquire again, further, whether it was in the psychic state that was theirs that they would become disciples to Christ.

S1

The mystery of our Lord that was hidden in his Father from worlds and from generations has been revealed in his appearance; and the election of his holy apostles before the foundations of the world has been known in his gospel; and concerning the tribes that were distant from his hope, it has been revealed to them and he has drawn them near to him.

cf. Lk 1.26–38 (S2); cf. Eph 3.9 (S1); cf. Eph 2.11–13 (S1)
COMING FORTH OF CHRIST: Jn 16.28: Grk. *exelthōn ek tou Patros*. Calling of the disciples: Mt 4.18–22.

6.78

S2

The equivalent of the body is that which is equal to it in mixture.

S1

[Same as S2]

This keph. forms a pair with 6.80. Nearly everywhere Syr. *muzāgā* corresponds to Grk. *poiōtes*, but here the alternative meaning, "mixture," makes more sense, hence we presuppose an original Grk. *krasis*, paralleled by the Greek and Syriac for *Reflections* 17. The human body was thought to consist of earth (see 1.68) in mixture with other elements. More difficult is Syr. *peḥmeh*, which

452 EVAGRIUS OF PONTUS

has a wide range of meanings: copy, comparison, equal, likeness. Our understanding of this word here and at 6.80 is informed by 6.79, which concerns the incarnation of Christ as fully human and fully divine, against those who might deny the reality of the human body of Christ (as in 6.77). Any material object that shares with the human body its peculiar mixture of the elements is an instance of that class of bodies, not accurately conveyed by a concise English translation of this kephalaion.

6.79

S2

The body of Christ is of the same nature as our body, and his soul is of the nature of our souls, but the *logos* that is essentially in him is coessential with the Father.

S1

The body of Christ is of the same nature as our body; also, his soul is from the nature of our souls. So also his divinity is coessential with the Father.

The body and soul of Christ are Syr. *bar kyana'*, connatural, with ours; but the Logos in him is Syr. *bar 'itutha'*, likely Grk. *ousiōdes*, essentially *homoousios*, with the Father. Cf. 4.9; 5.69; 6.14.

6.80

S2

The equivalent of rational substance is that which is equal to it in knowledge.

S1

The equivalent of the rational nature is that which is equal to it in knowledge.

See 6.78.

KEPHALAIA GNOSTIKA 453

6.81

S2

Just as it is not possible for a rational nature to be with the body outside of the world, so also it is not possible [for it] to be outside of the body in the world.

S1

Just as it is not possible for a rational nature to exist with the body outside the world, so it is not possible for the rational nature to be outside the flesh in the new world.

Cf. Origen, *Contra Celsum* 7.32 on the need for a body in this aeon.

6.82

S2

It is said that God is in the bodily nature like an architect in the things that have come into existence from him, and like him, it is said that he would be in a statue if he happened to have made for himself a statue of wood.

S1

Thus it is said that God lives in his creation as a builder in his house.

God like an architect: Job 38.1–41 and cf. 1 Cor 3.10, where Paul is a "skilled architect"; and as Demiurge: Plato, *Timaeus* 28a6, and Plotinus, *Enneads* 2.3.18.15; 1.5.2.7.

6.83

S2

It is said that the mind sees those things that it knows, and that it does not see those things that it does not know, and because of this it is not all the thoughts that are forbidden to it by the knowledge of God, but only those that attack it from anger and desire, and that are against nature.

454 EVAGRIUS OF PONTUS

S1

It is said that the mind sees those things that it knows, and does not see those things that it does not know, and because of this the knowledge of God does not prohibit all the thoughts, but only those that attack it from either anger or desire.

> The nous is changed by what it observes (2.83) and must therefore avoid observing whatever is against nature (3.59), thus diverting it from its true origin (1.50; 6.20; 6.85) and destiny (3.9).

6.84

S2

The angering part of the soul is joined with the heart, where is its intelligence, and the desiring part is joined with the flesh and blood, if it is necessary for us to "put far from the heart anger, and from the flesh, malice"

S1

Anger slithers in the heart, and desire of the flesh, in the blood. Because of this, we have been commanded to "put anger far from the heart and to make evil depart from the flesh."

Eccl 11.10

> Cf. Sch. 72 on Eccl 11.10; cf. *Thoughts* 4. On the heart: *Prak.* 46.

6.85

S2

If all the powers we have in common with the beasts are bodily in nature, then it is clear that anger and desire do not seem to have been created with rational nature before the movement.

S1

If we have in common with animals desire and anger, it is evident that those creatures have not been created with us at the beginning of our creation. Rather, they burst in upon upon the rational nature after the movement.

This keph. resembles a syllogism (see 1.11) that lacks two middle claims, that the only powers we share with the beasts are anger and desire, and that no bodily nature preexisted the movement. On THE MOVEMENT: 1.50–51.

6.86

Greek

The holy angels teach some with a word, others they convert through dreams, others they chasten by nocturnal terrors, and others they restore to virtue through blows.

Vat. gr. 2028, tenth/eleventh century (Géhin 1996, p. 65)

S2

Holy angels instruct some human beings by a word, and they convert others by means of dreams, and others they chasten by means of terrors at night, and they turn the rest back to virtue by blows.

S1

Among people, holy angels instruct some with a word, and they convert others with dreams, and others they chasten with fear, and they turn back others to virtue with blows.

Angels "instruct" humans and minister divine providence: *Prak.* 24 (angels "suggest" and demons "exhort").

6.87

S2

The mind, according to the word of Solomon, is joined with the heart, but the light that rises upon it is thought to be from the perceptible head.

S1

The mind, according to the word of Solomon, dwells in the heart, and intelligence in the brain.

456 EVAGRIUS OF PONTUS

This chapter forms a pair with 6.84. Cf. Sch. 10 on Ps 39.13; Sch. 14 on Ps 72.21; Sch. 11 on Eccl 2.14 the head of the wise one. Solomon and the heart as the site of knowledge: Sch. 68 on Eccl 9.1.1–2; Cf: the heart: *Prak.* 46; the head: *Prak.* pr.2. *Kardia* as *nous*: Sch. 9 at 30.14.

6.88

S2

It was not the holy angels alone fighting with us for our salvation, but also the stars themselves, if in the days of Barak they made war from heaven with Sisera.

S1

It was not only the holy angels fighting with us for our salvation, but also the saints, our companions, who also are assistants in the gospel of our Lord.

cf. Jgs 5.20 (S2)

S1 has dropped the reference to Jgs 5.20 and turned the stars into saints, to avoid the theme—inherited from Origen and condemned by anathema 6 of 543—that the stars are rational beings. On stars: 3.37.

6.89

S2

Just as in this world our Lord was "the firstborn from the house of the dead," so also in the world to come he will be "the firstborn of many brothers."

S1

Just as in this world, it is our Lord "the firstborn who rose from the house of the dead," thus also in the world to come he will be "the firstborn with many brothers."

Col 1.18; Rom 8.29

HOUSE OF THE DEAD: Col 1.18 Peshitta. FIRSTBORN: 2.36; coheirs: 3.72.

KEPHALAIA GNOSTIKA   457

6.90

S2

Everyone who is made worthy of spiritual knowledge will assist the holy angels, and will lead back rational souls from evil to virtue and from ignorance to knowledge.

S1

Everyone who by the grace of our Lord is made worthy of the knowledge of the spirit is with diligence assisting the holy angels as they take rational souls from evil to virtue and from ignorance to the knowledge of the truth.

Cf. Sch. 164 on Prv 17.17. Assisting the angels: 6.76, 86; *Prak.* 24, 76; *Gn.* 50.

Epilogue

S2

Examine our words, brothers, and explain zealously the symbols of the centuries, of the number of the six days of creation.

S1

Examine our words, brothers, expound them with worthy thought to those who possess this sign which is placed by us in this number of six centuries, a mystery of the number six, of our generations.

EXAMINE: *Gn.* 43; CREATION: 5.89.

Epilogue 2

S2

Finished are the six centuries of Evagrius the Blessed.

S1

Finished is the sixth century, which lacks ten chapters.

458   EVAGRIUS OF PONTUS

Finished are the six centuries of kephalaia of knowledge, which were spoken by Evagrius the Blessed.

This secondary epilogue was added by the Syriac translators. S1 has supplied two epilogues, one for the sixth century and the second for the entire work.

Bibliography

Bunge, Gabriel. "Encore une fois: Hénade ou monade? Au sujet de deux notions-clés de la terminologie technique d'Évagre le pontique." *Adamantius* 15 (2009): 9–42.

Bunge, Gabriel. "Hénade ou Monade? Au sujet de deux notions centrales de la terminologie évagrienne." *Le Muséon* 102 (1989): 69–91.

Casiday, Augustine. *Reconstructing the Theology of Evagrius Ponticus: Beyond Heresy.* Cambridge: Cambridge University Press, 2013.

Chiaradonna, Ricardo. "Porphyry and Iamblichus on Universals and Synonymous Predication." *Documenta e studi sulla Tradizione Filosofica Medievale* 18 (2007): 123–140.

Corrigan, Kevin. *Evagrius and Gregory: Mind, Soul and Body in the 4th Century.* Ashgate Studies in Philosophy & Theology in Late Antiquity. Farnham and Burlington: Ashgate, 2009.

Cribiore, Raffaella. *Gymnastics of the Mind: Greek Education in Hellenistic and Roman Egypt.* Princeton, NJ: Princeton University Press, 2001.

Davis, Stephen J. "Evagrius Ponticus at the Monastery of the Syrians: Newly Documented Evidence for an Arabic Reception History." In *Heirs of the Apostles: The Story of Arabic Christianity*, edited by D. Bertaina, S. Keating, M. N. Swanson, and A. Treiger, 347–92. Leiden; Boston: Brill, 2018.

Devreesse, Robert. *Les anciens commentateurs grecs de l'Octateuque et des Rois: [Fragments tirés des chaînes].* Studi e testi 201. Città del Vaticano: Biblioteca apostolica vaticana, 1959.

Diekamp, Franz. *Doctrina patrum de incarnatione verbi; Ein griechisches Florilegium aus der Wende des siebenten und achten Jahrhunderts.* Münster in Westf.: Aschendorffsche Verlagsbuchhandlung, 1907.

Elior, Rachel. *Three Temples: On the Emergence of Jewish Mysticism.* Oxford: Littman Library, 2005.

Elm, Susanna. *Virgins of God: The Making of Asceticism in Late Antiquity.* Oxford Classical Monographs. Oxford; New York: Clarendon Press, 1996.

Furrer-Pilliod, Christiane. *Oroi kai ypographai: Collections alphabétiques de définitions profanes et sacrées.* Studi e testi (Biblioteca apostolica vaticana) 395. Città del Vaticano: Biblioteca apostolica Vaticana, 2000.

Géhin, Paul. "En marge de la constitution d'un repertorium Evagrianum Syriacum: Quelques remarques sur l'organisation en corpus des oeuvres d'Évagre." *Parole de l'Orient* 35 (2010): 285–301.

Géhin, Paul. "Evagriana d'un Manuscrit Basilien (*Vaticanus Gr. 2028; Olim Basilianus 67*)." *Le Muséon* 109 (1996): 59–85.

Géhin, Paul. "La tradition arabe d'Évagre le Pontique." *Collectanea Christiana Orientalia* 3 (2006): 83–104.

Géhin, Paul. "Les Collections de *Kephalaia* Monastiques: Naissance et succès d'un genre entre création originale, plagiat et florilège." In *The Minor Genres of Byzantine Theological Literature*, edited by Antonio Rigo, 1–50. Studies in Byzantine History and Civilization 8. Turnhout: Brepols, 2013.

460 BIBLIOGRAPHY

Géhin, Paul, ed. *Scholies aux Proverbes*. Sources chrétiennes 340. Paris: Éditions du Cerf, 1987.

Géhin, Paul, Claire Guillaumont, and Antoine Guillaumont, eds. *Sur les pensées*. Sources chrétiennes 438. Paris: Cerf, 1998.

Gribomont, Jean. "Ps.-Basil, Epistula 8." In *Le lettere*, edited by Marcella Forlin Patrucco, 84–112. Corona Patrum 11. Torino: Società editrice internazionale, 1983.

Gronewald, M., ed. *Didymos der Blinde. Psalmenkommentar*. Part 5. Papyrologische Texte und Abhandlungen 12. Bonn: Habelt, 1970.

Guillaumont, Antoine, ed. *Les six centuries des "Kephalaia gnostica": Édition critique de la version syriaque commune et édition d'une nouvelle version syriaque, intégrale, avec une double traduction française*. Patrologia Orientalis 28. Paris: Firmin-Didot, 1958.

Guillaumont, Antoine, and Claire Guillaumont. "Les versions orientales et le texte grec des Lettres d'Evagre le Pontique." In *Langues orientales anciennes philologie et linguistique*, 3:151–62. Louvain: Peeters, 1991.

Guillaumont, Antoine. *Les "Képhalaia gnostica" d'Évagre le Pontique et l'histoire de l'origénisme chez les grecs et chez les syriens*. Publications de la Sorbonne série patristica Sorbonensia 5. Paris: Eds. du Seuil, 1962.

Guillaumont, Antoine. *Un philosophe au désert: Evagre le Pontique*. Textes et traditions 8. Paris: Vrin, 2004.

Guillaumont, Antoine, and Claire Guillaumont, eds. *Le gnostique, ou, A celui qui est devenu digne de la science*. Sources chrétiennes 356. Paris: Éditions du Cerf, 1989.

Guillaumont, Claire, and Antoine Guillaumont, eds. *Traité pratique, ou, Le moine*. 2 vols. Sources chrétiennes 170–71. Paris: Éditions du Cerf, 1971.

Hausherr, Irénée. "Nouveaux fragments grecs d'Évagre le Pontique." *Orientalia Christiana Periodica* 5 (1939): 229–33.

Hoek, Annewies van den. *Clement of Alexandria and His Use of Philo in the Stromateis: An Early Christian Reshaping of a Jewish Model*. Supplements to Vigiliae Christianae v. 3. Leiden; New York: Brill, 1988.

Kalvesmaki, Joel. "Evagrius in the Byzantine Genre of Chapters." In *Evagrius and His Legacy*, edited by Joel Kalvesmaki and Robin Darling Young, 257–87. South Bend, IN: University of Notre Dame Press, 2016.

Kalvesmaki, Joel, "Evagrius the Cappadocian: Redating the *Kephalaia Gnostika*." *Journal of Early Christian Studies* 31, no. 4 (2023): forthcoming.

Kalvesmaki, Joel. *The Theology of Arithmetic: Number Symbolism in Platonism and Early Christianity*. Hellenic Studies 59. Washington DC: Center for Hellenic Studies, 2013.

Kramer, J. *Didymos der Blinde: Kommentar zum Ecclesiastes*, pt. 3. Papyrologische Texte und Abhandlungen 13. Bonn: Habelt, 1970.

Kugel, James. *Traditions of the Bible: A Guide to The Bible As It Was at the Start of the Common Era*. Harvard: University Press, 1998.

Lampe, G. W. H. *A Patristic Greek Lexicon*. Oxford: Clarendon Press, 1961.

Larsen, Lillian I., and Samuel Rubenson. *Monastic Education in Late Antiquity: The Transformation of Classical Paideia*. Cambridge: University Press, 2018.

Lavenant, René. *La lettre à Patrikios de Philoxène de Mabboug*. Patrologia Orientalis 30.5. Paris: Firmin-Didot, 1963.

Layton, Richard A. *Didymus the Blind and His Circle in Late-Antique Alexandria: Virtue and Narrative in Biblical Scholarship*. Urbana: University of Illinois Press, 2004.

LeMoine, F. J. "Jerome's Gift to Women Readers." In *Shifting Frontiers in Late Antiquity*, edited by Ralph W. Mathisen and Hagith S. Sivan, 230–41. Aldershot, Hampshire; Brookfield, VT: Variorum, 1996.

BIBLIOGRAPHY   461

Muyldermans, Joseph. *À travers la tradition manuscrite d'Evagre le pontique: Essai sur les manuscrits grecs conservés à la Bibliothèque Nationale de Paris*. Bibliothèque du Muséon 3. Louvain: Bureaux du Muséon, 1932.

Muyldermans, Joseph. "Evagriana." *Le Muséon. Revue d'Études Orientales* 44 (1931): 37–68.

Muyldermans, Joseph. *Evagriana: Extrait de La Revue* Le Muséon, *Vol. 44, Augmenté de Nouveax Fragments Grecs Inédits*. Paris: Paul Geuthner, 1931.

Neyt, François, ed. and trans. *Barsanuphe et Jean de Gaza, Correspondance*, vol. 2, pt. 2, *Aux cénobites, Lettres 399–616*. Sources chrétiennes 451. Paris: Éditions du Cerf, 2001.

Pitra, J. B. *Analecta sacra spicilegio Solesmensi parata*. Paris: A. Jouby et Roger, 1876.

Ramelli, Ilaria L. E. *Evagrius's Kephalaia Gnostika: A New Translation of the Unreformed Text from the Syriac*. Atlanta: SBL Press, 2015.

Regnault, L., and J. de Préville. *Dorothée de Gaza. Oeuvres spirituelles*. Sources chrétiennes 92. Paris: Éditions du Cerf, 1963.

Remes, Pauline. *Neoplatonism*. Berkeley: University of California Press, 2008.

Remijsen, S. *The End of Greek Athletics in Late Antiquity*. Greek Culture in the Roman World. Cambridge: University Press, 2015.

Richard, Marcel. "Les fragments du commentaire de S. Hippolyte sur les Proverbes de Salomon." *Le Muséon* 78, nos. 1–2 (1965): 257–290.

Rondeau, Marie-Josèphe, Paul Géhin, and Matthieu Cassin, eds. *Scholies aux Psaumes*, vol. 1, *Psaumes 1–70*; vol. 2, *Psaumes 71–150*. Sources chrétiennes 614–15. Paris: Les Éditions du Cerf, 2021.

Rorem, Paul, and John C. Lamoreaux. *John of Scythopolis and the Dionysian Corpus: Annotating the Areopagite*. Oxford Early Christian Studies. Oxford: Clarendon, 1998.

Scherer, Jean. Le commentaire o'Origène sur Rom. III. 5–V. 7, d'après les extraits du papyrus no. 88748 du Musée du Caire et les fragments de la Philocalie et du Vaticanus gr. 762: Essai de reconstitution du texte et de la pensee des tomes V et VI du "Commentaire sur l'épitre aux romains." Bibliothèque d'Étude T. 27. Cairo: Impr. de l'Institut français d'archéologie orientale, 1957.

Schwartz, Eduard, and Johannes Straub. Acta conciliorum oecumenicorum. Vol. 4, Concilium universale Constantinopolitanum sub Iustiniano habitum. Berlin: De Gruyter, 1971.

Sicherl, Martin. "Ein Neuplatonischer Hymn unter den Gedichten Gregors von Nazianzen." In *Neoplatonic and Byzantine Studies Presented to Leendert Gerrit Westerink at 75*, ed. John Duffy et al., 61–83. Buffalo: Arethusa, 1988.

Stewart, Columba. "Imageless Prayer and the Theological Vision of Evagrius Ponticus." *Journal of Early Christian Studies* 9, no. 2 (2001): 173–204.

Young, Robin Darling, and Hovsep Karapetian, ed. and trans. *Evagrius Letters in Armenian Translation*. Corpus Scriptorum Christianorum Orientalium 704. Louvain: Peeters, 2022.

Watts, Edward Jay. *Hypatia: The Life and Legend of an Ancient Philosopher*. Women in Antiquity. New York: Oxford University Press, 2017.

Wolf, Johann Christoph. *Anecdota graeca sacra et profana: Ex codicibus manu exaratis nunc primum in lucem edita, versione Latina donata et notis illustrata*. 4 vols. Hamburg: Apud Theodorum Christophorum Felginer, 1722.

Select Writings of Evagrius

Listed below are select editions and translations of the works of Evagrius that are cited in this book. Entries are alphabetized by abbreviation, followed by the fuller English title and in parentheses the number assigned by the *Clavis Patrum Graecorum*. Editions cited may contain the work only in part or only in a particular version.

Readers interested in a detailed account of all of Evagrius' known works (including spuria) and all the editions of those works are encouraged to consult Joel Kalvesmaki, ed., *The Guide to Evagrius Ponticus*, available at http://evagriusponticus.net/corpus.htm.

Antirr. = *Antirrhetikos* (CPG 2434)

Brakke, David. *Talking Back: A Monastic Handbook for Combating Demons*. Cistercian Studies 229. Collegeville, MN: Cistercian Publications, 2009.
Frankenberg, W., ed. *Euagrius Ponticus*, 472–545. Abhandlungen der Königlichen gesellschaft der wissenschaften zu Göttingen. Philologisch-historische klasse, n.F., 13, no. 2. Berlin: Weidmannsche buchhandlung, 1912.
O'Laughlin, Michael. "Antirrheticus (Selections)." In *Ascetic Behavior in Greco-Roman Antiquity: A Sourcebook*, edited by Vincent L. Wimbush, 243–62. Studies in Antiquity and Christianity. Minneapolis: Fortress Press, 1990.
Sims-Williams, Nicholas. *The Christian Sogdian Manuscript C2*. Schriften Zur Geschichte Und Kultur Des Alten Orients. Berliner Turfantexte 12. Berlin: Akademie-Verlag, 1985.

Thirty-Three Chapters (CPG 2442)

PG 40:1264d–68b, 1858.
Sinkewicz, Robert E., ed. *Evagrius of Pontus: The Greek Ascetic Corpus*, 224–27. Oxford: Oxford University Press, 2003.

Cherubim = *On the Cherubim* (CPG 2459)

Muyldermans, Joseph. "Sur les séraphins et Sur les chérubins d'Évagre le Pontique dans les versions syriaque et arménienne." *Le Muséon: Revue d'Études Orientales* 59 (1946): 367–79.

Disc. = *The Disciples of Evagrius* (CPG 2483)

Géhin, Paul, ed. *Chapitres des disciples d'Évagre*. Sources chrétiennes 514. Paris: Cerf, 2007.

464 SELECT WRITINGS OF EVAGRIUS

Eight Thoughts = The Eight Spirits of Wickedness (CPG 2451)

Bigot, Émery, ed. *Palladii episcopi helenopolitani De vita s. Johannis Chrysostomi dialogus: Accedunt homilia Sancti Johannis chrysostomi in laudem Diodori, Tarsensis episcopi, Acta Tarachi, Probi et andronici, Passio Banifatii Romani, Evagrius de octo cogitationibus, Nilus de octo vitiis*. Lutetiae Parisiorum: Apud viduam Edmundi Martini, 1680.

Muyldermans, Joseph, ed. *Evagriana syriaca: Textes inedits du British Museum et de la Vaticane*, 55–59. Bibliothèque du Muséon 31. Louvain: Publications universitaires, 1952.

PG 79:1145–64, 1863.

Sinkewicz, Robert E., ed. *Evagrius of Pontus: The Greek Ascetic Corpus*, 66–90. Oxford: Oxford University Press, 2003.

Eulogios = Treatise to the Monk Eulogius or To Eulogius on the Confession of Thoughts and Counsel in Their Regard (CPG 2447)

PG 79:1093d–1140a, 1863.

Sinkewicz, Robert E., ed. *Evagrius of Pontus: The Greek Ascetic Corpus*, 12–59. Oxford: Oxford University Press, 2003.

Fogielman, Charles-Antoine, ed. *A Euloge: Les vices opposés aux vertus*. Sources chrétiennes 591. Paris: Les Éditions du Cerf, 2017.

Exh. Monks = Exhortations to Monks / Counsel to Monks (CPG 2454)

Joest, Christoph, ed. *Ad monachos; Ad virginem; Institutio ad monachos = Der Mönchsspiegel; Der Nonnenspiegel; Ermahnungen an Mönche*. Fontes Christiani 51. Freiburg im Breisgau: Herder, 2012.

PG 79:1235–40, 1863.

Sinkewicz, Robert E., ed. *Evagrius of Pontus: The Greek Ascetic Corpus*, 217–23. Oxford: Oxford University Press, 2003.

Foundations = Hypotyposeis / Principles of the Monastic Life (CPG 2441)

Casiday, Augustine, ed. *Evagrius Ponticus*, 81–88. New York: Routledge, 2006.

Muyldermans, Joseph, ed. *Evagriana syriaca: Textes inedits du British Museum et de la Vaticane*, 31–33. Bibliothèque du Muséon 31. Louvain: Publications universitaires, 1952.

Nicodemus the Hagiorite and Saint Makarios, eds. *Φιλοκαλία τῶν νηπτικῶν συνερανισθεῖσα παρὰ τῶν ἁγίων καὶ θεοφόρων πατέρων ἡμῶν ἐν ᾗ διὰ τῆς κατὰ τὴν Πρᾶξιν καὶ Θεωρίαν Ἠθικῆς Φιλοσοφίας ὁ νοῦς καθαίρεται, φωτίζεται, καὶ τελετοῦται*. 3rd ed. 5 vols. Athens: Ἀστήρ, 1957.

PG 40:1252d–64c, 1858.

Sinkewicz, Robert E., ed. *Evagrius of Pontus: The Greek Ascetic Corpus*, 1–11. Oxford: Oxford University Press, 2003.

SELECT WRITINGS OF EVAGRIUS 465

Gn. = Gnostikos (CPG 2431)

Frankenberg, W., ed. *Euagrius Ponticus*, 546–53. Abhandlungen der Königlichen gesellschaft der wissenschaften zu Göttingen. Philologisch-historische klasse, n.F., 13, no. 2. Berlin: Weidmannsche buchhandlung, 1912.
Guillaumont, Antoine, and Claire Guillaumont, eds. *Le gnostique, ou, A celui qui est devenu digne de la science.* Sources chrétiennes 356. Paris: Éditions du Cerf, 1989.

Instructions (Prov.) / Proverbs and their Interpretation (CPG 2477)

Muyldermans, Joseph. "Evagriana." *Le Muséon: Revue d'Études Orientales* 44 (1931): 37–68.
Muyldermans, Joseph. *Evagriana syriaca: Textes inedits du British Museum et de la Vaticane,* 135–38, 165–67. Bibliothèque du Muséon 31. Louvain: Publications universitaires, 1952.

Just = Just and the Perfect / The Just and the Perfect (CPG 2465)

Muyldermans, Joseph, ed. *Evagriana syriaca: Textes inedits du British Museum et de la Vaticane,* 105–9, 142–46. Bibliothèque du Muséon 31. Louvain: Publications universitaires, 1952.

KG = Kephalaia gnostika (CPG 2432)

Frankenberg, W., ed. *Euagrius Ponticus*, 422–71. Abhandlungen der Königlichen gesellschaft der wissenschaften zu Göttingen. Philologisch-historische klasse, n.F., 13, no. 2. Berlin: Weidmannsche buchhandlung, 1912.
Guillaumont, Antoine, ed. *Les six centuries des "Kephalaia gnostica": Édition critique de la version syriaque commune et édition d'une nouvelle version syriaque, intégrale, avec une double traduction française.* Patrologia Orientalis 28. Paris: Firmin-Didot, 1958.
O'Laughlin, Michael. "Origenism in the Desert: Anthropology and Integration in Evagrius Ponticus." PhD dissertation, Harvard Divinity School, 1987.
Ramelli, Ilaria L. E. *Evagrius's Kephalaia Gnostica: A New Translation of the Unreformed Text from the Syriac.* Writings from the Greco-Roman World. Atlanta: SBL Press, 2015.

Letter on Faith / Epistula Fidei (CPG 2439)

Bunge, Gabriel, ed. *Briefe aus der Wüste.* Sophia 24. Trier: Paulinus-Verlag, 1986.
Casiday, Augustine, ed. *Evagrius Ponticus*, 45–58. London; New York: Routledge, 2006.
Frankenberg, W., ed. *Euagrius Ponticus*, 620–35. Abhandlungen der Königlichen gesellschaft der wissenschaften zu Göttingen. Philologisch-historische klasse, n.F., 13, no. 2. Berlin: Weidmannsche buchhandlung, 1912.
Gribomont, Jean. "Ps.-Basil, Epistula 8." In *Le lettere*, edited by Marcella Forlin Patrucco, 84–112. Corona Patrum 11. Torino: Società editrice internazionale, 1983.
PG 32:245–68, 1857.

466 SELECT WRITINGS OF EVAGRIUS

Letter to Melania (CPG 2438)

Casiday, Augustine, ed. *Evagrius Ponticus*, 63–77. New York: Routledge, 2006.

Ferguson, Everett. *Forms of Devotion: Conversion, Worship, Spirituality, and Asceticism*, 272–310. Recent Studies in Early Christianity 5. New York: Garland, 1999.

Frankenberg, W., ed. *Euagrius Ponticus*, 612–19. Abhandlungen der Königlichen gesellschaft der wissenschaften zu Göttingen. Philologisch-historische klasse, n.F., 13, no. 2. Berlin: Weidmannsche buchhandlung, 1912.

Parmentier, M. "Evagrius of Pontus' Letter to Melania." *Bijdragen* 46 (1985): 2–38.

Vitestam, Gösta. *Seconde partie du traité, qui passe sous le nom de "La grande lettre d'Évagre le Pontique à Mélanie l'Ancienne."* Scripta minora regiae societatis humaniorum litterarum Lundensis 3. Lund: Glerrup, 1964.

Letters / 62 Letters (CPG 2437)

Bunge, Gabriel, ed. *Briefe aus der Wüste*. Sophia 24. Trier: Paulinus-Verlag, 1986.

Casiday, Augustine, ed. *Evagrius Ponticus*, 59–62. New York: Routledge, 2006.

Frankenberg, W., ed. *Euagrius Ponticus*, 564–611. Abhandlungen der Königlichen gesellschaft der wissenschaften zu Göttingen. Philologisch-historische klasse, n.F., 13, no. 2. Berlin: Weidmannsche buchhandlung, 1912.

Géhin, Paul. "Nouveaux fragments grecs des lettres d'Évagre." *Revue d'Histoire des Textes* 24 (1994): 117–47.

Guillaumont, Claire. "Fragments grecs inédits d'Évagre le Pontique." In *Texte und Textkritik: Eine Aufsatzsammlung*, edited by Johannes Irmscher, Franz Paschke, Kurt Treu, and Jürgen Dummer, 209–21. Texte und Untersuchungen zur Geschichte der altchristlichen Literatur 133. Berlin: Akademie-Verlag, 1987.

Young, Robin Darling. "Cannibalism and Other Family Woes in Letter 55 of Evagrius of Pontus." In *The World of Early Egyptian Christianity: Language, Literature, and Social Context; Essays in Honor of David W. Johnson*, edited by James E. Goehring and Janet Timbie, 130–39. CUA Studies in Early Christianity. Washington DC: Catholic University of America Press, 2007.

Young, Robin Darling, and Hovsep Karapetian, ed. and trans. *Evagrius Letters in Armenian Translation*. Corpus Scriptorum Christianorum Orientalium 704. Louvain: Peeters, 2022.

Masters and Disciples / On Masters and Disciples (CPG 2449)

Unpublished

Maxims 1 / Parenetikos (CPG 2443)

PG 79:1235–40, 1863.

Sinkewicz, Robert E., ed. *Evagrius of Pontus: The Greek Ascetic Corpus*, 228–30. Oxford: Oxford University Press, 2003.

SELECT WRITINGS OF EVAGRIUS 467

Maxims 2 / Spiritual Chapters Alphabetized (CPG 2444)

Muyldermans, Joseph, ed. *Evagriana syriaca: Textes inedits du British Museum et de la Vaticane*, 33. Bibliothèque du Muséon 31. Louvain: Publications universitaires, 1952.

PG 40:1268c–69b, 1858.

Sinkewicz, Robert E., ed. *Evagrius of Pontus: The Greek Ascetic Corpus*, 230–31. Oxford: Oxford University Press, 2003.

Maxims 3 / Other Sentences (CPG 2445)

PG 40:1269b–d, 1858.

Elter, Antonio, ed. *Gnomica*. Leipzig: Teubner, 1892

Sinkewicz, Robert E., ed. *Evagrius of Pontus: The Greek Ascetic Corpus*, 231–32. Oxford: Oxford University Press, 2003.

Monks = Chapters to Monks (CPG 2435)

Driscoll, Jeremy, ed. *Evagrius Ponticus: Ad Monachos*. Ancient Christian Writers 59. New York: Newman Press, 2003.

Joest, Christoph, ed. *Ad monachos; Ad virginem; Institutio ad monachos = Der Mönchsspiegel; Der Nonnenspiegel; Ermahnungen an Mönche*. Fontes Christiani 51. Freiburg im Breisgau: Herder, 2012.

Leclercq, Jean. "L'ancienne version latine des Sentences d'Évagre pour les Moines." *Scriptorium* 5 (1951): 195–213.

Mühmelt, Martin. "Zu der neuen lateinischen Übersetzung des Mönchsspiegels des Euagrius." *Vigiliae Christianae* 8 (1954): 101–3.

PG 40:1277–82, 1858.

Sinkewicz, Robert E., ed. *Evagrius of Pontus: The Greek Ascetic Corpus*, 115–31. Oxford: Oxford University Press, 2003.

Prak. = Praktikos (CPG 2430)

Bamberger, John Eudes, ed. *The Praktikos: Chapters on Prayer*. Cistercian Studies Series 4. Spencer, MA: Cistercian Publications, 1970.

Guillaumont, Claire, and Antoine Guillaumont, eds. *Traité pratique, ou, Le moine*. 2 vols. Sources chrétiennes 170–71. Paris: Éditions du Cerf, 1971.

Nicodemus the Hagiorite and Saint Makarios, eds. *Φιλοκαλία τῶν νηπτικῶν συνερανισθεῖσα παρὰ τῶν ἁγίων καὶ θεοφόρων πατέρων ἡμῶν ἐν ᾗ διὰ τῆς κατὰ τὴν Πρᾶξιν καὶ Θεωρίαν Ἠθικῆς Φιλοσοφίας ὁ νοῦς καθαίρεται, φωτίζεται, καὶ τελετοῦται.* 3rd ed. 5 vols. Athens: Ἀστήρ, 1957.

PG 40:1220c–1236c, 1858.

Sinkewicz, Robert E., ed. *Evagrius of Pontus: The Greek Ascetic Corpus*. Oxford: Oxford University Press, 2003.

Tugwell, Simon, ed. *Praktikos and On Prayer*. Oxford: Faculty of Theology, 1987.

468   SELECT WRITINGS OF EVAGRIUS

Prayer = *Chapters on Prayer* (CPG 2452)

Bamberger, John Eudes, ed. *The Praktikos: Chapters on Prayer*. Cistercian Studies Series 4. Spencer, MA: Cistercian Publications, 1970.

Casiday, Augustine, ed. *Evagrius Ponticus*, 185–201. New York: Routledge, 2006.

Hausherr, Irénée. "Le *De oratione* d'Évagre le Pontique en syriaque et en arabe." *Orientalia Christiana Periodica* 5 (1939): 7–71.

Muyldermans, Joseph, ed. *Evagriana syriaca: Textes inedits du British Museum et de la Vaticane*, 41–43. Bibliothèque du Muséon 31. Louvain: Publications universitaires, 1952.

Nicodemus the Hagiorite and Saint Makarios, eds. Φιλοκαλία τῶν νηπτικῶν συνερανισθεῖσα παρὰ τῶν ἁγίων καὶ θεοφόρων πατέρων ἡμῶν ἐν ᾗ διὰ τῆς κατὰ τὴν Πρᾶξιν καὶ Θεωρίαν Ἠθικῆς Φιλοσοφίας ὁ νοῦς καθαίρεται, φωτίζεται, καὶ τελετοῦται. 3rd ed. 5 vols. Athens: Ἀστήρ, 1957.

PG 79:1165a–1200c, 1863.

Sinkewicz, Robert E., ed. *Evagrius of Pontus: The Greek Ascetic Corpus*, 183–209. Oxford: Oxford University Press, 2003.

Tugwell, Simon, ed. *Praktikos and On Prayer*. Oxford: Faculty of Theology, 1987.

Reflections = *Skemmata* (CPG 2433)

Frankenberg, W., ed. *Euagrius Ponticus*, 452–67. Abhandlungen der Königlichen gesellschaft der wissenschaften zu Göttingen. Philologisch-historische klasse, n.F., 13, no. 2. Berlin: Weidmannsche buchhandlung, 1912.

Muyldermans, Joseph. "Evagriana." *Le Muséon: Revue d'Études Orientales* 44 (1931): 37–68.

Muyldermans, Joseph. "Sur les séraphins et *Sur les chérubins* d'Évagre le Pontique dans les versions syriaque et arménienne." *Le Muséon: Revue d'Études Orientales* 59 (1946): 367–79.

Sinkewicz, Robert E., ed., *Evagrius of Pontus: The Greek Ascetic Corpus*, 210–16. Oxford: Oxford University Press, 2003.

Sch on Eccl = Scholia on Ecclesiastes (CPG 2458.5)

Géhin, Paul, ed. *Scholies à l'Ecclésiaste*. Sources chrétiennes 397. Paris: Éditions du Cerf, 1993.

Sch on Prv = Scholia on the Proverbs (CPG 2456 = CPG 2458.4)

Géhin, Paul, ed. *Scholies aux Proverbes*. Sources chrétiennes 340. Paris: Éditions du Cerf, 1987.

Sch on Ps = Scholia on the Psalms (CPG 2455)

PG 12:1054–1686, passim; 27:60–545, passim, 1862.

Pitra, J. B. *Analecta sacra spicilegio Solesmensi parata*, 2:444–83; 3:1–364. Paris: A. Jouby et Roger, 1876.

SELECT WRITINGS OF EVAGRIUS 469

Sch on Ps = Scholia on the Psalms (CPG 2455)

Rondeau, Marie-Josèphe, Paul Géhin, and Matthieu Cassin, eds. *Scholies aux Psaumes I, Psaumes 1–70*. Sources chrétiennes 614. Paris: Les Éditions du Cerf, 2021.
Rondeau, Marie-Josèphe, Paul Géhin, and Matthieu Cassin, eds. *Scholies aux Psaumes II, Psaumes 71–150*. Sources chrétiennes 615. Paris: Les Éditions du Cerf, 2021.

Thoughts = *On the Thoughts* (CPG 2450)

Casiday, Augustine, ed. *Evagrius Ponticus*, 89–116. New York: Routledge, 2006.
Géhin, Paul, Claire Guillaumont, and Antoine Guillaumont, eds. *Sur les pensées*. Sources chrétiennes 438. Paris: Cerf, 1998.
Nicodemus the Hagiorite and Saint Makarios, eds. *Φιλοκαλία τῶν νηπτικῶν συνερανισθεῖσα παρὰ τῶν ἁγίων καὶ θεοφόρων πατέρων ἡμῶν ἐν ᾗ διὰ τῆς κατὰ τὴν Πρᾶξιν καὶ Θεωρίαν Ἠθικῆς Φιλοσοφίας ὁ νοῦς καθαίρεται, φωτίζεται, καὶ τελετοῦται*. 3rd ed. 5 vols. Athens: Ἀστήρ, 1957.
Sinkewicz, Robert E., ed. *Evagrius of Pontus: The Greek Ascetic Corpus*, 136–82. Oxford: Oxford University Press, 2003.

Vices = *On the Vices Opposed to the Virtues* (CPG 2448)

PG 79:1140b–44d, 1863.
Sinkewicz, Robert E., ed. *Evagrius of Pontus: The Greek Ascetic Corpus*, 60–65. Oxford: Oxford University Press, 2003.

Virgin = *Chapters to a Virgin* (CPG 2436)

Casiday, Augustine, ed. *Evagrius Ponticus*, 165–71. New York: Routledge, 2006.
Frankenberg, W., ed. *Euagrius Ponticus*, 562–65. Abhandlungen der Königlichen gesellschaft der wissenschaften zu Göttingen. Philologisch-historische klasse, n.F., 13, no. 2. Berlin: Weidmannsche buchhandlung, 1912.
Joest, Christoph, ed. *Ad monachos; Ad virginem; Institutio ad monachos = Der Mönchsspiegel; Der Nonnenspiegel; Ermahnungen an Mönche*. Fontes Christiani 51. Freiburg im Breisgau: Herder, 2012.
Mühmelt, Martin. "Zu der neuen lateinischen Übersetzung des Mönchsspiegels des Euagrius." *Vigiliae Christianae* 8 (1954): 101–3.
PG 40:1185–88, 1858.
Sinkewicz, Robert E., ed. *Evagrius of Pontus: The Greek Ascetic Corpus*, 131–36. Oxford: Oxford University Press, 2003.

Quotations and Direct Allusions

In the index below, entries marked with ⁺ indicate paraphrases; those with *, direct allusions; all other entries are verbatim quotations of one or more words.

Old Testament (Septuagint)

The sequence and names of Old Testament books follows that of the Rahlfs edition of the Septuagint, as well as that the versification of that edition.

Gn

1

27: *KG* 6.45 (S1)

2

2: *KG* 3.68* (S2)
7: *KG* 3.71
9: *KG* 3.56; 5.69*
10: *KG* 5.72*

3

19: *KG* 5.35

11

4–9: *KG* 4.53*

16

KG 1.32*

17

KG 1.32*
12: *KG* 6.7*

28

12–13: *KG* 4.43*

32

7: *Prak.* 26

25

17: *KG* 4.63*
23–30: *Gn.* 46
30: *KG* 2.86*

26

35: *Gn.* 46

28

4: *KG* 4.48*, 56*, 69*, 75*, 79*
31: *KG* 4.66*
33–34: *KG* 4.66*
36: *KG* 4.52*
42: *KG* 4.72*

29

2: *KG* 4.28*
13: *KG* 4.32*, 36

33

3: *KG* 3.67

36

29: *KG* 4.66*

37

10–16: *Gn.* 46

Ex

12

38: *KG* 4.64*

19

3: *KG* 5.40*
9: *KG* 5.13*

20

21: *KG* 5.16*

22

29: *KG* 5.10*

23

10–11: *KG* 5.8*

24

11: *KG* 5.39* (S1)

Lv

8

9: *KG* 4.48*

11

2–19: *Gn.* 20
22: *Prak.* 38

Nm

6

3: *KG* 5.44*

15

32–36: *KG* 4.26*

24

17–19: *Gn.* 21

472 QUOTATIONS AND DIRECT ALLUSIONS

32
1–5: *KG* 6.47* (S2)
35
11: *KG* 4.82

Dt
18
11: *KG* 6.61
32
9: *KG* 1.31*
33: *KG* 5.44
33
1: *KG* 2.56*

Josh
1
14–15: *KG* 6.47* (S2)
5
2–3: *KG* 6.66*
13
1: *KG* 5.36*
20
2–3: *KG* 4.82
4–6: *KG* 4.83*

Jgs
5
20: *KG* 6.88* (S2)
6
19–24: *KG* 4.45* (S1)
7
5–7: *Prak.* 17
13
15–21: *KG* 4.45*
16
19–21: *KG* 5.45*

1 Kgdms/1 Sam
28
7–20: *KG* 6.61*

2 Kgdms/2 Sam
6
10–11: *Gn.* 38
14
20: *KG* 1.23*

Ps
1
3: *KG* 5.67
5
12: *KG* 3.36 (Grk.)

9
17: *KG* 6.74
10
2: *Prak.* 50
17
39: *Prak.* 72
18
11: *KG* 3.64*
23
3: *KG* 6.1 (S1)
7: *KG* 5.77*
26
2: *Prak.* 72
32
2: *KG* 6.48*
35
10: *KG* 5.67
41
6: *Prak.* 27
44
8: *KG* 4.21
62
4: *KG* 1.73
67
31: *KG* 6.27 (S2)
77
25: *KG* 1.23
80
10: *KG* 5.49
85
9: *KG* 6.27
90
6: *Prak.* 12
91
4: *KG* 6.48*
103
15: *Prak.* ep
24: *KG* 1.14; 2.70
107
3: *KG* 6.48*
115
3: *KG* 3.89
118
103: *KG* 3.64*
125
6: *Prak.* 90
126
1: *Prak.* pr.2
141
8: *KG* 4.70
144
3: *KG* 1.71 (S2)

QUOTATIONS AND DIRECT ALLUSIONS   473

146

5: *KG* 1.71 (S1)

Prv

3

18: *Prak.* pr.7

4

23: *KG* 6.52

9

2: *KG* 5.32*

14

9: *KG* 3.9 (S2)

20

27: *KG* 4.67 (S2)

Eccl

1

5: *Gn.* 20

2

14: *KG* 1.72

3

1: *Gn.* 17

8

8: *Gn.* 25

11

10: *KG* 6.84

12

3: *KG* 2.50

Job

1

15: *KG* 2.55 (S2)

40

19: *KG* 6.36
25: *KG* 5.37*

41

25: *KG* 6.36

Wis

11

20: *Gn.* 17

13

5: *KG* 1.87 (Grk.)

Jon

1

5: *Gn.* 34

Hb

3

2: *KG* 4.11

Mal

3

20: *Prak.* ep; *KG* 3.52; 4.29 (S2)

Is

1

19: *KG* 1.23

14

12: *Prak.* pr.2

Ezek

16

15–34: *Gn.* 20

New Testament

Mt

3

12: *KG* 2.26*

5

13–14: *Gn.* 3
14: *KG* 5.74*
26: *KG* 4.34

6

25: *Gn.* 38

7

6: *Prak.* pr.9

9

2–7: *KG* 6.64*

10

34: *KG* 6.6

11

27: *KG* 3.1*

12

43–45: *KG* 5.30*

13

25: *Gn.* 44

14

15–21: *KG* 4.57* (S2)

15

32–38: *KG* 4.57* (S2)

16

19: *KG* 4.40

17

1–8: *KG* 4.23*

19

21: *Prak.* 97
29: *KG* 4.42*

20

6: *KG* 4.26

474 QUOTATIONS AND DIRECT ALLUSIONS

21

12–13: *Gn.* 24

22

32: *KG* 6.61

24

29: *KG* 4.29 (S2)
35: *KG* 1.20 (S1)

25

1–13: *Gn.* 7

Mk

4

28: *KG* 1.24*

16

19: *KG* 2.89*; 4.21* (S2)

Lk

1

26–38: *KG* 6.77* (S2)

11

24–26: *KG* 5.30*
26: *KG* 4.59*

12

22: *Gn.* 38
59: *KG* 4.34

13

32: *KG* 1.90; 3.9 (S2); 4.26

14

10: *Gn.* 29

16

1–2: *KG* 1.60*
3: *KG* 5.33* (S2)
5–8: *KG* 5.33* (S1)
8: *KG* 1.60*
19–20: *KG* 1.40*
31: *KG* 1.40*

17

21: *KG* 5.30

19

17–19: *KG* 6.24

20

36: *KG* 6.24 (S1)

22

30: *KG* 2.60*
31: *KG* 1.25*

Jn

1

32–34: *KG* 4.27*

2

1–10: *KG* 4.57* (S2)

4

21–24: *Prak.* 12

5

22: *KG* 1.65 (S2)
44: *Prak.* pr.3

7

24: *KG* 2.59* (S2)

8

23: *KG* 4.17*

9

1–7: *KG* 4.57* (S2)

11

25: *KG* 6.7*
49–51: *Gn.* 21

14

6: *KG* 5.43*

17

3: *KG* 4.42

Ac

1

11: *KG* 6.56*
24: *Prak.* 46

2

5–13: *KG* 4.54* (S2)

9

15: *Prak.* 93

10

11–16: *KG* 4.46*

Rom

1

19: *KG* 4.2

2

29: *KG* 4.12* (Grk.)

5

14: *KG* 5.1; 6.3* (S2)

8

15: *KG* 6.51
17: *KG* 3.72*; 4.8
29: *KG* 2.36; 6.34 (S2), 89

9

5: *KG* 6.14 (S1)

11

33: *KG* 4.30*

12

13: *KG* 1.66

13

14: *Prak.* 53

1 Cor

3

6–7: *Prak.* ep
7: *KG* 6.30* (S1)
16–17: *KG* 5.84*

QUOTATIONS AND DIRECT ALLUSIONS 475

6

18: *KG* 1.66
19–20: *KG* 5.84*

7

1: *Prak.* pr.5
31: *KG* 1.26

9

27: *Gn.* 37

13

9: *KG* 5.3 (S1)
12: *KG* 5.3 (S1)
13: *Prak.* 38

15

25: *KG* 6.15
27: *KG* 6.70*
28: *KG* 6.33
41: *KG* 3.37
42: *KG* 3.25 (S1)
45: *KG* 3.71
52: *KG* 3.40*, 47, 54 (S2)
53–54: *KG* 3.33*

2 Cor

4

10: *Prak.* pr.6

11

14: *KG* 3.47* (S1)

Gal

4

21–31: *KG* 1.32*

Eph

2

11–13: *KG* 6.77* (S1)

3

9: *KG* 6.77* (S1)
10: *KG* 1.43; 2.2, 21; 3.11, 81 (S1); 4.7; 5.84
18–19: *KG* 2.58*

4

8: *KG* 2.55 (S1)
10: *KG* 6.76
26: *Prak.* 21

5

19: *Prak.* 71

6

16: *KG* 5.31*
17: *KG* 5.28*, 34*

Phil

2

9: *KG* 6.27 (S2)

10: *KG* 3.79*
13: *KG* 1.77* (S1)

3

21: *KG* 6.34 (S2)

Col

1

15: *KG* 2.23 (S1)
18: *KG* 4.24; 6.89
19: *KG* 6.14 (S1)

2

11: *KG* 6.7*

1 Thes

2

6: *Prak.* 13

5

2: *KG* 3.73
17: *Prak.* 49

2 Thes

1

5: *KG* 1.82; 2.59* (S2); 3.47 (S1), 68
(S1); 6.43 (S1), 47 (S1)

1 Tm

2

4: *Gn.* 22

3

15: *Gn.* 45

4

5: *KG* 3.74

2 Tm

3

7: *KG* 6.62

4

7: *KG* 3.60*; 5.3* (S1)
8: *KG* 1.75; 2.77* (S1); 3.40* (S1),
47* (S1)

Heb

2

14: *KG* 4.13

9

2: *KG* 2.86*

12

14: *Gn.* 13
22: *KG* 5.6

476 QUOTATIONS AND DIRECT ALLUSIONS

Jas
1
    22–24: *KG* 4.55

1 Pt
2
    5: *KG* 5.53*
4
    5: *KG* 1.82

1 Jn
1
    5: *KG* 1.35

Rev
1
    5: *KG* 4.24
22
    12: *KG* 1.82

Aristotle

3b24–25: *KG* 1.1⁺
8b27–30: *KG* 6.21*
10b12–14: *KG* 1.2⁺

Cross References

This index lists passages discussed in the notes.

Bible

Gn

1
  KG 1.29; 4.4
  1: *KG* 1.39; 5.63
  14: *KG* 2.70
  15–16: *KG* 2.90
  20–27: *KG* 1.53
  26: *Gn.* 50; *KG* 5.20; 6.73

2
  2: *KG* 3.68
  3: *KG* 4.44; 5.67
  5: *KG* 5.33
  7: *KG* 5.20
  9: *Prak.* pr 7
  10: *KG* 1.83
  10-4: *KG* 5.72
  13: *KG* 1.83
  20: *KG* 1.53; 2.66
  21: *Prak.* 14

3
  KG 1.57
  19: *KG* 5.35
  24: *KG* 5.28

5
  3: *KG* 2.80

7
  19–20: *KG* 1.53

8
  21: *KG* 3.85

13
  Prak. 26

14
  Prak. 26
  18: *KG* 5.32

15
  12: *Prak.* 14
  20: *KG* 5.71

17
  1: *KG* 4.41
  25: *KG* 6.7

18
  1: *KG* 4.41
  6: *KG* 4.28
  19: *KG* 5.43

27
  3: *KG* 6.6

32
  2: *Prak.* 28
  4-33.16: *Prak.* 26
  6: *Prak.* 26
  7: *Prak.* 26
  22–31: *KG* 4.41

38
  KG 4.12

46
  KG 5.6

50
  24: *KG* 5.36

Ex

1
  KG 2.50

3
  1: *KG* 2.64
  2: *KG* 1.30
  14: *KG* 2.5

8
  20–32: *KG* 2.86

9
  23–25: *KG* 3.66

12
  11: *Prak.* pr 5
  38: *KG* 4.64

13
  21–22: *KG* 5.13

17
  KG 5.67

19
  3ff.: *KG* 5.40
  9: *KG* 5.13

478 CROSS REFERENCES

20

8–11: *KG* 4.44
21: *KG* 5.16

23

10–11: *KG* 5.8
30: *KG* 4.40

24

6: *KG* 5.32

25

30: *KG* 2.86

26

35: *Gn.* 46

28

4: *KG* 4.48, 79
28: *KG* 5.80
42: *KG* 4.72

29

13: *KG* 4.36

30

26: *KG* 3.43

33

2: *KG* 4.40

34

33: *KG* 2.20

36

34–38: *KG* 4.48

39

27–31: *KG* 4.48
28: *KG* 4.72

40

9: *KG* 2.57

Lv

1

1–17: *KG* 2.57

8

7: *KG* 4.79
7–9: *KG* 4.48
9: *KG* 4.48

11

12–19: *Gn.* 20

15

16–17: *Prak.* 55

16

3: *KG* 2.57

19

31: *KG* 5.87

Nm

4

6–14: *KG* 4.69

10

8: *KG* 3.40

12

KG 4.47
3: *Prak.* 38

15

32–36: *KG* 4.26

20

2–13: *KG* 5.67

35

11: *KG* 4.82

Dt

2

11: *KG* 5.71
20: *KG* 5.71
21: *KG* 5.71

3

11: *KG* 5.71
13: *KG* 5.71

4

24: *KG* 1.30

6

4: *KG* 1.1

11

10–11: *KG* 4.64
23: *KG* 4.40

15

9: *Prak.* 25

19

1–13: *KG* 4.82

23

11–12: *Prak.* 55

32

17: *Prak.* 5
33: *KG* 5.44

33

1: *KG* 2.56

Josh

13

1: *KG* 5.36
6: *KG* 4.40

14

6: *KG* 2.56

15

8: *KG* 5.71

17

15: *KG* 5.71

20

2–3: *KG* 4.82
4–6: *KG* 4.83

23

1: *KG* 5.36

CROSS REFERENCES 479

Jgs

5

  20: *KG* 6.88

13

  1–5: *KG* 5.36

16

  KG 5.45
  3: *KG* 5.80

1 Kgdms/1 Sam

10

  1: *KG* 3.43
  32–33: *KG* 5.68

14

  50: *Gn.* 38

16

  13: *KG* 3.43

17

  8: *KG* 5.68
  10: *KG* 5.68

23

  27: *KG* 5.30

28

  KG 6.61

32–33

  45: *KG* 5.68

2 Kgdms/2 Sam

2–3

  Gn. 38

6

  10–11: *Gn.* 38

14

  20: *KG* 1.23

21

  15–22: *KG* 5.68

22

  36: *KG* 5.31

23

  13: *KG* 5.71

3 Kgdms/1 Kgs

7

  KG 2.50
  8: *KG* 2.50
  22: *KG* 2.50

18

  44: *KG* 5.13

19

  13: *Prak.* pr 6
  19: *Prak.* pr 6

4 Kgdms/2 Kgs

2

  8: *Prak.* pr 6
  11: *KG* 2.51
  13: *Prak.* pr 6

4

  29: *Prak.* pr 7

9

  6: *KG* 3.43

14

  Prak. pr 6

19

  28: *KG* 5.37

21

  13: *KG* 2.77

1 Paral/1 Chron

1–25

  KG 6.3

15

  18: *Gn.* 38

23

  14: *KG* 2.56

2 Paral/2 Chron

1

  2–3: *KG* 2.86
  16: *KG* 2.86

13

  12: *KG* 3.40
  14: *KG* 3.40

30

  16: *KG* 2.56

Ezr

3

  2: *KG* 2.56

Tb

6

  17: *KG* 5.78

2 Mc

1

  24: *KG* 6.32

6

  4: *Gn.* 24

4 Mc

2

  9: *Prak.* ep

480 CROSS REFERENCES

3
   12: *KG* 5.65
11
   5: *KG* 6.32

Job

5
   23: *KG* 1.53
6
   7: *KG* 5.78
15
   14: *Prak.* 84
16
   10: *Prak.* 33
17
   9: *Prak.* pr 4
38
   1–41: *KG* 6.82
40
   25: *KG* 5.37
40–41
   KG 4.85
41
   1–2: *KG* 5.37

Ps

1
   KG 2.56
   3: *KG* 5.13
3
   3: *KG* 5.31
6
   7: *Prak.* 27
9
   6: *KG* 2.77
10
   2: *KG* 1.65
15
   10: *KG* 6.40
18
   11: *Gn.* 25
19
   1: *KG* 2.70
23
   3: *KG* 2.37
32
   15: *Prak.* 47
34
   2: *KG* 5.31
   16: *Prak.* 33
36
   28: *KG* 6.40

41
   Prak. 27
44
   KG 2.4
50
   19: *KG* 4.22
   20: *KG* 5.82
57
   5: *Prak.* 20; *KG* 5.44
58
   12: *KG* 5.65
60
   3: *Prak.* 12
68
   10: *KG* 3.43
69
   9: *KG* 3.43
72
   15: *KG* 4.89
74
   7–10: *KG* 5.77
77
   25: *KG* 1.23
79
   24–25: *KG* 5.9
80
   10: *KG* 5.49
81
   6: *KG* 4.51; 5.81
87
   7: *KG* 2.44
88
   13: *KG* 4.23
90
   KG 2.56
   6: *Prak.* 12, 36; *KG* 4.73
   13: *KG* 4.17
91
   KG 2.56
93
   11: *Prak.* 11
   14: *KG* 6.40
95
   8: *KG* 1.60
   11: *KG* 3.68
101
   1: *Prak.* 12
102
   2–4: *KG* 3.89
   15: *Prak.* 29
103
   24: *KG* 2.70

CROSS REFERENCES 481

104

  4: *KG* 1.68

108

  10: *KG* 5.14

109

  19: *KG* 4.79

111

  1: *KG* 5.3

113

  3: *KG* 3.60

116

  13: *KG* 2.44

117

  19–20: *KG* 5.77

118

  28: *Prak.* 12
  103: *Gn.* 25

141

  2: *KG* 2.57

Prv

1

  6: *Gn.* 44
  21: *KG* 2.57

2

  1: *Gn.* 14
  5: *KG* 1.33

3

  18: *Prak.* pr 7; *KG* 3.56
  19: *KG* 1.14
  34: *Prak.* 14

5

  23: *KG* 6.8

6

  4: *Prak.* 12

7

  12: *KG* 2.57

8

  3: *KG* 2.57
  22–31: *KG* 1.14

9

  2: *KG* 5.32
  10: *KG* 6.37

15

  1: *Prak.* 11

21

  14: *Prak.* 26

22

  2: *Gn.* 1
  14: *KG* 4.85

24

  5: *KG* 2.56

25

  20: *Prak.* 47

26

  15: *KG* 3.56

27

  16: *Gn.* 46
  22: *KG* 5.49

30

  24–28: *KG* 4.51

31

  24: *KG* 4.79

Eccl

1

  5: *Gn.* 20

3

  1: *Gn.* 17

7

  25: *KG* 4.62

12

  7: *Prak.* 52

SS

4

  9: *KG* 2.29

Wis

1

  4: *Prak.* pr 7; *KG* 4.68
  14: *KG* 5.63

7

  25–26: *KG* 2.1

11

  20: *Gn.* 17; *KG* 5.63

13

  5: *KG* 1.87

Sir

4

  16: *KG* 6.8

22

  13: *Prak.* 12

24

  26: *KG* 1.83

29

  5: *Prak.* 12

50

  2: *Gn.* 24

482 CROSS REFERENCES

Is

5
1–6: *Prak.* ep
6
2: *Gn.* 14; *KG* 3.48
11
1: *KG* 6.8
14
12: *Prak.* pr 2; *KG* 2.64
24
1–3: *KG* 2.17
27
1: *KG* 5.37
13: *Prak.* pr 1
37
29: *KG* 5.37
40
3: *KG* 5.43
9: *KG* 5.40
21: *KG* 5.50
41
26: *KG* 5.50
44
6: *KG* 5.87
48
6: *KG* 3.42
59
17: *KG* 5.34
60
1: *KG* 6.16
61
1–2: *KG* 4.1
3: *Prak.* 12
66
24: *KG* 3.18

Jer

2
18: *KG* 1.83
5
14: *KG* 1.30
6
16: *Prak.* 91
17
7–8: *KG* 5.13
8: *KG* 4.1
10: *Prak.* 46
51
25: *KG* 2.17

Bar

3
1: *Prak.* 12

Ezek

1
10: *Gn.* 14
27: *KG* 2.26
4
10–11: *Prak.* 94
9
2–3: *KG* 4.79
16
15–34: *Gn.* 20
20
28: *KG* 3.85

Dn

1
12: *Prak.* 94
16: *Prak.* 94
2
28: *KG* 3.42
7
15: *Prak.* 12
10
13: *KG* 3.41
21: *KG* 3.41
12
2–3: *KG* 3.37
3: *KG* 4.31
13: *KG* 5.50

Jl

2
20: *Gn.* 46

Mi

4
2: *KG* 5.40

Hb

3
2: *KG* 4.11

Zec

9
9: *KG* 1.75
13
9: *KG* 3.18

Mal

2
7: *Gn.* 14
3
20: *Prak.* ep; *KG* 2.70

Mt

1
9–13: *Prak.* 57
18–23: *Prak.* 57

3
4: *KG* 4.79
11: *KG* 4.39
16: *KG* 4.27

4
1–11: *Prak.* 5
16: *KG* 5.14
18–22: *KG* 6.77

5
3–11: *KG* 3.86
8: *Introduction* A Profile of the Syriac
    Translations
13–14: *Gn.* 3
14: *KG* 5.74
24: *Prak.* 20
26: *KG* 4.34

6
2: *KG* 3.40
6: *Prak.* 62
10: *KG* 2.30
13: *Prak.* 45
18: *Prak.* 8
19: *KG* 3.90
20: *KG* 4.39
25: *Gn.* 38; *KG* 3.8
33: *Prak.* 3

7
6: *Prak.* pr 9
7–8: *Prak.* 58; *KG* 1.14
12: *Gn.* 24
22: *Prak.* 5

8
9: *KG* 4.51
28–34: *KG* 5.9
29: *KG* 6.8
31: *KG* 3.90

9
34: *Prak.* 5; *KG* 4.65

10
18: *KG* 4.62
25: *KG* 2.86
34: *KG* 6.6
42: *KG* 5.32

11
10: *KG* 5.43
18: *Prak.* 5
19: *KG* 4.1
25: *Gn.* 14

12
1: *Prak.* 19
12: *KG* 4.44
24: *KG* 2.86
32: *KG* 1.11; 5.3

13
25: *Gn.* 44
31: *KG* 2.49
36–44: *KG* 5.41
38: *Prak.* 58

14
26: *Prak.* 46

15
11: *KG* 5.9
11–20: *KG* 3.75

16
19: *KG* 4.40

17
1–9: *KG* 2.4
2: *KG* 2.90
11: *KG* 2.13

18
15: *Gn.* 50

19
4: *KG* 5.50
6: *Prak.* 52

21
12–13: *Gn.* 24
33: *Prak.* 19

22
32: *KG* 6.61

24
2: *KG* 2.43

35: *KG* 1.20; 5.39

25
46: *KG* 6.8

26
6–13: *KG* 6.15
7: *KG* 3.43
39–42: *KG* 2.44

28
20: *KG* 3.74

Mk

1
10: *KG* 4.27

3
20–30: *KG* 2.86

4
11–12: *KG* 2.86
28–31: *KG* 1.24

484 CROSS REFERENCES

6

3: *KG* 4.76

7

22: *Prak.* 14

9

4: *KG* 3.18
34: *Gn.* 26

10

38–39: *KG* 2.44

12

27: *KG* 6.61
39: *KG* 1.1

14

3–9: *KG* 6.15
36: *KG* 2.44

16

19: *KG* 2.12

Lk

1

52: *KG* 4.31
78–79: *KG* 6.16
79: *KG* 5.14

2

8–20: *KG* 6.2

3

22: *KG* 4.27

4

17–21: *KG* 4.1

5

17–39: *KG* 4.76

7

8: *KG* 4.51
14: *KG* 6.38
35: *KG* 4.1
36–50: *KG* 6.15

10

18: *KG* 2.64
19: *KG* 4.17

11

26: *Prak.* 45

12

22: *KG* 3.8
42–43: *KG* 1.60
49: *KG* 2.57

13

4: *Prak.* 19

15

26: *Prak.* 96

16

1–8: *KG* 1.60
14: *Prak.* 9
19–31: *KG* 2.65

17

3: *Prak.* 25
21: *KG* 5.12

18

8: *Prak.* 5
22: *Prak.* 97

20

20: *KG* 5.18

21

23: *Prak.* 11

22

17: *KG* 5.32
20: *KG* 5.32

24

37: *Prak.* 46
42: *KG* 2.44

Jn

1

KG 1.29
1: *Gn.* 40; *KG* 1.39
1–18: *KG* 2.22
3: *KG* 5.20
14: *KG* 3.30
32: *KG* 3.30; 4.27

2

17: *KG* 3.43

3

16: *KG* 6.42
23: *KG* 3.85

4

14: *KG* 5.67
52: *Prak.* 96

5

Prak. 13
21: *KG* 5.20
22: *KG* 1.65
24: *KG* 5.20
44: *Prak.* pr 3

6

40: *KG* 4.81

8

19: *Prak.* 95

10

1: *Prak.* 5
7–9: *KG* 5.77
34–35: *KG* 4.51

11

11: *KG* 5.73
25: *KG* 5.20
49–51: *Gn.* 21

12

1–8: *KG* 6.15

CROSS REFERENCES   485

14

17: *Prak.* 22
31: *KG* 4.65

6: *KG* 5.43

15

2: *Prak.* pr 6

16

6: *Prak.* 10
28: *KG* 6.77

19

32–34: *KG* 5.32

22

19: *KG* 6.39

Ac

1

11: *KG* 6.56
24: *Prak.* 46

2

2–4: *KG* 4.39, 40
4–13: *KG* 4.35
5: *Prak.* 84

3

21: *KG* 2.13

5

13: *KG* 6.19
21: *Prak.* pr 9

7

54: *Prak.* 33

8

22: *KG* 3.75

10

10: *Prak.* 14
11: *KG* 4.46

15

3: *KG* 2.13
8: *Prak.* 46
16: *KG* 5.22

16

1–5: *Gn.* 6

17

19: *Prak.* 96

22

17: *Prak.* 14

23

1: *KG* 5.53
20: *Prak.* 96

24

16: *KG* 5:53

Rom

1

KG 4.2
10: *KG* 5.51

18: *Prak.* 11
19–20: *KG* 4.2
21: *Prak.* 23
26: *Prak.* 47

2

5: *KG* 4.5

3

25: *KG* 4.63

3–7

KG 4.2

4

1: *KG* 4.40

5

3–4: *Gn.* 28
4–5: *Prak.* pr 8
14: *KG* 4.65
17: *KG* 4.65

6

6: *KG* 6.40
8: *Prak.* 18

7

5: *Prak.* 47

8

13: *KG* 4.9
17: *KG* 4.4, 39
18: *Prak.* 47
19–20: *KG* 2.36
27: *Prak.* 46
29: *KG* 2.36
38: *KG* 3.29

9

16: *Prak.* 33

10

4: *KG* 2.20

11

34: *KG* 2.74

12

11: *KG* 1.30

13

14: *Prak.* 53

15

17: *KG* 1.28

16

10: *Prak.* 28
15: *KG* 2.44

·1 Cor

1

5: *KG* 2.8; 4.30
22: *KG* 4.14
24: *KG* 2.1; 3.32

2

4: *KG* 1.38; 6.44
16: *KG* 2.74

486 CROSS REFERENCES

3

1: *Prak.* pr 2
6: *Prak.* ep
6–8: *KG* 5.13
10: *KG* 6.82
12–15: *KG* 3.39
16–17: *KG* 5.84
18–23: *KG* 6.22, 40

4

1: *Gn.* 30, 44; *KG* 5.33

5

5: *KG* 4.14

6

1–8: *Gn.* 8
3: *KG* 3.46
9: *KG* 4.39
16: *Prak.* 75
18: *Prak.* 8
19: *KG* 3.75
19–20: *KG* 5.84

7

1: *KG* 4.79

8

10: *KG* 4.25

9

11: *Prak.* 32
13: *Prak.* pr 9
19: *Gn.* 50
22: *Gn.* 50
24–25: *KG* 1.75

10

1–4: *KG* 5.13
11: *KG* 6.8
18: *Prak.* 8
20ff.: *Prak.* 5

11

19: *Prak.* 28
24–25: *Gn.* 14

12

KG 4.40

13

1: *KG* 4.35; 6.3
9: *KG* 5.3
12: *Prak.* 64; *KG* 3.15, 17; 4.47, 55; 5.3, 64
13: *Prak.* 38

14

KG 2.49

15

KG 1.24; 2.4; 3.25, 47, 77; 6.58
4: *KG* 4.24
10: *Prak.* pr 2
23: *KG* 4.24

27: *KG* 6.70
28: *KG* 1.86; 2.75; 6.15
31: *Prak.* 29
34: *KG* 4.17
35–49: *KG* 3.37
36–44: *KG* 2.25
40–49: *KG* 2.80
42: *KG* 6.58
44: *KG* 1.90; 4.24; 6.23
49: *KG* 4.24
51–53: *KG* 2.4
51–58: *KG* 2.4
53–54: *KG* 4.24

2 Cor

1

5: *Prak.* 47
6: *Prak.* 72
22: *KG* 4.12

2

1: *Prak.* 10
7: *Prak.* 10
14: *Prak.* 23

3

18: *KG* 2.4

4

6: *KG* 6.16
8: *Prak.* 72
10: *Prak.* pr 6

5

4–21: *KG* 4.58
5: *KG* 4.12
8–9: *KG* 3.1
10: *KG* 2.90; 6.57
17: *KG* 6.40

6

1: *KG* 6.22

7

5: *Prak.* 72

10

5: *KG* 5.74
10–15: *Prak.* 15

11

3: *KG* 5.1
14: *KG* 4.67
27: *Prak.* 15

12

7: *Prak.* 25

13

8: *Prak.* 64; *KG* 5.64

CROSS REFERENCES 487

Gal

3

27: *KG* 3.3; 6.28
28: *KG* 4.51

4

7: *KG* 2.7

5

22–23: *Prak.* pr 8

6

10: *KG* 5.73

Eph

1

10: *KG* 2.30
11–18: *KG* 1.18
14: *KG* 4.12

2

7: *KG* 4.39
12: *Prak.* pr 3
19: *KG* 5.73
19–22: *KG* 6.39
20: *KG* 6.39

3

2: *KG* 2.30
9: *KG* 2.30
9–10: *Prak.* 15
10: *KG* 1.14, 43; 3.81; 4.7; 5.23, 84
18: *KG* 2.69
18–19: *KG* 2.58

4

8: *KG* 2.55
9: *KG* 2.71; 4.80
22–24: *KG* 6.40
31: *Prak.* 11

5

1: *KG* 6.51
1–2: *Prak.* 35
14: *KG* 1.38; 3.73
19: *Prak.* 71
22–32: *KG* 5.1

6

4: *KG* 6.8
11: *Prak.* 83
16: *KG* 5.31
17: *KG* 5.28, 34

Phil

1

25: *Prak.* 59

2

6–11: *KG* 4.9
15: *KG* 2.90

3

14: *Prak.* 32
20: *Prak.* pr 3

Col

1

12: *KG* 1.18
15: *KG* 2.36
15–17: *KG* 4.58
18: *KG* 2.36; 6.39
24: *KG* 6.39

2

3: *KG* 5.63
11–13: *KG* 6.40
14: *KG* 2.7; 6.40
14–15: *KG* 6.40
17: *KG* 5.14

3

5: *Prak.* pr 6, 47
8: *Prak.* 11
16: *Prak.* 71

1 Thes

1

3: *Prak.* 15

2

6: *Prak.* pr 3, 13

3

4: *Prak.* 72

4

3: *Prak.* 8
16: *KG* 3.40; 5.4

5

Prak. 49
2: *KG* 3.73
8: *KG* 5.34
16–18: *Prak.* 69

2 Thes

1

7: *Prak.* 50, 72

2

12: *Prak.* 92
19: *KG* 1.75

5

14: *Prak.* 92

1 Tm

1

9: *Prak.* 70
17: *Prak.* 95

488 CROSS REFERENCES

2

  4: *KG* 6.59
  8: *Prak.* 11
  13–14: *KG* 5.1

3

  9: *Prak.* 19; *KG* 5.53
  15: *Gn.* 45

4

  15: *Prak.* 59

5

  8: *KG* 5.73

6

  9: *Prak.* 19
  10: *Prak.* 9
  20: *Gn.* 1

2 Tm

1

  3: *KG* 5.53

2

  26: *Prak.* 19

3

  2: *Prak.* 9
  7: *KG* 6.62

4

  1: *KG* 2.84
  7: *KG* 3.60
  8: *KG* 1.75; 2.77

Ti

1

  12: *Prak.* 7

2

  12: *Prak.* 24

8

  20–22: *Prak.* 24

Heb

1

  3: *KG* 2.23
  7: *KG* 1.30, 68; 2.68; 5.18
  14: *KG* 2.7; 5.18

2

  5: *KG* 1.11; 4.38; 5.3
  9: *Prak.* 47
  10: *KG* 6.14

3

  11: *Prak.* 11; *KG* 3.68
  15: *KG* 1.60

4

  3: *Prak.* 11
  9–10: *KG* 4.44
  12: *Prak.* 46; *KG* 6.6
  14: *KG* 5.46

5

  7: *KG* 5.46
  13–14: *KG* 3.10

6

  5: *KG* 1.11; 5.3

7

  15: *KG* 5.32

9

  2: *KG* 2.86
  5: *KG* 5.14

10

  1: *KG* 5.14

11

  9: *KG* 5.30
  34: *Prak.* 98
  37: *Prak.* pr 6

12

  18: *KG* 5.16
  29: *KG* 1.30

13

  11: *Prak.* 98
  12: *Prak.* 98
  19: *KG* 2.13

Jas

1

  8: *KG* 3.39
  11: *Gn.* 50
  22–25: *KG* 5.2
  23: *KG* 5.64

2

  9: *KG* 4.10
  19: *Prak.* 5
  26: *Prak.* 52

3

  2: *KG* 4.10
  15: *KG* 5.11

1 Pt

1

  7: *KG* 3.18
  8: *Prak.* 12
  11: *Prak.* 47
  24: *Gn.* 50

3

  1: *Gn.* 50

CROSS REFERENCES 489

4

    5: *KG* 2.84

5

    4: *KG* 1.75

2 Pt

1

    4: *KG* 2.17
    10: *KG* 4.10

2

    4: *KG* 3.18
    15–16: *Gn.* 21
    21: *KG* 5.22

3

    11–12: *KG* 2.17

1 Jn

2

    13: *KG* 5.50
    14: *KG* 5.50
    15: *KG* 4.25

4

    14: *KG* 3.30

5

    17: *Prak.* 36
    20: *KG* 5.20

Jude

9

    KG 3.41; 5.4

11

    Gn. 21

Rev

1

    8: *KG* 4.39; 5.20
    16: *KG* 5.28
    19: *KG* 3.42

2

    1: *Gn.* 47
    2: *Prak.* 15
    8: *Gn.* 47
    10: *KG* 1.75
    12: *KG* 5.28
    14: *Gn.* 21
    16: *KG* 5.28
    17ff.: *KG* 3.55
    26: *KG* 5.50

3

    1: *Gn.* 47
    7: *Gn.* 47
    20: *KG* 4.83

4

    1: *KG* 3.40
    6–9: *Gn.* 14
    8: *KG* 3.48

5

    8: *KG* 2.57
    11: *KG* 4.74
    13: *KG* 4.74

6

    8: *Prak.* 95; *KG* 5.28

7

    14: *Gn.* 47

8

    3–4: *KG* 2.57
    6–13: *KG* 3.40, 66
    12: *Gn.* 47

9

    1: *KG* 3.40

10

    1: *KG* 5.13
    2: *KG* 2.20
    7: *KG* 3.40; 6.42

11

    15: *KG* 3.40

12

    1: *KG* 5.29
    7: *KG* 5.68
    7–12: *KG* 3.41
    10: *KG* 4.83

13

    1–10: *KG* 4.65

14

    13: *Prak.* 15
    14: *KG* 5.13
    17: *KG* 4.53

15

    KG 5.39
    4: *KG* 6.27

16

    KG 1.65
    14: *Prak.* 5

17

    6: *KG* 5.29

19

    2: *Prak.* 8
    15: *KG* 5.28
    21: *KG* 5.28

20

    1–10: *Prak.* 5
    14: *KG* 1.58

21

    1–4: *KG* 5.39
    6: *KG* 5.67
    10: *KG* 5.6

490   CROSS REFERENCES

12: *KG* 4.53
14: *KG* 4.53
21–22
    KG 5.77, 84
22
    1–7: *KG* 5.72
    2: *KG* 5.67
    13: *KG* 5.87
    13–21: *KG* 5.20

Ancient Authors

1 Enoch
    KG 6.3

Acts of Archelaus
    KG 3.87; 4.60

Aeschylus
Eumenides
    KG 5.17

Alexander of Aphrodisias
Commentary on Aristotle's Metaphysics
    KG 1.7; 3.14

Anathemas of 553
    KG 1.77; 2.17

Anatolius of Laodicea
Theology of Arithmetic
    KG 1.7

Anthony
Letters
    Prak. 1, 55

Antipatrus
On Definitions
    Gn. 27

Apollodorus
Fragments
    KG 2.58

Apostolic Tradition
    KG 3.71

Aristotle
Categories
    Prak. 45; *Gn.* 41; ; *KG* 1.4, 20; 5.62;
        6.21, 72

Eudaemonian Ethics
    Prak. 5, 18; *Gn.* 30
History of Animals
    KG 4.37; 6.37
Metaphysics
    Prak. 2, 45, 87; *Gn.* 14, 27; *KG* 1.7, 55,
        67; 4.3, 51, 62, 71, 81, 90; 6.10, 73
Nicomachean Ethics
    Prak. pr 3, 5, 35, 45, 48, 73, 98; *Gn.* 27;
        KG 1.5, 35, 64; 6.21
On Breathing
    KG 4.37
On Generation and Corruption
    KG 1.4
On Interpretation
    Prak. 40, 47
*On Youth and Old Age, on Life and Death, on
Breathing*
    KG 4.37
On the Generation of Animals
    KG 3.76
On the Soul
    Prak. 11, 37, 39, 40, 48; *KG* 1.36, 67; 2.9;
        4.37, 62, 84
On the World
    KG 1.4
Parts of Animals
    KG 4.37
Physics
    Prak. 2; *KG* 4.51; 6.73
Politics
    Prak. 58; *KG* 4.51
Posterior Analytics
    Gn. 1
Prior Analytics
    Prak. 18; *Gn.* 41
Rhetoric
    Prak. pr 3, 56
Sense and the Sensible
    KG 4.37
Topics
    Gn. 41

Athanasius
Against the Arians
    Prak. 1
Apology
    Prak. pr 9
Festal Letters
    KG 1.83; 4.35
Letter to Amoun
    Prak. 55
Letter to Marcellinus
    Prak. pr 2
Life of Anthony
    4: *Prak.* 14

CROSS REFERENCES 491

6: *Prak.* 33
7: *Prak.* 5
11: *Prak.* 50
14: *Prak.* pr 3, 10
19: *Prak.* 29
20: *Prak.* 86
23: *KG* 4.35
43: *Prak.* 56
55: *Prak.* 13, 21
63: *Prak.* 39; *KG* 5.78
72: *Prak.* 92
77: *Prak.* 81
91: *Prak.* pr 6
On Virginity
    Prak. pr 2; *KG* 3.85

Augustine

Customs of the Manichaeans
    KG 3.50, 59
On Heresies
    KG 4.60

Barsanouphios and John

Letters
    KG 2.64, 69

Basil of Caesarea

Against Eunomius
    Prak. 3, 87; *Gn.* 26
Hexaemeron
    Prak. 71; *KG* 5.14
Homilies on Julitta
    Prak. 55
Homilies on Psalms
    Prak. pr 5, 15
Homily
    Gn. 28
Letters
    Prak. 1, 5, 21; *Gn.* 45; *KG* 1.35, 78;
    3.90
Longer Rules
    Prak. pr 6, 5, 29; *Gn.* 8; *KG* 3.90
Pay Attention to Yourself
    Prak. 25; *Gn.* 45
Shorter Rules
    Prak. 55

Caelius Aurelianus

On Chronic Diseases
    Prak. 55

Cassian

Institutes
    Prak. pr 1, pr 3

Cicero

Dream of Scipio
    KG 3.37
Tusculan Disputations
    Prak. 56, 58

Clement of Alexandria

Excerpts from Theodotus
    KG 2.36; 4.43, 52; 5.1, 18; 6.60
Fragments
    KG 5.18
On Providence
    Gn. 48
Paidagogos
    1: *Prak.* 1, 6, 22, 87, 92; *Gn.* 33; *KG* 1.43,
    81; 3.67; 4.11, 14, 74
    2: *Prak.* pr 3, 7, 13, 96; *Gn.* 44
    3: *Prak.* pr 9; *KG* 4.58
    26: *KG* 3.3
    62: *Gn.* 7
Prophetic Eclogues
    Prak. 59; *KG* 2.34; 5.10
Protreptikos
    1: *Prak.* 27, 71; *KG* 6.46
    3: *KG* 3.50
    6: *Prak.* pr 9
    8: *KG* 3.73
    9: *KG* 1.38
    10: *Prak.* pr 3
    12: *KG* 4.1
    98: *KG* 5.1
Stromateis
    1: *Prak.* pr 3, pr 9, 1, 38, 57, 98; *Gn.* 26;
    KG 1.15; 4.1, 90; 5.18; 6.10
    2: *Prak.* pr 2, pr 7, pr 8; *KG* 2.26; 4.3; 6.54
    3: *KG* 1.12; 2.32; 5.1
    4: *Prak.* pr 1, pr 2, 68
    5: *Prak.* 52; *Gn.* 32, 34, 41, 44; *KG* 1.15,
    35, 61; 3.90; 4.22, 48, 52, 56; 5.10
    6: *Prak.* 2, 32; *Gn.* 1, 44; *KG* 1.67; 4.10; 5.8
    7: *Prak.* 1, 2, 13, 81; *Gn.* 3, 6, 8, 22, 23, 38;
    KG 3.3, 65; 4.25, 47, 50, 65; 6.8, 15
    8: *Prak.* 40; *Gn.* 49
Who Is the Rich Man
    Prak. pr 3; *Gn.* 3, 30; *KG* 4.30

Clementine Homilies

    KG 1.67

Cyril of Alexandria

Commentary on Romans
    KG 2.17

492 CROSS REFERENCES

Cyril of Jerusalem
Catech.
    KG 3.71
    KG 4.14, 25

Damascius
On Principles
    KG 6.11

Democritus
Fragments
    Prak. 4

Didascalia Apostolorum
    Prak. 55

Didymus the Blind
Commentary on Ecclesiastes
    KG 4.71
Commentary on Ps 20 and 21
    KG 1.89
Commentary on Zechariah
    KG 1.83
Trinity
    KG 4.14

Diogenes Laertius
Lives of the Philosophers
    Gn. 17, 27

Dionysius of Alexandria
Canonical Letters
    Prak. 55

Dionysius the Areopagite
Divine Names
    Gn. 41
Ecclesiastical Hierarchy
    KG 2.78; 5.11

Divisiones Aristoteleae
    KG 1.7

Doctrina patrum de incarnatione verbi
    KG 4.16; 6.31, 32

Dorotheus
Didaskaliai
    KG 4.76

Empedocles
Fragments
    KG 1.4

Epictetus
Discourses
    Prak. 20, 88
Manual
    Prak. 6, 37

Epicurus
Letters
    Prak. pr 8, 2, 7

Epiphanius
On Gems
    KG 4.52
Panarion
    Prak. 1, 5; *Gn.* 1; *KG* 1.78; 4.65; 5.18

Epiphanius, pseudo-
Homilies on Resurrection of Christ
    KG 4.64

Eusebius
Church History
    Prak. pr 1, pr 3, pr 9; *KG* 1.78; 4.54, 61
Commentary on Psalms
    KG 1.67; 4.23
Demonstration of the Gospel
    KG 4.9
Praise of Constantine
    Prak. 27
Preparation of the Gospel
    Prak. 1; *KG* 4.51

Evagrius
Antirrhetikos
    Prak. 5, 42, 48; *KG* 5.28, 30, 36; 6.53
    1: *Prak.* 7, 16, 54
    2: *Prak.* 8, 80; *KG* 6.37
    3: *Prak.* 9; *Gn.* 7, 8
    4: *Prak.* 5, 10, 59, 94; *KG* 5.12
    5: *Prak.* 11, 26, 91; *Gn.* 28, 32
    6: *Prak.* 12, 27, 29; *Gn.* 28; *KG* 1.74; 5.15
    7: *Prak.* 13, 31
    8: *Prak.* 14, 46, 51; *KG* 4.67
Disciples of Evagrius
    KG 1.90
    1: *KG* 1.22, 70
    2: *KG* 1.89
    5: *KG* 2.36

8: *KG* 2.68
11: *KG* 1.57
12: *KG* 1.57
14: *KG* 1.89; 2.55
15: *Prak.* 99
19: *Prak.* 18
25: *KG* 2.87
26: *KG* 1.22
29: *KG* 6.4
30: *KG* 1.73; 5.63
31: *KG* 2.34
35: *Gn.* 49; *KG* 3.28
52: *KG* 5.30
78: *KG* 5.15
87: *Gn.* 23
93: *KG* 2.9
96: *KG* 1.64
123: *KG* 1.87
148: *Prak.* 100
155: *Gn.* 23, 33
183: *Prak.* 94
192: *KG* 4.43

Eight Thoughts
1: *Prak.* 7, 16; *Gn.* 37; *KG* 2.1; 4.64; 5.74
2: *Prak.* 57; *KG* 5.9, 17; 6.53
3: *KG* 1.75; 2.10
4: *Prak.* 8, 24; *KG* 2.57; 3.90; 4.53; 5.13
5: *KG* 4.50
6: *KG* 1.68; 4.67, 68
7: *Prak.* 9, 13; *KG* 1.70
8: *Prak.* pr 7; *KG* 5.4, 40
9: *Prak.* 11; *Gn.* 5
10: *Prak.* 11
11: *Prak.* 10, 19
15: *Prak.* 31
16: *KG* 3.86
17: *Prak.* 14
18: *Prak.* 33; *Gn.* 28

Eulogius
2: *Prak.* 74
5: *Prak.* 22; *KG* 4.67
6: *Prak.* 11
7: *Prak.* 10; *Gn.* 39; *KG* 1.82
8: *Prak.* 13, 28
10: *Prak.* 24; *KG* 3.48; 5.74
11: *Prak.* 22, 75; *KG* 4.53
12: *KG* 1.78
14: *Prak.* 31
16: *KG* 3.90
17: *KG* 1.57
18: *Prak.* 16
19: *Prak.* 8, 15, 52
21: *Prak.* 93; *KG* 3.86
22: *Prak.* 5, 58

23: *Prak.* 35, 81; *KG* 4.18
24: *Prak.* 24, 50, 61; *Gn.* 24; *KG* 3.1
27: *KG* 6.56, 68
28: *KG* 4.60
29: *KG* 1.75
30: *KG* 4.50; 5.29
31: *KG* 1.5; 5.38
32: *Prak.* 15

Exhortation to Monks
1: *Prak.* 14
2: *Gn.* 9, 37; *KG* 2.1; 4.53

Foundations
3: *Gn.* 38
4: *Prak.* 9
5: *Prak.* 95; *Gn.* 11
8: *KG* 4.50
9: *Prak.* 24; *Gn.* 36; *KG* 1.82; 3.18; 5.4

Letter on Faith
KG 3.1; 4.19
1: *KG* 4.71
2: *KG* 4.50
3: *Prak.* 45, 89; *KG* 5.30, 74
5: *KG* 1.7
7: *KG* 1.17; 2.3; 4.19; 5.62
9: *Prak.* 30; *Gn.* 27; *KG* 1.1, 22
11: *KG* 2.12
13: *KG* 3.28
14: *KG* 6.53
15: *Prak.* 1; *Gn.* 14; *KG* 4.13
19: *KG* 3.73
21: *Prak.* pr 8; *Gn.* 40; *KG* 2.87; 3.83
22: *KG* 2.1; 4.81; 6.2
23: *KG* 3.17, 19, 28; 4.74
24: *Prak.* 2
25: *KG* 1.7; 5.49
29: *KG* 1.4
31: *KG* 3.28
36: *KG* 1.39
38: *Prak.* 46
39: *KG* 3.64
40: *Prak.* 15

Letter to Melania
KG 1.17, 24; 3.1
3: *KG* 1.64
7: *KG* 2.12
22: *KG* 1.7; 6.33
23: *KG* 2.17
26: *KG* 1.50, 65; 2.37; 3.28, 60, 70; 5.25
27: *KG* 1.22; 4.74
28: *KG* 4.29
32: *Gn.* 11
35: *Prak.* 92
39: *KG* 2.18
51: *KG* 2.32

494 CROSS REFERENCES

65: *KG* 2.2
66: *KG* 1.89; 4.50
Letters
  2: *Prak.* ep; *KG* 4.67
  3: *KG* 1.22
  4: *KG* 4.12; 5.74
  6: *Prak.* 41; *KG* 5.37
  8: *Prak.* 13; *Gn.* 49
  12: *Prak.* 100; *KG* 2.1
  16: *Prak.* 9, 47
  17: *Prak.* 91
  18: *Prak.* 29
  19: *Prak.* 38, 49
  23: *KG* 3.9, 65; 6.24
  25: *Gn.* 11, 31; *KG* 1.31; 3.43, 48; 4.53
  27: *Prak.* 38; *Gn.* 5, 7, 46; *KG* 5.32;
      6.36, 53
  29: *KG* 1.89; 2.44, 47; 4.68
  30: *KG* 3.53, 59
  33: *Gn.* 8
  37: *KG* 6.57
  39: *Prak.* 6; *KG* 1.74; 5.15, 39
  41: *KG* 5.8
  42: *Gn.* 28
  43: *Prak.* 15; *KG* 1.40; 2.8
  46: *Prak.* ep
  47: *Gn.* 6, 33
  48: *Gn.* 9
  51: *KG* 1.25
  52: *KG* 5.17
  56: *Prak.* 20, 38; *KG* 2.34; 4.38; 5.11,
      26, 44
  57: *KG* 3.78
  58: *Gn.* 50; *KG* 1.73; 5.30
  59: *KG* 1.39, 40
  61: *KG* 4.90
  62: *Gn.* 4
Masters and Disciples
  Gn. 5
  32: *KG* 4.38
  78: *Gn.* 33
Maxims 1
  KG 1.36
  6: *KG* 1.75
  18: *Prak.* 16
Maxims 2
  KG 1.36
  7: *KG* 2.1
  9: *KG* 5.84
  22: *KG* 1.75
Maxims 3
  5: *Gn.* 39
  17: *KG* 3.56
  25: *KG* 1.75

Monks
  1: *Prak.* 15; *KG* 1.18; 2.7; 3.72
  3: *Prak.* pr 8, 81, 84
  8: *KG* 6.41
  10: *Prak.* 27
  11: *Prak.* 16
  12: *Prak.* pr 4
  13: *KG* 3.90
  15: *Prak.* 25, 26
  23: *Prak.* 24; *KG* 2.55
  27: *Prak.* 28
  34: *Prak.* 48
  39: *Prak.* 74; *KG* 4.74; 5.9
  40: *KG* 2.38
  43: *Prak.* 2
  48: *Prak.* 41
  52: *KG* 4.60, 67
  54: *KG* 1.82
  55: *Prak.* 28
  59: *Prak.* 47
  60: *KG* 1.75
  61: *Prak.* 14
  62: *Gn.* 28
  64: *KG* 1.83
  68: *Prak.* 73
  70: *KG* 6.53
  72: *Gn.* 25
  74: *Gn.* 30
  98: *Prak.* 15
  102: *Prak.* 17, 94
  107: *KG* 2.34
  109: *Gn.* 5
  110: *KG* 2.16
  111: *KG* 5.38
  118: *Prak.* 1; *KG* 1.73; 2.44
  119: *Gn.* 14, 47
  121: *Gn.* 1
  124: *KG* 4.29
  126: *Gn.* 43
  129: *KG* 4.64
  132: *Gn.* 48
On the Seraphim
  25: *KG* 3.48
Prayer
  KG 1.22, 75
  1: *Gn.* 6, 11; *KG* 2.57; 5.38
  3: *KG* 5.53
  4: *KG* 2.64
  7: *Prak.* 30
  12: *Prak.* 74; *KG* 1.82
  13: *Prak.* 25
  17: *Prak.* 63; *KG* 6.47
  21: *Prak.* 20
  27: *KG* 2.28; 6.17

CROSS REFERENCES   495

30: *Prak.* 24, 80
31: *KG* 1.63
36: *Gn.* 29; *KG* 1.78
37: *Gn.* 28; *KG* 1.76; 3.58
38: *Prak.* 85
39: *KG* 5.76
40: *Prak.* 100
42: *Prak.* 4
44: *KG* 4.7
46: *Prak.* 61
47: *Prak.* 44
50: *Prak.* 41
54: *KG* 1.86
62: *KG* 4.50
63: *Gn.* 4
64: *Gn.* 5
67: *Prak.* 64
68: *Gn.* 45
69: *KG* 1.89
73: *Prak.* 13, 64
74: *KG* 1.74
75: *KG* 5.15
81: *KG* 2.30
82: *Prak.* pr 2
83: *Prak.* 15, 49, 82
84: *KG* 1.64
85: *Prak.* 69
86: *Prak.* 15
94: *Prak.* 99; *KG* 5.77
95: *KG* 4.67
104: *KG* 4.33
114: *KG* 1.29
117: *KG* 3.86
118: *Prak.* 57
119: *KG* 3.15
120: *Prak.* 62
122: *KG* 3.1
128: *KG* 3.90; 5.13
134: *Prak.* 7, 44
139: *KG* 3.90; 4.67
152: *KG* 4.86

Reflections
   KG 6.14, 78
1: *KG* 4.27
2: *Prak.* 64; *Gn.* 45; *KG* 1.22, 74; 5.15, 39
3: *Prak.* 57
5: *KG* 3.56
6: *KG* 2.83; 4.44; 5.83
8: *Prak.* 42
9: *Prak.* 11
11: *KG* 1.67
14: *KG* 5.41
15: *KG* 3.59
16: *Prak.* 2

20: *KG* 5.26
21: *Prak.* 74
22: *Prak.* 25
23: *Prak.* 11
24: *KG* 2.5
25: *Prak.* 64
30: *KG* 4.74
32: *Gn.* 1
40: *Prak.* 14
43: *Prak.* 11
45: *Prak.* 75
46: *Prak.* 24, 30
47: *Prak.* 43
52: *KG* 5.39
57: *Prak.* 13, 31
59: *Prak.* 39

Scholia on Ecclesiastes
1.1 (Sch. 1): *KG* 3.1
1.2 (Sch. 2): *KG* 1.73; 3.14; 4.71; 5.2
1.11 (Sch. 3): *KG* 1.78; 6.15
2.10 (Sch. 8): *KG* 3.12; 4.13
2.10. (Sch. 8): *KG* 3.44
2.11 (Sch. 10): *KG* 1.49, 50
2.14 (Sch. 11): *KG* 1.14; 6.87
2.22 (Sch. 12): *KG* 1.49
3.10–13 (Sch. 15): *KG* 1.32, 87; 2.10;
      3.24, 59; 5.12, 13, 41, 57, 60
3.15 (Sch. 19): *KG* 1.73
3.19–22 (Sch. 21): *KG* 1.17
4.1 (Sch. 23): *Prak.* 14; *KG* 2.59
4.4 (Sch. 25): *KG* 6.36
4.5 (Sch. 26): *Prak.* pr 3; *KG* 1.32
4.6 (Sch. 27): *KG* 1.63
4.8 (Sch. 28): *Prak.* 18; *KG* 6.51
4 (Sch. 33): *KG* 4.34
5.1 (Sch. 35): *Gn.* 27
5.7–11 (Sch. 38): *Prak.* 24, 58; *KG* 1.23;
      2.60, 74; 5.7, 18, 41; 6.24
5.12 (Sch. 39): *Gn.* 14
5.13 (Sch. 40): *KG* 3.24
5.14–15 (Sch. 41): *KG* 1.32
5.17–19 (Sch. 42): *KG* 4.30
6.1–6 (Sch. 46): *KG* 3.28
6.10–12 (Sch. 52): *KG* 4.60
7.8 (Sch. 57): *KG* 4.55
9.1.1–2 (Sch. 68): *KG* 6.87
11.10 (Sch. 72): *KG* 6.84
13.10–13 (Sch. 15): *KG* 3.64

Scholia on Proverbs
1.1 (Sch. 1): *KG* 1.32, 78
1.1 (Sch. 2): *Gn.* 48; *KG* 4.5
1.3 (Sch. 4): *KG* 6.54
1.7 (Sch. 5): *KG* 5.57; 6.55
1.9 (Sch. 7): *Gn.* 19; *KG* 1.51, 75

496 CROSS REFERENCES

1.13 (Sch. 8): *KG* 3.28
1.13 (Sch. 9): *KG* 5.28, 34
1.20 (Sch. 12): *KG* 4.64; 5.77
1.32 (Sch. 16): *KG* 3.74, 76; 4.13
2.3 (Sch. 19): *Prak.* 25
2.12 (Sch. 22): *KG* 3.4
2.21 (Sch. 26): *KG* 3.28
3.1 (Sch. 27): *KG* 4.55
3.5 (Sch. 28): *KG* 2.48
3.8 (Sch. 29): *KG* 2.9
3.18 (Sch. 32): *Prak.* pr 7; *KG* 3.56; 4.68; 6.8
3.18 (Sch. 31): *KG* 2.34
3.19–20 (Sch. 33): *KG* 1.14, 57; 2.58, 70; 3.78
3.24–25 (Sch. 36): *KG* 3.39
3.34 (Sch. 39): *Prak.* 14
3.35 (Sch. 40): *KG* 1.18; 3.72
4.9 (Sch. 44): *KG* 1.75
4.10 (Sch. 45): *KG* 5.43
4.18 (Sch. 49): *KG* 3.44
4.27 (Sch. 53): *Gn.* 46; *KG* 1.5
5.3–4 (Sch. 55): *KG* 1.89
5.8 (Sch. 59): *KG* 2.48; 5.43
5.9 (Sch. 60): *Prak.* 20
5.11 (Sch. 61): *Gn.* 14
5.14 (Sch. 62): *KG* 1.39, 40; 2.65
6.1 (Sch. 69): *KG* 1.32
6.4 (Sch. 70): *Prak.* 12
6.8 (Sch. 72): *Gn.* 25; *KG* 1.20, 73; 3.64
6.19 (Sch. 78): *KG* 6.27, 51, 53
6.20–22 (Sch. 79): *KG* 1.73
6.30–31 (Sch. 84): *Gn.* 43
7.4 (Sch. 88): *KG* 3.38
7.6 (Sch. 90): *KG* 4.68
7.15 (Sch. 94): *KG* 4.55
8.3 (Sch. 99): *KG* 4.64; 6.21, 64
8.10–11 (Sch. 101): *KG* 6.51
8.13 (Sch. 102): *Prak.* 14
9.2 (Sch. 103): *KG* 1.23, 32; 3.10, 12
9.2 (Sch. 104): *Gn.* 47; *KG* 2.44; 5.32
9.3 (Sch. 105): *KG* 1.14; 2.35
9.5 (Sch. 107): *KG* 3.10
9.12 (Sch. 112): *KG* 1.89
9.13 (Sch. 113): *KG* 2.80; 3.37
10.3 (Sch. 118): *Gn.* 6; *KG* 6.15, 33, 70
10.18 (Sch. 120): *KG* 2.30
10.27 (Sch. 122): *KG* 3.44
10.30 (Sch. 123): *Prak.* 3; *KG* 1.67, 70
11.17 (Sch. 127): *Prak.* 49; *KG* 1.49
11.21 (Sch. 128): *KG* 3.55
11.30 (Sch. 132): *KG* 3.56; 4.1
13.22 (Sch. 134): *KG* 3.65; 4.5; 6.24
14.9 (Sch. 136): *KG* 3.9
16.14 (Sch. 145): *KG* 6.8

17.2 (Sch. 153): *Gn.* 30; *KG* 1.32; 2.58, 69; 3.10, 38; 5.33; 6.64
17.4 (Sch. 154): *Prak.* 25
17.6 (Sch. 155): *KG* 2.8
17.13 (Sch. 158): *KG* 3.89
17.14 (Sch. 159): *KG* 1.89
17.16 (Sch. 161): *KG* 6.47
17.17 (Sch. 163): *KG* 4.74; 6.51
17.17 (Sch. 164): *KG* 5.7; 6.90
17.25 (Sch. 169): *KG* 6.51
18.13 (Sch. 182): *Gn.* 20
18.14 (Sch. 183): *KG* 3.28
18.16 (Sch. 184): *Prak.* 70; *KG* 2.30; 6.21
19.4 (Sch. 189): *Prak.* 56; *KG* 2.30, 60; 5.7
19.11 (Sch. 194): *Gn.* 33
19.16 (Sch. 198): *KG* 2.48
19.17 (Sch. 199): *KG* 3.12
19.19 (Sch. 200): *KG* 1.73
19.23 (Sch. 202): *KG* 1.14
19.24 (Sch. 203): *Prak.* pr 3
20.1 (Sch. 206): *KG* 5.44
20.4 (Sch. 208): *KG* 5.8, 83
20.9 (Sch. 210): *Prak.* 100; *KG* 1.17; 4.1; 6.27, 51, 65
20.10 (Sch. 214): *Gn.* 24
20.12 (Sch. 215): *KG* 4.60
20.27 (Sch. 221): *KG* 4.67
21.3 (Sch. 222): *KG* 4.22
21.19 (Sch. 224): *KG* 3.44
21.22 (Sch. 229): *KG* 5.74
21.23 (Sch. 230): *Prak.* 49
22.10 (Sch. 240): *KG* 2.35
22.11–12 (Sch. 241): *Gn.* 6; *KG* 1.32
22.14 (Sch. 243): *KG* 4.85
22.16 (Sch. 245): *KG* 3.90
22.17 (Sch. 246): *KG* 4.55
22.20 (Sch. 247): *Prak.* 1
22.28 (Sch. 249): *KG* 3.48; 4.29
23.6–8 (Sch. 252): *KG* 1.32
23.18 (Sch. 256): *Prak.* 81
23.22 (Sch. 258): *KG* 1.74; 5.15
23.33 (Sch. 263): *KG* 2.7
24.6 (Sch. 266): *KG* 1.10
24.7 (Sch. 267): *KG* 5.77
24.9–10 (Sch. 268): *KG* 5.5; 6.8
24.11 (Sch. 269): *Gn.* 23
24.13 (Sch. 270): *Gn.* 25; *KG* 3.64
24.22 (Sch. 275): *KG* 1.65, 70; 2.75; 3.38; 6.67
24.22 (Sch. 276): *KG* 5.28
24.27 (Sch. 291): *KG* 5.39, 41
24.27 (Sch. 292): *KG* 4.68
24.31 (Sch. 293): *KG* 5.82
25.2 (Sch. 299): *KG* 4.75

CROSS REFERENCES 497

25.17 (Sch. 310): *Prak.* 49; *KG* 1.32; 2.10, 83; 3.28
26.3 (Sch. 319): *Prak.* pr 7; *KG* 6.8
27.23–24 (Sch. 340): *Prak.* 25
27.25 (Sch. 341): *KG* 2.30, 59; 5.40
28.4 (Sch. 343): *KG* 5.82
28.17 (Sch. 351): *KG* 4.34
28.19 (Sch. 352): *KG* 5.33
28.21 (Sch. 353): *KG* 4.55
28.22 (Sch. 354): *KG* 1.32
28.28 (Sch. 355): *KG* 3.18
29.11 (Sch. 363): *Gn.* 44; *KG* 2.59
29.18 (Sch. 364): *Prak.* pr 7; *KG* 4.61
29.26 (Sch. 370): *KG* 2.75; 3.46
30.4 (Sch. 282): *KG* 3.60
30.4 (Sch. 282a): *KG* 3.24
30.4 (Sch. 284): *KG* 3.60
30.9 (Sch. 287b): *KG* 3.12; 4.13
30.9 (Sch. 288): *KG* 2.7; 3.72
31.15 (Sch. 374): *KG* 3.44
31.18 (Sch. 375): *KG* 2.34; 4.25
31.19 (Sch. 376): *KG* 2.34
31.21 (Sch. 377): *Prak.* 61; *KG* 3.39
31.22 (Sch. 378): *Gn.* 48; *KG* 1.73; 2.34
31.24 (Sch. 379): *KG* 4.46

Scholia on Psalms
1.1 (Sch. 2): *Prak.* 2
1.3 (Sch. 5): *KG* 3.56
1.5 (Sch. 8): *KG* 1.17; 3.48
1.5 (Sch. 10): *KG* 3.48, 50
2.12 (Sch. 4): *Prak.* 78
3.4 (Sch. 2): *KG* 2.2
3.5 (Sch. 3): *KG* 5.40
3.7 (Sch. 4): *KG* 3.59
4.3 (Sch. 3): *KG* 5.13
4.5 (Sch. 4): *KG* 3.90
4.6 (Sch. 5): *KG* 4.22
4.7 (Sch. 6): *KG* 3.24, 48
5.12 (Sch. 11): *KG* 3.36
6.8 (Sch. 4): *Prak.* 20; *Gn.* 5; *KG* 5.27
7.13 (Sch. 6): *KG* 5.28
9.5 (Sch. 2): *KG* 4.11
9.16 (Sch. 20): *KG* 6.15
9.18 (Sch. 7): *KG* 6.8
9.35 (Sch. 17): *KG* 5.8
9.37 (Sch. 20): *Prak.* 2
10.2 (Sch. 3): *Prak.* 50
10.2 (Sch. 2): *KG* 2.34; 6.53
12.5 (Sch. 3): *Prak.* 76
13.7 (Sch. 7): *KG* 2.55
13.7 (Sch. 6): *KG* 5.6; 6.49
14.1 (Sch. 1): *KG* 5.40
15.2 (Sch. 1): *KG* 3.59
15.9 (Sch. 4): *Gn.* 19

16.11 (Sch. 5): *KG* 3.28
16.13 (Sch. 7): *Prak.* 24; *KG* 2.12; 5.7, 13, 18; 6.24
17.7 (Sch. 4): *KG* 5.84
17.13 (Sch. 7): *KG* 5.28
17.16 (Sch. 9): *KG* 5.72
17.17–18 (Sch. 10): *KG* 4.17
17.21 (Sch. 12): *KG* 1.79
17.37 (Sch. 19): *KG* 2.12
17.38 (Sch. 21): *Prak.* 72
17.48 (Sch. 35): *Prak.* 38
17.49 (Sch. 25): *Prak.* 20; *KG* 5.44
18.2 (Sch. 1): *KG* 3.44
20.12 (Sch. 5): *KG* 3.59
21.29 (Sch. 14): *KG* 6.15
22.4 (Sch. 3): *Prak.* pr 7
22.5 (Sch. 4): *Gn.* 6
23.6 (Sch. 3): *Prak.* 24
23.7 (Sch. 4): *KG* 5.77
24.17–18 (Sch. 9): *Prak.* 32
24.20 (Sch. 11): *Prak.* 81; *Gn.* 28
25.2 (Sch. 1): *Prak.* pr 5, 38; *Gn.* 14
25.6 (Sch. 4): *KG* 2.57
26.2 (Sch. 1): *KG* 1.23
26.3 (Sch. 2): *KG* 5.30
26.6 (Sch. 5): *KG* 4.22
26.12 (Sch. 8): *KG* 3.90
27.2 (Sch. 2): *KG* 5.84
27.5 (Sch. 3): *KG* 3.44
29.8 (Sch. 7): *KG* 1.23
30.3 (Sch. 2): *KG* 4.82
30.9 (Sch. 6): *Prak.* 20
30.10 (Sch. 7): *Prak.* 20; *Gn.* 5; *KG* 5.27
30.22 (Sch. 14): *KG* 5.74, 82
31.14 (Sch. 10): *Prak.* 23
32.2 (Sch. 3): *KG* 2.34; 6.46
33.19 (Sch. 11): *KG* 4.22
34.11 (Sch. 8): *KG* 5.84
36.7 (Sch. 4): *KG* 6.68
36.9 (Sch. 8): *KG* 3.28
36.11 (Sch. 11): *Prak.* 2
36.20 (Sch. 18): *KG* 4.26
36.23 (Sch. 19): *KG* 2.34
36.25 (Sch. 20): *Gn.* 28; *KG* 6.40
36.25 (Sch. 21): *KG* 1.39
36.27 (Sch. 24): *KG* 6.54
37.12 (Sch. 8): *Gn.* 28
37.17 (Sch. 10): *Prak.* 76
38.14 (Sch. 10): *Prak.* 2
39.13 (Sch. 10): *KG* 6.87
42.3 (Sch. 2): *KG* 5.40
43.6 (Sch. 4): *KG* 2.34
43.11 (Sch. 6): *KG* 1.66
43.21 (Sch. 13): *KG* 1.89

498 CROSS REFERENCES

44.5 (Sch. 5): *KG* 2.12
44.6 (Sch. 6): *Prak.* 81
44.8 (Sch. 7): *KG* 3.85; 4.18, 21
44.10 (Sch. 8): *KG* 2.2; 5.2
45.2 (Sch. 1): *Prak.* 17
45.5 (Sch. 3): *KG* 5.2, 28, 74
47.11 (Sch. 6): *KG* 2.12
48.15 (Sch. 10): *KG* 3.9, 65; 6.24
49.4 (Sch. 3): *KG* 2.84
49.14 (Sch. 6): *KG* 4.22
49.22 (Sch. 11): *KG* 3.28
50.20 (Sch. 6): *KG* 5.82
54.7 (Sch. 2): *KG* 2.6; 3.56
54.10 (Sch. 3): *KG* 4.35, 53
54.24 (Sch. 12): *KG* 3.44
55.3 (Sch. 1): *KG* 4.33
56.9 (Sch. 5): *KG* 6.46
56.11 (Sch. 6): *KG* 5.13
57.5 (Sch. 3): *Prak.* 38
62.4 (Sch. 2): *KG* 1.73
62.11 (Sch. 5): *KG* 4.33
64.8 (Sch. 3): *KG* 5.17
64.10 (Sch. 5): *Gn.* 19
64.10 (Sch. 4): *KG* 4.30
65.6 (Sch. 3): *KG* 5.17
67.5 (Sch. 3): *KG* 3.28, 60
67.6 (Sch. 4): *KG* 5.8
67.19 (Sch. 13): *KG* 2.55
67.24 (Sch. 15): *Gn.* 14
67.32 (Sch. 19): *KG* 1.83; 4.64; 6.49
67.34 (Sch. 21): *KG* 3.60
67.35 (Sch. 22): *KG* 5.13
68.5 (Sch. 4): *KG* 1.23
68.13 (Sch. 8): *KG* 5.44
68.15 (Sch. 9): *KG* 4.33
68.36 (Sch. 23): *KG* 6.49
70.11 (Sch. 4): *Gn.* 28; *KG* 6.40
70.20 (Sch. 8): *KG* 4.33
72.20 (Sch. 13): *KG* 6.40
72.21 (Sch. 14): *Prak.* pr 5; *KG* 6.87
72.23 (Sch. 15): *KG* 1.70
73.19 (Sch. 9): *Prak.* 20; *KG* 1.53
74.4 (Sch. 1): *KG* 3.44
75.4 (Sch. 3): *KG* 6.53
76.14 (Sch. 9): *KG* 5.43
76.15 (Sch. 10): *KG* 1.14
76.16 (Sch. 11): *KG* 2.12
76.17 (Sch. 13): *Prak.* 38
76.21 (Sch. 15): *Gn.* 13; *KG* 1.15; 6.10
77.25 (Sch. 10): *Prak.* 24; *KG* 1.23; 3.10
77.34 (Sch. 14): *KG* 6.40
77.45 (Sch. 18): *KG* 2.86
77.54 (Sch. 23): *KG* 5.40

78.7 (Sch. 2): *KG* 5.70
79.18 (Sch. 8): *KG* 2.12
80.10 (Sch. 4): *KG* 5.49
82.13 (Sch. 3): *KG* 1.18
83.3 (Sch. 1): *KG* 1.74; 5.84
83.12 (Sch. 12): *Gn.* 19
86.2 (Sch. 1): *KG* 5.6
88.2 (Sch. 4): *KG* 2.22
88.13 (Sch. 8): *KG* 4.23
88.21 (Sch. 11): *Gn.* 7; *KG* 1.89; 3.43; 4.18; 6.15
88.32 (Sch. 17): *KG* 4.68
88.46 (Sch. 22): *Gn.* 28
88.49 (Sch. 23): *Gn.* 17
88.51 (Sch. 24): *KG* 1.23
89.3 (Sch. 1): *Gn.* 28
89.4 (Sch. 2): *KG* 2.87
89.17 (Sch. 9): *Gn.* 3
90.6 (Sch. 4): *KG* 4.73
91.4 (Sch. 2): *KG* 2.34; 6.46
91.7 (Sch. 3): *Prak.* 81
91.8 (Sch. 4): *KG* 4.26
92.1 (Sch. 1): *KG* 6.15, 33, 70
92.4 (Sch. 3): *KG* 5.17
93.6 (Sch. 4): *KG* 5.8
93.6 (Sch. 3): *KG* 5.8
93.18 (Sch. 9): *Gn.* 28
94.4 (Sch. 1): *KG* 2.12
94.11 (Sch. 7): *KG* 3.68
95.4 (Sch. 2): *Prak.* 83
95.8 (Sch. 4): *KG* 4.22
96.1 (Sch. 1): *KG* 5.17
96.3 (Sch. 2): *KG* 4.26
96.4 (Sch. 7): *KG* 5.13
98.5 (Sch. 2): *KG* 5.48
98.7 (Sch. 4): *KG* 5.13
99.4 (Sch. 1): *KG* 5.77
100.5 (Sch. 5): *Prak.* 89
101.14 (Sch. 8): *KG* 5.6
102.1 (Sch. 1): *Prak.* 46; *KG* 2.9
102.5 (Sch. 6): *KG* 6.40
102.18 (Sch. 13): *KG* 4.55
103.9 (Sch. 8): *KG* 4.33
103.13 (Sch. 11): *KG* 5.13
104.31 (Sch. 16): *KG* 2.86
104.37 (Sch. 19): *Gn.* 4
105.5 (Sch. 3): *KG* 1.17
106.3 (Sch. 1): *KG* 3.60
106.4 (Sch. 2): *KG* 5.74
106.10 (Sch. 4): *Gn.* 5
106.16 (Sch. 7): *KG* 5.80
106.28–29 (Sch. 13): *KG* 5.17
106.29 (Sch. 15): *KG* 5.17

CROSS REFERENCES 499

107.3 (Sch. 2): *KG* 6.46
107.5 (Sch. 3): *Prak.* pr 2; *KG* 5.13
108.9 (Sch. 7): *KG* 5.8
109.2 (Sch. 1): *KG* 6.38
109.3 (Sch. 2): *Prak.* pr 2; *KG* 6.39
110.3 (Sch. 2): *KG* 4.30
111.4 (Sch. 4): *Gn.* 30
112.3 (Sch. 1): *KG* 3.44, 60
112.9 (Sch. 4): *KG* 6.60
113.4 (Sch. 2): *KG* 2.30; 6.19
113.12–15 (Sch. 6): *KG* 1.36
114.2 (Sch. 1): *KG* 3.44
114.7 (Sch. 3): *Prak.* 73; *KG* 4.44
115.2 (Sch. 2): *KG* 4.90
117.27 (Sch. 8): *KG* 3.56
118.7 (Sch. 5): *KG* 3.82; 4.33; 6.49
118.28 (Sch. 13): *Prak.* 12
118.37 (Sch. 17): *KG* 5.43
118.47 (Sch. 20): *Prak.* pr 3
118.55 (Sch. 22): *Gn.* 42
118.61 (Sch. 25): *KG* 4.34
118.61 (Sch. 26): *KG* 4.55
118.70 (Sch. 30): *KG* 1.40
118.75 (Sch. 34): *Gn.* 26
118.85 (Sch. 37): *Gn.* 4
118.98 (Sch. 43): *KG* 1.65
118.103 (Sch. 45): *KG* 3.64
118.109 (Sch. 48): *Gn.* 26
118.128 (Sch. 57): *Prak.* 5
118.140 (Sch. 63): *KG* 4.26
118.147 (Sch. 67): *KG* 3.44
118.155 (Sch. 69): *KG* 4.68
118.159 (Sch. 72): *Gn.* 1
118.161 (Sch. 74): *KG* 1.67
118.164 (Sch. 76): *KG* 4.44; 5.83
123.7 (Sch. 3): *Prak.* 19
125.1 (Sch. 1): *KG* 2.55
125.5 (Sch. 3): *Prak.* 90; *KG* 1.39
126.1 (Sch. 2): *Prak.* 1; *KG* 5.84
126.2 (Sch. 3): *KG* 1.38
129.4–5 (Sch. 4): *Prak.* 81
131.1 (Sch. 1): *Prak.* pr 4; *Gn.* 5
131.5 (Sch. 2): *KG* 2.34
131.7 (Sch. 5): *KG* 5.48
132.2 (Sch. 2): *KG* 3.43
132.2 (Sch. 4): *KG* 3.43, 85
134.6 (Sch. 2): *KG* 4.33
134.7 (Sch. 5): *KG* 1.24
134.7 (Sch. 3): *KG* 5.13
134.12 (Sch. 6b): *Prak.* 2, 3; *KG* 5.30
135.6 (Sch. 3): *KG* 1.39; 2.80; 3.37;
    4.64; 6.49
135.23 (Sch. 4): *KG* 1.17

136.7 (Sch. 4): *KG* 1.39
137.1 (Sch. 1): *Prak.* 49
138.2 (Sch. 1): *KG* 6.21
138.7 (Sch. 3): *KG* 1.89
138.11 (Sch. 4): *Gn.* 17; *KG* 3.90
138.16 (Sch. 8): *Prak.* 92; *Gn.* 48; *KG*
    1.23; 2.34, 84; 3.58
138.22 (Sch. 12): *Gn.* 28
138.23 (Sch. 13): *KG* 1.17
139.3 (Sch. 1): *Prak.* 12
139.6 (Sch. 3): *Prak.* 12; *Gn.* 42
139.11 (Sch. 6): *KG* 4.26
140.2 (Sch. 1): *KG* 2.83
140.5 (Sch. 3): *KG* 3.43
140.9 (Sch. 5): *KG* 5.37
141.4 (Sch. 1): *Gn.* 42
141.5 (Sch. 2): *Prak.* 49
141.6 (Sch. 3): *KG* 1.14
141.7 (Sch. 4): *Gn.* 42
141.8 (Sch. 5): *KG* 4.70
143.1 (Sch. 1): *KG* 5.38
143.7 (Sch. 5): *Prak.* pr 3; *Gn.* 43
144.1 (Sch. 1): *KG* 1.23; 2.34
144.3 (Sch. 2): *Prak.* 87; *KG* 2.46; 3.63
144.20 (Sch. 7): *KG* 6.40
147.1–2 (Sch. 1): *KG* 5.6, 80; 6.49
147.3 (Sch. 3): *KG* 1.39; 6.60
147.5 (Sch. 5): *KG* 6.25
148.4 (Sch. 3): *KG* 3.44
148.4 (Sch. 4): *KG* 5.67
148.14 (Sch. 5): *KG* 2.34
149.1 (Sch. 1): *KG* 6.40
149.6 (Sch. 2): *KG* 5.28
149.8 (Sch. 3): *KG* 3.44
150.2 (Sch. 3): *KG* 6.46
150.4 (Sch. 7): *KG* 5.2

Thirty-Three Chapters
    KG 1.36
    1: *KG* 1.73
    9: *Prak.* 14
    19: *KG* 4.51
    31: *KG* 2.30
Thoughts
    1: *Prak.* 14, 16, 84, 99
    2: *Prak.* 11, 39, 43, 48; *KG* 2.83
    3: *Gn.* 33, 34
    4: *Prak.* 54; *Gn.* 7, 14; *KG* 1.63, 75; 2.30;
        4.60; 5.12, 17; 6.84
    5: *Prak.* 47; *KG* 2.86; 5.44
    6: *Prak.* 24; *KG* 3.8
    7: *Prak.* pr 6, 29, 46, 51; *KG* 2.75
    8: *Prak.* 100; *Gn.* 16; *KG* 2.30; 4.69;
        5.83; 6.2, 8

500 CROSS REFERENCES

9: *Prak.* 11, 12, 15; *KG* 1.68; 5.74
10: *Prak.* 81; *Gn.* 28
11: *Prak.* 43; *KG* 1.82; 3.86
12: *Gn.* 30
14: *Prak.* 13
15: *Prak.* 31, 60; *KG* 6.21, 55
16: *Prak.* 11; *Gn.* 37, 44; *KG* 3.90; 4.7
17: *Prak.* 24; *KG* 1.74, 84, 85; 2.64; 5.15, 40, 41
18: *Prak.* 18
19: *Prak.* 5, 11, 100; *KG* 3.59, 78, 82; 5.30, 76
20: *KG* 5.29
21: *Prak.* 14, 100; *KG* 1.78; 5.44
22: *Prak.* 22; *Gn.* 24
23: *Prak.* 87; *KG* 3.89; 5.9; 6.41
24: *Prak.* 20, 64; *KG* 1.17
25: *Prak.* 16, 40, 48, 49, 68; *KG* 1.32, 55; 2.35
26: *Prak.* 15, 54; *KG* 1.78, 85; 2.9, 10; 5.17
27: *Prak.* pr 4, 11, 15; *KG* 3.68
28: *KG* 4.5
29: *Prak.* 64, 66; *KG* 2.6; 3.56; 4.27
31: *KG* 1.22, 39, 40
32: *Prak.* 20; *Gn.* 8
33: *KG* 2.35; 3.30; 6.25
34: *KG* 1.49; 5.28; 6.36
35: *Prak.* 16, 49, 94; *KG* 1.5; 4.12
37: *KG* 3.90
38: *KG* 3.3; 6.42
39: *Prak.* 64; *KG* 1.22; 5.39; 6.40
40: *KG* 3.24
41: *KG* 2.34
42: *KG* 1.73; 2.5, 29; 5.13

Vices

1: *KG* 1.78; 4.53
2: *KG* 4.12
3: *KG* 3.86
4: *KG* 5.13
5: *KG* 2.1
6: *KG* 1.75
7: *Prak.* 13
8: *KG* 4.67

Virgin

5: *Prak.* 49
6: *Prak.* 20; *Gn.* 11
14: *KG* 5.9
24: *Prak.* 48
26: *KG* 4.50
33: *KG* 5.2
39: *Prak.* 27

40: *Prak.* 15
41: *Prak.* 26
43: *Gn.* 7
47: *KG* 1.75
48: *Prak.* 71
54: *Prak.* 24; *Gn.* 45; *KG* 5.15
55: *Prak.* 3; *KG* 4.29

Galen

Anatomical Procedures
    KG 4.32
On the Formation of the Fetus
    KG 3.76
Protreptikos
    Prak. 14

Gospel of Philip
    KG 3.89

Gregory of Nazianzus

Letters
    Prak. pr 3, 52, ep
Orations
    2: *Prak.* 13; *Gn.* 15
    6: *Prak.* 38
    9: *Prak.* 27
    10: *KG* 4.18
    14: *KG* 4.14
    21: *Gn.* 44, 46
    23: *Prak.* pr 3; *KG* 6.10, 13
    27: *Prak.* 52; *KG* 5.51
    28: *Prak.* 87; *Gn.* 26, 41, 49, 50; *KG* 3.30; 5.40
    29: *Gn.* 41; *KG* 5.26
    30: *Gn.* 50; *KG* 4.18
    31: *KG* 1.35; 5.3; 6.4
    34: *KG* 4.14
    39: *Prak.* 81
    40: *Prak.* pr 5, 3
    41: *KG* 4.54
    43: *Gn.* 45
    45: *KG* 4.11, 25
Poems
    Prak. 3, 11, 15, 21, 71

Gregory of Nyssa

Against Eunomius
    Prak. 97; *Gn.* 26
Catechetical Oration
    Prak. pr 6, pr 9
De sancto Theodoro
    Gn. 50

CROSS REFERENCES   501

Homilies on the Song of Songs
 Prak. 19; *KG* 3.17; 4.50
Inscriptions on the Psalms
 KG 6.46
Life of Moses
 Prak. pr 5, pr 6 , 87; *KG* 4.48, 56; 5.17
On Virginity
 Gn. 49; *KG* 3.17
On the Dead
 KG 4.50
On the Lord's Prayer
 KG 4.72
On the Soul and the Resurrection
 KG 2.25

Herodotus
Histories
 KG 4.64

Hippocrates
On Generation
 Prak. 17
On the Regimen
 Prak. 54

Hippocrates, pseudo-
Letter to Ptolemy
 KG 2.9

Hippolytus
Commentary on Psalms
 KG 5.49
Determination of the Date of Easter
 KG 6.72
Fragments
 KG 5.49; 6.72
Refutation
 KG 2.26

History of the Monks of Egypt
 Prak. 17; *Gn.* 48

Homer
Iliad
 Prak. pr 5

Hymn to God
 KG 3.30

Hypotyposis of the Archons
 KG 5.1

Iamblichus
Chaldean Theology
 KG 6.11
Pythagorean Way of Life
 Gn. 49; *KG* 4.22

Irenaeus
Heresies
 Gn. 1

Jerome
Fragments
 KG 5.6
Letters
 Prak. 54; *KG* 4.11

John Chrysostom
De sancto Meletio Antiocheno
 Gn. 50
Homilies on 1 Corinthians
 Prak. 97
Homilies on 1 Timothy
 Gn. 1
Homilies on 2 Corinthians
 KG 4.14
Homilies on 2 Timothy
 Prak. pr 3
Homilies on John
 Prak. 1
Homilies on Psalms
 Prak. pr 9
On the Incomprehensibility of God
 Prak. 87
On the Priesthood
 Prak. 13; *KG* 4.52
On the Statues
 Prak. 97

John of Damascus
Dialogues against Manichaeans
 KG 6.4

Josephus
Antiquities of the Jews
 Gn. 38

Julian
Oration
 Gn. 6

Julian the Emperor

Letter to the Athenians
    Gn. 26

Justin Martyr

Dialogue
    KG 4.61

Juvenal

Saturnalia
    Prak. pr 2

Leontius of Byzantium

Against Nestorius and Eutychius
    KG 4.50

Letter to Diognetus

    KG 4.64

Libanius

Oration
    Prak. 27

Life of Adam and Eve

    KG 6.8

Macarius

Sermon
    KG 4.50

Macarius of Egypt

Letter to His Sons
    Prak. 29

Mani

Kephalaia of the Teacher
    KG 3.52, 55, 56

Marcus Aurelius

To Himself
    Prak. 37

Melito of Sardis

On the Pasch
    KG 6.27

Nemesius

On the Nature of Humanity
    Prak. 37; KG 1.67

Nicomachus of Gerasa

Introduction to Arithmetic
    Gn. 49; KG 6.13

Nyssa

Homilies on the Song of Songs
    Prak. 4

Oribasius

Synopsis
    Prak. 56

Origen

Commentary on 1 Corinthians
    KG 6.22
Commentary on Ephesians
    KG 4.14
Commentary on Ezek
    Gn. 34
Commentary on Genesis
    KG 2.70; 3.58
Commentary on John
    1: KG 1.17; 2.1; 3.58, 65; 4.45; 6.8, 20
    2: Prak. pr 9; KG 3.28; 4.23; 5.75
    6: Prak. 30, 59; KG 1.83; 4.9; 5.43;
        6.1, 15
    10: KG 5.18
    13: KG 4.6, 28; 5.6
    19: KG 4.65; 5.51
    20: KG 1.61; 5.48
    28: Prak. 13; KG 6.8
    32: Prak. ep
Commentary on Matthew
    4: KG 1.61
    12: KG 4.23, 28, 41
    13: Prak. pr 2; KG 4.40
    14: Prak. 52
    15: KG 4.54
    17: KG 4.30
Commentary on Psalms
    KG 3.28
Commentary on Romans
    KG 1.86; 3.18; 4.34, 42, 71; 6.34
Commentary on the Song of Songs
    Prak. pr 9, 1; KG 1.13
Contra Celsum
    1: KG 1.82; 2.36
    2: Prak. 22; KG 1.17; 4.64, 90; 5.48
    3: Prak. 1, 3; KG 3.1
    4: Prak. pr 2; Gn. 34; KG 1.21, 40, 61; 4.53
    5: Prak. pr 1; KG 1.24, 65; 2.25; 4.54

6: *Prak.* pr 9; *Gn.* 19, 36; *KG* 1.49; 4.47; 5.48, 51
7: *Prak.* 14; *KG* 1.33; 4.22, 37, 74; 6.81
8: *Prak.* pr 3; *Gn.* 48; *KG* 1.67; 2.36; 3.50

Dialogue with Heracleides
    KG 1.61

Exhortation to Martyrdom
    KG 3.41

First Principles
    KG 2.78; 5.11
1: *Prak.* 24; *KG* 1.12, 17, 50, 61, 67, 87; 2.1, 30, 68; 3.37, 73, 79; 4.11, 38; 6.4, 10
2: *Prak.* pr 2, 24; *Gn.* 39, 46, 50; *KG* 1.24, 30, 49, 65, 89; 2.17, 29, 74; 3.9; 4.18, 30, 58; 5.48, 51, 85; 6.8, 17
3: *Prak.* 28; *Gn.* 16, 28, 48; *KG* 3.82; 4.38, 57; 5.89; 6.34
4: *Gn.* 25; *KG* 1.81; 3.64

Fragments
    KG 1.40; 5.6

Homilies on Exodus
1: *KG* 1.24
6: *KG* 4.48
7: *KG* 1.17
8: *KG* 5.40
9: *Prak.* pr 1; *Gn.* 46; *KG* 4.52, 72; 5.80
13: *Prak.* pr 6; *KG* 4.56

Homilies on Ezek
    Prak. 32; *KG* 6.56

Homilies on Genesis
    Gn. 34; *KG* 1.17; 2.1; 3.52; 4.54

Homilies on Jeremiah
    Prak. 5; *Gn.* 23, 44; *KG* 2.26; 3.18; 4.28

Homilies on Jgs
    KG 5.30

Homilies on Joshua
    Prak. 15; *KG* 4.12; 5.71, 74

Homilies on Leviticus
    KG 4.22
3: *KG* 4.32
5: *KG* 4.36
6: *KG* 4.48, 56
7: *KG* 4.46
8: *KG* 4.57
13: *Prak.* ep; *KG* 4.25

Homilies on Luke
    Gn. 29

Homilies on Numbers
4: *Gn.* 14
10: *Gn.* 38; *KG* 2.57; 4.63
11: *KG* 1.89; 6.4

13: *Gn.* 21
14: *Gn.* 21
18: *Prak.* 15

Homilies on Psalms
    Prak. 55; *KG* 1.83; 3.1, 3; 6.22

Homilies on the Song of Songs
    KG 1.38

Homilies on the Witch of Endor
    KG 3.82

Letters
    Prak. pr 1

On Prayer
    KG 3.41; 4.42
1: *Prak.* 49
2: *Prak.* 12
14: *KG* 4.11
19: *KG* 3.82
20: *Prak.* 24
21: *Prak.* 62
24: *Prak.* 30
28: *Prak.* 8
29: *KG* 1.65
45: *Prak.* 11

Philokalia
    KG 1.65; 6.43

Select Passages on Psalms
    Prak. 55

Selections on Job
    KG 4.14

Palladius

Lausiac History
2: *Prak.* pr 1
10: *Gn.* 30
11: *Gn.* 48
18: *Prak.* 29
25: *Prak.* 14
26: *Prak.* 58
38: *Prak.* 7, 40, 95; *Gn.* 26

Philo

Allegorical Commentary on Genesis
    KG 1.61

Allegories of the Law
    Prak. 38, 46; *KG* 1.83; 3.37, 56

Dreams
    KG 3.37

Giants
    Prak. 98

Life of Moses
    Prak. pr 1, 1 , 87; *KG* 4.22, 48

504 CROSS REFERENCES

On Monarchy
    KG 4.56
On Planting
    KG 2.32, 48
On Sacrifice
    Prak. 98
On the Confusion of Tongues
    KG 4.53
On the Creation of the World
    Prak. 38; KG 1.15, 61; 2.58; 3.28;
       4.50; 5.1
On the Decalogue
    Gn. 39
On the Migration of Abraham and On
    the Virtues
    Prak. 61; KG 6.8
Questions on Exodus
    Prak. pr 1, pr 5
Special Laws
    Prak. 6, 17, 38; KG 4.22
That God Is Unchangeable
    Gn. 23; KG 1.70
That the Worse Attacks the Better
    Gn. 39

Philodemus

Fragments
    Prak. 56
On Signs
    Prak. 56
On the Gods
    Prak. 56
Rhetoric
    Gn. 6

Philoxenus of Mabbug

Letter to Patrikios
    Gn. 25

Plato

Cratylus
    KG 4.90
Gorgias
    Prak. 27, 96
Ion
    KG 2.34
Laws
    Prak. 9, 50, 96; KG 5.17
Letters
    Gn. 44
Menas
    Prak. 27

Parmenides
    KG 1.43
Phaedo
    KG 4.90; 5.14
Phaedrus
    Prak. 4, 52; Gn. 17; KG 1.67; 2.6; 3.56;
       5.73, 90; 6.15
Politics
    Prak. 50; Gn. 1
Republic
    Prak. pr 3, 9, 21, 29, 55, 57, 86; Gn. 23, 26;
       KG 1.64, 67; 3.58; 4.90; 5.8, 14, 74
Symposium
    Prak. 14; Gn. 50; KG 1.43; 3.58; 4.50
Theaetetus
    Prak. 56; KG 1.1; 4.43, 71
Timaeus
    Gn. 50; KG 1.61; 3.57, 58; 6.82

Plotinus

Enneads
    1: Prak. 75; Gn. 26; KG 1.21, 71; 5.57,
      62, 90
    2: KG 1.30, 70; 5.12; 6.82
    3: Prak. 37, 52; Gn. 48; KG 4.50
    4: Prak. 50; KG 3.14, 28; 4.67
    5: KG 1.64; 2.2; 5.22
    6: Prak. 14; Gn. 50; KG 1.1; 3.57; 4.9;
      5.39, 73; 6.10

Plutarch

De communibus notitiis adversus Stoicos
    Prak. 15
Dion
    Prak. 27
Septem sapientium convivium
    KG 1.67

Polybius

History
    Gn. 39

Porphyry

Commentary on Ptolemy's Harmony
    KG 1.3
Isagoge
    Gn. 41; KG 1.20, 70
Launching Points to the Intelligibles
    Prak. 2, 52, 85; KG 1.67; 3.28; 5.22, 58
Letter to Anebo
    KG 4.22, 37

CROSS REFERENCES 505

Life of Plotinus
    KG 3.53
Life of Pythagoras
    KG 4.51
On Abstinence
    KG 3.50
    2: *Prak.* 5; *Gn.* 41; *KG* 2.52; 3.8, 30;
        4.22, 35, 37
    26: *KG* 3.14
    31: *KG* 2.2
On the Cave of the Nymphs
    KG 5.14

Rufinus

Church History
    KG 4.22

Scholasticus

Church History
    KG title.

Seneca

Letters to Lucilius
    Prak. 1, 29
On Anger
    Prak. 11
On Benefits
    Gn. 39

Serapion

Against the Manichaeans
    KG 3.55

Severus of Antioch

Letters
    Gn. 41

Socrates Scholasticus

Church History
    Gn. 45

Strabo

Geography
    Prak. 98

Testament of Job

    KG 6.3

Themistius

Paraphrase de anima
    Prak. 4

Thunder—Perfect Intellect

    KG 3.89

Xenophon

Anabasis
    Prak. 59
Cyropaedeia
    Prak. 57

Zeno

On the Passions
    Prak. 6

Index

For the benefit of digital users, indexed terms that span two pages (e.g., 52–53) may, on occasion, appear on only one of those pages.

abandonment of evil, second renunciation of, 198–99
abyss, demons' fear of, 185
accidents, 186
accommodation in teaching, 102–4
actions
  good or bad, 89
  material knowledge and, 225
Adam, 357
adultery and fornication of Jerusalem, 115–16
aeons, 32, 189–90, 192, 193
air, 166, 191–92
akēdia, 20, 35, 41, 53
  demon of, 40, 49, 52, 347
  eight passions, 36
Alexander, Origen on Temple visit of, 23–24
Alexandria, Platonic philosophy of teachers of, 2–3
allegorical interpretations, of scripture, 4, 5, 128–29
almsgiving, gnostic, 104–5
altars
  knowledge three, 354–55
  three, 236–37
Ammonius Saccas, 2–3
analogy
  grain, 232–33
  wheat, 220–21
anathemas, 63, 214–15, 216–17, 312–13
Anatolius, addressee of *Praktikos*, 1–2, 1n.1, 3, 9, 14, 23–24, 29–30, 98
angelic thoughts, 85
angels, 49–50, 258, 279, 289–90, 296, 360–61, 428. *See also* archangel
  anger and conduct of, 325–26
  festival with, 361–62
  honoring of, 384
  instruction by, 455
  ranks of, 362–63
  rejoicing of, 83
  saints as, 347
  salvation and, 456
  sight of, 446

thēoria of, 360
anger, 36
  angelic conduct and, 325–26
  blinding of mind and, 371–72
  demon and, 272
  demon of, 331
  desire and, 454–55
  gnostic freedom from, 102–3
  interpretation of gnostic and, 106–7
  monks and, 96–97
  soul and, 454
  temptations of, 62
  thoughts, 35–36, 39–40, 47–52
  wine of dragons and, 382–83
angering soul
  courage in, 89–90
  endurance in, 89–90
annulment, of four elements of soul, 157–58
anointing, 314–15
  intelligible, 312–13
apatheia (health of mind and soul), 14–15, 20, 28–29, 200
  dreams and, 72–73
  kingdom of heaven and, 32
  proof of, 77–78
  state approaching, 73–77
  symbols of, 77–80
  wings of, 210–11
apokatasasis, 214–15
Arabic version
  Gnostikos absence of, 11–12
  of *KG*, 12–13
  of *Praktikos*, 10
archangel, 359
archetype, image of, 144–45
Aristotle, 16–19, 50, 90, 125
  on passions of soul, 66
  syllogism from, 147–48
Armenian translation
  of *Gnostikos*, 10, 12n.27
  of *Praktikos*, 10
arrow, intelligible, 438
arts, 168, 231

508   INDEX

askēsis (training), 2–3
Athanasius, Moses and, 140
avaricious people, 125

Babai the Great, 13
baptism, 299
bared hands, 25–26
Basil of Caesarea ("Basil the
    Cappadocian"), 138–39
begetting, 301, 311–12, 425–27
being in self, 149–51
beings. *See also* rational beings
    divine book and *thēoria* of, 409
    father and *thēoria* of, 425
    second, 187
    thēoria of, 210, 276, 314–15, 365–66
belt, 315–16, 350
    of monk, 26–27
blade of stone, circumcision and, 445
blasphemy, 339
    demon of, 69
    demons causing, 64–65
blinded mind, 76–77
bodies
    of demons, 161–62, 401
    spiritual, 154–55
bodiless nature
    bodily nature and, 297, 308–9
    passing of body and, 244–45
bodily nature, 261, 313–14, 338, 436
    bodiless nature and, 297, 308–9
    goodness of, 293–94
body, 179, 241. *See also* spiritual bodies
    bodiless and passing of, 244–45
    change of, 440–41
    demon, 161–62
    equal, 215
    knowledge of God and evil, 283
    passing away, form of, 164
    passion of, 58, 126
    in potentia and, 179
    resurrection of, 368
    soul and, 69–70, 180
    thēoria about, 239
    thickness, 242
    transfer into, 265–66
body of Christ, 452
bread, rational nature, 376–77
breathing of animals, 325

captivity, 235
Casiday, Augustine, 13n.32
Cassian, John, 14–15

Categories (Aristotle), *KG* Century One
    and, 148–49
change, 159, 209–10, 259, 282
    blink of eye and, 279–80
    body, 440–41
    Didymus on, 209–10
    inner, 159
    sinners and, 281–82
Chapters of Knowledge, *Kephalaia gnostika*, 146
chariot of knowledge, 233–34
cherubs, names of, 283–84
children, 311
    flesh and blood of, 310
christ versus Christ, 255–56
Christ, 255–56, 303–4, 416
    angelic appearance of, 327–28
    body absence of, 418–19
    coming forth of, 451
    cornerstone of, 430
    death of, 431–32
    essential knowledge and, 417–18
    feet of, 417
    high priest of, 384
    imprinting of, 427
    inheritance of, 292–93, 304–5
    inscribing of letters by, 285
    judgment seat of, 440
    just judgment of, 237–38
    knowable, 304
    knowledge of, 219
    ladder of Jacob and, 328–29
    rational beings and unity of, 257
    table of, 238
    three miracles of, 337
    worship of, 384–85
Christianity, 30–32
church, hearers in, 358
circumcision, 309–10, 389–404, 412, 445
cities, 373
    authority over, 422
    intelligible, 398–99
Clement of Alexandria, 16–19, 101, 125
clothing,
    anxiety over, 131–32
    in form of cross, 26
    monastic, 23–29
cloud
    intelligible, 362–65
    intelligible dark, 366
coat or cloak, 315–16, 344, 348
commandments, 212, 378, 427
comprehension, temptation and, 123–24
condemnation. *See* anathemas

INDEX   509

conscience, gnostic, 132
constant prayer, 67–68
contemplation. *See thēoria*
contingency, meanings by, 160
contrariety, 148–49, 150
copyist note, in *Praktikos (To a Monk)*, 30–31
cornerstone, Christ as, 430
corruption, 184, 225, 414
cosmos, intelligible, 380
courage
  in angering part of soul, 89–90
  Gregory of Nazianzus on virtues, 136–38
cowl, 24–25
creation, 457
cross, intelligible, 429
crown of justice, spiritual knowledge, 196–97
crucifixion, 430–31
cups or vessels, 374–75

day of Lord, 293
deadbolt, intelligible, 402
death
  immortality and, 185–86, 188
  soul after, 211
deep pit, demons and, 353–54
deficient soul, 262–63
definitions, matters and, 112–13
demonic songs, 81
demonic stench, passion and, 60
demons, 34–35, 154, 183, 234, 296, 367–68
  alliance of evil, 64
  anger, 331
  anger and, 272
  bodies of, 161–62, 401
  choke-holds of, 81–82
  deep pit and, 353–54
  fear of abyss by, 185
  fight against monks, 63–64
  merciless, 322
  monks' knowledge of, 68
  movement of passions by, 428
  objects and, 66–67
  opposed to each other, 74–75
  recognition of, 63
  of sexual lust, 69, 74–75
  sight of, 446
  slander of gnostic by, 301–2
  sleep and, 423
  soul's approach to virtue and, 75
demonstration of Holy Spirit, 432
desires
  anger and, 454–55
  monks and, 96–97

provisions for, 70
desiring soul
  love in, 89–90
  self-restraint in, 89–90
  temperance in, 89–90
Didymus the Blind, 16–19
  on change, 209–10
  logoi about providence of
    God and, 141–43
diet, Saint Paul and regime of, 130–31
Dionysius Bar Salibi, *KG* commentary by, 13
disgraceful people, words of, 116–17
disputing, without knowledge, 120–21
distinctions, 245
distraction
  prayers without, 77
  singing psalms without, 79–80
disturbance
  pathē, 1–2
  symptoms of, 61
divine book, *thēoria* of beings and, 409
divine scripture and testimonies, of
  Gnostikos, 114
dreams
  apatheia during, 72–73
  fantasies of, 71
  images seen in, 71–72
dyad, 415

earth, 166
  destruction of, 319–20
  things on, 162
earthly deeds, first renunciation of, 198
Ecclesiastical History (Socrates
  Scholasticus), 11
Egypt, 406–7
  soul and exodus from, 444
  symbol of evil, 435–36
ekstasis, 43
elements, 166, 191–92, 213, 266–67, 423–24
  annulment and, 157–58
  four corners and four, 330–31
Elijah as saint, 316
emotions. *See pathēma*
encounters with people, 107
end of world, 407
endurance, in angering soul, 89–90
English translations, of *Praktikos*, 1
ephod, 315–16, 337, 348
epinoia, 159, 182, 412
equal bodies, 215
eschaton, 319–20
essence, 338

510 INDEX

essential knowledge, 281, 349, 403
angels and, 428
Christ from, 417–18
father and, 424–25
Eucharist, 230, 251–52
Eudaemonian Ethics (Aristotle), 125
Eve, 357
everywhere and nowhere, God's
presence, 177–78
evil, 286–87
abandonment of, 198–99
burning of thoughts, 275
Egypt as symbol of, 435–36
existence of, 174–76
hating of, 300
impurity from, 294
knowledge of God and body as, 283
by nature and soul, 161
perfect fullness of, 240
virtue and movement, 182
virtues and, 176–77
exegesis, of Evagrius
allegorical scripture interpretations in, 4, 5
biblical commentaries in scholia form, 4
compositional method of, 4
exhortation, text about, 115–16
existence of evil, 174–76
extremes, mean compared to, 150–51

faculty of senses, 171–72
faith, 298
father, 411
essential knowledge of, 424–25
knowledge of Trinity and, 425
thēoria of beings, 425
fear
demon of abyss, 185
of Christ, 417
of God, 28–29, 429
of Hades, 185
festival with angels, 361–62
final judgment, 260, 276
final trumpet, 276, 290
fire, 166–67, 191–92, 222
firstborn, 314, 362, 430
of dead, 316–17
first good, 147–48
first renunciation of earthly deeds, 198
first trumpet, 290
fishhook, intelligible, 377
five senses, 158, 226
food, anxiety over, 131–32
four corners, four elements and, 330–31

four elements
four corners and, 330–31
soul annulment of, 157–58
freedom, gnostics' from anger, 102–3
Friday, 205
friends, 398

garments, 259–60
gates, intelligible, 400–1
Gennadius of Marseilles, 11–12
gifts
Holy Spirit, 323–24
resentment and, 51–52
Gihon river, 201
gnostic. *See gnōstikos*
Gnostic Trilogy, 1
annotations for, 16–19
collections of, 8–9
Latin translation, 7
manuscripts, text and ancient translations
in, 7–13
Praktikos Greek *intact* survival in, 7
quotations from, 9–10
reading of today, 19–21
references for, 15–16
Gnostikos. See specific topics
gnōstikos (gnostic), 1–2
accommodation in teaching of, 102–4
almsgiving of, 104–5
anger and interpretation of knowledge, 106–7
Clement of Alexandria on Christian teachers
and, 2–3
conscience of, 132
demons slander of, 301–2
freedom from anger of, 102–3
knowledge of, 305
legal dispute involvement by, 105–6
nature of, 399–400
Origen use of, 2–3
sacred scripture restriction to advanced, 5
sadness and unfriendliness of, 117–18
seeing of, 99–100
sin of, 135–36
temptation of, 135
God. *See also* image of God; Lord; sacrifices to
God; *specific attributes of*
architect of, 453
body as evil and knowledge of, 283
descent to Sheol, 350–51
Didymus and providence of, 141–43
grace of, 298, 355
judgment of, 274–75
knowable of, 303–4

knowledge of, 166–82, 203
Life of Anthony on illiteracy and knowledge of, 92–93
living and, 442
mind and teaching of, 284
mirror of goodness of, 207
modes associated with, 419–20
presence of, 177–78
providence of, 432
rational beings and, 303
rational beings and sanctification by, 293–94
recent and new, 385–86
rest of, 291
seeing, 371
sleep metaphor and, 173
thoughtless speaking about, 122–23
gospel book, 95
grace of God, 298, 355
grain analogy, 232–33
Greek Bible, scripture from, 4
Greek fragments, *Kephalaia gnostika*, 7–9, 12
Gregory of Nazianzus, 16–19, 90–91, 134
    on *theōria* virtues of prudence, courage, moderation, and justice, 136–38
Gregory of Nyssa, 16–19
Guillaumont, Antoine, 8n.11, 8n.13, 9n.16, 12n.27
    KG discovery by, 13
    on salt and light, 101
Guillaumont, Claire, 8n.13, 9n.16, 10–11, 12n.27
    KG discovery by, 13
    on salt and light, 101

Hades, 413. *See also* Sheol
    fear of, 185
hand of Lord, 214
harp, 433–34
healing, 127–28
    intelligible, 444
    of mind, 273
    of soul, 84–85
health of mind and soul. *See apatheia*
hearers in church, 358
heavenly powers
    minds of, 258
    providence and, 450–51
    ranks of, 247
heir
    with Christ, 306–7
    heirship, 349–50
    inheritance and, 307
helmet, intelligible, 376

hidden star, 321
high priest, 383–84
    Christ as, 384
holy knowledge, life and, 195
Holy Mountain, of Jerusalem, 23–24
holy mysteries, love of monks and, 97
holy powers, 223, 238, 330, 418
Holy Spirit, 242–43
    demonstration of, 432
    gift of, 323–24
    by means of Moses, 242–43
    resurrection and, 295–96
Holy Trinity, 133–34, 216, 231–32, 234, 263, 270, 271–72, 334–35, 354, 388–89, 392, 396, 411, 414, 415–16, 445–46
    knowledge of, 192–93, 197–98, 291
    living mind and, 292
    partial vision of, 358–59
    peace and tranquility of, 189–90
    worship of, 386
holy unity, natural knowledge and, 194, 204
holy water, Holy Trinity and, 396
Horeb, Moses on, 239–40
house of dead, *KG* Chapter Six on, 456
humanity in image of God, 433
humans
    angel ranks and state of, 362–63
    inability to see angels, demons 446
    ranks of, 269–70
    soul and embryological development of, 294–95
    three lives of, 223–24
humility, 24, 56, 73, 346, 359
    abandonment and, , 123
    of anger, 350
    comprehension and, 123
    temptation and, 123
    vainglory and, 74

ignorance, 88–89, 235, 260, 300–1, 319–20
    feigning, 118
    knowledge and, 197, 201–2
    limited, 288–89
    practical concepts, 88–89
    separation from, 199
image. *See also* image of God
    body of soul and house, 343–44
    engraving of, 144–45
image of God, 219, 271, 448–49
    humanity in, 433
immaterial knowledge, 239, 264
immortality, 94–95, 271–72
    death and, 185–86, 188

512 INDEX

impassibility, 378
impassioned, 348–49
impassioned mind, 202
imperfect mind, 260–61
impurity, 352–53
  evil and, 294
incorporeals, 179, 192–93, 196, 340–41,
    353, 354
  intellections of, 388
  knowledge of, 374–75
  land of, 76
  nature of, 297
  thēoria of, 243–44
infinite knowledge, 300–1
inheritance
  of Christ, 292–93, 304–5
  heir and, 307
  of saints, suffering and, 159
in the beginning (phrase), 393
in potentia
  body and, 179
  in soul, 180
instructions, 60–70
  by angels, 455
  body without soul, 69–70
  constant prayer, 67–68
  demon of sexual lust and blasphemy against
      God, 69
  demons and objects, 66–67
  demons causing blasphemy, 64–65
  levels of, 129
  provision for desires, 70
  recognition of demons, 63
  symptoms of disturbance, 61
  temptations for anger, 62
  travel, 61–62
instrument of soul
  KG, 190–91
  thēoria (contemplation or observation)
      and, 248
intellection of incorporeals, 388
intellection of matter, 448
intellection of world, 192–93, 222, 223
intelligible anointing, 312–13
intelligible arrow, 438
intelligible city, 398–99
intelligible cloud, 364–65
intelligible cosmos, 380
intelligible cross, 429
intelligible dark cloud, 366
intelligible deadbolt, 402
intelligible fishhook, 377
intelligible gates, 400–1

intelligible healing, 444
intelligible helmet, 376
intelligible Israel, 447
intelligible leaf, 334–35
intelligible matters, 227
intelligible moon, rational nature and, 282–83
intelligible mountain, 379
intelligible nations, 410
intelligible Philistine, 395–96
intelligible shield, 374
intelligible stars, rational nature and, 288
intelligible sun, rational nature and, 278
intelligible sword, 372
intelligible temple, 404–5
intelligible things, mind and, 439
intelligible wall, 403
intelligible warrior, 397
intermediaries, 156
interpretation
  allegorical, of scripture, 4, 5
  allegory and spiritual, 128–29
  anger and knowledge, 107
  discussion and, 121–22
  existent things multiple, 132–33
  things said, 111–12
Israel, 167
  intelligible, 447
  new, 341–42

Jacob's ladder, Christ and, 328–29
Jerusalem, 406–7
  adultery and fornication of, 115–16
  coming down from heaven of, 360
  Holy Mountain of, 23–24
  resurrection of soul and, 369
Jesus, moral teachings of, 3
judgment, 129–30, 245–46
  of Christ, just, 237–38
  different, 245–46
  final, 260, 276
  of God, 274–75, 434
  just and, 280–81
  last, 246
  of living and dead, 250–51, 449
  providence and, 141–43, 370
  seat of Christ, 253, 440
justice
  Gregory of Nazianzus on *thēoria* virtue
      of, 136–38
  in soul, 89–90

katastasis, 43, 420–21
kephalaia, 11

INDEX   513

defined, 1
as majority of work of Evagrius, 6–7
of Mani, 7
kephalaia, 1–2, 3
Kephalaia gnostika (KG), 1, 11–12, 29–30, 146–458. *See also specific topics*
  Century Two, 207–54
  Century Three, 255–302
  Century Four, 303–56
  Century Five, 357–408
  Century Six, 409–58
  Chapters of Knowledge, 146
  Six Hundred Prognostic Problems, 146
  translations of, 12–13
The Kephalaia of the Teacher (Mani), 7
key to kingdom of heaven, 327
KG. See Kephalaia gnostika
kingdom of God, 33
kingdom of heaven, 178, 373–74, 421
  apatheia and, 32
  key to, 327
knowable of Christ, 304
knowable of God, 303–4
knowledge, 188. *See also* spiritual knowledge
  actions and material, 225
  chariot of, 233–34
  Christ and, 219
  emptying of, 244
  essential, 281
  failed and declined, 335
  first and second, 406
  first kind of, 208
  four in, 160
  gnostic, 305
  gnostic anger and interpretation of, 106–7
  high, 312
  Holy Trinity, 192–93, 197–98, 291
  ignorance and, 197, 201–2
  immaterial, 239, 264
  incorporeals and, 374–75
  infinite, 300–1
  knowledge begetting, 249
  life and holy, 195
  light of mind and, 196
  limited, 288–89
  magnet and, 225
  natural, 194, 204
  from outside, *logoi* and, 101–2
  priority of, 192
  protection of, 106
  pure, 305–6
  rational beings growth of, 225
  spiritual *thēoria*, 267, 268

  three altars of, 354–55
  truth and, 217–18, 277
  knowledge of God, 181–82, 203, 355–56, 419, 424
  body as evil and, 283
  submission and, 446
  sweetness of, 289
  knowledge of Trinity, father and, 425

Lake Mareotis, 96
land of promise, 377
languages
  gift of, 323–24
  tongues and, 336
last judgment, 246
Latin version, of *Praktikos*, 9–10
leaf, intelligible, 334–35
left behind, being, 229–30
legal disputes, gnostic involvement in, 105–6
Letter on Faith (Evagrius), 2, 6
letters, of Evagrius, 6
  to Anatolius, 1–2, 1n.1, 3, 9, 14, 23–24, 29–30
Letter to Melania (Evagrius), 6
life, holy knowledge and, 195
Life of Anthony, on illiteracy and knowledge of God, 92–93
light, 169–70
light of mind, knowledge and, 196, 200
lobe of liver sacrifice, 315–16, 321–22
logismoi (malign thoughts), 1–2
logoi (reasons of *praktikos*), 99–100, 133, 279–80, 284
  Didymus and providence of God, 141–43
  knowledge from outside and, 101–2
logos, 20, 133, 307
  on judgment, 129–30
  understanding and, 422
longing, 332–33
Lord
  day of, 293
  hand of, 214
  mind of, 346–47
love, 85–86, 87, 202–3
  in desiring soul, 89–90
  monks and holy mysteries of, 97
luminaries, 243, 253

Macarius the Egyptian, 93–94
magnet, knowledge as, 225
malign thoughts. *See logismoi*
Mani, 7, 284
Manichaeism, 280
man of God, 235–36

514 INDEX

manuscripts of *Praktikos (To a Monk)*, 9, 9n.16
material knowledge, actions and, 225
material objects, *theoria* of, 391–92
Maximus the Confessor, 11
mean, extremes compared to, 150–51
meanings by contingency, 160
memory, undisturbed, 79
mercy seat, 341
mind, 221, 438–39
　anger and blinding of, 371–72
　creation of world in, 380–81
　God as teacher of, 284
　head of soul and, 383
　heavenly powers, 258
　Holy Trinity and, 270
　Holy Trinity and living, 292
　impassioned, 202
　imperfect, 260–61
　intelligible things and, 439
　knowledge and light of, 196, 200
　naked, 258–59
　nearness of Lord and, 346–47
　organs of sense and, 230–31
　particular path of, 232
　passions removed from, 363–64, 365–66
　perfect, 261–62
　power of, 391, 401–2
　pure, 387, 407–8
　resurrection of, 370
　Solomon and, 455–56
　spiritual knowledge and healing of, 273
　spiritual knowledge as wings of, 284–85
　sterile, 441–42
　unity of, 271
　war against passions by, 86–87
miracles of Christ, 337
mirror, 393–94
　of goodness of God, 207
　of virtues, 336
mixture, 451–52
moderation, Gregory of Nazianzus on *theoria*,
　virtue of, 136–38
monks, 98
　consent to thoughts by, 83
　demons' knowledge by, 68
　desires and anger of, 96–97
　eating with women, 95
　five reasons of, 96
　gospel book, 95
　immortality, 94–95
　Lake Mareotis, 96
　Life of Anthony on illiteracy and knowledge of
　　God, 92–93

love and holy mysteries of, 97
Macarius the Egyptian, 93–94
paths of, 92
sayings of Holy, 91–98
temptations for, 82–83
vessel of election, 93
moon, rational nature and intelligible, 282–83
moral training. *See askēsis*
Moses
　Athanasius and, 140
　Horeb and, 239–40
　theoria of, 316
mothers, 233
mountain
　intelligible, 379
　of Transfiguration, 316
movement, evil, virtue and, 182
moving of passion, 58–59
multiform movement of rational beings, 369–70
mysteries, 444–45
　sharing of, 119

naked mind, 258–59, 265, 292
names, 182, 220, 227
　cherub, 283–84
nations, perceptible and intelligible, 410
natural knowledge, holy unity and, 194, 204
natural system, 273–74
nature. *See physikē*; rational nature
Nilus of Ancyra, 8–9, 11
nourishment, 249, 252–53, 258
numbers, 152
　five, 157–58, 228
　forty and fifty, 229
　four, 157–58, 228–29
numerical triad, 415–16

observation. *See theoria*
oil and perfumed oil, 299
oil-lamp sacrifice in temple, 315–16, 317
On the Virtues and the Vices (Aristotle), 90
operations, of passion, 57
organon of soul, 265–66, 278–79
Origen, 2–3, 5, 16–19
　on Temple visit by Alexander, 23–24
　on wisdom literature, 31–32
origin, 182–84
orphans, support of, 361

paced learning, 124
paideia, 3–4
Pantaenus, 2–3
Paradise, 413

INDEX 515

partial vision, Holy Trinity, 358–59
passible power, 263–64
passing away
  body, form of, 164
passing of body
  bodiless nature and, 244–45
passion, 10, 56–60
  of body, 58
  body and soul, 126
  demonic stench and, 60
  demons and movement of, 428
  free from, 100
  mind and war against, 86–87
  mind without, 363–64, 365–66
  moving of, 58–59
  on operations of, 57
  sensations of, 59–60
  of soul, 57–58
  soul and, 437
Passion, 228
passions in soul, symbols of, 65–66
path, intelligible, 381–82
pathē (disturbances afflicting soul), 1–2
pathēma (emotions), 66
path of mind, 232
patience, 237–38
Paul (saint), 3, 130–31
peace and tranquility, 378–79
  Holy Trinity and, 189–90
pectoral, 315–16, 342
Pentecost, 228, 229, 324
people
  avaricious, 125
  words of disgraceful, 116–17
perceptibility, 200, 389–90
perceptible nations, 410
perceptible words, 421
perfect fullness, of evil, 240
perfect mind, 261–62
perfect soul, 263–64
Philistines
  intelligible, 395–96
  slaves of, 377
Philo, 2–3
physikē (nature), 108, 113–14, 143–44
  first and second, 405
  spiritual knowledge on, 167–68
  thēoria of, 268–69
pillar of truth, Basil the Cappadocian, 138–39
place of knowledge, 396–97
place of refuge, 352
Plato, 16–19
  on first good and substance, 147–48

tripartite soul and, 91
Platonic philosophy
  of Alexandria teachers, 2–3
  in exegesis, 4
pleasures, 332
  through senses, 212–13
pledge, 310–11
pleonasm, 15
Plotinus, 2–3
Porphyry, 16–19
practical concepts, 80–91
  angelic thoughts, 85
  demonic choke holds, 81–82
  demonic songs, 81
  good or bad actions, 89
  healing of soul, 84–85
  ignorance, 88–89
  love, 85–86, 87
  practice of virtues, 84
  rational soul, 88, 89–90
  rejoicing of angels, 83
  rest and repose, 82
  seeds of virtue, 91
  soul activity exercising, 86
  virtues, 84, 87
  war against passion by mind, 86–87
practice. *See praktikē*
practiced ones. *See praktikos*
praktikē (practice), 108, 113–14, 143–44
  one who, 394
  thēoria and, 156
praktikos (practiced one)
  logoi of, 99–100
  understanding of, 99–100
Praktikos (To a Monk). *See specific topics*
prayers
  constant, 67–68
  without distraction, 77
  mind resistant to, 78
pride
  remedies, 56
  thoughts (Eight Thoughts), 35–36, 43, 56
priest, secrecy of, 109–11
priestly symbols
  belt, 315–16, 350
  coat or cloak, 315–16, 344, 348
  ephod, 315–16, 337, 348
  lobe of liver, 315–16, 321–22
  pectoral, 315–16, 342
  petalon, 315–16, 342
  priestly trousers, 315–16, 346
  propitiatory, 315–16, 341
  sacrificial fat, 315–16, 324

516 INDEX

priestly symbols (*cont.*)
  temple oil-lamp, 315–16, 317
  turban, 315–16, 331–32
  unleavened bread, 315–16, 319
primary *thēoria*, 164–65
priority of knowledge, 192
prison-house, 323
promise of hundredfold, 328
propitiatory, 315–16, 341
Proverbs, Origen scholia on, 5
providence
  God's, 432, 441
  heavenly powers and, 450–51
  judgment and, 141–43, 370
prudence
  Gregory of Nazianzus on *thēoria* virtue
    of, 136–38
  in rational soul, 89–90
psalms, singing without distraction for, 79–80
psaltery, 434–35
pure conscience, spiritual sacrifice of, 387–88
pure knowledge, 305–6
pure mind, 387, 407–8, 443–44
purification, fiery, 318
purity of soul, 344–45

ranks, 399
  angels and, 362–63
  heavenly powers, 247–53
  human, 269–70
rational beings, 188–89, 197–98, 216–17
  first movement of, 266
  God and, 303
  growth of knowledge of, 225
  multiform movement of, 369–70
  sanctification by God of, 293–94
  unity of Christ and, 257
  wealth of God and, 326–27
rational bodies, 246
rational nature, 149, 156, 204–5, 215, 217,
    338, 452–53
  bread of, 376–77
  intelligible moon as, 282–83
  intelligible stars as, 288
  intelligible sun as, 278
  return to, 419
  sign of trees and, 395
  three parts of, 342
rational soul, 88, 89–90
  prudence in, 89–90
  spiritual sense and, 172–73
  understanding in, 89–90
  wisdom in, 89–90

reasons. *See logoi*
references, for *Gnostic Trilogy*, 15–16
  biblical quotations and, 15
  Bunge numeration system for, 16
rejoicing of angels, 83
remedies, 10, 43–56
  akēdia, 52–54
  anger, 47–52
  gluttony, 45
  logismoi, 1–2
  love of money, 46, 49
  pride, 56
  sadness, 46–47
  sexual lust, 45
  vainglory, 54–56
renunciation
  first, 198
  second, 198–99
  third, 199
rest and repose, 82
  God and, 291
resurrection, 412
  body and, 368
  Holy Spirit and, 295–96
  mind and, 370
  soul and, 369
return (*apokatastasis*), 214–15
right hand, 253
river
  four, 397–98
  Gihon, 201

sabbath, 329
sacrifices to God, 315
sacrifice to demons, 315–16
sacrificial fat, 315–16, 324
sadness, 36
  remedies, 46–47
  thoughts, 35–36, 38–39, 46–47
  unfriendliness of gnostic or, 117–18
saints
  angels of, 347
  inheritance of, 159
salt
  gnostic likeness to, 100–1
  Guillaumont, C., and Guillaumont, A., on
    light and, 101
salvation
  angels and, 456
  ways of, 165
sanctification, rational beings and God, 293–94
scholia, of Evagrius, 4, 6
  on Ecclesiastes, 6

INDEX 517

on Job, 6
on Proverbs, 6
on Psalms, 6, 8
scripture
allegorical interpretations of, 4, 5, 128–29
Evagrius on, 5
from Greek Bible, 4
restriction to advanced *gnōstikos*, 5
testimonies and divine, 114
seat of the mind, 420–21
second beings, 187
Second Council of Constantinople, 9, 214–15.
See also anathemas
second renunciation, of abandonment of
evil, 198–99
second things, *thēoria* of, 207–8, 214–15, 218,
238, 266, 287–88, 299–300, 313–14, 333–34
secrecy, of priest, 109–11
seeds of virtues, 91, 173–74
self
being in, 149–51
engendering of, 153
numbers in, 152
separation of, 153
self-controlled persons, 79
self-restraint, in desiring soul, 89–90
sensations, 390–91
eye of, 222
of passion, 59–60
sense perceptions, 169
organ of, 170–71
senses, 249–50
faculty of, 171–72
failure of, 345
five, 158, 226
mind and organs of, 230–31
organs of, 250
pleasures through, 212–13
soul and, 343
separation from ignorance, third renunciation
and, 199
separation of self, 153
Serapion, spiritual knowledge and, 141
Severus of Antioch, 134
sexual lust, 36
demon of, 69, 74–75
shadows, 365
sheepskin, 27
Sheol, 175, 185, 287, 350–51, 413
shield, intelligible, 374
showbread, 251–52
sign,
revelation of, 339–40

sin, of gnostic, 135–36
sinful soul, 269
sinners, change of, 281–82
Six Hundred Prognostic Problems, *KG*, 146
skills, 156–57
slander, 126–27
of gnostic by demons, 301–2
sleep, 70–73
apatheia during dreams, 72–73
demons and, 423
fantasies of dreams, 71
Gnostikos and, 70
God and metaphor of, 173
images seen in dreams in, 71–72
Socrates Scholasticus, 11
songs, demonic, 81
soul
anger and, 454
angering, 89–90
annulment of four elements of, 157–58
body and, 180
body without, 69–70
after death, 211
deficient, 262–63
demons and virtue approach of, 75
desiring, 89–90
evils in nature and, 161
exercising of activity of, 86
exodus from Egypt and, 444
healing of, 84–85
human embryological development
and, 294–95
image of house and body of, 343–44
instrument of, 190–91
irrational part of, 78–79
justice in, 89–90
mind as head of, 383
organon of, 265–66, 278–79
passion in, 437
passion of, 57–58, 126
peaceful states of, 73–74
perfect, 263–64
in potentia in, 180
purity of, 344–45
rational, 88, 89–90
resurrection of, 369
senses and, 343
sinful, 269
sterile, 443
symbols of passions in, 65–66
thēoria of instrument of, 248
tripartite, 89–91
wealth of, 211–12

518 INDEX

spiritual bodies, 154–55, 267–68, 278–79
   thēoria of, 210
spiritual circumcision, 309–10
spiritual knowledge, 457
   crown of justice and, 196–97
   healing of mind and, 273
   just and, 194
   nature and, 167–68
   Serapion and, 141
   thēoria of, 277
   wings of mind and, 284–85
spiritual sacrifice, pure conscience
   and, 387–88
spiritual sense, 226
   rational soul and, 172–73
spiritual *thēoria*, 267, 268
staff, 27–28
stars, 274
   hidden, 321
   intelligible, 288
state, 199, 270
   angelic and archangelic, 247, 325–26,
    362, 363
   Aristotle on distinction of, 50
   excellence, of rational soul, 202–3
   fall from *katastasis*, 43
   of final blessedness, 260
   impassible, 369, 378
   katastasis and, 63, 420–21
   kosmikos, 65
   "little *apatheia*," 76
   of mind, 20
   positive, 20
   of rational soul, 319, 337, 381
   of rational soul and virture, 420
   thēoria and, 264, 288
   thymos and, 47
   of turmoil, 275
   visible manifestation of, 66
state approaching *apatheia*, 73–77
   blinded mind, 76–77
   demon of vainglory and sexual lust, 74–75
   demons and soul advance to virtue, 75
   demons opposed to each other, 74–75
   land of incorporeals, 76
   peaceful states of soul, 73–74
   perfect *apatheia*, 75–76
steward, 375–76
   parable of wise, 186–87
subjection, submission compared to, 447
submission
   knowledge of God and, 446
   subjection compared to, 447

substance
   first good and, 147–48
   Plato on first good and, 147–48
suffering, inheritance of saints and, 159
sun, rational nature and intelligible, 278
survival, in Greek, 7
sword, intelligible, 372
symbolism
   of east and west, 287
   festal, 228
   marital, 374
   number, 152, 313–14
symbols of *apatheia*, 77–80
   irrational part of soul, 78–79
   prayer resistant to mind, 78
   prayers without distraction, 77
   proof of *apatheia*, 77–78
   psalm-singing without distraction, 79–80
   self-controlled persons, 79
   undisturbed memory, 79
   virtues, 80
Syriac translations, 8–9
   of *Gnostikos*, 11–12, 14
   of *KG*, 12–13, 14
   manuscript witnesses to, 17*t*
   of *Praktikos*, 9–10, 10n.20, 14
   profile of, 13–15

table of Christ, 238
teaching, 24–25
   accommodation in, 103–4
   Jesus and Paul moral, 3
   mind and God, 284
   writers about true, 307–8
temperance, in desiring soul, 89–90
temple
   intelligible, 404–5
   oil-lamp sacrifice in, 315–16, 317
Temple, Origen on Alexander visit to, 23–24
temptation
   comprehension and, 123–24
   of gnostic, 135
   of monk, 82–83
temptations
   of anger, 62
testimonies, divine scripture and, 114
tetrad, 414–15
theologikē (words about God), 108, 113–14
thēoria (contemplation or observation),
   20, 192–93
   of angels, 360
   of beings, 210, 276, 314–15, 365–66
   bodies and, 239

INDEX 519

divine book and beings, 409
father and beings, 425
Gregory of Nazianzus on prudence, courage,
    moderation, justice virtues of, 136–38
Holy Trinity and, 449–50
immaterial, 351–52
incorporeals and, 243–44
instrument of soul and, 248
knowledge of, 192–93
material objects and, 391–92
material things and, 224
nature, 268–69
practice and, 156
primary, 164–65
second things, 207–8, 214–15, 218, 238, 266,
    287–88, 299–300, 313–14, 333–34
spiritual, 267, 268
spiritual knowledge, 277
of this world, 409–10
types of, 265
things on earth, 162
third renunciation, separation from ignorance
    and, 199
thoughtless speaking, about God, 122–23
thoughts
    angelic, 85
    on angels, 85
    burning of evil, 275
    logismoi, 1–2
    monks' consent to, 83
thoughts (Eight Thoughts), 10, 35–43
    akēdia, 35–36, 40–41, 52–54
    anger, 35–36, 39–40, 47–52
    gluttony, 35–37, 45
    love of money, 35–36, 38, 46, 49
    pride, 35–36, 43, 56
    sadness, 35–36, 38–39, 46–47
    sexual lust, 35–36, 37, 45
    vainglory, 35–36, 42–43, 54–56
three altars, of knowledge, 354–55
time, 252, 414
times, customs, and laws, understanding of, 111
To a Monk. See Praktikos
tongues and languages, 336
torment, 184, 264–65, 359
transfer, 248
translations. *See also* Armenian translation;
    Syriac translation
    Gnostic Trilogy, 7–13
    of *KG*, 12–13
    Praktikos English, 1
translators, of *Gnostic Trilogy*, 16t
travel, instructions on, 61–62

treatises, of Evagrius, 6
    To Eulogius, 6
    Foundations of the Monastic Life, 6
    About Thoughts, 6
tree imagery, 303, 395
trials, 164
tripartite soul, 89–91
    Gregory of Nazianzus and, 90–91
trouble, 275
truth
    knowledge of, 217–18, 277
turban, 315–16, 331–32

uncreated, 411–12
understanding
    of *praktikos*, 99–100
    in rational soul, 89–90
under the earth, 296–97
undifferentiated things, 241
unity, 180–81, 197–98, 257, 262, 318–19, 394–
    95. *See also* holy unity
    mind and, 271
    rational beings and Christ, 257
unleavened bread sacrifice, 315–16, 319

vainglory, 36, 405–6
    demons of, 74–75
vessels of election, 93
vestment, 28, 29
virtues, 80, 84, 87, 190, 287–88, 420–21. *See
    also* soul
    demons and soul advance to, 75
    evil and, 176–77
    Gregory of Nazianzus on prudence, courage,
        moderation, and justice *thēoria*, 136–38
    mirror of, 336
    movement, evil and, 182
    practice of, 84
    seeds of, 91, 173–74
    speaking to youth about works of, 108–9
virtue
    state of rational soul and, 420
vision, 439–40

wall, intelligible, 403
war against passion by mind, 86–87
warrior, intelligible, 397
water, 166, 191–92
waves, 367
ways of salvation, 165
wealth of God, 320, 326–27
wealth of soul, 211–12
wheat analogy, 220–21

520 INDEX

Who Is the Rich Man (Clement), 101, 125
widows, support of, 361
wine of dragons, anger as, 382–83
wings of *apatheia*, 210–11
wings of mind, spiritual knowledge
    and, 284–85
wisdom, 269–70, 297, 306, 436–37
    full of variety, 306
    of God, 218, 387
    in rational soul, 89–90
wisdom literature
    Evagrius on, 5
    Origen on, 31–32
wise steward parable, 186–87
women, 95
words about God. *See theologikē*
world
    composition of, 190–91
    end of, 407

intellection of, 192–93
mind creation of, 380–81
natural system of, 273–74
perfect departure from, 431
thēoria of this, 409–10
worship
    Christ, 384–85
    Holy Trinity, 386
writers about true teachings, 307–8
writings, 286
writings, of Evagrius, 6–7
    of kephalaia, 6
    of letters, 6
    of scholia, 6
    of treatises, 6

youth, works of virtue of, 108–9

Zion, 406–7